The Yorkshire County Cricket Club Limited

Registered Number 28929R

YEARBOOK
2022

124th EDITION

Editor:
GRAHAM HARDCASTLE

Production Editor:
JAMES M. GREENFIELD

Records and Statistics
Yorkshire First Eleven:
JOHN T POTTER

Yorkshire Second Eleven:
HOWARD CLAYTON

Official Photographers:
SIMON WILKINSON, ALEX WHITEHEAD
ALLAN McKENZIE and WILL PALMER. *SWpix.com*
and JOHN HEALD

Published by
THE YORKSHIRE COUNTY CRICKET CLUB LTD
EMERALD HEADINGLEY CRICKET GROUND
LEEDS LS6 3BU
Tel: 0344 504 3099 Fax: 0113 278 4099
Internet: http://www.yorkshireccc.com
e-mail: cricket@yorkshireccc.com

TELEPHONE AND FAX NUMBERS

EMERALD HEADINGLEY CRICKET GROUND
Tel: 0344 504 3099
Fax: 0113 278 4099

NORTH MARINE ROAD, SCARBOROUGH **Tel: 01723 365625**
Fax: 01723 364287

SHIPTON ROAD, YORK   **Tel: 01904 623602**

ST GEORGE'S ROAD, HARROGATE **Tel: 01423-525000**

© The Yorkshire County Cricket Club Ltd 2022

All rights reserved. Please note that no part of this publication may be reproduced or transmitted in any form or by any means, electronic or mechanical, including photocopying, recording or any information storage and retrieval system now known or to be invented without permission in writing from the publisher.

Produced by:

Great Northern Books
PO Box 1380, Bradford, BD5 5FB
www.greatnorthernbooks.co.uk

ISBN: 978-1-914227-27-1

CONTENTS

	Page
Telephone numbers of Yorkshire grounds	2
Patrons, Honorary Life Members and Vice-Presidents	4
Officials of the Club	5
Yorkshire's Most Difficult Year — Lord Patel	7
Fixtures — 2022	10
Mission for The Dazzler — Darren Gough	15
Ottis Gibson Hits The Ground Running — Graham Hardcastle	17
New Faces on the Bench	19
Historic Link With Lahore Qalandars — Graham Hardcastle	21
Golden Girl With Yorkshire Legends — Graham Hardcastle	23
First Class Review of 2021 — Andrew Bosi	30
Colts Thrive in Royal London Cup — Graham Hardcastle	33
County Age Groups 2021	37
Northern Diamonds Review of 2021 — Kevin Hutchinson	39
Headingley The Ground Where England Win — Paul Edwards	43
Yorkshire Men and Women Superchargers — Graham Hardcastle	47
Disability Icon Set for the Aussies — Graham Hardcastle	49
Quickie Sets Sights on Paralympics — Graham Hardcastle	52
Yorkshire Pair Through England's Door — Graham Hardcastle	54
Adil Rashid Superstar	56
Qalandars Boost for Rising Batter	57
100 Years Ago — Anthony Bradbury	59
50 Years Ago — Anthony Bradbury	67
Bicentenary of a Slow Birth — Jeremy Lonsdale	76
Book Reviews — Graham Hardcastle	80
Obituaries — Graham Hardcastle, David Warner and John T Potter	83
First Class Highlights of 2021 — John T Potter	95
LV= Insurance County Championship 2021 — Scorecards, Tables, Match Pictures and Reports By Andrew Bosi, Graham Hardcastle, John T Potter, Simon Wilkinson, Alex Whitehead, Allan McKenzie and Will Palmer	101
Patto's Amazing Repeat Show — David Warner	133
Vitality Blast 2021	135
Blow That Shocked The World — Graham Hardcastle	165
Royal London One-Day Cup 2021	166
Northern Diamonds 2021	180
Charlotte Edwards Cup 2021	181
Rachael Heyhoe-Flint Trophy 2021	199
Yorkshire Second Eleven Highlights of 2021	219
Records Section	226

Colour Plates — Facing Pages 32 and 256

PATRONESS

THE DUCHESS OF KENT

PATRONS

DAVID LASCELLES, EARL OF HAREWOOD   LORD HAWKE
The EARL OF MEXBOROUGH

HONORARY LIFE MEMBERS

Mr J G BINKS
Mr H D BIRD, OBE,
Hon. D (Univ) LLD
Sir GEOFFREY BOYCOTT
Mr D BYAS
Mr D GOUGH

Mr R A HUTTON
Mr D S LEHMANN
Mr D E V PADGETT
Mr R K PLATT
Mr S R TENDULKAR
Mr M P VAUGHAN, OBE

PRESIDENT

Mr G A COPE

VICE-PRESIDENTS

Mrs J BAIRSTOW
Mr B BOUTTELL
Mr I M CHAPPELL
Mr M COWAN
Mr D S HALL, CBE, TD
Mr R A HILLIAM
Mr S J MANN
Mr K H MOSS MBE

Mr J W T MUSTOE
Mr D M RYDER
Mr R A SMITH, TD, DL
Mr W B STOTT
Mr K TAYLOR
Mr A L VANN
Mr D WARNER
Mr J D WELCH

Officials of the Yorkshire County Cricket Club

President

T R Barker	1863
M J Ellison	1864-97
Lord Hawke	1898-1938
Rt Hon Sir F S Jackson	1939-1947
T L Taylor	1948-1960
Sir W A Worsley Bart	1961-1973
Sir K Parkinson	1974-1981
N W D Yardley	1981-1983
The Viscount Mountgarret	1984-1989
Sir Leonard Hutton	1989-1990
Sir Lawrence Byford QPM, LLD, DL	1991-1999
R A Smith TD, LLB, DL	1999-2004
David Jones CBE	2004-6
Robert Appleyard	2006-8
Brian Close CBE	2008-10
Raymond Illingworth CBE	2010-12
Geoffrey Boycott OBE	2012-13
Harold 'Dickie' Bird OBE	2014-15
John H Hampshire	2016-17
Richard A Hutton	2017-18
Geoff A Cope	2018-

Chairman

A H Connell, DL	1971-1979
M G Crawford	1980-1984
H R Kirk	1984-1985
B Walsh, QC	1986-1991
Sir Lawrence Byford CBE, QPM, LLD, DL	1991-1998
K H Moss MBE	1998-2002
G A Cope	2002
R A Smith TD, LLB, DL	2002-5
C J Graves	2005-15
S J Denison	2015-18
R A Smith TD, LLB, DL	2018-20
C N R Hutton	2020-21
Lord K Patel	2021-

Secretary

Geo Padley	1863
J B Wostinholm	1864-1902
F C (Sir Fredk.) Toone	1903-1930
J H Nash	1931-1971
J Lister	1972-1991
D M Ryder	1991-2002

Company Secretary

B Bouttell	2002-5
C Hartwell	2011-14
P Hudson	2014-

Officials of the Yorkshire County Cricket Club

Captain

R Iddison	1863-1872	J V Wilson	1960-1962
J Rowbotham	1873	D B Close	1963-1970
L Greenwood	1874	G Boycott	1971-1978
J Rowbotham	1875	J H Hampshire	1979-1980
E Lockwood	1876-1877	C M Old	1981-1982
T Emmett	1878-1882	R Illingworth	1982-1983
Hon M B (Lord) Hawke	1883-1910	D L Bairstow	1984-1986
E J R H Radcliffe	1911	P Carrick	1987-1989
Sir A W White	1912-1918	M D Moxon	1990-1995
D C F Burton	1919-1921	D Byas	1996-2001
Geoff Wilson	1922-1924	D S Lehmann	2002
A W Lupton	1925-1927	A McGrath	2003
W A Worsley	1928-1929	C White	2004-6
A T Barber	1930	D Gough	2007-8
F E Greenwood	1931-1932	A McGrath	2009
A B Sellers	1933-1947	A W Gale	2010-16
N W D Yardley	1948-1955	G S Ballance	2017-18
W H H Sutcliffe	1956-1957	S A Patterson	2018-
J R Burnet	1958-1959	D J Willey	2020-
			(T20 only)

Treasurer

M J Ellison	1863-1893	M G Crawford	1963-1979
M Ellison, jun.	1894-1898	J D Welch	1980-1984
Chas Stokes	1899-1912	P W Townend	1984-2002
R T Heselton	1913-1931		
A Wyndham Heselton	1932-1962		

Chief Executive

C D Hassell	1991-2002	Colin J Graves	2012-13
Colin J Graves	2002-5	Mark Arthur	2013-21
Stewart Regan	2006-10		

Chair looks forward from club's most difficult year

YORKSHIRE WILL BECOME SHINING EXAMPLE TO SPORT

By Lord Patel

2021 was the most difficult year in the history of Yorkshire County Cricket Club. While the world grappled with the ongoing impact of the pandemic the club became synonymous with institutional racism and appeared on the front pages for all the wrong reasons. We have been rocked to our foundations.

I was honoured to be appointed Chair in November 2021, but I was also very aware that the rebuild — forging real and lasting change — could not happen overnight.

Out of adversity, however, I truly believe that there is real opportunity — to become a shining example, leading the way for the rest of the sport by creating a scalable model on diversity and inclusion and creating a space that is welcoming and celebratory of people from all backgrounds. We have started the journey but cannot forget what brought us here.

The brave, shocking testimony of Azeem Rafiq in November was a moment that will resonate across cricket, and more widely, for years to come. The words of Azeem, and many other whistleblowers across the UK and internationally, remain a clear call to the sport that change is urgent, unavoidable, and long overdue.

I am a proud Yorkshireman. I know how important this club is for the community, the cricketing family and all who are associated with it.

From day one, I committed to listen, to learn, and to take action. Since that day, as a club we have made some difficult decisions — indeed, some of which have been criticised — but all with the clear and singular purpose of addressing the wrongs of the past and doing what is right. I want to make all of us proud of this club, from the youngest ambitious player picking up their first bat to our oldest and most venerable member who has watched us for a lifetime.

I firmly believe that Yorkshire County Cricket Club has made significant progress on the long journey to win back pride, as we aim to become that beacon to which the rest of the sport can aspire.

The hosting of international cricket is vital to the future survival of the club. Following the suspension of Headingley's hosting rights in November, we have worked night and day to get this sanction overturned. This has included developing a culture of equity, diversity and inclusion, adapting a zero-tolerance policy to discrimination and ensuring Headingley is a welcoming environment for everyone, amongst other things.

The ECB's decision to overturn the suspension in February was welcomed, and testimony to the change that has occurred. Clearly, we are only at the start of this journey, but I am confident that we will continue in the right direction over the coming weeks and months.

I must express a debt of gratitude to our members whose passion for the club and desire to see it reformed has shone through since I first started. Be it the number of supportive letters and emails I have received, the fantastic attendance and engaging questions at the Members' Forum in January or the overwhelming support in calling an EGM in March, it's clear to see that there is a strong desire to see this club build back stronger.

Our new partnership with the Lahore Qalandars and Multiply Momentum Titans marks a really exciting new era. It presents an opportunity to build relationships with two of the best franchises in the world, providing development opportunities for players present and future and take key learnings from their systems and processes.

Clearly, a vitally important component is in the way we identify and nurture talent and our early plans in this space are incredibly exciting, and I believe a real first for cricket in England.

As you will have seen, we have now assembled a new coaching and support team — spearheaded by Darren Gough and Ottis Gibson. It's been heartening to see the large numbers of high-quality candidates that have applied for these roles and, following a very thorough recruitment process, we are delighted with the support team we have in place for this season.

The Northern Diamonds continue to be a source of pride for the region, having reached two finals in 2021. An increase in full-time contracted players from five to eight is another step in the right direction and I'm looking forward to seeing if the team can go one step further in 2022 and claim some silverware.

While we still have a long road and a lot of hard work ahead, the potential prize is great; a once in a generation opportunity not only to transform the game in Yorkshire, but also provide a model for learning and change — both in cricket and across the world of sport.

All dressed up and somewhere to go: Wicket-keeper Harry Duke models the new LV= Insurance County Championship shirt, which will be worn in 2022. Yorkshire are delighted to have entered into a three-year partnership with world-renowned kit manufacturers Kukri Sports.

COUNTY FIXTURES — 2022

LV= INSURANCE COUNTY CHAMPIONSHIP
(All four-day matches)

Date			Opponents	Venue
Thu	14-17	April	Gloucestershire	Bristol
Thu	21-24	April	Northamptonshire	Northampton
THU	**28-1**	**APRIL/MAY**	**KENT**	**HEADINGLEY**
Thu	5-8	May	Essex	Chelmsford
THU	**12-15**	**MAY**	**LANCASHIRE**	**HEADINGLEY**
THU	**19-22**	**MAY**	**WARWICKSHIRE**	**HEADINGLEY**
Sun	12-15	June	Hampshire	Southampton
MON	**11-14**	**JULY**	**SURREY**	**SCARBOROUGH**
Tue	19-22	July	Somerset	Taunton
MON	**25-28**	**JULY**	**HAMPSHIRE**	**SCARBOROUGH**
Mon	5-8	September	Lancashire	Old Trafford
MON	**12-15**	**SEPTEMBER**	**ESSEX**	**HEADINGLEY**
Tue	20-23	September	Surrey	The Oval
MON	**26-29**	**SEPTEMBER**	**GLOUCESTERSHIRE**	**HEADINGLEY**

VITALITY BLAST (Twenty20)
(All matches floodlit except where stated)

WED	**25**	**MAY**	**WORCESTERSHIRE**	**HEADINGLEY**
Fri	27	May	Lancashire	Old Trafford
SUN	**29**	**MAY**	**LEICESTERSHIRE (NOT FLOODLIT)**	**HEADINGLEY**
TUE	**31**	**MAY**	**DERBYSHIRE**	**HEADINGLEY**
FRI	**3**	**JUNE**	**DURHAM**	**HEADINGLEY**
MON	**6**	**JUNE**	**NOTTINGHAMSHIRE**	**HEADINGLEY**
WED	**8**	**JUNE**	**LANCASHIRE**	**HEADINGLEY**
Fri	10	June	Birmingham Bears	Edgbaston
Fri	17	June	Durham	Riverside
Sat	18	June	Derbyshire (not floodlit)	Chesterfield
Thu	23	June	Worcestershire	Worcester
Fri	24	June	Northamptonshire	Northampton
FRI	**1**	**JULY**	**BIRMINGHAM BEARS**	**HEADINGLEY**
Sun	3	July	Leicestershire (not floodlit)	Leicester
Wed	6-9	July	Quarter-Finals	TBC
Sat	*16*	*July*	*Finals Day*	*Edgbaston*

ROYAL LONDON ONE-DAY CUP (50 Overs)

TUE	**2**	**AUGUST**	**NORTHAMPTONSHIRE**	**YORK**
THU	**4**	**AUGUST**	**LANCASHIRE**	**YORK**
SUN	**7**	**AUGUST**	**WORCESTERSHIRE**	**SCARBOROUGH**
Wed	10	August	Glamorgan	Cardiff
Wed	17	August	Essex	Chelmsford
Fri	19	August	Kent	Canterbury
Sun	21	August	Derbyshire	Chesterfield
TUE	**23**	**AUGUST**	**HAMPSHIRE**	**SCARBOROUGH**
Fri	26	August	Quarter-Finals	TBC
Tue	30	August	Semi-Finals	TBC
Sat	*17*	*September*	*Final*	*Trent Bridge*

OTHER MATCHES

SAT	2-4	APRIL	LEEDS/BRADFORD UCCE	.......WEETWOOD
			(University Three-Day Friendly)	
Sun	31	July	Northumberland	....................TBC
			(National County 50-Over Friendly).	

INTERNATIONAL MATCHES PLAYED AT HEADINGLEY

THU	23-27	JUNE	THIRD TEST	...ENGLAND v. NEW ZEALAND
SUN	24	JULY	ODI	............ENGLAND v. SOUTH AFRICA

SECOND ELEVEN CHAMPIONSHIP
(All four-day matches)

MON	**2-5**	**MAY**	**LANCASHIRE**	....................**HOME, TBC**
SUN	**8-11**	**MAY**	**KENT**	............................**HOME, TBC**
Mon	20-23	June	Durham	.............................Richmondshire
Mon	27-30	June	Nottinghamshire	.... Nottinghamshire Sports Club, Lady Bay
MON	**4-7**	**JULY**	**ESSEX**	...........................**HOME, TBC**
Mon	11-14	July	Derbyshire	..................................Chesterfield
MON	**18-21**	**JULY**	**LEICESTERSHIRE**	...............**HOME, TBC**
Mon	12-15	September	Lancashire	....Blackpool

SECOND ELEVEN TWENTY20

Mon	16	May	Durham *(Two games)*	.................Away, TBC
MON	**23**	**MAY**	**LANCASHIRE**	....................**HOME, TBC**
WED	**25**	**MAY**	**LEICESTERSHIRE**	...............**HOME, TBC**
Fri	27	May	Derbyshire *(Two games)*	.................Chesterfield
Mon	30	May	Leicestershire	.....................................Leicester
Wed	1	June	Lancashire	....Blackpool
FRI	**3**	**JUNE**	**NOTTINGHAMSHIRE** *(Two games)*	.**WEETWOOD**
Thurs	9	June	Finals Day	....Arundel

Further fixtures and venues are to be confirmed.
Please visit www.yorkshireccc.com for more details

YORKSHIRE IN VITALITY WOMEN'S T20 (Group One North)

Mon	18	April	10.30am: North East Warriors	............................TBC
			1.30pm: Cumbria	
Sun	24	April	10.30am: Derbyshire	..................................TBC
			1.30pm: Nottinghamshire	
Mon	2	May	11.00am: Northern Rep XI	..........................TBC
			3.00pm: Lancashire	

THE HUNDRED, PRESENTED BY CAZOO

All fixture dates, aside from the first two which are standalone men's games, are men's and women's double-headers.

Date			Opponents	Venue
Fri	5	August	Manchester Originals	..................Old Trafford
TUE	**9**	**AUGUST**	**TRENT ROCKETS**	............**HEADINGLEY**
Thu	11	August	Oval Invincibles	..........................The Oval
SUN	**14**	**AUGUST**	**LONDON SPIRIT**	....**HEADINGLEY**
Fri	19	August	Birmingham Phoenix	....................Edgbaston
SUN	**21**	**AUGUST**	**MANCHESTER ORIGINALS**	...**HEADINGLEY**
Fri	26	August	Welsh Fire	....Cardiff
WED	**31**	**AUGUST**	**SOUTHERN BRAVE**	...........**HEADINGLEY**
Fri	2	September	Eliminator	..................................Southampton
Sat	3	September	Final	....Lord's

CHARLOTTE EDWARDS CUP (TWENTY 20)
NORTHERN DIAMONDS

Sat	14	May	Loughborough Lightning	Loughborough
Wed	18	May	Thunder	Sale
SAT	**21**	**MAY**	**SOUTHERN VIPERS**	**TBC**
SUN	**29**	**MAY**	**THUNDER**	**HEADINGLEY**
WED	**1**	**JUNE**	**LOUGHBOROUGH LIGHTNING**	**RIVERSIDE**
Sat	4	June	Southern Vipers	Southampton
Sat	11	June	Finals Day	Northampton

RACHAEL HEYHOE FLINT TROPHY (50 OVERS)
NORTHERN DIAMONDS

Sat	2	July	Thunder	Sale
SAT	**9**	**JULY**	**SUNRISERS**	**HEADINGLEY**
Sat	16	July	Central Sparks	Worcester
SAT	**23**	**JULY**	**LOUGHBOROUGH LIGHTNING**	**RIVERSIDE**
Fri	9	September	South East Stars	Beckenham
Sun	11	September	Western Storm	Taunton
SAT	**17**	**SEPTEMBER**	**SOUTHERN VIPERS**	**HEADINGLEY**
Wed	21	September	Qualifier	TBC
Sun	25	September	Final	Lord's

YORKSHIRE ACADEMY IN THE YPL NORTH LEAGUE

SAT	**23**	**APRIL**	**HARROGATE**	**WEETWOOD**
Sat	30	April	Woodhouse Grange	Woodhouse Grange
Mon	2	May	Driffield Town	Driffield
SAT	**7**	**MAY**	**CASTLEFORD**	**WEETWOOD**
Sat	14	May	York	Clifton Park
Sat	21	May	Sessay	Sessay
SAT	**28**	**MAY**	**BEVERLEY TOWN**	**WEETWOOD**
Sat	4	June	Scarborough	North Marine Road
SAT	**11**	**JUNE**	**CLIFTON ALLIANCE**	**WEETWOOD**
Sat	18	June	Sheriff Hutton Bridge	Sheriff Hutton Bridge
SAT	**25**	**JUNE**	**DRIFFIELD TOWN**	**WEETWOOD**
Sat	2	July	Acomb	Acomb
Sat	9	July	Harrogate	Harrogate
SAT	**16**	**JULY**	**WOODHOUSE GRANGE**	**WEETWOOD**
Sat	23	July	Castleford	Castleford
SAT	**30**	**JULY**	**YORK**	**WEETWOOD**
SAT	**6**	**AUGUST**	**SESSAY**	**WEETWOOD**
Sat	13	August	Beverley Town	Beverley
SAT	**20**	**AUGUST**	**SCARBOROUGH**	**WEETWOOD**
Sat	27	August	Clifton Alliance	Clifton All, York
MON	**29**	**AUGUST**	**SHERIFF HUTTON BRIDGE**	**WEETWOOD**
SAT	**3**	**SEPTEMBER**	**ACOMB**	**WEETWOOD**

THE COMPETITIONS EXPLAINED

LV= INSURANCE COUNTY CHAMPIONSHIP

After two summers of trialling the Conference system — three groups of six — it is back to two divisions for 2022.

Division One consists of eight teams, each playing each other home and away. The top team will be crowned the county champions.

Division Two consists of 10 teams, each also playing 14 games but not everyone home and away.

There is a two up, two down promotion and relegation system in place between the two divisions. Divisions are based on the 2019 finishing positions, pre-Coronavirus and the Conference experiment.

Yorkshire are in Division One, while Warwickshire are defending champions. There is no Bob Willis Trophy in 2022.

VITALITY BLAST

The counties are split into two regional groups of nine, with 14 games. Yorkshire will play the majority of their opponents home and away, but not all.

The top four teams in each table advance to the quarter-finals ahead of the traditional Finals Day, still at Edgbaston but in July this year.

The top two teams — four in total across the North and South — all win the right to host their quarter-final. Kent are the reigning champions

ROYAL LONDON ONE-DAY CUP

The counties have been split into two non-regionalised groups of nine. Each will play eight matches — four at home, four away.

The top three in each table advance to the knockout stages. The top team qualifies direct to the semi-final, while the second and third teams play each other in an effective quarter-final. The winners advance to the semi-final, with the final played at Trent Bridge.

Glamorgan are the defending champions.

THE HUNDRED, PRESENTED BY CAZOO

The ECB's new competition and new format is entering its second year. Each game will be 100 balls per side, both for the men and the women, with a number of different playing conditions within that.

In a regular campaign both genders play eight group fixtures, including their closest rivals twice. The Northern Superchargers usually play the Manchester Originals twice. For this summer alone, however, the women play only six group fixtures due to a busy schedule including England's involvement in the Commonwealth Games, so only the men will play the Originals twice in 2022.

Rounds one and two this summer are stand-alone men's fixtures before the remaining six are all men's and women's double headers.

The top team after the group stage advances directly into the final, while the second and third-placed teams play off in an Eliminator for the right to advance to the final.

The reigning men's champions are Southern Brave, while Oval Invincibles won the women's event in 2021.

RACHAEL HEYHOE FLINT TROPHY

The 50-over competition played between the eight women's Regional Centres of Excellence is into its third year.

Each team plays everybody else once in the group stage — non-regionalised. The Diamonds have four away games and three at home

The finals series is exactly the same as the Hundred. The top team after the group stage advances directly to the September 25 final, while the second and third-placed teams play off for the right to fight for the trophy. Southern Vipers have won both RHFT titles so far.

CHARLOTTE EDWARDS CUP

The women's regional T20 competition is into its second year, with South East Stars the 2021 winners.

The eight regions are split into two non-regionalised groups of four, with six group games — three at home and three away.

The champions will be decided at Finals Day.

The best-placed group winner advances directly to the final. Beforehand, the other group winner plays the best second-placed team as a means to qualify for the final.

Talent identification mission for The Dazzler

HOPES HIGH FOR ON-FIELD SUCCESS THIS SEASON

By Darren Gough, Interim Managing Director of Cricket

Excited to be back: ex-Yorkshire and England ace takes the helm.

I'm thrilled to be back at Yorkshire, having spent some of my fondest years here, from coming through the Academy to returning as captain in 2007.

The opportunity to be the Managing Director of Cricket was one I couldn't turn down, and I'm here to make a difference at this club.

Under very unique circumstances, my first job was to be a calming influence on our players following a very difficult period. I moved to put an interim team of coaches in place for the New Year to ensure that training could resume.

I'd like to thank Tim Boon, Paul Shaw, Cookie Patel, Ryan Sidebottom, Martin Speight, David Wainwright, Steve Harmison and Richard Waite, who have all helped us through this period. You will have seen that we advertised for a variety of permanent positions, and we had over 200 applicants across the coaching and medical roles. We followed a rigorous recruitment process, which included a points-based system and rounds of sifting through CVs and covering letters. This involved independent people to ensure the process was as inclusive as possible.

We were delighted that, following an interview process with eight potential candidates for the Head Coach role, the panel unanimously decided that Ottis Gibson was the best person for the job. Ottis has enjoyed a long and successful coaching career, winning a T20 World Cup as Head Coach of West Indies, an *Ashes* series as Bowling Coach of England and most recently spells with South Africa and Bangladesh. He has international playing experience, having played two Tests and 15 ODIs, and has represented Durham, Glamorgan and Leicestershire.

Ottis's knowledge and passion for county cricket was a huge factor in the decision to appoint him. His overall responsibility will be for performance and management of the first team, and he will be supported by two assistant coaches, Kabir Ali and Ali Maiden.

Following some exciting meetings with Sameen Rana, the Chief Operating Officer at Lahore Qalandars, we were delighted to agree a ground-breaking partnership with the Pakistan Super League team. As part of the partnership we have signed Haris Rauf for the first six Championship games. Haris has not played much red-ball cricket, but he is a serious talent with a lot of pace, and is hungry to improve his cricket in all formats. Haris will be a great addition to our squad.

We were also delighted to extend this partnership to South African franchise, the Momentum Multiply Titans. What excites me the most is the prospect of information sharing, player and coach development opportunities and a vast array of other components that will come from these partnerships.

Our pre-season has included time training in a marquee at Weetwoodas as well as a tour to Dubai in March. We feel this should give our players the optimum preparation for competitive action, with a couple of tough away games to look forward to at the start of the season at Bristol and Northampton.

Youth cricket is a big passion of mine and there is a lot going on at this moment. We are looking at how our county age-group systems are run, and have carried out a listening exercise with the parents and players from the boys' and girls' teams. We are focusing on how we can make our systems better, more inclusive and affordable for all.

We will be undertaking a new talent-identification programme this summer to find special talent that has been missed through our systems over the past three or four years. Hopefully, this will provide a good opportunity for many young players around the county.

My hopes are high for success on the field this season. We have a large and talented squad, but there are always uncertainties around what players will be available due to England commitments. Young players Matthew Fisher and Harry Brook have recently received international call-ups and could join England regulars such as Jonny Bairstow, Adil Rashid, Joe Root, Dawid Malan and Dom Bess. This makes it difficult to prepare with the uncertainty around availability, but it's certainly a positive that our players go on to play for England.

There are lots of reasons to be optimistic heading into this season, and I'm excited for what the future holds. I'm very much looking forward to seeing you all at the various grounds around Yorkshire, and hope that you enjoy a great summer of cricket.

Coach sees the ingredients to bake Yorkshire success

OTTIS GIBSON AIMS TO HIT THE GROUND RUNNING

By Graham Hardcastle

Ottis Gibson has set out his aims for Yorkshire in 2022, with the new coach in charge at Headingley admitting: "The ingredients are there for us to have some success, for sure."

Gibson has taken over from Andrew Gale, inheriting a very solid base to work from. While no trophy was secured in 2021 there were encouraging signs, notably in the Royal London Cup when a side shorn of many senior players due to the Hundred qualified for the knockouts. The performances of the younger players indicated a bright future.

"The squad assembled is a very good one," Gibson said in his first head coaching role with a county. "There is a really good mix of young and senior players. When the England players are available you have the Test captain, Jonny, Dawid Malan, Adil, David Willey and Dom Bess. Adam Lyth is also an international. Then, the younger players are very talented as well. That is one of the things that really drew me to the job."

Gibson is a two-time international coach with his home nation, the West Indies, and also South Africa, winning the T20 World Cup with the West Indies in 2012.

Appointed in late January, he officially started work with Yorkshire only on March 1 due to a prior agreement to be bowling coach for Multan Sultans in the Pakistan Super League through February, but soon shortly after his appointment he spoke on the phone with Steve Patterson and in person with T20 captain David Willey, a colleague at Multan.

"I have said this to David and Steve, 'I want to win'. That's my nature," continued the affable Bajan. "My career has been stacked with winning trophies and trying to win tournaments, World Cups, whatever. I'm sure everybody at the club wants to win, but not without making the environment enjoyable for everybody. The aim is to win the County Championship, the Blast, the one-day Cup. Every tournament we enter we want to win it for Yorkshire CCC."

Gibson references the environment, and his appointment follows a host of cricketing department departures on the back of accusations of discriminatory behaviour by former off-spinner Azeem Rafiq.

Gibson in his pomp: the Durham paceman peppers Dominic Cork, of Lancashire and England, in 2006.

Gibson, who still lives in Durham — the county he played for immediately prior to retirement in 2007, said: "It's obviously been a difficult time for everybody. A lot has happened. We have to try and make sure we clear what happened and make sure it doesn't happen again.

"That's part of my job and Darren's (Gough) and Lord Patel's. Everybody's in fact. I'm happy to be a part of that, to have those conversations and to make sure the dressing room environment is a healthy one for everybody to operate in.

"One of the key things about cricket is it affords you the opportunity to make friendships you wouldn't may be otherwise make. I still have friendships with people from when I played in South Africa in 1991.

"That is something I'm looking forward to over the next couple of years at Yorkshire, making friendships but having those honest conversations in the dressing room. We have to make sure it is a healthy place for players to come in and express themselves, play cricket and entertain the supporters who pay good money to sit in the stands and watch us."

Whatever tasks he faces with Yorkshire, it is clear the former international fast bowler is hugely excited about what lies ahead.

"Yorkshire is a huge club on the cricketing landscape in England," he said. "To get the opportunity to be the head coach there is unbelievable. I'm really looking forward to getting started and getting stuck in.

"The thing with Multan came before Yorkshire, so I wanted to fulfil that commitment. But a large part of me wanted to be at Yorkshire immediately, getting going."

NEW FACES ON THE BENCH

Kabir Ali — Assistant Coach

The former England seamer who played for Worcestershire, Hampshire and Lancashire and took exactly 500 first-class wickets during a 15-year playing career which ended in 2015.

Ali, right, played his only Test Match against South Africa at Headingley in 2003, and played the first of 14 One-Day-Internationals at the same venue, against Zimbabwe, later that summer.

The 41-year-old from a cricket-mad Birmingham family has since been work-

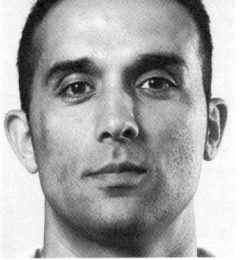

ing in a variety of bowling consultancy roles around the world, including with Royal Challengers Bangalore at the Indian Premier League.

He has been working with Warwickshire recently, and is the co-founder and director of cricket at the South Asian Cricket Academy, where his cousin Moeen is president.

Alastair Maiden — Assistant Coach

A Stourbridge-born former Durham University batter, Maiden, left, also played Minor Counties cricket for Staffordshire and Northumberland, making 10 first-class appearances with a best of 211 not out opening the batting in a University fixture for Durham against Somerset at Taunton in April 2005.

He has previously worked at both Durham as their second-team coach and Leicestershire as the head of their Academy, from where he joins after just over two years in position.

The 39-year-old was also the assistant coach of England's senior women's team for four years, including when they famously won the one-day World Cup on home soil in 2017.

Tom Smith — Second Team Coach

Arrives at Headingley with a reputation as one of the brightest coaching talents in England at present. The former Lancashire captain's near 300-game playing career was cut short in 2016 due to a long-standing back issue.

His move into coaching started as an assistant with Lancashire Thunder women in 2017. Tom, right, also held a similar position with England women that year. Now aged 36, he was appointed as Leicestershire's second-team coach at the start of 2018, and has since transitioned into their first-team assistant and bowling coach.

Player Awards 2021

Northern Diamonds. Players' Player of the Year: Linsey Smith; Fans' Player of the Year and Batter of the Year: Sterre Kalis; Bowler of the Year: Jenny Gunn; Fielder of the Year: Hollie Armitage.

Yorkshire Academy. Players' Player of the Year: Ciara Boaden; Coaches' Player of the Year: Emma Marlow.

Yorkshire Player of the Year. Players' Player of the Year, Members' Player of the Year, Young Player of the Year and Fielder of the Year: Harry Brook.

Yorkshire Academy. Player of the Year: Will Luxton

Howard Clayton Second XI Performance of the Year: George Hill (207 v. Gloucestershire at Bristol, Championship).

Yorkshire CCC departures

Senior management: Roger Hutton (Chair), Mark Arthur (Chief executive).

Coaches: Martyn Moxon (Director of Cricket), Andrew Gale (First Team Coach), Rich Pyrah (Assistant/Bowling Coach), Paul Grayson (Batting Coach), Ian Dews (Academy Director/Second Team coach), Richard Damms (Academy Head Coach).

Players: Mathew Pillans, Josh Poysden (both released at the end of their contracts).

Talent shared in historic link with Lahore Qalandars

YORKSHIRE SCHOLARSHIPS GIVE OPPORTUNITY TO ALL

By Graham Hardcastle

Yorkshire will this summer offer four new scholarships to two male and two female cricketers. As part of a countywide search for undiscovered talent the county, in partnership with Pakistan Super League champions Lahore, are opening the opportunity to all aged 18 or over.

In December they announced a link-up with Lahore as part of a vision to improve access to the sport. A friendly match between the two sides was pencilled in for January before being postponed due to Coronavirus restrictions, but the two clubs are planning many activities, including the chance for young players to train at both Headingley and in Lahore.

Talent sharing will also take place. Harry Brook has just played in the most recent edition of the PSL for Lahore, while fast bowler Haris Rauf will be a Yorkshire overseas player this summer.

The county are particularly keen to emulate Lahore's famous player development programme, from which Rauf was discovered having been brought in for trial after playing tape-ball cricket while working as a shop salesman in Rawalpindi.

Yorkshire chair Lord Patel said: "The work the Lahore Qalandars do, both on and off the pitch, is remarkable and can serve as a benchmark for clubs around the world – ours included – for how best to spot, foster and support talent at all levels in the game of cricket.

"The player-development programme is an incredible achievement – breaking the mould for how teams can be created within our sport, and demonstrating that through offering access and support great cricketing talent can be found from all backgrounds.

"Over the coming months this, coupled with scholarships and new opportunities and experiences for Academy players, will represent an exciting step toward a Yorkshire CCC that is welcoming and supportive to all."

The first Yorkshire-wide trials will give players the chance to impress a selection panel led by interim managing director of cricket Darren Gough, who will be joined by representatives from the Qalandars coaching team. The most talented players will be divided into four teams to play a Finals Day. From these games the best four cricketers — male and female — will be chosen for scholarships with YCCC, including the opportunity to travel to Lahore and train at the Qalandars' elite high performance centre.

Lahore's chief operating officer, Sameen Rana, said: "We are delighted to have built a partnership with Yorkshire.

"Our PDP has been an essential tool to discovering new talent in Pakistan and opening up the sport to those who previously felt unable to access it. We are looking forward to sharing our learnings as the partnership develops."

Lahore already have a similar link-up with the Melbourne Stars in Australia's Big Bash. During the most recent BBL the Stars fielded a trio of Qalandars as overseas players in Rauf, fellow fast bowler Ahmed Daniyal and spinner Syed Faridoun.

HARIS RAUF: Key signing

When announcing the partnership with Lahore, Gough said: "I am thrilled to welcome the exceptionally talented Haris Rauf to our club. I am also excited by the opportunity to learn from the inspirational player-development programme.

"I have spoken in the past about my passion for developing accessible pathways to cricket. For many people from a background like mine, cricket isn't seen as an option, with the associated costs and access to facilities creating real barriers to entry.

"This partnership is an opportunity to take the blueprint the Qalandars has developed to such a success and work with them to define how that can be used to provide access for potential players from across Yorkshire."

Gough's opposite number at Lahore is, likewise, a former international fast bowler in Aqib Javed.

He added: "The way in which we have worked and continue to work with clubs around the world when it comes to exchanging players should be a model that many clubs look to follow. It allows for increased diversity, the sharing of skills and expertise and all of these lead to positive cultures in which excellence thrives."

In February it was announced that the Titans from South Africa had also joined to make the partnership a three-way one.

All-round Diamond's shine may never be matched

GOLDEN GIRL WHO STANDS WITH YORKSHIRE LEGENDS

Special Feature By Graham Hardcastle

Katherine Brunt. Yorkshire and England legend. *Hero* and *inspiration* are two other words which spring to mind when describing a fast bowling all-rounder who has sailed past 500 career wickets and racked up over 5,000 runs in her 18-year career and is still going strong.

Brunt's achievements in the game include County Championship, Ashes and World Cup triumphs added to countless individual records and honours, giving her a rightful place among the plethora of *White Rose* greats celebrated in the men's game. Legend!

The women's game hasn't been given the prominence it so richly deserves in cricketing circles down the years, but things are changing for the better. The first edition of the Hundred was played last summer in front of huge crowds, and 2022 promises to be another landmark year for Brunt and co, who are not only bidding to achieve success on the field, but also pave the way for stars of the future. Hero and inspiration!

In the past few months Brunt has been featuring in the *Ashes* in Australia and the one-day World Cup in New Zealand. England lost the *Ashes*, while the result of the World Cup was unknown at the time of publication of this Yearbook. In July she plans to play for England when T20 cricket is introduced into the Commonwealth Games in Birmingham for the first time.

This seemed the perfect time to sit down with the Barnsley-born superstar and delve deeply into a remarkable career and life: "I'm the youngest of six, but I grew up with my brother, Daniel, who is the next youngest," she says. "He was three-and-a-half years older than me, which is a decent amount between a boy and a girl. He was also stronger and taller. He was the person who was always there.

"The others, there's quite a decent gap between us. I barely know my eldest brother. He's 50, and moved away quite quickly. The others were sort of around, but too old for me to play with. But Daniel was the one, and luckily he was quite athletic.

"He's 6'2, strong and loves all sports — the type of lad who can turn his hand to anything. He plays off scratch at golf. In terms of an inspiration, he was it, and he was the kick-starter for the career I've had in many ways. Always aspiring to be better than someone who is off

Brunt the bowler: Katherine in action at Headingley in 2021 against Central Sparks in the Rachael Heyhoe Flint Trophy.
(Photo: Will Palmer)

scratch at golf is a decent aspiration!

"I was always losing, was always second fiddle and would always be annoyed at losing. But I got damn close.

"It would be everything. Fighting, wrestling, playing basketball in the garden, one hand one bounce. Anything we did, I wanted to be better than him. It was a really good challenge for me.

"I was good at football as well, and played a bit for Barnsley at one stage. It was all against lads. There were no girls anywhere. I started to think I was weird.

"I'm not posh. Whereas Nat (Sciver, her fiancee and England teammate) played tennis and hockey I never played any of that or netball or volleyball because they weren't at my school. I was playing the rough and ready stuff like football and rugby, cricket. And when I did it was always with the lads. That was very challenging."

While it may not be in competition with her brother Daniel, Brunt does now play golf in her spare time, as a lot of cricketers do. Fellow Yorkshire star Lauren Winfield-Hill is a keen golfer, to name just one.

"My brother did ask me whether I had a handicap," she chuckled. "I don't, because I'm here, there and everywhere all year round, and don't have time to join a club and dedicate myself to getting a handicap. But I've been lucky enough to play some amazing courses. In January (2021) we played at Jack's Point in Queenstown, when we were touring New Zealand. That was absolutely unbelievable. Even the pros say it's solid to play on. It was so open and hilly and the views were amazing."

So, let's get stuck into the cricket, starting with her Yorkshire career. Brunt's first recorded appearance wearing the *White Rose* came in September 1999, an Under-15s 30-over final against East Sussex at Milton Keynes. Brunt opened the bowling in a nine-wicket win, returning 0-31 from six overs. Salliann Briggs, currently head coach of the Tasmanian and Hobart Hurricanes women's teams, opened the batting for Yorkshire that day. "I'm not sure whether that would have been my first game or not," she said. "I asked my mum recently, 'When was it that I started playing for Yorkshire?' One of the earliest photos I have is when I was playing at Ampleforth College. I think I was about 14."

Ampleforth College and Briggs are a part of Brunt's journey, given it amusingly brought about one of her nicknames, Nunny. As part of a prank during a residential cricket trip for which Katherine was blamed she was carted off by the monks in charge: "Everyone thought I'd been taken away to repent my sins, so that's where the nickname came from."

When you delve into Brunt's career some statistics stand out. England's leading one-day international wicket-taker with 163, for example, a haul which is the fourth best in the world. One which catches the eye is that she has played exactly 100 times across List A and T20 for Yorkshire's senior side, the last of which came at the start of 2019. She claimed 95 wickets and scored 2,048 runs, but that statistic does not include Yorkshire Diamonds or Northern Diamonds appearances.

More importantly, however, she helped to secure a County Championship title in 2015, resulting in a trip to Buckingham Palace to receive the trophy from the late HRH The Duke of Edinburgh.

"I've got loads of great memories, but that's the one," she recalled. "Yorkshire had been in the Premiership, then had seven retirements. So we went down to Division Two and then Three. I was part of the rebirth.

"The previous squad had done something stupid like win seven titles in a row, but all retired at once, and things went downhill. But we fought back up the leagues to win it. We'd been on this massive journey from being amazing to having to rebuild and win the Championship again.

"We took it from Kent, who would win it every year. The day at the Palace was really amazing. I loved it."

Another highlight for Brunt was her first appearance at Headingley: "I can't even remember the game," she admitted. "It was just that I got to play at Headingley, which was a massive ambition of mine."

This brings us back to an earlier comment about the women's game not getting the prominence it deserves. Of those 100 Yorkshire appearances none were at Headingley and only two at current county headquarters — Hove and Canterbury. According to *CricketArchive* her first career appearance at Headingley came in the opening game of the Kia Super League in 2016 while playing for the Yorkshire Diamonds.

"The treatment of the women's game hasn't been right across most of the counties," she said. "Thankfully, it has improved, and significantly over the last couple of years. I'm happy with the direction it's going, but it's been long overdue."

Brunt the batter: Katherine swings for four in her innings of 43 against Central Sparks at Headingley in the Rachael Heyhoe Flint Trophy. *(Photo: Will Palmer)*

Talking of the Kia Super League's first season, Brunt claimed a hat-trick in a Yorkshire Diamonds win over Lancashire Thunder at Old Trafford: "That was good fun," she smiled. "It's always nice beating Lancashire, and contributing made it even better."

Brunt's near 250-game England career started with a Test Match debut against New Zealand in August 2004 at Scarborough. She claimed three wickets in a weather-affected draw. Since then, she has won everything there is to win at international level — aside from Commonwealth Games gold. That will be achieved this summer with a bit of luck.

At the time of writing Brunt has taken 312 international wickets across all formats, added to 1,695 runs. She has bests of 6-69 and 72 not out in Test and ODIs respectively. A three-time England Cricketer of the Year, an ICC ranked No.1 bowler in the world in 2011, she was in the first group of England women's players centrally contracted in 2014.

"It's the proudest thing I've ever done in my life," she said of her international career. "I'm not a mother yet, and I don't know when that will be. But I've had the time of my life from when I set out with England as an 18 or 19-year-old. I didn't look back from that moment on. I set out to be the best in the world at what I did, and I also set out to achieve certain things, which I've done.

"I've got lots of different memories with lots of different feelings. The 2017 (one-day) World Cup final win against India at Lord's was one of those unbelievable, wow things. We'd all worked ridiculously hard to get to that moment, and it wasn't by chance. I don't think we've ever worked as hard as we did leading up to that tournament.

"When we won it in 2009 we just happened to be the best team in the world, and knew it. Whereas in 2017 we weren't the best team in the world. What we were was the hardest-working team in the world. We knew we would have a good shot. What happened on that day, winning it in front of a sold-out Lord's, was more of an outer-body experience.

"The proudest moment for myself would probably be my first Ashes Test Match, a draw at Hove in 2005. I didn't know what international cricket was all about then, the stress and anxiety that comes with it. I was just a kid, and was free and was doing my best."

In her second Ashes Test, a few weeks later at Worcester, she claimed career-best match figures of 9-52, and scored 52 batting at 10 in the first innings of a victory: "I got nine wickets in the match and should have had 12. I had two dropped catches and a really shocking lbw decision turned down."

The tone of her voice indicates frustration to this day: "Absolutely," she conceded. "It took away the one 10-for I would probably ever get in Test cricket. The pitches we play on are like the M25 now. I remember every decision I was never given."

Brunt has not had things easy. It has not been far from the exact opposite. She has battled constantly against injury, mainly to her back, and she had to miss the 2007-8 series Down Under. But she continues to steam in with an enviable determination to win games for her country and now the Northern Diamonds and be the best cricketer she can be.

"I think that goes back to just being that eight-year-old kid being slapped about at school and those battles with my brother and stuff," she said. "I just have this huge amount of resilience and robustness that I haven't actually seen in many people. I'm glad that I went through all of that crap because it's definitely given me what I needed to get through a long and hard career. I don't know how far I would have got without that. It's probably my favourite attribute, I guess."

Brunt describes that attribute as a "super power". She does so when discussing comparisons between herself and fiancee, Nat, who, aged 29, is also one of the world's best all-rounders.

"Neither of us like being compared because I'm a bowling all-rounder and she's a batting all-rounder," said Brunt before discussing those super powers. "I'm robust and resilient, a hard fighter. She's more like an assassin, and is a great leader. She also has the patience of a saint — all of which will make her England's next captain, I have no doubt."

The pair first crossed paths at Loughborough University, with Brunt recalling: "It's been about 10 years since she came on the scene, and I

How it all began: Katherine with red-capped brother Daniel

coached her when she first did. When she was at Loughborough I was head coach of the women's side there. I coached her, Amy Jones, Beth Langston, Tammy Beaumont, Lauren, all these lot.

"One of the coaches said to me, 'Have you seen this Natalie Sciver, she bowls around 70mph?' I said, 'Oh, we'll see about that!' I saw her in her first trial, and said, 'She doesn't bowl 70mph, what's he on about?' I knew he was just trying to wind me up.

"But I could still see how much talent she had, and knew she was one I would be looking out for and would be hot on my tail. Straightaway, we all became really good friends, which has remained with us being in the England squad together.

"From that moment on, definitely fitness and physically, I tried to be better than them all the time. I managed that up until about two years ago when I started to slow down. It was important for me because I needed that fire up my backside."

At 36 Brunt is clearly coming to the closing stages of her career. But has there been a specific time earmarked to hang up the boots?

"Never!" she laughed before taking a more considered tone. "I've literally thought one thing, and then another, and it just changes. I said I would never play in another 50-over World Cup because it's so hard and draining. And I spent the winter preparing for one. Then I thought I would be this T20 specialist who retires from ODIs and Tests. But that didn't happen either. Then the Commonwealth Games came along, and I thought, 'That would be so cool to play in the very first one'. Things keep happening like the Hundred. I thought, 'Well, I've got to be a part of that as well'. It's hard to walk away from these things.

"I guess you could say I have my eye on the Commonwealth Games as the time to sit down. We'll see. I've changed my mind many times."

One thing is clear: her personal relationship has helped to extend her career: "I would say so, yes," Brunt said. "She's one of the main reasons I'm around. If she wasn't here I'd be on my own for eight months of the year, and I'm needy. I can't cope with that.

"I don't think this would work for a lot of people. Myself and Nat are in each other's pockets all day every day. There is literally no time apart. A lot of couples wouldn't be able to cope with that. But it just works for us. We don't argue, we don't need time apart. We are very lucky. And that's what makes playing in the same team so awesome. We just love each other's company. I think we surprise a lot of the team, actually. I think the coaches worry that on a big tour like the Ashes we'll have this massive argument and won't speak to each other, we'll both play rubbish and we'll lose. But it never happens."

What comes next after her England career? Nothing is set in stone aside from continuing to indulge her passion for property development.

"I've been doing a lot of property developing for the last eight years," she said. "It was after my last major surgery that I had a wake-up call and had to find something really quick outside the game.

"I have got my level-three coaching qualification, but I soon realised that my passion didn't really lie in most sides of coaching. I like the specific side of it where I'd get a couple of 16 or 17-year-olds who had some natural talent and really wanted to play for England. I've done coaching with people who see it as more of a hobby, and I'm less passionate about that. I'd rather do consultancy or mentoring.

"I'm not sure I could go full time unless it was a job like the Diamonds coach or the Superchargers. I'm not definitely saying, 'No'. But my passion lies in property. It was hard to find something I love as much as cricket. You can't match it, but you can get close."

What about the possibility of returning to play for the Northern Diamonds post her international career? "If I did that it would be as a leg-spinner. I'm all right, you know. I can't say whether I would or not, because sometimes when you retire you retire."

Whenever Brunt does retire it will be a sad moment for Yorkshire and England Cricket. Equally, it will be time to celebrate and sing from the rooftops about a player whose achievements will be difficult to match.

Review of the Year 2021

HIGH HOPES DOWN THE DRAIN, BUT AWARDS FLOW TO BROOK

By Andrew Bosi

A year of steady progress ended in disappointment with defeats against a side also rebuilding in Nottinghamshire and one which leapfrogged Yorkshire to take both the Championship and Bob Willis Trophy titles in Warwickshire.

No side won more matches in the Conference section of the Championship than Yorkshire's five, and they were the only county to qualify for the first division and knockout stages of the Vitality Blast and Royal London one-day Cup. The achievement in the RL50, including victory over eventual winners Glamorgan to seal their knockout progression, was perhaps the greatest of these, given the loss of so many players to the Hundred. Younger players made headway, and some, notably George Hill and Harry Duke, carried this into the Championship.

Harry Brook made great strides with 1,283 runs across four-day and T20 cricket, and won all manner of end-of-season awards, including being named as Yorkshire's Members' and Players' Player of the Year. He was also the club's Young Player of the Year, gaining similar awards from the Professional Cricketers Association and the Cricket Writers Club. Jordan Thompson was the only player to score 400 runs and take 40 wickets in the County Championship.

Matthew Fisher recorded his best figures, 9-64 against Somerset at Scarborough, and Ben Coad and Steve Patterson were reliable if not quite as potent as in previous seasons. The slip cordon of Tom Kohler-Cadmore, Adam Lyth and Brook was the finest in the country, bringing off some stunning catches.

Had Yorkshire won against Hampshire at the Ageas Bowl in the opening round of the late-season Division One campaign, when bad light prevented a rampant Thompson from taking the 10th wicket, the loss to Warwickshire would not have ended their title hopes, instead providing the intensity in that last game which seemed to bring out the best in the side. Yorkshire came from behind in several games, and the ability to seize the day bodes so well for the future.

Yorkshire struggled in the opening game, first to finish off Glamorgan's first innings and, after the batting failed, lost both opening

Great strides: Harry Brook, who dominated the award presentations after his Championship and T20 batting in 2021, runs and dives to catch Derbyshire's Matthew Critchley off Dom Bess in their Vitality Blast clash at Headingley.

bowlers — Coad and Fisher — to injury. A better second-innings performance secured a draw after snow had curtailed play on day three.

Patterson and company then won their two games in the south against Kent and Sussex — sadly, still no supporters were allowed due to Coronavirus protocols — but the defining moment was surely the one-run win at home to Northamptonshire when the day was well and truly seized. The wickets were shared among the bowlers, but the run-out of Northamptonshire captain Ricardo Vasconcelos, effected by David Willey, and Patterson's cool head at the end to remove Wayne Parnell were decisive in this narrowest of wins.

Weather ruined the next two games, although the presence of Joe Root with a sublime 99 on a tricky pitch at Cardiff was the difference between the two sides and raised hopes of a win even after the loss of time, only for more rain to limit the last day to a single session.

Yorkshire paid dearly for the decision to bat first at Old Trafford, but again fought hard from an almost impossible position, and might have saved the game had Coad not been adjudged caught close to the end.

Sussex's over-reliance on youth may have contributed to their fourth-day collapse. They seemed well on top on day one, but the tail failed to wag next day, and Yorkshire secured maximum batting points thanks to a rare appearance from Dawid Malan, who brilliantly made 199.

Yorkshire then completed a second double, this time over Northamptonshire at Wantage Road. Again, they came from behind, Hill alone offering resistance and the home side on course for a big lead at the end of day one. A better performance in the field limited that to 12 runs, but again the new ball undermined Yorkshire before Harry Brook backed up the excellent work of Dom Bess to turn the game with the first of two summer centuries. The target for the hosts was only 206, but the force was with Yorkshire after this innings, and they prevailed. Bess's first-innings 7-43 represented Yorkshire's best figures by a spinner since Phil Carrick took 7-35 against Glamorgan at Sheffield in 1978.

With other results going Yorkshire's way, they topped the group and were assured of Division One status.

The loss of much time due to rain and then drainage problems cost Yorkshire dear in the return *Roses* fixture, because the only points to be carried forward were those secured against the side going through with them. Defeat at Old Trafford meant their five wins counted for little and they began in Division One with the fewest points of anybody.

But they dominated Hampshire on their home ground. And when they beat Somerset in two days they had leapt from bottom of the table to top. Then came the disappointment against Warwickshire at Headingley to end their chances of silverware. For the final round some England players were allowed to appear for their counties, while all five of Yorkshire's red-ball internationals were not. Patterson and Gary Ballance were also missing through injury and illness, handing Coad the honour of leadership. Lyth's welcome return to form and his third century of the season, which propelled him to the head of the runs chart with 819, restored pride from being bowled out for 73 in the first innings.

In many ways the passage to the quarter finals of the Blast was the smoothest of the three qualifications. Frequent team changes were forced on the side. Jonny Bairstow, Mark Stoneman, Lockie Ferguson, Adil Rashid and Matthew Waite appeared, none of whom played in the Championship. Yorkshire secured a home tie against Sussex, although the use of Headingley for the Hundred meant they played it at the Riverside, Chester-le-Street. They seemed to have posted a winning score, 177-5, only for uncharacteristic lapses in the field to cost them dear. The wait for a place in Finals Day goes on for another year. Curiously, while Northern teams dominated the top 10 places in the Championship all four quarter-finals went south.

While journalists with an enthusiasm for the game enjoyed a long season of gripping cricket, the Covid restrictions and other events limited the amount of cricket available to the spectator. Yorkshire were by no means worst affected. Ask members of Essex, Durham and Middlesex. But, though the format of the Championship provided a compelling finale for those in Division One the desire to win produced some bowler-friendly pitches so that few games went into the final session on the fourth day. So it is back to two divisions in 2022.

RECORD-BREAKER: Joe Root on the way to his 121 in the Third Test v. India at Headingley. In the calendar year 2021 the England Test captain scored 1,708 Test runs, the most by an Englishman. Only Pakistan's Mohammad Yousuf and West Indian Sir Viv Richards have scored more. Root registered two double-hundreds, including one in his 100th Test against India at Chennai at the start of the year, and four further centuries, ensuring he was named ICC Test Cricketer of the Year.

RUEING THE ROOT: Joe holds his head as younger brother Billy, right, gets his bowling away to complete a century for Glamorgan in Yorkshire's opening 2021 County Championship fixture at Headingley.

SUPERSTAR: Leg-spinning magician Adil Rashid reached two career milestones during England's five-match January T20 series against the West Indies in Barbados. In the first game he played his 200th international across all formats, and in the last bagged his 300th international wicket. Rashid is ranked the world's fourth best T20 bowler by the ICC.

WINTER WONDERLAND: Groundsmen rush on to cover the Headingley square as snow forces the early abandonment of the third day of the opening-round County Championship game against Glamorgan on April 10.

AND BREATHE: What a victory! Steve Patterson and his teammates celebrate the winning wicket of Wayne Parnell as Yorkshire beat Northamptonshire by one run in a thriller at Headingley in May.

SAFE HANDS: Tom Kohler-Cadmore helps Ben Coad to dismiss Australian Travis Head with a catch at first slip in Yorkshire's June Championship win over Sussex at Headingley as Harry Duke watches.

NORTHERN DIAMONDS 2021: The squad lines up for the Rachael Heyhoe Flint Trophy Final v. Southern Vipers at Northampton. Back row, left to right: Phil Lee (sports psychologist); James Carr (Director of Cricket); Beth Langston, Phoebe Graham, Leah Dobson, Linsey Smith, Hollie Armitage, Jenny Gunn, Katie Levick, Ami Campbell, Jen McDowell (Media Support); Harrison Allen (team analyst) and Danielle Hazell (head coach). Front row: Sarah Hattie (head physio); Richard Waite (performance coach); Bess Heath, Ella Telford, Rachel Slater, Rachel Hopkins, Sterre Kalis and Isaac Leung (head of strength and conditioning). *(Photo: DAVID VOKES)*

BUCKET LIST TON: Yorkshire hero Lauren Winfield-Hill, who had always dreamt of scoring a century on her home ground at Headingley. She achieves it with a superb 110 in a narrow opening-day Rachael Heyhoe-Flint Trophy defeat for Northern Diamonds v. Central Sparks.

ON THE ATTACK: Bess Heath, one of four newly contracted Northern Diamonds professionals for 2022, bats for Yorkshire women in a T20 friendly v. North East Warriors at Harrogate. **BELOW:** England wicket-keeping legend Sarah Taylor nearly hangs on to a stunner on debut for Northern Diamonds v. South East Stars. Taylor came out of retirement to answer the call following the injury and unavailability of Bess Heath and Lauren Winfield-Hill. *(Photos: JOHN HEALD)*

YORKSHIRE COLTS THRIVE IN SHORN RL CUP SQUAD

By Graham Hardcastle

Yorkshire's Royal London Cup campaign of 2021 may be looked back on in years to come as vitally important, given the exposure it gave to a raft of up-and-coming players.

No silverware, but definite signs of encouragement as the Vikings made it to the knockout stages of a 50-over competition shorn of many senior players across all counties due to the Hundred being played at the corresponding time. A defeat at Essex in the semi-final eliminator tie — an effective quarter-final — came two days after a remarkable victory over eventual champions Glamorgan at Cardiff.

The likes of Harry Duke, George Hill, Will Luxton and Matthew Revis — there are others to add to that list — all shone and demonstrated that they have the ability to prosper at first-team level.

In many ways the month-long competition between July 22 and August 19 was as settled a period of the summer as there was for Yorkshire's young players. Coronavirus had a significant impact on both the Academy's Yorkshire Premier League North campaign and the Second-team programme.

The Seconds reached Finals Day in their T20 competition, only to be beaten in the semi-final by hosts Sussex at Arundel. Sussex fielded a team including Phil Salt, Travis Head, Ravi Bopara, Stuart Meaker and Mitch Claydon, while Yorkshire's experience was limited to Ben Coad, Duanne Olivier and Mat Pillans. There was no 50-over competition, while the Championship programme was disrupted by Coronavirus issues, with matches cancelled or interrupted.

The Academy had to curtail their involvement in the YPL North, playing no matches beyond July 31. They finished second in the table, decided by average points per completed game, behind champions Castleford with eight wins from 13 games.

The Seconds started the summer with a Championship game against Gloucestershire at Bristol, a drawn fixture which saw Will Fraine and Hill share a brilliant 224 for the third wicket as the visitors recorded a first-innings total of 602-8 declared. Fraine made 186 and Hill 207 to underpin the county's highest-ever total at second-team level.

"I think we genuinely made the best of what cricket we had," outgoing Academy head coach Richard Damms said in summary of the chal-

Record-breakers: George Hill, left, and Will Fraine who shared a stand of 224 for the third wicket for Yorkshire v. Gloucestershire in the Second Eleven Championship at Bristol as the visitors amassed their highest-ever total of 602-8 declared. Hill made 207 and Fraine 186

lenges faced at second-team and Academy level and the quality of cricket produced. Yorkshire were without 10 senior players in the Royal London Cup because of the Hundred — Bairstow, Kohler-Cadmore, Lyth, Rashid, Root, Willey, Malan, Brook, Fisher and Thompson. Head coach Andrew Gale was also part of the Northern Superchargers coaching team, leaving his assistant, Rich Pyrah, to take charge.

There were two groups and three qualifiers from each. The top two teams went through directly to the semi-final, while the second and third teams in each group played off for the right to face them. Yorkshire won four of eight group games, lost two and had two rained-off No Results.

Yorkshire lost their opening game against Surrey at Scarborough before bouncing back superbly with a victory over Leicestershire at Grace Road. Wicket-keeper Duke opened the batting, and brilliantly led a chase of 328 with 125 off 130 balls, helped out chiefly by Hill's unbeaten 90. They shared 172 for the third wicket.

At 19 years and 322 days, Duke — in only his second one-day game — was the youngest Yorkshire player to make a List A century since Sachin Tendulkar at 19 years, 100 days against Lancashire in 1992. Matthew Waite had claimed his maiden five-wicket haul, 5-59 in Leicestershire's innings.

A No Result against Northamptonshire at Scarborough followed, but with enough time for 18-year-old Academy captain Will Luxton to hit an

Wicket-keeper on the chase: Harry Duke, whose 125 off 130 balls and stand of 172 with George Hill snatched victory at Leicester

excellent rearguard 68 off 85 balls to help them to a recovery from 69-6 to 222 all out. Rain came with Northamptonshire 2-0 after five balls of their reply.

A rain-affected loss to Somerset at Taunton was followed by a high-scoring win over Warwickshire at York's Clifton Park. Matthew Waite crashed 42 off 16 to lift Vikings to 320-7, hitting three fours and three sixes as the last over from Ethan Brookes went for a whopping 32.

The Bears replied with a battling 281, including three wickets apiece for Ben Coad and Hill. In Yorkshire's innings Hill (64) Gary Ballance (54) and Jonny Tattersall (70) contributed significantly.

There was minimal play in a No Result against Nottinghamshire at the same venue before rain disrupted the following game against Derbyshire at Chesterfield. But not enough to prevent Yorkshire from securing a 10-over win to put them on course for the knockout stages. Derbyshire posted a competitive 108-6, only for Fraine to crash a sensational 69 off 32 balls to make the target look minute. On the way to that total the opener reached 50 off 19 — the Vikings' fastest half-century in List A cricket.

Yorkshire knew that a win against Glamorgan at Cardiff in their final Group B fixture would give them a great chance of finishing third and qualifying for the knockouts. A defeat would eliminate them, while there was an outside chance they could fail to qualify even with a win if results and net run-rate went against them elsewhere.

What followed was one of the most remarkable games of the summer.

On a turgid pitch the Vikings, invited to bat, recovered from 88-4 and 132-7 to post a competitive 230 all out, which was underpinned by Tattersall's calming 53 and Waite's busy 44 down the order.

In reply Glamorgan looked in an unassailable position at 180-1 in the 42nd over, but they lost seven wickets for 43 in a collapse which saw Hill claim 3-49 from 10 overs of medium pace change-ups. At 226-8

Yorkshire had won by four runs to set up a trip to Chelmsford. Three more wins and this young side would be champions.

It wasn't to be, as a strong Essex side fielding Sir Alastair Cook, Tom Westley, Ryan ten Doeschate, Adam Wheater and Simon Harmer sealed a relatively straightforward win. Young opener Josh Rymell's 121 — his maiden first-team century — underpinned 317-7 before Yorkshire were bowled out for 188 inside 39 overs in reply.

Coach Pyrah said: "To qualify for that Essex game ahead of some counties who had full-strength teams available was great. But, for me, the biggest positive was young cricketers playing in the first team and performing.

Run to earth: Matthew Waite, who bagged his maiden five-for v. Leicestershire Foxes

"We all know these lads have talent. They can play as much second-team cricket as they want, but 10 or so games in the first team in a month is absolutely invaluable. And it wasn't as if it was just one or two of them who performed. Everyone carried us through at some point.

"I remember the game at Chesterfield against Derby. That really stood out for me. It rained and got down to a 10-over game. We were unsure whether to bat or bowl. So we asked a couple of the lads and they said, 'Just let them get what they want, and we'll chase it down'. For young players to talk like that is amazing, and shows they have no fear.

"I firmly believe that from every single game, win or lose, there were positives. We lost the toss both games at Scarborough, where it nibbles around early and then flattens out. But we rebuilt through the likes of Matty Revis and Will Luxton. Not only that, the lads grew as people as well as players, which was really special to see.

"From a wider perspective, it wasn't just development for Yorkshire. It was development for players around the country, which is great for English cricket moving forwards. I definitely would give the competition the thumbs up!"

COUNTY AGE GROUPS 2021

The summer was again affected by Coronavirus cases among Yorkshire and opposing players and staff, resulting in many cancellations.

Under 10s: Thirteen inter and county matches were played, a mixture of 30-35 over and T20 games. George Lamb, with 61 not out v. Staffordshire, Jack Kettleborough 51 (retired) v. Warwickshire, and Freddie Long 5-2 v. Warwickshire were the standout performances.

Under 11s: Twenty-three games were played across the Tykes (11) and Phoenix (12) teams at this level, a mixture of 35-40 over games and T20s. Louis Veazay, with 57 v. Nottinghamshire, Safiullah Abrar 5-19 v. Phoenix, Oliver Shepherd 75 v. Nottinghamshire, Alex Davis 5-5 v. Tykes were the standout performances.

Under 12s: The Tykes and Phoenix teams played nine games apiece, a mixture of 40-45 overs and T20 games. The highlight of the season was the Rugby School Festival, where Yorkshire were beaten by Warwickshire in a close encounter on the final day having won their previous matches.

Under 13s: Twenty-three games were played. Like the Under 12s, the highlight of the programme was the Rugby School Festival, where a loss to Nottinghamshire was followed by wins against Essex, Staffordshire and Warwickshire. Standout performances were Aarush Shinde's 106 v. Northumberland and 100 not out v. Cumbria, Peter Greenfield 100 not out v. Staffordshire and Arjun Samanth 8-22 v. Cumbria.

Under 14s: A busy schedule saw the 21 games played across a 25-day period, a mixture of two-day, 50-over and T20 matches. Several players made the step-up to play in the Under 15s and Futures teams. The outstanding performances came from Will Bennison with 192 v. Warwickshire and 5-47 v. Lancashire.

Under 15s: Seventeen games, this programme being the worst affected by Covid cancellations. There were a number of standout performances, the best coming from Rohan Ratnalingham with 125 not out v. Durham and Josh Hen-Boisen 5-14 v. Northumberland. Several Under 15s progressed to play for the Futures side.

Futures: This was a new concept aimed at providing cricket for boys who had left the Under 15s and CAG system but whom it was felt could be late developers. It would also give younger players more chance to develop. Fifteen games were played, the outstanding performances being Nico Nicola's 158 v. Warwickshire and Will Bennison 8-48 v.

Warwickshire. Eight players went on to represent Yorkshire's Academy/Under 18s side.

In early 2022 Yorkshire's head of county age-group cricket, Jim Love, the former Yorkshire and England batter, moved into a newly created role as a mentor and advisor to the Academy at Headingley.

James Martin, the Yorkshire Cricket Board's head of region for East Yorkshire, has replaced Love on an interim basis until September, when a permanent position will be advertised.

Record-breaking Kohler-Cadmore

Tom Kohler-Cadmore, left, enjoyed a memorable December as his sides claimed silverware in both the Abu Dhabi T10 League and the (Sri) Lanka Premier League.

And the Yorkshire batter was very much to the fore.

Playing for Deccan Gladiators, he scored 96 in Abu Dhabi, the highest score in the competition's five-season history. He was Deccan's leading run-scorer with 288 in 12 matches.

He went straight to Sri Lanka, and posted the highest score of the entire campaign, a 92, playing for winners Jaffna Kings. He scored fifties in both finals.

Double help for England

There was Yorkshire and Northern Diamonds representation in Australia either side of Christmas in England's second string squads as they helped the senior teams to prepare for their Ashes series. Yorkshire duo Harry Brook and Matthew Fisher travelled Down Under before Christmas with the Lions, while Beth Langston toured Australia in the New Year with Women's A.

Ex-Yorkshire trio honoured

The Marylebone Cricket Club announced Honorary Life Memberships including former Yorkshire overseas players Damien Martyn (2003), Morne Morkel (2008) and Herschelle Gibbs (2010). Also honoured was England's Sarah Taylor, who played a handful of games for Northern Diamonds last summer.

Pride and frustration for Northern Diamonds

ALWAYS THE BRIDESMAIDS... BUT NEXT TIME THE BRIDES?

By Kevin Hutchinson

The Diamonds can reflect on their first full season of competition with a great deal of pride and just a hint of frustration. Pride that they reached the final of the Charlotte Edwards Cup, a brand-new T20 competition featuring the eight regional centres of excellence introduced for the women's game in 2021 and, in a repeat of last season, appeared in the final of the 50-over Rachael Heyhoe Flint Trophy. Frustration from the fact that the trophy cabinet still awaits its first silverware.

Unlike the Covid-restricted and hastily organised competition of 2020 a fully structured calendar was set out for the professional women's game, the domestic competitions bisected mid-season by the Hundred.

The squad remained largely unchanged, and in the early matches newly appointed captain Hollie Armitage was able to call on the services of England trio Lauren Winfield-Hill, Katherine Brunt and Nat Sciver. Despite a first-ever Diamonds century from opener Winfield-Hill, also her first in any cricket on her home ground at Headingley, their RHF Trophy campaign began with a defeat at home to Central Sparks.

A four-wicket haul by Brunt proved crucial as the side squared their record with a narrow victory at Loughborough-based Lightning, and a second away game saw them bowl out Sunrisers for 53 at Cambridge, where Brunt was again in the wickets — her 3-11 marginally bettered by 3-10 from former international teammate Jenny Gunn, who would go on to finish as the side's leading wicket-taker in the competition.

The first half of the 50-over competition ended with a thrilling finish at Headingley, where the home side clinched a third straight win with four balls to spare against South East Stars. This time Gunn demonstrated her value as an all-rounder with a half-century to go alongside a similar effort from Linsey Smith and Sterre Kalis (76) as the Diamonds emerged victorious from a perilous position midway through their innings. Kalis would finish the competition as one of the leading run-scorers with 290 at an average of 41.42.

The England players had departed for international duties by this time, but a legend of the game in Sarah Taylor would drop in for a handful of games following an injury to regular wicket-keeper Bess Heath. Taylor would come out of the best part of two years of retirement to

Caught and bowled: left-armer Linsey Smith does it all herself to despatch Western Storm's Nat Wraith in the Diamonds' Charlotte Edwards Cup clash at Chester-le-Street

debut against the Stars as she warmed up for duties in the Hundred.

As attention switched to the new T20 competition, which saw the team grouped alongside Western Storm, Thunder and Sunrisers in the opening round-robin group stage, their results followed a similar pattern to those in the longer format.

An opening defeat at home against Thunder was followed by victory at Chelmsford against the Sunrisers. And, in their last game before the break for the Hundred, they produced a stunning performance at Taunton, beating Western Storm off the last ball with the final pair at the wicket — after Alex MacDonald had claimed her season's best 4-17.

When the regional campaign resumed a second win over the Sunrisers was followed by a four-wicket reverse against Western Storm, meaning a place at the three-team Finals Day rested on the final round of matches. Gunn turned in another excellent performance of 4-15 to restrict Thunder to under 100 at Chester, after which Heath scored an unbeaten 58 off 40 balls to capture a run-rate-based bonus point and secure a place at Hampshire's Ageas Bowl.

The returning Winfield-Hill (65) and Gunn (4-26) might well have shared the Player of the Match award, which Winfield-Hill took following semi-final success against Southern Vipers by 18 runs. That set up a final against South East Stars, but despite a half-century from captain Armitage her side were unable to post a defendable target and lost with two overs to spare.

There was no time for the team to dwell on the result, as they returned to action in the longer format five days later. They bounced back with a Smith (5-34) inspired victory against Western Storm at Chester-le-Street, where Armitage passed 50 for the second time in a week.

A thumping victory at the same venue against Thunder left them assured of a place in the knockout stages with a game to spare, and in what turned out to be a preview of the final they lost out to the Southern Vipers at Southampton the following weekend. A win there would have advanced them directly to the final. Instead, they had to contend with a semi-final eliminator clash with Central Sparks at Scarborough.

Ami Campbell's performances had been somewhat muted going into that Sparks game, which offered the Diamonds their first visit to North Marine Road. It saw the batter come into her own with a run-a-ball 76 as her side swept into the final.

The left-hander carried her form into the final against Vipers three days later, again passing 60, and Beth Langston, the side's leading wicket-taker in the competition with 13, added two early victims to her tally. But for the pair and their teammates the day would end in heartache as Vipers recovered from 109-7 to chase 184 with two balls to spare.

Whether 2021 was a success or a failure will be judged a few years down the line. Only then will we know if being runners-up twice was the height of the team's achievements, or merely provided them with a springboard to success...clearly realistic given the Diamonds head into 2022 with eight full-time contracted professionals, more than any other region, after Yorkshire paid for two on top of the ECB-funded six.

YORKSHIRE had 10 T20 friendlies scheduled through April and May, though six of those against North East Warriors (May 3) and Lancashire (May 9 and 16) were abandoned due to wet weather.

In the four games played two were lost, and two won. The wins were secured over Cumbria at Arnside on April 25, Hollie Armitage enjoying a day to remember with runs and wickets. In the morning game, a nine-wicket win, she claimed 2-18 from four overs of leg-spin and hit 71 not out, opening the batting. In the afternoon fixture, a 99-run success, she hit 64 and returned 3-7 from four overs.

Sunday April 18, 2021, Welbeck CC
Yorkshire (58-7) lost to Nottinghamshire (135-5) by 77 runs
Yorkshire (73) lost to Nottinghamshire (74-2) by eight wickets

Sunday April 25, 2021, Arnside CC
Yorkshire (122-1) beat Cumbria (121-3) by nine wickets
Yorkshire (174-5) beat Cumbria (75-7) by 99 runs

Bradford Under-15s girls made it a September day to remember by winning at Lord's.

Teams representing hubs from Bradford, the Cotswolds, Manchester and Slough all took part in the MCC's National Foundation competition Finals Day at the Home of Cricket, with Bradford crowned champions in glorious fashion on September 20. They comfortably defended their 20-over total of 135-3 in the final on the main square against the Cotswolds, having beaten teams from Sheffield and Hull to qualify.

Batsmen are out: Lauren Winfield-Hill pulls the old word

BATTING FOR CHANGE

Lauren Winfield-Hill has welcomed the terminology change from *batsman* to *batter* as the MCC try to promote equality across the game. The change, which will be game-wide, men's as well women's, came about last September.

"It's one of those things where, because we've become so accustomed to the terminology within the game, you don't quite realise the impact it has," said the England, Yorkshire and Northern Diamonds star. "I think it's not necessarily for this generation, but the generation to come — to show that the game's always evolving."

Winfield-Hill is a fabulous ambassador for the women's game, regularly speaking about its rapid growth during the inaugural Hundred campaign when she was captaining the Headingley-based Northern Superchargers. The 31-year-old, who came through the ranks at Stamford Bridge, recalled the quandary her teammates found themselves in, highlighting the need for change.

"I remember when I was a junior growing up, I played all my cricket with the boys. There was no such things as girls' teams, really. It would be something the boys would say, 'Is it batsman, what do we call you?'

"At the time, it was never something which particularly bothered me. But if the boys are unsure whether it's the right terminology to use or not it does suggest there's any uneasy nature of calling a female a batsman."

Trio of centuries for Yorkshire's Test captain Root

HEADINGLEY — THE GROUND WHERE ENGLAND WIN

By Paul Edwards

All cricketers look back with fond satisfaction on the times when everything went swimmingly. Even the humblest fourth-team club reserves can recall Saturdays when runs streamed from their bats or their deliveries befuddled opponents. The knowledge that such experiences are shared with the greatest players in the world is one of sport's charms. For a few brief moments you, too, can be Joe Root.

But reality obtruded upon such dreams last August, when spectators were reminded of the chasm that divides us from those we can only watch. Root's trio of centuries in successive Tests against India revealed England's captain to be at the peak of even his considerable powers. Fittingly, the last of those hundreds was scored at Headingley, and it helped England to square the five-match series after their defeat in a very great Test match at Lord's.

It should be noted in passing that when this *Yearbook* appears the result of the series will not be known. India lead 2-1, and the final match is scheduled to be played at Edgbaston in July, nearly 11 months after the first game at Trent Bridge. The final Test at Old Trafford last September was cancelled due to Coronavirus issues and rescheduled.

The 2021 Headingley Test did not offer a climax anything like as gripping as that provided by Ben Stokes and Jack Leach against Australia almost two years previously. The whole match was completed in less than 10 sessions, and Virat Kohli did not dispute the merit of England's innings and 76-run triumph. Yet not even the tightest Yorkshireman thought himself short-changed, especially if he had a ticket for day one when India were dismissed for 78 and England's openers had built a 42-run lead by the close.

Almost inevitably, James Anderson was at the heart of things. After Kohli opted to bat first, a reasonable decision given the conditions, Anderson took three wickets in his first 31 balls, swinging and seaming the ball just enough to take three thin edges, one of them that of Kohli. It was another of those precious hours when spectators could reflect that they were seeing one of the finest cricketers our game has produced. Rohit Sharma and Ajinkya Rahane tried to rebuild the innings, but

Rahane succumbed to Craig Overton just before lunch, and his was the first of seven wickets to fall for 22 runs in 15 overs.

All the England seamers made important breakthroughs, and Jos Buttler grabbed five catches.

This was to be a match in which everyone on the winning side did something; no English cricketer would be embarrassed to swig his beer on Saturday afternoon.

Given the sort of opportunity they can scarcely have envisaged after being outfought at Lord's, England seized it with unaccustomed ruthlessness.

Haseeb Hameed made his first half-century in a Test Match in England and had helped Rory Burns to take England to 120-0 at stumps. Rarely is a day's cricket so absolutely one-sided, and nothing happened in the next three sessions to divert the course of the contest.

Form of his life: Yorkshire's England captain, Joe Root, pulls handsomely during his innings of 121 against India at Headingley

Burns was bowled by the excellent Mohammed Shami early on Thursday morning, and Hameed's increasingly ponderous progress towards a first Test century was halted on 68 when he was deceived by Ravi Jadeja's turn. By then, though, Dawid Malan was marking his return to five-day cricket after a three-year absence by backcutting the ball between slips and gully in characteristic fashion, and he was now joined by Root, who batted with easy perfection.

The pair put on 139 for the third wicket, and by the end of their partnership it was plain that India would have to bat exceptionally well to save the game. Root reached his century off 124 balls, a dozen of which he had hit to the boundary with little apparent effort. Almost none of his runs were scored in the classical "V" but a cricket field is composed of many such sectors and the English captain's favourite areas in red-ball

Happy return: Ollie Robinson, who had been released by Yorkshire seven years previously, receives the Player of the Match Award at Headingley after his second five-for of the 2021 Test series against India

cricket have long been the covers, mid-wicket and just backward of square on the off side. Although Root was one of five dismissed by India's willing bowlers after tea on the second day, England's lead was 345 at the close.

The result, though, was still in doubt, and the third day's play did little to resolve the matter. An outstanding slip catch by Jonny Bairstow removed KL Rahul just before lunch, only for Sharma and Cheteshwar Pujara to drop their anchors, seemingly oblivious to the view that their side's bulkheads were breached and the ship was taking in water.

Nothing came easy to England's bowlers that Friday afternoon. Sharma's was the only other wicket to fall and even that required the help of DRS. Spectators arrived for the fourth day's play with every expectation of watching three full sessions.

Instead, they saw England complete their victory in a mere 19.3 overs with the new ball.

Ollie Robinson, who had known some unhappy days when he was on the staff at Headingley, took five wickets for the second time in the series and thus secured his place on the plane for the forthcoming Ashes tour. Having been released by Yorkshire seven years previously, it was a sweet return for the man who only realised how much he wanted to be a professional cricketer when his career was in doubt.

Overton also bowled well, and finished with match figures of 6-61. Overshadowed by Anderson in the first innings and Robinson in the second, the Somerset bowler at least took the last wicket when Mohammed Siraj nicked him to Bairstow.

"Roooot!" bayed the happy crowd. One saw their point.

Third LV= Test Match
England v. India

Played at Emerald Headingley, Leeds, on August 25, 26, 27 and 28, 2021
England won by an innings and 76 runs at 12.43 pm on the Fourth Day
Toss won by India

Close of play: First Day, England 120-0 (Burns 52*, Hameed 60*); Second Day, England 423-8 (Overton 24*, Robinson 0*); Third Day, India 215-2 (Pujara 91*, Kohli 45*)

INDIA

	First Innings		Second Innings	
R G Sharma, c Robinson b Overton	19	lbw b Robinson	59
K L Rahul, c Buttler b Anderson	0	c Bairstow b Overton	8
C A Pujara, c Buttler b Anderson	1	lbw b Robinson	91
* V Kohli, c Buttler b Anderson	7	c Root b Robinson	55
A M Rahane, c Buttler b Robinson	18	c Buttler b Anderson	10
§ R R Pant, c Buttler b Robinson	2	c Overton b Robinson	1
R A Jadeja, lbw b Curran	4	c Buttler b Overton	30
Mohammed Shami, c Burns b Overton	0	b Ali	6
I Sharma, not out	8	c Buttler b Robinson	2
J J Bumrah, lbw b Curran	0	not out	1
Mohammed Siraj, c Root b Overton	3	c Bairstow b Overton	0
Extras lb 11, nb 5	16	Extras b 4, lb 4, w 2, nb 5	15
Total	78	Total	278

FoW: 1-1 (Rahul), 2-4 (Pujara), 3-21 (Kohli), 4-56 (Rahane), 5-58 (Pant),
1st 6-67 (R G Sharma), 7-67 (M Shami), 8-67 (Jadeja), 9-67 (Bumrah), 10-78 (M Siraj)
FoW: 1-34 (Rahul), 2-116 (R G Sharma), 3-215 (Pujara), 4-237 (Kohli), 5-239 (Rahane),
2nd 6-239 (Pant), 7-254 (M Shami), 8-257 (I Sharma), 9-278 (Jadeja), 10-278 (M Siraj)

	O	M	R	W		O	M	R	W
Anderson	8	5	6	3	Anderson	26	11	63	1
Robinson	10	3	16	2	Robinson	26	6	65	5
Curran	10	2	27	2	Overton	18.3	6	47	3
Ali	2	0	4	0	Curran	9	1	40	0
Overton	10.4	5	14	3	Ali	14	1	40	1
					Root	6	1	15	0

ENGLAND

R J Burns, b Mohammed Shami		61
H Hameed, b Jadeja		68
D J Malan, c Pant b Mohammed Siraj		70
* J E Root, b Bumrah		121
J M Bairstow, c Kohli b Mohammed Shami		29
§ J C Buttler, c I Sharma b Mohammed Shami		7
M M Ali, c sub (A Patel) b Jadeja		8
S M Curran, c sub (M A Agarwal) b M Siraj		15
C Overton, lbw b Mohammed Shami		32
O E Robinson, b Bumrah		0
J M Anderson, not out		0
Extras b 8, lb 4, w 1, nb 8		21
Total		432

FoW: 1-135 (Burns), 2-159 (Hameed), 3-298 (Malan), 4-350 (Bairstow), 5-360 (Buttler),
6-383 (Root), 7-383 (Ali), 8-418 (Curran), 9-431 (Overton), 10-432 (Robinson)

	O	M	R	W
I Sharma	22	0	92	0
Bumrah	27.2	10	59	2
Mohammed Shami	28	8	95	4
Mohammed Siraj	23	3	86	2
Jadeja	32	8	88	2

Man of the match: O E Robinson

Umpires: A G Wharf and R A Kettleborough Scorers: J T Potter and J R Virr
Third: R K Illingworth Fourth: M J Saggers Match Referee: B C Broad

The Northern Superchargers

YORKSHIRE MEN AND WOMEN SHINE IN THE HUNDRED

By Graham Hardcastle

Men's and women's Northern Superchargers teams achieved similar results in 2021, winning three matches apiece.

The men finished fifth out of eight teams and the women sixth.

Lauren Winfield-Hill's side went into their last group fixture against Birmingham Phoenix at Headingley in mid-August knowing a win would qualify them for the Eliminator clash at the Oval — an effective semi-final. They lost by 14 as Phoenix advanced instead.

Dousing the Fire: Superchargers Jemimah Rodrigues on her way to 92 not out against the Welsh.

All match days were double headers, and in the evening the men's side, captained by David Willey, were already out of finals contention. They lost heavily to a Birmingham side who were to be beaten in the final by Southern Brave. The Phoenix women lost their Eliminator clash with eventual champions Oval Invincibles.

The Superchargers men won games against Oval Invincibles and Manchester Originals at Headingley. Sandwiched in between was victory over London Spirit at Lord's.

The women won Headingley home games against Welsh Fire, their opening game of the tournament, and the eventual champions from the Oval. They also beat Katherine Brunt's Trent Rockets.

Standout individual contributions came from Willey with 81 not out in the win at Lord's and India batting star Jemimah Rodrigues, whose sensational 92 not out doused the Fire.

Driving to the top: Yorkshire's Harry Brook, who was the men's leading run-scorer with 189 from five appearances.

In the men's victory over the Originals at Headingley the Superchargers posted 200-5, thanks largely to 71 not out from wicket-keeper John Simpson. It was the only score of 200 or more in the entire competition.

Yorkshire batter Harry Brook was the men's leading run-scorer with 189 from five appearances, while Northern Diamonds left-arm spinner Linsey Smith led the way with the ball for the women, taking nine wickets from seven games.

In early 2022 men's coach Darren Lehmann stepped down as head coach, citing Coronavirus restrictions as a large part of his decision, given the travelling involved from Australia. Former Essex and England wicketkeeper James Foster was appointed as his replacement.

Women's coach Dani Hazell remained in charge and was looking for a stronger team performance.

More players are the prize for award-winner

DISABILITY ICON WANTS FRESH CRACK AT THE AUSSIES

By Graham Hardcastle

If you ever want advice from someone about making the best out of a challenging situation Yorkshire disability bowling star Alex Jervis may be the perfect person to ask.

Jervis, a 26-year-old adopted Yorkshireman from Worksop, has been an integral part of the county's set-up for 14 years and has been around the England Learning Disability squad for much of the last 10.

Unfortunately, as with all walks of life, Coronavirus put a spanner in the works. There were no international series played such as the *Ashes*, in which Jervis made his England debut Down Under in 2015 and was part of the squad who won the most recent series in 2019.

So the seamer had to concentrate his efforts elsewhere.

Thankfully, Yorkshire Cricket was at the heart of those efforts, helping to further develop opportunities for others and raising awareness of disability cricket. One of the main things he did was to ensure Yorkshire's hardball D40 (deaf) team played their first fixtures for a number of years.

He helped to organise and coach players as well as raising vital funds.

Jervis also learned sign language to ensure strong communication with players, while also helping out with recruitment. "As soon as I got involved in disability cricket, my vision was A, how long can I go for? B, looking at the coaching side," he explained. "Because of Covid the coaching side has been my main focus.

"We've had no international cricket, so that's not been on my radar. The Yorkshire D40 side, I'm very proud to have helped get them back playing. "A lot of players left because there was a change in rules and they weren't eligible.

"So we have been trying to build up a new squad to get into the Disability League, which we did last year. Through some contacts I know I got seven new deaf players to join the squad."

In October he was honoured by the Lord's Taverners, winning their Disability Cricketer of the Year award for 2021. "I wasn't expecting it to be honest," Jervis, whose life outside of cricket sees him work in Tesco's distribution centre, reflected. "All I have been trying to do since I got into the England team is to give back to the game that has given me so much.

"I want to get people onto the same pathway as me, whether that's at Yorkshire or with England — just get more people involved in disability cricket.

"I'm not here to win awards. It's mainly about trying to get more people involved in cricket. Whether that's at club level, county level or internationals, I don't care.

"I just want more people playing cricket.

Disability Cricketer of the Year: Alex Jervis receives his award at October's Cricket Writers Club lunch. He is joined by fellow award winner, Sophia Dunkley, the England women's star.

"Getting the award all started when this time last year I decided that I was going to do a 100-mile bike ride to raise money for some new kit for us at Yorkshire.

"I moved clubs to Blyth in Nottinghamshire three games into last year. Before I went there I helped out with their clubhouse refurbishment. On my days off work I fitted some carpet tiles for them. They were also having their car park retarmaced. So I helped moving the tarmac as well."

A man of many talents, hey!

But his main talent remains his seam bowling. Jervis first played for Nottinghamshire aged 11, but quickly moved to Yorkshire because of the better opportunities on offer: "There was a better pathway into the Yorkshire team and then the England set-up."

He debuted for England in Australia in 2015. "It's quite an interesting story about how I got into the England set-up," continued the big Sheffield Steelers Ice Hockey fan. "My dad enquired about it, and realised on the Thursday that I needed to be there on the Friday. I ended up playing two trial games of indoor cricket, and it went from there.

"I've still got a photo of that 2015 series on my wall, and my dad has got my first playing shirt for England up on his wall. It was a fantastic series. One of my highlight performances was in the Disability Premier League, which has been introduced by the ECB to almost run alongside the Hundred.

"I took 4-2 from 2.2 overs while playing for the England BlackCats at Loughborough in September. My best figures were 5-46 in the first ODI of a tri-series in Cheshire against South Africa in 2017.

"I had been told I would play the first game, miss the second and they would take the rest of the series from there. But it was hard for them to drop me after that. Hitting my first six in an England shirt was also fun!"

Jervis, LD team-mate Rob Hewitt, Gordon Laidlaw and Liam Thomas are among the prominent Yorkshire players across the England disability set-up. Laidlaw has just retired, but he plans to continue with the county.

"It's in a very good place at the moment," Jervis said of Yorkshire's disability cricket.

After all the good work of the last couple of years Jervis has another task on the horizon — to down the Aussies once more: "It was only recently that I've found out there is an international tour this year, with three of the four England impairment squads going to Australia in June.

"The squads going are the blind, the learning disability and the hearing impaired. The only squad not going, but they are back in training, is the physical disability lads. I think there's something else in the pipeline for them.

"We had our first training session since February 2019 as a group just before Christmas, and we usually have two years of planning for a tour like Australia. But we have to get it all into four months."

Yorkshire's World Cup starlet

Batting starlet Will Luxton, left, was an ever-present in England Under-19s' impressive run to the World Cup final in the Caribbean through January and February.

The Young Lions reached the February 6 final in Antigua, only for India to beat them by four wickets as they successfully chased down 190.

Luxton, aged 18 at the time, batted in the middle order and posted 156 runs in six matches, including three scores in the 40s. His best was an unbeaten 47 in England's quarter-final win over South Africa.

Fast bowler Ben Cliff, an Academy teammate of Luxton's, was also in the squad, but did not play.

All-round sports star on track of the two Ps...

THE QUICKIE WITH AN EYE TO FIELD PARALYMPICS

By Graham Hardcastle

Meet the Yorkshire disability all-round star who is chasing the two Ps: *Promotion* and the *Paralympics*. William Baxter, 26, is a sportsman of some repute.

A right-arm fast bowler who will be central to the Yorkshire D40 team's hopes of promotion this summer, he is also a world leader in athletics with an eye on Paris 2024 or Los Angeles 2028.

"I like to play lots of different sports, but cricket is my favourite," said the Doncaster-born quick whose ability to swing the ball is one of his main assets. William is deaf, and has cerebral palsy.

WILLIAM BAXTER
Fantastic life through cricket

He communicated for this article through his father, Tony.

"When I was little I watched my brothers, James and Thomas, play cricket and dreamt of following them," he continued.

William has worked as an assistant greenkeeper at Doncaster Golf Club and volunteered on the ground staff at Doncaster Rovers FC pre the Coronavirus pandemic. But cricket was the sport which caught his attention. He plays his club cricket in the Lincolnshire County League for Haxey seconds — a team within the Doncaster postcode — and counts a 2019 clash against Brigg Town as his career highlight.

"It was my first five-wicket haul for Haxey, all bowled: 5-28 from 11.2 overs," he recalled. "Brigg had won the league the year before. We're big rivals, and we bowled them out for 69."

His first match of 2022 will be for Haxey on April 23 before Yorkshire's fixtures start in May. "We look like we have a strong team this year, with lots of new players and better training than we've had in the past," he said. "Cheshire and Shropshire both have strong teams as well, so they look like they will be our rivals."

England learning-disability bowler Alex Jervis said the county's disability programme was in a good place. Baxter points to the hard work put in by Owen Jervis, Alex's father, and others such as Mark Atkins and Russ Ingram, and says: "I agree with Alex. "The teams have been built up well over the last few years after a few problems here and there."

He would like to follow in the footsteps of Jervis and play international cricket: "I would like to play for England in the future, but the PD (physical disability) squad only play T20s at the moment, and I would say I'm better suited to the longer format," he said.

"My batting is an area which needs to improve. I need to be more like Ben Stokes. He can change a game on his own, so I'd like to be more like him if I can. I've watched him a few times live, including at the World Cup against Afghanistan at Old Trafford in 2019."

Baxter, who received the 2013 Yorkshire Cricket Board Disability Achiever of the Year Award, has already represented the North of England. And he is no stranger to the international stage, given he also excels at discus and shot-put.

"I was able to break the national records for shot-put and discus last year," he said. "And I recorded the number one mark in the world at F36 for discus last year. I would love to go to the Paralympics and the World Games. I have been in the Cerebral Palsy World Games, which is below the Paralympics, and got three gold medals.

"I was also drafted in at the last minute to the 4x100m relay team and got a silver in that, which I was really happy with."

Baxter is on the Paralympic development programme for Great Britain, but admits: "The discus, which is my best event, hasn't been chosen in my category for Paris 2024. If I improve a lot with the shot-put Paris is possible. But Los Angeles in 2028 is more realistic.

"My coach has said that I won't be a mature thrower for another 10 years yet. It takes a lot of time to develop. So there is plenty of time.

"Bowling and shot-put require different actions with the body. So the better I get at bowling the worse my shot-put gets. But I have a new strength and conditioning coach who is trying to work on maintaining my strength for both disciplines."

That is a fairly scary prospect for batters across the Lincolnshire League and in county cricket, with Baxter keen to add to the 100-plus wickets he has to his name on the *PlayCricket* website.

"He loves his stats," added father Tony. "Cricket has just been fantastic for William. It's given him confidence, focus and friendships. A lot of joy. He's had a fantastic life through cricket."

Dream come true, says Player of the Year Brook

YORKSHIRE PAIR KNOCK OPEN ENGLAND DOOR

By Graham Hardcastle

Harry Brook described his England senior debut against the West Indies in January as a "dream come true", with fellow Yorkshire star Matthew Fisher hoping to follow suit.

Brook was handed his first international appearance in a T20 in Barbados in January, while Fisher gained Test selection for a March tour against the island nation.

Brook, 23, played in the third of five T20s at the Kensington Oval on January 26, making a middle-order 10 in a defeat. He was drafted in as a late replacement for injured captain Eoin Morgan after some excellent 2021 form for his county and in the Hundred for the Northern Superchargers.

A product of the Burley-in-Wharfedale club, he said: "As a young lad growing up, trying to be a pro cricketer, cricket in the family and always on my doorstep, making my England debut was a massive honour and a dream come true.

"The whole tour was a phenomenal experience – really good fun – and to be able to get my cap out there was a really proud moment for me and my family."

MATTHEW FISHER
Set for debut cap

Ironically, it was a similar situation for Fisher as well, but Brook's grandparents once placed a bet on the then whipper-snapper to one day play for England. His grandfather died in 2012, but his grandma has been able to cash in.

Brook laughed: "I don't know the details or what the odds were or anything like that. I think my gran's a bit too tight to tell me."

At time of writing a bet placed by Fisher's mother and brothers for him to do the same had yet to be won because he had been selected only for the late-March three-Test series and not yet handed his debut cap.

Fisher, 24, said: "It's what I've worked for since I was seven, when I started playing and fell in love with the game. To get picked for England in Test cricket is all I've ever wanted to do.

"I'm obviously not there yet, but this is the next hurdle. Hopefully, I might get a chance out there to get my first England cap, which is something no one can ever take away from me. It's incredibly exciting. I went on the Lions trip before Christmas and bowled really nicely. Andrew Strauss has said in the media that I was the most impressive bowler in the party. He wasn't there, so it's been fed back to him. That was nice."

Fisher did not have the standout 2021 summer which Yorkshire Player of the Year Brook did, but he claimed 18 of his 20 County Championship wickets in the final four matches of the summer, including nine in the win over Somerset at Scarborough.

"There are going to be people around the country — you hear it all the time — who are saying, 'I'm not sure he deserves to get picked'. But I think my selection is more on potential, with one eye on the future," continued the man selected to tour ahead of Stuart Broad and James Anderson. "Wickets-wise, there are perhaps players out there who deserve it more than me. But, attributes-wise, I think there are certain things they look for in Test cricket, and they obviously see my game fitting into that. It's really nice that they've picked me, and I just want to try and repay that now."

Alex Lees, a former teammate of Brook and Fisher at Yorkshire, was also selected for the Test tour. The left-handed opener has enjoyed a profitable time since leaving Headingley for Durham in 2018.

Both Fisher and Lees tragically lost their fathers as teenagers, with Fisher adding: "I'm chuffed to bits that Leesy's got the call as well. We've never really spoken in detail about that kind of stuff (their late fathers) but we kind of have that nod to each other that we know what we've both been through."

ADIL RASHID — SUPERSTAR

Adil Rashid, Yorkshire's leg-spinning magician, brought up two significant milestones during England's five-match T20 series against the West Indies in Barbados in January.

In the first game Rashid played his 200th international across all formats, and in the last he claimed his 300th international wicket.

What a career it has been for a precocious talent from Bradford.

Aged only 18 when he took six wickets on his Yorkshire debut in a Championship match against Warwickshire at Scarborough in 2006, he has gone on to become one of the world's very best spin bowlers.

Above all the personal statistics the most important came in 2019 as he helped England to a sensational one-day World Cup win on home soil, claiming 3-54 in the semi-final win over Australia at Edgbaston as his best performance among 11 wickets in as many appearances.

A two-time Championship winner with Yorkshire in 2014 and 2015, Rashid had been named as the Professional Cricketers' Association and Cricket Writers' Club's Young Player of the Year in 2007.

He is ranked the fourth best T20 bowler in the world by the ICC, with all of the top five being wrist spinners: Wanindu Hasaranga is No. 1, followed by Tabraiz Shamsi, Adam Zampa, Rashid and Rashid Khan.

Rash, or Dilly if you prefer, has been batting right down the order for England in limited-overs cricket, though his 10 first-class hundreds with the *White Rose* on his chest point to a very, very capable batter.

Both his one-day and T20 international debuts came in 2009 before the first of 19 Test matches came in 2015.

It is a shame that we have not seen more of him in a Test shirt for England, though that should not detract from a special career which has seen him bamboozle many of the world's top batters with his skill. Virat Kohli is a player high up on that list. Rashid, an expert exponent of the googly, is heavily involved in local charity work and has been honoured with the Freedom of the City of Bradford.

He played alongside managing director of Yorkshire Cricket Darren Gough on his T20 debut for the county in the summer of 2008. And Gough, along with every other Yorkshire fan, will want to see this soon to be 34-year-old bowling genius back in county colours this summer.

His domestic appearances have been limited in recent years, but he played five Vitality Blast games last year.

Yorkshire has much cause to congratulate Adil Rashid.

First beneficiary sets his sights on Yorkshire shirt

QALANDERS LINK BOOST FOR RISING BATTER

By Graham Hardcastle

Under-15s batting star Shahzaib Sayeed has admitted his delight at becoming the first beneficiary of Yorkshire's link-up with Lahore Qalanders, training in Pakistan through a fortnight in February.

Sayeed, a product of Mount CC, now plays for New Rover in Leeds and dreams of becoming a professional player in the future.

"I want to score plenty of runs for Yorkshire," said the left-hander who made a Roses half-century on county debut for the Under-13s side.

The 15-year-old combined a family trip to Lahore with a handful of training sessions at the Qalandars' High Performance Centre.

**SHAHZAIB SAYEED
Pride and passion**

"I had five sessions with them, and it was a really good experience," he said. "My game and my confidence have risen because of it. The facilities were beautiful, and all the coaches there and students were really helpful."

Sayeed was given leave of absence from school to travel to Lahore to see his sick mother and, thanks to help from Lord Patel and Qalandars' chief operating officer Sameen Rana, was able to include some cricket.

"We have supported the Qalandars since the Pakistan Super League started," revealed the Thornhill Community Academy student — a prefect and potential head boy.

"Our family links are to Lahore, and they are our side. We love to follow them. Unfortunately, we didn't have the time to go to a PSL game, as I wanted to spend time with my mum. Hopefully, I can get to one in the future."

In a social media video filmed by the Qalandars, Sayeed spoke about how he has refined his grip and stance at the crease and worked hard on improving his cut shot: "I felt really comfortable with the changes they have helped me make. "The bowlers there were around 140kmph, and were bowling as fast as they could. "With my old technique I might have got hit or been late on the ball. But I was able to get to the ball much faster, and was able to play with soft hands.

"The bowlers, the students of the Academy, were open age. Some were my age, but others were 20 or even 26 and 27. It's given me a lot of confidence ahead of this season. Hopefully, I can score a lot of runs and keep going because cricket's my passion.

"I want to be a professional."

Sayeed counts Joe Root and Ben Stokes as his cricketing heroes, and hopes to get to Headingley this summer to see Lahore speedster Haris Rauf play in a Yorkshire shirt.

"I'm really thankful to Yorkshire for giving me this opportunity," he said. "The coaches at Yorkshire have been wonderful with me. Hopefully, I will get another chance to go over to the Qalandars."

Sayeed's father, Mohammed, who says his son "lives and breathes cricket", echoed those thanks to the county. "It was fantastic," he said. "The people at the Qalandars were brilliant, and the coaching was really beneficial for Shahzaib.

"I would very much recommend any other boys and girls to go and visit if they get the chance, because the experience they will get is first-class. Yorkshire are a wonderful county, and what they do for the kids is unbelievable. It was really good for Shahzaib to go over to the Qalandars and get a different perspective on his game for a couple of weeks."

Line-up of the young ones...

Yorkshire Academy Squad 2022: Harry Allinson, Ben Cliff, Clark Doughney, Noah Kelly, Noah Priestley, Yash Vagadia, Matthew Weston.

Yorkshire Emerging Players Programme 2022: George Booth, Harry Finch, Josh Hoyle, Charlie McMurren, Louie Owens.

Northern Diamonds Academy 2022: Madeleine Atkinson, Ciara Boaden, Mary Butler, Abi Glenn, Grace Hall, Trudy Johnson, Lucy Lindley, Emma Marlow, Ellie Nightingale, Harriet Robson, Lizzie Scott, Bethany Slater, Ellie Tiffin, Phoebe Turner, Jessica Woolston and Emily Whiting.

100 Years Ago — The Season of 1922

STEAMROLLER DRIVES INTO FOUR-YEAR GOLDEN AGE

By Anthony Bradbury

In 1922 Yorkshire started a run of four years of consecutive Championship success. They steamrollered many opponents to substantial defeats and won 19 Championship games, losing only twice. Individual counties played between 22 and 30 matches, so the Championship was decided on a percentage basis, based on points achieved as against points possible. Yorkshire in attaining 107 points from a possible 145 had a percentage of 73.79, marginally ahead of Nottinghamshire who had lost three more games.

To lose a match was not to incur much, if any, of a points penalty.

Under the rather gentle captaincy of Mr Geoffrey Wilson, who was happy to defer to the views of Wilfred Rhodes, Yorkshire were a settled side. In their first 14 games up to July 1 the team was unchanged — Holmes, Sutcliffe, Oldroyd, R Kilner, Rhodes, Robinson, N Kilner, Wilson, Macaulay, Dolphin and Waddington. When Geoffrey Wilson succumbed to appendicitis during a *Roses* match in August, Rockley Wilson returned as captain, and earlier Maurice Leyland and Arthur Mitchell (once) came into the side as replacements for the out-of-form Norman Kilner. Both Leyland and Mitchell later had highly productive careers with Yorkshire.

Yorkshire won their opening six first-class matches by huge margins, including their very first match against Glamorgan, where the margin was an innings and 258 runs and where Yorkshire had scored 404-2 declared. There were some very weak counties in 1922, and to illustrate that point Yorkshire used only 16 players including three amateurs in the whole Championship. Glamorgan in eight fewer games used 38 players, of whom 31 were amateur.

One extraordinary innings win for Yorkshire was at Hull against Sussex. The visitors, who had a good side, were bowled out for 95 (Rhodes 6-43) and then on a damp wicket Yorkshire were all out for 125. Yorkshire were not troubled. In the next 14.4 overs Sussex were dismissed for 20, and Abe Waddington with, as *Wisden* stated, "bewildering swerve and great pace off the wicket" took in seven overs seven wickets for six runs. The Sussex 20 is the lowest score made against

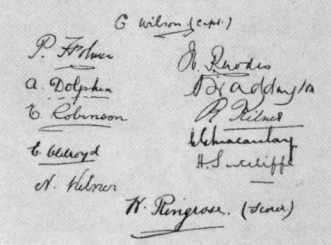

Yorkshire in the last 100 years. Sussex were to make a bold effort to exact revenge in the return match at Hove.

> To Messrs. ROWNTREE & CO., LTD.,
> YORK. August, 1922.
>
> Rowntree's Toffee has made a great Hit. We have all made a Test of it, and we think it easily heads the Toffee Championship Table. It is beautifully smooth and silky — and, like the perfect pitch, it is never too sticky for our batsmen or too hard for our bowlers. We shall never "run out" of Rowntree's.
>
> *[signatures: G. Wilson (capt.), P. Holmes, A. Dolphin, E. Robinson, E. Oldroyd, N. Kilner, W. Rhodes, R. Kilner, Waddington, Macaulay, H. Sutcliffe, W. Ringrose (scorer)]*

Yorkshire batted first, and the pitch was awkward. Having reached 18 without loss, Yorkshire then lost 10 wickets for 24 runs and their total of 42 remains their lowest against Sussex.

Maurice Tate and H E Roberts each took 5-20 for Sussex, but when Sussex batted they were out for 95, and after Yorkshire revived in their second innings Sussex again collapsed, so Yorkshire won by 92 runs. It was never as easy as it may now seem.

There were two drawn games that caused controversy. Agreement had been reached that close of play on the third day at Harrogate against Essex would be early so that Yorkshire could catch an afternoon train to Maidstone. No one had remembered that an extra half hour could be claimed if that would achieve a result. When Essex had nine second innings wickets down at the agreed time the Yorkshire professionals, perhaps thinking of the win bonus, wanted to play the extra half hour. Captain Wilson disagreed, and the players left the field.

There was a dressing room protest, and procrastination in getting changed. So the train was missed — and Wilson (and his professionals) did not reach Maidstone until breakfast time next day! Wilson later wrote: "I feel personally that any match, however serious it might be, and however much may depend upon the result, should be played in the most friendly spirit. The result should be second in importance."

The Yorkshire crowd might not have agreed with this early example of *The Spirit of Cricket*.

The second draw arose in gripping circumstances in the Old Trafford *Roses* match. Yorkshire gained a first-innings lead of four runs, which would gain them two points in a drawn game. No first-innings points were available in a game lost. In their second innings Yorkshire needed five runs off the last over to win and their final pair were at the wicket. Rhodes was batting and Cecil Parkin was bowling. Neville Cardus later wrote "The crowd sat in dumb futility, all aching eyes but helpless. The

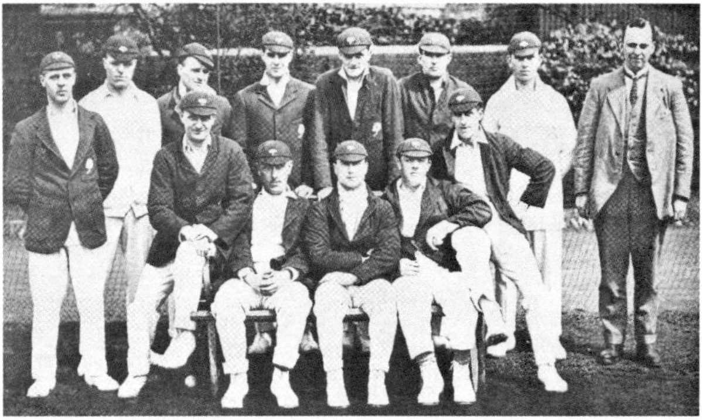

Yorkshire 1922. Back row, left to right: E Oldroyd, N Kilner, R Kilner, H Sutcliffe, G G Macaulay, A Waddington, M Leyland, and F Nottingham (scorer). Front row: Emmott Robinson, W Rhodes, G Wilson (captain) A Dolphin and P Holmes. *(Photo: Ron Deaton Archive)*

tension seemed to have a low throbbing sound." Parkin bowled five balls, which Rhodes patted back to him, and just a single was taken off the last ball. The match was drawn with Yorkshire four short of victory. To Rhodes, drawing a *Roses* match with a first-innings lead and two points was more important than the risk of losing and no points at all.

Oldroyd, with 1,534 Championship runs, headed the batting averages at 45.11. Sutcliffe, who made 232 in a Surrey game, was close behind. Holmes had made a brace of double-centuries in separate matches against Warwickshire, and he joined Oldroyd, Sutcliffe, Rhodes and Roy Kilner in scoring over 1,000 runs. Yorkshire took 500 wickets against their opponents — Rhodes, Macaulay, Roy Kilner, Waddington and E R Wilson averaging between 12.71 and 18.45 and taking 499 of those wickets. The 500th was surprisingly taken by Herbert Sutcliffe.

No international cricket was played that summer, but George Macaulay was chosen for the Players against the Gentlemen at Lord's. Arthur Dolphin had a benefit, raising a satisfactory total of £1,891. The Committee Report noted the "the usual custom of investing two-thirds of this amount in the name of the Club's trustees." Lord Hawke was very much a dominant President, and the professionals were not to be trusted with their own money. The membership of 5,000 and more were listed name by name in the Annual Report with a note that Lady and Youth members were not entitled to attend or vote at meetings.

How times have changed.

100 Years Ago

YORKSHIRE'S FIRST CLASS HIGHLIGHTS OF 1922

Wins by an innings (10)

Yorkshire (495) defeated Warwickshire (99 and 125) by an innings and 271 runs at Huddersfield

Glamorgan (78 and 68) lost to Yorkshire (404-2 dec) by an innings and 258 runs at Cardiff Arms Park *

Worcestershire (111 and 90) lost to Yorkshire (421) by an innings and 220 runs at Dudley *

Leicestershire (97 and 114) lost to Yorkshire (410) by an innings and 199 runs at Bramall Lane, Sheffield **

Yorkshire (342) defeated Northamptonshire (69 and 88) by an innings and 185 runs at Leeds

Yorkshire (453-2 dec) defeated Warwickshire (123 and 178) by an innings and 152 runs at Birmingham

Glamorgan (161 and 165) lost to Yorkshire (429-7 dec) by an innings and 103 runs at Leeds

Middlesex (138 and 180) lost to Yorkshire (339-7 dec) by an innings and 21 runs at Lord's

Sussex (95 and 20) lost to Yorkshire (125) by an innings and 10 runs at Hull

Gloucestershire (134 and 87) lost to Yorkshire (228) by an innings and 7 runs at Dewsbury **

* and ** consecutive matches

Win by 200 or more runs (1)

Yorkshire (147 and 314-4 dec) defeated Derbyshire (130 and 80) by 251 runs at Derby

Win by 10 wickets (3)

Hampshire (272 and 44) lost to Yorkshire (293 and 25-0) at Bournemouth

Kent (163 and 131) lost to Yorkshire (273 and 24-0) at Leeds

Northamptonshire (81 and 42) lost to Yorkshire (112 and 12-0) at Northampton

Totals of 400 and over (7)

539-5 dec v. Surrey at The Oval
495-5 dec v. Warwickshire at Huddersfield
453-2 dec v. Warwickshire at Birmingham
429-7 dec v. Glamorgan at Leeds
421   v. Worcestershire at Dudley *
410   v. Leicestershire at Bramall Lane, Sheffield
404-2 dec v. Glamorgan at Cardiff Arms Park *

* Consecutive matches

Opponents dismissed for under 100 (20)

- 20 v. Sussex at Hull 2nd innings **
- 42 v. Northamptonshire at Northampton — 2nd innings *
- 44 v. Hampshire at Bournemouth
- 58 v. Gloucestershire at Fry's Ground, Bristol
- 68 v. Glamorgan at Cardiff Arms Park — 2nd innings *
- 69 v. Northamptonshire at Leeds — 1st innings *
- 72 v. Cambridge University at Cambridge *
- 74 v. Nottinghamshire at Nottingham ***
- 78 v. Glamorgan at Cardiff Arms Park — 1st innings *
- 80 v. Derbyshire at Derby *
- 81 v. Northamptonshire at Northampton — 1st innings *
- 83 v. Sussex at Hove — 2nd innings
- 87 v. Gloucestershire at Dewsbury ***
- 88 v. Northamptonshire at Leeds — 2nd innings *
- 90 v. Worcestershire at Dudley *
- 95 v. Sussex at Hull — 1st innings **
- 95 v. Sussex at Hove —1st innings
- 97 v. Leicestershire at Bramall Lane, Sheffield ***
- 99 v. Warwickshire at Huddersfield
- 99 v. Derbyshire at Bramall Lane, Sheffield **

*, ** and *** *consecutive matches*

Century Partnerships (21)

For the 1st wicket (4)

145	P Holmes and H Sutcliffe	v. Warwickshire at Huddersfield
143	P Holmes and H Sutcliffe	v. Kent at Maidstone
123	P Holmes and H Sutcliffe	v. MCC at Scarborough
100	P Holmes and H Sutcliffe	v. Middlesex at Lord's

For the 2nd wicket (4)

333	P Holmes and E Oldroyd	v. Warwickshire at Birmingham
224	P Holmes and E Oldroyd	v. Glamorgan at Cardiff Arms Park
196	H Sutcliffe and E Oldroyd	v. Surrey at The Oval
104	H Sutcliffe and E Oldroyd	v. Kent at Leeds

For the 3rd wicket (2)

176	E Oldroyd and R Kilner	v. Derbyshire at Derby
173	H Sutcliffe and R Kilner	v. Surrey at The Oval

For the 4th wicket (5)

205	E Oldroyd and R Kilner	v. Worcestershire at Dudley
160	E Oldroyd and W Rhodes	v. Leicestershire at Bramall Lane, Sheffield
129	R Kilner and W Rhodes	v. Middlesex at Leeds
114	H Sutcliffe and R Kilner	v. Hampshire at Bournemouth
107	H Sutcliffe and W Rhodes	v. Nottinghamshire at Nottingham

For the 5th wicket (1)

165	E Oldroyd and W Rhodes	v. Glamorgan at Leeds

For the 6th wicket (2)

122 *	P Holmes and N Kilner	v. Warwickshire at Huddersfield
109	R Kilner and N Kilner	v. Northamptonshire at Leeds

For the 7th wicket (1)

111	E Robinson and G G Macaulay	v. The Rest at The Oval

For the 8th wicket (2)

192 *	W Rhodes and G Wilson	v. Essex at Harrogate
103	W Rhodes and A Dolphin	v. The Rest at The Oval

Centuries (20)

P Holmes (5)
- 220 * v. Warwickshire at Huddersfield
- 209 v. Warwickshire at Birmingham
- 138 v. Glamorgan at Cardiff Arms Park
- 129 v. Middlesex at Lord's
- 107 v. Kent at Maidstone

E Oldroyd (5)
- 151 * v. Glamorgan at Cardiff Arms Park
- 143 v. Glamorgan at Leeds
- 138 * v. Warwickshire at Birmingham
- 128 v. Leicestershire at Bramall Lane, Sheffield
- 121 v. Worcestershire at Dudley

W Rhodes (4)
- 110 v. Glamorgan at Leeds
- 108 * v. Essex at Harrogate
- 106 v. Hampshire at Bournemouth
- 105 v. Middlesex at Leeds

H Sutcliffe (3)
- 232 v. Surrey at The Oval
- 114 v. Surrey at Bradford
- 101 * v. MCC at Scarborough

R Kilner (2)
- 124 v. Northamptonshire at Leeds
- 117 v. Worcestershire at Dudley

G G Macaulay (1)
- 101 * v. Essex at Harrogate

5 wickets in an innings (31)

A Waddington (10)
- 8- 34 v. Northamptonshire at Leeds
- 8- 35 v. Hampshire at Bradford
- 8- 39 v. Kent at Leeds
- 7- 6 v. Sussex at Hull
- 7- 31 v. Derbyshire at Derby
- 5- 35 v. Gloucestershire at Dewsbury
- 5- 39 v. Worcestershire at Bradford
- 5- 52 v. Kent at Maidstone — 2nd innings
- 5- 97 v. Nottinghamshire at Bramall Lane, Sheffield
- 5-106 v. Kent at Maidstone — 1st innings

G G Macaulay (8)
- 7- 47 v. Gloucestershire at Dewsbury — 1st innings
- 6- 8 v Northamptonshire at Northampton — 1st innings
- 6- 12 v. Glamorgan at Cardiff Arms Park
- 5- 23 v Northamptonshire at Northampton — 2nd innings
- 5- 29 v. Gloucestershire at Dewsbury — 2nd innings
- 5- 30 v. Leicestershire at Bramall Lane, Sheffield
- 5- 31 v. Middlesex at Lord's
- 5- 67 v. Surrey at Bradford

R Kilner (5)
- 6- 13 v. Hampshire at Bournemouth
- 6- 22 v. Essex at Harrogate — 2nd innings
- 5- 14 v. Nottinghamshire at Nottingham
- 5- 29 v. Essex at Harrogate — 1st innings
- 5- 38 v. Middlesex at Leeds

5 wickets in an innings *(Continued)*

W Rhodes (5)
- 6- 13   v. Sussex at Hove
- 6- 43   v. Sussex at Hull
- 5- 12   v. Warwickshire at Birmingham
- 5- 24   v. Worcestershire at Dudley
- 5- 24   v. Gloucestershire at Fry's Ground, Bristol

E Robinson (2)
- 5- 20   v. Nottinghamshire at Nottingham
- 5- 36   v. Leicestershire at Bramall Lane, Sheffield

E R Wilson (1)
- 5- 91   v. Surrey at The Oval

10 wickets in a match (8)

A Waddington (4)
- 11- 57   (4-26 and 7-31)   v. Derbyshire at Derby
- 11- 69   (8-35 and 3-34)   v. Hampshire at Bradford
- 11- 72   (8-39 and 3-33)   v. Kent at Leeds
- 10- 158 (5-106 and 5-52)   v Kent at Maidstone

R Kilner (2)
- 11- 51   (5-29 and 6-22)   v. Essex at Harrogate
- 10- 90   (4-77 and 6-13)   v. Hampshire at Bournemouth

G G Macauley (2)
- 12- 76   (7-47 and 5-29)   v. Gloucestershire at Dewsbury
- 11- 31   (6 - 8 and 5-23)   v. Northamptonshire at Northampton

3 catches in an innings (9)

A Dolphin (2)
- 3   v. Glamorgan at Leeds
- 3   v. Leicestershire at Bramall Lane, Sheffield

E Robinson (2)
- 3   v. Lancashire at Bramall Lane, Sheffield
- 3   v. Leicestershire at Bramall Lane, Sheffield

G G Macauley (1)
- 3   v. Derbyshire at Derby

R Kilner (1)
- 3   v. Hampshire at Bournemouth

E Oldroyd (1)
- 3   v. Surrey at The Oval

H Sutcliffe (1)
- 3   v. Sussex at Hull

A Waddingham (1)
- 3   v. The Rest at The Oval

3 dismissals in an innings (2)

A Dolphin (2)
- 4 (1ct, 3st)   v. Cambridge University at Cambridge
- 3 (1ct, 2st)   v. Sussex at Hove

5 catches in a match (none)

Debut (1)
In First Class cricket (1): A Mitchell

Cap awarded (1): G Wilson

100 YEARS AGO
YORKSHIRE AVERAGES 1922
ALL FIRST-CLASS MATCHES

Played 33   Won 20   Lost 2   Drawn 11

County Championship: Played 30   Won 19   Lost 2   Drawn 9

BATTING AND FIELDING *(Qualification 10 completed innings)*

Player	M.	I.	N.O.	Runs	H.S.	100s	50s	Avge	ct/st
H Sutcliffe	33	47	5	1909	232	3	12	45.45	20
E Oldroyd	33	45	6	1690	151*	5	8	43.33	18
W Rhodes	33	40	6	1368	110	4	5	40.23	27
P Holmes	33	47	3	1614	220*	5	3	36.68	10
R Kilner	33	43	3	1132	124	2	6	28.30	24
E Robinson	33	40	7	730	57*	0	3	22.12	30
G Wilson	24	22	6	323	49*	0	0	20.18	9
N Kilner	16	16	1	290	69	0	2	19.33	5
G G Macaulay	32	31	5	453	101*	1	2	17.42	28
A Dolphin	31	29	9	318	50	0	1	15.90	40/17
M Leyland	14	17	1	220	29	0	0	13.75	7
A Waddington	33	29	8	149	25*	0	0	7.09	43

Also batted

A Mitchell	2	2	0	31	29	0	0	15.50	1
E R Wilson	10	12	6	43	13*	0	0	7.16	2
W R Allen	2	2	0	13	9	0	0	6.50	4
H D Badger	1	2	1	6	6*	0	0	6.00	0

BOWLING
(Qualification 10 wickets)

Player	Overs	Mdns	Runs	Wkts	Avge	Best	5wI	10wM
W Rhodes	698	272	1232	100	12.32	6- 13	5	0
G G Macaulay	802.4	205	1785	130	13.73	7- 47	8	2
E R Wilson	237	100	346	23	15.04	5- 91	1	0
R Kilner	1005.1	383	1640	107	15.32	6- 13	5	2
A Waddington	886.4	198	2090	132	15.83	8- 34	10	4
E Robinson	545.5	192	1020	52	19.61	5- 20	2	0

Also bowled

P Holmes	4	1	5	1	5.00	1- 5	0	0
H Sutcliffe	2.4	0	11	1	11.00	1- 3	0	0
H D Badger	20	5	34	0	—	0- 15	0	0
E Oldroyd	5	1	21	0	—	0- 21	0	0
M Leyland	4	1	11	0	—	0- 11	0	0

50 Years Ago — The Season of 1972

TRIPPED AT B&H LAST FENCE BY THE TWO EX-YORKIES

By Anthony Bradbury

The 1971 season had resulted in a very poor performance in the County Championship with Yorkshire finishing 13th. That year was the first in which Geoffrey Boycott had been captain. Surely matters would improve in 1972? The prognosis was not over optimistic.

There remained divisions in the dressing-room, with a number of senior players openly hostile to the captain and younger players anxious and concerned. The stability of the club administration had been affected by the retirement of long-serving Secretary John H Nash and the arrival of his successor, Joe Lister. Doug Padgett, a source of quiet diplomacy within the first team, was now to be the second eleven captain and not readily available to help to calm troubled waters. A past Editor of this *Yearbook*, Derek Hodgson, was to write of the start of 1972 that the "dressing room was as factional as an Italian court of the Renaissance".

So how did playing matters develop?

The start of the season was rather good. The shadows of one-day cricket and the introduction of the Benson and Hedges competition had resulted in first-class Championship cricket being reduced from 24 to 20 games. By the end of the eighth game Yorkshire were top of the Championship table, though with only two wins and six drawn matches. Both Boycott and Hampshire had by then each scored two centuries. Tony Nicholson, Richard Hutton and Chris Old had all had some good bowling analyses. But then disaster struck.

Boycott received a bad finger injury which led him to miss a host of games, and the batting rather collapsed. There were big consecutive losses to Northamptonshire, Surrey and Lancashire — the last two by an innings and more — and Yorkshire slid down the table. There was a small revival in August when both Surrey and Middlesex were well beaten, and Andrew Dalton in that second match scored a wonderful 128 and then 49. No one else on either side reached 40 in an innings. To illustrate the fickle fortunes of cricket Dalton's scores in his next game were 0 and 1, the last run he was to score for his county. He retired from first-class cricket in September.

Towards the end of the season Boycott had returned, and he made four more centuries including 204 not out of 310-7 declared against

Spot the new Secretary: Joe Lister, who came from Worcestershire to succeed John Nash in 1972, is pictured back row extreme left on his first-class debut for Yorkshire at the County Ground, Bristol, against Gloucestershire on May 8-11, 1954. Yorkshire won by 80 runs with No. 5 Joe scoring 11 in the first innings — c Graveney b Cook — and 16 in the second — b Lambert. Sir Leonard Hutton is acting captain in the absence of Norman Yardley, and there is a big smile on the face of Bob Appleyard, back row third from left, returning for his first county match after two years of treatment for tuberculosis. The doctors had told his wife that he would never play for Yorkshire again. Back row, left to right: Lister, Raymond Illingworth, Brian Close, Appleyard, Roy Booth and Freddie Trueman. Front row: Vic Wilson, Johnny Wardle, Hutton, Willie Watson and Frank Lowson.
(Photo: Ron Deaton Archive)

Leicestershire. In 10 Championship games he scored 1,156 runs at 96.33. For players who batted in 10 or more games the next highest average at 30.58 was that of John Hampshire. None of Richard Lumb, Barrie Leadbeater, Hutton or Philip Sharpe scored a century, and their averages were all in the 20s. Bowlers Old, Nicholson and all-rounder Hutton did well, each with over 50 wickets, but the spinners fell away. Again Geoff Cope had his action questioned, and was not permitted to play from early July, and Don Wilson, in his benefit year, lost control and was dropped. Left-arm spinner Mike Bore and off-spinner Chris Clifford, in his only season with Yorkshire, did not progress. Because of Boycott's injury and Wilson's loss of form the captaincy occasionally

Captain caught: Yorkshire's early-season 1972 match against the touring Australians at Bradford was abandoned after the first day was lost to rain, so it was decided to play two one-day warm-up games instead. Both ended in no results, but Geoffrey Boycott picked up a century in the first before Australian skipper Ian Chappell was caught at slip by Philip Sharpe off Don Wilson for 17, above. The wicket-keeper is David Bairstow. *(Photo: Mick Pope Archive)*

passed to Philip Sharpe and once to Tony Nicholson. None of this was very settling, and only two players, Hutton and the lively David Bairstow, played in every game.

Yorkshire ultimately were 10th in the Championship — three places better than in 1971 but hardly satisfactory. When Bill Bowes, the once great fast bowler who had turned to journalism, prepared a review of the season for *Wisden* he wrote of missed opportunities for bonus batting points that could have put Yorkshire into a mid-table position, and while recognising the success of Boycott — "heavy atmosphere, green-top wickets, wet pitches, crumbling pitches, they all come alike to him", he

JOE LISTER: As members will remember him in the office

ANDY DALTON: Walked from a Yorkshire career

(Photos: Ron Deaton Archive)

added: "He is the sheet anchor of the side, but never the powerhouse".

Yet clearly Boycott did need better batting support.

With the new Benson & Hedges Cup the county had a good run of success. They started with a nine-wicket win over Lancashire, and only lost one regional game. In the semi-final they easily beat Gloucestershire, and they must have fancied their chances against Leicestershire in the final. But with Boycott still out with injury Yorkshire in 55 overs could manage only 135-9 and were easily beaten by five wickets. It did not help that Leicestershire were shrewdly captained by Raymond Illingworth and that their top scorer, Balderstone, was an ex-Yorkshire player.

In the Gillette Cup Yorkshire were eliminated in their first match, but they did rather better in the popular John Player League, winning 10 of their 16 games. They finished fourth to Kent, who won only one more game but to whom Yorkshire had lost by nine wickets. Barrie Leadbeater had a handsome average of 55 in that competition to top other Yorkshire players. The Second XI did head the Minor Counties table but, despite having a team which had or would include 10 first-class players, lost to Bedfordshire in the Challenge Match.

Off the field Yorkshire secured a modest financial surplus for the year. Yet the club's assets, without the ownership of any ground, were minimal, consisting just of cars and office furniture, and their liabilities were less than £10,000.

That all portrays a very different picture to 50 years later. For 1973 there were, as always, renewed hopes of better days ahead.

50 Years Ago

YORKSHIRE'S FIRST CLASS HIGHLIGHTS OF 1972

Win by an innings (1)

    Yorkshire (345-8 dec) defeated Glamorgan (86 and 135) by an innings and 124 runs at Scarborough

Totals of 400 and over (none)

Opponents dismissed for under 100 (3)

60	v. Warwickshire at Bramall Lane, Sheffield	86	v. Glamorgan at Scarborough
		97	v. Gloucestershire at Middlesbrough

Century Partnerships (3)

For the 1st wicket (2)

  181   G Boycott and R G Lumb   v. Hampshire at Southampton
  119   G Boycott and P J Sharpe   v. Lancashire at Leeds

For the 3rd wicket (1)

  109   G Boycott and J H Hampshire   v. Somerset at Taunton

Centuries (9)

G Boycott (6))

- 204 * v. Leicestershire at Leicester
- 122 * v. Somerset at Taunton
- 121   v. Essex at Chelmsford
- 105   v. Lancashire at Leeds
- 105   v. Hampshire at Southampton
- 100   v. Nottinghamshire at Worksop

J H Hampshire (2)

- 111   v. Glamorgan at Scarborough
- 103   v. Middlesex at Lord's

A J Dalton (1)

- 128   v. Middlesex at Leeds

5 wickets in an innings (11

A G Nicholson (4)

- 7- 49 v. Lancashire at Leeds
- 5- 32 v. Glamorgan at Scarborough
- 5- 49 v. Derbyshire at Chesterfield
- 5- 55 v. Gloucestershire at Middlesbrough

C M Old (3)

- 6- 69 v. Kent at Bradford
- 5- 26 v. Derbyshire at Bramall Lane, Sheffield
- 5- 39 v. Worcestershire at Bramall Lane, Sheffield

R A Hutton (2)

- 5- 27 v. Glamorgan at Scarborough
- 5- 72 v. Somerset at Taunton

5 wickets in an innings *(Continued)*

G A Cope (1)
- 6- 40   v. Oxford University at Harrogate

C C Clifford (1)
- 5- 70   v. Surrey at The Oval

10 wickets in a match (none)

3 catches in an innings (8)

D L Bairstow (5)
- 4   v. Northamptonshire at Northampton 1st innings
- 3   v. Derbyshire at Chesterfield
- 3   v. Glamorgan at Scarborough
- 3   v. Northamptonshire at Northampton 2nd innings
- 3   v. Kent at Bradford

J H Hampshire (2)
- 3   v. Glamorgan at Scarborough
- 3   v. Warwickshire at Bramall Lane, Sheffield

R G Lumb (1)
- 5   v. Gloucestershire at Middlesbrough

3 dismissals in an innings (none)

5 catches in a match (3)

D L Bairstow (1)
- 7 (4 + 3)   v. Northamptonshire at Northampton

J H Hampshire (1)
- 5 (2 + 3)   v. Glamorgan at Scarborough

R G Lumb (1)
- 6 (1 + 5)   v. Gloucestershire at Middlesbrough

Debut (1

In First Class cricket: C C Clifford

Caps awarded (None)

LIST A HIGHLIGHTS OF 1972

Wins by 9 wickets (2)

Lancashire (82) lost to Yorkshire (84-1) at Bradford — Benson & Hedges Cup
Minor Counties North (170-9) lost to Yorkshire (173-1) at Middlesbrough
— Benson & Hedges Cup

Totals of 200 and over (1)

211-4   v. Northamptonshire at Bramall Lane, Sheffield (won)
— John Player League

Opponents dismissed for under 100 (3)

82   v. Lancashire at Bradford — Benson & Hedges Cup
85   v. Sussex at Bradford — Benson & Hedges Cup
90   v. Gloucestershire at Tewkesbury — John Player League

Match aggregates of 400 and over (1)

412   Yorkshire (211-4) defeated Northamptonshire (201-8) at Bramall Lane, Sheffield
— John Player League

Century Partnerships (4)

For 1st wicket (1)

    129   P J Sharpe and B Leadbeater v. Minor Counties North at Middlesbrough
                                                            — Benson & Hedges Cup

For 2nd wicket (1)

    109   G Boycott and B Leadbeater v. Australians at Bradford

For 3rd wicket (1)

    109   B Leadbeater and R G Lumb v. Northamptonshire at Bramall Lane, Sheffield
                                                            — John Player League

For 6th wicket (1)

    110   B Leadbeater and C Johnson v. Nottinghamshire at Hull
                                                                       — John Player League

Centuries (2)

  G Boycott (1)

    105   v. Australians at Bradford

  J H Hampshire (1)

    106 * v. Lancashire at Manchester — John Player League

4 wickets in an innings (7)

  A G Nicolson (4)

      6-27 v. Minor Counties North at Middlesbrough — Benson & Hedges Cup
      6-36 v. Somerset at Bramall Lane, Sheffield — John Player League
      5-17 v. Nottinghamshire at Hull — John Player League
      4-26 v. Derbyshire at Chesterfield — Benson & Hedges Cup

  R A Hutton (1)

      4-18 v. Surrey at The Oval — John Player League

  C M Old (1)

      5-38 v. Northamptonshire at Bramall Lane, Sheffield — John Player League

  D Wilson (1)

      5-26 v. Lancashire at Bradford — Benson & Hedges Cup

3 catches in an innings (4)

  D L Bairstow (4)

      3   v. Derbyshire at Chesterfield — Benson & Hedges Cup
      3   v. Sussex at Bradford — Benson & Hedges Cup
      3   v. Leicestershire at Lord's — Benson & Hedges Cup
      3   v. Hampshire at Bradford — John Player League

3 dismissals in an innings (None)

List A Debuts (none)

50 YEARS AGO

YORKSHIRE AVERAGES 1972

ALL FIRST-CLASS MATCHES

Played 21 Won 4 Lost 5 Drawn 12 Abandoned 1

County Championship: Played 20 Won 4 Lost 5 Drawn 11

BATTING AND FIELDING (*Qualification 10 completed innings*)

Player	M.	I.	N.O.	Runs	H.S.	100s	50s	Avge	ct/st
G Boycott	10	17	5	1156	204*	6	4	96.33	5
J H Hampshire	18	28	2	805	111	2	4	30.96	19
R G Lumb	14	22	0	611	79	0	4	27.77	14
B Leadbeater	19	31	3	761	71	0	2	27.17	6
P J Sharpe	11	17	0	370	53	0	1	21.76	10
R A Hutton	21	30	4	544	57*	0	1	20.92	15
C Johnson	20	28	4	409	53	0	1	17.04	9
C M Old	15	21	3	302	64	0	1	16.77	6
P J Squires	8	14	0	210	64	0	1	15.00	3
D L Bairstow	21	27	4	284	52*	0	1	12.34	42/5
A G Nicholson	18	19	8	114	31	0	0	10.36	3
D Wilson	14	19	2	157	25	0	0	9.23	4

Also played

A J Dalton	3	4	0	178	128	1	0	44.50	0
H P Cooper	7	10	4	97	47	0	0	16.16	4
M K Bore	9	6	1	49	15	0	0	9.80	0
J D Woodford	2	4	0	36	18	0	0	9.00	0
G A Cope	9	7	3	29	8*	0	0	7.25	4
C C Clifford	11	12	4	39	12*	0	0	4.87	5
A L Robinson	1	0	0	0	—	0	0	—	0

BOWLING (*Qualification 10 wickets*)

Player	Overs	Mdns	Runs	Wkts	Avge	Best	5wI	10wM
C M Old	378.5	106	931	54	17.24	6-69	3	0
G A Cope	221.5	97	407	23	17.69	6-40	1	0
A G Nicholson	547.3	152	1203	62	19.40	7-49	4	0
R A Hutton	413.3	87	1109	54	20.53	5-27	2	0
H P Cooper	200.1	45	495	24	20.62	4-37	0	0
C C Clifford	266.5	103	666	26	25.61	5-70	1	0
D Wilson	271	84	731	21	34.80	4-83	0	0
M K Bore	239	106	531	15	35.40	3-56	0	0

Also bowled

J H Hampshire	24	10	34	3	11.33	3-22	0	0
A L Robinson	21	7	42	0	—	0-19	0	0
C Johnson	12	4	31	0	—	0-7	0	0
J D Woodford	7	2	42	0	—	0-42	0	0

50 YEARS AGO

YORKSHIRE AVERAGES 1972

LIST A

Played 25 Won 15 Lost 8 No Result 2 Abandoned 1

John Player League: 4th (17) Benson & Hedges Cup: Losing Finalist
Gillette Cup: Round 1

BATTING AND FIELDING *(Qualification 10 completed innings)*

Player	M.	I.	N.O.	Runs	H.S.	100s	50s	Avge	ct/st
G Boycott	17	17	4	599	105	1	3	46.07	8
B Leadbeater	23	22	5	641	86*	0	3	37.70	2
R A Hutton	25	19	6	297	61	0	1	22.84	8
C Johnson	24	14	4	218	51*	0	1	21.80	6
J H Hampshire	23	21	1	413	106*	1	0	20.65	1
P J Sharpe	17	17	0	256	89	0	1	17.06	8

Also played

H P Cooper	14	7	6	44	10*	0	0	44.00	1
R G Lumb	8	7	1	171	56	0	2	28.50	3
A J Dalton	3	3	0	53	29	0	0	17.66	1
P J Squires	9	9	1	123	46	0	0	15.37	1
J D Woodford	21	14	5	136	43*	0	0	15.11	7
C M Old	24	13	4	107	30	0	0	11.88	5
M K Bore	3	1	0	10	10	0	0	10.00	0
D Wilson	17	6	1	30	12*	0	0	6.00	5
D L Bairstow	25	11	2	50	21	0	0	5.55	29/1
A G Nicholson	20	6	2	22	10	0	0	5.50	4
A L Robinson	1	0	0	0	—	0	0	—	0
G A Cope	1	0	0	0	—	0	0	—	0

BOWLING *(Qualification 4 wickets)*

Player	Overs	Mdns	Runs	Wkts	Avge	Best	4wI	RPO
A G Nicholson	167.5	35	466	39	11.94	6-27	4	2.77
D Wilson	115	27	379	24	15.79	5-26	0	3.29
J D Woodford	163.1	27	559	29	19.27	3-14	0	3.42
C M Old	195.3	34	585	28	20.89	5-38	1	2.99
H P Cooper	101.5	10	304	13	23.38	2-17	0	2.98
R A Hutton	187.5	29	603	24	25.12	4-18	1	3.21

Also bowled

A L Robinson	8	0	40	1	40.00	1-40	0	5.00
M K Bore	11	3	43	1	43.00	1-43	0	3.90
C Johnson	2	0	8	0	—	0 -8	0	4.00
B Leadbeater	3	0	10	0	—	1-10	0	3.33
G A Cope	4	1	9	0	—	0 9	0	2.25

Bicentenary of slow birth for the 'county'

WHY DID IT TAKE YORKSHIRE SO LONG TO CATCH UP?

By Jeremy Lonsdale

Two hundred years ago, on August 26, 1822, the first major game was played on the new ground at Darnall in Sheffield, between 15 of Sheffield and Nottingham. A large crowd attended, although the game is memorable less for Sheffield's heavy defeat than the collapse of a temporary stand. During the decade Sheffield became the centre of Yorkshire cricket with a second ground opening at Darnall in 1824, and another at Hyde Park in 1826. All venues were enclosed, allowing the owners to charge admission to watch some of the best players of the day.

Yet despite these developments it would be more than 40 years before Yorkshire County Cricket Club was established in 1863, and even longer before a truly representative county side played regularly. Even with talented players like Marsden, Dearman, Vincent, Chatterton and Sampson, Yorkshire cricket took several decades to reach the standards of southern counties, raising the question — why did it take so long?

In the early years of recorded cricket in Yorkshire — from the 1760s to the late 1820s — the game developed in localised pockets, with minimal cross-over between parts of the county. The strongest areas were around Sheffield and Leeds and among some towns and villages in the North Riding. Playing cricket at this time generally involved limited travel and occasional fixtures with the same opponents. Grounds were mostly rudimentary. Thus, cricket in Yorkshire was a pale imitation of that played in parts of the South.

Towards the end of the 1820s there are indications that a cross-county perspective was growing. Whether this was a sign of easier travel, greater confidence in local cricket, or a desire to emulate increasingly visible developments elsewhere is hard to say. Perhaps some noticed reports of teams with unofficial and misleading titles like *Nottinghamshire* and *Leicestershire*. Or were inspired by the first county side to visit Yorkshire — Sussex, which played All England at Sheffield in 1827.

Possibly influenced by such developments, some clearly had a Yorkshire-wide perspective. In 1828 an article in a Sheffield paper hoped Yorkshire would "form a common club for the county". This

Where it all began: the new ground at Darnall in the 1820s.
(Photo: Mick Pope Archive)

would "make the best players known to each other; it would enable them to concentrate their strength, and by the collection of a small contribution produce an adequate fund to pay certain players (whose circumstances render it necessary) for practising, make up stake money, travelling expenses etc."

Such thoughts coincided with the start of connections between cricketers in different parts of the county. In August 1829 Sheffield Wednesday

Token to get in

travelled to Ripon for the first time. Some of the Sheffield cricketers openly showed their contempt for what they considered "unsophisticated" local players, but Ripon still won by 18 runs, and the reputation of cricketers in the north of Yorkshire increased.

County-wide developments continued. In 1830 a match was played between Sheffield Wednesday and a side referred to as "Yorkshire", although only three men — from Doncaster and Ripon — were not from Sheffield. In 1832 a "Grand Yorkshire Cricket Match" was played at Leeds between Sheffield and "Twenty-Two chosen Men of all Yorkshire". The 22 were selected from some of the most significant clubs in Yorkshire — Leeds, Thirsk, Ripon, Bedale, Harewood and Yarm — but the difficulties of arranging a cross-county side were clear. Thirteen did not turn up, and replacements were selected on the ground.

A big step forward was the first "county"match, when Yorkshire played Norfolk in 1833, followed by similar contests in 1834 and 1836.

A fixture with Sussex was also held in 1835. However, the following year, the organiser, W H Woolhouse, announced that the cost of bringing together men from across Yorkshire was not covered by gate receipts. The risk for those organising big matches was made worse because the standard — particularly of bowling — was still lower than in the south. In 1838 one of Sheffield's finest players, James Dearman, was easily beaten twice by Kent's Alfred Mynn at single-wicket, making Yorkshire cricketers nervous about taking on men from elsewhere.

Thereafter, it was nearly a decade before sides with the name *Yorkshire* played occasional games with Manchester, Kent, Lancashire, Surrey, Sheffield and, from 1846, the All England Eleven. The restart of "county" fixtures was linked to the revival of Sheffield cricket, which had been in a slump in the early 1840s.

The story of the development of county-level cricket in Yorkshire is one of slow progress. There were few matches before 1861, although not every proposed fixture appears to have taken place. In 1850 games with Surrey and Kent were mentioned, but did not happen. In 1852 possible matches with Nottinghamshire and Surrey, with Surrey the following year, and one with Nottinghamshire in 1855 also came to nothing, suggesting Sheffield was struggling to find the necessary financial backing. Yorkshire cricketers concentrated on popular inter-town matches.

In 1855 Sheffield Cricket Club offered a "Cricketers County Champion Challenge Cup" for competition between four "recognised cricketing counties". This was to celebrate the opening of the new ground at Bramall Lane, but did not take place due to existing obligations. Instead, Yorkshire played Sussex for the first time for 20 years, but were well beaten as Wisden made a memorable 148.

After this resounding defeat no further matches by a county side were played in the 1850s, and Yorkshire did not take on All England Eleven between 1856 and 1860. The shortcomings in Yorkshire cricket were clear. Local bowling had been considered weak since the early 1840s, and Yorkshire batsmen had struggled to play "the extraordinary straight bowling" of Wisden and Grundy.

Despite this, observers highlighted the array of talent in the county, which raises the question of why those leading Yorkshire cricket struggled to exploit what was available. One charge was that the side was too narrowly selected. Sheffield undoubtedly had very capable players, and results in games with the rest of the county provided some justification for so many Sheffield men appearing in the Yorkshire side. Nevertheless, some considered there was Sheffield bias in team selection and better men from elsewhere were ignored.

Many professionals also needed to be working, rather than practising — and so not earning — as members of a county side. Many had commitments inside and outside cricket, and probably did not want to break long-term contracts to play in occasional matches.

The cricket of the day revolved around individuals. Whether it was professionals contracted to specific clubs for the summer, men contesting single-wicket matches, or the "given men" employed by teams to take on the touring elevens, the focus was on single players, rather than sides of exclusive contractors. This worked against the formation of a county team.

There were other challenges. Some believed that, unlike the Sussex and Surrey teams, Yorkshire players did not practise enough together, and so were less familiar with each other's strengths and weaknesses. Developments at Bramall Lane after 1855 may have preoccupied the leading lights of Sheffield cricket. The new ground gave Sheffield cricket a solid base, but created significant financial demands. It is also possible that some in Yorkshire cricket were not happy with so many professionals playing in the strongest sides. Efforts were made, especially in York, to put out "gentlemen" sides to play the All England Eleven. And the heavy defeat by Sussex in 1855 may have had an impact. Those concerned with Yorkshire's reputation may have been unwilling to risk further defeats until they could find better bowlers.

In the end the one common factor was money. Organising fixtures against southern counties was expensive and risky. It was cheaper to play within Yorkshire or host matches against touring sides. For many years the responsibility appears to have been beyond even the resources of the strongest centre of Yorkshire cricket — Sheffield. However, from 1858 renewed efforts were made to raise more funds to play important county games there. In 1861 the Public Match Fund, a distinct sum separate from that financing particular clubs, got things moving, and in 1863 it was with some trepidation that Yorkshire County Cricket Club was formed and began to harness the talents from across the county.

HENRY 'HARRY' SAMPSON
(Photo: Mick Pope Archive)

Jeremy Lonsdale has written four books on Yorkshire cricket history.

Book Review

TRIUMPHS AND TROUBLES IN PRE-WAR GOLDEN AGE

By Graham Hardcastle

**A Game Divided: Triumphs and troubles in Yorkshire cricket in the 1920s   By Jeremy Lonsdale   *(shop.acscricket.com £15*

When writing for this *Yearbook* Jeremy continues to come up trumps with his wonderful historical pieces on Yorkshire. It will be no surprise, therefore, to learn that his latest book on the county is a cracker.

A Game Divided: Triumphs and troubles in Yorkshire cricket in the 1920s was published in 2020, and is his third in a series looking back through the history at Headingley.

It is Lonsdale's fourth book in all on Yorkshire, the other a biography of former all-rounder and captain Tom Emmett.

Published by The Association of Cricket Statisticians and Historians, this latest book was nominated for the Cricket Writers Book of the Year award in 2021.

The 1920s was a period of significant success for Yorkshire, the Championship won four times on the run between 1922-1925. A team including Holmes, Kilner, Leyland, Rhodes, Robinson and Sutcliffe only lost 20 matches through the whole decade.

However, as the title suggests, it wasn't all great cricket and silverware to polish. The game was divided.

There were fallouts between amateur players and professionals, of which counties were made up of both at the time, and fierce battles between the northern and southern teams among many other things. Lonsdale attributes some of this discontent to the fact that a tense nation had only just come out of the First World War.

He starts this book with a chapter on a mid-season table-topping clash between Yorkshire and Middlesex at Bramall Lane, Sheffield. It was a fixture which saw the hosts wanting to exact revenge after an early season defeat at Lord's, and brought about an unsavoury atmosphere as the home crowd sensed Middlesex blood.

Continuing to explore the acrimony through the body of the book, Lonsdale ends with a chapter exploring the quality of this team in a chapter entitled *A Great Side?*

One thing is for sure, this is A Great Book! It can be purchased for £15 from *shop.acscricket.com* among many other places.

Wilfred Rhodes – The Triumphal Arch
Von Krumm Publishing

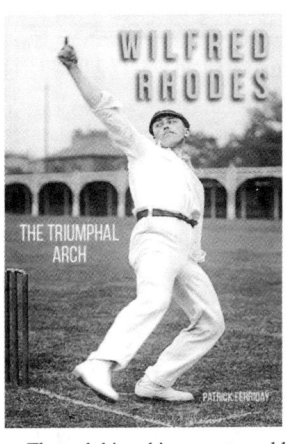

By Patrick Ferriday
Standard Edition £25

Wilfred Rhodes was, is (and always will be) the most prolific player first-class cricket has ever known. No one played more games, took more wickets or batted more often. Yet war took four seasons from him.

A *Wisden* cricketer in his debut season, he represented England for the last time 32 years later at the age of 52. In his first game he bowled to Grace and in his last to Bradman: he was *The Triumphal Arch* between the game's two most famous players.

The man from Kirkheaton was a giant of the game, and not just for the records he broke and still holds.

Through his achievements and longevity he became a part of the fabric of society in Yorkshire and beyond for 32 years. Forty years after retiring he was still giving interviews, totally blind and having outlived all his contemporaries.

The words of Alfred Pullin, *Old Ebor*, upon Rhodes's retirement:

He bestrides the world of bat and ball like a Colossus. Historians a hundred years hence will be trying to prove the man never existed – that he is a glorious myth, invented by a county that was mad on cricket and its supremacy therein. His feats already wear the aspect of legend; and we can imagine future pundits, who pride themselves on their commonsense and superstition, pointing to the fact that in 1926, when he was reputed to have won a Test match for England at the Oval, he was nearing his 49th birthday, and at the time of his retirement was a grandfather.

The thing sounds too absurd for belief, and future ages may be too sceptical to believe it. Here, nevertheless, we put it on record that the thing is true.

The book contains 408 pages, with 146 pictures, many previously unseen, courtesy of the Rhodes family archive and Yorkshire Cricket Foundation.

Standard edition – £25. Limited edition signed by granddaughter Margaret Garton and author of cricket books David Frith contains a CD of an extended interview between Rhodes and Frith from 1970 – £75.

Available from *www.vonkrummpublishing.co.uk* and all usual outlets.

Brook hits first century of 2022

Harry Brook scored an unbeaten 115 during Yorkshire's opening game of 2022, a two-day pre-season friendly against Gloucestershire in Dubai in March.

Gloucester batted on day one and made 326-4 before Yorkshire responded with 293-2, a total underpinned by Brook's century before he retired to give others valuable time at the crease.

Will Fraine enjoyed a profitable four-game first-class spell playing in Zimbabwe through January and February, where he represented the Eagles team. The 25-year-old from Huddersfield posted scores of 45, 88 and 85 in his favoured opener's position.

Wainwright champion skipper

Former Yorkshire all-rounder David Wainwright led Castleford to the Yorkshire Premier League North title, their maiden crown, while it was a similar case in the YPL South League as Appleby Frodingham celebrated maiden success at that level. There were title retentions in the Bradford League and the North Yorkshire South Durham Leagues as Woodlands and Richmondshire claimed silverware.

Scorecard — Page 179

Obituary

RAYMOND ILLINGWORTH CBE

By Graham Hardcastle

An integral figure in the Yorkshire team which won seven titles in the 1960s, including six County Championships, Raymond Illingworth CBE died at the age of 89 on Christmas Eve.

An *Ashes*-winning captain Down Under in 1970-71, his contribution to Farsley Cricket Club will never, ever be forgotten in that neck of the woods.

His first-class and List A playing career spanned between 1951 and 1983 for Yorkshire, Leicestershire and England, winning titles for all those teams as captain.

In 1957 he completed a seasonal "double", passing 1,000 first-class runs and 100 wickets, for the first of five times in his career.

He later became a highly successful and respected coach, administrator and broadcaster, while continuing to be heavily involved at Farsley, where he was president at the time of his death.

Leader, legend, a national icon. Raymond Illingworth in off-spin mode
(Photo: Mick Pope Archive)

The Bradford League said in tribute: "Over more than 70 years he maintained a strong bond with the club. There aren't many top players who have given back so much to their club after playing at the top level. You were just as likely to see him preparing the pitch as chasing sponsors or selling raffle tickets, usually sporting his trademark shorts."

An off-spinning all-rounder, "Illy" played 61 Tests and three ODIs.

He captained England in the first ever one-day international against Australia at Melbourne in early 1971, and his final one-day international came shortly after his 41st birthday against New Zealand at Old Trafford in 1973, the same year he was awarded a CBE. He remains the oldest to have played in that format.

He took 122 Test wickets, including a best analysis of 7-29, and scored 1,836 Test runs with two centuries. His first-class career brought him 24,134 runs and 2,072 wickets.

Above all the personal statistics, he would have been much happier with the silverware he won — seven Championship titles with Yorkshire and lastly the Sunday League title as county captain in 1983, having returned to Headingley from Leicestershire, where he had nurtured a young David Gower.

He left Yorkshire for Grace Road in 1969 because cricket chairman Brian Sellers would not agree to him being given a three-year contract, but he accepted an offer to return to Headingley as cricket manager in 1979 when Yorkshire were going through a troublesome period due to a combination of poor results and the Geoffrey Boycott controversy.

During the 1982 season, aged 50, he replaced Chris Old as Yorkshire captain, and in the following year led them to the John Player (Sunday) League title. But he could not prevent them from finishing bottom of the County Championship table for the first time in the club's history.

Illingworth's post playing career is best known for becoming England's chair of selectors in 1994 followed by roles as coach and manager. He was a well known voice on the BBC's cricket coverage.

One of his daughters, Diane, is married to former Yorkshire batter Ashley Metcalfe. He also leaves behind Victoria. In November, he revealed he was battling oesophageal cancer. His wife, Shirley, had died a year earlier following her own battle against cancer.

Yorkshire chair Lord Kamlesh Patel said: "I am saddened to hear of the death of Ray, one of Yorkshire's and England's greatest players. He will be fondly remembered by fans of cricket across the county and the nation. My heart goes out to his family and all who knew him."

Former Yorkshire opening batter Bryan Stott, who spent his entire county career playing alongside Illingworth, said: "All of us who grew up with Raymond knew him as a good team man with a marvellous cricketing brain. He could read a wicket better than anyone, and was a tremendously tough competitor.

"From those early days when he first scored a century for Farsley it was obvious that he was a great player in the making. He was also a good person to know, and all the qualities that Raymond possessed don't always come together in the same person."

Yorkshire president Geoff Cope, who took over from Illingworth as the county's premier off-spinner, said: "Raymond was without doubt one of Yorkshire's greatest cricketers of all time and one of their finest all-rounders. It would not be unreasonable to link him with the likes of

George Hirst and Wilfred Rhodes in what he achieved for Yorkshire. Coming in at six he could get you out of any trouble you may be in and, of course, if the ball turned he was among the very best of spinners.

"He went on to become a very successful captain for England and Leicestershire, but he never forgot where it all began, and served Farsley Cricket Club in so many ways throughout his life."

RAYMOND (RAY) ILLINGWORTH
FIRST-CLASS CRICKET FOR YORKSHIRE 1951 TO 1968
and 1982 TO 1983
FIRST-CLASS CRICKET FOR LEICESTERSHIRE 1969 TO 1978

Born: Pudsey June 8, 1932 Died: December 24, 2021
Right-hand batsman. Right-arm off-break bowler
Debut for Yorkshire: v. Hampshire at Leeds May 19, 1951
Last played: v. Essex at Chelmsford September 10, 1983
Yorkshire Cap: August 5, 1955

YORKSHIRE BATTING AND FIELDING

Season	M	I	NO	Runs	HS	Avge	100s	50s	Ct
1951	1	1	0	56	56	56.00	0	1	0
1952	4	3	1	38	17*	19.00	0	0	1
1953	34	40	11	823	146*	28.37	1	2	11
1954	24	33	5	426	59	15.21	0	2	14
1955	26	33	6	980	138	36.29	2	5	20
1956	34	46	8	755	78	19.86	0	4	12
1957	31	48	9	1193	97	30.58	0	8	15
1958	29	42	8	613	81*	18.02	0	2	8
1959	27	44	12	1490	162	46.56	4	4	24
1960	28	41	7	906	86	26.64	0	4	21
1961	31	46	4	1029	75	24.50	0	7	20
1962	35	55	8	1610	127	34.25	3	8	28
1963	20	27	5	592	107*	26.90	1	0	14
1964	33	44	9	1301	135	37.17	2	7	17
1965	31	47	8	916	90	23.48	0	3	25
1966	25	36	8	666	98*	23.78	0	2	20
1967	23	30	8	718	68*	32.63	0	4	6
1968	26	30	8	717	100*	32.59	1	3	15
1982	13	6	2	86	33	21.50	0	0	3
1983	21	16	4	71	16	5.91	0	0	11
	496	668	131	14986	162	27.90	14	66	285

YORKSHIRE BOWLING

Seasons	Matches	Overs	Mdns	Runs	Wkts	Avge	Best	5wI	10wM
1951	1	0	0	0	0	—	—	0	0
1952	4	57	14	121	4	30.25	3-33	0	0
1953	34	813.2	240	2023	75	26.97	7-22	2	0
1954	24	309.3	93	683	25	27.32	8-69	1	1
1955	26	541.1	182	1229	40	30.72	4-15	0	0
1956	34	620.5	204	1348	103	13.08	6-15	5	1
1957	31	766.2	271	1753	92	19.05	9-42	5	1
1958	29	626.2	198	1390	81	17.16	7-49	6	0
1959	27	830.5	267	1931	92	20.98	5-35	2	0
1960	28	871.3	374	1689	98	17.23	8-70	7	1
1961	31	1025	415	2080	120	17.33	8-50	9	1
1962	35	1047.2	412	2195	116	18.92	7-40	8	0
1963	20	437.5	165	917	49	18.71	6-13	3	0
1964	33	1012.4	374	2131	122	17.46	7-49	7	1
1965	31	819	346	1560	94	16.59	8-20	6	0
1966	25	767.1	292	1515	96	15.78	6-30	8	1
1967	23	681	272	1289	78	16.52	7- 6	5	2
1968	26	696.5	251	1414	105	13.46	7-73	5	2
1982	13	223.4	65	587	9	65.22	2-32	0	0
1983	21	411.5	137	951	32	29.71	4-48	0	0
	496	12,551	4572	26,806	1431	18.73	9-42	79	11

Centuries (14)

1953	146*	v. Essex	at Hull
1955	116	v. Essex	at Southend on Sea
	138	v. MCC	at Scarborough
1959	150	v. Essex	at Colchester
	162	v. Indians	at Sheffield
	122	v. Sussex	at Hove
	105*	v. MCC	at Scarborough
1962	107	v. Warwickshire	at Sheffield
	127	v. Surrey	at The Oval
	115	v. Hampshire	at Bournemouth
1963	107*	v. Warwickshire	at Birmingham
1964	135	v. Kent	at Dover
	103	v. MCC	at Scarborough
1968	100*	v. Leicestershire	at Sheffield

5 wickets in an innings (79)

1953	6-29	v. Kent	at Dover
	7-22	v. Hampshire	at Bournemouth
1954	8-69	v. Surrey	at The Oval
1956	6-15	v. Scotland	at Hull
	5-62	v. Somerset	at Harrogate
	5-48	v. Lancashire	at Manchester
	6-26	v. Worcestershire	at Bradford
	5-41	v. MCC	at Scarborough
1957	5-61	v. Kent	at Tunbridge Wells
	5-52	v. Leicestershire	at Hull
	6-62	v. Hampshire	at Bournemouth
	9-42	v. Worcestershire	at Worcester
	5-31	v. Glamorgan	at Cardiff Arms Park
1958	5-37	v. Northamptonshire	at Northampton
	6-91	v. Surrey	at The Oval

5 wickets in an innings *(Continued)*

1958	7-49	v. Essex	at Middlesbrough
	5-51	v. Derbyshire	at Leeds
	6-69	v. Glamorgan	at Swansea
	5-56	v. MCC	at Scarborough
1959	5-38	v. Surrey	at Bradford
	5-35	v. Middlesex	at Scarborough
1960	5-55	v. Lancashire	at Leeds
	5-77	v. Essex	at Colchester
	5-45	v. Leicestershire	at Leicester
	5-26	v. South Africans	at Sheffield
	8-70	1st innings v. Glamorgan	at Swansea
	7-53	2nd innings v. Glamorgan	at Swansea
	6-53	v. MCC	at Scarborough
1961	5-12	v. Cambridge University	at Cambridge
	6-51	v. Nottinghamshire	at Hull
	8-50	v. Lancashire	at Manchester
	7-54	v. Warwickshire	at Middlesbrough
	5-51	v. Somerset	at Hull
	5-57	v. Gloucestershire	at Scarborough
	6-86	v. Kent	at Dover
	7-39	1st innings v. Hampshire	at Bournemouth
	5-63	2nd innings v. Hampshire	at Bournemouth
1962	5-31	v. Glamorgan	at Bradford
	5-64	v. Warwickshire	at Sheffield
	7-40	v. Northamptonshire	at Northampton
	5-33	v. Surrey	at Sheffield
	5-63	v. Gloucestershire	at Bristol
	6-26	v. Essex	at Sheffield
	5-52	v. Kent	at Middlesbrough
	5-10	v. Sussex	at Scarborough
1963	5-35	v. Warwickshire	at Scarborough
	5-13	v. Leicestershire	at Scarborough
	6-13	v. Leicestershire	at Leicester
1964	6-30	v. Oxford University	at Oxford
	6-50	v. Middlesex	at Leeds
	5-40	v. Glamorgan	at Swansea
	7-89	v. Nottinghamshire	at Scarborough
	7-49	1st innings v. Kent	at Dover
	7-52	2nd innings v. Kent	at Dover
	7-62	v. Surrey	at The Oval
1965	6-67	v. Cambridge University	at Cambridge
	6-39	v. Northamptonshire	at Northampton
	8-20	v. Worcestershire	at Leeds
	5-62	v. Warwickshire	at Sheffield
	5-39	v. Nottinghamshire	at Nottingham
	5-52	v. Leicestershire	at Leeds
1966	5-75	v. Gloucestershire	at Bristol
	5-96	1st innings v. Leicestershire	at Leicester
	6-30	2nd innings v. Leicestershire	at Leicester
	6-66	v. Warwickshire	at Birmingham
	5-42	v. Sussex	at Leeds
	5-54	v. Nottinghamshire	at Worksop
	5-33	v. Lancashire	at Manchester
	5-55	v. Kent	at Harrogate
1967	6-34	v. Worcestershire	at Hull
	6-52	1st innings v. Leicestershire	at Leicester
	5-27	2nd innings v. Leicestershire	at Leicester

5 wickets in an innings *(Continued)*

	1967	7-58	1st innings v. Gloucestershire	at Harrogate
		7- 6	2nd innings v. Gloucestershire	at Harrogate
	1968	6-44	v. Warwickshire	at Middlesbrough
		5-26	v. Middlesex	at Leeds
		6-81	v. Glamorgan	at Sheffield
		6-42	v. Worcestershire	at Sheffield
		7-37	v. MCC	at Scarborough

LEICESTERSHIRE BATTING AND FIELDING

Season	M	I	NO	Runs	HS	Avge	100s	50s	Ct
1969-78	176	237	56	5,341	153*	29.50	4	23	84

LEICESTERSHIRE BOWLING

Seasons	Matches	Overs	Mdns	Runs	Wkts	Avge	Best	5wI	10wM
1969-78	176	3,618.2	1,232	7544	372	20.27	8-38	14	0

TEST MATCHES FOR ENGLAND
BATTING AND FIELDING

Seasons	M	I	NO	Runs	HS	Avge	100s	50s	Ct
1958	1	1	1	3	3*	—	0	0	0
1959	2	3	1	118	50	59.00	0	1	5
1959/60	5	8	1	92	41*	13.14	0	0	1
1960	4	6	2	81	37	20.25	0	0	1
1961	2	3	0	28	15	9.33	0	0	5
1962	1	1	1	2	2*	—	0	0	0
1962/63	5	6	0	125	46	20.83	0	0	4
1965	1	0	0	0	—	—	0	0	0
1966	2	3	0	7	4	2.33	0	0	2
1967	4	6	1	41	12	8.20	0	0	2
1968	3	4	0	51	21	12.75	0	0	1
1969	6	9	1	253	113	31.62	1	1	7
1970/71	8	13	1	391	53	32.58	0	1	6
1971	6	9	0	242	107	26.88	1	0	4
1972	5	8	2	194	57	32.33	0	1	6
1973	6	10	0	208	65	20.80	0	1	1
	61	90	11	1836	113	23.24	2	5	45

BOWLING

Seasons	Matches	Overs	Mdns	Runs	Wkts	Avge	Best	5wI	10wM
1958	1	45	18	59	3	19.66	2-20	0	0
1959	2	85	33	124	4	31.00	2-16	0	0
1959/60	5	196	61	383	4	95.75	2-46	0	0
1960	4	77	32	146	6	24.33	3-15	0	0
1961	2	55.3	17	126	3	42.00	2-110	0	0
1962	1	34	14	81	1	81.00	1-54	0	0
1962/63	5	99.2	31	204	6	34.00	4-34	0	0
1965	1	35	14	70	4	17.50	4-42	0	0
1966	2	63	24	165	4	41.25	2-22	0	0
1967	4	200.3	93	324	23	14.08	6-29	1	0
1968	3	183.2	82	291	13	22.38	6-87	1	0
1969	6	194.3	75	372	15	24.80	4-37	0	0
1970/71	8	230.4	55	451	10	45.10	3-39	0	0
1971	6	205.3	79	364	13	28.00	5-70	1	0
1972	5	88	28	197	7	28.14	2-32	0	0
1973	6	196.4	59	450	6	75.00	3-50	0	0
	61	1989	715	3807	122	31.20	6-29	3	0

ALL FIRST-CLASS MATCHES

Matches	Innings	NO	Runs	HS	Avge	100s	50s	Ct/St
787	1073	213	24134	162	28.06	22	106	446

Overs	Maidens	Runs	Wkts	Avge	Best	5Wi	10Wm
19643.2	6879	42020	2072	20.27	9-42	104	11

LIST A: YORKSHIRE 1963 TO 1968 AND 1982 TO 1983
LIST A: LEICESTERSHIRE 1969 TO 1978

Yorkshire debut: Gillette Cup v. Nottinghamshire at Middlesbrough May 22, 1963
Last played: John Player League v. Derbyshire at Bradford August 28, 1983

YORKSHIRE BATTING AND FIELDING

Season	M	I	NO	Runs	HS	Avge	100s	50s	Ct
1963-64	2	2	1	34	23	34.00	0	0	1
1965	4	2	1	51	45	51.00	0	0	3
1966-68	4	4	3	63	32*	63.00	0	0	1
1982	13	4	3	6	2*	6.00	0	0	4
1983	18	3	3	17	9*	—	0	0	5
	41	15	11	171	45	42.75	0	0	14

YORKSHIRE BOWLING

Seasons	Matches	Overs	Mdns	Runs	Wkts	Avge	Best	4wI
1963-64	2	6.2	1	9	1	9.00	1- 6	0
1965	4	24.4	2	58	5	11.60	5-29	1
1966-68	4	15	1	54	1	54.00	1-23	0
1982	13	77	6	299	8	37.37	2-36	0
1983	18	120	16	373	25	14.92	4- 6	1
	41	243	26	793	40	19.82	5-29	2

4 wickets in an innings (2)

| 1965 | 5-29 | v. Surrey | at Lord's |
| 1983 | 4- 6 | v. Middlesex | at Hull |

ENGLAND BATTING AND FIELDING

Season	M	I	NO	Runs	HS	Avge	100s	50s	Ct
1970/71	1	1	0	1	1	1.00	0	0	0
1973	2	1	0	4	4	4.00	0	0	1
	3	2	0	5	5	2.50	0	0	1

ENGLAND BOWLING

Seasons	Matches	Balls	Mdns	Runs	Wkts	Avge	Best	4wI
1970/71	1	64	1	50	3	16.66	3-50	0
1973	2	66	1	34	1	34.00	1-34	0
	3	130	2	84	4	21.00	3-50	0

ALL LIST A MATCHES
BATTING, FIELDING AND BOWLING

M	I	NO	Runs	HS	Avge	100s	50s	Ct	Balls	M	Runs	Wkts	Avge	Best
218	144	55	2380	79	26.74	0	4	58	8097	170	4686	186	25.19	5-20

DR KEITH HOWARD OBE

Dr Keith Howard OBE, left, a generous benefactor of the arts and sports in West Yorkshire and whose Bingley-based Emerald Group acquired the naming rights of Headingley between 2018 and late 2021, died on August 12 last year, aged 89.

Dr Howard was one of Yorkshire CCC's most ardent supporters. In March 2011, as chairman of the trustees of the Emerald Foundation, he performed the opening ceremony for the £300,000 Yorkshire Cricket Museum, which the foundation had funded.

Manchester-born, he was brought up in Horsforth, and it was while a scholar at Leeds Grammar School that he developed a passion for cricket and rugby.

He played league cricket for over 60 years. In his first competitive game for Horsforth Hall Park in the Airedale and Wharfedale Junior League, he bowled Rawdon's Brian Close for a duck! It was the start of a long-lasting friendship until Brian's death in 2015.

Keith was a good enough fast bowler to attract Yorkshire's attentions. In early spring 1948, on Herbert Sutcliffe's recommendation, he was invited to a session at Headingley to select players for the forthcoming Yorkshire Federation Southern Tour.

He was one of three pace bowlers instructed by coach Arthur Mitchell to bowl at Close, but Mitchell made up his mind which of them to take on the tour as soon as one clean bowled the up-and-coming star. The name of the dark-haired youngster was Fred Trueman.

Having forged a hugely successful career in academia and industry, Keith formed the print firm Emerald in 1967 with a group of academic colleagues from the University of Bradford. The business developed into a now global brand with over 450 employees worldwide.

Dr Howard stepped down as chairman in 2017, though he remained a board member.

His generous patronage was not limited to Headingley. He was president of Opera North, which has also received substantial backing from the Emerald Foundation, as has the Grand Theatre in Leeds.

David Warner

SIDNEY FIELDEN

Sidney Fielden, right, Yorkshire's long-standing Public Relations chair, died on December 18, aged 88.

A former detective sergeant in Barnsley and Doncaster, Sidney was an eloquent and persuasive speaker who dedicated countless hours of service to YCCC.

He and his wife, Maureen, lived at Skellow, Doncaster, and he joined Yorkshire's committee as the Doncaster representative in 1981.

By then he had become closely associated with the Yorkshire Reform Group, who were sympathetic with what they saw as the poor treatment of Geoffrey Boycott by the club.

When a special general meeting was held at Harrogate over Boycott's sacking Sidney was among a number of speakers whose argument against the decision was so powerful it brought down the committee and resulted in fresh elections and the opening batter's reinstatement.

Although he later changed his views on this controversy, Sidney continued to involve himself heavily in the welfare of the club's members and became close friends with several "establishment" figures, including Bob Appleyard.

Considered something of a rebel at the start of his committee involvement, he didn't serve immediately on any of the subcommittees. But, with the changing tide, he was elected Public Relations chair in 1984. The following year he switched to the Grounds and Membership committee, but returned as PR chair in 1986 and remained in that role until briefly resigning from the General Committee in 1998.

In 1999 he returned to the General Committee as a South District representative and joined the Marketing and Membership subcommittee until the committee system was abolished in 2003. It was replaced by the Board, which was originally made up of the "Gang of Four" in Robin Smith as chair, Colin Graves (chief executive), Brian Bouttell (director of finance) and Geoff Cope (director of cricket).

In recognition of his service he was made a Yorkshire vice-president.

During his time on the committee Sidney also served on the Management Committee — formed in 1987 and first chaired by Viscount Mountgarret and later Sir Lawrence Byford.

Sidney was a lifelong Methodist and well-known local preacher.

David Warner

BERNARD BROOKE

Bernard Brooke, left, who was Yorkshire's oldest known surviving player, died on April 19, 2021, aged 91. Born in Newsome, Huddersfield, on March 3, 1930.

Brooke played in two matches for Yorkshire in 1950, and although that was the extent of his first class career he was still able to boast two notable scalps with his fast bowling.

On his debut against MCC at Lord's he shared the new ball with Alec Coxon and later in the innings had Bill Edrich caught behind by Don Brennan for 129, Yorkshire going on to lose by nine wickets. In the match which immediately followed he dismissed D B Carr, but again finished on the losing side as Yorkshire were beaten by eight wickets.

Brooke, a founder member of the Yorkshire CCC Players' Association, enjoyed a distinguished career as a professional with several clubs in the Huddersfield and Bradford Leagues.

Olivier returns to the Tests

Duanne Olivier returned to Test cricket with South Africa at the start of the year having initially retired ahead of 2019 to take up a Kolpak contract with Yorkshire. Olivier's status changed to overseas ahead of 2021 — as a result of Brexit — opening up the opportunity to play for his country once more. He played against India at home and New Zealand away in January and February, taking eight wickets in three appearances.

SHANE WARNE AND ROD MARSH

Shane Warne died of a suspected heart attack on March 4, aged 52, while on holiday in Thailand. The legendary Australian leg-spin bowler took 708 wickets in a 15-year Test career which ended in early 2007. He remains the second highest wicket-taker in Test history.

A multiple-*Ashes* winner and a World Cup champion, Melburnian Warne remained a prominent figure in the game as a respected commentator and pundit with Sky Sports among others.

He was also the coach of the London Spirit men's team in the *Hundred* and a long time opponent and friend of Yorkshire's managing director of cricket, Darren Gough.

Only three of Warne's Test wickets came in a trio of Test appearances at Headingley, while he claimed 21 wickets in six County Championship matches against Yorkshire while playing as an overseas player for Hampshire in the 2000, 2006 and 2007 seasons.

Warne, a proficient Australian Rules footballer in his youth — plus a keen tennis player and golfer, made his Test debut in 1992 and retired in early 2007 on the back of a 5-0 *Ashes* victory on home soil.

His death rocked the cricketing world, and came just hours after the passing of another Australian great, Rod Marsh, who also died of a suspected heart attack. Marsh, who was 74, claimed 355 dismissals behind the stumps in a career spanning from 1970 to 1984.

Marsh famously played in the 1981 *Ashes* Test at Headingley and put £5 on England, then down and out, at 500-1 to turn things around.

He went on to be an England Academy coach and a selector for the senior team, holding similar roles within Australian Cricket.

It says everything about Warne in particular that towards the end of the fifth *Ashes* Test at the Oval in 2005 a section of the English support interrupted their celebrations in the stands to salute him by chanting: "We only wish you were English'.

Both men will be missed greatly by the cricketing family worldwide.

Next Page: Shane Warne at Headingley in 2006 as captain of Hampshire appeals for a wicket in their County Championship match v. Yorkshire.

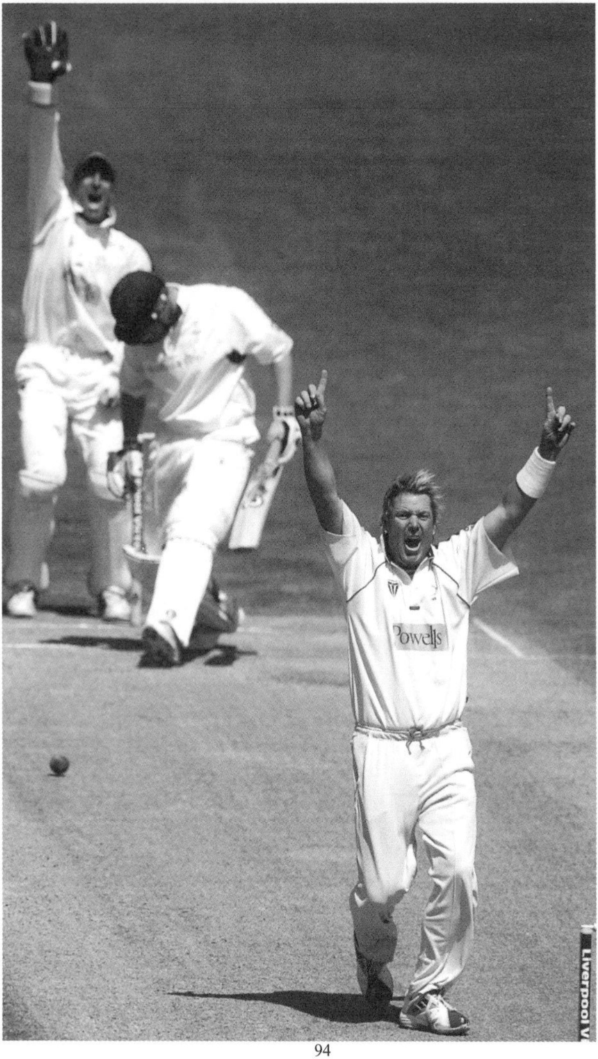
Powells
Liverpool V

YORKSHIRE'S FIRST-CLASS HIGHLIGHTS OF 2021

Wins by an innings (2)

Somerset (134 and 141) lost to Yorkshire (308) by an innings and 33 runs at Scarborough

Sussex (313 and 215) lost to Yorkshire (558) by an innings and 30 runs at Leeds

Win by 200 runs (1)

Yorkshire (379 and 330-5 dec) defeated Kent (265 and 244) by 200 runs at Canterbury

Totals of 400 and over (1)

558   v. Sussex at Leeds

Century Partnerships (7)

For 2nd wicket (2)

121	G C H Hill and T Kohler-Cadmore	v. Hampshire at West End, Southampton
103	A Lyth and T Kohler-Cadmore	v. Nottinghamshire at Nottingham

For 3rd wicket (2)

180	D J Malan and G S Ballance	v. Sussex at Leeds
119	A Lyth and J E Root	v. Kent at Canterbury

For 4th wicket (2)

131	A Lyth and H C Brook	v. Glamorgan at Leeds
102	G S Ballance and H C Brook	v. Kent at Leeds

For 9th wicket (1)

118   J E Root and S A Patterson   v. Glamorgan at Cardiff

Centuries (8)

A Lyth (3)
- 153   v. Nottinghamshire at Nottingham
- 116   v. Kent at Canterbury
- 115 *   v. Glamorgan at Leeds

H C Brook (2)
- 118   v. Somerset at Scarborough
- 113   v. Northamptonshire at Northampton

G S Ballance (1)
- 101 *   v. Hampshire at West End, Southampton

D J Malan (1)
- 199   v. Sussex at Leeds

J E Root (1)
- 101   v. Kent at Canterbury

5 wickets in an innings (5)

D M Bess (2)
- 7 -43   v, Northamptonshire at Northampton
- 6 -53   v. Sussex at Hove

M D Fisher (1)
- 5 -42   v. Somerset at Scarborough

J A Thompson (1)
- 5 -52   v. Warwickshire at Leeds

D J Willey (1)
- 5 -61   v. Kent at Canterbury

10 wickets in a match (none)

3 catches in an innings (12)

H G Duke (6)
- 6   v. Nottinghamshire at Nottingham
- 3   v. Sussex at Leeds
- 3   v. Hampshire at West End, Southampton
- 3   v. Somerset at Scarborough
- 3   v. Warwickshire at Leeds — 1st innings
- 3   v. Warwickshire at Leeds — 2nd innings

A Lyth (2)
- 3   v, Kent at Leeds
- 3   v. Sussex at Leeds

T Kohler-Cadmore (2)
- 3   v. Northamptonshire at Leeds
- 3   v. Lancashire at Manchester

J A Tattersall (2)
- 3   v. Kent at Canterbury
- 3   v. Northamptonshire at Leeds

5 catches in a match (5)

H G Duke (3)
- 6 (3 + 3) v. Warwickshire at Leeds
- 6 (6 + 0) v. Nottinghamshire at Nottingham
- 5 (3 + 2) v Sussex at Leeds

T Kohler-Cadmore (1)
- 5 (3 + 2) v. Northamptonshire at Leeds

J A Tattersall (1)
- 5 (3 + 2) v. Kent at Canterbury

3 dismissals in an innings (none)

Debuts (2)
In First Class cricket (1): H G Duke
In First Class cricket for Yorkshire (1): S A Northeast

Capped (1): H C Brook

FIRST CLASS FACTFILE
LV= COUNTY CHAMPIONSHIP 2021

Compiled by John T Potter

Versus GLAMORGAN at Leeds
1. Glamorgan last played a Championship match at Leeds in 2012.
2. First Class debut for J P McIlroy.
3. Championship debut for C Z Taylor.
4. T van der Gugten's 85 not out was his highest First Class score.
5. Glamorgan's second-innings unbroken fifth-wicket partnership of 212 between W T Root and C B Cooke was their highest against Yorkshire.
6. A Lyth passed 11,000 First Class runs during his second innings.

Versus KENT at Canterbury
1. J L Denly passed 12,550 First Class runs during his second innings.
2. D I Stevens took his 550th First Class wicket when he dismissed D M Bess in Yorkshire's first innings.
3. D J Willey's 5-61 in Kent's second innings was his first First Class five-wicket haul in an innings for Yorkshire.

Versus SUSSEX at Hove
1. Yorkshire last played a Championship match at Hove in 2015.
2. J J Carson's 5-85 was his best First Class bowling analysis.
3. G S Ballance passed 8,000 First Class runs for Yorkshire.
4. D M Bess took his 150th First Class wicket when he dismissed S van Zyl in Sussex's second innings. Bess's 6-53 in Sussex's second innings was his first First Class five-wicket haul in an innings for Yorkshire.

Versus NORTHAMPTONSHIRE at Leeds
1. Northamptonshire last played a Championship match at Leeds in 2014.
2. Yorkshire's one-run victory was their second in Championship matches and third in First Class cricket. The other Championship match was against Middlesex at Bradford in 1976. Yorkshire's other one-run victory margin was against Loughborough UCCE at Leeds in 2007, S A Patterson taking the final wicket in that match just as he did against Northamptonshire. In the match against Loughborough UCCE R M Pyrah scored his maiden First Class century, and and A Lyth made his First Class debut.

LV= COUNTY CHAMPIONSHIP FACTFILE *(Continued)*

Versus KENT at Leeds

1. N N Gilchrist made his Championship debut.
2. Weather played a large part in this match, with no play on the third day and play on the last day did not start until 2.45pm. A total of 624 minutes were lost to the weather.

Versus GLAMORGAN at Cardiff

1. Yorkshire last played a Championship match at Cardiff in 1998, when they they won by 114 runs. It was a match with fond memories for all-rounder G M Hamilton, who struck 79 and 70 and took 5-69 and 5-43.
2. H G Duke made his First Class debut.
3. Yorkshire's ninth-wicket partnership of 118 between J E Root and S A Patterson was the county's highest against Glamorgan.
4. The weather again played a large part, with no play on the first day and play on the last did not start until 4.15pm. A total of 791 minutes were lost.

Versus LANCASHIRE at Manchester

1. G C H Hill made his Championship debut.
2. H G Duke scored his maiden First Class fifty.
3. B O Coad took his 150th Championship wicket when he dismissed K K Jennings.
4. S Mahmood took his maiden five-wicket haul in an innings in First Class matches with 5-47 in Yorkshire's second innings.
5. Lancashire's last victory over Yorkshire by an innings had been at Old Trafford in 1972.

Versus SUSSEX at Leeds

1. Sussex last played a Championship match at Leeds in 2015.
2. A G H Orr and D K Ibrahim made their First Class debuts.
3. D J Malan's 199 equalled his highest Championship score.
4. J A Atkin's 5-98 was his maiden First Class five-wicket haul in an innings.
5. D M Bess took his 100th Championship wicket when he dismissed D Ibrahim in Sussex's second innings.
6. The last time Yorkshire did the double over Sussex was in 1959.

LV= COUNTY CHAMPIONSHIP FACTFILE *(Continued)*

Versus NORTHAMPTONSHIRE at Northampton

1. Yorkshire had last played a Championship match at Northampton in 2014.
2. S A Northeast made his First Class debut for Yorkshire.
3. G C H Hill's 71 in Yorkshire's first innings was his maiden First Class fifty.
4. D M Best's 7-43 in Northamptonshire's first innings was a First Class career best.
5. Yorkshire completed the double over Northamptonshire as they had in 2014.

Versus LANCASHIRE at Leeds

1. Championship debuts for G P Balderson and D J Leech.
2. No play on the second or fourth days.

Versus HAMPSHIRE at West End, Southampton

1. A Lyth with 6 in his first innings reached a total of 10,000 Championship runs.
2. G S Ballance scored his seventh century against Hampshire, the most by any Yorkshire player.
3. In Hampshire's second innings M S Crane and J M Vince never changed ends during their fifth-wicket partnership, which started after 56.2 overs and finished on 81.5 overs. Vince did not change ends until his 113th ball, ball 1 of over 95.

Versus SOMERSET at Scarborough

1. M D Fisher's 5-41 in Somerset's first innings was his First Class career best.
2. Yorkshire had last defeated Somerset by an innings at Scarborough in 2000.

Versus WARWICKSHIRE at Leeds

1. First Class debut for J G Bethell.
2. C R Woakes passed 6,000 First Class runs during his first innings.
3. S A Patterson took his 450th First Class wicket during Warwickshire's first innings. All of his wickets have been for Yorkshire.
4. J A Thompson's 5-52 in Warwickshire's second innings was his maiden five-wicket haul in a Championship match.
5. Warwickshire had last won at Leeds in a Championship match in 2011.

LV= COUNTY CHAMPIONSHIP FACTFILE *(Continued)*
Versus NOTTINGHAMSHIRE at Nottingham

1. H G Duke with six dismissals, all caught, in Nottinghamshire's first innings became only the ninth Yorkshire wicket-keeper to achieve this. D L Bairstow is the only one to have captured seven victims in an innings.
2. J A Thompson took his 50th Championship wicket when he dismissed J D M Evison in Nottinghamshire's first innings.
3. A Lyth passed 11,000 First Class runs for Yorkshire during his second innings.
4. This was Nottinghamshire's first Championship win against Yorkshire at Nottingham since 2008.

LV= Insurance County Championship 2021

Captain: S A Patterson

* Captain

§ Wicket-Keeper

Figures in brackets ( ) indicate position in Second Innings batting order, where different from First Innings

DETAILS OF PLAYERS WHO APPEARED FOR YORKSHIRE IN 2021

Player	Date of Birth	Birthplace	First-Class debut for Yorkshire	Date Capped
S A Patterson	October 3, 1983	Beverley	August 3, 2005	May 16, 2012
A Lyth	September 25, 1987	Whitby	May 16, 2007	Aug 22, 2010
G S Ballance	November 22, 1989	Harare, Zimbabwe	July 11, 2008	Sept 4, 2012
J E Root	December 30, 1990	Sheffield	May 10, 2010	Sept 4, 2012
D J Willey	February 28, 1990	Northampton	May 1, 2016	Aug 13, 2016
B O Coad	January 10, 1994	Harrogate	June 20, 2016	Sept 18, 2018
T Kohler-Cadmore	April 19, 1994	Chatham	July 3, 2017	Feb 28, 2019
D Olivier	May 9, 1992	Groblersdal, South Africa	March 31, 2019	Mar 31, 2019
D J Malan	September 3, 1987	Roehampton	August 1, 2020	Aug 1, 2020
D M Bess	July 22, 1997	Exeter	May 14, 2019	Apr 8. 2021
H C Brook	February 22, 1999	Keighley	June 26, 2016	Sept 5, 2021
M D Fisher	November 9, 1997	York	April 19, 2015	
J A Tattersall	December 15, 1994	Harrogate	June 20, 2018	
W A R Fraine	June 13, 1996	Huddersfield	June 3, 2019	
J A Thompson	October 9, 1996	Leeds	June 10, 2019	
M L Revis	November 15, 2001	Steeton	September 16, 2019	
T W Loten	January 8, 1999	York	September 23, 2019	
D J Leech	January 10, 2001	Middlesbrough	August 8, 2020	
G C H Hill	January 24, 2001	Keighley	August 15, 2020	
H G Duke	September 6, 2001	Wakefield	May 13, 2021	
S A Northeast	October 16, 1989	Ashford	July 4, 2021	

LV= County Championship — Group Three
Yorkshire v. Glamorgan

Played at Headingley, Leeds, on April 8, 9, 10 and 11, 2021
Match drawn at 5.15pm on the Fourth Day

Toss won by Yorkshire   Glamorgan 14 points, Yorkshire 11 points
Close of play: First Day, Glamorgan 310-8 (van der Gugten 80*, Hogan 40*); Second Day, Glamorgan 68-4 (W T Root 25*, Cooke)*; Third Day, Glamorgan 161-4 (Root 77*, Cooke 57*)

GLAMORGAN

First Innings		Second Innings	
N J Selman, b Coad	4	c Tattersall b Coad	0
D L Lloyd, b Fisher	4	c Brook b Coad	16
A Balbirnie, lbw b Patterson	16	c Brook b Olivier	5
W T Root, c Tattersall b Coad	43	not out	110
K S Carlson, c Lyth b Olivier	55	c Tattersall b Coad	0
*§ C B Cooke, c Kohler-Cadmore b Patterson	1	not out	102
C Z Taylor, b Fisher	9		
D A Douthwaite, b Coad	57		
T van der Gugten, not out	85		
M G Hogan, c Patterson b Coad	54		
J P McIlroy, lbw b Patterson	0		
Extras lb 2	2	Extras lb 8	8
Total	330	Total (4 wkts dec)	241

Bonus points — Glamorgan 3, Yorkshire 3
FoW: 1-8 (Selman), 2-12 (Lloyd), 3-29 (Balbirnie), 4-111 (Carlson), 5-112 (Cooke),
1st 6-128 (Taylor), 7-132 (Root), 8-254 (Douthwaite), 9-326 (Hogan), 10-330 (McIlroy).
2nd: 1-0 (Selman), 2-17 (Balbirnie), 3-29 (Lloyd), 4-29 (Carlson)

	O	M	R	W		O	M	R	W
Coad	26	5	94	4	Coad	7	3	18	3
Fisher	21	3	78	2	Olivier	14	4	33	1
Patterson	23.4	8	51	3	Patterson	14	6	30	0
Olivier	19	6	69	1	Bess	25.4	3	83	0
Bess	9	1	23	0	Root	5	0	20	0
Root	3	0	13	0	Brook	13	1	49	0

YORKSHIRE

First Innings		Second Innings	
A Lyth, lbw b Douthwaite	52	not out	115
T Kohler-Cadmore, c Cooke b Hogan	11	c Cooke b van der Gugten	4
T W Lotan, b Hogan	0	lbw b Hogan	9
J E Root, c Douthwaite b Taylor	16	c Balbirnie b Douthwaite	13
H C Brook, lbw b Lloyd	40	c Root b Hogan	60
§ J A Tattersall, lbw b van der Gugten	15	not out	15
D M Bess, not out	38		
M D Fisher, c Cooke b McIlroy	6		
* S A Patterson, c Selman b Lloyd	3		
B O Coad, c Taylor b Douthwaite	5		
D Olivier, c Cooke b Taylor	3		
Extras nb 4	4	Extras lb 5, nb 2	7
Total	193	Total (4 wkts)	223

Bonus points — Glamorgan 3
FoW: 1-19 (Kohler-Cadmore), 2-31 (Loten), 3-79 (Lyth), 4-79 (Root), 5-129 (Tattersall),
1st 6-149 (Brook), 7-160 (Fisher), 8-167 (Patterson), 9-175 (Coad), 10-193 (Olivier).
2nd: 1-19 (Kohler-Cadmore), 2-32 (Loten), 3-47 (Root), 4-178 (Brook)

	O	M	R	W		O	M	R	W
Hogan	13	4	50	2	van der Gugten	13	4	35	1
van der Gugten	12	3	48	1	Hogan	13	2	32	2
Root	2	0	6	0	Douthwaite	9	1	35	1
McIlroy	9	4	12	1	McIlroy	6	2	26	0
Douthwaite	11	3	39	2	Taylor	19	4	62	0
Taylor	4.2	1	16	2	Root	6	0	28	0
Lloyd	7	1	22	2					

Umpires: P K Baldwin and R J Warren   Scorers: J T Potter and J R Virr

Yorkshire v. Glamorgan

Lyth keeps out the cold

Landmark century: Adam Lyth on the way to his match saving 115 not out

Yorkshire were outplayed by a side who finished bottom of the Central Group in the 2020 shortened Bob Willis Trophy, and were grateful to Adam Lyth's 25th first-class century for steering them to an 11-point draw.

Lyth began his journey to 115 not out just after midday on day four when Glamorgan had set a 379 target in a minimum of 76 overs.

Yorkshire slipped to 47-3 before he and Harry Brook (60) united to save the game by sharing 131 through most of the afternoon. But this Group Three opener will be remembered largely for other reasons.

Only 32 overs were possible at the start of day three due to snow, which arrived at 12.55pm and quickly covered the Headingley outfield in a scene which screamed February rather than fielding at fine-leg. At that stage Glamorgan were 161-4 in their second innings and leading by 298. So, Yorkshire were grateful for the icy intervention.

The hosts started day three reporting muscle injuries for new-ball duo Ben Coad (pectoral) and Matthew Fisher (abdominal). They would not bowl again in a game played in good batting conditions. Coad had claimed seven wickets; four in the first innings, three in the second.

Glamorgan, invited to bat, were reduced to 29-3 and 132-7 on day one, but recovered to 330 early on day two thanks to half-centuries for Kiran Carlson, Dan Douthwaite, Timm van der Gugten (85 not out) and Michael Hogan.

Lyth top-scored with 52 in Yorkshire's 193 reply, with new signing Dom Bess adding 38 unbeaten as the 181 follow-on target was reached with nine wickets down.

The great subplot, Joe Root versus younger brother Billy, was won by Billy. Test captain Joe scored 16 and 13, while Billy posted 43 and a superb 110 not out. Joe was even the bowler when the left-hander worked two off his pads to reach three figures on the fourth morning.

LV= County Championship — Group Three
Kent v. Yorkshire

Played at Spitfire Ground, St Lawrence Canterbury, on April 15, 16, 17 and 18, 2021
Yorkshire won by 200 runs on the Fourth Day

Toss won by Yorkshire   Yorkshire 23 points, Kent 5 points

Close of play: First Day, Yorkshire 358-8 (Willey 25*, Patterson 34*); Second Day, Yorkshire 6-0 (Lyth 6*, Kohler-Cadmore 0*); Third Day, Kent 33-2 (Bell-Drummond 24*, Milnes 0*)

YORKSHIRE

First Innings		Second Innings	
A Lyth, c Robinson b Milnes	97	c Cox b Milnes	116
T Kohler-Cadmore, c Robinson b Stevens	11	c Cox b Stewart	3
T W Loten, c Robinson b Podmore	27	lbw b Milnes	21
J E Root, c Robinson b Milnes	11	b Denly	101
H C Brook, lbw b Cummins	54	not out	66
§ J A Tattersall, c Stevens b Leaning	11		
D M Bess, lbw b Stevens	36		
J A Thompson, c Robinson b Stevens	34	(6) b Denly	6
D J Willey, not out	37		
* S A Patterson, c sub (F J Klaassen) b Milnes	38		
D Olivier, b Stevens	5		
Extras b 5, lb 8, nb 2	15	Extras b 4, lb 5, nb 8	17
Total	379	Total (5 wkts dec)	330

Bonus points — Yorkshire 4, Kent 3

FoW: 1st 1-28 (Kohler-Cadmore), 2-124 (Loten), 3-143 (Root), 4-150 (Lyth), 5-219 (Brook), 6-240 (Tattersall), 7-292 (Bess), 8-299 (Thompson), 9-362 (Patterson), 10-379 (Olivier)
2nd 1-24 (Kohler-Cadmore), 2-99 (Loten), 3-218 (Lyth), 4-314 (Root), 5-330 (Thompson)

	O	M	R	W		O	M	R	W
Podmore	10	1	53	1	Milnes	18	1	68	2
Stevens	19.2	3	60	4	Stewart	10	1	32	1
Milnes	21	3	76	3	Stevens	9	1	41	0
Cummins	18	1	92	1	Cummins	14	0	48	0
Stewart	17	5	50	0	Denly	13.2	0	61	2
Denly	14	6	27	0	Leaning	11	0	71	0
Leaning	6	3	8	1					

KENT

First Innings		Second Innings	
* D J Bell-Drummond, lbw b Willey	13	b Willey	24
J M Cox, lbw b Patterson	38	b Willey	0
Z Crawley, b Olivier	1	c Lyth b Thompson	4
J L Denly, lbw b Patterson	17	(5) c Tattersall b Thompson	30
J A Leaning, c Tattersall b Patterson	0	(6) c Kohler-Cadmore b Thompson	0
§ O G Robinson, c Tattersall b Thompson	44	(7) c Tattersall b Olivier	28
D I Stevens, lbw b Brook	52	(8) c Root b Willey	47
G Stewart, c Tattersall b Olivier	40	(9) not out	8
M E Milnes, not out	26	(4) lbw b Willey	78
M L Cummins, c Kohler-Cadmore b Olivier	13	lbw b Willey	12
H W Podmore absent injured		absent injured	
Extras b 7, lb 14	21	Extras b 8, lb 5	13
Total	265	Total	244

Bonus points — Kent 2, Yorkshire 3

FoW: 1st 1-18 (Bell-Drummond), 2-25 (Crawley), 3-59 (Denly), 4-59 (Leaning), 5-86 (Cox), 6-156 (Robinson), 7-205 (Stevens), 8-247 (Stewart), 9-265 (Cummins)
FoW: 2nd 1-13 (Cox), 2-33 (Crawley), 3-34 (Bell-Drummond), 4-86 (Denly), 5-86 (Leaning), 6-148 (Robinson), 7-223 (Milnes), 8-224 (Stevens), 9-244 (Cummins)

	O	M	R	W		O	M	R	W
Willey	14	4	47	1	Willey	16.4	3	61	5
Olivier	18.1	1	55	3	Olivier	18	2	57	1
Patterson	18	3	43	3	Thompson	12	6	24	3
Thompson	16	2	52	1	Patterson	14	5	23	0
Bess	9	1	32	0	Bess	23	10	57	0
Brook	12	4	15	1	Brook	2	0	6	0
					Root	3	1	3	0

Umpires: I J Gould and M J Saggers   Scorers: L A R Hart and A L Bateup

Kent v. Yorkshire
White Rose Canterbury tale...

Second-innings centuries for Adam Lyth and Joe Root and a match-clinching five-wicket haul for new-ball seamer David Willey underpinned a hugely impressive 200-run victory.

Given the below-par performance against Glamorgan, adding to a mounting injury list boasting Ballance, Coad, Fisher and Waite, Kent were marginal favourites.

A county whose development in four-day cricket has been strong in recent years, they fielded Test batter Zak Crawley and veteran all-rounder Darren Stevens, both announced as *Wisden* Cricketers of the Year.

But from the end of day one Yorkshire dominated, and clinched a hard-fought and deserved 23-point win midway through the final day's evening session. Opener Lyth scored 97 in the first innings and 116 in the second, while Test captain Joe Root made 100 in the second on an attritional pitch.

Yorkshire opted to bat, and were 124-1 shortly before lunch, only to slip to 240-6, including Harry Brook's 54 — he also made a swashbuckling 66 in the second. Thirties from Jordan Thompson, Dom Bess, Willey and Steve

DAVID WILLEY Underpinned two century-makers

Patterson — the last two shared 63 for the ninth wicket - boosted the total to 379. Three wickets apiece for Patterson and Duanne Olivier limited Kent to 265, with seamer Harry Podmore unable to bat following a first-day side injury.

Yorkshire started their second innings late on day two, leading by 114, and Lyth continued his fabulous early form with a second Championship century in as many matches, sharing 119 for the third wicket with Root. Day three was paused for 80 minutes for the Duke of Edinburgh's funeral, and Yorkshire declared midway through the evening on 330-5. Kent, chasing 445, slipped to 86-5 before lunch on day four, only for nightwatchman Matt Milnes (78) to resist.

Yorkshire needed four wickets at tea — three with Podmore not batting — and excellent Willey claimed them all, including Milnes. Former Yorkshire batter Jack Leaning made a pair for the hosts.

LV= County Championship — Group Three
Sussex v. Yorkshire

Played at 1st Central County Ground, Hove, on April 22, 23, 24 and 25, 2021
Yorkshire won by 48 runs on the Fourth Day

Toss won by Yorkshire
Yorkshire 19 points, Sussex 4 points
Close of play: First Day, Sussex 118-3 (Haines 71*, Clark 7*); Second Day, Yorkshire 163-5 (Ballance 36*, Patterson 4*); Third Day, Sussex 136-6 (Brown 26*)

YORKSHIRE

First Innings		Second Innings	
A Lyth, c Clark b Garton	42	lbw b Robinson	66
T Kohler-Cadmore, b Garton	17	st Brown b Carson	21
G S Ballance, c Garton b Hunt	18	lbw b Carson	74
J E Root, lbw b Garton	5	c Brown b Carson	5
H C Brook, b Rawlins	14	c Brown b Garton	12
§ J A Tattersall, c Brown b Hunt	7	c Garton b Carson	8
D M Bess, c Brown b Rawlins	17	(8) lbw b Robinson	19
J A Thompson, lbw b Carson	5	(9) c Thomason b Robinson	13
D J Willey, c and b Robinson	13	(10) not out	28
* S A Patterson, c Brown b Robinson	3	(7) b Garton	12
D Olivier, not out	1	lbw b Carson	21
Extras b 2, lb 6	8	Extras b 9, lb 7, nb 10	26
Total	150	Total	305

Bonus points — Sussex 3

FoW: 1-60 (Lyth), 2-61 (Kohler-Cadmore), 3-75 (Root), 4-102 (Ballance), 5-102 (Brook),
1st   6-126 (Bess), 7-126 (Tattersall), 8-140 (Thompson), 9-149 (Patterson), 10-150 (Willey)
FoW: 1-90 (Kohler-Cadmore), 2-96 (Lyth), 3-113 (Root), 4-124 (Brook), 5-157 (Tattersall),
2nd 6-194 (Patterson), 7-226 (Ballance), 8-251 (Thompson), 9-254 (Bess), 10-305 (Olivier)

	O	M	R	W		O	M	R	W
Robinson	7.5	1	17	2	Robinson	24	5	73	3
Hunt	11	3	45	2	Crocombe	11	3	22	0
Crocombe	4	0	19	0	Carson	39.4	7	85	5
Garton	11	4	25	3	Garton	14	2	69	2
Carson	11	1	24	1	Rawlins	15	2	40	0
Rawlins	6	2	12	2					

SUSSEX

First Innings		Second Innings	
A D Thomason, c Brook b Thompson	20	b Bess	10
T J Haines, b Bess	86	c Tattersall b Thompson	37
S van Zyl, c Kohler-Cadmore b Olivier	16	b Bess	24
H T Crocombe, c Tattersall b Olivier	0	(10) c Willey b Bess	4
T G R Clark, b Olivier	33	(4) c Brook b Bess	6
§ * B C Brown, lbw b Patterson	37	(5) b Thompson	46
D M W Rawlins, c Root b Olivier	2	(6) c Kohler - Cadmore b Bess	0
G H S Garton, c Kohler-Cadmore b Patterson	14	(7) c Tattersall b Bess	21
O E Robinson, b Patterson	0	(8) lbw b Patterson	6
J J Carson, b Patterson	0	(9) c Lyth b Root	18
S F Hunt, not out	0	not out	2
Extras lb 5, nb 8	13	Extras b 6, lb 2, nb 4	12
Total	221	Total	186

Bonus points — Sussex 1, Yorkshire 3

FoW: 1-60 (Thomason), 2-104 (van Zyl), 3-104 (Crocombe), 4-168 (Clark), 5-168 (Haines),
1st   6-179 (Rawlins), 7-212 (Brown), 8-212 (Robinson), 9-212 (Carson), 10-221 (Garton)
FoW: 1-45 (Thomason), 2-64 (Haines), 3-81 (Clark), 4-86 (van Zyl), 5-86 (Rawlins),
2nd 6-136 (Garton), 7-145 (Robinson), 8-180 (Carson), 9-180 (Brown), 10-186 (Crocombe)

	O	M	R	W		O	M	R	W
Willey	9	0	35	0	Olivier	4	0	23	0
Olivier	15	2	61	4	Thompson	11	2	31	2
Patterson	12.3	3	26	4	Willey	2	0	13	0
Root	4	0	6	0	Bess	29.5	9	53	6
Bess	25	6	55	1	Patterson	12	3	32	1
Thompson	11	3	33	1	Root	11	3	26	1

Umpires: I D Blackwell and P R Pollard   Scorers: G J Irwin and P Elford

Sussex v. Yorkshire
Bess spins his winning way

"That's what great teams do — they find a way," Hove match-clincher Dom Bess said after Yorkshire had secured back-to-back away wins.

Confidence was building as a victory at Kent, summed up as "hard yakka" by coach Andrew Gale, was followed by a 48-run 19-point success.

It started with Yorkshire bowled out for 150 and losing all 10 wickets for 90 having won the toss. Only Adam Lyth (42) reached 20.

From then on Yorkshire took charge. The Sussex lead was limited to 71 by four wickets apiece for Duanne Olivier and Steve Patterson, the South African setting the tone and the captain mopping up the tail.

DOM BESS: Superb 6-53

Yorkshire's second innings started shortly after lunch on day two, and Lyth's fluent 66 moved him to within a couple of hits of 500 runs for the season. Gary Ballance top-scored with 74 in his first first-class appearance since late 2019. Sussex's Irish off-spinner Jack Carson claimed career-best figures of 5-85, including the cheap wicket of Joe Root. caught behind driving on a pitch showing increasing signs of turn.

The key moment came through the later stages of the third morning and just into the afternoon when 10th-wicket pair David Willey and Olivier shared a stand of 51, pushing the target up to 235. A game which had been in the balance was tipped definitely towards Yorkshire.

It would now take something special for a young and inexperienced Sussex side to counter the threat of Test offie Bess, even though he had taken only his first wicket of the season in the first innings. So it proved.

A theme of this fixture was early success with the bat before wickets in clusters. The Martlets reached 45-0 before Bess bowled Aaron Thomason — the first of five wickets before the close. At 136-6 Sussex need 99 more on day four. Ben Brown's 46 threatened a surprise, but Patterson, Root, Jordan Thompson and Bess, who completed a superb 6-53, all struck to guide Yorkshire to the Group Three summit.

LV= County Championship — Group Three
Yorkshire v. Northamptonshire

Played at Headingley, Leeds, on April 29 and 30 and May 1 and 2, 2021
Yorkshire won by 1 run at 3.45pm on the Fourth Day

Toss won by Northamptonshire Yorkshire 20 points, Northamptonshire 4 points

Close of play: First Day, Northamptonshire 36-0 (Curran 14*, Vasconcelos 21*); Second Day, Yorkshire 43-3 (Ballance 8*, Patterson 0*); Third Day, Northamptonshire 94-4 (Procter 20*, Zaib 1*)

YORKSHIRE

First Innings		Second Innings	
A Lyth, b Sanderson	0	c Taylor b Berg	27
T Kohler-Cadmore, b Berg	42	c Vasconcelos b Sanderson	0
W A R Fraine, lbw b Berg	11	lbw b Parnell	3
G S Ballance, c Curran Parnell	4	c Curran Parnell	16
H C Brook, lbw b Parnell	0	(6) c Keogh b Parnell	39
§ J A Tattersall, c Berg b Sanderson	26	(7) c Vasconcelos b Taylor	18
D M Bess, c Kerrigan b Berg	56	(8) lbw b Sanderson	32
J A Thompson, b Parnell	17	(9) c Vasconcelos b Kerrigan	37
D J Willey, c Vasconcelos b Parnell	12	(10) not out	41
* S A Patterson, c Vasconcelos b Parnell	9	(5) lbw b Parnell	4
D Olivier, not out	0	b Parnell	11
Extras b 19, lb 9, w 1	29	Extras b 12, lb 6, w 1	19
Total	206	Total	247

Bonus points — Yorkshire 1, Northamptonshire 3

FoW: 1-0 (Lyth), 2-66 (Fraine), 3-76 (Ballance), 4-76 (Brook), 5-80 (Kohler-Cadmore),
1st 6-137 (Tattersall), 7-160 (Thompson), 8-186 (Willey), 9-206 (Bess), 10-206 (Patterson).
FoW: 1-12 (Kohler-Cadmore), 2-25 (Fraine), 3-35 (Lyth), 4-55 (Ballance), 5-60 (Patterson),
2nd 6-86 (Tattersall), 7-145 (Bess), 8-149 (Brook), 9-214 (Thompson), 10-247 (Olivier).

	O	M	R	W		O	M	R	W
Sanderson	21	8	48	2	Sanderson	21	8	37	2
Taylor	14	5	34	0	Taylor	15	4	45	1
Parnell	15.3	4	64	5	Parnell	17.4	2	79	5
Berg	13	6	32	3	Berg	12	4	47	1
					Kerrigan	13	4	21	1

NORTHAMPTONSHIRE

First Innings		Second Innings	
B J Curran, c Brook b Patterson	15	lbw b Thompson	9
§ * R S Vasconcelos, c Kohler-Cadmore b Patterson	47	run out (Willey)	41
C O Thurston, c Lyth b Thompson	13	lbw b Thompson	0
R I Keogh, c Kohler-Cadmore b Patterson	1	c Kohler-Cadmore b Willey	5
L A Procter, c Brook b Thompson	4	c Tattersall b Willey	27
S A Zaib, b Willey	55	c Kohler-Cadmore b Olivier	25
T A I Taylor, b Bess	50	lbw b Patterson	1
W D Parnell, c Kohler-Cadmore b Willey	16	c Tattersall b Patterson	33
G K Berk, not out	11	c Tattersall b Willey	16
S C Kerrigan, c Lyth b Willey	8	c Lyth b Olivier	12
B W Sanderson, c Tattersall b Thompson	4	not out	4
Extras b 5, lb 5	10	Extras b 24, lb 17, nb 4	45
Total	234	Total	218

Bonus points — Northamptonshire 1, Yorkshire 3

FoW: 1-47 (Curran), 2-76 (Thurston), 3-76 (Vasconcelos), 4-81 (Keogh), 5-81 (Procter),
1st 6-173 (Taylor), 7-199 (Zaib), 8-217 (Parnell), 9-229 (Kerrigan), 10-234 (Sanderson).
FoW: 1-9 (Curran), 2-17 (Thurston), 3-38 (Keogh), 4-74 (Vasconcelos), 5-115 (Procter),
2nd 6-136 (Taylor), 7-146 (Zaib), 8-178 (Berg), 9-206 (Kerrigan), 10-218 (Parnell).

	O	M	R	W		O	M	R	W
Willey	18	5	43	3	Patterson	25.5	5	53	2
Thompson	18.5	6	58	3	Thompson	14	2	51	2
Patterson	18	9	35	3	Willey	18	4	39	3
Olivier	16	2	56	0	Olivier	14	2	33	2
Brook	3	1	8	0	Bess	2	1	1	0
Bess	15	6	24	1					

Umpires: N G B Cook and D J Millns Scorers: J T Potter and J R Virr

Yorkshire v. Northamptonshire
Skipper Patterson is the one

A game which displayed batting, bowling and fielding frailties produced compelling drama and a conclusion for the ages as Yorkshire extended their impressive run of results.

For only the second time in Championship history the county won by one run as Northamptonshire fell agonisingly short of a 220 target.

Steve Patterson claimed the winning wicket as the fixture's star, South African all-rounder Wayne Parnell, edged behind to a relieved Jonny Tattersall following a composed 33 to add to five wickets in each innings.

Homing in: Yorkshire's Jonny Tattersall catches Luke Procter from the bowling of David Willey

The finish brought up two thoughts. The only way this Sunday evening conclusion could have been better would have been for an expectant crowd to be present. And how big a hole will Patterson, 37 at the time, leave in Yorkshire's team when he retires?

Northamptonshire, who chose to bowl, always held the advantage. But it was never anything but slender in conditions always favouring the bowlers. Yorkshire made 206 on day one, including 56 for Dom Bess — the contest's highest score. David Willey, Jordan Thompson and Patterson all claimed three wickets in the visitors' 234 reply, but while Yorkshire had recovered from 80-5 Northamptonshire advanced from 81-5. The hosts pouched seven slip catches in the innings.

Yorkshire's early season batting struggles continued as they slipped to 86-6 in their second innings on day three, a lead of only 48, but Willey hit three sixes against his former county in an unbeaten 41 from No. 10 to help to engineer a total of 247 and that 220 target.

Northamptonshire entered the last day on 94-4, needing 126, with Willey having brilliantly run out opener and captain Ricardo Vasconcelos the night before. A few catches went down on day four, interrupted by 50 minutes of afternoon rain with the visitors at 206-9 still needing 14. At 3.45pm Patterson dramatically secured a third successive win to cement second place in Group Three behind Lancashire.

LV= County Championship — Group Three
Yorkshire v. Kent

Played at Headingley, Leeds, on May 6, 7, 8 and 9, 2021
Match drawn at 5.20pm on the Fourth Day

Toss won by Yorkshire   Kent 14 points, Yorkshire 13 points

Close of play: First Day, Kent 224-7 (O'Riordan 4*, Gilchrist 3*); Second Day, Yorkshire 240-5 (Ballance 91*, Bess 4*); Third Day, no play

KENT

* D J Bell-Drummond, c Brook b Coad	4
J M Cox, c Lyth b Patterson	20
Z Crawley, c Root b Patterson	90
J L Denly, c Lyth b Thompson	3
J A Leaning, c Lyth b Brook	47
§ O G Robinson, c Thompson b Coad	38
D I Stevens, c Tattersall b Coad	9
M K O'Riordan, b Olivier	40
N N Gilchrist, b Thompson	9
M L Cummins, not out	28
M R Quinn, c and b Bess	1
Extras b 4, lb 8, nb 4	16
Total	305

Bonus points — Kent 3, Yorkshire 2   Score at 110 overs: 300-8

FoW: 1-4 (Bell-Drummond), 2-46 (Cox), 3-65 (Denly), 4-144 (Crawley), 5-206 (Leaning),
1st   6-216 (Robinson), 7-217 (Stevens), 8-244 (Gilchrist), 9-304 (O'Riordan), 10-305 (Quinn)

	O	M	R	W
Coad	22	4	53	3
Thompson	23	11	41	2
Patterson	21	7	58	2
Olivier	18	1	77	1
Bess	22.3	4	56	1
Brook	4	2	2	1
Root	1	0	6	0

YORKSHIRE

A Lyth, c Cummins b Stevens	23
T Kohler-Cadmore, b Gilchrist	14
G S Ballance, run out (O'Riordan)	96
J E Root, c Robinson b Quinn	41
H C Brook, lbw b Gilchrist	59
§ J A Tattersall, c Robinson b Denly	1
D M Bess, b Stevens	15
J A Thompson, c Robinson b Gilchrist	18
* S A Patterson, c Robinson b Gilchrist	2
B O Coad, not out	33
D Olivier, c O'Riordan b Leaning	7
Extras lb 2, nb 10	12
Total	321

Bonus points — Yorkshire 3, Kent 3

FoW: 1-39 (Lyth), 2-48 (Kohler-Cadmore), 3-131 (Root), 4-233 (Brook), 5-236 (Tattersall),
1st   6-246 (Ballance), 7-256 (Bess), 8-269 (Patterson), 9-304 (Thompson), 10-321 (Olivier)

	O	M	R	W
Cummins	17	2	77	0
Stevens	22	10	48	2
Quinn	23	8	42	1
Gilchrist	18	3	74	4
O'Riordan	8	2	31	0
Leaning	7.3	1	21	1
Denly	10	2	26	1

Umpires: P J Hartley and R A Kettleborough   Scorers: J T Potter and J R Virr

Yorkshire v. Kent

Coad the sting in the tail

This was a far cry from the hullaballoo of a week earlier when Yorkshire edged past Northamptonshire.

The weather won and a draw was inevitable from the moment day three was washed out.

This fifth-round fixture, which marked the halfway stage of the Championship's initial group phase,

Clean sweep: Gary Ballance, who was to be run out four short of his century

failed to get out of the first innings, with England Test players present and past Zak Crawley and Gary Ballance making 90 and 96.

Steve Patterson opted to bowl, but Kent's resistance on a slowish pitch left honours even at the close of day one, the visitors on 224-7, thanks largely to Crawley's 90 and 47 from Yorkshire exile Jack Leaning. Ben Coad claimed three wickets on his return after three games out with a pectoral-muscle problem, while Patterson had Crawley chipping to cover to end a battling innings injected with elegance.

Lower-order hitting early on day two pushed Kent to 305, and Yorkshire responded with 240-5 at the close, including Ballance's unbeaten 91. This was his highest first-class score since July 2019 following illness and injury, and he was short of career century No. 41.

Saturday's play was abandoned just after 11am, and a wet outfield delayed the start of day four until 2.45pm. That meant the Sunday afternoon and evening, exactly a week on from the Northamptonshire drama, was turned into a pursuit of bonus points alone.

That was actually quite entertaining. Ballance was run out for 96 by a direct hit at the striker's end from Marcus O'Riordan at backward point, while Kent's 20-year-old seamer, Nathan Gilchrist, impressed with 4-74 in his second first-class appearance.

The key moment was Coad's unbeaten 33, helping Yorkshire to recover from 269-8 at tea to post 321 and secure a third batting point. Coad shared 35 for the ninth wicket with Jordan Thompson, and crashed four fours in his first 12 balls. Yorkshire retained second place in Group Three, seven points behind Lancashire.

LV= County Championship — Group Three
Glamorgan v. Yorkshire

Played at Sophia Gardens, Cardiff, on May 13, 14, 15 and 16, 2021
Match drawn at 5.10pm on the Fourth Day

Toss won by Yorkshire   Yorkshire 12 points, Glamorgan 11 points
Close of play: First Day, no play; Second Day, Yorkshire 69-4 (Root 34*, Bess 4*;); Third Day, Glamorgan 108-3 (Lloyd 40*, Carlson 44*)

First Innings	GLAMORGAN	Second Innings	
J M Cooke, lbw b Thompson	5	c Duke b Coad	6
D L Lloyd, b Patterson	31	lbw b Coad	40
M Labuschagne, lbw b Coad	10	b Thompson	0
W T Root, c and b Brook	23	lbw b Brook	13
K S Carlson, c Kohler-Cadmore b Patterson	4	not out	88
* § C B Cooke, lbw b Brook	3	not out	8
D A Douthwaite, lbw b Brook	0		
M G Neser, c Lyth b Thompson	24		
A G Salter, not out	24		
T van der Gugten, c Kohler-Cadmore b Patterson	9		
M G Hogan, c Root b Willey	7		
Extras b 8, lb 1	9	Extras b 4, lb 5	9
Total	149	Total (4 wkts)	164

Bonus points — Yorkshire 3

FoW: 1st: 1-11 (J M Cooke), 2-34 (Labuschagne), 3-69 (Lloyd), 4-73 (Carlson), 5-73 (Root), 6-73 (Douthwaite), 7-82 (C B Cooke), 8-117 (Neser), 9-128 (van der Gugten), 10-149 (Hogan)
2nd: 1-16 (J M Cooke), 2-17 (Labuschagne), 3-43 (Root), 4-117 (Lloyd)

	O	M	R	W		O	M	R	W
Coad	12	2	40	1	Coad	9	3	16	2
Thompson	13	4	33	2	Thompson	13	2	44	1
Willey	7.5	0	25	1	Patterson	7	0	36	0
Patterson	13	3	27	3	Brook	4	0	14	1
Brook	8	2	15	3	Willey	7	0	45	0

YORKSHIRE

A Lyth, c Carlson b Neser	0
T Kohler-Cadmore, b Hogan	1
G S Ballance, c J M Cooke b Neser	7
J E Root, b Douthwaite	99
H C Brook, lbw b Neser	11
D M Bess, c Lloyd b Neser	20
§ H G Duke, c J M Cooke b Neser	0
J A Thompson, lbw b Hogan	12
D J Willey, c J M Cooke b Douthwaite	3
* S A Patterson, not out	47
B O Coad, c Neser b Salter	0
Extras b 18, lb 10, nb 2	30
Total	230

Bonus points — Yorkshire 1, Glamorgan 3

FoW: 1st: 1-0 (Lyth), 2-6 (Kohler-Cadmore), 3-10 (Ballance), 4-36 (Brook), 5-78 (Bess), 6-78 (Duke), 7-91 (Thompson), 8-111 (Willey), 9-229 (Root), 10-230 (Coad)

	O	M	R	W
Neser	15	5	39	5
Hogan	16	5	42	2
van der Gugten	18	3	37	0
Lloyd	8	2	28	0
Douthwaite	8	1	22	2
Labuschagne	3	0	13	0
Salter	7.5	1	21	1

Umpires: N J Llong and M J Saggers   Scorers: A K Hignell and K Probert

Glamorgan v. Yorkshire

Majestic Root brightens sky

Joe Root's majestic 99 brightened a rainy Cardiff draw. Yorkshire's first first-class trip to Wales since 2012 ended in similar fashion to Colwyn Bay nine years ago.

Only 34 overs were bowled then, while here the equivalent of two full days were lost, including an opening day washout.

Play took place on a seam-bowling-friendly surface, and both sides had dominant spells as wicketkeeper Harry Duke debuted for Yorkshire.

Three wickets apiece for Steve Patterson, who won the toss, and Harry Brook helped to bowl the hosts out for 149 when play started on day two, with medium-pacer Brook's 3-15 his first-class best. Patterson claimed his 400th Championship wicket in his 150th match.

JOE ROOT: One of his best

Opener David Lloyd top-scored with 31 after Ben Coad had trapped prolific Australian Marnus Labuschagne lbw for 10. Yorkshire slipped to 69-4 before the close and 111-8 in the early stages of day three, with Aussie seamer Michael Neser claiming five wickets on home debut. Then, Root starred with one of his best county innings.

He may have fallen short of a 32nd career first-class century, but this 199-ball effort was worth many more. He expertly navigated seam, swing and uneven bounce, and shared 118 for the ninth wicket with Patterson, whose unbeaten 47 contributed to an 81-lead at 230.

Jordan Thompson bowled Labuschagne for a duck with a beauty of a nip-backer as Glamorgan slipped to 43-3 second time around. They started day four at 4.15pm on 108-3, leading by 21, and impressive youngster Kiran Carlson reached 88 not out in 13 overs of play as the hosts reached 164-4, a lead of 83 when the players shook hands 55 minutes later.

Energetic Duke, 19, claimed a catch and impressed greatly behind the stumps, despite posting a golden duck. Yorkshire's 12-point haul took them five clear of Lancashire at the top of Group Three after six games (three wins, three draws). But the *Red Rose* had a game in hand.

LV= County Championship — Group Three
Lancashire v. Yorkshire

Played at Emirates Old Trafford, Manchester, on May 27, 28, 29 and 30, 2021

Lancashire won by an innings and 79 runs at 5.40 pm on the Fourth Day

Toss won by Yorkshire   Lancashire 22 points, Yorkshire 1 point

Close of play: First Day, Lancashire 95-1 (Jennings 22*, Wells 11*); Second Day, Lancashire 350-6 (Bohannon 47*, Lamb 4*); Third Day, Yorkshire 85-2 (Fraine 6*, Patterson 2*)

YORKSHIRE

First Innings		Second Innings	
A Lyth, c Lamb b Bailey	4	c Wells b Parkinson	39
T Kohler-Cadmore, lbw b Bailey	10	lbw b Mahmood	32
W A R Fraine, c Vilas b Mahmood	10	b Mahmood	6
H C Brook, run out (Davies)	0	(5) lbw b Parkinson	52
G C H Hill, c Livingstone b Bailey	2	(6) b Bailey	18
D M Bess, c Lamb b Wood	3	(7) c Livingstone b Parkinson	46
§ H G Duke, c Vilas b Bailey	52	(8) b Wood	29
J A Thompson, c Jennings b Wood	10	(9) c Vilas b Mahmood	14
* S A Patterson, b Parkinson	27	(4) b Mahmood	8
B O Coad, not out	32	c Vilas b Mahmood	0
D Olivier, c Wells b Lamb	10	not out	0
Extras b 1, nb 8	9	Extras b 14, lb 3, nb 10	27
Total	159	Total	271

Bonus points — Lancashire 3

FoW: 1-4 (Lyth), 2-9 (Fraine), 3-9 (Brook), 4-11 (Hill), 5-21 (Bess), 6-21 (Kohler-Cadmore),
1st   7-40 (Thompson), 8-117 (Patterson), 9-121 (Duke), 10-159 (Olivier)

FoW: 1-72 (Lyth), 2-82 (Kohler-Cadmore), 3-87 (Fraine), 4-92 (Patterson), 5-151 (Hill),
2nd   6-180 (Brook), 7-238 (Duke), 8-271 (Thompson), 9-271 (Coad), 10-271 (Bess)

	O	M	R	W		O	M	R	W
Bailey	14	11	6	3	Bailey	19	11	30	1
Mahmood	15	2	49	1	Mahmood	26	9	47	5
Lamb	11.1	3	26	2	Parkinson	41.2	17	61	3
Wood	11	2	51	2	Livingstone	22	5	58	0
Parkinson	13	3	26	1	Lamb	14	6	23	0
					Wood	13	5	35	1
					Wells	1	1	0	0

LANCASHIRE

K K Jennings, c Kohler-Cadmore b Coad		114
A L Davies, c Duke b Olivier		52
L W P Wells, c Kohler-Cadmore b Thompson		60
J J Bohannon, not out		127
L S Livingstone, c Olivier b Thompson		6
* § D J Vilas, c Kohler-Cadmore b Coad		35
L Wood, c Duke b Thompson		7
D J Lamb, c Patterson b Bess		61
T E Bailey, b Hill		12
S Mahmood, run out (Hill/Duke)		0
M W Parkinson	Did not bat	
Extras b 11, lb 10, nb 14		35
Total (9 wkts dec)		509

Bonus points — Lancashire 3, Yorkshire 1   Score at 110 overs: 324-5

FoW: 1-71 (Davies), 2-246 (Jennings), 3-246 (Wells), 4-252 (Livingstone), 5-309 (Vilas), 6-340 (Wood), 7-490 (Lamb), 8-506 (Bailey), 9-509 (Mahmood)

	O	M	R	W
Coad	26	12	65	2
Thompson	25	5	86	3
Patterson	27	11	46	0
Olivier	24	4	95	1
Bess	43.4	10	120	1
Brook	17	4	37	0
Hill	11	2	39	1

Umpires: S J O'Shaughnessy and A G Wharf   Scorers: C Rimmer and G L Morgan

Lancashire v. Yorkshire

Thorny *Red Rose* triumph

HARRY DUKE: Maiden Championship 50

Yorkshire fell 40 balls short of holding on for a draw, but in truth they couldn't argue with the end result — defeat by an innings and 79 runs.

It was their first Championship loss against Lancashire for 10 years and the first in Manchester since 2000.

The Yorkshire batting was depleted, highlighted by the late withdrawal of Gary Ballance with a calf injury, but that did not excuse their first morning collapse 40-7 after Steve Patterson had won his sixth toss.

The top six aggregated only 19 runs before Harry Duke led a recovery either side of lunch with a determined 52 in only his second game. Patterson made 27 and Ben Coad 32 unbeaten, but 159 represented nothing more than respectability.

From tea on day one to mid-afternoon on day three Group Three leaders Lancashire showed Yorkshire, also unbeaten coming into this seventh-round fixture, just how to bat on an abrasive surface offering little help for bowlers. Opener Keaton Jennings and Josh Bohannon batted for more than five-and-a-half hours for centuries — 114 and 127 — to underpin the *Red Rose's* 509-9 declared, a lead of 350.

Yorkshire, for whom Jordan Thompson took three wickets, would have to bat for a minimum of 152 overs to save their skins, and they made a pretty good fist of things. Brook matched Duke's day one 52, while Dom Bess posted 46 and took time out of the game after the visitors had fallen to 92-4 inside the opening half hour of day four.

Seamer Saqib Mahmood claimed his maiden first-class five-for, and leg-spinner Matthew Parkinson added three wickets, including Bess caught at slip, to spark home celebrations and give Lancashire a 24-point lead at the top of the table. The game was played in front of crowd for the first time since September 2019.

Live streaming did a brilliant job of filling the void while spectators were shut out by the Coronavirus pandemic. Lancashire had 589,000 views on their live stream across the four days of this match, while their previous average for home games in 2021 was 150,000.

LV= County Championship — Group Three
Yorkshire v. Sussex

Played at Headingley, Leeds, on June 3, 4, 5 and 6, 2021
Yorkshire won by an innings and 30 runs at 6.14 pm on the Fourth Day

Toss won by Yorkshire   Yorkshire 23 points, Sussex 4 points
Close of play: First Day, Sussex 267-5 (Brown 126*, Ibrahim 37*); Second Day, Yorkshire 272-2 (Malan 103*, Ballance 74*); Third Day; Sussex 38-0 (Orr 23*, Haines 12*)

SUSSEX

	First Innings		Second Innings	
A G H Orr, c sub (D Olivier) b Brook	15	b Bess	67
T J Haines, c Brook b Willey	2	c Lyth b Bess	24
S van Zyl, c Duke b Thompson	15	c Duke b Thompson	0
A D Thomason, c Malan b Thompson	40	c Lyth b Bess	52
T M Head, c Duke b Thompson	14	c Kohler-Cadmore b Coad	18
*§ B C Brown, c Duke b Coad	127	b Patterson	22
D Ibrahim, c Brook b Coad	55	c Lyth b Bess	0
J J Carson, not out	10	c Thompson b Willey	5
S C Meaker, b Patterson	9	c Brook b Willey	0
H T Crocombe, lbw b Willey	1	c Duke b Willey	0
J A Atkins, run out (Willey)	2	not out	10
Extras b 11, lb 8, nb 4	23	Extras b 4, lb 11, nb 2	17
Total	313	Total	215

Bonus points — Sussex 3, Yorkshire 2   Score at 110 overs: 308-7

FoW: 1-8 (Haines), 2-25 (van Zyl), 3-38 (Orr), 4-68 (Head), 5-175 (Thomason),
1st   6-269 (Brown), 7-296 (Ibrahim), 8-310 (Meaker), 9-311 (Crocombe), 10-313 (Atkins)
FoW: 1-60 (Haines), 2-61 (van Zyl), 3-125 (Orr), 4-164 (Head), 5-180 (Thomason),
2nd   6-180 (Ibrahim), 7-187 (Carson), 8-187 (Meaker), 9-187 (Crocombe), 10-215 (Brown)

	O	M	R	W		O	M	R	W
Coad	26	7	64	2	Coad	20	11	43	1
Willey	21	3	83	2	Willey	19	10	26	3
Thompson	24	8	53	3	Thompson	24	6	55	1
Patterson	25.3	11	42	1	Bess	35	15	51	4
Brook	8	1	24	1	Patterson	9.4	1	21	1
Bess	11	2	28	1	Lyth	6	2	4	0

YORKSHIRE

A Lyth, b Atkins	48
T Kohler-Cadmore, lbw b Ibrahim	25
D J Malan, b Carson	199
G S Ballance, c Brown b Carson	77
H C Brook, c Brown b Atkins	49
D M Bess, c Brown b Meaker	8
§ H G Duke, lbw b Atkins	54
J A Thompson, c Meaker b Atkins	42
D J Willey, not out	8
* S A Patterson, c and b Carson	8
B O Coad, b Atkins	1
Extras b 9, lb 11, w 3, nb 16	39
Total	558

Bonus points — Yorkshire 5, Sussex 1   Score at 110 overs: 419-5

FoW: 1-83 (Kohler-Cadmore), 2-95 (Lyth), 3-275 (Ballance), 4-374 (Brook), 5-402 (Bess),
       6-459 (Malan), 7-535 (Duke), 8-542 (Thompson), 9-555 (Patterson), 10-558 (Coad)

	O	M	R	W
Crocombe	16	1	80	0
Atkins	26	2	98	5
Meaker	23	0	103	1
Ibrahim	21	3	72	1
Carson	43	7	124	3
Haines	7	1	18	0
Head	9	0	43	0

Umpires: R J Bailey and G D Lloyd   Scorers: J T Potter and J R Virr

Yorkshire v. Sussex

Patterson does it again

Serene: Dawid Malan, who so nearly became the first Yorkshire batter to score two double-hundreds in successive first-class innings.

A week after losing by an innings with 40 balls left at Old Trafford Yorkshire gained redemption as they beat Sussex by an innings with only 32 balls left.

This was the first men's match played before a crowd at Headingley since September 2019.

Skipper Steve Patterson was again the match clincher. He took the winning wicket when the hosts beat Northamptonshire by one run in early May, and here he bowled opposition captain Ben Brown to hand the hosts a fourth win and move them to within four points of Lancashire at the Group Three summit. Patterson's contribution was decisive, but others will take the headlines.

Dawid Malan's serene 199 on a slow pitch underpinned a first-innings 558 as they replied to young Sussex's 313 early on day two. He shared 177 for the third wicket with Gary Ballance and narrowly missed out on becoming the first Yorkshire batter to score two double-hundreds in as many first-class innings. This was his first appearance since posting 219 in the August 2020 Bob Willis Trophy draw against Derbyshire.

Yorkshire's victory chance looked to have gone despite securing a lead of 245 on first innings after tea on day three.

Sussex opener Ali Orr, aged 20 and on debut, posted a steadfast 67, supplemented by Aaron Thomason's similar 52. They helped their side to 165-4 at tea on day four with 35 overs remaining, but five wickets fell for seven runs as they slipped from 180-4 to 187-9. David Willey and Dom Bess (4-51) brilliantly shared all five in a crazy five overs, with Thomason caught at slip driving at Bess to open the door.

Record breaker: In Sussex's first innings debutant all-rounder Dan Ibrahim, aged 16 years and 299 days, became the youngest player to score a fifty in Championship history with 55.

LV= County Championship — Group Three
Northamptonshire v. Yorkshire

Played at the County Ground, Wantage Road, Northampton, on July 4, 5 and 6, 2021
Yorkshire won by 53 runs at 5.04pm on the Third Day

Toss won by Yorkshire   Yorkshire 19 points, Northamptonshire 3 points

Close of play: First Day, Northamptonshire 61-2 (Vasconcelos 32*, Berg 0*); Second Day, Yorkshire 159-6 (Brook 76*, Thompson 6*)

YORKSHIRE

First Innings		Second Innings	
A Lyth, c Vasconcelos b Sanderson	0	c Vasconcelos b Sanderson	5
G C H Hill, lbw b Keogh	71	b Kerrigan	13
S A Northeast, c Vasconcelos b Taylor	3	st Vasconcelos b Kerrigan	1
G S Ballance, c Thurston b Kerrigan	22	lbw b Kerrigan	26
H C Brook, c Sanderson b Kerrigan	7	c Zaib b Kerrigan	113
D M Bess, c Vasconcelos b Berg	10	lbw b Parnell	10
§ H G Duke, lbw b Taylor	5	b Kerrigan	13
J A Thompson, lbw b Parnell	22	c Vasconcelos b Sanderson	6
* S A Patterson, c Zaib b Keogh	3	c Gay b Sanderson	10
B O Coad, b Parnell	0	c and b Taylor	8
D Olivier, not out	0	not out	0
Extras b 5, lb 8, nb 2	15	Extras b 8, lb 4	12
Total	158	Total	217

Bonus points — Northamptonshire 3

FoW: 1-4 (Lyth), 2-21 (Northeast), 3-65 (Ballance), 4-91 (Brook), 5-112 (Bess),
1st   6-126 (Duke), 7-142 (Hill), 8-142 (Patterson), 9-153 (Coad), 10-158 (Thompson)
FoW: 1-22 (Hill), 2-24 (Northeast), 3-24 (Lyth), 4-64 (Ballance), 5-105 (Bess),
2nd   6-140 (Duke), 7-167 (Thompson), 8-189 (Patterson), 9-207 (Coad), 10-217 (Brook)

	O	M	R	W		O	M	R	W
Sanderson	12	6	24	1	Sanderson	20	4	70	3
Berg	10	0	37	1	Berg	3	0	12	0
Taylor	11	6	14	2	Kerrigan	30.2	12	39	5
Parnell	11.3	4	26	2	Keogh	16	2	41	0
Kerrigan	13	2	36	2	Taylor	9	1	25	1
Keogh	7	4	8	2	Parnell	5	1	18	1

NORTHAMPTONSHIRE

First Innings		Second Innings	
* § R S Vasconcelos, c Duke b Bess	55	lbw b Patterson	10
E N Gay, lbw b Bess	21	c Northeast b Bess	8
S C Kerrigan, c Ballance c Patterson	1	(10) c Duke b Olivier	29
G K Berg, c Patterson b Bess	8	(8) c Northeast b Coad	0
C O Thurston, c Duke b Bess	4	(3) c Ballance b Patterson	1
R I Keogh, c Lyth b Olivier	9	(4) c Brook b Bess	6
S A Zaib, lbw b Bess	11	(6) c Lyth b Olivier	9
T A I Taylor, not out	42	(7) lbw b Coad	40
W D Parnell, lbw b Bess	0	run out (Thompson/Duke)	3
B W Sanderson, c Lyth b Bess	5	(11) lbw b Olivier	0
L A Procter, absent		(5) not out	42
Extras b 1, lb 9, nb 4	14	Extras lb 4	4
Total	170	Total	152

Bonus points — Yorkshire 3

FoW: 1-54 (Gay), 2-61 (Kerrigan), 3-88 (Berg), 4-93 (Thurston), 5-106 (Vasconcelos),
1st   6-110 (Keogh), 7-146 (Zaib), 8-150 (Parnell), 9-170 (Sanderson)
FoW: 1-17 (Vasconcelos), 2-19 (Thurston), 3-19 (Gay), 4-28 (Keogh), 5-43 (Zaib),
2nd   6-97 (Taylor), 7-97 (Berg), 8-103 (Parnell), 9-152 (Kerrigan), 10-152 (Sanderson)

	O	M	R	W		O	M	R	W
Coad	7	0	35	0	Coad	9	2	33	2
Thompson	7	1	18	0	Patterson	11	2	22	2
Bess	24.4	11	43	7	Bess	24	9	59	2
Patterson	16	3	47	1	Olivier	8	1	34	3
Olivier	7	1	17	1					

Umpires: T Lungley and B V Taylor   Scorers: J T Potter and A C Kingston

Northamptonshire v. Yorkshire
The Brook and Bess show

Harry Brook played one of the knocks of the summer, 113 off 178 balls, in the second innings as Yorkshire again recovered from early troubles to claim their fifth win, go top of Group Three by two points from Lancashire and secure qualification for the late-summer top group.

They elected to bat on a used pitch and were bowled out for 158 on day one, including George Hill's composed 71 opening the batting for the first time since schools cricket at Sedbergh.

Two wickets for left-arm spinner Simon Kerrigan indicated where most of the assistance for bowlers would be, a theory strengthened as Yorkshire fought back late on day one and into day two, which Northamptonshire started at 61-2.

Dom Bess claimed a career best 7-43. He ousted home captain Ricardo Vasconcelos for 55 as Northamptonshire claimed a slender advantage at 170-9. Luke Procter missed day two due to a family bereavement.

HARRY BROOK: 113 despite virus alert

England off-spinner Bess took advantage of turn and uneven bounce as Yorkshire claimed valuable momentum from another fightback, having failed to register a batting bonus point for the fourth time in nine games. The visitors fell to 64-4, but they started day three on 159-6 with Brook unbeaten on 76.

There was a brief thought Brook would not be able to resume his innings after news broke of seven positive Coronavirus cases in England's one-day international squad, hence a new squad having to be picked two days out from the series opener against Pakistan.

Any players called up were pulled out of ongoing games across the country, and Brook's recent *T20* form put him in the frame. But he moved to a 168-ball century, the third of his first-class career in a total of 217 all out, so setting a 206 target.

It was one Northamptonshire rarely threatened. Yorkshire's four-man attack of Ben Coad, Steve Patterson, Bess and Duanne Olivier (3-34), shared the wickets to complete victory late on day three.

LV= County Championship — Group Three
Yorkshire v. Lancashire

Played at Headingley, Leeds, on July 11, 12, 13 and 14, 2021
Match drawn at 10.00am on the Fourth Day

Toss won by Yorkshire — Lancashire 11 points, Yorkshire 8 points

Close of play: First Day, Lancashire 273-2 (Wells 35*, Bohannon 7*); Second Day, no play; Third day, Lancashire 411-2 (Wells 97*, Bohannon 74*); Fourth Day, no play

LANCASHIRE

K K Jennings, c and b Thompson		132
A L Davies, lbw b Thompson		84
L W P Wells, not out		97
J J Bohannon, not out		74
* § D J Vilas		
R P Jones		
S J Croft		
G P Balderson	Did not bat	
T E Bailey		
J M Blatherwick		
J M Anderson		
Extras b 12, lb 11, w 1		24
Total (2 wkts)		411

Bonus points — Lancashire 3   Score at 110 overs: 342-2

FoW: 1-163 (Davies), 2-256 (Jennings)

	O	M	R	W
Coad	24	4	53	0
Leech	17	1	79	0
Thompson	20	5	76	2
Patterson	25	4	94	0
Brook	6	2	7	0
Bess	23.2	3	76	0
Hill	4	1	3	0

YORKSHIRE

A Lyth
G C H Hill
S A Northeast
G S Ballance
H C Brook
D M Bess
§ H G Duke
J A Thompson
* S A Patterson
B O Coad
D J Leech

Umpires: I J Gould and N J Llong   Scorers: J T Potter and C Rimmer

Yorkshire v. Lancashire

Unhappiest of endings

Cruel blow: Dominic Leech is tended by Yorkshire and Lancashire medical staff after dislocating his left knee as he collided with the concrete base of the West Stand.

This was a week Yorkshire would rather forget. Only 119.2 overs were bowled in a fixture originally scheduled for Scarborough as rain and a wet outfield ruined the final Group Three meeting between the two counties already qualified for the late-summer top group. Lancashire dominated what play was possible on day one after Steve Patterson opted to bowl under an overcast sky. Keaton Jennings and Alex Davies shared 163 either side of lunch in otherwise excellent batting conditions.

Jennings, with 132, became the 13th Lancashire player to post two *Roses* centuries in the same season, and Davies (84) played a more than useful support act. Jordan Thompson removed both, the only Yorkshire successes of the match, on what was to be the only full day. Monday's second day was washed out, and day three was delayed until 12pm due to a wet outfield. Then Luke Wells reached 97 not out and Josh Bohannon an unbeaten 74 to share an unbroken 155 for the third wicket and leave Yorkshire without a bowling point. This was crucial, Yorkshire carrying forward 4.5 points to Lancashire's 16.5.

Dom Leech suffered a dislocated left knee as he collided with the concrete base of the West Stand, and after a 15-minute delay for treatment umpires Ian Gould and Nigel Llong took the players off. They inspected safety concerns surrounding the bowlers' run-ups, and did not return. Day four was abandoned at 10am.

LV= County Championship — Division One
Hampshire v. Yorkshire

Played at The Ageas Bowl, West End, Southampton,
on August 30 and 31 and September 1 and 2, 2021
Match drawn at 6.23pm on the Fourth Day

Toss won by Hampshire
Yorkshire 12 points, Hampshire 11 points
Close of play: First Day, Yorkshire 197-6 (Bess 45*, Thompson 15*); Second Day, Yorkshire 34-1 (Hill 10*, Kohler-Cadmore 16*); Third Day, Hampshire 26-2 (Weatherley 16*, Crane 0*)

First Innings	YORKSHIRE	Second Innings	
A Lyth, lbw b Abbott	6	c McManus b Wheal	7
G C H Hill, lbw b Abbott	31	c McManus b Holland	55
T Kohler-Cadmore, c McManus b Abbott	20	c Dawson b Crane	89
G S Ballance, c Weatherley b Dawson	42	not out	101
H C Brook, b Wheal	13	c Gubbins b Vince	12
D M Bess, b Barker	54	(7) c McManus b Barker	0
§ H G Duke, c Weatherley b Wheal	12	(8) not out	1
J A Thompson, b Wheal	15	(6) c Vince b Barker	33
M D Fisher, lbw b Crane	17		
* S A Patterson, not out	9		
B O Coad, lbw b Crane	0		
Extras b 4, lb 16, nb 4	24	Extras b 4, lb 5, w 3, nb 2	14
Total	243	Total (6 wkts dec)	312

Bonus points — Yorkshire 1, Hampshire 3
FoW: 1-13 (Lyth), 2-60 (Hill), 3-84 (Kohler-Cadmore), 4-114 (Brook), 5-138 (Ballance),
1st 6-159 (Duke), 7-197 (Thompson), 8-215 (Bess), 9-239 (Fisher), 10-243 (Coad)
FoW: 1-7 (Lyth), 2-128 (Hill), 3-206 (Kohler-Cadmore), 4-236 (Brook), 5-295 (Thompson),
2nd 6-296 (Bess)

	O	M	R	W		O	M	R	W
Barker	26	6	52	1	Barker	18	5	39	2
Abbott	20	6	47	3	Wheal	4	1	16	1
Wheal	24	8	47	3	Holland	12	4	21	1
Holland	15	9	21	0	Dawson	35	7	104	0
Dawson	16	2	38	1	Crane	12	1	68	1
Crane	5.1	0	18	2	Vince	6	0	55	1

First Innings	HAMPSHIRE	Second Innings	
J J Weatherley, c Duke b Fisher	1	lbw b Thompson	43
I G Holland, lbw b Coad	0	c Brook b Coad	3
T P Alsop, b Bess	12	c Ballance b Bess	7
N R T Gubbins, c Brook b Coad	15	(5) c and b Fisher	6
* J M Vince, c Hill b Fisher	49	(6) lbw b Thompson	42
L A Dawson, lbw b Thompson	11	(7) lbw b Fisher	0
§ L D McManus, c Duke b Bess	7	(8) b Thompson	8
K H D Barker, c Kohler-Cadmore b Thompson	2	(9) c Duke b Thompson	4
M S Crane, c Lyth b Thompson	4	(4) c Lyth b Fisher	28
K J Abbott, not out	21	not out	9
B T J Wheal, c Duke b Coad	12	not out	0
Extras b 15, lb 8, nb 6	29	Extras b 8, lb 13, nb 6	27
Total	163	Total (9 wkts)	177

Bonus points — Yorkshire 3
FoW: 1-1 (Holland), 2-1 (Weatherley), 3-16 (Gubbins), 4-86 (Vince), 5-93 (Alsop),
1st 6-109 (Dawson), 7-113 (Barker), 8-121 (McManus), 9-123 (Crane), 10-163 (Wheal)
FoW: 1-9 (Holland), 2-26 (Alsop), 3-74 (Weatherley), 4-86 (Gubbins), 5-120 (Crane),
2nd 6-124 (Dawson), 7-138 (McM++anus), 8-159 (Barker), 9-177 (Vince)

	O	M	R	W		O	M	R	W
Coad	12.3	4	29	3	Coad	16	9	16	1
Fisher	10	4	28	2	Fisher	21	8	42	3
Patterson	9	4	14	0	Thompson	17	11	18	4
Thompson	12	3	35	3	Bess	33	21	43	1
Bess	19	4	34	2	Lyth	7	6	2	0
					Patterson	17	10	27	0
					Hill	4	1	8	0

Umpires: N J Llong and J D Middlebrook
Scorers: J T Potter and A C Mills

Hampshire v. Yorkshire

The dark moment title went

A superb game ended in disappointment as bad light precluded Jordan Thompson from seeking a fifth wicket in the second innings, with injured Hampshire bowlers Kyle Abbott (ankle) and Brad Wheal (knee) seeing out the last 46 balls against spin to secure a draw.

Inserted on a pitch so green spectators were unsure where the best view lay, Yorkshire batted with determination for 243 in nearly four sessions.

Several batters made starts without going on, the highest score achieved by Dom Bess, who completed 54 on the second morning. Missing out a second batting point was disappointing, but a pre-lunch burst saw both Ben Coad and Matthew Fisher rewarded (29-3).

James Vince and Tom Alsop navigated challenging conditions, but Yorkshire dried up the runs. Vince lost patience and perished to Fisher for 49.

**JORDAN THOMPSON
Robbed by the light**

Only a last-wicket stand of 40 between Abbott and Wheal reduced the deficit below 100. Yorkshire faced a tricky final hour of day two, losing only Adam Lyth. Next day, George Hill (55) and Tom Kohler-Cadmore for a season's best 89 batted soundly against an attack shorn of its most dangerous two pace bowlers.

Left-arm spinner Liam Dawson bowled unchanged from just before the close to the final over of the third afternoon, and once the remaining seamers were spent Gary Ballance capitalised. On the ground where he has scored four previous first-class centuries Ballance added an aggressive fifth in 85 balls and finished with 101 to set an improbable 393 target. Yorkshire had 115 overs to seal victory.

Two wickets before the close bode well, but nightwatchman Mason Crane frustrated Yorkshire for 197 balls. Only when the second new ball was taken did the *White Rose* look capable of winning. Thompson chipped away at the wickets, but bad light left Bess and Lyth tasked with taking the last wicket. They couldn't do it. Coach Andrew Gale feared it could prove the moment which cost his side the Championship.

LV= County Championship — Division One
Yorkshire v. Somerset

Played at North Marine Road, Scarborough, on September 5 and 6, 2021
Yorkshire won by an innings and 33 runs at 6.50pm on the Second Day

Toss won by Somerset   Yorkshire 22 points, Somerset 3 points
Close of play: First Day, Yorkshire 159-5 (Brook 79*, Duke 4*)

SOMERSET

	First Innings		Second Innings	
* T B Abell,	c Duke b Fisher	2	b Fisher	14
T A Lammonby,	c Brook b Willey	8	c Brook b Willey	0
Azhar Ali,	b Thompson	24	c Lyth b Fisher	1
J C Hildreth,	c Lyth b Hill	24	lbw b Fisher	2
G A Bartlett,	c Duke b Hill	4	lbw b Fisher	0
§ S M Davies,	c Kohler-Cadmore b Fisher	15	c Kohler-Cadmore b Hill	25
T Banton,	c Duke b Thompson	0	c Lyth b Bess	10
B G F Green,	not out	13	b Thompson	32
M J Leach,	c Lyth b Fisher	4	c Lyth b Bess	26
J H Davey,	lbw b Fisher	4	not out	5
M de Lange,	b Fisher	22	b Thompson	21
	Extras b 8, lb 6	14	Extras b 4, lb 1	5
	Total	134	Total	141

Bonus points — Yorkshire 3

FoW: 1-2 (Abell), 2-14 (Lammonby), 3-64 (Hildreth), 4-68 (Bartlett), 5-68 (Azhar Ali),
1st   6-68 (Banton), 7-86 (Davies), 8-100 (Leach), 9-108 (Davey), 10-134 (de Lange)
FoW: 1-2 (Lammonby), 2-7 (Azhar Ali), 3-17 (Hildreth), 4-17 (Bartlett), 5-18 (Abell),
2nd   6-45 (Davies), 7-69 (Davies), 8-111 (Leach), 9-115 (Green), 10-141 (de Lange)

	O	M	R	W		O	M	R	W
Fisher	11	4	41	5	Fisher	9	5	23	4
Willey	7	3	22	1	Willey	9	1	40	1
Patterson	6	2	9	0	Patterson	12	5	18	0
Thompson	11	4	36	2	Thompson	8.5	1	32	3
Hill	7	2	12	2	Hill	5	2	11	1
					Bess	8	3	12	2

YORKSHIRE

A Lyth,	c Davies b de Lange	0
G C H Hill,	c Hildreth b Davey	29
T Kohler-Cadmore,	c Abell b Davey	1
G S Ballance,	c Abell b Davey	32
H C Brook,	c Abell b Green	118
D M Bess,	st Davies b Leach	10
§ H G Duke,	b Davey	9
J A Thompson,	c Lammonby b de Lange	57
D J Willey,	c and b de Lange	23
M D Fisher,	not out	15
* S A Patterson,	c Azhar Ali b de Lange	0
	Extras b 8, lb 4, nb 2	14
	Total	308

Bonus points — Yorkshire 3, Somerset 3

FoW: 1-1 (Lyth), 2-16* (Kohler-Cadmore retired hurt), 2-51 (Hill), 3-51 (Kohler-Cadmore),
4-89 (Ballance), 5-122 (Bess), 6-179 (Duke), 7-230 (Brook), 8-285 (Thompson),
9-296 (Willey), 10-308 (Patterson)

	O	M	R	W
Davey	28	9	72	4
de Lange	25.3	8	55	4
Abell	17	1	57	0
Lammonby	8	1	43	0
Green	9	3	29	1
Leach	16	3	40	1

Umpires: R T Robinson and R A White   Scorers: J T Potter and L M Rhodes

Yorkshire v. Somerset
Match ball for Fisher

MATTHEW FISHER: Chief destroyer with nine wickets

Somerset took first use of Scarborough's pitch as first-class cricket returned to the East Coast for the first time since 2019.

After a reasonable start they were blown away for 134. The chief destroyer was Matthew Fisher, whose 5-41 was a career best. Yorkshire lost half their wickets in surpassing this total on day one (159-6), but only Harry Brook remained of the top order with 79.

Dom Bess will have been particularly miffed to fall to his former Somerset spin twin, Jack Leach. With David Willey replacing Ben Coad from the draw at Hampshire, Yorkshire had a strong lower order. Brook, awarded his first-team cap on the field before the fixture's opening over, rewarded Yorkshire with his fourth career century, the second against these opponents and third made in testing conditions. He was well supported by Harry Duke and Jordan Thompson, the second and last batter in the match to pass 50. Yorkshire secured a third batting point with the last pair together.

Somerset's second innings started with 44 overs remaining on day two, and they needed a sound start to erase a deficit of 174 and bat into the fourth day to have any hope of salvaging a draw. It was no real surprise they failed to achieve it as Fisher again found just enough movement to bamboozle the top order. His opening spell brought four wickets for two runs, thus being more devastating than his earlier career-best figures.

There seemed no way back from 18-5. Although an eighth-wicket stand absorbed 14 overs it ended in time for Yorkshire to claim the extra half hour, closing out the game with the day's last-but-one ball when Thompson bowled Marchant de Lange. Ben Green's 32 was Somerset's highest score of the match.

Bess exacted revenge on Leach, while Thompson's three-wicket burst at the end reinforced his growing reputation. Yorkshire jumped from bottom of Division One to top, albeit briefly while other fixtures were being completed.

LV= County Championship — Division One
Yorkshire v. Warwickshire

Played at Headingley, Leeds, on September 12, 13, 14 and 15, 2021
Warwickshire won by 106 runs at 12.11pm on the Fourth Day

Toss won by Yorkshire   Warwickshire 19 points, Yorkshire 3 points
Close of play: First Day, Yorkshire 95-8 (Ballance 51*, Patterson 1*); Second Day, Yorkshire 50-3 (Ballance 21*); Third Day, no play

WARWICKSHIRE

First Innings		Second Innings	
* W M H Rhodes, c Duke b Coad	13	b Patterson	12
D P Sibley, lbw b Patterson	11	c Duke b Thompson	45
C G Benjamin, b Patterson	9	c Lyth b Thompson	3
S R Hain, c Bess b Coad	0	c Duke b Thompson	0
M J Lamb, b Patterson	16	b Patterson	0
§ M G K Burgess, c Bess b Coad	66	c Brook b Fisher	37
C R Woakes, lbw b Patterson	9	c Duke b Patterson	0
T T Bresnan, lbw b Hill	4	lbw b Coad	36
J G Bethell, c Duke b Patterson	15	b Fisher	8
C N Miles, c Duke b Coad	0	not out	17
L C Norwell, not out	4	c Malan b Thompson	13
Extras b 4, lb 4	8	Extras b 4, lb 1	5
Total	155	Total	176

Bonus points — Yorkshire 3
FoW: 1-24 (Sibley), 2-24 (Rhodes), 3-24 (Hain), 4-48 (Benjamin), 5-55 (Lamb),
1st 6-71 (Woakes), 7-103 (Bresnan), 8-133 (Bethell), 9-134 (Miles), 10-155 (Burgess)
FoW: 1-23 (Rhodes), 2-26 (Benjamin), 3-26 (Hain), 4-27 (Lamb), 5-97 (Sibley),
2nd 6-97 (Woakes), 7-108 (Burgess), 8-130 (Bethell), 9-163 (Bresnan), 10-176 (Norwell)

	O	M	R	W		O	M	R	W
Coad	11.4	0	48	4	Coad	17	6	26	1
Fisher	10	3	38	1	Fisher	13	1	48	2
Patterson	14	3	34	4	Patterson **	12.5	3	27	2
Thompson	5	0	24	0	Thompson	15.4	3	52	5
Hill	2	0	3	1	Hill	3	0	14	0
					Brook **	0.1	0	4	0

** Patterson was unable to complete his 13th over, which was finished by Brook.

YORKSHIRE

First Innings		Second Innings	
A Lyth, lbw b Norwell	1	c Bresnan b Miles	14
G C H Hill, lbw b Norwell	4	c Bresnan b Woakes	1
D J Malan, c Bethell b Woakes	9	c Bresnan b Norwell	12
G S Ballance, b Miles	58	c Hain b Woakes	21
H C Brook, lbw b Woakes	15	c Bresnan b Woakes	9
D M Bess, b Norwell	1	(7) lbw b Bresnan	4
§ H G Duke, lbw b Norwell	7	(8) c and b Miles	8
J A Thompson, c Rhodes b Miles	5	(6) c Bresnan b Norwell	18
M D Fisher, c Bresnan b Miles	0	not out	13
* S A Patterson, b Norwell	7	c Bresnan b Miles	5
B O Coad, not out	0	c Rhodes b Norwell	2
Extras lb 2	2	Extras lb 8, nb 2	10
Total	108	Total	117

Bonus points — Warwickshire 3
FoW: 1-5 (Hill), 2-5 (Lyth), 3-27 (Malan), 4-63 (Brook), 5-64 (Bess),
1st 6-76 (Duke), 7-91 (Thompson), 8-93 (Fisher), 9-108 (Patterson), 10-108 (Ballance)
FoW: 1-1 (Hill), 2-18 (Lyth), 3-50 (Malan), 4-50 (Ballance), 5-69 (Brook),
2nd 6-82 (Bess), 7-95 (Duke), 8-105 (Thompson), 9-114 (Patterson), 10-117 (Coad)

	O	M	R	W		O	M	R	W
Woakes	12	3	40	3	Woakes	14	6	26	3
Norwell	14	6	27	4	Norwell	15.3	4	38	3
Bresnan	7	2	18	0	Miles	11	2	34	3
Miles	9.5	3	21	3	Bresnan	9	5	11	1

Umpires: N J Llong and N A Mallender   Scorers: J T Potter and M D Smith

Yorkshire v. Warwickshire
Done by a Yorkshireman

STEVE PATTERSON: Six wickets and injury for the skipper

Yorkshire's proliferation of seamers who can bat have prospered since Tim Bresnan departed for Warwickshire midway through 2020...

...but here he reminded Yorkshire of his capabilities with six first-slip catches as the home side forlornly chased 224, key wickets and a valuable late-order second-innings contribution of 36 that put victory and, more importantly, the Championship title beyond Yorkshire's reach.

The cancellation of England's Old Trafford Test against India enabled Dawid Malan for Yorkshire and Chris Woakes for the Bears to feature. The pitch was tailor-made for Woakes. Although for the second week running Yorkshire had dismissed their opponents by 2pm on day one, a failure to hit the straps at the start of their reply was to prove costly. Yorkshire were reasonably placed at 63-3 in reply, 92 in arrears, but five wickets in the evening gloom transferred the initiative to the visitors.

When Gary Ballance was last out next day for 58 Yorkshire trailed by 47. They fought back commendably with four wickets for as many runs as Sam Hain collected a king pair. Dom Sibley and Michael Burgess, mainstay of the first innings with an aggressive match-high 66, produced the biggest partnership of the match — 70 for the fifth wicket from 27-4, but four wickets restored hope.

Warwickshire led by 177 with two wickets remaining, but Bresnan's stand of 33 with Craig Miles took that well beyond 200, leaving Yorkshire needing the highest score of the match to win. Steve Patterson suffered a hamstring injury during the later stages of Warwickshire's innings. The last ball of day three and the first over of day four, after a washed-out day two, ended Yorkshire's hopes with the loss of Malan and Ballance to Bresnan catches (50-4), Malan's a one-handed stunner. The remaining six wickets were blown away before lunch to leave Yorkshire contemplating only their second defeat in 19 first-class fixtures.

LV= County Championship — Division One
Nottinghamshire v. Yorkshire

Played at Trent Bridge, Nottingham, on September 21, 22, 23 and 24, 2021
Nottinghamshire won by 5 wickets at 1.35pm on the Fourth Day

Toss won by Yorkshire   Nottinghamshire 21 points, Yorkshire 3 points
Close of play: First Day, Nottinghamshire 292-9 (Evison 58*, Paterson 0*); Second Day, Yorkshire (following on) 169-3 (Lyth 74*); Third Day, Nottinghamshire 42-1 (Slater 15*, Duckett 23*)

NOTTINGHAMSHIRE

First Innings		Second Innings	
B T Slater, c Duke b Hill	18	not out	79
H Hameed, c Duke b Fisher	23	c Lyth b Coad	4
B M Duckett, c Bess b Hill	7	b Thompson	54
J M Clarke, c Lyth b Coad	109	c Kohler-Cadmore b Bess	10
*S J Mullaney, c Duke b Coad	31	b Coad	9
§T J Moores, c Duke b Thompson	9	c Fraine b Coad	7
L A Patterson-White, c Duke b Coad	16	not out	4
J D M Evison, lbw b Thompson	58		
B A Hutton, c Duke b Revis	9		
L J Fletcher, c Thompson b Revis	4		
D Paterson, not out	4		
Extras b 2, lb 4, nb 2	8	Extras b 4, lb 3	7
Total	296	Total (5 wkts)	174

Bonus points — Nottinghamshire 2, Yorkshire 3

FoW: 1-45 (Hameed), 2-47 (Slater), 3-70 (Duckett), 4-119 (Mullaney), 5-147 (Moores), 6-173
1st   (Patterson-White), 7-270 (Clarke), 8-282 (Hutton), 9-292 (Fletcher), 10-296 (Evison)
2nd   1-9 (Hameed), 2-107 (Duckett), 3-130 (Clarke), 4-143 (Mullaney), 5-163 (Moores)

	O	M	R	W		O	M	R	W
Coad	25	7	75	3	Coad	17	0	58	3
Fisher	18	3	69	1	Fisher	8	1	26	0
Thompson	20.3	6	55	2	Thompson	8	0	42	1
Hill	9	3	32	2	Bess	12	2	35	1
Revis	9	2	19	2	Hill	3	1	6	0
Bess	11	1	27	0					
Brook	5	1	13	0					

YORKSHIRE

First Innings		Second Innings	
A Lyth, lbw b Hutton	4	c Moores b Evison	153
G C H Hill, c Hameed b Fletcher	5	run out (sub [C G Harrison])	34
T Kohler-Cadmore, b Fletcher	0	lbw b Patterson-White	49
W A R Fraine, c Moores b Fletcher	12	(5) lbw b Hutton	3
H C Brook, c Moores b Evison	12	(6) c Hutton b Paterson	42
J A Thompson, lbw b Evison	16	(7) c Duckett b Mullaney	31
M L Revis, c Hutton b Evison	12	(8) c Clarke b Paterson	34
D M Bess, c Hutton b Evison	12	(9) lbw b Hutton	8
§H G Duke, b Paterson	0	(10) lbw b Hutton	7
M D Fisher, c Moores b Paterson	4	(4) lbw b Paterson	0
*B O Coad, not out	0	not out	3
Extras b 4, lb 2, nb 2	8	Extras b 20, lb 12	32
Total	73	Total	396

Bonus points — Nottinghamshire 3

FoW: 1-5 (Hill), 2-6 (Kohler-Cadmore), 3-21 (Lyth), 4-21 (Fraine), 5-45 (Thompson),
1st   6-45 (Revis), 7-60 (Brook), 8-63 (Duke), 9-73 (Bess), 10-73 (Fisher)
FoW: 1-65 (Hill), 2-168 (Kohler-Cadmore), 3-169 (Fisher), 4-182 (Fraine), 5-261 (Brook),
2nd   6-335 (Thompson), 7-347 (Lyth), 8-356 (Bess), 9-368 (Duke), 10-396 (Revis)

	O	M	R	W		O	M	R	W
Fletcher	8	3	31	3	Fletcher	23	7	68	0
Hutton	7	3	12	1	Hutton	34	8	101	3
Paterson	7.2	1	11	2	Evison	28	6	78	1
Evison	7	3	13	4	Paterson	21.2	5	39	3
					Mullaney	19	3	50	1
					Patterson-White	17	6	28	1

Umpires: R J Bailey and R A Kettleborough   Scorers: J T Potter and R Marshall

Nottinghamshire v. Yorkshire

Lyth throws back message

Yorkshire's quartet of England players were unavailable ahead of winter international commitments, while captain Steve Patterson was absent with his hamstring injury and Gary Ballance reported illness just hours before the toss.

Ben Coad was named Yorkshire's seventh summer captain across all formats as the county pursued an unlikely Bob Willis Trophy final place.

A victory was required plus other results to go Yorkshire's way, but the former rarely looked like being achieved. Coad won the toss and bowled on a pitch as green as the outfield. In the first hour they beat the bat without luck before three wickets fell in each session. A let-off for Joe Clarke on 59 proved costly, and he reached a century before the close, when Nottinghamshire were 291-9.

A third batting point, required to

ADAM LYTH: Valiant 153

realistically keep their own title hopes alive, was spurned by the hosts early on day two, but their bowlers did not show the disappointment as Yorkshire slumped to 73 all out shortly after lunch, medium-pacer Joey Evison taking four wickets.

Having been asked to follow-on 223 behind, Adam Lyth led a valiant response to reward supporters with two more days in the sunshine and post his third century of the season — having been told he would be dropped due to a barren mid-season before Ballance's late withdrawal. A century stand for the second wicket with Tom Kohler-Cadmore (49) ended in the last-but-one over of the day.

Only Lyth passed 50, but stands of 79 and 74 with Harry Brook and Jordan Thompson extended Yorkshire's lead beyond 100 before wickets began to fall after tea on day three. Matthew Revis added a useful 43 to Lyth's outstanding 153, setting Nottinghamshire 174 to get in 11 overs and a day. Coad struck once before the close. Had Ben Slater been held in the slips on 19 at the start of day four a tense finish might have ensued...but he made 79, and only four more wickets were taken.

LV= COUNTY CHAMPIONSHIP 2021

PCF = Points carried forward from Group Stage to Divisional Stage

GROUP 1

	P	W	L	D	Abdn	BAT	BOWL	Ded	Points	PCF
1 Nottinghamshire	10	4	2	4	0	26	29	0	151	5.0
2 Warwickshire	10	4	1	5	0	17	25	1	145	21.0
3 Durham	10	3	2	5	0	17	30	3	132	4.0
4 Essex	10	3	2	5	0	15	26	0	129	19.0
5 Worcestershire	10	1	3	6	0	24	21	0	109	18.5
6 Derbyshire	10	0	5	5	0	10	23	1	72	9.5

Deduction (Ded):

Warwickshire	1 point deducted for slow over-rate against Derbyshire on June 3
Durham	2 points deducted for slow over-rate against Warwickshire on July 4
Durham	1 point deducted for slow over-rate against Nottinghamshire on July 11
Derbyshire	1 point deducted for slow over-rate against Warwickshire on June 3

GROUP 2

	P	W	L	D	Abdn	BAT	BOWL	Ded	Points	PCF
1 Somerset	10	4	1	5	0	26	26	8	148	18.5
2 Hampshire	10	4	2	4	0	23	26	0	145	8.5
3 Gloucestershire	10	5	3	2	0	14	21	0	131	12.0
4 Surrey	10	2	2	6	0	19	24	0	123	13.0
5 Leicestershire	10	2	4	4	0	22	25	0	111	11.5
6 Middlesex	10	2	7	1	0	14	30	1	84	13.0

Deduction (Ded):

Somerset	8 points deducted for breaching ECB Pitch Regulations during home County Championship match against Essex in 2019
Middlesex	1 point deducted for slow over-rate against Leicestershire on July 11

GROUP 3

	P	W	L	D	Abdn	BAT	BOWL	Ded	Points	PCF
1 Lancashire	10	4	1	5	0	22	24	0	150	16.5
2 Yorkshire	**10**	**5**	**1**	**4**	**0**	**14**	**23**	**0**	**149**	**4.5**
3 Glamorgan	10	2	2	6	0	18	29	0	127	11.5
4 Northamptonshire	10	3	3	4	0	22	21	0	123	16.0
5 Kent	10	0	3	7	0	15	26	0	97	11.0
6 Sussex	10	1	5	4	0	18	28	0	94	12.0

LV= COUNTY CHAMPIONSHIP 2021

PBF = Points brought forward from Group Stage to Division Stage

DIVISION 1

	P	W	L	D	Abdn	BAT	BOWL	Ded	PBF	Points
1 Warwickshire	4	2	1	1	0	6	10	0	21.0	77.0
2 Lancashire	4	2	1	1	0	7	10	0	16.5	73.5
3 Nottinghamshire	4	3	1	0	0	8	12	0	5.0	73.0
4 Hampshire	4	2	1	1	0	1	12	0	8.5	61.5
5 Yorkshire	**4**	**1**	**2**	**1**	**0**	**4**	**12**	**0**	**4.5**	**44.5**
6 Somerset	4	0	4	0	0	3	11	1	18.5	31.5

Deduction (Ded):

Somerset 1 point deducted for slow over-rate against Warwickshire on September 21

DIVISION 2

This division decided on Average Points (Av Pts)

	P	W	L	D	Abdn	BAT	BOWL	Ded	PBF	Points	Av Pts
1 Essex	4	3	0	1	0	9	12	0	19.0	96.0	19.2
2 Gloucestershire	4	3	1	0	0	4	12	0	12.0	76.0	15.2
3 Durham	3	1	1	1	0	7	9	0	4.0	44.0	11.0
4 Northamptonshire	4	1	2	1	0	3	11	0	16.0	54.0	10.8
5 Surrey	3	0	1	2	0	6	5	0	13.0	40.0	10.0
6 Glamorgan	4	0	3	1	0	8	7	0	11.5	34.5	6.9

DIVISION 3

	P	W	L	D	Abdn	BAT	BOWL	Ded	PBF	Points
1 Kent	4	4	0	0	0	7	12	0	11.0	94.0
2 Middlesex	4	3	1	0	0	7	12	0	13.0	80.0
3 Worcestershire	4	2	2	0	0	5	12	0	18.5	67.5
4 Leicestershire	4	1	2	1	0	9	10	0	11.5	54.5
5 Derbyshire	4	1	2	1	0	8	10	0	9.5	51.5
6 Sussex	4	0	4	0	0	12	6	0	12.0	30.0

YORKSHIRE AVERAGES 2021

COUNTY CHAMPIONSHIP

Played 14　　Won 6　　Lost 3　　Drawn 5

BATTING AND FIELDING
(Qualification 10 completed innings)

Player	M.	I.	N.O.	Runs	H.S.	100s	50s	Avge	ct/st
G S Ballance	10	14	1	594	101*	1	4	45.69	3
A Lyth	14	22	1	819	153	3	3	39.00	25
H C Brook	14	22	1	797	118	2	5	37.95	17
G C H Hill	7	11	0	263	71	0	2	23.90	1
D M Bess	14	20	1	399	56	0	2	21.00	4
J A Thompson	13	20	0	411	57	0	1	20.55	4
T Kohler-Cadmore	11	18	0	353	89	0	1	19.61	21
H G Duke	9	13	1	197	54	0	2	16.41	31/0
S A Patterson	13	17	2	191	47*	0	0	12.73	3

Also played

D J Malan	2	3	0	220	199	1	0	73.33	2
D J Willey	6	8	4	165	41*	0	0	41.25	1
J E Root	5	8	0	291	101	1	1	36.37	4
M L Revis	1	2	0	34	34	0	0	17.00	0
J A Tattersall	5	8	1	101	26	0	0	14.42	16/0
T W Loten	2	4	0	57	27	0	0	14.25	0
M D Fisher	5	7	2	55	17	0	0	11.00	1
B O Coad	10	13	5	84	33*	0	0	10.50	0
D Olivier	7	11	0	61	21	0	0	10.16	1
W A R Fraine	3	6	0	35	11	0	0	5.83	1
S A Northeast	2	2	0	4	3	0	0	2.00	2
D J Leech	1	0	0	0	—	0	0	—	0

BOWLING
(Qualification 10 wickets)

Player	Overs	Mdns	Runs	Wkts	Avge	Best	5wI	10wM
M D Fisher	121	29	393	20	19.65	5 -41	1	0
J A Thompson	329.5	91	949	46	20.63	5 -52	1	0
B O Coad	287.1	79	766	35	21.88	4 -48	0	0
D J Willey	148.3	30	479	20	23.95	5 -61	1	0
S A Patterson	364	111	815	32	25.46	4 -26	0	0
D M Bess	405.4	122	912	28	32.57	7 -43	2	0
D Olivier	175.1	26	610	18	33.88	4 -61	0	0

Also bowled

M L Revis	9	2	19	2	9.50	2 -19	0	0
G C H Hill	48	12	128	7	18.28	2 -12	0	0
H C Brook	82.1	18	194	7	27.71	3 -15	0	0
J E Root	27	4	74	1	74.00	1 -26	0	0
A Lyth	13	8	6	0	—	0 - 2	0	0
D J Leech	17	1	79	0	—	0 -79	0	0

PATTO'S AMAZING REPEAT SHOW

By David Warner

Skipper Steve Patterson was the hero of the hour last May when he had Wayne Parnell caught behind by Jonny Tattersall to bring Yorkshire a pulsating one-run victory over Northamptonshire in the gripping LV= Insurance County Championship match at Headingley.

But 14 years earlier, in May 2007, Patterson had been under the spotlight for bowling an even more incredible over to bring Yorkshire a one-run triumph over Loughborough MCCU at the same venue.

Although the result of that match was of little consequence compared to the clash with Northamptonshire, it looked as if Yorkshire were heading for an embarrassing defeat when Patterson prepared to bowl the last scheduled over with the students needing 10 with two wickets in hand.

Eight runs off his first four deliveries left Yorkshire staring down the barrel, but Patterson then yorked both Steven Wheeler and last man Tom Parsons to squeeze the hosts home by the skin of their teeth.

The win over Northamptonshire was only Yorkshire's second by one run in the Championship and their third overall. And I have seen all three, thanks last season to the wonders of live online streaming.

The first was against Middlesex at Bradford Park Avenue in 1976, and that was also a storyline straight out of the pages of *Boy's Own*.

Middlesex were nine down in their second innings and still requiring five to win when Clive Radley came out to bat with his arm in a sling after breaking a finger while fielding much earlier in the game and taking no further part until now.

It looked as if Middlesex were about to scrape home until Radley left his crease and was smartly stumped by David Bairstow, Jonny's dad. And the bowler? None other than Yorkshire's president Geoff Cope, whose off-spin brought him match figures of 11-167.

YORKSHIRE CCC SQUAD 2022

Player	Date of Birth	Birthplace	Role
S A Patterson (Captain)	October 3, 1983	Beverley	RAMF, RHB
J M Bairstow	September 26, 1989	Bradford	RHB, WK
G S Ballance	November 22, 1989	Harare, Zim	LHB
D M Bess	July 22, 1997	Exeter	OS, RHB
B D Birkhead	October 28, 1998	Halifax	RHB, WK
H C Brook	February 22, 1999	Keighley	RHB, RM
B O Coad	January 10, 1994	Harrogate	RAMF, RHB
H G Duke	September 6, 2001	Wakefield	RHB, WK
M D Fisher	November 9, 1997	York	RAMF, RHB
W A R Fraine	June 13, 1996	Huddersfield	RHB
G C H Hill	January 24, 2001	Airedale	RAMF, RHB
T Kohler-Cadmore	August 19, 1994	Chatham	RHB
D J Leech	January 10, 2001	Middlesbrough	RAMF, RHB
T W Loten	January 8, 1999	York	RHB, RAMF
W A Luxton	May 6, 2003	Keighley	RHB
A Lyth	September 25, 1987	Whitby	LHB, OS
D J Malan	September 3, 1987	Roehampton	LHB, LS
D Olivier (overseas)	May 9, 1992	Groblersdal, SA	RAF, RHB
A U Rashid	February 17, 1988	Bradford	LS, RHB
H Rauf (Overseas)	November 7, 1993	Rawalpindi, Pak	RAF, RHB
M L Revis	November 15, 2001	Keighley	RHB, RAMF
J E Root	December 30, 1990	Sheffield	RHB, OS
J W Shutt	June 24, 1997	Barnsley	OS, RHB
H A Sullivan	December 17, 2002	Leeds	SLA, LHB
J R Sullivan	August 4, 2000	Leeds	LB, RHB
J A Tattersall	December 15, 1994	Harrogate	RHB, WK
J A Thompson	October 9, 1996	Leeds	RAMF, LHB
M J Waite	December 24, 1998	Leeds	RAMF, RHB
J H Wharton	February 1, 2001	Huddersfield	RHB
D J Willey (T20 Captain)	February 28, 1990	Northampton	LAMF, LHB

NB: Will Luxton, Matthew Revis, Harry and Josh Sullivan and James Wharton are all on rookie contracts for 2022.

YORKSHIRE'S VITALITY BLAST HIGHLIGHTS OF 2021

WINNERS: **Kent Spitfires** (167-7) defeated Somerset (142-9) by 25 runs

Totals of 150 and over (9)

240-4	v. Leicestershire at Leeds (won)
224-3	v. Northamptonshire at Leeds (won)
216-6	v. Worcestershire at Worcester (won)
191-5	v. Worcestershire at Leeds (won)
180-4	v. Lancashire at Leeds (won)
177-7	v. Sussex at Chester-le-Street (lost)
174-5	v. Derbyshire at Leeds (won)
173	v. Leicestershire at Leicester (lost)
161-6	v. Durham at Chester-le-Street (lost)

Match aggregates of 350 and over (6)

462	Yorkshire (240-4) defeated Leicestershire (222-8) by 18 runs at Leeds
380	Leicestershire (207-3) defeated Yorkshire (173) by 34 runs at Leicester
370	Yorkshire (191-5) defeated Worcestershire (179-5) by 12 runs at Leeds
366	Yorkshire (224-3) defeated Northamptonshire (142) by 82 runs at Leeds
355	Yorkshire (177-7) lost to Sussex (178-5) by 5 wickets at Chester-le-Street
351	Yorkshire (180-4) defeated Lancashire (171-8) by 9 runs at Leeds

Century Partnerships (3)

For 1st wicket (1)

113   A Lyth and J M Bairstow v. Leicestershire at Leeds

For 3rd wicket (1)

146   J M Bairstow and T Kohler-Cadmore v. Worcestershire at Worcester

For 6th wicket (1)

141 *   H C Brook and J A Thompson v. Worcestershire at Leeds

Century (1)

J M Bairstow (1)

    112   v. Worcestershire at Worcester

4 wickets in an innings (2)

L J Ferguson (1)

    4 -24   v. Lancashire at Leeds

J A Thompson (1)

    4 -44   v. Durham at Chester-le-Street

3 catches in an innings (1)

A Lyth (1)

    3   v. Lancashire at Leeds

3 dismissals in an innings (none)

Debuts (4)

T20 (1): H G Duke
For Yorkshire (3): L J Ferguson, M D Stoneman and S A Northeast

Vitality T20 Blast — North Group
Yorkshire v. Birmingham Bears

Played at Headingley, Leeds, on June 10, 2021
Yorkshire won by 6 wickets

Toss won by Yorkshire · Yorkshire 2 points, Birmingham Bears 0 points

BIRMINGHAM BEARS
E J Pollock, c Ferguson b Willey	1
A J Hose, c Lyth b Waite	22
*W M H Rhodes, c Lyth b Waite	0
S R Hain, c Fraine b Willey	59
D R Mousley, c Kohler-Cadmore b Thompson	22
C R Brathwaite, c and b Thompson	3
§ M G K Burgess, c and b Thompson	4
T T Bresnan, c Bairstow b Ferguson	23
C N Miles, not out	5
D R Briggs, not out	0
J B Lintott Did not bat	
Extras lb 3, w 2	5
Total (8 wkts, 20 overs)	144

FoW: 1-6 (Pollock), 2-6 (Rhodes), 3-29 (Hose), 4-62 (Mousley), 5-73 (Brathwaite), 6-89 (Burgess), 7-138 (Bresnan), 8-141 (Hain)

	O	M	R	W
Willey	4	0	27	2
Waite	4	1	36	2
Thompson	4	0	23	3
Ferguson	4	0	29	1
Rashid	4	0	26	0

YORKSHIRE
A Lyth, c Miles b Briggs	5
§ J M Bairstow, b Briggs	34
D J Malan, c Lintott b Bresnan	23
T Kohler-Cadmore, not out	31
H C Brook, c Hain b Brathwaite	24
W A R Fraine, not out	19
J A Thompson	
*D J Willey	
A U Rashid Did not bat	
M J Waite	
L H Ferguson	
Extras lb 4, w 7	11
Total (4 wkts, 18.3 overs)	147

FoW: 1-6 (Lyth), 2-64 (Malan), 3-69 (Bairstow), 4-118 (Brook)

	O	M	R	W
Briggs	4	0	28	2
Mousley	2	0	14	0
Brathwaite	4	0	30	1
Bresnan	3.3	0	25	1
Lintott	4	0	34	0
Miles	1	0	12	0

Man of the Match: J A Thompson

Umpires: D J Millns and C M Watts   Scorers: J T Potter and A J Ruffles

Yorkshire v. Birmingham Bears

Bairstow starts with a bang

Jonny Bairstow top-scored with 34 off 22 balls as Yorkshire eased to a 145 target to begin their North Group campaign with a bang.

Bairstow shared 59 for the second wicket with England colleague Dawid Malan, but both fell in the seventh and ninth overs — Malan for 23 — (69-3) before Tom Kohler-Cadmore, Harry Brook and Will Fraine saw their side home with nine balls left.

Jordan Thompson equalled a career-best 3-23 from four overs of seam as the Bears stuttered to 144-8, including Sam Hain's 59 off 41. Matthew Waite had Will Rhodes and Adam Hose caught off miscues as Birmingham slipped to 29-3 inside four overs having been inserted. Hain, who went in at 6-2 and hit three sixes, shared 33 for the fourth wicket with Dan Mousley and 49 for the seventh with former home favourite Tim Bresnan, who made 23 to advance the Bears from 89-6 in the 13th over on a true pitch.

JONNY BAIRSTOW: Three sixes

All-rounders Waite and Thompson outshone Adil Rashid and New Zealand debutant Lockie Ferguson as all the Bears wickets were caught. Waite opened the bowling and returned a career best 2-36. Thompson dismissed West Indian Carlos Brathwaite cheaply with a superb caught and bowled effort.

Yorkshire lost Adam Lyth after four balls to Danny Briggs's left-arm spin, but Bairstow slog-swept him for six over mid-wicket in the third over. Making his first Blast appearance since Finals Day 2016, Bairstow also pulled Bresnan for two sixes. When Bairstow chopped on to Briggs in the ninth over the Vikings slipped to 69-3, but they never realistically looked like faltering in front of a 4,000 crowd.

Kohler-Cadmore and Brook (24) shared 49 before Brook fell to Brathwaite: 118-4 after 16.1 overs. Kohler-Cadmore finished 31 not out before Fraine crashed 19 off eight balls, including the winning runs.

Vitality T20 Blast — North Group
Durham v. Yorkshire

Played at Emirates Riverside, Chester-le-Street, on June 11, 2021

Durham won by 20 runs

Toss won by Yorkshire

Durham 2 points, Yorkshire 0 points

DURHAM

G Clark, c Willey b Ferguson	34
D G Bedingham, c Malan b Thompson	11
B A Raine, c Fraine b Thompson	5
* C T Bancroft, c Bairstow b Ferguson	15
S R Dickson, c Willey b Rashid	8
§ E J H Eckersley, c Thompson b Waite	16
P Coughlin, c Kohler-Cadmore b Thompson	21
B A Carse, c Brook b Thompson	51
L Trevaskis, not out	9
Extras b 1, lb 1, w 3, nb 6	11
Total (8 wkts, 20 overs)	181

S G Borthwick, M J Potts   Did not bat

FoW: 1-43 (Clark), 2-48 (Raine), 3-54 (Bedingham), 4-67 (Dickson), 5-89 (Bancroft), 6-95 (Eckersley), 7-132 (Coughlin), 8-181 (Carse).

	O	M	R	W
Willey	3	0	38	0
Waite	4	0	37	1
Ferguson	4	0	31	2
Thompson	4	0	44	4
Rashid	4	0	19	1
Lyth	1	0	10	0

YORKSHIRE

A Lyth, c Bancroft b Potts	1
§ J M Bairstow, b Carse	67
D J Malan, b Trevaskis	10
T Kohler-Cadmore, c Potts b Raine	16
H C Brook, c Carse b Potts	41
W A R Fraine, c Coughlin b Raine	14
* D J Willey, not out	4
J A Thompson, not out	1
Extras lb 3, w 2, nb 2	7
Total (6 wkts, 20 overs)	161

A U Rashid, M J Waite, L H Ferguson   Did not bat

FoW: 1-11 (Lyth), 2-44 (Malan), 3-78 (Kohler-Cadmore), 4-102 (Bairstow), 5-154 (Brook), 6-157 (Fraine).

	O	M	R	W
Carse	3	0	26	1
Potts	4	0	28	2
Coughlin	4	0	42	0
Trevaskis	4	0	28	1
Borthwick	2	0	17	0
Raine	3	0	17	2

Man of the Match: B A Carse

Umpires: I D Blackwell and N A Mallender   Scorers: J T Potter and W R Dobson

Durham v. Yorkshire

Undone by the brave

A rattling 67 from Jonny Bairstow and a career best 4-44 from Jordan Thompson could not mask a below-par performance.

The visitors were undone by a brave Durham, the hosts recovering from 95-6 to set up a winning target of 182.

Thompson and New Zealand fast bowler Lockie Ferguson struck twice apiece as the hosts, invited to bat, slipped into deep trouble inside 13 overs. Vikings then encountered a belligerent 51 off 31 balls from soon-to-be England seamer Brydon Carse, who kept on swinging despite the loss of wickets. Carse shared stands of 37 for the seventh wicket with Paul Coughlin (21) and an unbroken 49 for the eighth with Liam Trevaskis.

JORDAN THOMPSON: Career best

Durham scored 41 runs in the last three overs.

Despite Thompson's four-for Adil Rashid could make a case for being Yorkshire's best bowler with 1-19 from his four overs of leg-spin. His wicket was that of Sean Dickson, brilliantly caught over his shoulder running back from cover towards mid-off by captain David Willey.

Bairstow then led the Vikings chase with nine fours and a six in 50 balls. Despite the cheap losses of Adam Lyth, Dawid Malan and Tom Kohler-Cadmore they were well placed at 102-3 in the 13th over with Bairstow unbeaten. Then he was bowled pulling at Carse, who would play a trio of one-day internationals approximately a month later.

Bairstow's dismissal proved a hammer blow. Harry Brook scored 41 off 27 with two sixes to keep slim hopes alive, but he fell to Matty Potts in the last-but-one over. Ben Raine was left defending a target of 25 off the last over, and he removed Will Fraine with the first ball (157-6).

Not even power duo Willey and Thompson could rescue things as Yorkshire (161-6) started their campaign with a win and this 20-run defeat having beaten Birmingham at Headingley 24 hours earlier.

Vitality T20 Blast — North Group
Yorkshire v. Leicestershire

Played at Headingley, Leeds, on June 15, 2021
Yorkshire won by 18 runs

Toss won by Yorkshire   Yorkshire 2 points, Leicestershire 0 points

YORKSHIRE

A Lyth, c Kimber b Parkinson	51
§ J M Bairstow, c Griffiths b Naveen ul Haq	82
D J Malan, st Inglis b Ackermann	6
* D J Willey, c Parkinson b Naveen ul Haq	44
W A R Fraine, not out	2
H C Brook, not out	48
T Kohler-Cadmore	
J A Thompson	
A U Rashid Did not bat	
M D Fisher	
L H Ferguson	
Extras b 2, lb 3, w 2	7
Total (4 wkts, 20 overs)	240

FoW: 1-113 (Lyth), 2-121 (Malan), 3-183 (Willey), 4-189 (Bairstow)

	O	M	R	W
Parkinson	4	0	31	1
Ackermann	4	0	31	1
Naveen ul Haq	4	0	49	2
Griffiths	3	0	60	0
Mike	2	0	21	0
Lilley	3	0	43	0

LEICESTERSHIRE

S Steel, c Brook b Willey	1
§ J P Inglis, c Thompson b Fisher	82
A M Lilley, b Ferguson	24
* C N Ackermann, c Willey b Thompson	32
R K Patel, c Ferguson b Fisher	21
L J Hill, c Fraine b Willey	10
L P J Kimber, c Lyth b Ferguson	10
B W M Mike, c Lyth b Willey	31
C F Parkinson, not out	2
Naveen ul Haq, not out	0
G T Griffiths Did not bat	
Extras lb 5, w 4	9
Total (8 wkts, 20 overs)	222

FoW: 1-6 (Steel), 2-55 (Lilley), 3-141 (Ackermann), 4-146 (Inglis), 5-158 (Hill) 6-175 (Patel), 7-214 (Kimber), 8-221 (Mike)

	O	M	R	W
Willey	4	0	44	3
Fisher	4	0	45	2
Thompson	3	0	39	1
Ferguson	4	0	28	2
Lyth	1	0	24	0
Rashid	4	0	37	0

Man of the Match: J M Bairstow

Umpires: P R Pollard and N J Pratt   Scorers: J T Potter and P J Rogers

Yorkshire v. Leicestershire
Gorging at the feast

Yorkshire won a remarkable game by 18 runs, just holding on as the Foxes almost chased down 241.

Leicestershire finished on 222-8 with openers Jonny Bairstow (45 balls) and Josh Inglis both hitting 82 for their sides.

The Vikings secured their second win in three in a match which saw 29 sixes hit. Records galore came from a contest boasting a combined 462 runs — equalling the Vitality Blast record.

Vikings amassed 240-4 before the Foxes gave them an almighty scare as Leeds-born Australian Inglis matched Bairstow's score off only 37 balls.

This was Yorkshire's third highest total in Blast history and included Adam Lyth's 51, 44 for David Willey and 48 not out for Harry Brook. Lyth's first run was his

DAVID WILLEY: One of 29 sixes in records bonanza

3,000th for all teams in T20 cricket. Leicester were far from out of it at 146-3 in the 13th over with opener Inglis unbeaten, but his departure, courtesy of a moment of magic, proved the key moment for the hosts.

Matthew Fisher removed him on his return from injury, but it was Jordan Thompson who took the credit with a brilliant one-handed catch on the deep cover boundary. Despite being born in Leeds and coming through the Yorkshire age-groups before his family emigrated to Perth when he was 15, this was his first appearance at Headingley. Funnily enough, he and Thompson had played junior league cricket together.

More later-order hitting, chiefly from Ben Mike with 31, took the target down to 31 off two overs with four wickets left and 23 off the last with three remaining. Lockie Ferguson brilliantly conceded only eight off the penultimate over as the New Zealander returned a superb 2-28 from four overs. Willey (3-44) comfortably saw it out in the last over.

This was the 20th time in T20 history that Yorkshire have scored 200 or more, 14 of them coming at Headingley.

Vitality T20 Blast — North Group
Worcestershire v. Yorkshire

Played at Blackfinch New Road, Worcester, on June 16, 2021

Yorkshire won by 94 runs

Toss won by Worcestershire   Yorkshire 2 points, Worcestershire 0 points

YORKSHIRE

§ J M Bairstow, c Wessels b Morris	112
A Lyth, c and b Pennington	2
D J Malan, b Dwarshuis	2
T Kohler-Cadmore, c Wessels b Dwarshuis	53
H C Brook, c Wessels b Dwarshuis	22
W A R Fraine, c Wessels b Dwarshuis	6
* D J Willey, not out	9
D M Bess, not out	2
M D Fisher	
A U Rashid Did not bat	
L H Ferguson	
Extras lb 3, w 5	8
Total (6 wkts, 20 overs)	216

FoW: 1-6 (Lyth), 2-10 (Malan), 3-156 (Kohler-Cadmore), 4-194 (Bairstow), 5-205 (Brook), 6-205 (Fraine)

	O	M	R	W
Ali	2	0	24	0
Pennington	3	0	32	1
Dwarshuis	4	0	31	4
Morris	4	0	46	1
Sodhi	4	0	53	0
Barnard	3	0	27	0

WORCESTERSHIRE

M H Wessels, c Kohler-Cadmore b Rashid	32
B L D'Oliveira, b Willey	0
* M M Ali, c Ferguson b Rashid	39
R A Whiteley, c sub (G S Ballance) b Willey	30
§ O B Cox, c Willey b Fisher	6
J D Libby, c and b Fisher	0
E G Barnard, b Bess	0
B J Dwarshuis, c Willey b Bess	0
I S Sodhi, c Lyth b Rashid	0
D Y Pennington, c Fisher b Ferguson	2
C A Morris, not out	2
Extras b 4, lb 4, w 1, nb 2	11
Total ((16.3 overs)	122

Note: T Kohler-Cadmore was wicket-keeper for all of this innings

FoW: 1-1 (D'Oliveira), 2-68 (Ali), 3-83 (Wessels), 4-110 (Cox), 5-111 (Libby), 6-112 (Barnard), 7-112 (Dwarshuis), 8-113 (Sodhi), 9-120 (Whiteley), 10-122 (Pennington)

	O	M	R	W
Willey	3	0	17	2
Fisher	3	0	15	2
Ferguson	2.3	0	20	1
Rashid	4	0	32	3
Bess	4	0	30	2

Man of the Match: J M Bairstow

Umpires: M J Saggers and R A White   Scorers: J T Potter and S M Drinkwater

Worcestershire v. Yorkshire

Stunning power of Bairstow

A stunning, powerful century from an injured Jonny Bairstow led Yorkshire to another victory as they posted 216-6 and beat 2018 champions Worcestershire by 94 runs at New Road.

Adil Rashid claimed three wickets and Dom Bess, Matthew Fisher and David Willey two apiece as the Rapids lost their last seven wickets for 12 to be bowled out for only 122.

Bairstow did not take the wicket-keeping gloves, having suffered a right ankle injury midway through his innings, meaning Tom Kohler-Cadmore deputised against his former county. Kohler-Cadmore (53 off 33 balls), contributed his first fifty of the season in any format.

Bairstow, with 112 off 51, was the star of the show, reaching his hundred off 48 balls, one slower than Ian Harvey's record 47-ball century against Derbyshire in 2005.

The Vikings, invited to bat, were in trouble at 10-2, but Bairstow and Kohler-Cadmore shared a record-breaking 146 for the third wicket inside 12 overs.

It was the county's second highest partnership in Blast history, falling just

JONNY BAIRSTOW
Star of the show

short of the 150 Adam Lyth and Willey put on against Northamptonshire in 2018. Bairstow was on five off 10 balls when he opted for a change of bat. From then on he almost middled everything.

He hit two sixes in as many balls off Dillon Pennington in the 13th over, the second clearing the stands at the New Road End. The locals reckoned it would have cleared even the New Road carriageway outside the ground and gone into the adjacent Cripplegate Park.

Willey struck early in defence, but the Vikings dropped Riki Wessels and Moeen Ali in the power play as the Rapids reached 45-1 after six overs. Rashid had Moeen caught at backward point for 39 — 68-2 in the ninth over — and from there it was realistically game up for the hosts, who crumbled quickly.

Vitality T20 Blast — North Group
Yorkshire v. Durham

At Headingley, Leeds, on June 18, 2021
Match abandoned without a ball bowled

Toss: None
Umpires: G D Lloyd and R T Robinson

Yorkshire 1 point, Durham 1 point
Scorers: J T Potter and W R Dobson

Yorkshire v. Derbyshire

Played at Headingley, Leeds, on June 20, 2021
Yorkshire won by 39 runs

Toss won by Derbyshire
Yorkshire 2 points, Derbyshire 0 points

YORKSHIRE

A Lyth, b van Beek	8
§ T Kohler-Cadmore, b Thomson	13
* J E Root, c Thomson b Scrimshaw	49
G S Ballance, c du Plooy b Scrimshaw	9
H C Brook, not out	48
W A R Fraine, c McKerr b Scrimshaw	10
J A Thompson, b Hudson-Prentice	21
M J Waite, not out	6
D M Bess	
M D Fisher Did not bat	
L H Ferguson	
Extras b 2, lb 1, w 7	10
Total (6 wkts, 20 overs)	174

FoW: 1-8 (Lyth), 2-29 (Kohler-Cadmore), 3-56 (Ballance), 4-113 (Root), 5-127 (Fraine), 6-167 (Thompson)

	O	M	R	W
van Beek	3	0	31	1
McKerr	2	0	21	0
Thomson	2	0	14	1
Hudson-Prentice	4	0	36	1
Critchley	4	0	31	0
Scrimshaw	4	0	30	3
Reece	1	0	8	0

DERBYSHIRE

L M Reece, c Thompson b Root	1
H R C Came, b Ferguson	21
* B A Godleman, c Bess b Waite	11
J L du Plooy, c and b Bess	9
M J J Critchley, c Brook b Bess	5
F J Hudson-Prentice, c Brook b Thompson	34
§ B D Guest, c Lyth b Bess	6
A T Thomson, c and b Thompson	28
L V van Beek, b Ferguson	2
C McKerr, not out	7
G L S Scrimshaw, b Ferguson	0
Extras b 1, lb 4, w 2, nb 4	11
Total (19 overs)	135

FoW: 1-3 (Reece), 2-35 (Came), 3-44 (Godleman), 4-49 (du Plooy), 5-69 (Critchley), 6-84 (Guest), 7-126 (Hudson-Prentice), 8-126 (Thomson), 9-135 (van Beek), 10-135 (Scrimshaw)

	O	M	R	W
Fisher	3	0	14	0
Root	2	0	19	1
Lyth	1	0	2	0
Thompson	2	0	25	2
Ferguson	4	0	21	3
Bess	4	0	21	3
Waite	3	0	28	1

Man of the Match: H C Brook

Umpires: P J Hartley and I N Ramage
Scorers: J T Potter and J M Brown

Yorkshire v. Derbyshire

The Falcons' wings clipped

Yorkshire clipped the wings of the Derbyshire Falcons to move top of the North Group table.

It was their fourth win in six games, this one by 39 runs, as captain Joe Root, Harry Brook, Dom Bess and Lockie Ferguson all contributed significantly.

Captain Root, back in county colours and deputising for the absent David Willey on England T20 duty, top-scored with 49 off 36 balls as the Vikings made 174-6, Brook unbeaten on 48. The Vikings, having been inserted, had to recover from 8-1 in the first over and 56-3 in the eighth, but Root and Brook, almost a case of master and apprentice, shared 57 in six overs for the fourth wicket before the visitors fell well short of their target — bowled out for 135 in 19 overs.

Getting out in front: Top-scorer Joe Root takes a turn as Vikings captain

While Root missed out on a sixth half-century in his last seven Blast innings dating back to July 2018 he took his tally of Blast runs to 378 in that time, including five half-centuries and averaging 75.59.

Bess and New Zealand overseas Ferguson finished with 3-21 apiece as Yorkshire secured a routine two points. Bess returned career-best figures in only his 10th T20 appearance, including a superb return catch tumbling to his right to get rid of the dangerous Leus du Plooy as Derbyshire slipped to 49-4 after nine overs of their chase.

Yorkshire were not only missing regular skipper Willey, because of Egland duty, but Jonny Bairstow, Dawid Malan and Adil Rashid as well.

Jordan Thompson hit two sixes and Brook and Matthew Waite one each in the last nine balls of the Vikings innings to significantly boost the total. Twenty-eight runs came off the last two overs, and when Root, with his off-spin, struck 10 balls into the Derbyshire chase — Luis Reece skewing high to point — the visitors were 3-1 and the writing was on the wall.

Vitality T20 Blast — North Group
Yorkshire v. Worcestershire

Played at Headingley, Leeds, on June 23, 2021
Yorkshire won by 12 runs

Toss won by Yorkshire   Yorkshire 2 points, Worcestershire 0 points

YORKSHIRE

§ J A Tattersall, c Libby b Pennington	6
A Lyth, c Morris b Pennington	7
* J E Root, lbw b Pennington	1
G S Ballance, c Barnard b Pennington	0
H C Brook, not out	83
G C H Hill, b Barnard	12
J A Thompson, not out	66

M J Waite
D M Bess   Did not bat
M D Fisher
L H Ferguson

Extras b 5, lb 3, w 6, nb 2 16
Total (5 wkts, 20 overs) 191

FoW: 1-13 (Lyth), 2-13 (Tattersall), 3-13 (Ballance), 4-15 (Root), 5-50 (Hill)

	O	M	R	W
Libby	1	0	8	0
Dwarshuis	4	0	30	0
Pennington	4	2	24	4
Morris	4	0	54	0
Sodhi	2	0	18	0
Barnard	3	0	28	1
D'Oliveira	2	0	21	0

WORCESTERSHIRE

M H Wessels, b Fisher	77
B L D'Oliveira, run out (Root)	2
T C Fell, c Tattersall b Ferguson	4
J D Libby, c Brook b Bess	5
* § O B Cox, not out	61
R A Whiteley, c Brook b Fisher	21
B J Dwarshuis, not out	3

E G Barnard
I S Sodhi   Did not bat
D Y Pennington
C A J Morris

Extras lb 4, nb 2 6
Total (5 wkts, 20 overs) 179

FoW: 1-11 (D'Oliveira), 2-35 (Fell), 3-50 (Libby), 4-118 (Wessels), 5-173 (Whiteley)

	O	M	R	W
Fisher	4	0	33	2
Root	2	0	17	0
Ferguson	4	0	32	1
Waite	3	0	26	0
Thompson	3	0	33	0
Bess	4	0	34	1

Man of the Match: J A Thompson

Umpires: S J O'Shaughnessy and N J Pratt   Scorers: J T Potter and S M Drinkwater

Yorkshire v. Worcestershire
Victory night to remember

This was undoubtedly a summer highlight. T20 games can often fade from memory pretty quickly, such are their frequency.

Not this one, as Yorkshire were indebted to the record-breaking heroics of Harry Brook and Jordan Thompson for an unbroken 141 for the sixth wicket to lead the recovery from 15-4 in beating the Rapids by 12 runs.

Electing to bat, the Vikings were all but goners at 15-4 in the fifth over and 18-4 after six following Dillon Pennington's fabulous first two overs.

Pennington struck three times in his first five balls and four times in his first eight without concession, including Joe Root lbw for one.

HARRY BROOK: 141 record stand with Jordan Thompson

Yorkshire's early campaign form had given them a confidence to suggest they were not yet out it. George Hill contributed 12 to help to steady the ship before Brook and Thompson, advancing from 50-5, wrote their names into the record books in scintillating style to underpin 191-5.

Both men posted their second career fifties and shared all 11 sixes in the Vikings innings as the wheels came off for Worcester. A stunning 158 runs came off the last 11 overs from 33-4 after nine, with Brook hitting superbly straight and Thompson peppering the stands on both sides of the wicket. Brook, dropped on two, top-scored with 83 not out off 54 balls, the unbeaten Thompson adding 66 off 28.

Their 56-ball partnership was a Blast record for the sixth wicket and the second highest for that wicket anywhere in the world. The highest was 61 between Andre Russell and Kennar Lewis for Jamaica in the 2018 Caribbean Premier League.

Riki Wessels's 77 off 45 balls led Worcester's spirited chase as they finished on 179-5, including captain Ben Cox's freewheeling 61 not out. Cox helped to take the target to 23 off the final over, bowled by Matthew Fisher, who earlier had yorked Wessels. Fisher struck again to despatch Whiteley and finish with 2-33.

Vitality T20 Blast — North Group
Leicestershire v. Yorkshire

Played at Uptonsteel County Ground, Leicester, on June 25, 2021
Leicestershire won by 34 runs

Toss won by Leicestershire   Leicestershire 2 points, Yorkshire 0 points

LEICESTERSHIRE

§ J P Inglis, c and b Root	16
S Steel, run out (Ballance>Bess)	32
A M Lilley, not out	99
* C N Ackermann, b Fisher	40
R K Patel, not out	4
L J Hill	
L P J Kimber	
B W M Mike Did not bat	
C F Parkinson	
Naveen ul Haq	
G T Griffiths	
Extras b 8, lb 1, w 5, nb 2	16
Total (3 wkts, 20 overs)	207

FoW: 1-24 (Inglis), 2-99 (Steel), 3-189 (Ackermann)

	O	M	R	W
Root	3	0	33	1
Fisher	4	0	44	1
Bess	4	0	21	0
Ferguson	4	0	35	0
Waite	2	0	24	0
Thompson	3	0	41	0

YORKSHIRE

§ J A Tattersall, c Patel b Parkinson	10
A Lyth, lbw b Parkinson	22
* J E Root, c Patel b Parkinson	15
G S Ballance, b Steel	34
H C Brook, c and b Griffiths	33
G C H Hill, c Lilley b Ackermann	5
J A Thompson, b Parkinson	0
M J Waite, c Ackermann b Naveen ul Haq	3
D M Bess, c Ackermann b Mike	24
M D Fisher, c Lilley b Mike	19
L H Ferguson, not out	0
Extras lb 2, w 6	8
Total (19.5 overs)	173

FoW: 1-33 (Tattersall), 2-34 (Lyth), 3-78 (Root), 4-93 (Ballance), 5-103 (Hill), 6-121 (Thompson), 7-127 (Brook), 8-137 (Waite), 9-165 (Fisher), 10-173 (Bess)

	O	M	R	W
Steel	4	0	21	1
Ackermann	3	0	34	1
Naveen ul Haq	4	0	34	1
Parkinson	4	0	35	4
Griffiths	4	0	38	1
Mike	0.5	0	9	2

Man of the Match: A M Lilley

Umpires: H M S Adnan and N L Bainton   Scorers: J T Potter and P J Rogers

Leicestershire v. Yorkshire
Foxes snare the Vikings

Yorkshire suffered their second loss of the season as the Foxes comfortably defended their imposing 207-3.

Arron Lilley smashed a career best 99 not out before the Vikings replied with 173 all out, left-arm spinner Callum Parkinson claiming 4-35.

An off night with the ball and in the field gave Yorkshire too much to do, losing by 34 runs with one ball remaining. Having lost the toss, anything which could go wrong seemingly did in good batting conditions.

Only Dom Bess with 0-21 from four overs could reflect on a job well done, the rest of Yorkshire's six-man attack going at more than 10 runs per over. Only seven overs in the Leicester innings were limited to single-figure scores.

Tormentor in chief was Lilley, the all-rounder who effectively bats as a pinch-hitter at No. 3 in this format. He clobbered nine fours and four sixes in 55 balls, falling narrowly short of a maiden century.

DOMINIC BESS: The only job that was well done

Lilley shared 75 for the second wicket with Scott Steel (32) from 24-1 and 90 for the third with captain Colin Ackermann (40) from 99-1.

Adam Lyth's 22 gave Yorkshire a bright start at 32-0 after three overs, but he and locum opening partner Jonny Tattersall were out to Parkinson in the fourth — caught at point and lbw. Tattersall was elevated to open due to the injury or unavailability of players such as Jonny Bairstow (England) and Tom Kohler-Cadmore (broken finger).

Parkinson had Joe Root caught at backward point off a full toss for 15: 78-3 in the ninth — and Yorkshire were falling behind the rate. The left-arm spinner also bowled Jordan Thompson for a duck, and when in-form Harry Brook offered a return catch to seamer Gavin Griffiths for five the visitors were 127-7 in the 16th over with a rare defeat all but signed and sealed.

Vitality T20 Blast — North Group
Yorkshire v. Northamptonshire

Played at Headingley, Leeds, on June 26, 2021
Yorkshire won by 82 runs

Toss won by Yorkshire   Yorkshire 2 points, Northamptonshire 0 points

YORKSHIRE

* A Lyth, b Taylor	25
M D Stoneman, lbw b Nabi	50
J A Thompson, c Taylor b Glover	74
H C Brook, not out	45
G S Ballance, not out	20
G C H Hill	
D M Bess	
M J Waite Did not bat	
§ J A Tattersall	
M D Fisher	
L H Ferguson	
Extras lb 3, w 5, nb 2	10
Total (3 wkts, 20 overs)	224

FoW: 1-34 (Lyth), 2-113 (Stoneman), 3-166 (Thompson)

	O	M	R	W
Nabi	4	0	23	1
Sanderson	3	0	42	0
Parnell	4	0	42	0
Taylor	3	0	47	1
Glover	3	0	29	1
White	2	0	23	0
Keogh	1	0	15	0

NORTHAMPTONSHIRE

R S Vasconcelos, c Lyth b Bess	16
* § A M Rossington, run out (Brook)	24
W D Parnell, c Ferguson b Bess	22
M Nabi, c Brook b Bess	4
R I Keogh, lbw b Waite	36
S A Zaib, c Stoneman b Thompson	4
C O Thurston, run out (Ballance)	4
T A I Taylor, c Thompson b Fisher	3
G G White, c Stoneman b Fisher	4
B W Sanderson, c Hill b Waite	9
B D Glover, not out	2
Extras b 6, lb 3, w 1, nb 4	14
Total (19.3 overs)	142

FoW: 1-45 (Rossington), 2-60 (Vasconcelos), 3-74 (Nabi), 4-78 (Parnell), 5-89 (Zaib), 6-102 (Thurston), 7-107 (Taylor), 8-111 (White), 9-135 (Keogh), 10-142 (Sanderson)

	O	M	R	W
Fisher	4	0	25	2
Waite	3.3	0	33	2
Lyth	2	0	21	0
Bess	4	0	17	3
Ferguson	4	1	20	2
Thompson	2	0	17	1

Man of the Match: J A Thompson

Umpires: J D Middlebrook and P R Pollard   Scorers: J T Potter and A C Kingston

Yorkshire v. Northamptonshire
Birthday with fireworks

Jordan Thompson made the most of being elevated to No. 3 by crashing a career-best 74, while debutant Mark Stoneman made 50 as Yorkshire sailed past 200 and hammered Northamptonshire by 82 runs.

Dom Bess also impressed with a career-best 3-17 from four overs as the Steelbacks slipped to 142 all out in 19.3 overs.

Thompson and Stoneman — who was celebrating his 34th birthday and *White Rose* debut having been signed on a short-term T20 loan from Surrey, underpinned the hosts' mammoth 224-3 as the second part of a T20 double header at Headingley. Earlier the Northern Diamonds had been beaten by Thunder.

Yorkshire took a significant step towards the Blast quarter-finals with a sixth win in nine, moving to 13 points. More impor-

JORDAN THOMPSON
Cracked career-best 74

tantly, they opened up a five-point gap to fifth-placed Lancashire, who were just outside the top four qualifying places.

Left-handers Stoneman and Thompson shared 79 for the second wicket to advance from 34-1 in the fifth over before Stoneman was trapped in front. It was the first of three half-century partnerships in the innings, with Thompson and Harry Brook adding 53 for the third wicket before Brook and Gary Ballance knocked up a quick-fire 58.

Brook made 45 not out and helped to take 27 runs off the last over. He and Ballance clobbered two sixes apiece, Stoneman falling the ball after reaching his 50 off 30 balls. Thompson reached his half-century in 27 balls, and in all hit three fours and seven sixes in 35.

Steelbacks were 60-1 after six overs, only to lose Ricardo Vasconcelos, Mohammad Nabi and Wayne Parnell to Bess and slip to 78-4 after nine overs. Vasconcelos was caught at cover, Nabi and Parnell in the deep, and from then it was one way traffic.

Vitality T20 Blast — North Group
Birmingham Bears v. Yorkshire

Played at Edgbaston, Birmingham, on June 30, 2021
Birmingham Bears won by 10 wickets

Toss won by Yorkshire Birmingham Bears 2 points, Yorkshire 0 points

YORKSHIRE

*A Lyth, b Brathwaite	19
M D Stoneman, c Hain b Brathwaite	4
J A Thompson, c Burgess b Bresnan	4
G S Ballance, c Lamb b Brathwaite	8
H C Brook, not out	28
G C H Hill, c Bresnan b Briggs	0
D M Bess, c Hain b Miles	2
§ J A Tattersall, st Burgess b Lintott	2
M J Waite, c Burgess b Miles	2
M D Fisher, c Rhodes b Miles	9
L H Ferguson, st Burgess b Briggs	2
Extras w 1	1
Total (15.5 overs)	81

FoW: 1-19 (Lyth), 2-23 (Thompson), 3-36 (Ballance), 4-36 (Stoneman), 5-38 (Hill), 6-42 (Bess), 7-52 (Tattersall), 8-55 (Waite), 9-71 (Fisher), 10-81 (Ferguson)

	O	M	R	W
Bresnan	2	0	21	1
Brathwaite	2	0	7	3
Briggs	3.5	0	12	2
Lintott	4	0	22	1
Miles	4	0	19	3

BIRMINGHAM BEARS

E J Pollock, not out	33
A J Hose, not out	46
*W M H Rhodes	
S R Hain	
M L Lamb	
C R Brathwaite	
§ M G K Burges Did not bat	
T T Bresnan	
C N Miles	
D R Briggs	
J B Lintott	
Extras w 1, nb 6	7
Total (0 wkts, 8.3 overs)	86

	O	M	R	W
Fisher	3	0	22	0
Ferguson	2.3	0	29	0
Waite	1	0	12	0
Thompson	1	0	14	0
Bess	1	0	9	0

Man of the Match: C R Brathwaite

Umpires: N L Bainton and T Lungley Scorers: J T Potter and M D Smith

Birmingham Bears v. Yorkshire
A record night to forget

This was a night when Yorkshire certainly did not have a Blast as an unwanted record tumbled in the second city.

Bowled out for 81 by Birmingham — their lowest ever total — they lost by 10 wickets with 69 balls remaining.

The Vikings suffered their third group-stage defeat following a batting performance littered with miscued shots as they were bowled out in 15.5 overs.

Having won the toss on a used hybrid pitch, stand-in skipper Adam Lyth raced out of the blocks. He took 15 runs off the first five balls from Tim Bresnan, including two fours and a six over cover...but that was as good as it got.

Four batters were out to miscued pull shots, while two were out stumped. One of those was last man Lockie Ferguson. Only Harry Brook with 28 not out reached 20. Lyth hit three boundaries and a six in his 19 off eight balls, but the rest combined only hit three fours and a six.

The seam of West Indian all-rounder Carlos Brathwaite returned 3-7 from two overs, while fellow seamer Craig Miles claimed 3-21 from four. Danny Briggs also struck twice.

ADAM LYTH: Opening six as good as it got

The silver lining was that Yorkshire were still well placed for quarter-final qualification. Birmingham started the night just outside the top four, so it was no surprise to see them attack the chase with all guns blazing in a bid to improve their net run-rate.

Openers Ed Pollock and Adam Hose dotted the i's and crossed the t's on the home win. Pollock finished 33 not out off 23 balls and Hose 46 unbeaten from 31 as the Bears moved into the top four.

Not only was the 81 Yorkshire's lowest ever total in Blast history, beating the 90-9 they posted in defeat at Durham in 2009, it was also the lowest ever total at Edgbaston. Also, there had only ever been nine lower totals anywhere in the competition's history.

Vitality T20 Blast — North Group
Yorkshire v. Lancashire

Played at Headingley, Leeds, on July 2, 2021
Yorkshire won by 9 runs

Toss won by Yorkshire
Yorkshire 2 points, Lancashire 0 points

YORKSHIRE

* A Lyth, c Jones b Wells	52
M D Stoneman, c Wells b Wood	2
J A Thompson, c Wells b Mahmood	5
H C Brook, not out	91
G S Ballance, st Vilas b Parkinson	2
G C H Hill, not out	19
D M Bess	
§ H G Duke	
M J Waite Did not bat	
M D Fisher	
L H Ferguson	
Extras b 3, lb 1, w 4, nb 2	9
Total (4 wkts, 20 overs)	180

FoW: 1-11 (Stoneman), 2-30 (Thompson), 3-107 (Lyth), 4-116 (Ballance)

	O	M	R	W
Croft	3	0	26	0
Mahmood	4	0	40	1
Wood	4	0	41	1
Parkinson	4	0	38	1
Wells	2	0	16	1
Hartley	3	0	16	0

LANCASHIRE

F H Allen, b Lyth	5
K K Jennings, c Brook b Bess	37
A L Davies, c Brook b Waite	13
* § D J Vilas, c Duke b Ferguson	1
R P Jones, not out	61
S J Croft, c Lyth b Fisher	41
L W P Wells, c Lyth b Ferguson	1
L Wood, b Ferguson	0
T W Hartley, c Lyth b Ferguson	0
S Mahmood	
M W Parkinson Did not bat	
Extras b 3, lb 1, w 2, nb 6	12
Total (8 wkts, 20 overs)	171

FoW: 1-13 (Allen), 2-32 (Davies), 3-34 (Vilas), 4-70 (Jennings), 5-155 (Croft), 6-171 (Wells), 7-171 (Wood), 8-171 (Hartley)

	O	M	R	W
Fisher	4	0	49	1
Lyth	3	0	18	1
Waite	2	0	17	1
Ferguson	4	0	24	4
Thompson	3	0	27	0
Bess	4	0	32	1

Man of the Match: H C Brook

Umpires: N G B Cook and B V Taylor   Scorers: J T Potter and C Rimmer
Third Umpire: B J Debenham

Yorkshire v. Lancashire
Hat-trick prunes *Red Rose*

This was a night to remember. Having lost by 10 wickets 48 hours earlier, Yorkshire responded with a first *Roses* Blast win in seven, dating back to 2017.

Harry Brook's scintillating unbeaten 91 led the Vikings to 180-4 before that total was narrowly defended. Lancashire recovered from 70-4 to need 20 off the last over and 10 off the last three balls against Lockie Ferguson.

But the New Zealand quick bowler claimed a stunning hat-trick, Yorkshire's first ever in T20 games, to win by nine runs.

Brook's career best came off 50 balls, including 10 fours and three sixes, after Adam Lyth elected to bat.

Yorkshire had lost five added to one abandonment since their last win against Lancashire four years ago, so the significance of this victory was much more than it leaving the

LOCKIE FERGUSON: Four wickets to stunning pace

Vikings with one foot in the quarter-finals. Yorkshire lost Mark Stoneman and Jordan Thompson to fall to 30-2 in the fifth over before Brook and Lyth (52 off 40) shared 77 inside nine overs, the skipper cracking on to his first 2021 Blast fifty.

From 107-2 in the 14th Lancashire dragged things back admirably, but Matthew Parkinson conceded 20 in the 17th, including two sixes over long-on for Brook to take the hosts to 140-4. Brook then hit the first three balls of the last over from Saqib Mahmood for four to build valuable momentum.

Lyth's off-spin bowled New Zealander Finn Allen, slog-sweeping in Lancashire's second over: 13-1. Matthew Waite and Ferguson struck, making it 34-3 in the sixth over, but Rob Jones and Steven Croft (41) superbly shared 85 from 70-4 in the 11th over, with Jones unbeaten on 61. They had been left too much to do by their top order, and Ferguson removed Luke Wells and Tom Hartley, superbly caught in the deep by Lyth, either side of Luke Wood being yorked, to send the full house wild.

Vitality T20 Blast — North Group
Nottinghamshire v. Yorkshire

Played at Trent Bridge, Nottingham, on July 9, 2021
Nottinghamshire won by 10 wickets

Toss won by Yorkshire   Nottinghamshire 2 points, Yorkshire 0 points

YORKSHIRE

* A Lyth, c Mullaney b Paterson		26
H C Brook, st Moores b Patel		0
J A Thompson, c Patel b Paterson		28
M J Waite, not out		3
S A Northeast, not out		0
G S Ballance		
G C H Hill		
D M Bes	Did not bat	
§ H G Duke		
M D Fisher		
J E Poysden		
Extras w 3		3
Total (3 wkts, 7 overs)		60

FoW: 1-1 (Brook), 2-55 (Lyth), 2-57 (Thompson)

	O	M	R	W
Patel	2	0	7	1
Carter	2	0	19	0
Fletcher	2	0	29	0
Paterson	1	0	5	2

NOTTINGHAMSHIRE

P D Trego, not out		29
A D Hales, not out		31
B T Slater		
§ T J Moores		
S R Patel		
* S J Mullaney		
L W James	Did not bat	
L J Fletcher		
C G Harrison		
M Carter		
D Paterson		
Extras b 2, w 3		5
Total (0 wkts, 3.4 overs)		65

	O	M	R	W
Bess	1	0	18	0
Fisher	1	0	11	0
Waite	1	0	16	0
Poysden	0.4	0	18	0

Man of the Match: S R Patel

Umpires: N J Llong and I N Ramage   Scorers: J T Potter and R Marshall

Nottinghamshire v. Yorkshire
Still short of last-eight berth

Yorkshire lost a rain-affected game by 10 wickets against the defending champions, meaning they were yet to seal a place in the quarter-finals.

The hosts easily chased a 61 target in a revised seven-over game to strengthen their position at the North Group's summit and secure their own qualification, winning with 20 balls remaining.

Yorkshire still required one point from their remaining two matches to join them. They posted 60-3, having won the toss, before rain arrived to delay a start from 6.30pm to 8.45pm.

And it just wasn't enough, thanks to some fireworks from home openers Peter Trego and Alex Hales.

JORDAN THOMPSON: A six to break shackles and top score

Yorkshire were unable to break the shackles of a tidy Outlaws bowling display led by wily left-arm spinner Samit Patel, who had form man Harry Brook stumped for a duck in the first over and finished with 1-7 from two overs. Acceleration came in the later stages of the innings, with Jordan Thompson top-scoring with 28 and Adam Lyth hitting 26. The pair shared 54 for the second wicket and hit a six apiece.

Nineteen runs came off Luke Fletcher in the sixth over, but it was key that Nottinghamshire bowled four overs which went for four, eight, three and five runs. South African seamer Dane Paterson removed both Lyth and Thompson, caught in the final over of the innings.

Trego hit three fours off former Somerset teammate Dom Bess as 18 came off the first over of the home chase, and it was a mountainous task from there for the Vikings. Trego led the way as he and Hales brought up their 50 partnership in 22 balls, finishing with 29 not out off 13.

Hales clobbered four sixes, including two off Josh Poysden in the fourth and final over to overtake Trego to 33 not out off 10. Yorkshire were hurt by New Zealand overseas fast bowler Lockie Ferguson's absence with a side strain.

Vitality T20 Blast — North Group
Lancashire v. Yorkshire

Played at Emirates Old Trafford, Manchester, on July 17, 2021
Lancashire won by 4 wickets

Toss won by Yorkshire   Lancashire 2 points, Yorkshire 0 points

YORKSHIRE

A Lyth, c Vilas b Wood	8
M D Stoneman, b Wood	2
* J E Root, c Vilas b Hurt	32
H C Brook, b Wells	22
G S Ballance, b Wood	31
W A R Fraine, not out	22
J A Thompson, c and b Wood	0
M J Waite, c Croft b Lamb	1
D M Bess, not out	4
§ H G Duke	
M D Fisher Did not bat	
Extras lb 1, w 1, nb 4	6
Total (7 wkts, 20 overs)	128

FoW: 1-10 (Lyth), 2-11 (Stoneman), 3-59 (Brook), 4-91 (Root), 5-101 (Ballance), 6-101 (Thompson), 7-110 (Waite)

	O	M	R	W
Croft	3	0	21	0
Hartley	3	0	16	0
Wood	4	0	20	4
Hurt	4	0	27	1
Lamb	3	0	17	1
Wells	3	0	26	1

LANCASHIRE

F H Allen, b Fisher	22
K K Jennings, c Root b Waite	15
A L Davies, run out (Thompson>Root)	13
* § D J Vilas, c Duke b Root	9
R P Jones, c Fisher b Bess	5
S J Croft, not out	26
L W P Wells, b Waite	30
D J Lamb, not out	11
L Wood	
T W Hartley Did not bat	
L J Hurt	
Extras	0
Total (6 wkts, 19 overs)	131

FoW: 1-37 (Jennings), 2-37 (Allen), 3-57 (Davies), 4-63 (Jones), 5-64 (Vilas), 6-118 (Wells)

	O	M	R	W
Fisher	3	0	30	1
Lyth	4	0	40	0
Waite	3	0	17	2
Root	4	0	20	1
Bess	4	0	19	1
Thompson	1	0	5	0

Man of the Match: L Wood

Umpires: I D Blackwell and R J Warren   Scorers: J T Potter and C Rimmer
Third Umpire: R J Bailey

Derbyshire v. Yorkshire

At The Incora County Ground, Derby, on July 18, 2021
Match cancelled

Lancashire v. Yorkshire

Roses come up together

Yorkshire's place in the quarter-finals had been secured a few days earlier because of the cancellation of their final group game at Derby.

The Falcons had Coronavirus issues in the camp, so the North Group was settled on an average-points-per-completed-game basis.

A top-two finish had also been secured, with the home quarter-final to be played at Durham's Emirates Riverside ground due to a clash of dates with the Headingley Test between England and India.

Yet Yorkshire's group stage ended in disappointment as they lost a low-scoring clash by four wickets with an over to spare when Lancashire chased 129 to also qualify.

A bowler-dominated game saw no batter from either side better Joe Root's 32 off 37 balls in the visitors' 128-7. Another Sheffield-born player, the Lightning's Luke Wood, claimed a career best 4-20 with his

JOE ROOT: Skipper, top scorer and a wicket

left-arm seamers as Yorkshire's innings included only one six from the blade of Gary Ballance after they had opted to bat.

Wood struck twice in two overs at either end of the innings. His first victim was Adam Lyth, brilliantly caught behind one-handed down the leg-side by Dane Vilas before he bowled Mark Stoneman: 11-2 in the third over. He later bowled Ballance and had Jordan Thompson caught and bowled in the 17th, leaving Yorkshire at 101-6.

Lancashire flew out of the blocks at 35-0 after two overs. The game looked done, but the visitors fought back impressively. New Zealander Finn Allen was bowled trying to scoop Matthew Fisher to leg as Lancashire lost five for 27 inside five overs, slipping to 64-5, including Root having Vilas caught behind sweeping.

Luke Wells (30) and Steven Croft (26 not out) shared 55 to steady the hosts through accumulation, and that was enough to leave Yorkshire with only one group-stage win on the road.

Vitality T20 Blast — First Quarter-Final
Yorkshire v. Sussex

Played at Emirates Riverside, Chester-le-Street, on August 24, 2021

Sussex won by 5 wickets

Toss won by Yorkshire

YORKSHIRE

A Lyth, c Jordan b Lenham	6
T Kohler-Cadmore, c Salt b Mills	55
*D J Willey, c Jordan b Mills	16
H C Brook, lbw b Rashid Khan	1
G S Ballance, c Rashid Khan b Garton	55
J A Thompson, c Rashid Khan b Mills	16
W A R Fraine, not out	6
M J Waite, b Jordan	3
M D Fisher, not out	0
§H G Duke	
A U Rashid Did not bat	
Extras b 1, lb 5, w 11, nb 2	19
Total (7 wkts, 20 overs)	177

FoW: 1-7 (Lyth), 2-31 (Willey), 3-33 (Brook), 4-118 (Ballance), 5-158 (Thompson), 6-166 (Kohler-Cadmore), 7-172 (Waite).

	O	M	R	W
Garton	4	0	44	1
Lenham	3	0	19	1
Mills	4	0	39	3
Rashid Khan	4	0	25	1
Beer	1	0	9	0
Jordan	4	0	35	1

SUSSEX

§P D Salt, c Lyth b Thompson	27
*L J Wright, b Rashid	54
R S Bopara, c Duke b Thompson	9
D M W Rawlins, b Fisher	27
D Wiese, c Lyth b Thompson	19
Rashid Khan, not out	27
C J Jordan, not out	7
G H S Garton	
W A T Beer Did not bat	
T S Mills	
A D Lenham	
Extras b 4, lb 2, w 2	8
Total (5 wkts, 19.4 overs)	178

FoW: 1-72 (Salt), 2-91 (Bopara), 3-111 (Wright), 4-135 (Rawlins), 5-156 (Wiese).

	O	M	R	W
Willey	4	0	35	0
Lyth	2	0	23	0
Fisher	3.4	0	33	1
Waite	2	0	18	0
Rashid	4	0	35	1
Thompson	4	0	28	3

Man of the Match: Rashid Khan

Umpires: P J Hartley and N J Llong   Scorers: J T Potter and W R Dobson

Third: P K Baldwin

Yorkshire v. Sussex — Quarter-Final
Shattered at the death

Sussex's Afghanistan spinner Rashid Khan starred with bat and not ball to shatter Yorkshire's hopes of reaching Finals Day.

Khan smashed a blistering unbeaten 27 off nine balls in pursuit of 178 to seal a five-wicket win with two balls remaining.

Yorkshire were chasing a third Finals

Fluent despatch: Top scores of 55 from Gary Ballance, above, and Tom Kohler-Cadmore were not enough as the Vikings went down by a knife edge

Day appearance to go with those in 2012 and 2016, but it wasn't to be following a pulsating quarter-final. Yorkshire were indebted to 55 apiece from Gary Ballance and opener Tom Kohler-Cadmore as they posted 177-7 on a true Riverside pitch with short boundaries, recovering from 33-3 after five overs.

Leg-spinner Khan's only wicket came early — Harry Brook lbw sweeping for one — but he was otherwise played comfortably, returning 1-25. Ballance and Kohler-Cadmore shared 85 in 10.1 overs for the fourth wicket: Ballance was fluent and pulled Khan for six to reach 50 in 34 balls, Kohler-Cadmore finding fluency late in his 47-ball fifty.

Both sides were sloppy in the field, dropping catches and letting balls through their legs, but it was the Vikings who were hurt the most.

While Khan was the star of the Sussex chase they were given a fast start by captain Luke Wright's 54 off 39. They were 53-0 after six overs, but Jordan Thompson's first of three wickets ended a 72-run opening stand in his first over, the ninth, when Phil Salt (27) found long-on.

The Vikings fought their way back well, with Adil Rashid bowling a sweeping Wright: 111-3 in the 14th over. When Matthew Fisher bowled Delray Rawlins, also for 27, Sussex needed 43 off 21 balls at 135-4.

Khan swung the game with some breathtaking hitting. He struck one particular six over long-on with an amazing lack of back swing and took David Willey for three fours in a crucial 19th over which cost 16.

Fisher was then unable to defend only six off the last over.

VITALITY BLAST in 2021

NORTH GROUP

		P	W	L	T	NR/A	PTS	NRR	PPG
1	Nottinghamshire Outlaws *	14	9	2	3	0	21	1.503	1.500
2	**Yorkshire Vikings ***	**13**	**7**	**5**	**0**	**1**	**15**	**0.305**	**1.153**
3	Lancashire Lightning *	14	7	5	1	1	16	0.205	1.142
4	Birmingham Bears *	14	7	6	0	1	15	0.006	1.071
5	Worcestershire Rapids	14	6	6	1	1	14	-0.629	1.000
6	Leicestershire Foxes	14	6	8	0	0	12	-0.019	0.857
7	Durham	14	5	8	0	1	11	-0.228	0.785
8	Derbyshire Falcons	12	4	7	1	0	9	-0.326	0.750
9	Northamptonshire Steelbacks	13	4	8	0	1	9	-0.871	0.692

North Group was decided on points per game (PPG) after Derbyshire's final two fixtures were cancelled, the squad self-isolating due to Covid19

SOUTH GROUP

		P	W	L	T	NR/A	PTS	NRR
1	Kent Spitfires *	14	9	4	0	1	19	0.657
2	Somerset *	14	8	4	0	2	18	0.371
3	Sussex Sharks *	14	6	3	0	5	17	0.479
4	Hampshire Royals *	14	6	5	0	3	15	0.388
5	Surrey	14	6	5	0	3	15	0.332
6	Gloucestershire	14	6	6	0	2	14	0.201
7	Essex Eagles	14	5	8	0	1	11	-0.468
8	Middlesex Panthers	14	4	9	0	1	9	-0.389
9	Glamorgan	14	3	9	0	2	8	-1.371

* *Qualified for the Quarter-Finals*

YORKSHIRE VIKINGS AVERAGES 2021

VITALITY BLAST

Played 14　　　Won 7　　　Lost 6　　　Abandoned 1

BATTING AND FIELDING

(Qualification 4 completed innings)

Player	M.	I.	N.O.	Runs	H.S.	100s	50s	Avge	ct/st
J M Bairstow	4	4	0	295	112	1	2	73.75	2/0
H C Brook	13	13	6	486	91*	0	2	69.42	9
T Kohler-Cadmore	6	5	1	168	55	0	2	42.00	3
J A Thompson	12	10	2	215	74	0	2	26.87	7
J E Root	4	4	0	97	49	0	0	24.25	2
G S Ballance	9	8	1	159	55	0	1	22.71	0
A Lyth	13	13	0	232	52	0	2	17.84	12
M D Stoneman	4	4	0	58	50	0	1	14.50	2
D J Malan	4	4	0	41	23	0	0	10.25	1
M J Waite	11	6	2	18	6*	0	0	4.50	0

Also played

Player	M.	I.	N.O.	Runs	H.S.	100s	50s	Avge	ct/st
D J Willey	5	4	2	73	44	0	0	36.50	5
W A R Fraine	7	7	4	79	22*	0	0	26.33	3
D M Bess	9	4	2	32	24	0	0	16.00	2
M D Fisher	11	3	1	28	19	0	0	14.00	3
G C H Hill	6	4	1	36	19*	0	0	12.00	1
J A Tattersall	4	3	0	18	10	0	0	6.00	1/0
L H Ferguson	10	2	1	2	2	0	0	2.00	4
S A Northeast	1	1	1	0	0*	0	0	—	0
A U Rashid	5	0	0	0	—	0	0	—	0
H G Duke	4	0	0	0	—	0	0	—	3/0
J E Poysden	1	0	0	0	—	0	0	—	0

BOWLING

(Qualification 4 wickets)

Player	Overs	Mdns	Runs	Wkts	Avge	Best	4wI	RPO
D M Bess	30	0	201	11	18.27	3-17	0	6.70
L H Ferguson	37	1	269	14	19.21	4-24	1	7.27
J A Thompson	30	0	296	14	21.14	4-44	1	9.86
D J Willey	18	0	161	7	23.00	3-44	0	8.94
M D Fisher	36.4	0	321	12	26.75	2-15	0	8.75
M J Waite	28.3	1	264	9	29.33	2-17	0	9.26
A U Rashid	20	0	149	5	29.80	3-32	0	7.45

Also bowled

Player	Overs	Mdns	Runs	Wkts	Avge	Best	4wI	RPO
J E Root	11	0	89	3	29.66	1-19	0	8.09
A Lyth	14	0	138	1	138.00	1-18	0	9.85
J E Poysden	0.4	0	18	0	—	0-18	0	27.00

Vitality T20 International — Match Two
England v. Pakistan

Played at Headingley, Leeds, on July 18, 2021
This was the first International T20 match played at Headingley
England won by 45 runs
Toss won by Pakistan

ENGLAND
J J Roy, c Mohammad Hafeez b Imad Wasim	10
* § J C Buttler, c Babar Azam b Mohammad Hasnain	59
D J Malan, c Azam Khan b Imad Wasim	1
M M Ali, c Babar Azam b Mohammad Hasnain	36
L S Livingstone, run out (Azam Khan/Haris Rauf)	38
J M Bairstow, c Fakhar Zaman b Shadab Khan	13
T K Curran, c Sohaib Maqsood b Mohammad Hasnain	9
C J Jordan, c Shadab Khan b Haris Rauf	14
A U Rashid, b Haris Rauf	2
S Mahmood, not out	3
M W Parkinson, b Shaheen Afridi	5
Extras lb 3, w 6, nb 1	10
Total (19.5 overs)	200

FoW: 1-11 (Roy), 2-18 (Malan), 3-85 (Ali), 4-137 (Buttler), 5-153 (Bairstow), 6-164 (Livingstone), 7-182 (Curran), 8-191 (Jordan), 9-191 (Rashid), 10-200 (Parkinson)

	O	M	R	W
Imad Wasim	4	0	37	2
Shaheen Afridi	3.5	0	28	1
Mohammad Hasnain	4	0	51	3
Haris Rauf	4	0	48	2
Shadab Khan	4	0	33	1

PAKISTAN
§ Mohammad Rizwan, c and b Rashid	37
* Babar Azam, c Malan b Mahmood	22
Sohaib Maqsood, st Buttler b Rashid	15
Mohammad Hafeez, c Bairstow b Ali	10
Fakhar Zaman, b Ali	8
Azam Khan, st Buttler b Parkinson	1
Imad Wasim, c Roy b Curran	20
Shadab Khan, not out	36
Shaheen Afridi, c Jordan b Mahmood	2
Haris Rauf, b Mahmood	0
Mohammad Hasnain, not out	0
Extras lb 1, w 3	4
Total (9 wkts, 20 overs)	155

FoW: 1-50 (Babar), 2-71 (Maqsood), 3-82 (Rizwan), 4-93 (Hafeez), 5-95 (Fakhar), 6-105 (Azam Khan), 7-142 (Imad), 8-147 (Shaheen), 9-154 (Haris)

	O	M	R	W
Rashid	4	0	30	2
Jordan	1	0	12	0
Curran	4	0	22	1
Mahmood	4	0	33	3
Ali	3	0	32	2
Parkinson	4	0	25	1

Man of the Match: M M Ali

Umpires: M J Saggers and A G Wharf Scorers: J R Virr and K N Hutchinson
Third: D J Millns Fourth: S J O'Shaughnessy Match Referee: W M Noon

England v. Pakistan

Blow that shocked the world

This was the first international staged at Headingley since 'that' Ashes Test in August 2019 when a boy from Durham left an indelible mark on the venue's rich history. This time a Lancastrian etched his name into LS6 folklore.

Liam Livingstone's contribution was nowhere near as significant as that of Ben Stokes in downing the Australians on that glorious Sunday afternoon when everything he touched turned to gold.

But, as Headingley staged its inaugural T20 international fixture the powerful right-hander from the wrong side of the Pennines turned heads — literally — in a big England win to level their three-match series with Pakistan at 1-1.

As England careered towards a score of 200 all out Livingstone smashed as big a six as you will ever see in a quickfire 38. Facing the pacey future Yorkshire overseas bowler Haris Rauf at the start of the 16th over, Livingstone walloped a full ball straight and high over the new North-

LIAM LIVINGSTONE
Cleared the stand

South Stand and onto the Rugby field. It led to world-wide acclaim and shock. Having been inserted in the sunshine, stand-in captain Jos Buttler delighted a sellout crowd with 59 off 39 balls at the top of the order as the hosts recovered from 18-2.

Amazingly, England will have been slightly disappointed with their total. From 137-4 in the 14th over they should have scored more, but young quick Mohammad Hasnain came back well and finished with 3-51, including Buttler's wicket. Pakistan made a brisk start to raise their hopes at 50-0 in the sixth over, though nobody bettered opener Mohammad Rizwan's 37 as a series of starts were not capitalised on.

Falling from 82-2 in the 11th over to 105-6 after 14 proved fatal to their chances, Saqib Mahmood claiming 3-33 and Adil Rashid, who opened the bowling on home turf, 2-30 as Pakistan finished on 155-9.

ROYAL LONDON ONE-DAY CUP HIGHLIGHTS OF 2021

Win by 100 or more runs (none)

Totals of 250 and over (2)

329-3	v. Leicestershire at Leicester (won)
320-7	v. Warwickshire at York (won)

Match aggregates of 450 and over (4)

656	Leicestershire (327-7) lost to Yorkshire (329-3) by 7 wickets at Leicester
601	Yorkshire (320-7) defeated Warwickshire (281) by 39 runs at York
505	Essex (317-7) defeated Yorkshire (188) by 129 runs at Chelmsford
456	Yorkshire (230) defeated Glamorgan (226-8) by 4 runs at Cardiff

Century Partnerships (2)

For 3rd wicket (1)

172	H G Duke and G C H Hill v. Leicestershire at Leicester

For 5th wicket (1)

110	G C H Hill and J A Tattersall v. Warwickshire at York

Century (1)

H G Duke
  125 v. Leicestershire at Leicester

4 wickets in an innings (4)

M W Pillans (2)
  4-26 v. Nottinghamshire at York
  4-57 v. Surrey at Scarborough

J R Sullivan (1)
  4-11 v. Derbyshire at Chesterfield

M J Waite (1)
  5-59 v. Leicestershire at Leicester

3 catches in an innings (none)

3 dismissals in an innings (none)

Debuts (7)

List A (6): H G Duke, G C H Hill, M L Revis, J W Shutt, W Luxton and J R Sullivan
For Yorkshire (1): D M Bess

Royal London One-Day Cup

FINAL TABLES 2021

WINNERS: **Glamorgan** (296-9) defeated Durham (238) by 58 runs

GROUP 1

		P	W	L	T	NR/A	PTS	NRR	PPG
1	Durham	8	6	1	0	1	13	0.921	1.625
2	Essex *	8	5	2	1	0	11	0.238	1.375
3	Gloucestershire *	7	4	3	0	0	8	0.094	1.142
4	Lancashire	8	3	2	1	2	9	0.014	1.125
5	Worcestershire	8	3	4	0	1	7	0.256	0.875
6	Hampshire	8	3	4	0	1	7	0.161	0.875
7	Sussex	8	2	4	0	2	6	-0.689	0.750
8	Middlesex	7	2	4	0	1	5	-0.286	0.714
9	Kent	8	1	5	0	2	4	-1.258	0.500

Group 1 was decided on points per game (PPG) after the Middlesex v. Gloucestershire fixture was cancelled due to a Covid19 outbreak

GROUP 2

		P	W	L	T	NR/A	PTS	NRR
1	Glamorgan	8	4	2	0	2	10	0.818
2	Surrey *	8	4	2	0	2	10	0.408
3	**Yorkshire ***	**8**	**4**	**2**	**0**	**2**	**10**	**-0.024**
4	Leicestershire	8	4	3	0	1	9	-0.428
5	Warwickshire	8	4	4	0	0	8	-0.025
6	Nottinghamshire	8	3	3	0	2	8	0.686
7	Somerset	8	3	3	0	2	8	-0.412
8	Northamptonshire	8	2	4	0	2	6	-0.412
9	Derbyshire	8	1	6	0	1	3	-0.558

* Qualified for the Quarter-Finals

Royal London One-Day Cup — Group B
Yorkshire v. Surrey

Played at North Marine Road, Scarborough, on July 22, 2021
Surrey won by 5 wickets

Toss won by Surrey

Surrey 2 points, Yorkshire 0 points

YORKSHIRE

W A R Fraine, b Atkinson	6
§ H G Duke, c David b Dunn	7
G S Ballance, c Patel b McKerr	39
G C H Hill, c Stoneman b Atkinson	15
J A Tattersall, c Smith b Atkinson	4
M L Revis, c Patel b McKerr	43
* D M Bess, c David b Moriarty	7
M J Waite, c and b Moriarty	13
MW Pillans, c Smith b Atkinson	10
B O Coad, c David b Patel	10
J W Shutt, not out	1
Extras lb 4, w 4, nb 2	10
Total (34.1 overs)	165

FoW: 1-9 (Fraine), 2-17 (Duke), 3-36 (Hill), 4-40 (Tattersall), 5-121 (Ballance), 6-128 (Revis), 7-130 (Bess), 8-151 (Pillans), 9-154 (Waite), 10-165 (Coad)

	O	M	R	W
Dunn	6	1	32	1
Atkinson	10	1	43	4
Patel	1.1	0	5	1
McKerr	7	0	36	2
Moriarty	10	2	45	2

SURREY

M D Stoneman, not out	73
* H M Amla, c Shutt b Pillans	29
B B A Geddes, b Pillans	0
§ J L Smith, c Ballance b Pillans	25
R S Patel, c Tattersall b Pillans	2
N M J Reiffer, b Bess	26
T H David, not out	8
A A P Atkinson	
C McKerr	Did not bat
M P Dunn	
D T Moriarty	
Extras b 1, lb 2, w 2	5
Total (5 wkts, 39.1 overs)	168

FoW: 1-59 (Amla), 2-59 (Geddes), 3-113 (Smith), 4-116 (Patel), 5-155 (Reiffer)

	O	M	R	W
Coad	8	1	25	0
Waite	5	0	16	0
Pillans	9	0	57	4
Bess	4.1	1	28	1
Revis	7	2	18	0
Hill	6	0	21	0

Umpires: P J Hartley and N A Mallender

Scorers: J T Potter and D Beesley

Royal London One-Day Cup — Group B
Leicestershire v. Yorkshire

Played at Uptonsteel County Ground, Leicester, on July 25, 2021
This was Yorkshire's 1,000th List A match played
Yorkshire won by 7 wickets

Toss won by Leicestershire   Yorkshire 2 points, Leicestershire 0 points

LEICESTERSHIRE

G H Rhodes, b Waite	8
R K Patel, c Ballance b Revis	24
M S Harris, c Ballance b Waite	127
* § L J H Hill, c Pillans b Waite	108
A M Lilley, c Bess Waite	15
L P J Kimber, c Tattersall b Waite	16
Rehan Ahmed, not out	7
B W M Mike, lbw b Coad	3
D Klein, not out	5
E Barnes	
C J C Wright Did not bat	
Extras b 4, lb 1, w 5, nb 4	14
Total (7 wkts, 50 overs)	327

FoW: 1-8 (Rhodes), 2-49 (Patel), 3-261 (Harris), 4-284 (Lilley), 5-307 (Hill), 6-314 (Kimber), 7-320 (Mike)

	O	M	R	W
Waite	8	0	59	5
Coad	8	1	46	1
Revis	6	0	35	1
Pillans	8	0	49	0
Bess	9	0	64	0
Shutt	4	0	23	0
Hill	7	0	46	0

YORKSHIRE

W A R Fraine, c Hill b Wright	45
§ H G Duke, b Barnes	125
G S Ballance, c Rhodes b Klein	43
G C H Hill, not out	90
J A Tattersall, not out	6
M L Revis	
J W Shutt	
* D M Bess Did not bat	
M J Waite	
M W Pillans	
B O Coad	
Extras b 2, lb 2, w 12, nb 4	20
Total (3 wkts, 47.5 overs)	329

FoW: 1-61 (Fraine), 2-147 (Ballance), 3-319 (Duke)

	O	M	R	W
Klein	10	0	65	1
Wright	8	0	48	1
Barnes	6.5	0	53	1
Rehan Ahmed	10	0	71	0
Lilley	3	0	19	0
Mike	5	0	32	0
Rhodes	5	0	37	0

Umpires: N G B Cook and B J Debenham   Scorers: J T Potter and P J Rogers

Royal London One-Day Cup — Group B
Yorkshire v. Northamptonshire

Played at North Marine Road, Scarborough, on July 28, 2021
No result

Toss won by Northamptonshire   Yorkshire 1 point, Northamptonshire 1 point

YORKSHIRE

W A R Fraine, c Thurston b C J White	28
§ H G Duke, b C J White	2
* G S Ballance, c Vasconcelos b Sanderson	2
G C H Hill, c and b C J White	3
J A Tattersall, c Vasconcelos b Taylor	14
M L Revis, c Vasconcelos b Taylor	8
W Luxton, b Parnell	68
M J Waite, b G G White	29
M W Pillans, c Parnell b Sanderson	40
S A Patterson, c Gay b Taylor	1
J W Shutt, not out	1
Extras b 8, lb 8, w 6, nb 4	26
Total (49.3 overs)	222

FoW: 1-7 (Duke), 2-18 (Ballance), 3-33 (Hill), 4-47 (Fraine), 5-60 (Tattersall), 6-69 (Revis), 7-121 (Waite), 8-214 (Luxton), 9-217 (Patterson), 10-222 (Pillans)

	O	M	R	W
C J White	10	1	38	3
Sanderson	9.3	0	35	2
Parnell	10	0	45	1
Taylor	10	0	64	3
G G White	10	1	24	1

NORTHAMPTONSHIRE

* § R S Vasconcelos, not out		1
E N Gay, not out		1
B J Curran		
R I Keogh		
S A Zaib		
C O Thurston		
W D Parnell	Did not bat	
T A I Taylor		
G G White		
B W Sanderson		
G G White		
Extras		0
Total (0 wkts, 0.5 overs)		2

	O	M	R	W
Waite	0.5	0	2	0

Umpires: N J Pratt and S J O'Shaughnessy   Scorers: J T Potter and A C Kingston

Royal London One-Day Cup — Group B
Somerset v. Yorkshire

Played at The Cooper Associates County Ground, Taunton, on August 1, 2021
Somerset won by 5 wickets

Toss won by Somerset   Somerset 2 points, Yorkshire 0 points

YORKSHIRE

W A R Fraine, c Drissell b Aldridge	23
§ H G Duke, c Davies b Davey	6
* G S Ballance, b Aldridge	10
G C H Hill, c Aldridge b Green	23
J A Tattersall, c Davies b Goldsworthy	0
M L Revis, not out	58
W Luxton, not out	31
M J Waite	
M W Pillans Did not bat	
B O Coad	
J W Shutt	
Extras b 4, w 3	7
Total (5 wkts, 20 overs)	158

FoW: 1-10 (Duke), 2-33 (Ballance), 3-51 (Fraine), 4-54 (Tattersall), 5-89 (Hill)

	O	M	R	W
Goldsworthy	4	0	17	1
Davey	4	0	31	1
Green	4	0	30	1
Aldridge	4	0	46	2
Baker	4	0	30	0

SOMERSET

§ S M Davies, c Revis b Coad	16
S J Young, c Ballance b Revis	25
J E K Rew, c Ballance b Shutt	20
J C Hildreth, not out	61
LP Goldsworthy, c Revis b Waite	21
E J Byrom, c Fraine b Waite	1
* B G F Green, not out	7
K L Aldridge	
G S Drissell Did not bat	
S Baker	
J H Davey	
Extras lb 3, w 3, nb 2	8
Total (5 wkts, 19.1 overs)	159

FoW: 1-22 (Davies), 2-53 (Young), 3-82 (Rew), 4-148 (Goldsworthy), 5-150 (Byrom)

	O	M	R	W
Coad	4	0	32	1
Waite	3.1	0	19	2
Revis	4	1	26	1
Pillans	4	0	38	0
Shutt	3	0	33	1
Hill	1	0	8	0

Umpires: M Burns and B V Taylor   Scorers: J T Potter and L M Rhodes

Royal London One-Day Cup — Group B
Yorkshire v. Warwickshire

Played at Clifton Park, York, on August 3, 2021
Yorkshire won by 39 runs

Toss won by Warwickshire   Yorkshire 2 points, Warwickshire 0 points

YORKSHIRE

W A R Fraine, c Burgess b Garett	0
§ H G Duke, run out (Pollock)	42
W Luxton, c Rhodes b Garrett	0
* G S Ballance, lbw b Mousley	54
G C H Hill, c Brookes b Carver	64
J A Tattersall, c Johal b Rhodes	70
M L Revis, c Yates b Johal	27
M J Waite, not out	42
B O Coad, not out	0
D Olivier	
J W Shutt Did not bat	
Extras b 4, lb 6, w 5, nb 6	21
Total (7 wkts, 50 overs)	320

FoW: 1-0 (Fraine), 2-0 (Luxton), 3-89 (Duke), 4-114 (Ballance), 5-224 (Hill), 6-265 (Tattersall), 7-287 (Revis).

	O	M	R	W
Garrett	7	1	24	2
Johal	9	0	42	1
Rhodes	5	0	48	1
Carver	10	0	64	1
Mousley	7	0	31	1
Bethell	5	0	28	0
Brookes	7	0	73	0

WARWICKSHIRE

E J Pollock, c Shutt b Waite	29
R M Yates, c Ballance b Waite	11
* W H M Rhodes, run out (Luxton)	37
§ M G K Burgess, b Hill	33
M J Lamb, c Olivier b Coad	14
D R Mousley, c Tattersall b Coad	61
J G Bethell, c Ballance b Olivier	66
E A Brookes, c Shutt b Hill	7
K Carver, c Dukes b Hill	0
G A Garrett, c Tattersall b Coad	1
M S Johal, not out	10
Extras lb 4, w 4, nb 4	12
Total (47.2 overs)	281

FoW: 1-22 (Yates), 2-49 (Pollock), 3-111 (Rhodes), 4-128 (Burgess), 5-134 (Lamb), 6-249 (Bethell), 7-269 (Brookes), 8-270 (Carver), 9-270 (Mousley), 10-281 (Garrett).

	O	M	R	W
Coad	9.2	3	30	3
Waite	9	0	69	2
Olivier	9	0	60	1
Shutt	4	0	32	0
Revis	6	0	39	0
Hill	10	0	47	3

Umpires: T Lungley and P R Pollard   Scorers: J T Potter and M D Smith

Royal London One-Day Cup — Group B
Yorkshire v. Nottinghamshire

Played at Clifton Park, York, on August 6, 2021
No result

Toss won by Yorkshire   Yorkshire 1 point, Nottinghamshire 1 point

NOTTINGHAMSHIRE

B T Slater, c Coad b Pillans	74
S G Budinger, c Duke b Pillans	71
* P D Trego, c Duke b Pillans	1
M Montgomery, not out	20
L W James, c Fraine b Pillans	3
L A Patterson-White, lbw b Sullivan	2
§ D Schadendorf, not out	4
B A Hutton	
F Singh Did not bat	
D Paterson	
T E Barber	
Extras lb 2, w 6, nb 2	10
Total (5 wkts, 33 overs)	185

FoW: 1-146 (Budinger), 2-152 (Slater), 3-152 (Trego), 4-158 (James), 5-165 (Patterson-White)

	O	M	R	W
Coad	7	0	35	0
Waite	6	0	38	0
Revis	4	0	24	0
Pillans	6	0	26	4
Sullivan	8	0	43	1
Hill	2	0	17	0

YORKSHIRE

W A R Fraine
§ H G Duke
W Luxton
* G S Ballance
G C H Hill
J A Tattersall
M L Revis
M J Waite
B O Coad
M W Pillans
J R Sullivan

Umpires: J D Middlebrook and R J Warren   Scorers: J T Potter and P R Clubley

Royal London One-Day Cup — Group B
Derbyshire v. Yorkshire

Played at Queen's Park, Chesterfield, on August 8, 2021
Yorkshire won by 8 wickets

Toss won by Yorkshire   Yorkshire 2 points, Derbyshire 0 points

DERBYSHIRE

H R C Came, c Ballance b Sullivan	28
M D Wagstaff, b Hill	22
T A Wood, c Fraine b Sullivan	9
§ B D Guest, st Duke b Sullivan	0
* A L Hughes, c Revis b Sullivan	0
F J Hudson-Prentice, not out	38
M H McKiernan, c Fraine b Waite	6
A K Dal, not out	0
A T Thomson	
R Rampaul Did not bat	
G L S Scrimshaw	
Extras b 1, lb 1, w 1, nb 2	5
Total (6 wkts, 10 overs)	108

FoW: 1-40 (Wagstaff), 2-49 (Wood), 3-50 (Guest), 4-50 (Hughes), 5-79 (Came), 6-104 (McKiernan)

	O	M	R	W
Coad	2	0	23	0
Waite	2	0	21	1
Revis	1	0	10	0
Pillans	2	0	31	0
Hill	1	0	10	1
Sullivan	2	0	11	4

YORKSHIRE

W A R Fraine, not out	69
M L Revis, c McKiernan b Rampaul	8
W Luxton, c Dal b Scrimshaw	20
* G S Ballance, not out	9
G C H Hill	
J A Tattersall	
§ H G Duke	
M J Waite Did not bat	
B O Coad	
M W Pillans	
J R Sullivan	
Extras lb 1, nb 2	3
Total (2 wkts, 8.4 overs)	109

FoW: 1-28 (Revis), 2-92 (Luxton)

	O	M	R	W
Hudson-Prentice	1.4	0	26	0
Rampaul	2	0	15	1
McKiernan	2	0	35	0
Scrimshaw	2	0	23	1
Thomson	1	0	9	0

Umpires: H M S Adnan and B J Debenham   Scorers: J T Potter and J M Brown

Royal London One-Day Cup — Group B
Glamorgan v. Yorkshire

Played at Sophia Gardens, Cardiff, on August 12, 2021

Yorkshire won by 4 runs

Toss won by Glamorgan Yorkshire 2 points, Glamorgan 0 points

YORKSHIRE

W A R Fraine, c Cullen b Hogan	25
§ H G Duke, b Salter	20
W Luxton, c Reingold b Weighell	12
*G S Ballance, b Reingold	12
G C H Hill, b Cooke	25
J A Tattersall, c Carlson b Hogan	53
M L Revis, c Cullen b Cooke	0
D M Bess, lbw b Weighell	6
M J Waite, c Root b Cooke	44
J R Sullivan, c Hogan b Weighell	6
B O Coad, not out	2
Extras lb 12, w 9, nb 4	25
Total (48.5 overs)	230

FoW: 1-32 (Fraine), 2-59 (Luxton), 3-70 (Duke), 4-88 (Ballance), 5-121 (Hill), 6-121 (Revis), 7-132 (Bess), 8-216 (Waite), 9-226 (Tattersall), 10-230 (Sullivan)

	O	M	R	W
Hogan	9	0	30	2
Carey	6	0	35	0
Weighell	9.5	0	55	3
Salter	10	1	34	1
Reingold	4	0	24	1
Cooke	10	1	40	3

GLAMORGAN

H D Rutherford, b Coad	58
N J Selman, c Ballance b Hill	92
S J Reingold, b Hill	25
*K S Carlson, b Hill	1
W T Root, b Revis	8
§ T N Cullen, c Hill b Waite	11
J M Cooke, c Tattersall b Revis	13
A G Salter, not out	8
M J Weighell, run out (Coad/Waite)	0
L J Carey, not out	0
M G Hogan Did not bat	
Extras b 3, w 7	10
Total (8 wkts, 50 overs)	226

FoW: 1-121 (Rutherford), 2-180 (Reingold), 3-182 (Carlson), 4-187 (Selman), 5-197 (Root), 6-215 (Cooke), 7-222 (Cullen), 8-223 (Weighell)

	O	M	R	W
Coad	10	2	30	1
Waite	8	1	31	1
Bess	10	0	45	0
Revis	8	0	43	2
Sullivan	4	0	25	0
Hill	10	0	49	3

Umpires: I D Blackwell and T Lungley Scorers: J T Potter and A K Higgnell

Royal London One-Day Cup — First Quarter-Final
Essex v. Yorkshire

Played at Cloudfm County Ground, Chelmsford, on August 14, 2021
Essex won by 129 runs

Toss won by Essex

ESSEX

J S Rymell, b Hill	121
A N Cook, c Revis b Waite	16
* T Westley, c Duke b Hill	33
F I N Khushi, b Hill	12
P I Walter, c Revis b Coad	33
R N ten Doeschate, c sub (B D Birkhead) b Revis	10
§ A J A Wheater, c Luxton b Coad	34
S R Harmer, not out	31
A S S Nijjar, not out	23
J H Plom	
B M J Allison Did not bat	
Extras lb 2, w 2	4
Total (7 wkts, 50 overs)	317

FoW: 1-26 (Cook), 2-86 (Westley), 3-108 (Khushi), 4-176 (Walter), 5-195 (ten Doeschate), 6-263 (Wheater), 7-267 (Rymell)

	O	M	R	W
Coad	10	0	64	2
Waite	9	0	65	1
Revis	7	0	34	1
Pillans	5	0	50	0
Bess	9	1	51	0
Hill	10	2	51	3

YORKSHIRE

W A R Fraine, c Allison b Harmer	31
§ H G Duke, b Plom	4
W Luxton, lbw b Nijjar	34
* G S Ballance, lbw b Westley	11
G C H Hill, c Plom b Harmer	2
J A Tattersall, b Nijjar	6
M L Revis, b Plom	42
D M Bess, c Rymell b Westley	6
M J Waite, st Wheater b Westley	31
M W Pillans, not out	11
B O Coad, c Walter b Plom	0
Extras lb 2, w 8	10
Total (38.4 overs)	188

FoW: 1-6 (Duke), 2-68 (Fraine), 3-73 (Luxton), 4-78 (Hill), 5-88 (Tattersall), 6-102 (Ballance), 7-125 (Bess), 8-171 (Revis), 9-179 (Waite). 10-188 (Coad)

	O	M	R	W
Plom	7.4	2	34	3
Allison	5	0	27	0
ten Doeschate	6	0	41	0
Harmer	8	1	25	2
Nijjar	6	0	26	2
Westley	6	0	33	3

Umpires: M Burns and B V Taylor   Scorers: J T Potter and A E Choat

YORKSHIRE VIKINGS AVERAGES 2021
ROYAL LONDON ONE-DAY CUP

Played 9   Won 4   Lost 3   No Result 2

BATTING AND FIELDING
(Qualification 4 completed innings)

Player	M.	I.	N.O.	Runs	H.S.	100s	50s	Avge	ct/st
M J Waite	9	5	1	159	44	0	0	39.75	0
G C H Hill	9	7	1	222	90*	0	2	37.00	1
W Luxton	7	6	1	165	68	0	1	33.00	1
W A R Fraine	9	8	1	227	69*	0	1	32.42	4
M L Revis	9	7	1	186	58*	0	1	31.00	5
H G Duke	9	7	0	206	125	1	0	29.42	4/1
G S Ballance	9	8	1	180	54	0	1	25.71	9
J A Tattersall	9	7	1	153	70	0	2	25.50	5
Also played									
M W Pillans	7	3	1	61	40	0	0	30.50	1
D M Bess	4	3	0	19	7	0	0	6.33	1
B O Coad	8	4	2	12	10	0	0	6.00	1
J R Sullivan	3	1	0	6	6	0	0	6.00	0
S A Patterson	1	1	0	1	1	0	0	1.00	0
J W Shutt	5	2	2	2	1*	0	0	—	3
D Olivier	1	0	0	0	—	0	0	—	1

BOWLING
(Qualification 4 wickets)

Player	Overs	Mdns	Runs	Wkts	Avge	Best	4wI	RPO
J R Sullivan	14	0	79	5	15.8	4-11	1	5.64
G C H Hill	47	2	249	10	24.90	3-47	0	5.29
M J Waite	51	1	320	12	26.66	5-95	1	6.27
M W Pillans	34	0	251	8	31.37	4-26	2	7.38
B O Coad	58.2	7	285	8	35.62	3-30	0	4.88
M L Revis	43	3	229	5	45.80	2-43	0	5.32
Also bowled								
D Olivier	9	0	60	1	60.00	1-60	0	6.66
J W Shutt	11	0	88	1	88.00	1-33	0	8.00
D M Bess	32.1	2	188	1	188.00	1-28	0	5.84

50 Over One-Day Friendly *(Not List A)*
Northumberland v. Yorkshire

Played at North Marine Road, Scarborough, on July 20, 2021
Yorkshire won by 9 wickets
Toss won by Northumberland

NORTHUMBERLAND

A Appleby, c Duke b Pillans	60
S J D Bell, c Waite b Bess	54
§ M J Richardson, c Fraine b Pillans	65
R D Pringle, c Tattersall b Bess	1
M J Allen, c Duke b Pillans	8
* T Cant, c Luxton b Waite	24
S J Tindale, b Waite	17
O McGee, c Duke b Waite	0
J Coughlin, not out	4
M Scott, not out	4
K Waterson Did not bat	
Extras b 2, lb 8, w 7	17
Total (8 wkts, 50 overs)	254

FoW: 1-99 (Appleby), 2-130 (Bell), 3-137 (Pringle), 4-148 (Allen), 5-210 (Cant), 6-243 (Tindale), 7-243 (McGee), 8-247 (Richardson)

	O	M	R	W
Waite	9	0	57	3
Coad	8	0	52	0
Shutt	10	1	53	0
Pillans	9	1	23	3
Hill	6	0	21	0
Bess	8	0	38	2

YORKSHIRE

W A R Fraine, not out	146
§ H G Duke, c Bell b Coughlin	52
M L Revis, not out	40
G C H Hill	
J A Tattersall	
W Luxton	
* D M Bess Did not bat	
M J Waite	
M W Pillans	
B O Coad	
J W Shutt	
Extras lb 10, w 5, nb 2	17
Total (1 wkt, 39.2 overs)	255

FoW: 1-144 (Duke)

	O	M	R	W
Coughlin	8	0	31	1
Waterson	6	0	31	0
Tindale	7	0	50	0
Scott	4	0	28	0
McGee	7	0	52	0
Pringle	4	0	23	0
Allen	2	0	21	0
Appleby	1.2	0	9	0

Umpires: G D Lloyd and N J Pratt   Scorers: J T Potter and J D Davidson

Yorkshire Premier Leagues Championship Final
Castleford v. Woodlands

Played at Headingley, Leeds, on September 18, 2021

Castleford won by 5 runs

Toss won by Castleford

CASTLEFORD

C F Hughes, b Brice	61
L Hyde, lbw b Brice	43
B Clark, lbw b Muhammad Bilal	34
* D J Wainwright, run out (Frankland)	29
C Hyde, c Muhammad Bilal b Kez Ahmed	15
C Briggs, run out (Frankland)	25
A Bourke, b Kez Ahmed	10
E Morrison, b Brice	2
§ A Kaye, b Brice	10
J Young, not out	5
M Rees, not out	2
Extras lb 2, w 2, nb 1	5
Total ((9 wkts, 50 overs)	241

FoW: 1-103 (L Hyde), 2-108 (Hughes), 3-157 (Wainwright), 4-181 (Clark), 5-191 (C Hyde), 6-210 (Bourke), 7-213 (Morrison), 8-232 (Briggs), 9-238 (Kaye)

	O	M	R	W
E Richardson	4	0	29	0
Muhammad Bilal	12	0	63	1
S Richardson	4	0	22	0
Brice	15	1	59	4
Kez Ahmed	15	2	66	2

WOODLANDS

S Frankland, c Kaye b Rees	8
T Jackson, c Kaye b Morrison	30
* C Garner, run out (Young)	32
L Collins, c Clark b Young	32
S Richardson, c Clark b Young	15
T Clee, c Hughes b Young	12
Muhammad Bilal, c and b C Hyde	19
§ G Finn, c Rees b Young	23
E Richardson, c Clark b Young	40
Kez Ahmed, not out	10
C Brice, not out	1
Extras lb 1, w 12	13
Total (9 wkts, 50 overs)	235

FoW: 1-16 (Frankland), 2-58 (Jackson), 3-108 (Collins), 4-111 (Garner), 5-132 (S Richardson), 6-149 (Clee), 7-159 (M Bilal), 8-223 (E Richardson), 9-225 Finn

	O	M	R	W
Rees	7	0	26	1
C Hyde	6	0	33	1
Morrison	14	1	55	1
Wainwright	7	0	36	0
Young	12	1	54	5
Hughes	4	0	30	0

Umpires: J Pitcher and S A Richardson Scorers: C Pearson and G Rees

NORTHERN DIAMONDS

Captain: Hollie Armitage
Director of Cricket: James Carr   Coach: Danielle Hazell
Academy Head Coach: Courtney Winfield-Hill

CHARLOTTE EDWARDS CUP 2021

Final: Northern Diamonds (138-4) lost to South East Stars (139-5) by 5 wickets

GROUP A	P	W	L	T	NR/A	PTS	NRR
1 South East Stars	6	5	1	0	0	21	1.050
2 Southern Vipers *	6	4	2	0	0	19	0.875
3 Central Sparks	6	3	3	0	0	12	-0.669
4 Lightning	6	0	6	0	0	0	-1.139

GROUP B	P	W	L	T	NR/A	PTS	NRR
1 **Northern Diamonds ***	**6**	**4**	**2**	**0**	**0**	**17**	**0.656**
2 Western Storm	6	4	2	0	0	17	0.182
3 Thunder	6	2	3	1	0	11	0.029
4 Sunrisers	6	1	4	1	0	6	-0.871

* Qualified for Semi-Final (One)

RACHAEL HEYHOE FLINT TROPHY 2021

Final: Northern Diamonds (188) lost to Southern Vipers (187-7) by 3 wickets

	P	W	L	T	NR/A	PTS	N R R
1 Southern Vipers	7	6	1	0	0	27	0.417
2 **Northern Diamonds ***	**7**	**5**	**2**	**0**	**0**	**23**	**1.182**
3 Central Sparks *	7	5	2	0	0	22	0.822
4 Lightning	7	3	4	0	0	13	0.274
5 South East Stars	7	3	4	0	0	13	-0.226
6 Western Storm	7	3	4	0	0	13	-0.462
7 Thunder	7	3	4	0	0	13	-0.620
8 Sunrisers	7	0	7	0	0	0	-1.598

* Qualified for Semi-Final (One)

NORTHERN DIAMONDS 2021 SQUAD (* denotes contracted player)

Player	Date of Birth	Birthplace	Role
H J Armitage (Captain) •	June 14, 1997	Huddersfield	RHB, LB
K H Brunt	July 2, 1985	Barnsley	RHB, RAF
L Dobson	June 10, 2001	Scarborough	RHB
J L Gunn •	May 9, 1986	Nottingham	RHB, RAMF
B A M Heath •	August 20, 2001	Chesterfield	RHB, WK
R H M Hopkins	July 19, 1992	Nottingham	RHB
S L Kalis •	August 30, 1999	Delft, Holland	RHB
B A Langston •	September 6, 1992	Harold Wood	RAF
K A Levick •	July 17, 1991	Sheffield	LB
N R Sciver	August 20, 1992	Tokyo, Japan	RHB, RAMF
L C N Smith •	March 10, 1995	Hillingdon	SLA
R Slater •	November 20, 2001	Glens Fallls, USA	LAM
E F Telford	April 5, 1999	Penrith	RAM
L Tipton	March 19, 2002	Sunderland	RHB
L Winfield-Hill	August 16, 1990	York	RHB, WK
A Glen	April 2, 2001		RHB, RAMF

NORTHERN DIAMONDS AVERAGES 2021

CHARLOTTE EDWARDS CUP

Played 8　　Won 5　　Lost 3

BATTING AND FIELDING
(Qualification 3 completed innings)

Player	M.	I.	N.O.	Runs	H.S.	100s	50s	Avge	ct/st
J L Gunn	8	6	3	97	27*	0	0	32.33	3
B A M Heath	5	5	1	103	58*	0	1	25.75	1/2
H J Armitage	8	8	2	141	59*	0	1	23.50	4
L Winfield-Hill	3	3	0	70	65	0	1	23.33	2
L Dobson	8	8	1	111	44*	0	0	15.85	2
S L Kalis	8	6	0	83	32	0	0	13.83	2
L C N Smith	8	5	0	45	30	0	0	9.00	6
A Campbell	3	3	0	20	15	0	0	6.66	2
R H M Hopkins	8	4	1	10	4*	0	0	3.33	0
Also batted									
B A Langston	2	2	1	57	46*	0	0	57.00	0
S J Taylor	3	2	1	54	43*	0	0	54.00	3/1
A L MacDonald	7	3	1	28	22	0	0	14.00	2
P C Graham	4	2	1	6	6*	0	0	6.00	3
R Slater	4	1	0	5	5	0	0	5.00	1
H L Fenby	1	1	0	0	0	0	0	0.00	1
K A Levick	8	3	3	15	7*	0	0	—	0
E F Telford	1	1	1	1	1*	0	0	—	0

BOWLING
(Qualification 3 wickets)

Player	Overs	Mdns	Runs	Wkts	Avge	Best	4wi	RPO
J L Gunn	28.3	1	165	13	12.69	4 -15	2	5.78
B A Langston	6	0	51	4	12.75	2 -19	0	8.50
R Slater	12	0	70	5	14.00	2 -16	0	5.83
A L MacDonald	26	0	127	9	14.11	4 -17	1	4.88
K A Levick	30	0	153	10	15.30	2 -19	0	5.10
L C N Smith	32	0	156	10	15.60	2 -12	0	4.87
P C Graham	13	0	79	4	19.75	2 -20	0	6.07
H J Armitage	9	0	71	3	23.66	2 -18	0	7.88
Also bowled								
H L Fenby	1	0	7	0	—	0 - 7	0	7.00

Charlotte Edwards Cup 2021 — Group B
Northern Diamonds v. Thunder

Played at Emerald Headingley, Leeds, on June 26, 2021
Thunder won by 12 runs

Toss won by Thunder   Thunder 4 points, Northern Diamonds 0 points

THUNDER

E L Lamb, c Kalis b Levick	58
G E B Boyce, c Gunn b Langston	0
§ E Threlkeld, c Fenby b Gunn	13
R E Duckworth, b Smith	1
N Brown, c Dobson b Graham	25
L Marshall, b Langston	2
L E Jackson, not out	7
D L Collins, not out	0
S Turner	
* A Hartley Did not bat	
H E Jones	
Extras lb 3, w 9	12
Total (6 wkts, 20 overs)	118

FoW: 1-8 (Boyce), 2-41 (Threlkeld), 3-44 (Duckworth), 4-107 (Lamb), 5-109 (Brown), 6-118 (Marshall)

	O	M	R	W
Fenby	1	0	7	0
Langston	4	0	32	2
Graham	4	0	18	1
Gunn	3	0	17	1
Levick	4	0	18	1
Smith	4	0	23	1

NORTHERN DIAMONDS

* H J Armitage, lbw b Lamb	20
L Dobson, c Lamb b Turner	8
A Campbell, lbw b Lamb	0
S L Kalis, st Threlkeld b Brown	32
J L Gunn, b Jones	6
B A Langston, c Hartley b Lamb	11
R H M Hopkins, b Lamb	1
L C N Smith, run out (Turner)	1
P C Graham, not out	6
H L Fenby, run out (Lamb)	0
K A Levick, not out	7
§ S J Taylor	
Extras lb 6, w 8	14
Total (9 wkts, 20 overs)	106

R H M Hopkins was a concussion replacement for S J Taylor at the start of the Northern Diamonds innings

FoW: 1-31 (Armitage), 2-31 (Campbell), 3-36 (Dobson), 4-63 (Gunn), 5-91 (Kalis), 6-92 (Hopkins), 7-93 (Langston), 8-93 (Smith), 9-94 (Fenby)

	O	M	R	W
Hartley	4	0	26	0
Jackson	1	0	17	0
Jones	4	0	17	1
Turner	4	1	4	1
Lamb	4	1	13	4
Brown	3	0	23	1

Umpires: J D Middlebrook and L Nenova   Scorers: K N Hutchison and V K Holliday

Northern Diamonds v. Thunder
A Lamb for the slaughter

It was very much a case of the Diamonds being a lamb to the slaughter on the opening day of the Charlotte Edwards Cup.

Thunder all-rounder Emma Lamb enjoyed one heck of a day as the visitors secured a 12-run victory in a low-scoring affair.

The first half of a T20 double header alongside the men — playing Northamptonshire — saw the Diamonds slip from a position of strength at 31-0 to 106-9 chasing 119.

Opener Lamb hit seven fours in a 43-ball 58 to drag Thunder up to 118-6 after they had elected to bat. Phoebe Graham and Katie Levick were excellent with 1-18 from their four-over spells as wickets were shared around. Beth Langston struck twice.

STERRE KALIS: Top score for the struggling hosts

Captain Hollie Armitage cracked four fours in 20 off 19 balls to start the chase, but things went downhill quickly. She was trapped lbw by Lamb's off-spin, her first of four victims in a four-over spell for only 13 runs. Armitage's dismissal left the score at 31-1 in the fifth, and the Diamonds lost nine for 63 as Lamb took a catch and affected a run-out.

The Diamonds' hopes were hurt by a concussion injury to wicket-keeping legend Sarah Taylor, who was substituted out at the mid-innings interval. With the last ball of the Thunder innings Taylor had been struck in the neck by a rising delivery from Langston and was replaced by Rachel Hopkins.

Only three Diamonds batters made it into double figures. Armitage was followed by Sterre Kalis with an innings top-score of 32, while Langston made 11.

As impressive as Lamb was, fledgling Thunder seamer Sophia Turner's four-over spell of 1-4 was equally important in putting the brakes on the home side after their healthy start to the chase. This was Thunder's first *Roses* win in regional cricket.

Charlotte Edwards Cup 2021 — Group B
Sunrisers v. Northern Diamonds

Played at The Cloudfm County Ground, Chelmsford, on July 2, 2021
Northern Diamonds won by 8 wickets

Toss won by Northern Diamonds — Northern Diamonds 4 points, Sunrisers 0 points

SUNRISERS

N D Dattani, b Gunn	1
A J Macleod, c and b Graham	13
G E Scrivens, lbw b Gunn	0
M K Villiers, c and b Graham	10
§ A D Carr, lbw b Levick	11
* K S Castle, c Taylor b Levick	9
J L Gardner, c Campbell b Gunn	42
K Speed, not out	26
M E W Rogers, not out	1
G K S Cole	
S Patel	
Extras lb 1, w 1, nb 1	3
Total (7 wkts, 20 overs)	116

FoW: 1-15 (Dattani), 2-15 (Scrivens), 3-15 (Macleod), 4-26 (Villiers), 5-41 (Carr), 6-48 (Castle), 7-112 (Gardner).

	O	M	R	W
Smith	4	0	21	0
Graham	4	1	20	2
Gunn	4	1	25	3
MacDonald	2	0	7	0
Armitage	2	0	19	0
Levick	4	0	23	2

NORTHERN DIAMONDS

* H J Armitage, st Carr b Villiers	14
L Dobson, not out	44
A Campbell, c Dattani b Scrivens	5
§ S J Taylor, not out	43
J L Gunn	
S L Kalis	
R H M Hopkins	
A L MacDonald	
L C N Smith	
P C Graham	
K A Levick	
Extras lb 2, w 9	11
Total (2 wkts, 16.2 overs)	117

FoW: 1-14 (Armitage), 2-30 (Campbell).

	O	M	R	W
Villiers	3	0	22	1
Dattani	3	0	16	0
Patel	2	0	20	0
Scrivens	3	0	22	1
Castle	3.2	0	19	0
Gardner	2	0	16	0

Umpires: J Ibbotson and I S McLelland   Scorers: P Parkinson and H M Hyde

Sunrisers v. Northern Diamonds

Clinical victory on the breeze

Clinical is an excellent way of describing the Diamonds as they bounced back from their opening defeat to breeze past Sunrisers for the second time in the summer, winning by eight wickets under the Chelmsford lights.

They elected to bowl, and Jenny Gunn claimed three wickets, while Phoebe Graham and Katie Levick impressed with two apiece as Sunrisers made a substandard 116-7 on a good pitch.

In many ways they were fortunate to get that many, given they had been 48-6 as comparisons were drawn

JENNY GUNN: Superbly set the tone with a double-wicket maiden

between the 50-over game the two had played at Cambridge a month earlier when Sunrisers were bowled out for 53. Credit to them: they more than doubled their score through a seventh-wicket partnership of 64 between Jo Gardner with 42 and Katherine Speed, 26 not out.

Earlier Gunn had set the tone superbly by bowling Naomi Dattani and trapping fellow opener Grace Scrivens lbw in a double-wicket maiden as the Sunrisers slipped to 15-2 in the third over.

In an explosive start to the pursuit Diamonds captain Hollie Armitage drove two boundaries and hoisted England off-spinner Mady Villiers over extra-cover for six in the opening over before falling for 14 off six balls. Ami Campbell, 30-2 in the fourth, followed before a dominant unbroken third-wicket partnership of 87 in 13 overs between Leah Dobson and fit-again Sarah Taylor secured the victory in grand style.

Both players, at either end of the experience spectrum, never looked like allowing Sunrisers into the game, with Dobson hitting two sixes in her 44 not out off 52 balls and Taylor busy for her unbeaten 43 off 35, including two fours in her first four balls.

Their respective scores were their best in Diamonds colours, a statistic more significant for 19-year-old Scarborough-born right-hander Dobson. The win was secured with 22 balls remaining.

Charlotte Edwards Cup 2021 — Group B
Western Storm v. Northern Diamonds

Played at The Cooper Associates County Ground, Taunton, on July 10, 2021
Northern Diamonds won by 1 wicket

Toss won by Northern Diamonds   Northern Diamonds 4 points, Western Storm 0 points

WESTERN STORM

F M K Morris, c Taylor b MacDonald	16
G M Hennessy, lbw b Smith	0
D R Gibson, c Smith b Gunn	12
*S N Luff, c Taylor b Graham	0
K L George, c Campbell b MacDonald	21
A C Griffiths, c Smith b MacDonald	11
§N A J Wraith, b Smith	20
L A Parfitt, c Graham b MacDonald	2
E M Edgcombe, st Taylor b Levick	7
N Harvey, not out	4
S Hutchins, not out	1
Extras lb 3, w 9	12
Total (9 wkts, 20 overs)	106

FoW: 1-1 (Hennessy), 2-21 (Gibson), 3-28 (Luff), 4-51 (Morris), 5-64 (George), 6-66 (Griffiths), 7-76 (Parfitt), 8-94 (Edgcombe), 9-103 (Wraith)

	O	M	R	W
Smith	4	0	15	2
Graham	4	0	31	1
Gunn	4	0	23	1
MacDonald	4	0	17	4
Levick	4	0	17	1

NORTHERN DIAMONDS

*H J Armitage, c Wraith b Edgcombe	5
L Dobson, c Harvey b Griffiths	12
A Campbell, c Gibson b Griffiths	15
§S J Taylor, run out (Griffiths)	11
A L MacDonald, b Gibson	6
S L Kalis, b Gibson	14
R H M Hopkins, lbw b Morris	2
L C N Smith, c Edgcombe b Harvey	5
J L Gunn, not out	27
P C Graham, b Harvey	0
K A Levick, not out	2
Extras w 11	11
Total (9 wkts, 20 overs)	110

FoW: 1-6 (Armitage), 2-33 (Campbell), 3-33 (Dobson), 4-55 (MacDonald), 5-62 (Taylor), 6-76 (Hopkins), 7-78 (Kalis), 8-93 (Smith), 9-96 (Graham)

	O	M	R	W
Edgcombe	2	0	14	1
Parfitt	1	0	8	0
Hennessy	1	0	11	0
Griffiths	4	1	28	2
Morris	4	0	23	1
Harvey	4	0	17	2
Gibson	4	0	9	2

Umpires: A C Harris and C M Watts   Scorers: Q L S Jones and K N Hutchinson

Western Storm v. Northern Diamonds

Gunn defies broken finger

Yorkshire's men had already snatched a one-run win in the County Championship against Northamptonshire, but this one-wicket victory for the Diamonds against the Storm was not far behind for drama.

You are always more likely to get such tight finishes in T20 cricket than the first-class arena. But, make no mistake, the Diamonds were on the ropes at 96-9 after 18.5 balls chasing 107.

A game which boasted some superb fielding from both sides saw no batter reach 30, with evergreen Diamonds all-rounder Jenny Gunn's match-clinching 27 not out the highest score.

ALEX MACDONALD: Crucial quartet of wickets for seamer

Gunn was dropped down the order to No. 9 — she came in at 78-7 after 15 overs — because of a fractured finger, but ended up hitting 12 of 13 runs in the last over from the medium pace of Alex Griffiths, including two boundaries. The second was lofted over mid-on to secure back-to-back victories immediately before the mid-season break for the start of the Hundred.

While Gunn will take the headlines for dragging the Diamonds out of trouble, as she so often does, Alex MacDonald's T20 career-best 4-17 with her skilful seamers was crucial. So was Sarah Taylor's contribution behind the stumps in the final appearance of her brief stay with the side, with two catches and a stumping. Her first catch, off Phoebe Graham's pace, was stunning to get rid of Storm captain Sophie Luff.

Diving to her right, Taylor parried a thick outside edge with her right hand before holding onto the catch in her left as she hit the turf.

MacDonald's haul included the wickets of Katie George and Griffiths caught in the 11th over as the Storm, invited to bat, slipped to 66-6. Thankfully for her, Gunn later ensured the second four-wicket haul of her T20 career contributed to a victory.

Charlotte Edwards Cup 2021 — Group B
Northern Diamonds v. Sunrisers

Played at Roseworth Terrace, Gosforth, on August 25, 2021
Northern Diamonds won by 19 runs

Toss won by Sunrisers Northern Diamonds 4 points, Sunrisers 0 points

NORTHERN DIAMONDS

*H J Armitage, c Gardner b Dattani	6
L Dobson, c Speed b Dattani	13
§ B A M Heath, c Griffith b Coppack	0
S L Kalis, b Scrivens	4
J L Gunn, c Rodgers b Coppack	2
L C N Smith, run out (Rogers>Gardner)	30
B A Langston, not out	46
R H M Hopkins, not out	4
P Graham	
K A Levick Did not bat	
A L MacDonald	
Extras lb 4, w 10, nb 1	15
Total (6 wkts, 20 overs)	120

FoW: 1-7 (Armitage), 2-10 (Heath), 3-23 (Dobson), 4-26 (Gunn), 5-32 (Kalis), 6-110 (Smith)

	O	M	R	W
Coppack	4	0	10	2
Scrivens	4	0	14	1
Dattani	3	1	24	2
Castle	3	0	20	0
Gole	2	0	15	0
Gardner	4	0	33	0

SUNRISERS

N D Dattani, c Armitage b Langston	9
C L Griffith, lbw b Langston	0
G E Scrivens, b Levick	11
J L Gardner, c Heath b MacDonald	31
F H Miller, b MacDonald	9
*K S Castle, b Armitage	0
§ M E W Rogers, c Smith b Armitage	6
K E Speed, not out	17
G K S Cole, not out	11
E Woodhouse	
K L Coppack Did not bat	
Extras w 6, nb 1	7
Total (7 wkts, 20 overs)	101

FoW: 1-10 (Dattani), 2-10 (Griffith), 3-44 (Scrivens), 4-63 (Gardner), 5-64 (Castle), 6-64 (Miller), 7-79 (Rogers)

	O	M	R	W
Smith	4	0	20	0
Langston	2	0	19	2
Graham	1	0	10	0
Gunn	3	0	17	0
Levick	2	0	6	1
MacDonald	4	0	11	2
Armitage	4	0	18	2

Umpires: P R Pollard and J Pratt Scorers: G Maddison and P Summerside

Northern Diamonds v. Sunrisers
Bitter-sweet for Langston

Beth Langston enjoyed a bitter-sweet day. Having starred with bat and ball to secure a hat-trick of Diamonds wins over the Sunrisers, she suffered a quad injury to rule her out of the next four regional fixtures.

Still, the seam-bowling all-rounder who had represented England A against the touring New Zealanders two days earlier can be satisfied she played the lead role in putting her side on course for Finals Day, courtesy of a 19-run win — their third in four Charlotte Edwards Cup games.

They were three points clear at the top of Group Two with two rounds remaining.

Having been inserted, the Diamonds were 32-5 in the 10th over as the seam of Naomi Dattani and Kate Coppack equally shared four wickets. Coppack bowled four overs straight with the new ball, returning 2-10. Only Leah Dobson (13) of the top five reached double figures before Langston united with sixth-wicket partner Linsey Smith to turn the game with a 78-run stand in just under 10 overs.

BETH LANGSTON: Top-scorer to miss next four games

Both players scored at better than a run-a-ball. Smith hit 30 off 25 balls with two fours, while Langston found the boundary six times in an unbeaten 46 off 38 to help to post 120-6. With that score against the struggling Sunrisers it was difficult to see any other result than a Diamonds victory. That view was strengthened two overs into the chase.

Langston snared openers Dattani and Cordelia Griffith in her first over: 10-2 after two. She then bowled her second over before hobbling off the field and leaving it to her teammates to wrap things up. They duly did so.

Jo Gardner struck the ball crisply for a middle order 31, but was afforded no support. Alex MacDonald, with 2-11 from four overs, and Hollie Armitage both struck twice as Sunrisers finished on 101-7.

Charlotte Edwards Cup 2021 — Group B
Northern Diamonds v. Western Storm

Played at Emirates Riverside, Chester-le-Street, on August 28, 2021
Western Storm won by 4 wickets

Toss won by Western Storm Western Storm 4 points, Northern Diamonds 0 points

NORTHERN DIAMONDS

L Dobson, run out (Gibson)	2
§ B A M Heath, c George b Parfitt	14
S L Kalis, c Hennessy b Harvey	12
*H J Armitage, run out (Griffiths)	5
J L Gunn, b Morris	18
L C N Smith, c Parfitt b Hennessy	7
R H M Hopkins, lbw b Harvey	3
A L MacDonald, b Morris	22
R Slater, lbw b Gibson	5
K A Levick, not out	6
E F Telford, not out	1
Extras lb 2, w 12, nb 1	15
Total (9 wkts, 20 overs)	110

FoW: 1-22 (Dobson), 2-30 (Heath), 3-45 (Armitage), 4-47 (Kalis), 5-56 (Smith), 6-62 (Hopkins), 7-98 (MacDonald), 8-103 (Gunn), 9-103 (Slater).

	O	M	R	W
Parfitt	4	0	20	1
Filer	1	0	11	0
Morris	4	0	24	2
Harvey	4	0	20	2
Gibson	3	0	18	1
Hennessy	4	0	15	1

WESTERN STORM

G M Hennessy, lbw b Smith	0
F M K Morris, b Slater	4
D R Gibson, b Slater	3
*S N Luff, not out	60
K L George, b Armitage	14
A C Griffiths, b Levick	4
§ N A J Wraith, c and b Smith	2
L A Parfitt, not out	20
N Harvey	
B Gammon	Did not bat
L Filer	
Extras lb 2, w 2	4
Total (6 wkts, 19.3 overs)	111

FoW: 1-0 (Hennessy), 2-6 (Morris), 3-14 (Gibson), 4-63 (George), 5-75 (Griffiths), 6-78 (Wraith).

	O	M	R	W
Smith	4	0	18	2
Slater	3	0	16	2
Gunn	3.3	0	18	0
Levick	4	0	24	1
MacDonald	4	0	20	0
Armitage	1	0	13	1

Umpires: J Naeem and N J Pratt Scorers: G Maddison and W R Dobson

Northern Diamonds v. Western Storm

Finals Day chance missed

RACHEL SLATER
Two wickets on debut

The last time the Diamonds made 110-9 against Storm they won a thriller by one-wicket. Not this time as they slipped to a four-wicket defeat and missed their first opportunity to qualify for Finals Day.

Only Alex MacDonald (22) reached 20 as the Diamonds, invited to bat, lost wickets regularly on the way to a total which proved competitive.

Spinners Fi Morris and Nicole Harvey impressed with two wickets apiece, while the seam of Georgia Hennessy really put the squeeze on as she returned an excellent 1-15 from four overs.

The visitors were sharp in the field, affecting two run-outs, as they replaced the Diamonds at the Group Two's summit with one round remaining.

The top team in the two groups would advance to Finals Day at Southampton the following weekend, with the best of them qualifying directly for the final.

The other group winner would then play the best second-placed finisher in a midday semi-final. The best second-placed team was looking likely to come from Group One, so the Diamonds would have to win Group Two. They went into the final round, against Thunder at Chester, on 12 points — a point behind Storm. With five points still available, Thunder could also qualify from third on 11.

For the Diamonds, they knew if Storm beat Sunrisers in their final game they would have to beat Thunder with a bonus point (five points) in order to top the group.

However, back to this Storm game: the Diamonds handed regional debuts to seamers Ella Telford and left-armer Rachel Slater, who with the new ball struck twice in her first two overs — Morris and Danielle Gibson bowled — as the score fell to 14-3. That became 78-6 in the 15th over, only for captain Sophie Luff's superb unbeaten 60 off 54 balls to seal victory with three balls remaining.

Charlotte Edwards Cup 2021 — Group B
Thunder v. Northern Diamonds

Played at Chester Boughton Hall CC on August 30, 2021
Northern Diamonds won by 8 wickets

Toss won by Northern Diamonds   Northern Diamond 5 points, Thunder 0 points

THUNDER

G E B Boyce, c MacDonald b Slater	12
D E Mullan, b Levick	14
§ E Threlkeld, c Kalis b Slater	1
L Marshall, b Smith	14
K L Cross, c MacDonald b Gunn	14
D L Collins, c Slater b Gunn	16
L E Jackson, c and b Gunn	8
A E Dyson, c Armitage b Gunn	0
H L Jones, not out	2
* A Hartley, st Heath b Smith	0
S Turner, not out	1
Extras lb 6, w 2	8
Total (9 wkts, 20 overs)	90

FoW: 1-20 (Boyce), 2-22 (Threlkeld), 3-47 (Marshall), 4-54 (Mullan), 5-68 (Cross), 6-83 (Jackson), 7-83 (Dyson), 8-87 (Collins), 9-89 (Hartley)

	O	M	R	W
Slater	4	0	22	2
Smith	4	0	12	2
Gunn	4	0	15	4
Levick	4	0	21	1
MacDonald	4	0	14	0

NORTHERN DIAMONDS

L Dobson, c Jackson b Dyson	20
§ B A M Heath, not out	58
L Winfield-Hill, b Jones	5
* H J Armitage, not out	7
J L Gunn	
L C N Smith	
R H M Hopkins	
A L MacDonald Did not bat	
R Slater	
K A Levick	
S L Kalis	
Extras lb 1, w 1	2
Total (2 wkts, 12.2 overs)	92

FoW: 1-46 (Dobson), 2-73 (Winfield-Hill)

	O	M	R	W
Cross	3	0	28	0
Jones	4	0	12	1
Jackson	1	0	11	0
Turner	2	0	15	0
Dyson	1	0	9	1
Hartley	1.2	0	16	0

Umpires: J Naeem and B V Taylor   Scorers: A M Cregan and A Lush

Thunder v. Northern Diamonds
Finals Day, here we come

This was one of the Diamonds' best performances of the summer, and what a time for it!

An eight-wicket victory with 42 balls to spare secured the bonus point needed to leapfrog Western Storm at the top of Group Two and qualify for Finals Day six days later, where they would play hosts Southern Vipers in the midday semi-final.

Not only this, but the Diamonds exacted revenge over Thunder for the Headingley defeat on the opening day of Charlotte Edwards Cup action. Then, England all-rounder Emma Lamb was their hero. Here, she was missing because of international duty.

Hero for the Diamonds was Jenny Gunn, who laid the founda-

BESS HEATH: Crashed 10 fours in her undefeated 58

tions for victory with a superb 4-15 from her four overs of seam. She removed former England teammate Kate Cross, and then ousted Laura Jackson, Alice Dyson and Danielle Collins in her last over, the 19th, as Thunder staggered to 90-9 having been inserted.

No batter made 20 as Rachel Slater and the left-arm spin of Linsey Smith claimed two wickets apiece. Smith conceded only 12 runs in a brilliant four-over spell which started with the new ball.

To achieve a bonus point a team must score at 1.25 times quicker than their opponents. This meant Diamonds had to chase 91 inside 16 overs to usurp the Storm, who had claimed a narrow victory over Sunrisers. It was done with plenty of time to spare and without a significant contribution from England one-day opener Lauren Winfield-Hill, batting at No.3 following a period of rest post the Hundred.

Winfield-Hill contributed only six to a chase which was lit up by wicket-keeper Bess Heath. Promoted up the order, Heath, 20, crashed 10 fours in 58 not out off 40 balls for her first regional half-century as the win was sealed in the 13th over.

Charlotte Edwards Cup 2021 — Only Semi-Final
Northern Diamonds v. Southern Vipers

Played at The Ageas Bowl, West End, Southampton, on September 5, 2021
Northern Diamonds won by 18 runs

Toss won by Northern Diamonds

NORTHERN DIAMONDS

L Dobson, run out (McCaughan)	1
§ B A M Heath, b Bell	9
L Winfield-Hill, b Adams	65
* H J Armitage, c Norris b Taylor	25
S L Kalis, b Elwiss	3
J L Gunn, not out	22
L C N Smith, c Scolfield b Norris	2
A L MacDonald, not out	0
R H M Hopkins	
R Slater Did not bat	
K A Levick	
Extras lb 3, w 5	8
Total (6 wkts, 20 overs)	135

FoW: 1-12 (Dobson), 2-16 (Heath), 3-75 (Armitage), 4-82 (Kalis), 5-114 (Winfield-Hill), 6-120 (Smith)

	O	M	R	W
Bell	4	0	15	1
Norris	4	0	29	1
Taylor	4	0	25	1
Scholfield	2	0	17	0
Elwiss	4	0	25	1
Adams	2	0	21	1

SOUTHERN VIPERS

* G L Adams, c Smith b Gunn	14
E M McCaughan, st Heath b Slater	13
G A Elwiss, c Winfield-Hill b Smith	9
P J Scholfield, b MacDonald	5
E L Windsor, c and b Smith	32
T G Norris, c Armitage b Levick	8
A Z Monaghan, lbw b Gunn	5
L K Bell, b Gunn	0
§ C E Rudd, c Dobson b Gunn	5
E R Chandler, run out (Hopkins/Heath)	4
C M Taylor, not out	2
Extras b 1, lb 3, w 16	20
Total (20 overs)	117

FoW: 1-29 (McCaughan), 2-33 (Adams), 3-41 (Scholfield), 4-59 (Elwiss), 5-75 (Norris), 6-99 (Monaghan), 7-99 (Bell), 8-110 (Windsor), 9-114 (Chandler), 10-117 (Rudd)

	O	M	R	W
Smith	4	0	18	2
Slater	4	0	18	1
Gunn	4	0	26	4
MacDonald	4	0	26	1
Levick	4	0	25	1

Player of the match: L Winfield-Hill

Umpires: A Y Harris and S Redfern   Scorers: R V Isaacs and I Thompson

Northern Diamonds v. Southern Vipers

One step from the silver

LAUREN WINFIELD-HILL: Smiting a six in her linchpin 49-ball 65

Lauren Winfield-Hill's brilliant 49-ball 65, backed by Jenny Gunn's all-round heroics, put the Diamonds one game away from a first piece of silverware as a region.

England's Winfield-Hill was the linchpin in 135-6 before the Vipers, who beat the Diamonds in last year's Rachael Heyhoe Flint final, got into a hole chasing in the midday semi-final.

Gunn claimed 4-26 from four overs in 117 all out. On a slow hybrid pitch Vipers fell from 29-0 to 41-3 and later 75-5 in the 15th over.

The Diamonds had been plunged into early trouble with the loss of openers Leah Dobson, run out at the non-striker's end from mid-off, and Bess Heath bowled by Lauren Bell: 16-2. But Winfield-Hill calmly led the revival, sharing a third-wicket stand of 59 with captain Hollie Armitage (25) and by the time she reached her fifty off 41 balls the Diamonds were 99-4 in the 17th. Shortly afterwards she hammered Georgia Adams's off-spin down the ground for the first of three sixes in the last three overs of the innings.

When Winfield-Hill was bowled trying to attack Adams the Diamonds were 114-5 after 17.5 overs, but 20 runs off the last two overs, including 16 off the last, gave them valuable momentum. Gunn crashed successive leg-side sixes in her unbeaten 22.

The Vipers' chase reached 24-0 after four overs, but they soon lost 3-12 in three overs, including Gunn's first wicket — Adams caught at short mid-wicket off a miscued pull: 41-3 in the eighth over.

Vipers went seven overs without a boundary from midway through the eighth over to midway through the 15th. In the 18th Gunn put the final nail in the Vipers coffin by trapping Alice Monaghan lbw and bowling Bell with successive deliveries: 99-7.

She then defended 25 off the last over, removing Carla Rudd. Linsey Smith had also returned a superb 2-18.

Charlotte Edwards Cup 2021 — Final
South East Stars v. Northern Diamonds

Played at The Ageas Bowl, West End, Southampton, on September 5, 2021
South East Stars won by 5 wickets
Toss won by Northern Diamonds

NORTHERN DIAMONDS

L Dobson, c Jones b Davidson-Richards	11
§ B A M Heath, run out (Jones)	22
L Winfield-Hill, lbw b Gibbs	0
*H J Armitage, not out	59
S L Kalis, c and b Smith	18
J L Gunn, not out	22
L C N Smith	
A L MacDonald	
R H M Hopkins Did not bat	
R Slater	
K A Levick	
Extras lb 1, w 5	6
Total (4 wkts, 20 overs)	138

FoW: 1-18 (Dobson), 2-22 (Winfield-Hill), 3-45 (Heath), 4-88 (Kalis)

	O	M	R	W
Capsey	4	0	30	0
Moore	4	0	20	0
Davidson-Richards	4	0	28	1
Gibbs	2	0	13	1
Smith	4	0	22	1
Gregory	2	0	24	0

SOUTH EAST STARS

*B F Smith, b Smith	37
A Cranstone, hit wicket b MacDonald	35
A R Capsey, not out	40
G J Gibbs, c Winfield-Hill b Levick	3
P A Franklin, c Gunn b Levick	0
A N Davidson-Richards, c Armitage b Macdonald	18
K E White, not out	1
E W S Jones	
K Moore Did not bat	
§ K M Chathli	
D L Gregory	
Extras w 5	5
Total (5 wkts, 18 overs)	139

FoW: 1-71 (Cranstone), 2-81 (Smith), 3-84 (Gibbs), 4-85 (Franklin), 5-136 (Davidson-Richards)

	O	M	R	W
Smith	4	0	29	1
Slater	1	0	14	0
Gunn	3	0	24	0
Levick	4	0	19	2
MacDonald	4	0	32	2
Armitage	2	0	21	0

Player of the match: A R Capsey

Umpires: S Bartlett and S Redfern   Scorers: R V Isaacs and I Thompson

South East Stars v. Northern Diamonds
Pipped at the last post

HOLLIE ARMITAGE: Captain's top score led fighting recovery

The Diamonds bid for Charlotte Edwards Cup glory fell at the final hurdle as South East Stars chased 139 to win by five wickets with two overs remaining.

Captain Hollie Armitage top-scored for the Diamonds with 59 not out as they recovered from 22-2 to 138-4.

The Stars, despite losing 4-14 at one stage to fall to 85-4, chased with a degree of comfort in the Southampton sunshine to end a hugely encouraging campaign on a disappointing note.

Stars openers Aylish Cranstone and Bryony Smith, their captain, set about the chase in dominant manner with 35 and 37 apiece, playing freely in sharing a defining 71 inside nine overs.

Both departed quickly afterwards in the loss of the four wickets. But 17-year-old England hopeful Alice Capsey steered her side home with a mixture of power and invention in 40 not out off 26 balls.

The Diamonds' innings bore similarities to the 135-6 they posted in the semi-final win over Vipers earlier in the day. This time, instead of Lauren Winfield-Hill, it was Armitage who anchored things with her first half-century of the summer. Jenny Gunn made a late 22 not out, but Winfield-Hill had been trapped lbw for a three-ball duck.

What looked like a competitive score at least was made to look considerably under par as openers Smith and, in particular, Cranstone flew out of the blocks. They posted 32-0 off the first three overs and 50-0 from six, with left-handed Cranstone 28 at that stage.

When Katie Levick had both Grace Gibbs and Phoebe Franklin caught in the deep within four balls in the 11th over to make it 85-4 there was a glimmer of hope, but 17-year-old Capsey, who made a name for herself in the Hundred with champions Oval Invincibles, ensured there were no further dramas in front of a Finals Day crowd of 1,270.

NEWLY CONTRACTED DIAMONDS

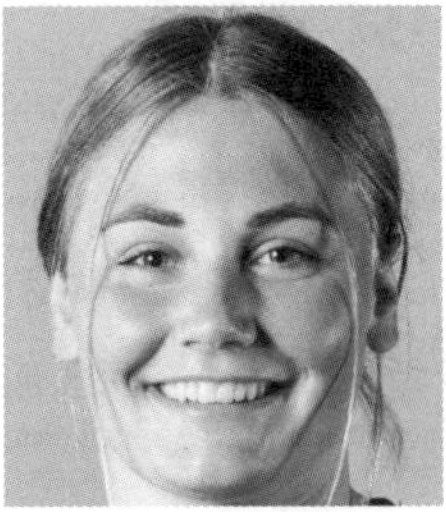

Bess Heath

Powerful wicket-keeper batter from Chesterfield, the 20-year-old started her county career with Derbyshire before moving to Yorkshire. Disruptive 2021 saw her suffer a hip injury early on before ending the summer in red-hot form with the bat. Turned down a trial with Worcester Warriors Rugby Union club not too long ago.

Sterre Kalis

Classy Dutch batter who has totalled 570 runs in both one-day and T20 cricket across the last two summers for the Diamonds. Aged 22, she has been their leading Rachael Heyhoe Flint Trophy (50-over) run-scorer in both 2020 and 2021 and has an international best of 126 not out in T20 cricket.

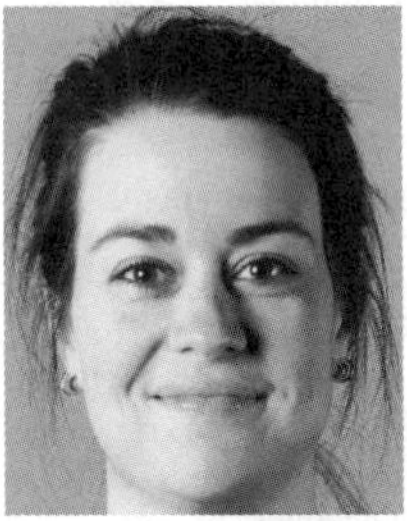

Katie Levick

Like Katherine Brunt and Lauren Winfield-Hill, Sheffield-born leg-spinner Levick is Yorkshire Cricket royalty. One of the most potent bowlers in English women's domestic cricket, the 30-year-old has taken 261 wickets from 198 career appearances in List A and T20s. Almost 140 of those appearances have come for Yorkshire.

Rachel Slater

Former Yorkshire age-group captain, left-arm swing bowler Slater made her Diamonds debut in August, taking two wickets inside her first two overs with the new ball in a T20 against Western Storm at Durham. Leeds-raised but born in New York State, the 20-year-old qualifies to play for the USA.

NORTHERN DIAMONDS AVERAGES 2021

RACHAEL HEYHOE-FLINT TROPHY

Played 9   Won 6   Lost 3

BATTING AND FIELDING
(Qualification 3 completed innings)

Player	M.	I.	N.O.	Runs	H.S.	100s	50s	Avge	ct/st
S L Kalis	9	8	1	290	76	0	2	41.42	2
B A Langston	9	6	2	141	59*	0	2	35.25	2
L Winfield-Hill	4	4	0	135	110	1	0	33.75	6/1
A Campbell	8	7	0	223	76	0	2	31.85	4
H J Armitage	9	9	2	197	68*	0	1	28.14	3
L C N Smith	8	5	2	82	37	0	0	27.33	1
J L Gunn	6	4	0	109	50	0	1	27.25	2
A L MacDonald	4	3	0	57	39	0	0	19.00	1
L Dobson	5	5	0	74	49	0	0	14.80	0
R H M Hopkins	4	4	0	43	20	0	0	10.75	0
K A Levick	8	3	0	11	8	0	0	3.66	0
Also batted									
B A M Heath	5	5	3	212	78*	0	2	106.00	4/1
K H Brunt	3	2	0	44	43	0	0	22.00	2
N R Sciver	3	3	1	26	10	0	0	13.00	2
R Slater	3	2	1	6	6*	0	0	6.00	0
S J Taylor	1	1	0	2	2	0	0	2.00	0
P C Graham	6	2	0	1	1	0	0	0.50	0
H L Fenby	1	1	1	2	2*	0	0	—	0
E F Telford	3	1	1	0	0*	0	0	—	1

BOWLING
(Qualification 3 wickets)

Player	Overs	Mdns	Runs	Wkts	Avge	Best	4wi	RPO
K H Brunt	27	9	75	9	8.33	4-23	1	2.77
K A Levick	59.1	5	190	12	15.83	4-34	1	3.21
J L Gunn	45	2	166	9	18.44	3-10	0	3.68
B A Langston	73.5	10	269	13	20.69	2-12	0	3.64
L C N Smith	73	10	286	12	23.83	5-34	1	3.91
H J Armitage	23	0	125	2	62.50	2-32	0	5.43
Also bowled								
P C Graham	49	2	250	6	41.66	3-44	0	5.10
R Slater	22	0	100	2	50.00	2-39	0	4.54
N R Sciver	23.2	2	101	2	50.50	2-24	0	4.32
E F Telford	14	0	98	0	—	0-17	0	7.00
A L MacDonald	3	0	21	0	—	0-21	0	7.00

Rachael Heyhoe-Flint Trophy 2021
Northern Diamonds v. Central Sparks

Played at Emerald Headingley, Leeds, on May 29, 2021
Central Sparks won by 2 wickets

Toss won by Central Sparks   Central Sparks 4 points, Northern Diamonds 0 points

NORTHERN DIAMONDS

§ L Winfield-Hill, c Fackrell b Butler	110
* H L Armitage, b Wong	13
N R Sciver, c E Jones b Arlott	7
S L Kalis, lbw b Glenn	36
K H Brunt, c Fackrell b Wong	43
A Campbell, c E Jones b Butler	4
J L Gunn, c A E Jones b Wong	17
A L Mac Donald, c A E Jones b Wong	13
B A Langston, c Glenn b Wong	13
L C N Smith, not out	1
K A Levick, c Davies b Russell	0
Extras lb 2, w 18. nb 2	22
Total (49.2 overs)	279

FoW: 1-20 (Armitage), 2-38 (Sciver), 3-150 (Kalis), 4-207 (Winfield-Hill), 5-211 (Campbell), 6-242 (Brunt), 7-257 (Macdonald), 8-277 (Gunn), 9-278 (Langston), 10-279 (Levick)

	O	M	R	W
Wong	10	1	49	5
Arlott	8	1	44	1
Russell	5.2	0	35	1
Butler	6	0	46	2
Glenn	10	1	35	1
E Jones	3	0	18	0
Fackrell	7	0	50	0

CENTRAL SPARKS

* E Jones, c Winfield-Hill b Brunt	0
G M Davies, lbw b Langston	0
M Kelly, c Brunt b Smith	31
§ A E Jones, c Campbell b Gunn	114
M Home, c Winfield-Hill b Smith	1
S Butler, c Gunn b Smith	3
S Glenn, not out	71
R A Fackrell, c Sciver b Langston	9
J E C M Wong, c and b Brunt	0
E L Arlott, not out	24
E A Russell Did not bat	
Extras b 12, lb 6, w 12	30
Total (8 wkts, 48.2 overs)	283

FoW: 1-6 (Davies), 2-6 (Jones), 3-109 (Kelly), 4-122 (Home), 5-134 (Butler), 6-164 (A E Jones), 7-194 (Fackrell), 8-196 (Wong)

	O	M	R	W
Brunt	9	3	41	2
Langston	8	2	26	2
Levick	4	0	30	0
Sciver	8.2	0	64	0
Gunn	10	0	50	1
Smith	9	0	54	3

Umpires: Hasan Adnan and J Naeem   Scorers: K N Hutchinson and V K Holliday

Northern Diamonds v. Central Sparks

Turnaround to disaster

Lauren Winfield-Hill's first career century at Headingley proved in vain as her England teammate, Amy Jones, matched her, and Sarah Glenn also starred to underpin a remarkable Central Sparks run chase in the opening game of the regional summer.

Brilliant Winfield-Hill opened the batting after the Diamonds had been inserted, scoring 110 off 126 balls. She reached three figures with one of her three sixes, a towering blow into the West Stand.

She received support from Sterre Kalis (36) and Katherine Brunt (43), and once she was out in the 42nd over at 207-4 the Diamonds were on course for a commanding 279 all out.

Highly-rated England fringe fast bowler Issy Wong claimed five wickets for the Sparks.

LAUREN WINFIELD-HILL
Brilliant century in vain

The drama was only just beginning. Openers Gwen Davies and Eve Jones fell for ducks inside the opening three overs before Amy Jones and Marie Kelly steadied the Sparks with a century stand to leave the chase at 109-2 in the 25th over.

Kelly's departure for 31 was the first of six wickets to fall for 87, three of them to the left-arm spin of Linsey Smith, who would benefit from a stunning one-handed catch from Jenny Gunn to help to remove Steph Butler. The Sparks slipped to 196-8, including the loss of Jones for a fine run-a-ball 114.

With 9.5 overs remaining the Sparks still needed 84 with two wickets left. It would not be stretching the truth to suggest that 95 times out of 100 it would be game over. This was one of those rarities.

Another of the raft of England internationals available for this game, leg-spinner Glenn walloped six sixes in 71 off 52 and shared an unbroken ninth-wicket stand of 87 with Emily Arlott (24). That the game was done with 10 balls remaining added to the jaw-dropping nature of the turnaround as the Diamonds were left licking their wounds after dominating most of the fixture.

Rachael Heyhoe-Flint Trophy 2021
Lightning v. Northern Diamonds

Played at Kibworth Cricket Club New Ground, Kibworth, on May 31, 2021
Northern Diamond won by 6 runs

Toss won by Lightning   Northern Diamonds 4 points, Lightning 0 points

NORTHERN DIAMONDS

§ L Winfield-Hill, c Higham b K E Bryce	2
* H L Armitage, c Gordon b K E Bryce	12
N R Sciver, c Beaumont b Munro	10
S L Kalis, b T M Graves	7
K H Brunt, c and b K E Bryce	1
A Campbell, c Kirk b T M Graves	9
J L Gunn, c Beaumont b K E Bryce	40
A L MacDonald, b Higham	39
B A Langston, c Freeborn b Y Graves	11
H L Fenby, not out	2
K A Levick, c S J Bryce b Higham	3
Extras b 1, lb 1, w 13	15
Total (45.5 overs)	151

FoW: 1-2 (Winfield-Hill), 2-28 (Sciver), 3-28 (Armitage), 4-30 (Brunt), 5-46 (Kalis), 6-50 (Campbell), 7-131 (Gunn), 8-144 (Langston), 9-146 (MacDonald), 10-151 (Levick)

	O	M	R	W
K E Bryce	8	2	16	4
Munro	7	1	21	1
Gordon	10	1	25	0
T M Graves	7	1	32	2
Higham	7.5	0	37	2
Y Graves	6	0	18	1

LIGHTNING

§ S J Bryce, b Brunt	0
T T Beaumont, lbw b Sciver	21
* K E Bryce, c Winfield-Hill b Brunt	1
§ A J Freeborn, c Winfield-Hill b Sciver	20
L F Higham, c Sciver b Levick	1
M L Kirk, lbw b Brunt	14
S Pai, lbw b Levick	9
T M Graves, c and b Langston	14
Y Graves, c Gunn b Brunt	19
K L Gordon, c Winfield-Hill b Langston	19
S Munro, not out	0
Extras b 1, lb 9, w 16, nb 1	27
Total (48.1 overs)	145

FoW: 1-0 (S J Bryce), 2-7 (K E Bryce), 3-51 (Freeborn), 4-57 (Higham), 5-57 (Beaumont), 6-75 (Pai), 7-92 (Kirk), 8-109 (T M Graves), 9-139 (Y Graves), 10-145 (Gordon)

	O	M	R	W
Brunt	10	3	23	4
Langston	8.1	0	32	2
Sciver	10	1	24	2
Levick	10	2	26	2
Gunn	9	0	23	0
Armitage	1	0	7	0

Umpires: J Ibbotson and M Newall   Scorers: K Gerrard and K Kilby

Lightning v. Northern Diamonds

Tiger Brunt bares her teeth

England stars present and past underpinned a thrilling Diamonds comeback victory over the Lightning in the leafy Leicestershire countryside.

Katherine Brunt's fabulous 4-23 from 10 overs steered a tigerish defence of a 152 target, while Nat Sciver and Jenny Gunn were also key contributors.

The Lightning, at 144-9, needed eight off two overs with one wicket remaining before seamer Beth Langston had Kirstie Gordon caught behind.

A top-order collapse left the Diamonds 50-6 inside 15 overs having been inserted, but ex-international Gunn hit a measured 40, the top-score in 151 all out.

Current England stars Brunt and Sciver then put the skids under the Lightning (57-5) with two wickets apiece, but the hosts held firm to set up a dramatic conclusion.

Other crucial Bank Holiday Monday contributors were Alex MacDonald (39), Katie Levick (2-26 from 10 overs of leg-spin) and Langston (2-32 from 8.1).

KATHERINE BRUNT
Fabulous 4-23

The medium-paced in-swing of captain Kathryn Bryce (4-16) and Teresa Graves had prospered for Lightning on a slow pitch, with most of the visitors top order caught. Seventh-wicket pair Gunn and MacDonald shared 81 inside 24 overs, playing similarly composed innings.

The Diamonds lost their last four for 20 before the defence was started ideally by spearhead Brunt, who uprooted Sarah Bryce's off-stump and had sister Kathryn caught behind: 7-2 in the third over.

England opener Tammy Beaumont was always going to be a key scalp. She shared 44 for the third wicket with Abi Freeborn, only to fall as one of three wickets for six runs. Sciver played her part in all, trapping Beaumont lbw for 21 as the score became 57-5.

Lightning slipped to 109-8 in the 39th over, only for Yvonne Graves and Gordon to heighten tensions by sharing 30. Brunt had Graves caught at mid-on in the 48th over before Langston struck the winning blow as Winfield-Hill caught Gordon.

Rachael Heyhoe-Flint Trophy 2021
Sunrisers v. Northern Diamonds

Played at F P Fenner's Ground, Cambridge, on June 5, 2021
Northern Diamonds won by 9 wickets

Toss won by Northern Diamonds   Northern Diamonds 5 points, Sunrisers 0 points

SUNRISERS

G F Scrivens, c Winfield-Hill b Langston	1
A J Macleod, lbw b Brunt	3
F C Wilson, c MacDonald b Gunn	6
C L Griffith, b Brunt	0
N D Dattani, b Langston	0
M K Villiers, b Brunt	1
*§ A D Carr, st Winfield-Hill b Smith	17
J L Gardner, b Gunn	0
K S Castle, b Gunn	0
G K S Gole, b Levick	11
K L Coppack, not out	4
Extras lb 4, w 6	10
Total (29.1 overs)	53

FoW: 1-5 (Macleod), 2-5 (Scrivens), 3-22 (Griffith), 4-15 (Dattani), 5-16 (Villiers), 6-23 (Wilson), 7-28 (Gardener), 8-36 (Castle), 9-45 (Carr), 10-53 (Gole)

	O	M	R	W
Langston	5	1	12	2
Brunt	8	3	11	3
Sciver	5	1	13	0
Gunn	6	1	10	3
Smith	5	3	3	1
Levick	0.1	0	0	1

NORTHERN DIAMONDS

§ L Winfield-Hill, c Carr b Coppack	7
* H L Armitage, not out	14
N R Sciver, not out	9
S L Kalis	
K H Brunt	
A Campbell	
J L Gunn Did not bat	
A L MacDonald	
B A Langston	
L C N Smith	
K A Levick	
Extras lb 6, w 18	24
Total (1 wkt, 7.4 overs)	54

FoW: 1-24 (Winfield-Hill)

	O	M	R	W
Dattani	2	0	22	0
Coppack	3	0	14	1
Castle	2	1	4	0
Gardner	0.4	0	8	0

Umpires: S M Bartlett and J Ibbotson   Scorers: Q L S Jones and A J Thurogood

Sunrisers v. Northern Diamonds

Carnage at Cambridge

It was carnage in Cambridge as the Diamonds won in double-quick time, bowling Sunrisers out for 53 inside 30 overs to win by nine wickets.

Katherine Brunt and Jenny Gunn were the destroyers in chief with three wickets apiece at the Fenner's University ground.

It was a miserable afternoon for the hosts, who went through the shortened 2020 season without victory and had started this campaign in the same fashion. Only two of their batters reached double figures, headed by captain Amara Carr's 17, while they conceded 24 extras in a meek defence.

As soon as Brunt and Beth Langston shared five wickets with the new ball, having elected to bowl, the Sunrisers never looked like recovering to post a competitive total. Brunt struck first in the fourth over, trapping Amy Macleod lbw before fellow opener Grace Scrivens fell in the next over, caught behind off Langston.

From then on it was a procession. Four Sunrisers batters, including England off-spinner Mady Villiers, fell for ducks. Two went to Gunn, who also dismissed Fran Wilson — another current England player — for six. The left-arm spin of Linsey Smith later chipped in with the wicket of top-scorer Carr, smartly stumped by Lauren Winfield-Hill.

JENNY GUNN
Double-quick victory

The Sunrisers highest partnership was just nine for the ninth wicket between Carr and Gayatri Gole.

The modest target presented no problems, with Winfield-Hill the only wicket to fall when she chased a wide one from opening bowler Kate Coppack and feathered behind for seven. Captain Hollie Armitage and Nat Sciver hit two boundaries apiece in not out scores of 14 and nine, but that tally of 24 extras, including 18 wides, proved the top score.

It was kind of apt, therefore, that the winning run came via a wide from Jo Gardner in the eighth over, handing the Diamonds their second win in three matches.

Rachael Heyhoe-Flint Trophy 2021
Northern Diamonds v. South East Stars

Played at Emerald Headingley, Leeds, on June 12, 2021
Northern Diamonds won by 3 wickets

Toss won by South East Stars   Northern Diamonds 4 points, South East Stars 0 points

SOUTH EAST STARS

* B F Smith, b Levick	31
A N Davidson-Richards, b Gunn	14
* C Brewer, lbw b Smith	25
§ K E White, b Langston	73
A R Capsey, c Campbell b Graham	21
A Cranstone, not out	42
G J Gibbs, b Gunn	1
P A Franklin, not out	28
§ KM Chathli	
D L Gregory Did not bat	
F R Davies	
Extras lb 1, w 14	15
Total (6 wkts, 50 overs)	250

FoW: 1-50 (Davidson-Richards), 2-50 (Smith), 3-106 (Brewer), 4-157 (Capsey), 5-196 (White), 6-203 (Gibbs).

	O	M	R	W
Langston	10	0	62	1
Graham	8	1	38	1
Gunn	9	1	45	2
Levick	7	0	30	1
Smith	10	0	31	1
MacDonald	3	0	21	0
Armitage	3	0	22	0

NORTHERN DIAMONDS

* H J Armitage, c Chathli b Davies	21
R H M Hopkins, lbw b Gibbs	12
S L Kalis, run out (Gibbs)	76
A L MacDonald, c Davidson-Richards b Gibbs	5
A Campbell, c Cranstone b Gregory	0
§ S J Taylor, b Gregory	2
J L Gunn, c Franklin b Smith	50
B A Langston, not out	59
L C N Smith, not out	7
P C Graham	
K A Levick Did not bat	
Extras lb 7, w 14, nb 1	22
Total (7 wkts, 49.2 overs)	254

FoW: 1-35 (Armitage), 2-58 (Hopkins), 3-64 (MacDonald), 4-65 (Campbell), 5-70 (Taylor), 6-160 (Gunn), 7-209 (Kalis).

	O	M	R	W
Davies	9.2	1	57	1
Davidson-Richards	7	0	49	0
Gibbs	8	0	40	2
Smith	10	0	40	1
Gregory	10	1	31	2
Franklin	2	0	16	0
Capsey	3	0	14	0

Umpires: T Lungley and J Naeem   Scorers: K N Hutchinson and V K Holliday

Northern Diamonds v. South East Stars

Thrilling comeback to the top

Beth Langston, Sterre Kalis and Jenny Gunn steered the Diamonds to the top of the table with a third win in four, as South East Stars came out the wrong end of another Headingley thriller.

The Diamonds won by three wickets with four balls to spare chasing 251 to replace Central Sparks at the summit.

Victory was unlikely at 70-5 in the 16th over of the chase after Kirstie White's 73 off 90 balls had underpinned the Stars' 250-6.

But Langston, Kalis and Gunn all scored crucial half-centuries, the aggressive Langston hitting the winning runs in the last over as she clubbed England seamer Freya Davies over mid-wicket. Dutch international Kalis top-scored with 76 off 106 balls, while Gunn made 50 off 70. They kick-started the recovery with a 90-run sixth-wicket stand before unbeaten Langston held her nerve as tensions increased, finishing with 59 off 53.

STERRE KALIS: Kick-started the recovery with fine 76

Sarah Taylor, warming up for the Hundred, returned to professional cricket after two years away and impressively stood in for wicket-keeping absentees Lauren Winfield-Hill (England duty) and Bess Heath (injured). In the final game before the beginning of other competitions Diamonds looked set for defeat when they lost four wickets for 12 to fall from 58-1 in the 11th.

Experienced White advanced the Stars after they had elected to bat in the sunshine. The Diamonds dropped three catches of varying difficulty: Taylor was responsible for the first in the contest's second over, when Alice Davidson-Richards edged Phoebe Graham behind on one. But, diving to her right, it would have been a stunner.

Gunn struck twice, but White harnessed power and invention to put Stars in command. That position was significantly strengthened inside 14 overs of the chase as the Diamonds slipped to 65-4, bringing Taylor in. She was bowled for two off an under-edged pull at Dani Gregory's leg-spin: 70-5...but then came the thrilling, successful fightback.

Rachael Heyhoe-Flint Trophy 2021
Northern Diamonds v. Western Storm

Played at Emirates Riverside, Chester-le-Street, on September 10, 2021
Northern Diamonds won by 7 wickets

Toss won by Northern Diamonds   Northern Diamonds 5 points, Western Storm 0 points

WESTERN STORM

F K M Morris, c Heath b Langston	30
G M Hennessy, b Langston	5
*S N Luff, b Smith	65
A C Griffiths, c Heath b Smith	36
D R Gibson, lbw b Levick	0
§N A J Wraith, b Smith	0
B Gammon, b Levick	0
C Skelton, b Smith	30
J L Roberts, b Smith	0
L Filer, run out (Telford/Heath)	0
S Hutchins, not out	0
Extras lb 2, w 15	17
Total ((38.1 overs)	183

FoW: 1-21 (Hennessy), 2-44 (Morris), 3-109 (Griffiths), 4-110 (Gibson), 5-111 (Wraith), 6-112 (Gammon), 7-173 (Skelton), 8-175 (Roberts), 9-183 (Filer), 10-183 (Luff)

	O	M	R	W
Langston	7	2	30	2
Telford	7	0	40	0
Graham	6	0	45	0
Smith	9.1	0	34	5
Gunn	1	0	7	0
Levick	8	0	25	2

NORTHERN DIAMONDS

L Winfield-Hill, lbw b Hennessy	16
*H J Armitage, not out	68
S L Kalis, lbw b Hutchins	32
L Dobson, lbw b Hutchins	16
§B A M Heath, not out	32
J L Gunn	
B A Langston	
L C N Smith Did not bat	
P Graham	
K A Levick	
E F Telford	
Extras lb 3, w 16, nb 1	20
Total (3 wkts, 31.1 overs)	184

FoW: 1-38 (Winfield-Hill), 2-97 (Kalis), 3-130 (Dobson)

	O	M	R	W
Filer	5	2	24	0
Gibson	2	0	14	0
Hennessy	8	0	35	1
Morris	3	0	27	0
Griffiths	3	0	19	0
Hutchins	5	0	27	2
Skelton	3	0	20	0
Roberts	2.1	0	15	0

Umpires: J D Middlebrook and L Nenova   Scorers: G Maddison and P Summerside

Northern Diamonds v. Western Storm

Smith has Storm in a spin

Linsey Smith claimed a fabulous career best 5-34 as the Diamonds clinically defeated Western Storm to take a significant step towards the RHF Trophy knockout stages.

Captain Hollie Armitage contributed an unbeaten 68 in a seven-wicket win chasing down 184.

Opposing skipper Sophie Luff top-scored with 65, though she was one of Smith's victims in her best ever List A performance.

Luff was one of four Storm batters bowled by the left-arm spinner, whose other scalp in her 9.1-over spell was a caught behind as the visitors slipped from strength at 109-2 in the 19th over to 183 all out inside 39.

LINSEY SMITH: Career-best 5-34 puts knockouts in sight

Luff was last out, with Beth Langston and Katie Levick both impressing with two wickets apiece. Storm, whose innings included four ducks having been inserted, were then always going to find it tough to defend their total. So it proved as classy Armitage led from the front, sealing victory with 18.5 overs to spare.

Armitage reached her fifty from 53 balls, and was unbeaten at the end, alongside Bess Heath (32 not out) to guide their side home with ease. It was their fourth victory in five games in the competition.

While only four Storm batters reached double figures, each of the Diamonds top five achieved that feat in a chase which never looked like faltering. England opener Lauren Winfield-Hill fell with the score at 38 in the sixth over before Armitage and Sterre Kalis shared 59 for the second wicket to turn the screw.

The Diamonds' scorecard had a very symmetrical look: in support of Armitage, who hit seven fours in her 69-ball innings, both Kalis and Heath made 32, while Winfield-Hill and Leah Dobson made 16.

This was the first 50-over fixture since mid-June following the completion of the Charlotte Edwards (T20) Cup and the Hundred. Success put the Diamonds just one more win away from a knockout berth.

Rachael Heyhoe-Flint Trophy 2021
Northern Diamonds v. Thunder

Played at Emirates Riverside, Chester-le-Street, on September 12, 2021
Northern Diamonds won by 105 runs

Toss won by Thunder   Northern Diamonds 5 points, Thunder 0 points

NORTHERN DIAMONDS
* H J Armitage, c Brown b Dyson	7
R H M Hopkins, c Threlkeld b Brown	20
S L Kalis, c Turner b Hartley	57
L Dobson, run out (Hartley)	9
A Campbell, c Marshall b Jones	48
§ B A M Heath, not out	78
L C N Smith, c Threlkeld b Hartley	6
B A Langston, not out	58
P Graham	
K A Levick Did not bat	
E F Telford	
Extras b 2, w 9	11
Total (6 wkts, 50 overs)	294

FoW: 1-18 (Armitage), 2-65 (Hopkins), 3-86 (Dobson), 4-122 (Kalis), 5-176 (Campbell), 6-203 (Smith)

	O	M	R	W
Jackson	10	1	59	0
Dyson	9	0	59	1
Brown	8.2	1	55	1
Jones	10	0	54	1
Lamb	2.4	1	8	0
Hartley	10	0	57	2

THUNDER
C E B Boyce, c Telford b Armitage	67
S A Smale, c Heath b Graham	12
§ E Threlkeld, lbw b Levick	13
D E Mullan, c Langston b Armitage	8
N Brown, run out (Armitage)	2
L Marshall, lbw b Levick	42
L E Jackson, b Levick	22
A E Dyson, c Armitage b Levick	3
H L Jones, not out	3
* A Hartley, not out	6
E L Lamb Did not bat	
Extras lb 3, w 8	11
Total (8 wkts, 50 overs)	189

FoW: 1-38 (Smale), 2-74 (Threlkeld), 3-99 (Mullan), 4-109 (Boyce), 5-111 (Brown), 6-166 (Jackson), 7-178 (Dyson), 8-180 (Marshall)

	O	M	R	W
Langston	7	3	12	0
Telford	5	0	41	0
Smith	10	2	26	0
Graham	10	0	41	1
Levick	10	0	34	4
Armitage	8	0	32	2

Umpires: H M S Adnan and J Ibbotson   Scorers: G Maddison and S Blacklock

Northern Diamonds v. Thunder

Red Rose wilts again

BESS HEATH: Brisk 78 not out helped Diamonds to the eliminator

Knockout cricket was secured on the back of a dominant batting display as the *Roses* rivals were hammered twice in a fortnight.

At the end of August the Diamonds had dispatched Thunder in the Charlotte Edwards Cup, and they did it again, courtesy of a trio of half-centuries and then four wickets for Katie Levick.

Having been inserted, Diamonds amassed 294-6 in an innings which was disrupted, but not shortened, by the Durham rain.

Bess Heath top-scored with a brisk 78 off 65 balls, her fifth score of 50 or more in List A cricket, while Sterre Kalis (57) and Beth Langston reached the same milestone. Langston's 58 not out came off 30 balls, and included seven boundaries to push the total from a good one to something completely beyond Thunder's reach.

Ami Campbell's 48, including the only two sixes of the innings, should not be forgotten.

Thunder's chances of success were undermined by a broken thumb suffered by England batting all-rounder Emma Lamb, a player who had already shone against the Diamonds during the summer. She was struck in her follow-through while bowling.

In reply, there was never any chance of a Thunder victory even though opener Georgie Boyce made an early 67. They were unable to gain any momentum, and lost wickets at regular intervals. When Boyce holed out off the leg-spin of Hollie Armitage the visitors were 109-4 early in the 33rd over and still 186 runs short.

Superb Levick's first wicket on the way to 4-34 from 10 overs was that of Ellie Threlkeld, trapped lbw to leave the score at 74-2. From there she bowled Laura Jackson, had Alice Dyson caught and trapped lbw Laura Marshall, the only Thunder batter to show any signs of aggression during a 40-ball 42.

The Diamonds had ensured themselves at least a place in the semi-final eliminator.

Rachael Heyhoe-Flint Trophy 2021
Southern Vipers v. Northern Diamonds

Played at The Ageas Bowl, West End, Southampton, on September 18, 2021
Southern Vipers won by 5 wickets

Toss won by Northern Diamonds   Southern Vipers 4 points, Northern Diamonds 0 points

NORTHERN DIAMONDS

* H J Armitage, b Elwiss	21
R H M Hopkins, c Elwiss b Norris	0
S L Kalis, st Rudd b Bouchier	23
L Dobson, run out (McCaughan)	49
A Campbell, c Adams b Bell	26
§ B A M Heath, run out (McCaughan)	71
L C N Smith, c Scolfield b Adams	37
B A Langston, b Bell	0
P Graham, b Scholfield	1
R Slater, lbw b Scholfield	0
E F Telford, not out	0
Extras b 2, lb 2, w 25	29
Total (48.3 overs)	257

FoW: 1-2 (Hopkins), 2-43 (Armitage), 3-56 (Kalis), 4-104 (Campbell), 5-170 (Dobson), 6-248 (Heath), 7-248 (Langston), 8-251 (Graham), 9-252 (Slater), 10-256 (Smith)

	O	M	R	W
Bell	10	2	29	2
Norris	7	0	57	1
Elwiss	10	2	43	1
Taylor	4	0	33	0
Scolfield	8	0	35	2
Bouchier	3	0	20	1
Adams	6.3	1	36	1

SOUTHERN VIPERS

* G L Adams, c Smith b Graham	67
E M McCaughan, run out (Heath)	2
M E Bouchier, c Armitage b Graham	40
G A Elwiss, not out	84
G H Lewis, lbw b Graham	39
E L Windsor, run out (Campbell)	1
P J Scholfield, not out	15
T G Norris	
§ C E Rudd Did not bat	
L K Bell	
C M Taylor	
Extras lb 1, w 10, nb 1	12
Total (5 wkts, 48.5 overs)	260

FoW: 1-7 (McCaughan), 2-74 (Bouchier), 3-163 (Adams), 4-225 (Lewis), 5-226 (Windsor)

	O	M	R	W
Langston	9	1	26	0
Slater	10	0	47	0
Graham	10	0	44	3
Smith	9.5	0	73	0
Telford	2	0	17	0
Armitage	8	0	52	0

Umpires: S McLelland and I N Ramage   Scorers: I Thompson and C Green

Southern Vipers v. Northern Diamonds

For want of key bowlers...

Only net run-rate separated regional cricket's top two sides ahead of the final round of group fixtures. The Diamonds narrowly led the way from the Vipers, the winner advancing directly through to the final a week later.

It was a repeat of last year's final, and it would be the Vipers, the defending champions, who would take the honours by five wickets with seven balls to spare.

Having elected to bat, the visitors, missing key bowlers Jenny Gunn, Katie Levick and Alex MacDonald through injury and unavailability, were reduced to 56-3 after 18 overs before an exhilarating recovery underpinned by Bess Heath, Leah Dobson (49) Linsey Smith (37) and Ami Campbell (26).

Heath played the lead role with 71 off 51 balls, her second successive score in the seventies, cracking eight fours and two sixes...but she was the first of the last five wickets to fall for eight runs, meaning the total of 256 all out was nothing more than competitive.

New-ball seamer Lauren Bell impressed with 2-29 from 10 overs.

The flow of both innings was similar — tough to score early on before acceleration. Vipers were 7-1 with the run-out of Ella McCaughan, but their strong top order comfortably reeled in the target.

PHOEBE GRAHAM
Three vital wickets

Captain and opener Georgia Adams made a measured 67, sharing half-century partnerships for the second and third wickets with England batters Maia Bouchier (40) and Georgia Elwiss. Fresh from a century in their last match, Elwiss posted an unbeaten 84 off 77 balls, and rarely looked in any trouble against an attack shorn of key wicket-takers.

Seamer Phoebe Graham impressed with 3-44 from her 10 overs, removing Adams, Bouchier and Irish international Gaby Lewis for 39, but the Vipers booked their place at Northampton. Would the Diamonds follow them there? They had to face Central Sparks at Scarborough in a midweek semi-final eliminator.

Rachael Heyhoe-Flint Trophy 2021 Eliminator
Northern Diamonds v. Central Sparks

Played at North Marine Road, Scarborough, on September 22, 2021
Northern Diamonds won by 6 wickets
Toss won by Central Sparks

CENTRAL SPARKS

*E Jones, c Kalis b Slater	9
M Kelly, lbw b Langston	0
D Perrin, c Campbell b Slater	1
G M Davies, lbw b Langston	42
T F Brookes, c Kalis b Smith	11
I Wong, lbw b Smith	0
§C A E Hill, c Campbell b Levick	14
R A Fackrell, not out	42
E L Arlott, not out	29
C K Boycott	
G K Davis Did not bat	
Extras lb 1, w 26	27
Total (7 wkts, 50 overs)	175

FoW: 1-1 (Kelly), 2-2 (Perrin), 3-35 (Jones), 4-67 (Brookes), 5-68 (Wong), 6-98 (Davies), 7-101 (Hill)

	O	M	R	W
Langston	10	1	29	2
Slater	8	0	39	2
Smith	10	2	25	2
Graham	9	0	44	0
Levick	10	1	25	1
Armitage	3	0	12	0

NORTHERN DIAMONDS

*H J Armitage, c Arlott b Davis	25
R H M Hopkins, c Hill b Arlott	11
S L Kalis, not out	41
L Dobson, b Arlott	0
A Campbell, c sub (G E A Potts) b Kelly	76
§B A M Heath, not out	6
L C N Smith	
B A Langston	
P Graham Did not bat	
R Slater	
K A Levick	
Extras b 1, lb 5, w 11	17
Total (4 wkts, 32.5 overs)	176

FoW: 1-33 (Armitage), 2-42 (Hopkins), 3-42 (Dobson), 4-158 (Campbell)

	O	M	R	W
Wong	3	0	30	0
Davis	10	0	35	1
Arlott	9	2	35	2
Boycott	3	0	23	0
Fackrell	4	0	20	0
Perrin	1	0	10	0
Kelly	1.5	0	9	1
Jones	1	0	8	0

Umpires: S Bartlett and R A White   Scorers: K N Hutchinson and V K Holliday

Northern Diamonds v. Central Sparks
Let's play that final again

Ami Campbell picked the perfect time to post her first half-century of a difficult summer as the Diamonds set up a repeat of last season's final against the Vipers.

The Northumbrian left-hander racked up 76 off 78 balls in a comfortable chase of 176, sealing the win by seven wickets with 17.1 overs remaining.

Campbell struggled for form at the start of 2021 before being struck down by Coronavirus during the Hundred, delaying her return to action until the closing weeks of the campaign.

Beth Langston, Rachel Slater and Linsey Smith claimed two wickets before 42 apiece for Gwen Davies and Ria Fackrell lifted the Sparks from 68-5 to 175-7. Diamonds then fell from 33-0 to 42-3 in reply before the aggressive Campbell and more reserved Sterre Kalis (42 not out) shared a telling 116 for the fourth wicket.

AMI CAMPBELL: Triumphant return after a tough summer

In-form Sparks captain Eve Jones elected to bat amid morning dew, and was one of three wickets to fall inside the opening 10 overs after miscuing a cut at Slater's left-arm seam to point: 35-3. Marie Kelly and Issy Wong were both trapped lbw for golden ducks, Wong as one of two wickets in three balls for left-arm spinner Smith in the 17th: 68-5.

Davies and Fackrell played in reserved fashion in their attempt to turn the tide, and they managed to gain respectability with the help of Emily Arlott's 29. Fackrell and Arlott shared an unbroken 74 for the eighth wicket, but it proved nowhere near enough against returns of 2-29 and 2-25 from Langston and Smith.

Captain Hollie Armitage got the chase off to a flyer with five fours in her first nine balls before falling for 25. England fringe seamer Arlott then struck twice as the score fell to 42-3 after nine overs, but that was as good as it got for Sparks, who were faced with a 51-ball fifty for top-scorer Campbell.

Rachael Heyhoe-Flint Trophy 2021 Final
Southern Vipers v. Northern Diamonds

Played at the County Ground, Wantage Road, Northampton, on September 25, 2021

Southern Vipers won by 3 wickets

Toss won by Northern Diamonds

NORTHERN DIAMONDS

* H J Armitage, b Scholfield	16
L C N Smith, c Lewis b Adams	31
S L Kalis, lbw b Adams	18
L Dobson, b Taylor	0
A Campbell, c Windsor b Elwiss	60
§ B A M Heath, lbw b Norris	25
J L Gunn, c Lewis b Adams	2
B A Langston, lbw b Adams	0
P Graham, b Taylor	0
K A Levick, c Rudd b Norris	8
R Slater, not out	6
Extras b 1, lb 4, w 11, nb 1	17
Total (49.2 overs)	183

FoW: 1-35 (Armitage), 2-72 (Smith), 3-73 (Dobson), 4-73 (Kalis), 5-112 (Heath), 6-115 (Gunn), 7-115 (Langston), 8-116 (Graham), 9-144 (Levick), 10-183 (Campbell)

	O	M	R	W
Bell	10	0	46	0
Norris	10	1	36	2
Elwiss	6.2	0	25	1
Scholfield	3	1	10	1
Taylor	10	0	26	2
Adams	10	1	35	4

SOUTHERN VIPERS

* G L Adams, b Langston	0
E M McCaughan, b Langston	0
M E Bouchier, st Heath b Levick	33
G A Elwiss, c Heath b Graham	14
G H Lewis, b Gunn	24
E L Windsor, not out	47
P J Scholfield, c Armitage b Gunn	9
§ C E Rudd, lbw b Gunn	0
T G Norris, not out	40
L K Bell	
C M Taylor	
Did not bat	
Extras lb 4, w 16	20
Total (7 wkts, 49.4 overs)	187

FoW: 1-0 (Adams), 2-6 (McCaughan), 3-47 (Elwiss), 4-62 (Bouchier), 5-93 (Lewis), 6-109 (Scholfield), 7-109 (Rudd)

	O	M	R	W
Langston	9.4	0	40	2
Slater	4	0	14	0
Graham	6	1	38	1
Gunn	10	0	31	3
Levick	10	2	20	1
Smith	10	2	40	0

Player of the Match: E L Windsor

Umpires: J Naeem and N J Pratt Scorers: Q L S Jones and H Vernon

Southern Vipers v. Northern Diamonds
Comebacks lead to dead end

The Diamonds were left contemplating another final defeat as Emily Windsor and Tara Norris staged a dramatic late rally to steal victory for the defending champions.

The Vipers looked like they had come up short in pursuit of 184 when Katie Levick (1-20) and Jenny Gunn (3-31) reduced them to 109-7.

Then Windsor, with 47, and Norris (40) shared an unbroken 78 to seal back-to-back titles by three wickets with two balls remaining.

While Norris added to two earlier wickets, Windsor was named player of the match after a number of Diamonds players had sunk to their knees following the winning blow.

Ami Campbell (60) scored a half-century for the second time in four days to drag Diamonds from 116-8 to 183, Georgia Adams taking 4-35 with her part-time off-spin.

Diamonds promoted Linsey Smith to open, and she solidly made 31 before becoming the first victim for

KATIE LEVICK: Leg-spin strangled the run-rate

Adams, the first of three wickets for one run: 73-4 in the 23rd over. Another collapse of four wickets for four runs followed. At 116-8 Diamonds were on the ropes, but left-handed Campbell struck four boundaries to reach 50 in 63 balls. By the time she holed out in the final over the last two wickets had accrued 67 and regained momentum.

The 183 total looked worth more when Beth Langston bowled Adams and Ella McCaughan for ducks to leave Vipers on 6-2. Maia Bouchier pulled the game's first six, but Phoebe Graham removed in-form Georgia Elwiss, caught behind for 14. Bouchier reached 33 before being stumped by Bess Heath off the leg-spin of Levick, who strangled the rate with Smith's help. With pressure mounting Jenny Gunn castled Gaby Lewis before having Paige Scholfield brilliantly caught by Hollie Armitage and trapping Carla Rudd first ball. Norris saved the hat-trick, and so began the match-winning stand from 109-7 in the 35th.

Second Eleven 2021

PLAYERS WHO APPEARED FOR YORKSHIRE SECOND ELEVEN IN 2021
(excluding First Eleven capped players)

Player	Date of Birth	Birthplace	Type
H G Duke*	September 6, 2001	Wakefield	RHB/WK
M D Fisher*	November 9, 1997	York	RHB/RMF
W A R Fraine*	June 13, 1996	Huddersfield	RHB/RM
G C H Hill*	January 24, 2001	Keighley	RHB/RMF
D J Leech*	January 10, 2001	Midddlesbrough	RHB/RMF
J W Shutt*	June 24, 1997	Barnsley	RHB/OB
J A Tattersall*	December 15, 1994	Knaresborough	RHB/LB
J A Thompson*	October 9, 1996	Leeds	LHB/RFM
M J Waite*	December 24, 1995	Leeds	RHB/RMF
H J J Allinson §	November 2, 2003	Harrogate	RH/LB
B D Birkhead	October 28, 1998	Halifax	RHB/WK
E F Booth §	October 19, 2001	Dewsbury	RHB/RFM
B M Cliff §	October 23, 2002	Halifax	RHB/RFM
T W Loten	January 8, 1999	York	RHB/RMF
W A Luxton §	May 6, 2003	Keighley	RHB
J Mukherjee §	January 8, 2002	Keighley	RHB/RM
M W Pillans	July 4, 1991	Westville, Kwa-Zulu Natal, South Africa	RHB/RF
J E Poysden	August 8, 1991	Shoreham-by-Sea, Sussex	LHB/LB
N J Priestley §	November 1, 2003	Halifax	LHB/RM
M L Revis	November 15, 2001	Steeton, Keighley	RHB/RM
HA Sullivan §	December 17, 2002	Leeds	LHB/SLA
J R Sullivan	August 4, 2000	Leeds	RHB/LB
Y Vagadia §	May 7, 2004	Newcastle upon Tyne	RHB/OB
M G Weston §	October 15, 2003	Huddersfield	LHB/OB
J H Wharton	February 1, 2001	Huddersfield	RHB/OB
S A Wisniewski §	October 2, 2001	Huddersfield	LHB/LCh

* Second Eleven cap

§ Debutants

SECOND ELEVEN HIGHLIGHTS OF 2021

CHAMPIONSHIP
Century partnerships (7)
For the 1st wicket (2)
270	by W A R Fraine and T Kohler-Cadmore	v. Worcestershire at Scarborough
111	by W A R Fraine and J H Wharton	v. Lancashire at Scarborough

For the 3rd wicket (4)
214	by WAR Fraine and GCH Hill	v. Gloucestershire at Bristol
131	by J H Wharton and M L Revis	v. Worcestershire at Scarborough
120	by H G Duke and J H Wharton	v. Warwickshire at Weetwood
104	by J H Wharton and JA Tattersall	v. Lancashire at Scarborough

For the 8th wicket (1)
116	by M J Waite and M L Revis	v. Essex at Billericay

Centuries (7

W A R Fraine (2)
  186 v. Gloucestershire at Bristol
  122 v. Worcestershire at Scarborough

G C H Hill (1)
  207 v. Gloucestershire at Bristol

M J Waite (1)
  170 v. Essex at Billericay

T Kohler-Cadmore (1)
  136 v. Worcestershire at Scarborough

H J J Allinson (1)
  126 v. Lancashire at Boughton Hall Avenue, Chester

B D Birkhead (1)
  101* v. Warwickshire at Weetwood

Ten wickets in a match: – There was no instances. D J Leech took seven wickets v. Essex at Billericay and T W Loten also took seven against Worcestershire at Scarborough

Five wickets in an innings (2)

T W Loten (1)
  5-19 v. Worcestershire at Scarborough

D J Leech (1)
  5-28 v. Essex at Billericay

Five victims in an innings: No wicket-keeper managed this feat in 2021. The best return was five catches in a match by J A Tattersall v. Derbyshire at Weetwood

Six catches at slip: T Kohler-Cadmore achieved this feat v. Worcestershire at Scarborough

T20 COMPETITION
Century Partnerships (1)
For the 2nd wicket (1)
169	H G Duke and G S Ballance	v. Lancashire at Aigburth, Liverpool

Centuries (1)

G S Ballance (1)
  125 v. Lancashire at Aigburth, Liverpool

This is Yorkshire`s highest individual score in the Second Eleven T20 competition
Yorkshire`s total of 237-5 is their highest ever team total in the competition

5 wickets in an innings:– No player achieved this feat. The best returns were 4-28 by J W Shutt v. Durham at Weetwood and 4-36 by M D Fisher v. Derbyshire at Derby

Five victims in an innings:– No player approached this milestone in 2021.

MISCELLANEOUS STATISTICS

1. Yorkshire's 602-8 dec against Gloucestershire in the Second Eleven Championship was the first time in 628 Second Eleven matches that they had registered a total over 600. The previous highest was 585-8 dec against Lancashire at Scarborough in 2017.
2. G C H Hill registered his maiden Second Eleven Championship century against Gloucestershire at Bristol. His final score of 207 is the 10th highest individual score ever registered in the Second Eleven Championship by a Yorkshire player.
3. The third-wicket stand of 224 by W A R Fraine and G C H Hill is Yorkshire's highest for that wicket against Gloucestershire and the highest for that wicket on either side.
4. D J Leech's 5-28 in Essex's second innings is his best Second Eleven Championship analysis and his first five-for in that competition. His previous best was 2-20 v. Nottinghamshire in 2019 at Harrogate. He took his last three wickets in four deliveries. His 5-28 is the best for Yorkshire against Essex in the Championship, beating Ryan Sidebottom's 5-35 at Pudsey Congs in 2003. The last four Essex second innings wickets fell in eight deliveries for one run
5. Yorkshire's eighth-wicket stand of 116 between M J Waite and M L Revis is the highest for that wicket for Yorkshire in 14 Championship fixtures against Essex. The previous best was 87 by C A Chapman and S Bartle at Southend in 1992

SECOND ELEVEN CHAMPIONSHIP AVERAGES 2021

Played 11   Won 3   Lost 1   Drawn 6

The match against Durham at Headingley was abandoned when Covid broke out among the Durham players and coaching staff.

BATTING AND FIELDING

(Qualification 5 innings)

Player	M.	I.	N.O.	Runs	H.S.	Avge	100s	50s	ct/st
W A R Fraine	6	8	0	497	186	62.12	2	1	8
H G Duke	5	7	2	282	67	56.40	0	3	8/1
G C H Hill	5	9	0	449	207	49.88	1	1	6
M J Waite	3	6	0	262	170	43.67	1	1	1
B D Birkhead	10	16	3	467	101*	35.92	1	2	20/3
J H Wharton	10	16	0	560	88	35.00	0	6	6
M D Fisher	3	5	1	106	77	26.50	0	1	-
M L Revis	9	14	2	287	53	23.91	0	1	6
J R Sullivan	6	6	2	95	33*	23.75	0	0	1
M W Pillans	5	6	0	119	44	19.83	0	0	1
T W Loten	9	12	0	197	92	16.41	0	1	4
D J Leech	8	7	2	45	17*	9.00	0	0	2
J W Shutt	7	7	4	15	8	5.00	0	0	4

SECOND ELEVEN CHAMPIONSHIP AVERAGES 2021 *(Continued)*

BATTING AND FIELDING *(Continued)*

Players with fewer than five innings

Player	M.	I.	N.O.	Runs	H.S.	Avge	100s	50s	ct/st
T Kohler-Cadmore	1	1	0	136	136	136.00	1	0	6
H J J Allinson	3	4	1	179	126	59.67	1	0	0
B O Coad	1	1	0	57	57	57.00	0	1	0
J A Tattersall	3	4	0	122	62	30.50	0	1	5
J Mukherjee	6	4	1	59	36	19.67	0	0	1
Y Vagadia	3	4	0	73	29	18.25	0	0	2
M G Weston	1	2	0	31	17	15.50	0	0	2
W A Luxton	2	4	1	46	22*	15.33	0	0	2
D Olivier	2	1	0	15	15	15.00	0	0	0
B M Cliff	3	3	0	29	13	9.67	0	0	0
J E Poysden	1	1	0	7	7	7.00	0	0	0
H A Sullivan	6	1	0	7	7	7.00	0	0	0
N J Priestley	1	2	0	10	9	5.00	0	0	0
G S Ballance	1	1	0	1	1	1.00	0	0	0
E F Booth	4	2	2	6	3*	—	0	0	2
S A Wisniewski	1	1	1	12	12*	—	0	0	0
S A Patterson	1	0	0	0	—	—	0	0	1

BOWLING

(Qualification 10 wickets)

Player	Overs	Mdns	Runs	Wkts	Avge	Best	5wI	10wM
T W Loten	100.2	30	284	17	16.70	5-19	1	0
J W Shutt	214.5	51	571	29	19.68	5-94	1	0
D J Leech	177.5	42	582	24	24.25	5-28	1	0
M L Revis	103.5	20	327	12	27.25	2-21	0	0

Also bowled

B O Coad	26	10	42	5	8.40	3-29	0	0
M J Waite	53	11	148	9	16.44	3-9	0	0
S A Patterson	18	10	34	2	17.00	2-26	0	0
B M Cliff	45.5	15	124	5	24.80	2-16	0	0
J Mukherjee	61	14	225	9	25.00	3-36	0	0
J E Poysden	27.1	3	100	4	25.00	2-35	0	0
M D Fisher	39	8	109	4	27.25	3-43	0	0
G C H Hill	81	21	239	8	29.87	3-21	0	0
D Olivier	46	13	127	4	31.75	2-36	0	0
H A Sullivan	132.2	38	296	9	32.88	4-36	0	0
Y Vagadia	23	6	66	2	33.00	1-22	0	0
M W Pillans	95	29	268	6	44.67	3-22	0	0
J R Sullivan	53	6	229	2	114.50	1-16	0	0
E F Booth	41	11	125	1	125.00	1-33	0	0
S A Wisniewski	12	2	33	0	—	—	0	0
N J Priestley	4	0	16	0	—	—	0	0
J H Wharton	0	0	5	0	—	—	0	0

SECOND ELEVEN CHAMPIONSHIP 2021

For 2021 the Championship reverted to one league of 18 teams, each team playing between seven and 12 games Final positions were decided on average points per game.

FINAL TABLE

		P	W	L	D	Aban	Bat	Bowl	Points	Average Points Per Match
1	Hampshire	9	7	1	1	0	16	27	163	18.111
2	Leicestershire	7	4	2	1	0	17	20	109	15.571
3	Durham	10	5	1	2	2	17	22	151	15.100
4	Middlesex	9	5	2	1	1	13	23	132	14.667
5	**Yorkshire**	**11**	**3**	**1**	**6**	**1**	**29**	**26**	**159**	**14.445**
6	Glamorgan	10	4	2	2	2	20	19	135	13.500
7	Worcestershire	8	3	2	2	1	18	15	105	13.125
8	Essex	9	3	3	2	1	22	25	118	13.111
9	Nottinghamshire	12	4	4	3	1	28	29	153	12.750
10	Lancashire	12	3	3	5	1	22	23	141	11.750
11	Gloucestershire	10	3	3	4	0	13	19	112	11.200
12	Northamptonshire	9	3	4	2	0	14	17	95	10.556
13	Somerset	9	3	5	1	0	10	25	91	10.111
14	Warwickshire	10	3	4	1	2	8	20	100	10.000
15	Surrey	8	1	3	3	1	13	17	78	9.750
16	Derbyshire	10	1	5	2	2	12	19	79	7.900
17	Sussex	9	0	6	3	0	21	17	62	6.889
18	Kent	8	0	6	1	1	9	18	43	5.375

The full scorecard for this historic match is reproduced on the next page, but pressures on pagination, the ever-increasing significance of the women's game and the Covid-enforced lack of a structure to the schedule at this level mean that it has not been possible to accommodate in the Yorkshire County Cricket Club Yearbook the full schedule of Second Eleven scorecards as in earlier years.

Second Eleven Championship
Gloucestershire v Yorkshire

Played at Bristol on April 19, 20, 21 and 22, 2021
Yorkshire won by an innings and 81 runs at 2.07pm on the Fourth Day

Toss won by Gloucestershir
Gloucestershire 3 points; Yorkshire 23 points
Close of play: First Day, Yorkshire 326-2 (Fraine 184, Hill 89; 97 overs); Second Day, Gloucestershire (1) 141-5 (Naish 36, Warner 1; 37 overs); Third Day, Gloucestershire (2) 123-2 (Taylor 39, Naish 31; 40 overs)

YORKSHIRE

W A R Fraine, b Hankins		186
J H Wharton, c Cockbain b Russell		30
G S Ballance, lbw Shaw		1
G C H Hill, c and b Hammond		207
M L Revis, b Hankins		3
B D Birkhead, c Barlow b Warner		35
M D Fisher, c Warner b Russell		11
§ H G Duke, not out		58
* J E Poysden, c Hankins b Taylor		7
D J Leech, not out		17
J W Shutt	Did not bat	
Extras b 21, lb 10, nb 16		47
Total (8 wkts dec, 156 overs)		602

FoW: 1-93 (Wharton), 2-113 (Ballance), 3-337 (Fraine), 4-347 (Revis), 5-438 (Birkhead), 6-457 (Fisher), 7-542 (Hill), 8-577 (Poysden)

	O	M	R	W
Shaw	13	6	37	1
Hankins	24	4	92	2
Barlow	14	3	51	0
Naish	9	1	35	0
Smith	31	7	81	0
Russell	22	3	92	2
Taylor	16	1	69	1
Hammond	15	1	79	1
Warner	10	1	23	1
Worgan	2	0	12	0

GLOUCESTERSHIRE

First Innings		Second Innings	
M A H Hammond, b Mukherjee	6	c Leech b Hill	32
* T M J Smith, c Revis b Shutt	16		
I A Cockbain, c Birkhead b Shutt	49	(3) lbw b Hill	91
J M R Taylor, lbw b Shutt	21	(4) c Birkhead b Revis	54
W I Naish, c Duke b Mukherjee	74	(2) b Fisher	11
O Meadows, b Poysden	0	(5) b Shutt	7
J D Warner, not out	39		
§ M R Trotman, c Revis b Shutt	2	c Shutt b Poysden	2
H J Hankins, c Birkhead b Shutt	17	c Loten b Shutt	5
A K Russell, c Duke b Mukherjee	9	c Hill b Poysden	0
G C H Barlow, c Duke b Poysden	25	(9) b Shutt	9
J L Worgan		not out	0
P P Choughule	Did not bat	(6) c Wharton b Shutt	5
Extras b 8, lb 1, w 1, nb 8	18	Extras b 22, lb 1, nb 6	29
Total (92.1 overs)	276	Total (83.1 overs)	245

FoW: 1st 1-10 (Hammond), 2-40 (Smith), 3-80 (Taylor), 4-119 (Cockbain), 5-120 (Meadows), 6-189 (Naish), 7-192 (Trotman), 8-216 (Hankins), 9-249 (Russell), 10-276 (Barlow)
FoW: 2nd 1-27 (Meadows), 2-56 (Hammond), 3-212 (Naish), 4-213 (Taylor), 5-218 (Choughule), 6-229 (Trotman), 7-235 (Warner), 8-240 (Hankins), 9-245 (Russell), 10-245 (Barlow)

	O	M	R	W		O	M	R	W
Leech	12	2	49	0	Fisher	6	1	16	1
Mukherjee	13	4	36	3	Leech	9	3	16	0
Shutt	35	8	94	5	Revis	9	2	16	1
Revis	9	1	26	0	Mukherjee	9	4	25	0
Hill	14	6	27	0	Hill	7	1	19	2
Poysden	9.1	0	35	2	Shutt	21.1	5	47	4
					Poysden	18	3	65	2
					Loten	4	1	18	0

Umpires: J W Llloyds and D R Turl
Scorers: C Jones and M W Turner

Yorkshire full substitute: T W Loten for G S Ballance (called up to the first team on Day 3)
Gloucestershire full substitute: M Shepherd for I A Cockbain (called up to the first team on Day 3)
Gloucestershire full substitute: P P Choughule for T M J Smith (called up to the first team on Day 3)
Gloucestershire full substitute: O Meadows for J Shaw (called up to the first team on Day 2)

SECOND ELEVEN T20 AVERAGES 2021

Played 10   Won 6   Lost 3   Tied 1

BATTING AND FIELDING
(Qualification 3 innings)

Player	M.	I.	N.O.	Runs	H.S.	Avge	Strike Rate	100s	50s	ct/st
G S Ballance	3	3	0	184	125	61.33	175.23	1	0	0
J A Tattersall	4	4	2	91	48*	45.50	128.16	0	0	2/1
H G Duke	3	3	1	77	59	38.50	120.31	0	1	1
G C H Hill	9	9	3	174	51*	29.00	123.40	0	1	3
D J Leech	7	4	2	55	25	27.50	125.00	0	0	4
M L Revis	9	9	1	205	50*	25.62	116.47	0	1	7
W A R Fraine	6	6	1	89	21	17.80	111.25	0	0	1
M J Waite	5	5	0	81	30	16.20	94.18	0	0	1
J E Poysden	8	4	2	28	13*	14.00	80.00	0	0	2
B D Birkhead	10	10	0	134	34	13.40	112.60	0	0	6/4
J R Sullivan	6	3	1	25	10*	12.50	138.88	0	0	1
T W Loten	6	3	1	23	11*	11.50	82.14	0	0	5
J H Wharton	9	7	0	66	28	9.42	103.12	0	0	4
M W Pillans	9	7	1	34	11*	5.67	91.89	0	0	2
M D Fisher	3	3	0	8	7	2.67	88.88	0	0	1

Also played

Player	M.	I.	N.O.	Runs	H.S.	Avge	Strike Rate	100s	50s	ct/st
W A Luxton	2	2	0	29	22	14.50	93.54	0	0	0
H C Brook	1	1	0	12	12	12.00	109.09	0	0	0
T Kohler-Cadmore	1	1	0	11	11	11.00	73.33	0	0	0
Y Vagadia	1	1	0	9	9	9.00	64.28	0	0	0
B O Coad	4	1	0	6	6	6.00	85.71	0	0	0
D Olivier	4	2	1	6	4	6.00	85.71	0	0	1
J A Thompson	1	1	0	3	3	3.00	42.85	0	0	0
J W Shutt	9	3	3	18	16*	—	72.00	0	0	1
D M Bess	1	0	0	0	0	—	—	0	0	0

BOWLING
(Qualification 5 wickets)

Player	Overs	Mdns	Runs	Wkts	Avge	Best	Strike Rate	Econ.	4wI
J W Shutt	31.3	0	203	16	12.68	4-28	12.43	6.12	1
M D Fisher	11	0	105	8	13.12	4-36	8.25	9.54	1
M J Waite	12	0	92	6	15.33	2-17	12.00	7.67	0
G C H Hill	13.5	0	108	7	15.42	2-11	11.85	7.80	0
J E Poysden	30.2	0	212	12	17.67	3-20	16.00	6.62	0
M W Pillans	25	0	180	7	25.71	3-29	21.42	7.20	0

Also bowled

Player	Overs	Mdns	Runs	Wkts	Avge	Best	Strike Rate	Econ.	4wI
J A Thompson	3	0	23	1	23.00	1-23	18.00	7.67	0
J R Sullivan	14.4	0	103	4	25.74	2-15	22.00	7.02	0
D Olivier	15	0	133	4	33.25	2-20	22.50	8.86	0
D J Leech	20	0	140	4	35.00	1-8	30.00	7.00	0
B O Coad	13	0	110	3	36.67	2-38	26.00	8.46	0
D M Bess	4	0	25	0	—	—	—	6.25	0
M L Revis	1	0	11	0	—	—	—	11.00	0
Y Vagadia	1	0	10	0	—	—	—	10.00	0

SECOND ELEVEN T20 IN 2021

Two matches versus the same opponents at the same venue on the same day.

SEMI-FINALS

Yorkshire (134-6)	lost to Sussex (137-1)	by 9 wickets
Warwickshire (155-7)	beat Middlesex (137)	by 18 runs

FINAL

Warwickshire (149-5)   beat Sussex (95)   by 54 runs

All matches played at Arundel Castle CC on June 24, 2021

NORTHERN GROUP FINAL TABLE

		P	W	T	L	NR	AB	Points	NRR	Bow SR
1	Durham	10	7	0	3	0	0	14	0.417	18.000
2	**Yorkshire**	**10**	**6**	**1**	**3**	**0**	**0**	**13**	**0.273**	**15.000**
3	Derbyshire	10	6	0	4	0	0	12	0.926	19.534
4	Leicestershire	10	4	0	6	0	0	8	-0.305	17.562
5	Lancashire	10	3	1	6	0	0	7	-0.478	17.088
6	Nottinghamshire	10	3	0	7	0	0	6	-0.887	16.955

NR =   No result
Ab =   Abandoned
NRR =   Net run rate
Bow SR =   Bowling Strike Rate

CENTRAL GROUP FINAL TABLE

		P	W	T	L	NR	AB	Points	NRR	Bow SR
1	Warwickshire	10	9	0	1	0	0	18	2.281	14.400
2	Gloucestershire	10	4	0	5	1	0	9	0.256	18.911
3	Worcestershire	10	4	0	5	1	0	9	-0.173	18.709
4	Northamptonshire	10	4	0	6	0	0	8	-0.567	19.776
5	Somerset	10	4	0	6	0	0	8	-0.761	17.328
6	Glamorgan	10	4	0	6	0	0	8	-1.134	19.913

SOUTHERN GROUP FINAL TABLE

		P	W	T	L	NR	AB	Points	NRR	Bow SR
1	Sussex	10	7	0	2	0	1	15	-0.048	17.607
2	Middlesex	10	5	0	3	0	2	12	0.594	16.473
3	Hampshire	10	4	1	3	0	2	11	0.669	16.038
4	Essex	10	4	0	5	0	1	9	-0.356	14.938
5	Surrey	10	3	1	6	0	0	7	0.106	17.145
6	Kent	10	3	0	7	0	0	6	-0.745	17.414

PREVIOUS WINNERS

2011	**Sussex**, who beat Durham by 24 runs
2012	**England Under-19s**, who beat Sussex by eight wickets
2013	**Surrey**, who beat Middlesex by six runs
2014	**Leicesterhire**, who beat Sussex by 11 runs
2015	**Middlesex**, who beat Kent by four wickets
2016	**Middlesex**, who beat Somerset by two wickets
2017	**Sussex**, who beat Hampshire by 24 runs
2018	**Lancashire**, who beat Essex by 25 runs
2019	**Glamorgan**, beat Hampshire by 1 run
2020	*No competition because of the Coronovirus epidemic*

RECORDS SECTION

All records in this section relate to First-Class Yorkshire matches except where stated

HONOURS

County Champions (34)
1867, 1870, 1893, 1896, 1898, 1900, 1901, 1902, 1905, 1908, 1912, 1919,
1922, 1923, 1924, 1925, 1931, 1932, 1933, 1935, 1937, 1938, 1939,
1946, 1959, 1960, 1962, 1963, 1966, 1967, 1968, 2001, 2014, 2015

Joint Champions (2)
1869, 1949

Promoted to Division 1
2005, 2012

Gillette Cup Winners (2)
1965, 1969

Cheltenham & Gloucester Trophy (1)
2002

Benson & Hedges Cup Winners (1)
1987

John Player Special League Winners (1)
1983

Fenner Trophy Winners (3)
1972, 1974, 1981

Asda Challenge Winners (1)
1987

Ward Knockout Cup (1)
1989

Joshua Tetley Festival Trophy (7)
1991, 1992 (Joint), 1993, 1994, 1996, 1997 and 1998

Tilcon Trophy Winners (2)
1978 and 1988

Pro-Arch Trophy (1)
2007-08

Emirates Airlines T20 (2)
2015 and 2016

Second Eleven Champions (4)
1977, 1984, 1991, 2003

Joint Champions (1)
1987

Minor Counties Champions (5)
1947, 1957, 1958, 1968, 1971

Under-25 Competition Winners (3)
1976, 1978, 1987

Bain Clarkson Trophy Winners (2)
1988 and 1994

Second Eleven Trophy (1)
2009

YORKSHIRE'S CHAMPIONSHIP CAPTAINS

1867 to 2019

* R Iddison (2)	1867, 1870
Lord Hawke (8)	1893, 1896, 1898, 1900, 1901, 1902, 1905, 1908
Sir Archibald White (1)	1912
D C F Burton (1)	1919
G Wilson (3)	1922, 1923, 1924
A W Lupton (1)	1925
F E Greenwood (2)	1931, 1932
A B Sellers (6)	1933, 1935, 1937, 1938, 1939, 1946
J R Burnet (1)	1959
J V Wilson (2)	1960, 1962
D B Close (4)	1963, 1966, 1967, 1968
D Byas (1)	2001
A W Gale (2)	2014, 2015

Joint Champions

* R Iddison (1)	1869
N W D Yardley (1)	1949

* R Iddison was captain when Yorkshire were Champion county, the County Championship starting in 1890.

RECORDS SECTION INDEX

Page

Champion Counties since 1873	229
Season-by-Season Record of all First-Class Matches	231
Analysis of Results	233
Highest and Lowest Match Aggregates	235
Large Margins of Victory	237
Heavy Defeats	239
Narrow Victories and Narrow Defeats	239
High Fourth Innings Scores	241
Tie Matches	242
Highest Scores By and Against Yorkshire	242
Lowest Scores By and Against Yorkshire	244
Individual Innings of 150 and over	246
Centuries By Current Players	256
Summary of Centuries For and Against Yorkshire	262
Four/Three Centuries in One Innings	263
Century in Each Innings	264
Highest Individual Scores For and Against Yorkshire	265
Carrying Bat Through Completed Innings	268
2,000 Runs in a Season and 1,000 Runs in a Season	269
Batsmen who have scored over 10,000 Runs	273
Batsmen who have scored centuries for and against Yorkshire	274
Record Partnerships For and Against Yorkshire	274
Century Partnerships	275
Fifteen Wickets or More in a Match	284
Ten Wickets in a Match	284
Ten Wickets in an Innings, Eight Wickets or More in an Innings	286
Six Wickets in an Innings at Less than Four Runs Each	291
Four Wickets in Four Balls	294
Best Bowling Analyses in a Match For and Against Yorkshire	295
Best Bowling Analyses in an Innings For and Against Yorkshire	297
Hat Tricks	299
200 Wickets in a Season and 100 Wickets in a Season	300
Bowlers who have Taken over 500 Wickets	302
Bowling Unchanged in a Match	302
Most Catches in an Innings/A Match/A Season/A Career	303
Most Dismissals in an Innings/A Match/A Season/A Career	304
The Double (All First-Class Matches)	305
Yorkshire Test Cricketers	307
Centuries for England	311
10 Wickets in a Match for England	314
Five Wickets in an Innings for England	314
Test Match Hat-Tricks	317
Test Matches at Leeds, 1899-2021	326
List of Yorkshire Players and Career Records	336
List A One-Day Records Section	361
List A Limited-Overs Career Records	390
Yorkshire One-Day International Cricketers	394
One-Day International Matches at Leeds, 1973-2019	397
Twenty20 Records Section	403
Twenty20 Career Records	415
Second Eleven Records	417

CHAMPION COUNTIES SINCE 1873

The County Championship

The County Championship was officially constituted in 1890, and before that Yorkshire were generally considered Champions by the Press in 1867 and 1870, and equal top in 1869. From 1873 the list was generally accepted in the form as it is today.

		Yorkshire's Position			Yorkshire's Position
1873	{ Gloucestershire / Nottinghamshire }	7th	1909	Kent	3rd
1874	Gloucestershire	4th	1910	Kent	8th
1875	Nottinghamshire	4th	1911	Warwickshire	7th
1876	Gloucestershire	3rd	**1912**	**Yorkshire**	**1st**
1877	Gloucestershire	7th	1913	Kent	2nd
1878	Middlesex	6th	1914	Surrey	4th
1879	Nottinghamshire/Lancashire	6th	**1919**	**Yorkshire**	**1st**
1880	Nottinghamshire	5th	1920	Middlesex	4th
1881	Lancashire	3rd	1921	Middlesex	3rd
1882	Nottinghamshire/Lancashire	3rd	**1922**	**Yorkshire**	**1st**
1883	Nottinghamshire	2nd	**1923**	**Yorkshire**	**1st**
1884	Nottinghamshire	3rd	**1924**	**Yorkshire**	**1st**
1885	Nottinghamshire	2nd	**1925**	**Yorkshire**	**1st**
1886	Nottinghamshire	4th	1926	Lancashire	2nd
1887	Surrey	3rd	1927	Lancashire	3rd
1888	Surrey	2nd	1928	Lancashire	4th
1889	{ Surrey/Lancashire / Nottinghamshire }	7th	1929	Nottinghamshire	2nd
			1930	Lancashire	3rd
1890	Surrey	3rd	**1931**	**Yorkshire**	**1st**
1891	Surrey	8th	**1932**	**Yorkshire**	**1st**
1892	Surrey	6th	**1933**	**Yorkshire**	**1st**
1893	**Yorkshire**	**1st**	1934	Lancashire	5th
1894	Surrey	2nd	**1935**	**Yorkshire**	**1st**
1895	Surrey	3rd	1936	Derbyshire	3rd
1896	**Yorkshire**	**1st**	**1937**	**Yorkshire**	**1st**
1897	Lancashire	4th	**1938**	**Yorkshire**	**1st**
1898	**Yorkshire**	**1st**	**1939**	**Yorkshire**	**1st**
1899	Surrey	3rd	**1946**	**Yorkshire**	**1st**
1900	**Yorkshire**	**1st**	1947	Middlesex	7th
1901	**Yorkshire**	**1st**	1948	Glamorgan	4th
1902	**Yorkshire**	**1st**	**1949**	**Yorkshire**/Middlesex	**1st**
1903	Middlesex	3rd	1950	Lancashire/Surrey	3rd
1904	Lancashire	2nd	1951	Warwickshire	2nd
1905	**Yorkshire**	**1st**	1952	Surrey	2nd
1906	Kent	2nd	1953	Surrey	12th
1907	Nottinghamshire	2nd	1954	Surrey	2nd
1908	**Yorkshire**	**1st**	1955	Surrey	2nd
			1956	Surrey	7th
			1957	Surrey	3rd

229

CHAMPION COUNTIES SINCE 1873 *(Continued)*

		Yorkshire's Position			*Yorkshire's Position*
1958	Surrey	11th	1990	Middlesex	10th
1959	**Yorkshire**	**1st**	1991	Essex	14th
1960	**Yorkshire**	**1st**	1992	Essex	16th
1961	Hampshire	2nd	1993	Middlesex	12th
1962	**Yorkshire**	**1st**	1994	Warwickshire	13th
1963	**Yorkshire**	**1st**	1995	Warwickshire	8th
1964	Worcestershire	5th	1996	Leicestershire	6th
1965	Worcestershire	4th	1997	Glamorgan	6th
1966	**Yorkshire**	**1st**	1998	Leicestershire	3rd
1967	**Yorkshire**	**1st**	1999	Surrey	6th
1968	**Yorkshire**	**1st**	2000	Surrey	3rd
1969	Glamorgan	13th	**2001**	**Yorkshire**	**1st**
1970	Kent	4th	2002	Surrey	9th
1971	Surrey	13th	2003	Sussex	Div 2, 4th
1972	Warwickshire	10th	2004	Warwickshire	Div 2, 7th
1973	Hampshire	14th	2005	Nottinghamshire	Div 2, 3rd
1974	Worcestershire	11th	2006	Sussex	Div 1, 6th
1975	Leicestershire	2nd	2007	Sussex	Div 1, 6th
1976	Middlesex	8th	2008	Durham	Div 1, 7th
1977	Kent/Middlesex	12th	2009	Durham	Div 1, 7th
1978	Kent	4th	2010	Nottinghamshire	Div 1, 3rd
1979	Essex	7th	2011	Lancashire	Div 1, 8th
1980	Middlesex	6th	2012	Warwickshire	Div 2, 2nd
1981	Nottinghamshire	10th	2013	Durham	Div 1, 2nd
1982	Middlesex	10th	**2014**	**Yorkshire**	**Div 1, 1st**
1983	Essex	17th	**2015**	**Yorkshire**	**Div 1, 1st**
1984	Essex	14th	2016	Middlesex	Div 1, 3rd
1985	Middlesex	11th	2017	Essex	Div 1, 4th
1986	Essex	10th	2018	Surrey	Div 1, 4th
1987	Nottinghamshire	8th	2019	Essex	Div 1, 5th
1988	Worcestershire	13th	*2020*	*No matches played due to Covid-19*	
1989	Worcestershire	16th	2021	Warwickshire	Div 1, 5th (6)

SEASON-BY-SEASON RECORD OF ALL FIRST-CLASS MATCHES PLAYED BY YORKSHIRE 1863-2021

Season	Played	Won	Lost	Drawn	Abd§	Season	Played	Won	Lost	Drawn	Abd§
1863	4	2	1	1	0	1921	30	17	5	8	0
1864	7	2	4	1	0	1922	33	20	2	11	0
1865	9	0	7	2	0	1923	35	26	1	8	0
1866	3	0	2	1	0	1924	35	18	4	13	0
1867	7	7	0	0	0	1925	36	22	0	14	0
1868	7	4	3	0	0	1926	35	14	0	21	1
1869	5	4	1	0	0	1927	34	11	3	20	1
1870	7	6	0	1	0	1928	32	9	0	23	0
1871	7	3	3	1	0	1929	35	11	2	22	0
1872	10	2	7	1	0	1930	34	13	3	18	2
1873	13	7	5	1	0	1931	33	17	1	15	1
1874	14	10	3	1	0	1932	32	21	2	9	2
1875	12	6	4	2	0	1933	36	21	5	10	0
1876	12	5	3	4	0	1934	35	14	7	14	0
1877	14	2	7	5	0	1935	36	24	2	10	0
1878	20	10	7	3	0	1935-6	3	1	0	2	0
1879	17	7	5	5	0	1936	35	14	2	19	0
1880	20	6	8	6	0	1937	34	22	3	9	1
1881	20	11	6	3	0	1938	36	22	2	12	0
1882	24	11	9	4	0	1939	34	23	4	7	1
1883	19	10	2	7	0	1945	2	0	0	2	0
1884	20	10	6	4	0	1946	31	20	1	10	0
1885	21	8	3	10	0	1947	32	10	9	13	0
1886	21	5	8	8	0	1948	31	11	6	14	0
1887	20	6	5	9	0	1949	33	16	3	14	0
1888	20	7	7	6	0	1950	34	16	6	12	1
1889	16	3	11	2	1	1951	35	14	3	18	0
1890	20	10	4	6	0	1952	34	17	3	14	0
1891	17	5	11	1	2	1953	35	7	7	21	0
1892	19	6	6	7	0	1954	35	16	3	16*	0
1893	23	15	5	3	0	1955	33	23	6	4	0
1894	28	18	6	4	1	1956	35	11	7	17	0
1895	31	15	10	6	0	1957	34	16	5	13	1
1896	32	17	6	9	0	1958	33	10	8	15	2
1897	30	14	7	9	0	1959	35	18	8	9	0
1898	30	18	3	9	0	1960	38	19	7	12	0
1899	34	17	4	13	0	1961	39	19	5	15	0
1900	32	19	1	12	0	1962	37	16	5	16	0
1901	35	23	2	10	1	1963	33	14	4	15	0
1902	31	15	3	13	1	1964	33	12	4	17	0
1903	31	16	5	10	0	1965	33	12	4	17	0
1904	32	10	2	20	1	1966	32	16	6	10	1
1905	33	21	4	8	0	1967	31	16	5	10	2
1906	33	19	6	8	0	1968	32	13	4	15	0
1907	31	14	5	12	2	1969	29	4	7	18	0
1908	33	19	0	14	0	1970	26	10	5	11	0
1909	30	12	5	13	0	1971	27	5	8	14	0
1910	31	11	8	12	0	1972	21	4	5	12	1
1911	32	16	9	7	0	1973	22	3	5	14*	0
1912	35	14	3	18	1	1974	22	6	7	9	0
1913	32	16	5	11	0	1975	21	11	1	9	0
1914	31	16	4	11	2	1976	22	7	7	8	0
1919	31	12	5	14	0	1977	23	7	5	11	1
1920	30	17	6	7	0	1978	24	10	3	11	1

SEASON-BY-SEASON RECORD OF ALL FIRST-CLASS MATCHES PLAYED BY YORKSHIRE 1863-2021 *(Contd.)*

Season	Played	Won	Lost	Drawn	Abd§	Season	Played	Won	Lost	Drawn	Abd§
1979	22	6	3	13	1	2000	18	7	4	7	0
1980	24	5	4	15	0	2001	16	9	3	4	0
1981	24	5	9	10	0	2002	16	2	8	6	0
1982	22	5	1	16	1	2003	17	4	5	8	0
1983	23	1	5	17	1	2004	16	3	4	9	0
1984	24	5	4	15	0	2005	17	6	1	10	0
1985	25	3	4	18	1	2006	16	3	6	7	0
1986	25	4	6	15	0	2007	17	5	4	8	0
1986-7	1	0	0	1	0	2008	16	2	5	9	0
1987	24	7	4	13	1	2009	17	2	2	13	0
1988	24	5	6	13	0	2010	18	6	2	10	0
1989	22	3	9	10	0	2011	17	4	6	7	0
1990	24	5	9	10	0	2012	17	5	0	12	0
1991	24	4	6	14	0	2013	17	8	2	7	0
1991-2	1	0	1	0	0	2014	17	8	1	8	0
1992	22	4	6	12	1	2015	18	12	1	5	0
1992-3	1	0	0	1	0	2016	18	5	4	9	0
1993	19	6	4	9	0	2017	15	5	5	5	0
1994	20	7	6	7	0	2018	13	5	5	3	2
1995	20	8	8	4	0	2019	15	6	4	5	0
1995-6	2	2	0	0	0	2020	5	3	0	2	0
1996	19	8	5	6	0	2021	14	6	3	5	0
1997	20	7	4	9	0		3664	1541	670	1453	40
1998	19	9	3	7	0						
1999	17	8	6	3	0						

* Includes one tie each season

§ All these matches were abandoned without a ball being bowled, except Yorkshire v. Kent at Harrogate, 1904, which was abandoned under Law 9. The two in 1914 and the one in 1939 were abandoned because of war. The four-day match, Yorkshire v. Essex at Leeds in 2018, was abandoned without a ball bowled, but each side received 5 points. All these matches are excluded from the total played.

Of the 1,541 matches won 526 have been by an innings margin, 89 by 200 runs or more, and 135 by 10 wickets. Of the 670 lost 114 have been by an innings margin, 17 by 200 runs or more, and 35 by 10 wickets.

ANALYSIS OF RESULTS VERSUS ALL FIRST-CLASS TEAMS 1863-2021

COUNTY CHAMPIONSHIP

Opponents	Played	Won	Lost	Drawn	Tied
Derbyshire	205	103	19	83	0
Durham	36	16	8	12	0
Essex	165	85	28	52	0
Glamorgan	113	53	13	47	0
Gloucestershire	200	102	43	55	0
Hampshire	176	75	20	81	0
Kent	204	86	40	78	0
Lancashire	263	79	53	131	0
Leicestershire	166	84	15	66	1
Middlesex	235	82	59	93	1
Northamptonshire	144	69	26	49	0
Nottinghamshire	259	93	48	118	0
Somerset	180	93	27	60	0
Surrey	248	87	69	92	0
Sussex	201	87	33	81	0
Warwickshire	195	87	33	75	0
Worcestershire	142	71	22	49	0
Cambridgeshire	8	3	4	1	0
Total	3140	1355	560	1223	2

OTHER FIRST-CLASS MATCHES

Opponents	Played	Won	Lost	Drawn	Tied
Derbyshire	3	1	1	1	0
Durham	1	1	0	0	0
Essex	2	2	0	0	0
Hampshire	1	0	0	1	0
Lancashire	13	5	3	5	0
Leicestershire	3	2	1	0	0
Middlesex	1	1	0	0	0
Nottinghamshire	3	2	1	0	0
Surrey	1	0	0	1	0
Sussex	2	0	0	2	0
Warwickshire	2	0	0	2	0
Totals	32	14	6	12	0
Australians	55	6	19	30	0
Indians	14	5	1	8	0
New Zealanders	10	2	0	8	0
Pakistanis	4	1	0	3	0
South Africans	17	1	3	13	0
Sri Lankans	3	0	0	3	0
West Indians	17	3	7	7	0
Zimbabweans	2	0	1	1	0
Bangladesh A	1	1	0	0	0
India A	2	0	0	2	0
Pakistan A	2	1	0	1	0
South Africa A	1	0	0	1	0
Totals	128	20	31	77	0

ANALYSIS OF RESULTS VERSUS ALL FIRST-CLASS TEAMS 1863-2021 *(continued.)*

Opponents	Played	Won	Lost	Drawn	Tied
Cambridge University/U C C E	88	42	17	29	0
Canadians	1	1	0	0	0
Combined Services	1	0	0	1	0
Durham MCCU	1	1	0	0	0
England XI's	6	1	2	3	0
Hon. M.B. Hawke's XI	1	0	1	0	0
International XI	1	1	0	0	0
Ireland	3	3	0	0	0
Jamaica	3	1	0	2	0
Leeds/Bradford MCCU	6	3	0	3	0
Liverpool and District*	3	2	1	0	0
Loughborough UCCE	2	1	0	1	0
MCC	155	55	40	60	0
Mashonaland	1	1	0	0	0
Matebeleland	1	1	0	0	0
Minor Counties	1	1	0	0	0
Oxford University	44	21	3	20	0
Philadelphians	1	0	0	1	0
Rest of England	16	4	5	7	0
Royal Air Force	1	0	0	1	0
Scotland**	11	7	0	4	0
South of England	2	1	0	1	0
C. I. Thornton's XI	5	2	0	3	0
United South of England	1	1	0	0	0
Western Province	2	0	1	1	0
Windward Islands	1	0	0	1	0
I Zingari	6	2	3	1	0
Totals	364	152	73	139	0
Grand Totals	3664	1541	670	1451	2

*Matches played in 1889, 1891, 1892 and 1893 are excluded. **Match played in 1878 is included

ABANDONED MATCHES (40)

1889	v. MCC at Lord's	1939	v. MCC at Scarborough (due to war)
1891 (2)	v. MCC at Lord's	1950	v. Cambridge University at Cambridge
	v. MCC at Scarborough		
1894	v. Kent at Bradford	1957	v. West Indians at Bradford
1901	v. Surrey at The Oval	1958 (2)	v. Nottinghamshire at Hull
1902	v. Leicestershire at Leicester (AR)		v. Worcestershire at Bradford
1904	v. Kent at Harrogate (Law 9 — now Law 10)	1966	v. Oxford University at Oxford
1907 (2)	v. Derbyshire at Sheffield	1967 (2)	v. Leicestershire at Leeds
	v. Nottinghamshire at Huddersfield		v. Lancashire at Manchester
1912	v. Surrey at Sheffield	1972	v. Australians at Bradford
1914 (2)	v. England at Harrogate (due to war)	1974	v. Hampshire at Bournemouth
	v. MCC at Scarborough (due to war)	1977	v. Gloucestershire at Bristol
1926	v. Nottinghamshire at Leeds	1978	v. Pakistan at Bradford
1927	v. Kent at Bradford	1979	v. Nottinghamshire at Sheffield (AP)
1930 (2)	v. Derbyshire at Chesterfield*	1982	v. Nottinghamshire at Harrogate
	v. Northamptonshire at Harrogate*	1983	v. Middlesex at Lord's
1931	v. Sussex at Hull	1985	v. Essex at Sheffield (AP)
1932 (2)	v. Derbyshire at Chesterfield	1987	v. Sussex at Hastings
	v. Kent at Sheffield	1992	v. Oxford University at Oxford
1937	v. Cambridge University at Bradford	2018	v. Leeds/Bradford MCCU at Leeds*
		2018	v. Essex at Leeds*

* Consecutive matches

ANALYSIS OF RESULTS ON GROUNDS IN YORKSHIRE USED IN 2021

FIRST-CLASS MATCHES

Ground	Played	Won	Lost	Drawn	Tied
Leeds Headingley 1891-2021	475	180 (37.89%)	83 (17.47%)	212 (44.63%)	0 (0.00%)
Scarborough North Marine Road 1874-2021	260	106 (40.77%)	40 (15.26%)	114 (43.85%)	0 (0.00%)

HIGHEST MATCH AGGREGATES – OVER 1,350 RUNS

Runs	Wkts	
1665	33	Yorkshire (351 and 481) lost to Warwickshire (601:9 dec and 232:4) by 6 wkts at Birmingham, 2002
1606	31	Yorkshire (438 and 363:5 dec) lost to Somerset (326 and 479:6) by 4 wkts at Taunton, 2009
1479	28	Yorkshire (405 and 333:4 dec) lost to Somerset (377 and 364:4) by 6 wkts at Taunton , 2010
1473	17	Yorkshire (600:4 dec. and 231:3 dec.) drew with Worcestershire (453:5 dec. and 189:5) at Scarborough, 1995.
1442	29	Yorkshire (501:6 dec. and 244:6 dec.) beat Lancashire (403:7 dec. and 294) by 48 runs at Scarborough, 1991.
1439	32	Yorkshire (536:8 dec. and 205:7 dec.) beat Glamorgan (482: 7 dec. and 216) by 43 runs at Cardiff, 1996.
1431	32	Yorkshire (388 and 312:6) drew with Sussex (398 and 333:6 dec) at Scarborough, 2011
1417	33	Yorkshire (422 and 193:7) drew with Glamorgan (466 and 336:6 dec) at Colwyn Bay, 2003
1406	37	Yorkshire (354 and 341:8) drew with Derbyshire (406 and 305:9 dec) at Derby, 2004
1400	32	Yorkshire (299 and 439: 4 dec.) drew with Hampshire (296 and 366:8) at Southampton, 2007
1393	35	Yorkshire (331 and 278) lost to Kent (377 and 407:5 dec) by 175 runs at Maidstone, 1994.
1390	34	Yorkshire (431:8 dec and 265:7) beat Hampshire (429 and 265) by 3 wkts at Southampton, 1995.
1390	33	Durham (573 and 124-3) beat Yorkahire (274 and 419) by 7 wkts at Scarborough, 2013.
1376	33	Yorkshire (531 and 158:3) beat Lancashire (373 and 314) by 7 wkts at Leeds, 2001
1376	20	Yorkshire (677: 7 dec.) drew with Durham (518 and 181:3 dec.) at Leeds, 2006
1374	36	Yorkshire (594: 9 dec. and 266:7 dec.) beat Surrey (344 and 170) by 346 runs at The Oval, 2007
1373	36	Yorkshire (520 and 114:6) drew with Derbyshire (216 and 523) at Derby, 2005
1364	35	Yorkshire (216 and 433) lost to Warwickshire (316 and 399:5 dec.) by 66 runs at Birmingham, 2006
1359	25	Yorkshire (561 and 138:3 dec.) drew with Derbyshire (412:4 dec. and 248:8) at Sheffield, 1996.
1359	30	Yorkshire (358 and 321) lost to Somerset (452 and 228:0) by 10 wkts at Taunton, 2011
1353	18	Yorkshire (377:2 dec. and 300:6) beat Derbyshire (475:7 dec. and 201:3 dec) by 4 wkts at Scarborough, 1990.

LOWEST MATCH AGGREGATES – UNDER 225 RUNS IN A COMPLETED MATCH

Runs	Wkts	
165	30	Yorkshire (46 and 37:0) beat Nottinghamshire (24 and 58) by 10 wkts at Sheffield, 1888.
175	29	Yorkshire (104) beat Essex (30 and 41) by an innings and 33 runs at Leyton, 1901.
182	15	Yorkshire (4:0 dec. and 88.5) beat Northamptonshire (4:0 dec. and 86) by 5 wkts at Bradford, 1931.
193	29	Yorkshire (99) beat Worcestershire (43 and 51) by an innings and 5 runs at Bradford, 1900.
219	30	Yorkshire (113) beat Nottinghamshire (71 and 35) by an innings and 7 runs at Nottingham, 1881.
222	32	Yorkshire (98 and 14:2) beat Gloucestershire (68 and 42) by 8 wkts at Gloucester, 1924.
223	40	Yorkshire (58 and 51) lost to Lancashire (64 and 50)

LOWEST MATCH AGGREGATES – UNDER 325 RUNS IN A MATCH IN WHICH ALL 40 WICKETS FELL

Runs	Wkts	
223	40	Yorkshire (58 and 51) lost to Lancashire (64 and 50) by 5 runs at Manchester, 1893.
288	40	Yorkshire (55 and 68) lost to Lancashire (89 and 76) by 42 runs at Sheffield, 1872.
295	40	Yorkshire (71 and 63) lost to Surrey (56 and 105) by 27 runs at The Oval, 1886.
303	40	Yorkshire (109 and 77) beat Middlesex (63 and 54) by 69 runs at Lord's, 1891.
318	40	Yorkshire (96 and 96) beat Lancashire (39 and 87) by 66 runs at Manchester, 1874.
318	40	Yorkshire (94 and 104) beat Northamptonshire (61 and 59) by 78 runs at Bradford, 1955.
319	40	Yorkshire (84 and 72) lost to Derbyshire (106 and 57) by 7 runs at Derby, 1878.
320	40	Yorkshire (98 and 91) beat Surrey (72 and 59) by 58 runs at Sheffield, 1893.
321	40	Yorkshire (88 and 37) lost to I Zingari (103 and 93) by 71 runs at Scarborough, 1877.
321	40	Yorkshire (80 and 67) lost to Derbyshire (129 and 45) by 27 runs at Sheffield, 1879.

LARGE MARGINS OF VICTORY – BY AN INNINGS AND OVER 250 RUNS

Inns and 397 runs	Yorkshire (548:4 dec.) beat Northamptonshire (58 and 93) at Harrogate, 1921
Inns and 387 runs	Yorkshire (662) beat Derbyshire (118 and 157) at Chesterfield, 1898.
Inns and 343 runs	Yorkshire (673:8 dec) beat Northamptonshire (184 and 146) at Leeds, 2003
Inns and 321 runs	Yorkshire (437) beat Leicestershire (58 and 58) at Leicester, 1908.
Inns and 314 runs	Yorkshire (356:8 dec) beat Northamptonshire (27 and 15) at Northampton, 1908. (Yorkshire's first match v. Northamptonshire).
Inns and 313 runs	Yorkshire (555:1 dec) beat Essex (78 and 164) at Leyton, 1932.
Inns and 307 runs	Yorkshire (681:5 dec.) beat Sussex (164 and 210) at Sheffield, 1897.
Inns and 302 runs	Yorkshire (660) beat Leicestershire (165 and 193) at Leicester, 1896.
Inns and 301 runs	Yorkshire (499) beat Somerset (125 and 73) at Bath, 1899.
Inns and 294 runs	Yorkshire (425:7 dec.) beat Gloucestershire (47 and 84) at Bristol, 1964.
Inns and 284 runs	Yorkshire (467:7 dec) beat Leicestershire (111 and 72) at Bradford, 1932.
Inns and 282 runs	Yorkshire (481:8 dec) beat Derbyshire (106 and 93) at Huddersfield, 1901.
Inns and 280 runs	Yorkshire (562) beat Leicestershire (164 and 118) at Dewsbury, 1903.
Inns and 271 runs	Yorkshire (460) beat Hampshire (128 and 61) at Hull, 1900.
Inns and 271 runs	Yorkshire (495:5 dec) beat Warwickshire (99 and 125) at Huddersfield, 1922.
Inns and 266 runs	Yorkshire (352) beat Cambridgeshire (40 and 46) at Hunslet, 1869.
Inns and 260 runs	Yorkshire (521: 7dec.) beat Worcestershire (129 and 132) at Leeds, 2007.
Inns and 258 runs	Yorkshire (404:2 dec) beat Glamorgan (78 and 68) at Cardiff, 1922. (Yorkshire's first match v. Glamorgan).
Inns and 256 runs	Yorkshire (486) beat Leicestershire (137 and 93) at Sheffield, 1895.
Inns and 251 runs	Yorkshire (550) beat Leicestershire (154 and 145) at Leicester, 1933.

LARGE MARGINS OF VICTORY – BY OVER 300 RUNS

389 runs	Yorkshire (368 and 280:1 dec) beat Somerset (125 and 134) at Bath, 1906.
370 runs	Yorkshire (194 and 274) beat Hampshire (62 and 36) at Leeds, 1904.
351 runs	Yorkshire (280 and 331) beat Northamptonshire (146 and 114) at Northampton, 1947.
346 runs	Yorkshire (594: 9 dec. and 266: 7 dec.) beat Surrey (344 and 179) at The Oval, 2007.
328 runs	Yorkshire (186 and 318:1 dec) beat Somerset (43 and 133) at Bradford, 1930.
328 runs	Yorkshire (280 and 277:7 dec) beat Glamorgan (104 and 105) at Swansea, 2001
320 runs	Yorkshire (331 and 353:9 dec) beat Durham (150 and 214) at Chester-le-Street, 2004
308 runs	Yorkshire (89 and 420) beat Warwickshire (72 and 129) at Birmingham, 1921
308 runs	Yorkshire (89 and 420) beat Warwickshire (72 and 129)
305 runs	Yorkshire (370 and 305:4 dec) beat Hampshire (227 and 143) at Leeds, 2015
305 runs	Yorkshire (282 and 263:4 dec) beat Nottinghamshire (94 and 146) at Scarborough 2016

LARGE MARGINS OF VICTORY – BY 10 WICKETS (WITH OVER 100 RUNS SCORED IN THE 4th INNINGS)

4th Innings

167:0 wkt	Yorkshire (247 and 167:0) beat Northamptonshire 233 and 180) at Huddersfield, 1948.
147:0 wkt	Yorkshire (381 and 147:0) beat Middlesex (384 and 142) at Lord's, 1896.
142:0 wkt	Yorkshire (304 and 142:0) beat Sussex (254 and 188) at Bradford, 1887.
139:0 wkt	Yorkshire (163:9 dec and 139:0) beat Nottinghamshire (234 and 67) at Leeds, 1932.
138:0 wkt	Yorkshire (293 and 138:0) beat Hampshire (251 and 179) at Southampton, 1897.
132:0 wkt	Yorkshire (328 and 132:0) beat Northamptonshire (281 and 175) at Leeds, 2005
129:0 wkt	Yorkshire (355 and 129:0) beat Durham MCCU (196 and 287) at Durham, 2011
127:0 wkt	Yorkshire (258 and 127:0) beat Cambridge University (127 and 257) at Cambridge, 1930.
119:0 wkt	Yorkshire (109 and 119:0) beat Essex (108 and 119) at Leeds, 1931.
118:0 wkt	Yorkshire (121 and 118:0) beat MCC (125 and 113) at Lord's, 1883.
116:0 wkt	Yorkshire (147 and 116:0) beat Hampshire (141 and 120) at Bournemouth, 1930.
114:0 wkt	Yorkshire (135 and 114:0) beat Hampshire (71 and 176) at Bournemouth, 1948.
114:0 wkt	Yorkshire (135 and 114:0) beat Hampshire (71 and 176)
105:0 wkt	Yorkshire (307 and 105:0) beat Worcestershire (311 and 100) at Worcester, 2015

HEAVY DEFEATS – BY AN INNINGS AND OVER 250 RUNS

Inns and 272 runs	Yorkshire (78 and 186) lost to Surrey (536) at The Oval, 1898.
Inns and 261 runs	Yorkshire (247 and 89) lost to Sussex (597: 8 dec.) at Hove, 2007.
Inns and 255 runs	Yorkshire (125 and 144) lost to All England XI (524) at Sheffield, 1865.

HEAVY DEFEATS – BY OVER 300 RUNS

433 runs	Kent (482-8 dec and 337-7 dec) defeated Yorkshire (269 and 117) at Leeds, 2019
376 runs	Essex (227 and 334-7 dec) defeated Yorkshire (111 and 74) at Chelmsford, 2017
324 runs	Yorkshire (247 and 204) lost to Gloucestershire (291 and 484) at Cheltenham, 1994.
305 runs	Yorkshire (119 and 51) lost to Cambridge University (312 and 163) at Cambridge, 1906.

HEAVY DEFEATS – BY 10 WICKETS (WITH OVER 100 RUNS SCORED IN THE 4th INNINGS)

4th Innings

228:0 wkt	Yorkshire (358 and 321) lost to Somerset (452 and 228:0) at Taunton, 2011
148:0 wkt	Yorkshire (83 and 216) lost to Lancashire (154 and 148:0) at Manchester, 1875.
119:0 wkt	Yorkshire (92 and 109) lost to Nottinghamshire (86 and 119:0 wkt) at Leeds, 1989.
108:0 wkt	Yorkshire (236 and 107) lost to Hampshire (236 and 108:0 wkt) at Southampton, 2008
100:0 wkt	Yorkshire (95 and 91) lost to Gloucestershire (88 and 100:0) at Bristol, 1956.

NARROW VICTORIES – BY 1 WICKET

Yorkshire (70 and 91:9) beat Cambridgeshire (86 and 74) at Wisbech, 1867.
Yorkshire (91 and 145:9) beat MCC (73 and 161) at Lord's, 1870.
Yorkshire (265 and 154:9) beat Derbyshire (234 and 184) at Derby, 1897.
Yorkshire (177 and 197:9) beat MCC (188 and 185) at Lord's, 1899.
Yorkshire (391 and 241:9) beat Somerset (349 and 281) at Taunton, 1901.
Yorkshire (239 and 168:9) beat MCC (179 and 226) at Scarborough, 1935.
Yorkshire (152 and 90:9) beat Worcestershire (119 and 121) at Leeds, 1946.
Yorkshire (229 and 175:9) beat Glamorgan (194 and 207) at Bradford, 1960.
Yorkshire (265.9 dec and 191:9) beat Worcestershire (227 and 227) at Worcester, 1961.
Yorkshire (329:6 dec and 167:9) beat Essex (339.9 dec and 154) at Scarborough, 1979.
Yorkshire (Innings forfeited and 251:9 beat Sussex (195 and 55.1 dec) at Leeds, 1986.
Yorkshire (314 and 150:9) beat Essex (200 and 261) at Scarborough, 1998.

NARROW VICTORIES – BY 5 RUNS OR LESS

By 1 run	Yorkshire (228 and 214) beat Middlesex (206 and 235) at Bradford, 1976.
By 1 run	Yorkshire (383 and inns forfeited) beat Loughborough UCCE (93: 3 dec. and 289) at Leeds, 2007.
By 1 run	Yorkshire (206 and 247) beat Northamptonshire (234 and 218) at Leeds, 2021
By 2 runs	Yorkshire (108 and 122) beat Nottinghamshire (56 and 172) at Nottingham, 1870.
By 2 runs	Yorkshire (304:9 dec and 135) beat Middlesex (225:2 dec and 212) at Leeds, 1985.
By 3 runs	Yorkshire (446:9 dec and 172:4 dec) beat Essex (300:3 dec and 315) at Colchester, 1991.
By 3 runs	Yorkshire (202 and 283) beat Somerset (224 and 258) at Taunton, 2017
By 5 runs	Yorkshire (271 and 147:6 dec) beat Surrey (198 and 215) at Sheffield, 1950.
By 5 runs	Yorkshire (151 and 176) beat Hampshire (165 and 157) at Bradford, 1962.
By 5 runs	Yorkshire (376:4 and 106) beat Middlesex (325:8 and 152) at Lord's, 1975
By 5 runs	Yorkshire (323:5 dec and inns forfeited) beat Somerset (inns forfeited and 318) at Taunton, 1986.

NARROW DEFEATS – BY 1 WICKET

Yorkshire (224 and 210) lost to Australian Imperial Forces XI (265 and 170:9) at Sheffield, 1919

Yorkshire (101 and 159) lost to Warwickshire (45 and 216:9) at Scarborough, 1934.

Yorkshire (239 and 184:9 dec.) lost to Warwickshire (125 and 302:9) at Birmingham, 1983.

Yorkshire (289 and 153) lost to Surrey (250:2 dec and 193:9) at Guildford, 1991.

Yorkshire (341 and Inns forfeited) lost to Surrey (39:1 dec and 306:9) at Bradford, 1992.

NARROW DEFEATS – BY 5 RUNS OR LESS

By 1 run	Yorkshire (135 and 297) lost to Essex (139 and 294) at Huddersfield, 1897.
By 1 run	Yorkshire (159 and 232) lost to Gloucestershire (164 and 228) at Bristol, 1906.
By 1 run	Yorkshire (126 and 137) lost to Worcestershire (101 and 163) at Worcester, 1968.
By 1 run	Yorkshire (366 and 217) lost to Surrey (409 and 175) at The Oval, 1995.
By 2 runs	Yorkshire (172 and 107) lost to Gloucestershire (157 and 124) at Sheffield, 1913.
By 2 runs	Yorkshire (179:9 dec and 144) lost to MCC (109 and 216) at Lord's, 1957.
By 3 runs	Yorkshire (126 and 181) lost to Sussex (182 and 128) at Sheffield, 1883.
By 3 runs	Yorkshire (160 and 71) lost to Lancashire (81 and 153) at Huddersfield, 1889.
By 3 runs	Yorkshire (134 and 158) lost to Nottinghamshire (200 and 95) at Leeds, 1923.
By 4 runs	Yorkshire (169 and 193) lost to Middlesex (105 and 261) at Bradford, 1920.
By 5 runs	Yorkshire (58 and 51) lost to Lancashire (64 and 50) at Manchester, 1893.
By 5 runs	Yorkshire (119 and 115) lost to Warwickshire (167 and 72) at Bradford, 1969.

HIGH FOURTH INNINGS SCORES – 300 AND OVER

By Yorkshire
To Win:	406:4	beat Leicestershire by 6 wkts at Leicester, 2005
	402:6	beat Gloucestershire by 4 wkts at Bristol, 2012
	400:4	beat Leicestershire by 6 wkts at Scarborough, 2005
	339:6	beat Durham by 4 wkts at Chester-le-Street, 2013
	331:8	beat Middlesex by 2 wkts at Lord's, 1910.
	327:6	beat Nottinghamshire by 4 wkts at Nottingham, 1990.*
	323:5	beat Nottinghamshire by 5 wkts at Nottingham, 1977.
	318:3	beat Glamorgan by 7 wkts at Middlesbrough, 1976.
	316:8	beat Gloucestershire by 2 wkts at Scarborough, 2012
	309:7	beat Somerset by 3 wkts at Taunton, 1984.
	305:8	beat Nottinghamshire by 2 wkts at Worksop, 1982.
	305:5	beat Hampshire by 5 wkts at West End, Southampton, 2015
	305:3	beat Lancashire by 7 wkts at Manchester, 1994.
	304:4	beat Derbyshire by 6 wkts at Chesterfield, 1959.
	300:4	beat Derbyshire by 6 wkts at Chesterfield, 1981.
	300:6	beat Derbyshire by 4 wkts at Scarborough, 1990.*
To Draw:	341:8	(set 358) drew with Derbyshire at Derby, 2004.
	333:7	(set 369) drew with Essex at Chelmsford, 2010
	316:6	(set 326) drew with Oxford University at Oxford, 1948.
	312:6	(set 344) drew with Sussex at Scarborough 2011
	316:7	(set 320) drew with Somerset at Scarborough, 1990.
	300:5	(set 392) drew with Kent at Canterbury, 2010
To Lose:	433	(set 500) lost to Warwickshire by 66 runs at Birmingham, 2006
	380	(set 406) lost to MCC. by 25 runs at Lord's, 1937.
	343	(set 490) lost to Durham by 146 runs at Leeds 2011
	324	(set 485) lost to Northamptonshire by 160 runs at Luton, 1994.
	322	(set 344) lost to Middlesex by 21 runs at Lord's, 1996.
	309	(set 400) lost to Middlesex by 90 runs at Lord's 1878.

*Consecutive matches

By Opponents:
To Win:	479:6	Somerset won by 4 wkts at Taunton, 2009
	472:3	Middlesex won by 7 wkts at Lord's, 2014
	404:5	Hampshire won by 5 wkts at Leeds, 2006
	392:4	Gloucestershire won by 6 wkts at Bristol, 1948
	364:4	Somerset won by 6 wkts at Taunton, 2010
	354:5	Nottinghamshire won by 5 wkts at Scarborough, 1990
	337:4	Worcestershire won by 6 wkts at Kidderminster, 2007
	334:6	Glamorgan won by 4 wkts at Harrogate, 1955
	329:5	Worcestershire won by 5 wkts at Worcester, 1979
	321:6	Hampshire won by 4 wickets at Leeds, 2017
	306:9	Surrey won by 1 wkt at Bradford, 1992
	305:7	Lancashire won by 3 wkts at Manchester, 1980
	302:9	Warwickshire won by 1 wkt at Birmingham, 1983

HIGH FOURTH INNINGS SCORES – 300 AND OVER *(Continued)*

By Opponents:

To Draw:	366:8	(set 443) Hampshire drew at Southampton, 2007.
	334:7	(set 339) MCC. drew at Scarborough, 1911.
	322:9	(set 334) Middlesex drew at Leeds, 1988.
	317:6	(set 355) Nottinghamshire drew at Nottingham, 1910.
	300:9	(set 314) Northamptonshire drew at Northampton, 1990.
To Lose:	370	(set 539) Leicestershire lost by 168 runs at Leicester, 2001
	319	(set 364) Gloucestershire lost by 44 runs at Leeds, 1987.
	318	(set 324) Somerset lost by 5 runs at Taunton, 1986.
	315	(set 319) Essex lost by 3 runs at Colchester, 1991.
	314	(set 334) Lancashire lost by 19 runs at Manchester, 1993.
	310	(set 417) Warwickshire lost by 106 runs at Scarborough, 1939.
	306	(set 413) Kent lost by 106 runs at Leeds, 1952.
	300	(set 330) Middlesex lost by 29 runs at Sheffield, 1930.

TIE MATCHES

Yorkshire (351:4 dec and 113) tied with Leicestershire (328 and 136) at Huddersfield, 1954.
Yorkshire (106:9 dec and 207) tied with Middlesex (102 and 211) at Bradford, 1973.

HIGHEST SCORES BY AND AGAINST YORKSHIRE

Yorkshire versus: —

Derbyshire: *By Yorkshire:*   *Against Yorkshire:*
In Yorkshire: 677:7 dec at Leeds 2013   491 at Bradford, 1949
Away: 662 at Chesterfield, 1898   523 at Derby, 2005

Durham:
In Yorkshire: 677:7 dec. at Leeds, 2006   573 at Scarborough, 2013
Away   589-8 dec at Chester-le-Street, 2014   507:8 dec at Chester-le-Street, 2016

Essex:
In Yorkshire: 516 at Scarborough, 2010   622:8 dec. at Leeds, 2005
Away: 555:1 dec. at Leyton, 1932   521 at Leyton, 1905

Glamorgan:
In Yorkshire: 580:9 dec at Scarborough, 2001   498 at Leeds, 1999
Away: 536:8 dec. at Cardiff, 1996   482:7 dec. at Cardiff, 1996

Gloucestershire:
In Yorkshire: 504:7 dec. at Bradford, 1905   411 at Leeds, 1992
Away: 494 at Bristol, 1897   574 at Cheltenham, 1990

Hampshire:
In Yorkshire: 593:9 dec. at Leeds 2016   498:6 dec at Scarborough, 2010
Away   585:3 dec at Portsmouth 1920   599:3 at Southampton, 2011

Kent:
In Yorkshire: 550:9 at Scarborough, 1995   537:9 dec at Leeds, 2012
Away: 559 at Canterbury, 1887   580: 9 dec. at Maidstone, 1998

Lancashire:
In Yorkshire: 590 at Bradford, 1887   517 at Leeds, 2007.
Away   616:6 dec at Manchester, 2014   537 at Manchester, 2005

Leicestershire:
In Yorkshire   562 { at Scarborough, 1901 / at Dewsbury, 1903   681:7 dec. at Bradford, 1996
Away: 660 at Leicester, 1896   425 at Leicester, 1906

HIGHEST SCORES BY AND AGAINST YORKSHIRE *(Continued)*

Yorkshire versus: —

Middlesex:	**By Yorkshire:**	**Against Yorkshire:**
In Yorkshire:	575:7 dec. at Bradford, 1899	527 at Huddersfield, 1887
Away	538:6 dec at Lord's, 1925	573:8 dec at Lord's, 2015
Northamptonshire:		
In Yorkshire:	673:8 dec. at Leeds, 2003	517:7 dec. at Scarborough, 1999
Away	546:3 dec at Northampton, 2014	531:4 dec at Northampton, 1996
Nottinghamshire:		
In Yorkshire:	572:8 dec at Scarborough, 2013	545:7 dec at Leeds, 2010
Away	534:9 dec at Nottingham, 2011	490 at Nottingham, 1897
Somerset:		
In Yorkshire:	525:4 dec. at Leeds, 1953	630 at Leeds, 1901
Away:	589:5 dec at Bath, 2001	592 at Taunton, 1892
Surrey:		
In Yorkshire:	582:7 dec. at Sheffield, 1935	516-7 dec at Leeds, 2017
Away:	704 at The Oval, 1899	634:5 dec at The Oval, 2013
Sussex:		
In Yorkshire:	681:5 dec. at Sheffield, 1897	566 at Sheffield, 1937
Away:	522:7 dec. at Hastings, 1911	597:8 dec. at Hove, 2007
Warwickshire		
In Yorkshire	561:7 dec at Scarborough 2007	482 at Leeds, 2011
Away:	887 at Birmingham, 1896	601:9 dec. at Birmingham, 2002
	(Highest score by a First-Class county)	
Worcestershire:		
In Yorkshire:	600: 4 dec. at Scarborough, 1995	572:7 dec. at Scarborough 2018
Away:	560:6 dec at Worcester, 1928	456:8 at Worcester, 1904
Australians:		
In Yorkshire:	377 at Sheffield, 1953	470 at Bradford, 1893
Indians:		
In Yorkshire:	385 at Hull, 1911	490:5 dec. at Sheffield, 1946
New Zealanders:		
In Yorkshire:	419 at Bradford, 1965	370:7 dec. at Bradford, 1949
Pakistanis:		
In Yorkshire:	433:9 dec. at Sheffield, 1954	356 at Sheffield, 1954
South Africans:		
In Yorkshire:	579 at Sheffield, 1951	454:8 dec at Sheffield, 1951
Sri Lankans:		
In Yorkshire:	314:8 dec. at Leeds, 1991	422:8 dec. at Leeds, 1991
West Indians:		
In Yorkshire:	312:5 dec. at Scarborough, 1973	426 at Scarborough, 1995
Zimbabweans:		
In Yorkshire:	298:9 dec at Leeds, 1990	235 at Leeds, 2000
Cambridge University:		
In Yorkshire:	359 at Scarborough, 1967	366 at Leeds, 1998
Away:	540 at Cambridge, 1938	425:7 at Cambridge, 1929
Durham MCCU:		
Away:	355 at Durham, 2011	287 at Durham, 2011
Leeds/Bradford MCCU:		
In Yorkshire	543-5 dec at Leeds, 2017	211 at Leeds, 2012
Away	489-8 dec at Weetwood, Leeds, 2019	219 at Weetwood, Leeds, 2019
Loughborough MCCU:		
In Yorkshire:	383:6 dec at Leeds, 2007	289 at Leeds, 2007

HIGHEST SCORES BY AND AGAINST YORKSHIRE *(Continued)*

Yorkshire versus: —

MCC: | **By Yorkshire:** | **Against Yorkshire:**
In Yorkshire: | 557:8 dec. at Scarborough, 1933 | 478:8 at Scarborough, 1904
Away: | 528:8 dec. at Lord's, 1919 | 488 at Lord's, 1919

Oxford University:
In Yorkshire: | 173 at Harrogate, 1972 | 190:6 dec at Harrogate, 1972
Away: | 468:6 dec. at Oxford, 1978 | 422:9 dec. at Oxford, 1953

LOWEST SCORES BY AND AGAINST YORKSHIRE

Yorkshire versus:

Derbyshire: | **By Yorkshire:** | **Against Yorkshire:**
In Yorkshire: | 50 at Sheffield, 1894 | 20 at Sheffield, 1939
Away: | 44 at Chesterfield, 1948 | 26 at Derby, 1880

Durham:
In Yorkshire: | 93 at Leeds, 2003 | 125 at Harrogate, 1995
Away: | 108 at Durham, 1992 | 74 at Chester-le-Street, 1998

Essex:
In Yorkshire: | 31 at Huddersfield, 1935 | 52 at Harrogate, 1900
Away: | 50 at Chelmsford, 2018 | 30 at Leyton, 1901

Glamorgan:
In Yorkshire: | 83 at Sheffield, 1946 | 52 at Hull, 1926
Away: | 92 at Swansea, 1956 | 48 at Cardiff, 1924

Gloucestershire:
In Yorkshire: | 61 at Leeds, 1894 | 36 at Sheffield, 1903
Away: | 35 at Bristol, 1959 | 42 at Gloucester, 1924

Hampshire:
In Yorkshire: | 23 at Middlesbrough, 1965 | 36 at Leeds, 1904
Away: | 96 at Bournemouth, 1971 | 36 at Southampton, 1898

Kent:
In Yorkshire: | 30 at Sheffield, 1865 | 39 { at Sheffield, 1882 / at Sheffield, 1936
Away: | 62 at Maidstone, 1889 | 63 at Canterbury, 1901

Lancashire:
In Yorkshire: | 33 at Leeds, 1924 | 30 at Holbeck, 1868
Away: | 51 { at Manchester, 1888 / at Manchester, 1893 | 39 at Manchester, 1874

Leicestershire: | **By Yorkshire:** | **Against Yorkshire:**
In Yorkshire: | 93 at Leeds, 1935 | 34 at Leeds, 1906
Away: | 47 at Leicester, 1911 | 57 at Leicester, 1898

Middlesex:
In Yorkshire: | 45 at Leeds, 1898 | 45 at Huddersfield, 1879
Away: | 43 at Lord's, 1888 | 49 at Lord's in 1890

Northamptonshire:
In Yorkshire: | 85 at Sheffield, 1919 | 51 at Bradford, 1920
Away | 64 at Northampton, 1959 | 15 at Northampton, 1908 (and 27 in first innings)

Nottinghamshire:
In Yorkshire: | 32 at Sheffield, 1876 | 24 at Sheffield, 1888
Away: | 43 at Nottingham, 1869 | 13 at Nottingham, 1901 (second smallest total by a First-Class county)

LOWEST SCORES BY AND AGAINST YORKSHIRE *(continued)*

Yorkshire versus:

Somerset: **By Yorkshire:**   **Against Yorkshire:**
In Yorkshire: 73 at Leeds, 1895   43 at Bradford, 1930
Away: 83 at Wells, 1949   35 at Bath, 1898

Surrey:
In Yorkshire: 54 at Sheffield, 1873   31 at Holbeck, 1883
Away: 26 at The Oval, 1909   44 at The Oval, 1935

Sussex:
In Yorkshire: 61 at Dewsbury, 1891   20 at Hull, 1922
Away: 42 at Hove, 1922   24 at Hove, 1878

Warwickshire:
In Yorkshire: 49 at Huddersfield, 1951   35 at Sheffield, 1979
Away: 54 at Birmingham, 1964   35 at Birmingham, 1963

Worcestershire:
In Yorkshire: 62 at Bradford, 1907   24 at Huddersfield, 1903
Away: 72 at Worcester, 1977   65 at Worcester, 1925

Australians:
In Yorkshire: 48 at Leeds, 1893   23 at Leeds, 1902

Indians:
In Yorkshire: 146 at Bradford, 1959   66 at Harrogate, 1932

New Zealanders:
In Yorkshire: 189 at Harrogate, 1931   134 at Bradford, 1965

Pakistanis:
In Yorkshire: 137 at Bradford, 1962   150 at Leeds, 1967

South Africans:
In Yorkshire: 113 at Bradford, 1907   76 at Bradford, 1951

Sri Lankans:
In Yorkshire: Have not been dismissed.   287:5 dec at Leeds, 1988
    Lowest is 184:1 dec at Leeds, 1991

West Indians:
In Yorkshire: 50 at Harrogate, 1906   58 at Leeds, 1928

Zimbabweans:
In Yorkshire: 124 at Leeds, 2000   68 at Leeds, 2000

Cambridge University:
In Yorkshire: 110 at Sheffield, 1903   39 at Sheffield, 1903
Away: 51 at Cambridge, 1906   30 at Cambridge, 1928

Durham MCCU:
Away: 355 at Durham, 2011   196 at Durham, 2011

Leeds/Bradford MCCU:
In Yorkshire   135 at Leeds, 2012   118 at Leeds, 2013
Away   118 at Weetwood, Leeds, 2019

Loughborough MCCU:
In Yorkshire   348:5 dec at Leeds, 2010   289 at Leeds, 2007

MCC:
In Yorkshire: 46 { at Scarborough, 1876
            at Scarborough, 1877   31 at Scarborough, 1877
Away: 44 at Lord's, 1880   27 at Lord's, 1902

Oxford University:
In Yorkshire: Have not been dismissed.
    Lowest is 115:8 at Harrogate, 1972   133 at Harrogate, 1972
Away: 141 at Oxford, 1949   46 at Oxford, 1956

INDIVIDUAL INNINGS OF 150 AND OVER

A complete list of all First Class Centuries up to and Including 2020 is to be found in the 2021 edition

J M BAIRSTOW (7)

205	v. Nottinghamshire	at Nottingham	2011
182	v. Leicestershire	at Scarborough	2012
186	v. Derbyshire	at Leeds	2013
161 *	v. Sussex	at Arundel	2014
219 *	v. Durham	at Chester-le-Street	2015
246	v. Hampshire	at Leeds	2016
198	v. Surrey	at Leeds	2016

G S BALLANCE (5)

174	v. Northamptonshire	at Leeds	2014
165	v. Sussex	at Hove	2015
203 *	v. Hampshire 2nd innings	at West End, Southampton	2017
194	v. Worcestershire	at Worcester	2018
159	v. Kent	at Canterbury	2019

W BARBER (7)

162	v. Middlesex	at Bramall Lane, Sheffield	1932
168	v. MCC	at Lord's	1934
248	v. Kent	at Leeds	1934
191	v. Sussex	at Leeds	1935
255	v. Surrey	at Bramall Lane, Sheffield	1935
158	v. Kent	at Bramall Lane, Sheffield	1936
157	v. Surrey	at Bramall Lane, Sheffield	1938

M G BEVAN (2)

| 153 * | v. Surrey | at The Oval | 1995 |
| 160 * | v. Surrey | at Middlesbrough | 1996 |

H D BIRD (1)

| 181 * | v. Glamorgan | at Bradford | 1959 |

R J BLAKEY (3)

204 *	v. Gloucestershire	at Leeds	1987
196	v. Oxford University	at Oxford	1991
223 *	v. Northamptonshire	at Leeds	2003

G S BLEWETT (1)

| 190 | v. Northamptonshire | at Scarborough | 1999 |

M W BOOTH (1)

| 210 | v. Worcestershire | at Worcester | 1911 |

G BOYCOTT (32)

165*	v. Leicestershire	at Scarborough	1963
151	v. Middlesex	at Leeds	1964
151*	v. Leicestershire	at Leicester	1964
177	v. Gloucestershire	at Bristol	1964
164	v. Sussex	at Hove	1966
220*	v. Northamptonshire	at Sheffield	1967
180*	v. Warwickshire	at Middlesbrough	1968
260*	v. Essex	at Colchester (Garrison Ground)	1970
169	v. Nottinghamshire	at Leeds	1971
233	v. Essex	at Colchester (Garrison Ground)	1971
182*	v. Middlesex	at Lord's	1971
169	v. Lancashire	at Sheffield	1971
151	v. Leicestershire	at Bradford	1971

INDIVIDUAL INNINGS OF 150 AND OVER *(Continued)*

G BOYCOTT *(Continued)*

204*	v. Leicestershire	at Leicester	1972
152*	v. Worcestershire	at Worcester	1975
175*	v. Middlesex	at Scarborough	1975
201*	v. Middlesex	at Lord's	1975
161*	v. Gloucestershire	at Leeds	1976
207*	v. Cambridge University	at Cambridge	1976
156*	v. Glamorgan	at Middlesbrough	1976
154	v Nottinghamshire	at Nottingham	1977
151*	v Derbyshire	at Leeds	1979
167	v Derbyshire	at Chesterfield	1979
175*	v Nottinghamshire	at Worksop	1979
154*	v Derbyshire	at Scarborough	1980
159	v Worcestershire	at Sheffield (Abbeydale Park)	1982
152*	v Warwickshire	at Leeds	1982
214*	v Nottinghamshire	at Worksop	1983
163	v Nottinghamshire	at Bradford	1983
169*	v Derbyshire	at Chesterfield	1983
153*	v Derbyshire	at Harrogate	1984
184	v Worcestershire	at Worcester	1985

T T BRESNAN (1)

169*	v. Durham	at Chester-le-Street	2015

G L BROPHY (1)

177*	v Worcestershire	at Worcester	2011

J T BROWN (8)

168*	v Sussex	at Huddersfield	1895
203	v Middlesex	at Lord's	1896
311	v Sussex	at Sheffield	1897
300	v Derbyshire	at Chesterfield	1898
150	v Sussex	at Hove	1898
168	v Cambridge University	at Cambridge	1899
167	v Australians	at Bradford	1899
192	v Derbyshire	at Derby	1899

D BYAS (5)

153	v Nottinghamshire	at Worksop	1991
156	v Essex	at Chelmsford	1993
181	v Cambridge University	at Cambridge	1995
193	v Lancashire	at Leeds	1995
213	v Worcestershire	at Scarborough	1995

D B CLOSE (5)

164	v Combined Services	at Harrogate	1954
154	v Nottinghamshire	at Nottingham	1959
198	v Surrey	at The Oval	1960
184	v Nottinghamshire	at Scarborough	1960
161	v Northamptonshire	at Northampton	1963

D DENTON (11)

153*	v Australians	at Bradford	1905
165	v Hampshire	at Bournemouth	1905
172	v Gloucestershire	at Bradford	1905
184	v Nottinghamshire	at Nottingham	1909
182	v Derbyshire	at Chesterfield	1910

INDIVIDUAL INNINGS OF 150 AND OVER *(Continued)*

D DENTON *(Continued)*

200*	v Warwickshire	at Birmingham	1912
182	v Gloucestershire	at Bristol	1912
221	v Kent	at Tunbridge Wells	1912
191	v Hampshire	at Southampton	1912
168*	v Hampshire	at Southampton	1914
209*	v Worcestershire	at Worcester	1920

A W GALE (4)

150	v. Surrey	at The Oval	2008
151*	v. Nottinghamshire	at Nottingham	2010
272	v. Nottinghamshire	at Scarborough	2013
164	v. Worcestershire	at Scarborough	2015

P A GIBB (1)

157*	v. Nottinghamshire	at Sheffield	1935

S HAIGH (1)

159	v. Nottinghamshire	at Sheffield	1901

L HALL (1)

160	v. Lancashire	at Bradford	1887

J H HAMPSHIRE (5)

150	v. Leicestershire	at Bradford	1964
183*	v. Sussex	at Hove	1971
157*	v. Nottinghamshire	at Worksop	1974
158	v. Gloucestershire	at Harrogate	1974
155*	v. Gloucestershire	at Leeds	1976

I J HARVEY (1)

209*	v. Somerset	at Leeds	2005

LORD HAWKE (1)

166	v. Warwickshire	at Birmingham	1896

G H HIRST (15)

186	v. Surrey	at The Oval	1899
155	v. Nottinghamshire	at Scarborough	1900
214	v. Worcestershire	at Worcester	1901
153	v. Leicestershire	at Dewsbury	1903
153	v. Oxford University	at Oxford	1904
152	v. Hampshire	at Portsmouth	1904
157	v. Kent	at Tunbridge Wells	1904
341	v. Leicestershire	at Leicester (Aylestone Road)	1905
232*	v. Surrey	at The Oval	1905
169	v. Oxford University	at Oxford	1906
158	v. Cambridge University	at Cambridge	1910
156	v. Lancashire	at Manchester	1911
218	v. Sussex	at Hastings	1911
166*	v. Sussex	at Hastings	1913
180*	v. MCC	at Lord's	1919

P HOLMES (16)

302*	v. Hampshire	at Portsmouth	1920
150	v. Derbyshire	at Chesterfield	1921
277*	v. Northamptonshire	at Harrogate	1921
209	v. Warwickshire	at Birmingham	1922

INDIVIDUAL INNINGS OF 150 AND OVER *(Continued)*

P HOLMES *(Continued)*

220*	v. Warwickshire	at Huddersfield	1922
199	v. Somerset	at Hull	1923
315*	v. Middlesex	at Lord's	1925
194	v. Leicestershire	at Hull	1925
159	v. Hampshire	at Southampton	1925
180	v. Gloucestershire	at Gloucester	1927
175*	v. New Zealanders	at Bradford	1927
179*	v. Middlesex	at Leeds	1928
275	v. Warwickshire	at Bradford	1928
285	v. Nottinghamshire	at Nottingham	1929
250	v. Warwickshire	at Birmingham	1931
224*	v. Essex	at Leyton	1932

L HUTTON (31)

196	v. Worcestershire	at Worcester	1934
163	v. Surrey	at Leeds	1936
161	v. MCC	at Lord's	1937
271*	v. Derbyshire	at Sheffield	1937
153	v. Leicestershire	at Hull	1937
180	v. Cambridge University	at Cambridge	1938
158	v. Warwickshire	at Birmingham	1939
280*	v. Hampshire	at Sheffield	1939
151	v. Surrey	at Leeds	1939
177	v. Sussex	at Scarborough	1939
183*	v. Indians	at Bradford	1946
171*	v. Northamptonshire	at Hull	1946
197	v. Glamorgan	at Swansea	1947
197	v. Essex	at Southend-on-Sea	1947
270*	v. Hampshire	at Bournemouth	1947
176*	v. Sussex	at Sheffield	1948
155	v. Sussex	at Hove	1948
167	v. New Zealanders	at Bradford	1949
201	v. Lancashire	at Manchester	1949
165	v. Sussex	at Hove	1949
269*	v. Northamptonshire	at Wellingborough	1949
156	v. Essex	at Colchester (Castle Park)	1950
153	v. Nottinghamshire	at Nottingham	1950
156	v. South Africans	at Sheffield	1951
151	v. Surrey	at The Oval	1951
194*	v. Nottinghamshire	at Nottingham	1951
152	v. Lancashire	at Leeds	1952
189	v. Kent	at Leeds	1952
178	v. Somerset	at Leeds	1953
163	v. Combined Services	at Harrogate	1954
194	v. Nottinghamshire	at Nottingham	1955

R A HUTTON (1)

189	v. Pakistanis	at Bradford	1971

R ILLINGWORTH (2)

150	v. Essex	at Colchester (Castle Park)	1959
162	v. Indians	at Sheffield	1959

Hon F S JACKSON (3)

160	v. Gloucestershire	at Sheffield	1898
155	v. Middlesex	at Bradford	1899
158	v. Surrey	at Bradford	1904

INDIVIDUAL INNINGS OF 150 AND OVER *(Continued)*

P A JAQUES (7)

243	v. Hampshire	at Southampton (Rose Bowl)	2004
173	v. Glamorgan	at Leeds	2004
176	v. Northamptonshire	at Leeds	2005
219	v. Derbyshire	at Leeds	2005
172	v. Durham	at Scarborough	2005
160	v. Gloucestershire	at Bristol	2012
152	v. Durham	at Scarborough	2013

R KILNER (5)

169	v. Gloucestershire	at Bristol	1914
206*	v. Derbyshire	at Sheffield	1920
166	v. Northamptonshire	at Northampton	1921
150	v. Northamptonshire	at Harrogate	1921
150	v. Middlesex	at Lord's	1926

T KOHLER-CADMORE (2)

176	v. Leeds/Bradford MCCU	at Weetwood, Leeds	2019
165*	v. Warwickshire	at Birmingham	2019

F LEE (1)

165	v. Lancashire	at Bradford	1887

A Z LEES (1)

275*	v. Derbyshire	at Chesterfield	2013

D S LEHMANN (13)

177	v. Somerset	at Taunton	1997
163*	v. Leicestershire	at Leicester	1997
182	v. Hampshire	at Portsmouth	1997
200	v. Worcestershire	at Worcester	1998
187*	v. Somerset	at Bath	2001
252	v. Lancashire	at Leeds	2001
193	v. Leicestershire	at Leicester	2001
216	v. Sussex	at Arundel	2002
187	v. Lancashire	at Leeds	2002
150	v. Warwickshire	at Birmingham	2006
193	v. Kent	at Canterbury	2006
172	v. Kent	at Leeds	2006
339	v. Durham	at Leeds	2006

E I LESTER (5)

186	v. Warwickshire	at Scarborough	1949
178	v. Nottinghamshire	at Nottingham	1952
157	v. Cambridge University	at Hull	1953
150	v. Oxford University	at Oxford	1954
163	v. Essex	at Romford	1954

M LEYLAND (17)

191	v. Glamorgan	at Swansea	1926
204*	v. Middlesex	at Sheffield	1927
247	v. Worcestershire	at Worcester	1928
189*	v. Glamorgan	at Huddersfield	1928
211*	v. Lancashire	at Leeds	1930
172	v. Middlesex	at Sheffield	1930
186	v. Derbyshire	at Leeds	1930
189	v. Middlesex	at Sheffield	1932
153	v. Leicestershire	at Leicester (Aylestone Road)	1932
166	v. Leicestershire	at Bradford	1932
153*	v. Hampshire	at Bournemouth	1932

INDIVIDUAL INNINGS OF 150 AND OVER *(Continued)*

M LEYLAND *(Continued)*

192	v. Northamptonshire	at Leeds	1933
210*	v. Kent	at Dover	1933
263	v. Essex	at Hull	1936
163*	v. Surrey	at Leeds	1936
167	v. Worcestershire	at Stourbridge	1937
180*	v. Middlesex	at Lord's	1939

E LOCKWOOD (1)

208	v. Kent	at Gravesend	1883

J D LOVE (4)

163	v. Nottinghamshire	at Bradford	1976
170*	v. Worcestershire	at Worcester	1979
161	v. Warwickshire	at Birmingham	1981
154	v. Lancashire	at Manchester	1981

F A LOWSON (10)

155	v. Kent	at Maidstone	1951
155	v. Worcestershire	at Bradford	1952
166	v. Scotland	at Glasgow	1953
259*	v. Worcestershire	at Worcester	1953
165	v. Sussex	at Hove	1954
164	v. Essex	at Scarborough	1954
150*	v. Kent	at Dover	1954
183*	v. Oxford University	at Oxford	1956
154	v. Somerset	at Taunton	1956
154	v. Cambridge University	at Cambridge	1957

R G LUMB (2)

159	v. Somerset	at Harrogate	1979
165*	v. Gloucestershire	at Bradford	1984

A LYTH (6)

248 *	v. Leicestershire	at Leicester	2012
230	v. Northamptonshire	at Northampton	2014
251	v. Lancashire	at Manchester	2014
202	v. Surrey	at The Oval	2016
194	v. Leeds/Bradford MCCU	at Leeds	2017
153	v. Nottinghamshire	at Nottingham	2021

D J MALAN (2)

219	v. Derbyshire	at Leeds	2020
199	v. Sussex	at Leeds	2021

D R MARTYN (1)

238	v. Gloucestershire	at Leeds	2003

A McGRATH (7)

165	v. Lancashire	at Leeds	2002
174	v. Derbyshire	at Derby	2004
165*	v. Leicestershire	at Leicester	2005
173*	v. Worcestershire	at Leeds	2005
158	v. Derbyshire	at Derby	2005
188*	v. Warwickshire	at Birmingham	2007
211	v. Warwickshire	at Birmingham	2009

INDIVIDUAL INNINGS OF 150 AND OVER *(Continued)*

A A METCALFE (7)

151	v. Northamptonshire	at Luton	1986
151	v. Lancashire	at Manchester	1986
152	v. MCC	at Scarborough	1987
216*	v. Middlesex	at Leeds	1988
162	v. Gloucestershire	at Cheltenham	1990
150*	v. Derbyshire	at Scarborough	1990
194*	v. Nottinghamshire	at Nottingham	1990

A MITCHELL (7)

189	v. Northamptonshire	at Northampton	1926
176	v. Nottinghamshire	at Bradford	1930
177*	v. Gloucestershire	at Bradford	1932
150*	v. Worcestershire	at Worcester	1933
158	v. MCC	at Scarborough	1933
152	v. Hampshire	at Bradford	1934
181	v. Surrey	at Bradford	1934

F MITCHELL (2)

194	v. Leicestershire	at Leicester	1899
162*	v. Warwickshire	at Birmingham	1901

M D MOXON (14)

153	v. Lancashire	at Leeds	1983
153	v. Somerset	at Leeds	1985
168	v. Worcestershire	at Worcester	1985
191	v. Northamptonshire	at Scarborough	1988
162*	v. Surrey	at The Oval	1989
218*	v. Sussex	at Eastbourne	1990
200	v. Essex	at Colchester (Castle Park)	1991
183	v. Gloucestershire	at Cheltenham	1992
171*	v. Kent	at Leeds	1993
161*	v. Lancashire	at Manchester	1994
274*	v. Worcestershire	at Worcester	1994
203*	v. Kent	at Leeds	1995
213	v. Glamorgan	at Cardiff (Sophia Gardens)	1996
155	v. Pakistan 'A'	at Leeds	1997

E OLDROYD (5)

151*	v. Glamorgan	at Cardiff	1922
194	v. Worcestershire	at Worcester	1923
162*	v. Glamorgan	at Swansea	1928
168	v. Glamorgan	at Hull	1929
164*	v. Somerset	at Bath	1930

D E V PADGETT (1)

161*	v. Oxford University	at Oxford	1959

R PEEL (2)

158	v. Middlesex	at Lord's	1889
210*	v. Warwickshire	at Birmingham	1896

A U RASHID (3)

157*	v. Lancashire	at Leeds	2009
180	v. Somerset	at Leeds	2013
159*	v. Lancashire	at Manchester	2014

INDIVIDUAL INNINGS OF 150 AND OVER *(Continued)*

W RHODES (8)

196	v. Worcestershire	at Worcester	1904
201	v. Somerset	at Taunton	1905
199	v. Sussex	at Hove	1909
176	v. Nottinghamshire	at Harrogate	1912
152	v. Leicestershire	at Leicester (Aylestone Road)	1913
167*	v. Nottinghamshire	at Leeds	1920
267*	v. Leicestershire	at Leeds	1921
157	v. Derbyshire	at Leeds	1925

P E ROBINSON (2)

150*	v. Derbyshire	at Scarborough	1990
189	v. Lancashire	at Scarborough	1991

J E ROOT (5)

160	v. Sussex	at Scarborough	2011
222 *	v. Hampshire	at Southampton (West End)	2012
182	v. Durham	at Chester-le-Street	2013
236	v. Derbyshire	at Leeds	2013

2013 innings consecutive

213	v.Surrey	at Leeds	2016

J W ROTHERY (1)

161	v. Kent	at Dover	1908

J A RUDOLPH (5)

220	v. Warwickshire	at Scarborough	2007
155	v. Somerset	at Taunton	2008
198	v. Worcestershire	at Leeds	2009
191	v. Somerset	at Taunton	2009
228*	v. Durham	at Leeds	2010

H RUDSTON (1)

164	v. Leicestershire	at Leicester (Aylestone Road)	1904

J J SAYERS (3)

187	v. Kent	at Tunbridge Wells	2007
173	v. Warwickshire	at Birmingham	2009
152	v. Somerset	at Taunton	2009

A B SELLERS (1)

204	v. Cambridge University	at Cambridge	1936

K SHARP (2)

173	v. Derbyshire	at Chesterfield	1984
181	v. Gloucestershire	at Harrogate	1986

P J SHARPE (4)

203*	v. Cambridge University	at Cambridge	1960
152	v. Kent	at Sheffield	1960
197	v. Pakistanis	at Leeds	1967
172*	v. Glamorgan	at Swansea	1971

G A SMITHSON (1)

169	v. Leicestershire	at Leicester	1947

W B STOTT (2)

181	v. Essex	Sheffield	1957
186	v. Warwickshire	Birmingham	1960

INDIVIDUAL INNINGS OF 150 AND OVER *(Continued)*

H SUTCLIFFE (39)

174	v. Kent	at Dover	1919
232	v. Surrey	at The Oval	1922
213	v. Somerset	at Dewsbury	1924
160	v. Sussex	at Sheffield	1924
255*	v. Essex	at Southend-on-Sea	1924
235	v. Middlesex	at Leeds	1925
206	v. Warwickshire	at Dewsbury	1925
171	v. MCC	at Scarborough	1925
200	v. Leicestershire	at Leicester (Aylestone Road)	1926
176	v. Surrey	at Leeds	1927
169	v. Nottinghamshire	at Bradford	1927
228	v. Sussex	at Eastbourne	1928
150	v. Northamptonshire	at Northampton	1929
150*	v. Essex	at Dewsbury	1930
173	v. Sussex	at Hove	1930
173*	v. Cambridge University	at Cambridge	1931
230	v. Kent	at Folkestone	1931
183	v. Somerset	at Dewsbury	1931
195	v. Lancashire	at Sheffield	1931
187	v. Leicestershire	at Leicester (Aylestone Road)	1931
153*	v. Warwickshire	at Hull	1932
313	v. Essex	at Leyton	1932
270	v. Sussex	at Leeds	1932
182	v. Derbyshire	at Leeds	1932
194	v. Essex	at Scarborough	1932
205	v. Warwickshire	at Birmingham	1933
177	v. Middlesex	at Bradford	1933
174	v. Leicestershire	at Leicester (Aylestone Road)	1933
152	v. Cambridge University	at Cambridge	1934
166	v. Essex	at Hull	1934
203	v. Surrey	at The Oval	1934
187*	v. Worcestershire	at Bradford	1934
200*	v. Worcestershire	at Sheffield	1935
212	v. Leicestershire	at Leicester (Aylestone Road)	1935
202	v. Middlesex	at Scarborough	1936
189	v. Leicestershire	at Hull	1937
165	v. Lancashire	at Manchester	1939
234*	v. Leicestershire	at Hull	1939
175	v. Middlesex	at Lord's	1939

W H H SUTCLIFFE (3)

171*	v. Worcestershire	at Worcester	1952
181	v. Kent	at Canterbury	1952
161*	v. Glamorgan	at Harrogate	1955

K TAYLOR (8)

168*	v. Nottinghamshire	at Nottingham	1956
159	v. Leicestershire	at Sheffield	1961
203*	v. Warwickshire	at Birmingham	1961
178*	v. Oxford University	at Oxford	1962
163	v. Nottinghamshire	at Leeds	1962
153	v. Lancashire	at Manchester	1964
160	v. Australians	at Sheffield	1964
162	v. Worcestershire	at Kidderminster	1967

T L TAYLOR (1)

| 156 | v. Hampshire | at Harrogate | 1901 |

INDIVIDUAL INNINGS OF 150 AND OVER *(Continued)*

J TUNNICLIFFE (2)

243	v. Derbyshire	at Chesterfield	1898
158	v. Worcestershire	at Worcester	1900

G ULYETT (1)

199*	v. Derbyshire	at Sheffield	1887

M P VAUGHAN (7)

183	v. Glamorgan	at Cardiff (Sophia Gardens)	1996
183	v. Northamptonshire	at Northampton	1996
161	v. Essex	at Ilford	1997
177	v. Durham	at Chester-le-Street	1998
151	v. Essex	at Chelmsford	1999
153	v. Kent	at Scarborough	1999
155*	v. Derbyshire	at Leeds	2000

E WAINWRIGHT (3)

171	v. Middlesex	at Lord's	1897
153	v. Leicestershire	at Leicester	1899
228	v. Surrey	at The Oval	1899

W WATSON (7)

153*	v. Surrey	at The Oval	1947
172	v. Derbyshire	at Scarborough	1948
162*	v. Somerset	at Leeds	1953
163	v. Sussex	at Sheffield	1955
174	v. Lancashire	at Sheffield	1955
214*	v. Worcestershire	at Worcester	1955
162	v. Northamptonshire	at Harrogate	1957

C WHITE (6)

181	v. Lancashire	at Leeds	1996
172*	v. Worcestershire	at Leeds	1997
186	v. Lancashire	at Manchester	2001
183	v. Glamorgan	at Scarborough	2001
161	v. Leicestershire	at Scarborough	2002
173*	v. Derbyshire	at Derby	2003

K S WILLIAMSON (1)

189	v. Sussex	at Scarborough	2014

B B WILSON (2)

150	v. Warwickshire	at Birmingham	1912
208	v. Sussex	at Bradford	1914

J V WILSON (7)

157*	v. Sussex	at Leeds	1949
157	v. Essex	at Sheffield	1950
166*	v. Sussex	at Hull	1951
223*	v. Scotland	at Scarborough	1951
154	v. Oxford University	at Oxford	1952
230	v. Derbyshire	at Sheffield	1952
165	v. Oxford University	at Oxford	1956

M J WOOD (5)

200*	v. Warwickshire	at Leeds	1998
157	v. Northamptonshire	at Leeds	2003
207	v. Somerset	at Taunton	2003
155	v. Hampshire	at Scarborough	2003
202*	v. Bangladesh 'A'	at Leeds	2005

INDIVIDUAL INNINGS OF 150 AND OVER *(Continued)*

N W D YARDLEY (2)

| 177 | v. Derbyshire | Scarborough | 1947 |
| 183* | v. Hampshire | Leeds | 1951 |

YOUNUS KHAN (2)

| 202* | v. Hampshire | Southampton (Rose Bowl) | 2007 |
| 217* | v. Kent | Scarborough | 2007 |

CENTURIES BY CURRENT PLAYERS

A complete list of all First-Class Centuries up to and including 2020 is to be found in the 2021 edition

J M BAIRSTOW (15)

205	v. Nottinghamshire	Nottingham	2011
136	v. Somerset	Taunton	2011
182	v. Leicestershire	Scarborough	2012
118	v. Leicestershire	Leicester	2012
107	v. Kent	Leeds	2012
186	v. Derbyshire	Leeds	2013
123	v. Leeds/Bradford	Leeds	2014
161*	v. Sussex	Arundel	2014
102	v. Hampshire	Leeds	2015
125*	v. Middlesex	Leeds	2015
219*	v. Durham	Chester-le-Street **	2015
108	v. Warwickshire	Birmingham **	2015

*(** consecutive innings)*

139	v. Worcestershire	Scarborough	2015
246	v. Hampshire	Leeds	2016
198	v. Surrey	Leeds	2016

G S BALLANCE (27)

111	v. Warwickshire	Birmingham	2011
121*	v. Gloucestershire	Bristol	2012
112	v. Leeds/Bradford MCCU	Leeds	2013
107	v. Somerset	Leeds	2013
141	v. Nottinghamshire	Scarborough	2013
112	v. Warwickshire	Leeds	2013
148	v. Surrey 1st inns	The Oval **	2013
108*	v. Surrey 2nd inns	The Oval **	2013
101	v. Leeds/Bradford MCCU	Leeds **	2014

*(** consecutive innings)*

174	v. Northamptonshire	Leeds	2014
130	v. Middlesex	Lord's	2014
165	v. Sussex	Hove	2015
105	v. MCC	Abu Dhabi	2016
132	v. Middlesex	Scarborough	2016
101*	v. Nottinghamshire	Scarborough	2016
120	v. Hampshire	Leeds	2017
108	v. Hampshire 1st innings	West End	2017
203*	v. Hampshire 2nd innings	West End	2017
109	v. Hampshire	West End	2018
104	v. Nottinghamshire	Nottingham	2018
194	v. Worcestershire	Worcester	2018
101*	v. Nottinghamshire	Nottingham	2019
148*	v. Hampshire	West End	2019
159	v. Kent	Canterbury	2019
100	v. Hampshire	Leeds	2019
111	v. Somerset	Leeds	2019
101*	v. Hampshire	West End	2021

FAST SIGNING: Rachel Slater, who broke into the Northern Diamonds' team in August and impressed enough to be offered a full-time contract for 2022. The American-born left-arm seamer, raised in Leeds, also qualifies to play for Scotland and represented them at the Commonwealth Games Qualifiers in Kuala Lumpur in January.

GETTING AHEAD WITH A CAP: Captain Steve Patterson presents Harry Brook with his 1st XI cap during Yorkshire's County Championship match v. Somerset at Scarborough. Brook won four end-of-season club Player of the Year awards and two further awards from the Professional Cricketers' Association and the Cricket Writers Club. Below, left to right: George Hill, Harry Duke and Dominic Leech receive their 2nd XI caps in Yorkshire's clash with Lancashire at Headingley.

MAGNIFICENT MALAN: England batter Dawid Malan on the way to a superb 199 in the first innings of the victory against Sussex at Headingley. He narrowly missed out on becoming the first Yorkshire player to score double centuries in successive first-class innings after one against Leicestershire in 2020.

CLOSE CALL: Adam Lyth just beats the throw in Yorkshire's Championship match v. Sussex at Headingley. He went on to 48, and Yorkshire won by an innings. **BELOW:** Adam takes an acrobatic catch to dismiss Sussex's Tom Haines off the bowling of Dom Bess. He notched up three centuries in the 2021 County Championship, finishing as Yorkshire's most prolific batter in that competition with 819 in 14 games.

THE COMING MAN: Pakistan and Lahore Qalandars fast bowler Haris Rauf starts the season with Yorkshire as an overseas player, bidding to help the county make a flying start to their Championship campaign. Rauf has made his name around the world in limited overs cricket, and had played in only four first-class matches, taking 16 wickets, before arriving at Headingley.

LEGEND HONOUR: Yorkshire and England's Ray Illingworth, whose death is reported in these pages, was Yorkshire President and himself a legend when he unveiled this plaque to mark Herbert Sutcliffe's birthplace cottage at Summerbridge.
(Photo: RON DEATON)

NEW KID ON THE BLOCK: Former England Under-19s all-rounder George Hill, opening the batting against Hampshire at the Ageas Bowl, enjoyed a hugely encouraging 2021 breakthrough with both bat and ball.

***

PRINCE HARRY: Wicket-keeper Harry Duke, 19, left, was handed his debut in a rainy Championship draw v. Glamorgan at Cardiff in mid-May.

He went on to score a half-century in the Roses four-day match and a Royal London Cup century v. Leicestershire.

***

CAPTAIN FANTASTIC: Hollie Armitage, who led Northern Diamonds to the finals of both the Charlotte Edwards Cup and the Rachael Heyhoe Flint Trophy. **BELOW:** Hollie, No. 57, is lost in the scrum after completing a superb diving catch in the Rachael Heyhoe Flint final. Sadly, the Diamonds were runners-up in both competitions.

WELL HELD: Yorkshire's Jonny Tattersall dives to catch Glamorgan's Billy Root off Ben Coad in his first innings of their Championship match at Headingley. Root hit 110 not out in the second.

HAPPY RETURN: *White Rose* all-rounder Jordan Thompson holds Lancashire centurion Keaton Jennings off his own bowling at Headingley.

OVERSEAS WINNER: Harry Brook, who in February helped Lahore Qalanders to win the Pakistan Super League, scoring a maiden T20 career century along the way.

CENTURIES BY CURRENT PLAYERS *(Continued)*

H C BROOK (4)

124	v. Essex	Chelmsford	2018
101	v. Somerset	Leeds	2019
113	v. Northamptonshire	Northampton	2021
118	v. Somerset	Scarborough	2021

W A R FRAINE (1)

106	v. Surrey	Scarborough	2019

T KOHLER-CADMORE (5)

106	v. Nottinghamshire	Nottingham	2018
105 *	v. Lancashire	Leeds	2018
176	v. Leeds/Bradford MCCU	Weetwood, Leeds	2019
102	v. Somerset	Leeds	2019
165 *	v. Warwickshire	Birmingham	2019

A LYTH (26)

132	v. Nottinghamshire	Nottingham	2008
142	v. Somerset	Taunton	2010
133	v. Hampshire	Southampton	2010
100	v. Lancashire	Manchester	2010
248 *	v. Leicestershire	Leicester	2012
111	v. Leeds/Bradford MCCU	Leeds	2013
105	v. Somerset	Taunton	2013
130	v. Leeds/Bradford MCCU	Leeds	2014
104	v. Durham	Chester-le-Street	2014
230	v. Northamptonshire	Northampton	2014
143	v. Durham	Leeds	2014
117	v. Middlesex	Scarborough	2014
251	v. Lancashire	Manchester	2014
122	v. Nottinghamshire	Nottingham	2014
113	v. MCC	Abu Dhabi	2015
111	v. Hampshire	Leeds	2016
106	v. Somerset	Taunton	2016
202	v. Surrey	The Oval	2016
114 *	v. Durham	Leeds	2016
194	v. Leeds/Bradford MCCU	Leeds	2017
100	v. Lancashire	Leeds	2017
134 *	v. Hampshire	Leeds	2018
103	v. Lancashire	Leeds	2020
115 *	v. Glamorgan	Leeds	2021
116	v. Kent	Canterbury	2021
153	v. Nottinghamshire	Nottingham	2021

D J MALAN (2)

219	v. Derbyshire	Leeds	2020
199	v. Sussex	Leeds	2021

A U RASHID (10)

108	v. Worcestershire	Kidderminster	2007
111	v. Sussex	Hove	2008
117 *	v. Hampshire	Basingstoke	2009
157 *	v. Lancashire	Leeds	2009
180	v. Somerset	Leeds	2013
110 *	v. Warwickshire	Birmingham	2013
103	v. Somerset	Taunton	2013

(2013 consecutive innings)

108	v. Somerset	Taunton	2014
159 *	v. Lancashire	Manchester	2014
127	v. Durham	Scarborough	2015

CENTURIES BY CURRENT PLAYERS *(Continued)*

J E ROOT (8)

160	v. Sussex	Scarborough	2011
222 *	v. Hampshire	Southampton (West End)	2012
125	v. Northamptonshire	Leeds	2012
182	v. Durham	Chester-le-Street	2013
236	v. Derbyshire	Leeds	2013
213	v. Surrey	Leeds	2016
130 *	v. Nottinghamshire	Nottingham	2019
101	v. Kent	Canterbury	2021

J A TATTERSALL (1)

135 *	v. Leeds/Bradford MCCU	Weetwood, Leeds	2019

J A TATTERSALL (1)

135 *	v. Leeds/Bradford MCCU	Weetwood, Leeds	2019

CENTURIES BY ALL PLAYERS 1863-2021
(Including highest score)

112	H Sutcliffe	313	v. Essex	at Leyton	1932
103	G Boycott	260*	v. Essex	at Colchester (Garrison Gd)	1970
85	L Hutton	280*	v. Hampshire	at Sheffield	1939
62	M Leyland	263	v. Essex	at Hull	1936
61	D Denton	221	v. Kent	at Tunbridge Wells	1912
60	P Holmes	315 *	v. Middlesex	at Lord's	1925
56	G H Hirst	341	v. Leicestershire	at Leicester (Aylestone Rd)	1905
46	W Rhodes	267 *	v. Leicestershire	at Leeds	1921
41	M D Moxon	274 *	v. Worcestershire	at Worcester	1994
39	A Mitchell	189	v. Northamptonshire	at Northampton	1926
37	E Oldroyd	194	v. Worcestershire	at Worcester	1923
34	J H Hampshire	183 *	v. Sussex	at Hove	1971
34	A McGrath	211	v. Warwickshire	at Birmingham	2009
33	D B Close	198	v. Surrey	at The Oval	1960
30	F A Lowson	259 *	v. Worcestershire	at Worcester	1953
29	D E V Padgett	161 *	v. Oxford University	at Oxford	1959
29	J V Wilson	230	v. Derbyshire	at Sheffield	1952
28	D Byas	213	v. Worcestershire	at Scarborough	1995
27	G S Ballance	203 *	v. Hampshire	at West End, Southampton	2017
27	W Barber	255	v. Surrey	at Sheffield	1935
26	D S Lehmann	339	v. Durham	at Leeds	2006
26	A Lyth	251	v. Lancashire	at Manchester	2014
26	W Watson	214 *	v. Worcestershire	at Worcester	1955
25	A A Metcalfe	216 *	v. Middlesex	at Leeds	1988
24	E I Lester	186	v. Warwickshire	at Scarborough	1949
23	J T Brown	311	v. Sussex	at Sheffield	1897
23	P J Sharpe	203 *	v. Cambridge University	at Cambridge	1960
22	R G Lumb	165 *	v. Gloucestershire	at Bradford	1984
22	J T Tunnicliffe	243	v. Derbyshire	at Chesterfield	1898
21	Hon F S Jackson	160	v. Gloucestershire	at Sheffield	1898
20	M P Vaughan	183	v. Glamorgan	at Cardiff (Sophia Gardens)	1996
	and	183	v. Northamptonshire	at Northampton	1996
19	A W Gale	272	v. Nottinghamshire	at Scarborough	2013
19	C White	186	v. Lancashire	at Manchester	2001
18	J A Rudolph	228 *	v. Durham	at Leeds	2010
18	E Wainwright	228	v. Surrey	at The Oval	1899
17	W B Stott	186	v. Warwickshire	at Birmingham	1960
17	N W D Yardley	183 *	v. Hampshire	at Leeds	1951
16	K Taylor	203 *	v. Warwickshire	at Birmingham	1961

CENTURIES BY ALL PLAYERS 1863-2021 *(Continued)*

16	M J Wood	207	v. Somerset	at Taunton	2003
15	J M Bairstow	246	v. Hampshire	at Leeds	2016
15	R Kilner	206 *	v. Derbyshire	at Sheffield	1920
15	G Ulyett	199 *	v. Derbyshire	at Sheffield	1887
15	B B Wilson	208	v. Sussex	at Bradford	1914
14	R Illingworth	162	v. Indians	at Sheffield	1959
13	J D Love	170 *	v. Worcestershire	at Worcester	1979
12	R J Blakey	223 *	v. Northamptonshire	at Leeds	2003
12	H Halliday	144	v. Derbyshire	at Chesterfield	1950
11	P A Jaques	243	v. Hampshire	at Southampton (Rose Bowl)	2004
11	A Z Lees	275 *	v. Derbyshire	at Chesterfield	2013
11	K Sharp	181	v. Gloucestershire	at Harrogate	1986
10	C W J Athey	134	v. Derbyshire	at Derby	1982
10	Lord Hawke	166	v. Warwickshire	at Birmingham	1896
10	F Mitchell	194	v. Leicestershire	at Leicester	1899
10	A U Rashid	180	v. Somerset	at Leeds	2013
9	D L Bairstow	145	v. Middlesex	at Scarborough	1980
9	M G Bevan	160 *	v. Surrey	at Middlesbrough	1996
9	L Hall	160	v. Lancashire	at Bradford	1887
9	J J Sayers	187	v. Kent	at Tunbridge Wells	2007
8	W Bates	136	v. Sussex	at Hove	1886
8	M J Lumb	144	v. Middlesex	at Southgate	2006
8	T L Taylor	156	v. Hampshire	at Harrogate	1901
7	J B Bolus	146 *	v. Hampshire	at Portsmouth	1960
7	E Robinson	135 *	v. Leicestershire	at Leicester (Aylestone Rd)	1921
7	P E Robinson	189	v. Lancashire	at Scarborough	1991
7	J E Root	236	v. Derbyshire	at Leeds	2013
6	E Lockwood	208	v. Kent	at Gravesend	1883
6	R Peel	210 *	v. Warwickshire	at Birmingham	1896
6	W H H Sutcliffe	181	v. Kent	at Canterbury	1952
5	T T Bresnan	169 *	v. Durham	at Chester-le-Street	2015
5	T Kohler-Cadmore	176	v. Leeds/Bradford MCCU	at Weetwood, Leeds	2019
5	C M Old	116	v. Indians	at Bradford	1974
4	H C Brook	124	v. Essex	at Chelmsford	2018
4	I Grimshaw	129 *	v. Cambridge University	at Sheffield	1885
4	S Haigh	159	v. Nottinghamshire	at Sheffield	1901
4	S N Hartley	114	v. Gloucestershire	at Bradford	1982
4	R A Hutton	189	v. Pakistanis	at Bradford	1971
4	J A Leaning	123	v. Somerset	at Taunton	2015
4	A B Sellers	204	v. Cambridge University	at Cambridge	1936
3	G L Brophy	177 *	v. Worcestershire	at Worcester	2011
3	P Carrick	131 *	v. Northamptonshire	at Northampton	1980
3	A J Dalton	128	v. Middlesex	at Leeds	1972
3	A Drake	147 *	v. Derbyshire	at Chesterfield	1911
3	F Lee	165	v. Lancashire	at Bradford	1887
3	G G Macaulay	125 *	v. Nottinghamshire	at Nottingham	1921
3	R Moorhouse	113	v. Somerset	at Taunton	1896
3	R M Pyrah	134 *	v. Loughborough MCCU	at Leeds	2010
3	J W Rothery	161	v. Kent	at Dover	1908
3	J Rowbotham	113	v. Surrey	at The Oval	1873
3	T F Smailes	117	v. Glamorgan	at Cardiff	1938
3	Younus Khan	217 *	v. Kent	at Scarborough	2007
2	M W Booth	210	v. Worcestershire	at Worcester	1911
2	D C F Burton	142 *	v. Hampshire	at Dewsbury	1919

CENTURIES BY ALL PLAYERS 1863-2021 *(Continued)*

2	K R Davidson	128	v. Kent	at Maidstone	1934
2	P A Gibb	157 *	v. Nottinghamshire	at Sheffield	1935
2	P J Hartley	127 *	v. Lancashire	at Manchester	1988
2	I J Harvey	209 *	v. Somerset	at Leeds	2005
2	C Johnson	107	v. Somerset	at Sheffield	1973
2	S A Kellett	125 *	v. Derbyshire	at Chesterfield	1991
2	N Kilner	112	v. Leicestershire	at Leeds	1921
2	D J Malan	219	v. Derbyshire	at Leeds	2020
2	B Parker	138 *	v. Oxford University	at Oxford	1997
2	A Sellers	105	v. Middlesex	at Lord's	1893
2	E Smith (Morley)	129	v. Hampshire	at Bradford	1899
2	G A Smithson	169	v. Leicestershire	at Leicester	1947
2	G B Stevenson	115 *	v. Warwickshire	at Birmingham	1982
2	F S Trueman	104	v. Northamptonshire	at Northampton	1963
2	C Turner	130	v. Somerset	at Sheffield	1936
2	D J Wainwright	104 *	v. Sussex	at Hove	2008
2	T A Wardall	106	v. Gloucestershire	at Gloucester (Spa Ground)	1892
1	Azeem Rafiq	100	v. Worcestershire	at Worcester	2009
1	A T Barber	100	v. England XI	at Sheffield	1929
1	H D Bird	181 *	v. Glamorgan	at Bradford	1959
1	T J D Birtles	104	v. Lancashire	at Sheffield	1914
1	G S Blewett	190	v. Northamptonshire	at Scarborough	1999
1	J A Brooks	109 *	v. Lancashire	at Manchester	2017
1	M T G Elliott	127	v. Warwickshire	at Birmingham	2002
1	T Emmett	104	v. Gloucestershire	at Clifton	1873
1	G M Fellows	109	v. Lancashire	at Manchester	2002
1	A J Finch	110	v. Warwickshire	at Birmingham	2014
1	W A R Fraine	106	v. Surrey	at Scarborough	2019
1	J N Gillespie	123 *	v. Surrey	at The Oval	2007
1	D Gough	121	v. Warwickshire	at Leeds	1996
1	A K D Gray	104	v. Somerset	at Taunton	2003
1	A P Grayson	100	v. Worcestershire	at Worcester	1994
1	F E Greenwood	104 *	v. Glamorgan	at Hull	1929
1	G M Hamilton	125	v. Hampshire	at Leeds	2000
1	P S P Handscomb	101 *	v. Lancashire	at Manchester	2017
1	W E Harbord	109	v. Oxford University	at Oxford	1930
1	R Iddison	112	v. Cambridgeshire	at Hunslet	1869
1	W G Keighley	110	v. Surrey	at Leeds	1951
1	R A Kettleborough	108	v. Essex	at Leeds	1996
1	B Leadbeater	140 *	v. Hampshire	at Portsmouth	1976
1	J S Lehmann	116	v. Somerset	at Leeds	2016
1	D R Martyn	238	v. Gloucestershire	at Leeds	2003
1	G J Maxwell	140	v. Durham	at Scarborough	2015
1	S E Marsh	125 *	v. Surrey	at The Oval	2017
1	J T Newstead	100 *	v. Nottinghamshire	at Nottingham	1908
1	L E Plunkett	126	v. Hampshire	at Leeds	2016
1	C A Pujara	133 *	v. Hampshire	at Leeds	2015
1	R B Richardson	112	v. Warwickshire	at Birmingham	1993
1	H Rudston	164	v. Leicestershire	at Leicester (Aylestone Rd)	1904
1	A Sidebottom	124	v. Glamorgan	at Cardiff (Sophia Gardens)	1977
1	I G Swallow	114	v. MCC	at Scarborough	1987
1	J A Tattersall	135 *	v. Leeds/Bradford MCCU	at Weetwood, Leeds	2019
1	S R Tendulkar	100	v. Durham	at Durham	1992
1	J Thewlis	108	v. Surrey	at The Oval	1868
1	C T Tyson	100 *	v. Hampshire	at Southampton	1921

CENTURIES BY ALL PLAYERS 1863-2021 *(Continued)*

1	H Verity	101	v. Jamaica	at Kingston (Sabina Park)	1935/36
1	A Waddington	114	v. Worcestershire	at Leeds	1927
1	W A I Washington	100 *	v. Surrey	at Leeds	1902
1	H Wilkinson	113	v. MCC	at Scarborough	1904
1	W H Wilkinson	103	v. Sussex	at Sheffield	1909
1	K S Williamson	189	v. Sussex	at Scarborough	2014
1	E R Wilson	104 *	v. Essex	at Bradford	1913
1	A Wood	123 *	v. Worcestershire	at Sheffield	1935
1	J D Woodford	101	v. Warwickshire	at Middlesbrough	1971

SUMMARY OF CENTURIES
FOR AND AGAINST YORKSHIRE 1863-2021

FOR YORKSHIRE				AGAINST YORKSHIRE		
Total	In Yorkshire	Away		Total	In Yorkshire	Away
111	66	45	**Derbyshire**	57	27	30
32	16	16	**Durham**	25	13	12
76	34	42	**Essex**	46	21	25
69	39	30	**Glamorgan**	25	15	10
87	41	46	**Gloucestershire**	53	27	26
102	44	58	**Hampshire**	61	27	34
84	37	47	**Kent**	64	32	32
118	59	59	**Lancashire**	119	59	60
97	52	45	**Leicestershire**	46	23	23
97	49	48	**Middlesex**	92	38	54
82	35	47	**Northamptonshire**	53	25	28
132	60	72	**Nottinghamshire**	88	33	55
106	54	52	**Somerset**	62	23	39
120	51	69	**Surrey**	114	41	73
91	43	48	**Sussex**	78	34	44
106	36	70	**Warwickshire**	75	29	46
75	32	43	**Worcestershire**	45	17	28
1	1	0	**Cambridgeshire**	0	0	0
1586	**749**	**837**	**Totals**	**1103**	**484**	**619**
9	9	0	**Australians**	16	16	0
9	9	0	**Indians**	7	7	0
8	8	0	**New Zealanders**	3	3	0
5	5	0	**Pakistanis**	1	1	0
9	9	0	**South Africans**	7	7	0
5	5	0	**Sri Lankans**	1	1	0
5	5	0	**West Indians**	6	6	0
1	1	0	**Zimbabweans**	0	0	0
3	3	0	**Bangladesh 'A'**	1	1	0
0	0	0	**India 'A'**	3	3	0
1	1	0	**Pakistan 'A'**	1	1	0
45	1	44	**Cambridge University**	20	2	18
2	2	0	**Combined Services**	0	0	0
1	0	1	**Durham MCCU**	1	0	1
4	3	1	**England XIs**	3	2	1
0	0	0	**International XI**	1	1	0
1	0	1	**Ireland**	0	0	0
3	0	3	**Jamaica**	3	0	3
10	8	2	**Leeds/Bradford MCCU**	0	0	0
1	0	1	**Liverpool and District**	0	0	0
2	2	0	**Loughborough MCCU**	1	1	0
1	0	1	**Mashonaland**	0	0	0
2	0	2	**Matabeleland**	1	0	1
54	38	16	**MCC**	52	34	18
39	0	39	**Oxford University**	11	0	11
6	0	6	**Rest of England**	15	0	15
9	5	4	**Scotland**	1	0	1
3	3	0	**C L Thornton's XI**	4	4	0
0	0	0	**Western Province**	1	0	1
1	1	0	**I Zingari**	1	1	0
239	**118**	**121**	**Totals**	**161**	**91**	**70**
1825	**867**	**958**	**Grand Totals**	**1264**	**575**	**689**

FOUR CENTURIES IN ONE INNINGS

1896 v. Warwickshire at Birmingham	F S Jackson	117
	E Wainwright	126
	Lord Hawke	166
	R Peel	*210

(First instance in First-Class cricket)

THREE CENTURIES IN ONE INNINGS

1884 v. Cambridge University at Cambridge	L Hall	116
	W Bates	133
	I Grimshaw	115
1887 v. Kent at Canterbury	G Ulyett	124
	L Hall	110
	F Lee	119
1897 v. Sussex at Sheffield	J T Brown	311
	J Tunnicliffe	147
	E Wainwright	*104
1899 v. Middlesex at Bradford	F S Jackson	155
	D Denton	113
	F Mitchell	121
1904 v. Surrey at The Oval	D Denton	105
	G H Hirst	104
	J Tunnicliffe	*139
1919 v. Gloucestershire at Leeds	H Sutcliffe	118
	D Denton	122
	R Kilner	*115
1925 v. Glamorgan at Huddersfield	P Holmes	130
	H Sutcliffe	121
	E Robinson	*108
1928 v. Middlesex at Lord's	P Holmes	105
	E Oldroyd	108
	A Mitchell	105
1928 v. Essex at Leyton	H Sutcliffe	129
	P Holmes	136
	M Leyland	*133
1929 v. Glamorgan at Hull	E Oldroyd	168
	W Barber	114
	F E Greenwood	*104
1933 v. MCC at Scarborough	H Sutcliffe	107
	A Mitchell	158
	M Leyland	133
1936 v. Surrey at Leeds	H Sutcliffe	129
	L Hutton	163
	M Leyland	*163
1937 v. Leicestershire at Hull	H Sutcliffe	189
	L Hutton	153
	M Leyland	*118
1947 v. Leicestershire at Leicester	L Hutton	137
	N W D Yardley	100
	G.A Smithson	169

THREE CENTURIES IN ONE INNINGS *(Continued)*

1971	v. Oxford University at Oxford	J H Hampshire R A Hutton A J Dalton	*116 101 111
1975	v. Gloucestershire at Bristol	G Boycott R G Lumb J H Hampshire	141 101 *106
1995	v. Cambridge University at Cambridge	M D Moxon D Byas M G Bevan	130 181 *113
2001	v. Leicestershire at Leeds	M J Wood M J Lumb D S Lehmann	102 122 104
2001	v. Glamorgan at Scarborough	C White M J Wood D Byas	183 124 104
2007	v. Surrey at The Oval	J A Rudolph T T Bresnan J N Gillespie	122 116 *123
2014	v. Leeds/Bradford MCCU at Leeds	A Lyth G S Ballance J M Bairstow	130 101 123
2016	v. Hampshire at Leeds	A Lyth J M Bairstow L E Plunkett	111 246 126
2019	v. Somerset at Leeds	G S Ballance T Kohler-Cadmore H C Brook	111 102 101

CENTURY IN EACH INNINGS

D Denton	107 and 109*	v. Nottinghamshire at Nottingham, 1906
G H Hirst	111 and 117*	v. Somerset at Bath, 1906
D Denton	133 and 121	v. MCC at Scarborough, 1908
W Rhodes	128 and 115	v. MCC at Scarborough, 1911
P Holmes	126 and 111*	v. Lancashire at Manchester, 1920
H Sutcliffe	107 and 109*	v. MCC at Scarborough, 1926
H Sutcliffe	111 and 100*	v. Nottinghamshire at Nottingham, 1928
E I Lester	126 and 142	v. Northamptonshire at Northampton, 1947
L Hutton	197 and 104	v. Essex at Southend, 1947
E I Lester	125* and 132	v. Lancashire at Manchester, 1948
L Hutton	165 and 100	v. Sussex at Hove, 1949
L Hutton	103 and 137	v. MCC at Scarborough, 1952
G Boycott	103 and 105	v. Nottinghamshire at Sheffield, 1966
G Boycott	163 and 141*	v. Nottinghamshire at Bradford, 1983
M D Moxon	123 and 112*	v. Indians at Scarborough, 1986
A A Metcalfe	194* and 107	v. Nottinghamshire at Nottingham, 1990
M P Vaughan	100 and 151	v. Essex at Chelmsford, 1999
Younus Khan	106 and 202*	v. Hampshire at Southampton, 2007
G S Ballance	148 and 108*	v. Surrey at The Oval, 2013
G S Ballance	108 and 203*	v. Hampshire at West End, 2017

HIGHEST INDIVIDUAL SCORES
FOR AND AGAINST YORKSHIRE

Highest For Yorkshire:
341 G H Hirst v. Leicestershire at Leicester, 1905
Highest Against Yorkshire:
318* W G Grace for Gloucestershire at Cheltenham, 1876

Yorkshire versus:

Derbyshire	For Yorkshire:	300 — J T Brown at Chesterfield, 1898
	Against:	270* — C F Hughes at Leeds, 2013
Most Centuries	For Yorkshire:	G Boycott 9
	Against:	K J Barnett and W Storer 4 each
Durham	For Yorkshire:	339 — D S Lehmann at Leeds, 2006
	Against:	221* — K K Jennings at Chester-le-Street, 2016
Essex	For Yorkshire:	313 — H Sutcliffe at Leyton, 1932
	Against:	219* — D J Insole at Colchester, 1949
Most Centuries	For Yorkshire:	H Sutcliffe 9
	Against:	F L Fane, K W R Fletcher, G A Gooch and D J Insole 3 each
Glamorgan	For Yorkshire:	213 — M D Moxon at Cardiff, 1996
	Against:	202* — H Morris at Cardiff, 1996
Most Centuries	For Yorkshire:	G Boycott, P Holmes and H Sutcliffe 5 each
	Against:	H Morris 5
Gloucestershire	For Yorkshire:	238 — D R Martyn at Leeds, 2003
	Against:	318*— W G Grace at Cheltenham, 1876
Most Centuries	For Yorkshire:	G Boycott 6
	Against:	W G Grace 9
Hampshire	For Yorkshire:	302* — P Holmes at Portsmouth, 1920
	Against:	300* — M A Carberry at Southampton, 2011
Most Centuries	For Yorkshire:	G S Ballance 7
	Against:	C P Mead 10
Kent	For Yorkshire:	248 — W Barber at Leeds, 1934.
	Against:	237 — D I Stevens at Leeds, 2019
Most Centuries	For Yorkshire:	A McGrath 6
	Against:	F E Woolley 5
Lancashire	For Yorkshire:	252 — D S Lehmann at Leeds, 2001
	Against:	225 — G D Lloyd at Leeds, 1997 (Non-Championship)
		206 — S G Law at Leeds, 2007
Most Centuries	For Yorkshire:	G Boycott and H Sutcliffe 9 each
	Against:	M A Atherton and C H Lloyd 6 each.
Leicestershire	For Yorkshire:	341 — G H Hirst at Leicester, 1905
	Against:	218— J J Whitaker at Bradford, 1996
Most Centuries	For Yorkshire:	H Sutcliffe 10
	Against:	J J Whitaker and C J B Wood 5 each
Middlesex	For Yorkshire:	315*— P Holmes at Lord's, 1925
	Against:	243*— A J Webbe at Huddersfield, 1887
Most Centuries	For Yorkshire:	P Holmes and H Sutcliffe 7 each
	Against:	M W Gatting 8

HIGHEST INDIVIDUAL SCORES FOR AND AGAINST YORKSHIRE *(continued)*

Yorkshire versus

Northamptonshire	*For Yorkshire:*	277* — P Holmes at Harrogate, 1921
	Against:	235 — A J Lamb at Leeds, 1990
Most Centuries	*For Yorkshire:*	H Sutcliffe 5
	Against:	W Larkins 5
Nottinghamshire	*For Yorkshire:*	285 — P Holmes at Nottingham, 1929
	Against:	251* — D J Hussey at Leeds, 2010
Most Centuries	*For Yorkshire:*	G Boycott 15
	Against:	R T Robinson 6
Somerset	*For Yorkshire:*	213 — H Sutcliffe at Dewsbury, 1924
	Against:	297 — M J Wood at Taunton, 2005
Most Centuries	*For Yorkshire:*	G Boycott 6
	Against:	L C H Palairet, IVA. Richards, M E Trescothick 5 each
Surrey	*For Yorkshire:*	255 — W Barber at Sheffield, 1935
	Against:	273 — T W Hayward at The Oval, 1899
Most Centuries	*For Yorkshire:*	H Sutcliffe 9
	Against:	J B Hobbs 8
Sussex	*For Yorkshire:*	311 — J T Brown at Sheffield, 1897
	Against:	274* — M W Goodwin at Hove, 2011
Most Centuries	*For Yorkshire:*	L Hutton 8
	Against:	C B Fry 7
Warwickshire	*For Yorkshire:*	275 — P Holmes at Bradford, 1928
	Against:	225 — D P Ostler at Birmingham, 2002
Most Centuries	*For Yorkshire:*	G Boycott and H Sutcliffe 8 each
	Against:	D L Amiss, H E Dollery, R B Kanhai and W G Quaife 4 each.
Worcestershire	*For Yorkshire:*	274* — M D Moxon at Worcester, 1994
	Against:	259 — D Kenyon at Kidderminster, 1956
Most Centuries	*For Yorkshire:*	M Leyland 6
	Against:	D Kenyon and G M Turner 5 each
Australians	*For Yorkshire:*	167 — J T Brown at Bradford, 1899
	Against:	193* — B C Booth at Bradford, 1964
Most Centuries	*For Yorkshire:*	G Boycott and D Denton 2 each
	Against:	N C O'Neill 2
Indians	*For Yorkshire:*	183* — L Hutton at Bradford, 1946
	Against:	244* — V S Hazare at Sheffield, 1946
Most Centuries	*For Yorkshire:*	M D Moxon 2
	Against:	V S Hazare, VMankad, PR Umrigar D K Gaekwad, G A Parkar and R Lamba 1 each
New Zealanders	*For Yorkshire:*	175 — P Holmes at Bradford, 1927
	Against:	126 — W M Wallace at Bradford, 1949
Most Centuries	*For Yorkshire:*	L Hutton and DB Close 2 each
	Against:	H G Vivian, WM Wallace and J G Wright 1 each
Pakistanis	*For Yorkshire:*	197 — P J Sharpe at Leeds, 1967
	Against:	139 — A H Kardar at Sheffield, 1954
Most Centuries	*For Yorkshire:*	P J Sharpe 2
	Against:	A H Kardar 1

HIGHEST INDIVIDUAL SCORES FOR AND AGAINST YORKSHIRE *(continued)*

Yorkshire versus

South Africans		*For Yorkshire:*	156 — L Hutton at Sheffield, 1951
		Against:	168 — I J Seidle at Sheffield, 1929
Most Centuries		*For Yorkshire:*	L Hutton 2
		Against:	H B Cameron, J D Lindsay, B Mitchell, D P B Morkel, I J Seidle, L J Tancred, C B van Ryneveld 1 each
Sri Lankans		*For Yorkshire:*	132 — M D Moxon at Leeds, 1988
		Against:	112 — S A R Silva at Leeds, 1988
Most Centuries		*For Yorkshire:*	K Sharp 2
		Against:	S A R Silva 1
West Indians		*For Yorkshire:*	112* — D Denton at Harrogate, 1906
		Against:	164 — S F A Bacchus at Leeds, 1980
Most Centuries		*For Yorkshire:*	M G Bevan, D Denton, L Hutton, R G Lumb and A A Metcalfe 1 each
		Against:	S F A Bacchus, C O Browne, S Chanderpaul P A Goodman, C L Hooper and G St A Sobers 1 each
Zimbabweans		*For Yorkshire:*	113 — M D Moxon at Leeds, 1990
		Against:	89 — G J Whittall at Leeds, 2000
Most Centuries		*For Yorkshire:*	M D Moxon 1
		Against:	None
Cambridge University		*For Yorkshire:*	207* — G Boycott at Cambridge, 1976
		Against:	171* — G L Jessop at Cambridge, 1899
			171 — P B H May at Cambridge, 1952
Most Centuries		*For Yorkshire:*	H Sutcliffe 4
		Against:	G M Kemp 2
Durham MCCU		*For Yorkshire:*	139 — J J Sayers at Durham, 2011
		Against:	127 — T Westley at Durham, 2011
Most Centuries		*For Yorkshire:*	J J Sayers 1
		Against:	T Westley 1
Leeds Bradford MCCU		*For Yorkshire:*	194 — A Lyth at Leeds, 2017
		Against:	69 — A MacQueen at Leeds, 2012
Most Centuries		*For Yorkshire:*	A Lyth, 3
Loughborough MCCU		*For Yorkshire:*	134* — R M Pyrah at Leeds, 2010
		Against:	107 — C P Murtagh at Leeds, 2007
Most Centuries		*For Yorkshire:*	R M Pyrah 1
		Against:	C P Murtagh 1
MCC		*For Yorkshire:*	180* — G H Hirst at Lord's, 1919
		Against:	214 — E H Hendren at Lord's, 1919
Most Centuries		*For Yorkshire:*	L Hutton 8
		Against:	R E S Wyatt 5
Oxford University		*For Yorkshire:*	196 — R J Blakey at Oxford, 1991
		Against:	201 — J E Raphael at Oxford, 1904
Most Centuries		*For Yorkshire:*	M Leyland 4
		Against:	A A Baig and Nawab of Pataudi (Jun.) 2 each

J B Hobbs scored 11 centuries against Yorkshire – the highest by any individual (8 for Surrey and 3 for the Rest of England).

Three players have scored 10 centuries against Yorkshire – W G Grace (9 for Gloucestershire and 1 for MCC). E H Hendren (6 for Middlesex, 3 for MCC and 1 for the Rest of England) and C P Mead (all 10 for Hampshire).

CARRYING BAT THROUGH A COMPLETED INNINGS

Batsman	Score	Total	Against	Season
G R Atkinson	30*	73	Nottinghamshire at Bradford	1865
L Hall	31*	94	Sussex at Hove	1878
L Hall	124*	331	Sussex at Hove	1883
L Hall	128*	285	Sussex at Huddersfield	1884
L Hall	32*	81	Kent at Sheffield	1885
L Hall	79*	285	Surrey at Sheffield	1885
L Hall	37*	96	Derbyshire at Derby	1885
L Hall	50*	173	Sussex at Huddersfield	1886
L Hall	74*	172	Kent at Canterbury	1886
G Ulyett	199*	399	Derbyshire at Sheffield	1887
L Hall	119*	334	Gloucestershire at Dewsbury	1887
L Hall	82*	218	Sussex at Hove	1887
L Hall	34*	104	Surrey at The Oval	1888
L Hall	129*	461	Gloucestershire at Clifton	1888
L Hall	85*	259	Middlesex at Lord's	1889
L Hall	41*	106	Nottinghamshire at Sheffield	1891
W Rhodes	98*	184	MCC at Lord's	1903
W Rhodes	85*	152	Essex at Leyton	1910
P Holmes	145*	270	Northamptonshire at Northampton	1920
H Sutcliffe	125*	307	Essex at Southend	1920
P Holmes	175*	377	New Zealanders at Bradford	1927
P Holmes	110*	219	Northamptonshire at Bradford	1929
H Sutcliffe	104*	170	Hampshire at Leeds	1932
H Sutcliffe	114*	202	Rest of England at The Oval	1933
H Sutcliffe	187*	401	Worcestershire at Bradford	1934
H Sutcliffe	135*	262	Glamorgan at Neath	1935
H Sutcliffe	125*	322	Oxford University at Oxford	1939
L Hutton	99*	200	Leicestershire at Sheffield	1948
L Hutton	78*	153	Worcestershire at Sheffield	1949
F A Lowson	76*	218	MCC at Lord's	1951
W B Stott	144*	262	Worcestershire at Worcester	1959
D E V Padgett	115*	230	Gloucestershire at Bristol	1962
G Boycott	114*	297	Leicestershire at Sheffield	1968
G Boycott	53*	119	Warwickshire at Bradford	1969
G Boycott	182*	320	Middlesex at Lord's	1971
G Boycott	138*	232	Warwickshire at Birmingham	1971
G Boycott	175*	360	Nottinghamshire at Worksop	1979
G Boycott	112*	233	Derbyshire at Sheffield	1983
G Boycott	55*	183	Warwickshire at Leeds	1984
G Boycott	55*	131	Surrey at Sheffield	1985
M J Wood	60*	160	Somerset at Scarborough	2004
J J Sayers	122*	326	Middlesex at Scarborough	2006
J J Sayers	149*	414	Durham at Leeds	2007
A Lyth	248*	486	Leicestershire at Leicester	2012

44 instances, of which L Hall (14 times), G Boycott (8) and H Sutcliffe (6) account for 28 between them.

The highest percentage of an innings total is 61.17 by H. Sutcliffe (104* v. Hampshire at Leeds in 1932) but P Holmes was absent ill, so only nine wickets fell.

Other contributions exceeding 55% are:

    59.48% G Boycott (138* v. Warwickshire at Birmingham, 1971)
    56.87% G Boycott (182* v. Middlesex at Lord's, 1971)
    56.43% H Sutcliffe (114* v. Rest of England at The Oval, 1933)
    55.92% W Rhodes (85* v. Essex at Leyton, 1910)

2,000 RUNS IN A SEASON

Batsman	Season	M	I	NO	Runs	HS	Avge	100s
G H Hirst	1904	32	44	3	2257	157	55.04	8
D Denton	1905	33	52	2	2258	172	45.16	8
G H Hirst	1906	32	53	6	2164	169	46.04	6
D Denton	1911	32	55	4	2161	137*	42.37	6
D Denton	1912	36	51	4	2088	221	44.23	6
P Holmes	1920	30	45	6	2144	302*	54.97	7
P Holmes	1925	35	49	9	2351	315*	58.77	6
H Sutcliffe	1925	34	48	8	2236	235	55.90	7
H Sutcliffe	1928	27	35	5	2418	228	80.60	11
P Holmes	1928	31	40	4	2093	275	58.13	6
H Sutcliffe	1931	28	33	8	2351	230	94.04	9
H Sutcliffe	1932	29	41	5	2883	313	80.08	12
M Leyland	1933	31	44	4	2196	210*	54.90	7
A Mitchell	1933	34	49	10	2100	158	53.84	6
H Sutcliffe	1935	32	47	3	2183	212	49.61	8
L Hutton	1937	28	45	6	2448	271*	62.76	8
H Sutcliffe	1937	32	52	5	2054	189	43.70	4
L Hutton	1939	29	44	5	2316	280*	59.38	10
L Hutton	1947	19	31	2	2068	270*	71.31	10
L Hutton	1949	26	44	6	2640	269*	69.47	9
F A Lowson	1950	31	54	5	2067	141*	42.18	5
D E V Padgett	1959	35	60	8	2158	161*	41.50	4
W B Stott	1959	32	56	2	2034	144*	37.66	3
P J Sharpe	1962	36	62	8	2201	138	40.75	7
G Boycott	1971	18	25	4	2221	233	105.76	11
A A Metcalfe	1990	23	44	4	2047	194*	51.17	6

1,000 RUNS IN A SEASON

Batsman		Runs scored	Runs scored	Runs scored
C W J Athey	(2)	1113 in 1980	1339 in 1982	—
D L Bairstow	(3)	1083 in 1981	1102 in 1983	1163 in 1985
J M Bairstow	(2)	1015 in 2011	1108 in 2015	—
G S Ballance	(3)	1363 in 2013	1023 in 2017	1014 in 2019
W Barber	(8)	1000 in 1932	1595 in 1933	1930 in 1934
		1958 in 1935	1466 in 1937	1455 in 1938
		1501 in 1939	1170 in 1946	—
M G Bevan	(2)	1598 in 1995	1225 in 1996	—
R J Blakey	(5)	1361 in 1987	1159 in 1989	1065 in 1992
		1236 in 1994	1041 in 2002	—
J B Bolus	(2)	1245 in 1960	1970 in 1961	—
M W Booth	(2)	1189 in 1911	1076 in 1913	—
G Boycott	(19)	1628 in 1963	1639 in 1964	1215 in 1965
		1388 in 1966	1530 in 1967	1004 in 1968
		1558 in 1970	2221 in 1971	1156 in 1972
		1478 in 1974	1915 in 1975	1288 in 1976
		1259 in 1977	1074 in 1978	1160 in 1979
		1913 in 1982	1941 in 1983	1567 in 1984
		1657 in 1985	—	—
J T Brown	(9)	1196 in 1894	1260 in 1895	1755 in 1896
		1634 in 1897	1641 in 1898	1375 in 1899
		1181 in 1900	1627 in 1901	1291 in 1903
D Byas	(5)	1557 in 1991	1073 in 1993	1297 in 1994
		1913 in 1995	1319 in 1997	—

1,000 RUNS IN A SEASON *(Continued)*

Batsman		Runs scored	Runs scored	Runs scored
D B Close	(13)	1192 in 1952	1287 in 1954	1131 in 1955
		1315 in 1957	1335 in 1958	1740 in 1959
		1699 in 1960	1821 in 1961	1438 in 1962
		1145 in 1963	1281 in 1964	1127 in 1965
		1259 in 1966	—	—
K R Davidson	(1)	1241 in 1934		
D Denton	(20)	1028 in 1896	1357 in 1897	1595 in 1899
		1378 in 1900	1400 in 1901	1191 in 1902
		1562 in 1903	1919 in 1904	2258 in 1905
		1905 in 1906	1128 in 1907	1852 in 1908
		1765 in 1909	1106 in 1910	2161 in 1911
		2088 in 1912	1364 in 1913	1799 in 1914
		1213 in 1919	1324 in 1920	—
A Drake	(2)	1487 in 1911	1029 in 1913	—
A W Gale	(2)	1076 in 2013	1045 in 2015	—
A P Grayson	(1)	1046 in 1994	—	—
S Haigh	(1)	1031 in 1904	—	—
L Hall	(1)	1120 in 1887	—	—
H Halliday	(4)	1357 in 1948	1484 in 1950	1351 in 1952
		1461 in 1953	—	—
J H Hampshire	(12)	1236 in 1963	1280 in 1964	1424 in 1965
		1105 in 1966	1244 in 1967	1133 in 1968
		1079 in 1970	1259 in 1971	1124 in 1975
		1303 in 1976	1596 in 1978	1425 in 1981
Lord Hawke	(1)	1005 in 1895	—	—
G H Hirst	(19)	1110 in 1896	1248 in 1897	1546 in 1899
		1752 in 1900	1669 in 1901	1113 in 1902
		1535 in 1903	2257 in 1904	1972 in 1905
		2164 in 1906	1167 in 1907	1513 in 1908
		1151 in 1909	1679 in 1910	1639 in 1911
		1119 in 1912	1431 in 1913	1655 in 1914
		1312 in 1919	—	—
P Holmes	(14)	1876 in 1919	2144 in 1920	1458 in 1921
		1614 in 1922	1884 in 1923	1610 in 1924
		2351 in 1925	1792 in 1926	1774 in 1927
		2093 in 1928	1724 in 1929	1957 in 1930
		1431 in 1931	1191 in 1932	—
L Hutton	(12)	1282 in 1936	2448 in 1937	1171 in 1938
		2316 in 1939	1322 in 1946	2068 in 1947
		1792 in 1948	2640 in 1949	1581 in 1950
		1554 in 1951	1956 in 1952	1532 in 1953
R Illingworth	(5)	1193 in 1957	1490 in 1959	1029 in 1961
		1610 in 1962	1301 in 1964	—
F S Jackson	(4)	1211 in 1896	1300 in 1897	1442 in 1898
		1468 in 1899	—	—
P A Jaques	(2)	1118 in 2004	1359 in 2005	—
S A Kellett	(2)	1266 in 1991	1326 in 1992	—
R Kilner	(10)	1586 in 1913	1329 in 1914	1135 in 1919
		1240 in 1920	1137 in 1921	1132 in 1922
		1265 in 1923	1002 in 1925	1021 in 1926
		1004 in 1927	—	—
T Kohler-Cadmore	(1)	1004 in 2019	—	—

1,000 RUNS IN A SEASON *(Continued)*

Batsman	Runs scored	Runs scored	Runs scored
A Z Lees	(2) 1018 in 2014	1285 in 2016	—
D S Lehmann	(5) 1575 in 1997	1477 in 2000	1416 in 2001
	1136 in 2002	1706 in 2006	
E I Lester	(6) 1256 in 1948	1774 in 1949	1015 in 1950
	1786 in 1952	1380 in 1953	1330 in 1954
M Leyland	(17) 1088 in 1923	1203 in 1924	1560 in 1925
	1561 in 1926	1478 in 1927	1554 in 1928
	1407 in 1929	1814 in 1930	1127 in 1931
	1821 in 1932	2196 in 1933	1228 in 1934
	1366 in 1935	1621 in 1936	1120 in 1937
	1640 in 1938	1238 in 1939	—
J D Love	(2) 1161 in 1981	1020 in 1983	—
F A Lowson	(8) 1678 in 1949	2067 in 1950	1607 in 1951
	1562 in 1952	1586 in 1953	1719 in 1954
	1082 in 1955	1428 in 1956	
M J Lumb	(1) 1038 in 2003	—	—
R G Lumb	(5) 1002 in 1973	1437 in 1975	1070 in 1978
	1465 in 1979	1223 in 1980	—
A Lyth	(3) 1509 in 2010	1619 in 2014	1153 in 2016
A McGrath	(3) 1425 in 2005	1293 in 2006	1219 in 2010
A A Metcalfe	(6) 1674 in 1986	1162 in 1987	1320 in 1988
	1230 in 1989	2047 in 1990	1210 in 1991
A Mitchell	(10) 1320 in 1928	1633 in 1930	1351 in 1932
	2100 in 1933	1854 in 1934	1530 in 1935
	1095 in 1936	1602 in 1937	1305 in 1938
	1219 in 1939		
F Mitchell	(2) 1678 in 1899	1801 in 1901	—
R Moorhouse	(1) 1096 in 1895	—	—
M D Moxon	(11) 1016 in 1984	1256 in 1985	1298 in 1987
	1430 in 1988	1156 in 1989	1621 in 1990
	1669 in 1991	1314 in 1992	1251 in 1993
	1458 in 1994	1145 in 1995	
E Oldroyd	(10) 1473 in 1921	1690 in 1922	1349 in 1923
	1607 in 1924	1262 in 1925	1197 in 1926
	1390 in 1927	1304 in 1928	1474 in 1929
	1285 in 1930		
D E V Padgett	(12) 1046 in 1956	2158 in 1959	1574 in 1960
	1856 in 1961	1750 in 1962	1380 in 1964
	1220 in 1965	1194 in 1966	1284 in 1967
	1163 in 1968	1078 in 1969	1042 in 1970
R Peel	(1) 1193 in 1896	—	—
W Rhodes	(17) 1251 in 1904	1353 in 1905	1618 in 1906
	1574 in 1908	1663 in 1909	1355 in 1910
	1961 in 1911	1030 in 1912	1805 in 1913
	1325 in 1914	1138 in 1919	1329 in 1921
	1368 in 1922	1168 in 1923	1030 in 1924
	1256 in 1925	1071 in 1926	
E Robinson	(2) 1104 in 1921	1097 in 1929	—
P E Robinson	(3) 1173 in 1988	1402 in 1990	1293 in 1991
J A Rudolph	(4) 1078 in 2007	1292 in 2008	1366 in 2009
	1375 in 2010	—	—

1,000 RUNS IN A SEASON *(Continued)*

Batsman	Runs scored	Runs scored	Runs scored
J J Sayers	(1) 1150 in 2009	—	—
A B Sellers	(1) 1109 in 1938	—	—
K Sharp	(1) 1445 in 1984	—	—
P J Sharpe	(10) 1039 in 1960	1240 in 1961	2201 in 1962
	1273 in 1964	1091 in 1965	1352 in 1967
	1256 in 1968	1012 in 1969	1149 in 1970
	1320 in 1973		
W B Stott	(5) 1362 in 1957	1036 in 1958	2034 in 1959
	1790 in 1960	1409 in 1961	—
H Sutcliffe	(21) †1839 in 1919	1393 in 1920	1235 in 1921
	1909 in 1922	1773 in 1923	1720 in 1924
	2236 in 1925	1672 in 1926	1814 in 1927
	2418 in 1928	1485 in 1929	1636 in 1930
	2351 in 1931	2883 in 1932	1986 in 1933
	1511 in 1934	2183 in 1935	1295 in 1936
	2054 in 1937	1660 in 1938	1416 in 1939

† First season in First-Class cricket – The record for a debut season.

Batsman	Runs scored	Runs scored	Runs scored
W H H Sutcliffe	(1) 1193 in 1955	—	—
K Taylor	(6) 1306 in 1959	1107 in 1960	1494 in 1961
	1372 in 1962	1149 in 1964	1044 in 1966
T L Taylor	(2) 1236 in 1901	1373 in 1902	—
S R Tendulkar	(1) 1070 in 1992	—	—
J Tunnicliffe	(12) 1333 in 1895	1368 in 1896	1208 in 1897
	1713 in 1898	1434 in 1899	1496 in 1900
	1295 in 1901	1274 in 1902	1650 in 1904
	1096 in 1905	1232 in 1906	1195 in 1907
C Turner	(1) 1153 in 1934	—	—
G Ulyett	(4) 1083 in 1878	1158 in 1882	1024 in 1885
	1285 in 1887	—	—
M P Vaughan	(4) 1066 in 1994	1235 in 1995	1161 in 1996
	1161 in 1998	—	—
E Wainwright	(3) 1492 in 1897	1479 in 1899	1044 in 1901
W A I Washington	(1) 1022 in 1902	—	—
W Watson	(8) 1331 in 1947	1352 in 1948	1586 in 1952
	1350 in 1953	1347 in 1954	1564 in 1955
	1378 in 1956	1455 in 1957	—
W H Wilkinson	(1) 1282 in 1908	—	—
B B Wilson	(5) 1054 in 1909	1455 in 1911	1453 in 1912
	1533 in 1913	1632 in 1914	—
J V Wilson	(12) 1460 in 1949	1548 in 1950	1985 in 1951
	1349 in 1952	1531 in 1953	1713 in 1954
	1799 in 1955	1602 in 1956	1287 in 1957
	1064 in 1960	1018 in 1961	1226 in 1962
A Wood	(1) 1237 in 1935	—	—
M J Wood	(4) 1080 in 1998	1060 in 2001	1432 in 2003
	1005 in 2005	—	—
N W D Yardley	(4) 1028 in 1939	1299 in 1947	1413 in 1949
	1031 in 1950	—	—

BATSMEN WHO HAVE SCORED OVER 10,000 RUNS

Player	M	I	NO	Runs	HS	Av'ge	100s
H Sutcliffe	602	864	96	38558	313	50.20	112
D Denton	676	1058	61	33282	221	33.38	61
G Boycott	414	674	111	32570	260*	57.85	103
G H Hirst	717	1050	128	32024	341	34.73	56
W Rhodes	883	1195	162	31075	267*	30.08	46
P Holmes	485	699	74	26220	315*	41.95	60
M Leyland	548	720	82	26180	263	41.03	62
L Hutton	341	527	62	24807	280*	53.34	85
D B Close	536	811	102	22650	198	31.94	33
J H Hampshire	456	724	89	21979	183*	34.61	34
J V Wilson	477	724	75	20548	230	31.66	29
D E V Padgett	487	774	63	20306	161*	28.55	29
J Tunnicliffe	472	768	57	19435	243	27.33	22
M D Moxon	277	476	42	18973	274*	43.71	41
A Mitchell	401	550	69	18189	189	37.81	39
P J Sharpe	411	666	71	17685	203*	29.72	23
E Oldroyd	383	509	58	15891	194	35.23	37
J T Brown	345	567	41	15694	311	29.83	23
W Barber	354	495	48	15315	255	34.26	27
R Illingworth	496	668	131	14986	162	27.90	14
D Byas	268	449	42	14398	213	35.37	28
G Ulyett	355	618	31	14157	199*	24.11	15
R J Blakey	339	541	84	14150	223*	30.96	12
A McGrath	242	405	29	14091	211	37.47	34
W Watson	283	430	65	13953	214*	38.22	26
F A Lowson	252	404	31	13897	259*	37.25	30
Lord Hawke	510	739	91	13133	166	20.26	10
R Kilner	365	478	46	13018	206*	30.13	15
D L Bairstow	429	601	113	12985	145	26.60	9
K Taylor	303	505	35	12864	203*	27.37	16
N W D Yardley	302	420	56	11632	183*	31.95	17
R G Lumb	239	395	30	11525	165*	31.57	22
E Wainwright	352	545	30	11092	228	21.53	18
S Haigh	513	687	110	10993	159	19.05	4
E I Lester	228	339	27	10616	186	34.02	24
A A Metcalfe	184	317	19	10465	216*	35.11	25
C White	221	350	45	10376	186	34.01	19
Hon F S Jackson	207	328	22	10371	160	33.89	21
J D Love	247	388	58	10263	170*	31.10	13
A Lyth	161	271	14	10046	251	39.08	22

PLAYERS WHO HAVE SCORED CENTURIES FOR AND AGAINST YORKSHIRE

Player		For	Venue	Season
C W J Athey (5)	114*	Gloucestershire	Bradford	1984
(10 for Yorkshire)	101	Gloucestershire	Gloucester	1985
	101*	Gloucestershire	Leeds	1987
	112	Sussex	Scarborough	1993
	100	Sussex	Eastbourne	1996
M G Bevan (1)	142	Leicestershire	Leicester	2002
(9 for Yorkshire)				
J B Bolus (2)	114	Nottinghamshire	Bradford	1963
(7 for Yorkshire)	138	Derbyshire	Sheffield	1973
D B Close (1)	102	Somerset	Taunton	1971
(33 for Yorkshire)				
M T G Elliott (1)	125	Glamorgan	Leeds	2004
(1 for Yorkshire)				
P A Gibb (1)	107	Essex	Brentwood	1951
(2 for Yorkshire)				
P A Jaques (1)	222	Northamptonshire	Northampton	2003
(7 for Yorkshire)				
N Kilner (2)	119	Warwickshire	Hull	1932
(2 for Yorkshire)	197	Warwickshire	Birmingham	1933
A Z Lees (1)	106	Durham	Chester-le-Street	2020
(11 for Yorkshire)				
M J Lumb (1)	135	Nottinghamshire	Scarborough	2013
(8 for Yorkshire)				
P J Sharpe (1)	126	Derbyshire	Chesterfield	1976
(23 for Yorkshire)				

RECORD PARTNERSHIPS FOR YORKSHIRE

1st wkt	555	P Holmes (224*)	and H Sutcliffe (313)	v. Essex at Leyton	1932
2nd wkt	346	W Barber (162)	and M Leyland (189)	v. Middlesex at Sheffield	1932
3rd wkt	346	J J Sayers (173)	and A McGrath (211)	v. Warwickshire at Birmingham	2009
4th wkt	372	J E Root (213)	and J M Bairstow (198)	v. Surrey at Leeds	2016
5th wkt	340	E Wainwright (228)	and G H Hirst (186)	v. Surrey at The Oval	1899
6th wkt	296	A Lyth (251)	and A U Rashid (159*)	v. Lancashire at Manchester,	2014
7th wkt	366*	J M Bairstow (219*)	and T T Bresnan (169*)	v. Durham at Chester-le-Street	2015
8th wkt	292	R Peel (210*)	and Lord Hawke (166)	v. Warwickshire at Birmingham	1896
9th wkt	246	T T Bresnan (116)	and J N Gillespie (123*)	v. Surrey at The Oval	2007
10th wkt	149	G Boycott (79)	and G B Stevenson (115*)	v. Warwickshire at Birmingham	1982

RECORD PARTNERSHIPS AGAINST YORKSHIRE

1st wkt	372	R R Montgomerie (127)	and M B Loye (205)	for Northamptonshire at Northampton	1996
2nd wkt	417	K J Barnett (210*)	and TA Tweats (189)	for Derbyshire at Derby	1997
3rd wkt	523	M A Carberry (300*)	and N D McKenzie (237)	for Hampshire at Southampton	2011
4th wkt	447	R Abel (193)	and T Hayward (273)	for Surrey at The Oval	1899
5th wkt	261	W G Grace (318*)	and W O Moberley (103)	for Gloucestershire at Cheltenham	1876
6th wkt	346	S W Billings (138)	and D I Stevens (237)	for Kent at Leeds	2019
7th wkt	315	D M Benkenstein (151)	and O D Gibson (155)	for Durham at Leeds	2006
8th wkt	178	A P Wells (253*)	and B T P Donelan (59)	for Sussex at Middlesbrough	1991
9th wkt	233	I J L Trott (161*)	and J S Patel (120)	for Warwickshire at Birmingham	2009
10th wkt	132	A Hill (172*)	and M Jean-Jacques (73)	for Derbyshire at Sheffield	1986

CENTURY PARTNERSHIPS FOR THE FIRST WICKET IN BOTH INNINGS

128	108	G Ulyett (82 and 91)	and L Hall (87 and 37)	v. Sussex at Hove	1885
		(First instance in First-Class cricket)			
138	147*	J T Brown (203 and 81*)	and J Tunnicliffe (62 and 63*)	v. Middlesex at Lord's	1896
		(Second instance in First-Class cricket)			
105	265*	P Holmes (51 and 127*)	and H Sutcliffe (71 and 131*)	v. Surrey at The Oval	1926
184	210*	P Holmes (83 and 101*)	and H Sutcliffe (111 and 100*)	v. Nottinghamshire at Nottingham	1928
110	117	L Hutton (95 and 86)	and W Watson (34 and 57)	v. Lancashire at Manchester	1947
122	230	W B Stott (50 and 114)	and K Taylor (79 and 140)	v. Nottinghamshire at Nottingham	1957
136	138	J B Bolus (108 and 71)	and K Taylor (89 and 75)	v. Cambridge University at Cambridge	1962
105	105	G Boycott (38 and 64)	and K Taylor (85 and 49)	v. Leicestershire at Leicester	1963
116	112*	K Taylor (45 and 68)	and J H Hampshire (68 and 67*)	v. Oxford University at Oxford	1964
104	104	G Boycott (117 and 49*)	and R G Lumb (47 and 57)	v. Sussex at Leeds	1974
134	185*	M D Moxon (57 and 89*)	and A A Metcalfe (216* and 78*)	v. Middlesex at Leeds	1988
118	129*	G S Ballance (72 and 73*)	and J J Sayers (139 and 53*)	v. Durham MCCU at Durham	2011

CENTURY PARTNERSHIPS FOR THE FIRST WICKET IN BOTH INNINGS BUT WITH CHANGE OF PARTNER

109		W H H Sutcliffe (82) and F A Lowson (46)
	143	W H H Sutcliffe (88) and W Watson (52) v. Canadians at Scarborough, 1954
109		G Boycott (70) and R G Lumb (44)
	135	G Boycott (74) and J H Hampshire (58) v. Northamptonshire at Bradford, 1977

CENTURY PARTNERSHIPS

FIRST WICKET (Qualification 200 runs)

555	P Holmes (224*) and H Sutcliffe (313) v. Essex at Leyton, 1932
554	J T Brown (300) and J Tunnicliffe (243) v. Derbyshire at Chesterfield, 1898
378	J T Brown (311) and J Tunnicliffe (147) v. Sussex at Sheffield, 1897
375	A Lyth (230) and A Z Lees (138) v. Northamptonshire at Northampton, 2014
362	M D Moxon (213) and M P Vaughan (183) v. Glamorgan at Cardiff, 1996
351	G Boycott (184) and M D Moxon (168) v. Worcestershire at Worcester, 1985
347	P Holmes (302*) and H Sutcliffe (131) v. Hampshire at Portsmouth, 1920
323	P Holmes (125) and H Sutcliffe (195) v. Lancashire at Sheffield, 1931
315	H Sutcliffe (189) and L Hutton (153) v. Leicestershire at Hull, 1937
315	H Sutcliffe (116) and L Hutton (280*) v. Hampshire at Sheffield, 1939
309	P Holmes (250) and H Sutcliffe (129) v. Warwickshire at Birmingham, 1931
309	C White (186) and M J Wood (115) v. Lancashire at Manchester, 2001
290	P Holmes (179*) and H Sutcliffe (104) v. Middlesex at Leeds, 1928
288	G Boycott (130*) and R G Lumb (159) v. Somerset at Harrogate, 1979
286	L Hutton (156) and F A Lowson (115) v. South Africans at Sheffield, 1951
282	M D Moxon (147) and A A Metcalfe (151) v. Lancashire at Manchester, 1986
281*	W B Stott (138*) and K Taylor (130*) v. Sussex at Hove, 1960
279	P Holmes (133) and H Sutcliffe (145) v. Northamptonshire at Northampton, 1919
274	P.Holmes (199) and H Sutcliffe (139) v. Somerset at Hull, 1923
274	P Holmes (180) and H Sutcliffe (134) v. Gloucestershire at Gloucester, 1927
272	P Holmes (194) and H Sutcliffe (129) v. Leicestershire at Hull, 1925
272	M J Wood (202*) and J J Sayers (115) v. Bangladesh 'A' at Leeds, 2005
270	A Lyth (143) and A Z Lees (108) v. Durham at Leeds, 2014
268	P Holmes (136) and H Sutcliffe (129) v. Essex at Leyton, 1928
267	W Barber (248) and L Hutton (70) v. Kent at Leeds, 1934
265*	P Holmes (127*) and H Sutcliffe (131*) v. Surrey at The Oval, 1926
264	G Boycott (161*) and R G Lumb (132) v. Gloucestershire at Leeds, 1976
253	P Holmes (123) and H Sutcliffe (132) v. Lancashire at Sheffield, 1919
248	G Boycott (163) and A A Metcalfe (122) v. Nottinghamshire at Bradford, 1983
245	L Hutton (152) and F A Lowson (120) v. Lancashire at Leeds, 1952
244	J A Rudolph (149) and J J Sayers (86) v. Nottinghamshire at Nottingham, 2009
241	P Holmes (142) and H Sutcliffe (123*) v. Surrey at The Oval, 1929
240	G Boycott (233) and P J Sharpe (92) v. Essex at Colchester, 1971
238*	P Holmes (126*) and H Sutcliffe (105*) v. Cambridge University at Cambridge, 1923
236	G Boycott (131) and K Taylor (153) v. Lancashire at Manchester, 1964
235	P Holmes (130) and H Sutcliffe (132*) v. Glamorgan at Sheffield, 1930
233	G Boycott (141*) and R G Lumb (90) v. Cambridge University at Cambridge, 1973
233	H Halliday (116) and W Watson (108) v. Northamptonshire at Northampton, 1948
231	M P Vaughan (151) and D Byas (90) v. Essex at Chelmsford, 1999
230	H Sutcliffe (129) and L Hutton (163) v. Surrey at Leeds, 1936
230	W B Stott (114) and K Taylor (140*) v. Nottinghamshire at Nottingham, 1957
228	H Halliday (90) and J V Wilson (223*) v. Scotland at Scarborough, 1951
228	G Boycott (141) and R G Lumb (101) v. Gloucestershire at Bristol, 1975
227	P Holmes (110) and H Sutcliffe (119) v. Leicestershire at Leicester, 1928
225	R G Lumb (101) and C W J Athey (125*) v. Gloucestershire at Sheffield, 1980
224	C W J Athey (114) and J D Love (104) v. Warwickshire at Birmingham, 1980
222	W B Stott (141) and K Taylor (90) v. Sussex at Bradford, 1958
221	P Holmes (130) and H Sutcliffe (121) v. Glamorgan at Huddersfield, 1925
221	M D Moxon (141) and A A Metcalfe (73) v. Surrey at The Oval, 1987
221	A Lyth (111) and A Z Lees (121) v. Leeds/Bradford MCCU at Leeds, 2013
219	P Holmes (102) and A Mitchell (130*) v. Somerset at Bradford, 1930
218	M Leyland (110) and H Sutcliffe (235) v. Middlesex at Leeds, 1925
218	R G Lumb (145) and M D Moxon (111) v. Derbyshire at Sheffield, 1981
210*	P Holmes (101*) and H Sutcliffe (100*) v. Nottinghamshire at Nottingham, 1928
210	G Boycott (128) and P J Sharpe (197) v. Pakistanis at Leeds, 1967
209	F A Lowson (115) and D E V Padgett (107) v. Scotland at Hull, 1956

CENTURY PARTNERSHIPS *(Continued)*

208	A Mitchell (85) and E Oldroyd (111) v. Cambridge University at Cambridge, 1929
207	A Mitchell (90) and W Barber (107) v. Middlesex at Lord's, 1935
206	G Boycott (118) and R G Lumb (87) v. Glamorgan at Sheffield, 1978
204	M D Moxon (66) and A A Metcalfe (162) v. Gloucestershire at Cheltenham, 1990
203	L Hutton (119) and F A Lowson (83) v. Somerset at Huddersfield, 1952
203	M D Moxon (117) and S A Kellett (87) v. Somerset at Middlesbrough, 1992
203	M D Moxon (134) and M P Vaughan (106) v. Matebeleland at Bulawayo, 1996
200*	P Holmes (107*) and H Sutcliffe (80*) v. Oxford University at Oxford, 1930

Note: P Holmes and H Sutcliffe shared 69 century opening partnerships for Yorkshire; G Boycott and R G Lumb 29; L Hutton and F A Lowson 22; M D Moxon and A A Metcalfe 21; J T Brown and J Tunnicliffe 19; H Sutcliffe and L Hutton 15; G Boycott and P J Sharpe 13, and L Hall and G Ulyett 12.

SECOND WICKET (Qualification 200 runs)

346	W Barber (162) and M Leyland (189) v. Middlesex at Sheffield, 1932
343	F A Lowson (183*) and J V Wilson (165) v. Oxford University at Oxford, 1956
333	P Holmes (209) and E Oldroyd (138*) v. Warwickshire at Birmingham, 1922
314	H Sutcliffe (255*) and E Oldroyd (138) v. Essex at Southend-on-Sea, 1924
311	A Z Lees (275*) and P A Jaques (139) v. Derbyshire at Chesterfield, 2013
305	J W.Rothery (134) and D Denton (182) v. Derbyshire at Chesterfield, 1910
302	W Watson (172) and J V Wilson (140) v. Derbyshire at Scarborough, 1948
301	P J Sharpe (172*) and D E V Padgett (133) v. Glamorgan at Swansea, 1971
288	H Sutcliffe (165) and A Mitchell (136) v. Lancashire at Manchester, 1939
280	L Hall (160) and F Lee (165) v. Lancashire at Bradford, 1887
266*	K Taylor (178*) and D E V Padgett (107*) v. Oxford University at Oxford, 1962
264	P A Jaques (152) and K S Williamson (97) v. Durham at Scarborough, 2013
261*	L Hutton (146*) and J V Wilson (110*) v. Scotland at Hull, 1949
260	R G Lumb (144) and K Sharp (132) v. Glamorgan at Cardiff, 1984
258	H Sutcliffe (230) and E Oldroyd (93) v. Kent at Folkestone, 1931
253	B B Wilson (150) and D Denton (200*) v. Warwickshire at Birmingham, 1912
248	H Sutcliffe (200) and M. Leyland (116) v. Leicestershire at Leicester, 1926
244	P. Holmes (138) and E Oldroyd (151*) v. Glamorgan at Cardiff, 1922
243	G Boycott (141) and J D Love (163) v. Nottinghamshire at Bradford, 1976
243	C White (183) and M J Wood (124) v. Glamorgan at Scarborough, 2001
237	H Sutcliffe (118) and D Denton (122) v. Gloucestershire at Leeds, 1919
237	M D Moxon (132) and K Sharp (128) v. Sri Lankans at Leeds, 1988
236	F A Lowson (112) and J V Wilson (157) v. Essex at Leeds, 1950
235	M D Moxon (130) and D Byas (181) v. Cambridge University at Cambridge, 1995
230	L Hutton (180) and A Mitchell (108) v. Cambridge University at Cambridge, 1938
230	M P Vaughan (109) and B Parker (138*) v. Oxford University at Oxford, 1997.
227	M J Wood (102) and M J Lumb (122) v. Leicestershire at Leeds, 2001
225	H Sutcliffe (138) and E Oldroyd (97) v. Derbyshire at Dewsbury, 1928
223	M D Moxon (153) and R J Blakey (90) v. Somerset at Leeds, 1985
222	H Sutcliffe (174) and D Denton (114) v. Kent at Dover, 1919
219	F S Jackson (155) and D Denton (113) v. Middlesex at Bradford, 1899
217	R G Lumb (107) and J D Love (107) v. Oxford University at Oxford, 1978
216	M P Vaughan (105) and D Byas (102) v. Somerset at Bradford, 1994
215	A W Gale (136) and A McGrath (99) v. Lancashire at Manchester, 2008
215	S E Marsh (125*) and A Z Lees (102) v. Surrey at The Oval, 2017
211	J A Rudolph (141) and A McGrath (80) v Nottinghamshire at Leeds, 2010
207	P A Jaques (115) and A McGrath (93) v. Essex at Chelmsford, 2004
206	J Tunnicliffe (102) and F S Jackson (134*) v. Lancashire at Sheffield, 1898
206	H Sutcliffe (187) and M Leyland (90) v. Leicestershire at Leicester, 1931
205	H Sutcliffe (174) and A Mitchell (95) v. Leicestershire at Leicester, 1933
205	G Boycott (148) and P J Sharpe (108) v. Kent at Sheffield, 1970
203	A T Barber (100) and E Oldroyd (143) v. An England XI at Sheffield, 1929
203	J J Sayers (187) and A McGrath (102) v. Kent at Tunbridge Wells, 2007
202*	W Rhodes (115*) and G H Hirst (117*) v. Somerset at Bath, 1906
202	G Boycott (113) and C W J Athey (114) v. Northamptonshire at Northampton, 1978

CENTURY PARTNERSHIPS *(Continued)*

THIRD WICKET (Qualification 200 runs)

346	J J Sayers (173) and A McGrath (211) v. Warwickshire at Birmingham, 2009
323*	H Sutcliffe (147*) and M Leyland (189*) v. Glamorgan at Huddersfield, 1928
317	A McGrath (165) and D S Lehmann (187) v. Lancashire at Leeds, 2002
310	A McGrath (134) and P A Jaques (219) v. Derbyshire at Leeds, 2005
301	H Sutcliffe (175) and M Leyland (180*) v. Middlesex at Lord's, 1939
293*	A A Metcalfe (150*) and P E Robinson (150*) v. Derbyshire at Scarborough, 1990
269	D Byas (101) and R J Blakey (196) v. Oxford University at Oxford, 1991
258*	J T Brown (134*) and F Mitchell (116*) v. Warwickshire at Bradford, 1901
253*	G S Ballance (101*) and J E Root (130*) v. Nottinghamshire at Nottingham, 2019
252	D E V Padgett (139*) and D B Close (154) v. Nottinghamshire at Nottingham, 1959
249	D E V Padgett (95) and D B Close (184) v. Nottinghamshire at Scarborough, 1960
248	C Johnson (102) and J H Hampshire (155*) v. Gloucestershire at Leeds, 1976
247	P Holmes (175*) and M Leyland (118) v. New Zealanders at Bradford, 1927
244	D E V Padgett (161*) and D B Close (144) v. Oxford University at Oxford, 1959
240	L Hutton (151) and M Leyland (95) v. Surrey at Leeds, 1939
237	J A Rudolph (198) and A McGrath (120) v. Worcestershire at Leeds, 2009
236	H Sutcliffe (107) and R Kilner (137) v. Nottinghamshire at Nottingham, 1920
236	M J Wood (94) and D S Lehmann (200) v. Worcestershire at Worcester, 1998
234*	D Byas (126*) and A McGrath (105*) v. Oxford University at Oxford, 1997.
233	L Hutton (101) and M Leyland (167) v. Worcestershire at Stourbridge, 1937
230	D Byas (103) and M J Wood (103) v. Derbyshire at Leeds, 1998
229	L Hall (86) and R Peel (158) v. Middlesex at Lord's, 1889
228	A Mitchell (142) and M Leyland (133) v. Worcestershire at Sheffield, 1933
228	W Barber (141) and M Leyland (114) v. Surrey at The Oval, 1939
228	J V Wilson (132*) and D E V Padgett (115) v. Warwickshire at Birmingham, 1955
226	D E V Padgett (117) and D B Close (198) v. Surrey at The Oval, 1960
224	J V Wilson (110) and D B Close (114) v. Cambridge University at Cambridge, 1955
224	G Boycott (140*) and K Sharp (121) v. Gloucestershire at Cheltenham, 1983
221	A Mitchell (138) and M Leyland (134) v. Nottinghamshire at Bradford, 1933
219	L Hall (116) and W Bates (133) v. Cambridge University at Cambridge, 1884
218	J A Rudolph (127) and A W Gale (121) v. Lancashire at Manchester, 2009
217	A McGrath (144) and J A Rudolph (129) v. Kent at Canterbury, 2008
216	R G Lumb (118) and J H Hampshire (127) v. Surrey at The Oval, 1975
215	A Mitchell (73) and M Leyland (139) v. Surrey at Bradford, 1928
213	E Oldroyd (168) and W Barber (114) v. Glamorgan at Hull, 1929
208	J V Wilson (157*) and E I Lester (112) v. Sussex at Leeds, 1949
206	A McGrath (105) and J A Rudolph (228*) v Durham at Leeds, 2010
205*	E Oldroyd (122*) and M Leyland (100*) v. Hampshire at Harrogate, 1924
205	F S Jackson (124) and D Denton (112) v. Somerset at Taunton, 1897
205	D E V Padgett (83) and D B Close (128) v. Somerset at Bath, 1959
204	M P Vaughan (113) and A McGrath (70) v. Essex at Scarborough, 2001
203	D Denton (132) and J Tunnicliffe (102) v. Warwickshire at Birmingham, 1905
203	A A Metcalfe (216*) and P E Robinson (88) v. Middlesex at Leeds, 1988
201	J Tunnicliffe (101) and T L Taylor (147) v. Surrey at The Oval, 1900
201	H Sutcliffe (87) and W Barber (130) v. Leicestershire at Leicester, 1938
200	M D Moxon (274*) and A P Grayson (100) v. Worcestershire at Worcester, 1994

FOURTH WICKET (Qualification 175 runs)

372	J E Root (213) and J M Bairstow (198) v. Surrey at Leeds, 2016
358	D S Lehmann (339) and M J Lumb (98) v. Durham at Leeds, 2006
330	M J Wood (116) and D R Martyn (238) v. Gloucestershire at Leeds, 2003
312	D Denton (168*) and G H Hirst (146) v. Hampshire at Southampton, 1914
299	P Holmes (277*) and R Kilner (150) v. Northamptonshire at Harrogate, 1921
272	D Byas (138) and A McGrath (137) v. Hampshire at Harrogate, 1996
271	B B Wilson (208) and W Rhodes (113) v. Sussex at Bradford, 1914
259	A Drake (115) and G H Hirst (218) v. Sussex at Hastings, 1911
258	J Tunnicliffe (128) and G H Hirst (152) v. Hampshire at Portsmouth, 1904

CENTURY PARTNERSHIPS (Continued)

258	P E Robinson (147) and D Byas (117) v. Kent at Scarborough, 1989
255	A W Gale (148) and J A Leaning (110) v. Nottinghamshire at Leeds, 2015
254	A W Gale (164) and J M Bairstow (139) v. Worcestershire at Scarborough, 2015
249	W B Stott (143) and G Boycott (145) v. Lancashire at Sheffield, 1963
247*	R G Lumb (165*) and S N Hartley (104*) v. Gloucestershire at Bradford, 1984
247	M Leyland (263) and L Hutton (83) v. Essex at Hull, 1936
238	D S Lehmann (216) and M J Lumb (92) v. Sussex at Arundel, 2002
233	D Byas (120) and P E Robinson (189) v. Lancashire at Scarborough, 1991
231	J E Root (236) and J M Bairstow (186) v. Derbyshire at Leeds, 2013
226	W H Wilkinson (89) and G H Hirst (140) v. Northamptonshire at Hull, 1909
225	C H Grimshaw (85) and G H Hirst (169) v. Oxford University at Oxford, 1906
212	B B Wilson (108) and G H Hirst (166*) v. Sussex at Hastings, 1913
212	G Boycott (260*) and J H Hampshire (80) v. Essex at Colchester, 1970
211	J V Wilson (120) and W Watson (108) v. Derbyshire at Harrogate, 1951
210*	A Mitchell (150*) and M Leyland (117*) v. Worcestershire at Worcester, 1933
210	E I. Lester (178) and W Watson (97) v. Nottinghamshire at Nottingham, 1952
207	D Byas (213) and C White (107*) v. Worcestershire at Scarborough, 1995
206	J A Rudolph (121) and A W Gale (150) v. Surrey at The Oval, 2008
205*	G Boycott (151*) and P J Sharpe (79*) v. Leicestershire at Leicester, 1964
205	E Oldroyd (121) and R Kilner (117) v. Worcestershire at Dudley, 1922
205	W Watson (162*) and E I Lester (98) v. Somerset at Leeds, 1953
205	A Lyth (111) and J M Bairstow (246) v. Hampshire at Leeds, 2016
204	A W Gale (148) and G S Ballance (90) v. Surrey at Leeds, 2013
201*	J H Hampshire (105*) and D B Close (101*) v. Surrey at Bradford, 1965
203	P A Jaques (160) and G S Ballance (121*) v. Gloucestershire at Bristol, 2012
201	W H H Sutcliffe (181) and L Hutton (120) v. Kent at Canterbury, 1952
200	J V Wilson (92) and W Watson (122) v. Somerset at Taunton, 1950
198	A A Metcalfe (138) and D Byas (95) v. Warwickshire at Leeds, 1989
198	A W Gale (124) and J M Bairstow (95) v. Durham at Chester-le-Street, 2014
197	N W D Yardley (177) and A Coxon (58) v. Derbyshire at Scarborough, 1947
197	A Lyth (248*) and J M Bairstow (118) v. Leicestershire at Leicester, 2012
196	M D Moxon (130) and D L Bairstow (104) v. Derbyshire at Harrogate, 1987
193	A Drake (85) and G H Hirst (156) v. Lancashire at Manchester, 1911
192	J V Wilson (132) and W Watson (105) v. Essex at Bradford, 1955
191	M Leyland (112) and C Turner (63) v. Essex at Ilford, 1938
190	A W Gale (125) and J A Leaning (76) v. Hampshire at West End, Southampton, 2015
188	H Myers (60) and G H Hirst (158) v. Cambridge University at Cambridge, 1910
188	G S Ballance (159) and J A Leaning (69) v. Kent at Canterbury, 2019
187	E Oldroyd (168) and F E Greenwood (104*) v. Glamorgan at Hull, 1929
187	K Taylor (203*) and W B Stott (57) v. Warwickshire at Birmingham, 1961
186	D S Lehmann (193) and D Byas (100) v. Leicestershire at Leicester, 2001
184	J H Hampshire (96) and R Illingworth (100*) v. Leicestershire at Sheffield, 1968
182*	E I Lester (101*) and W Watson (103*) v. Nottinghamshire at Bradford, 1952
180*	G Boycott (207*) and B Leadbeater (50*) v. Cambridge University at Cambridge, 1976
180	J Tunnicliffe (139*) and G H Hirst (108) v. Surrey at The Oval, 1904
179	J H Hampshire (179) and S N Hartley (63) v. Surrey at Harrogate, 1981
179	M D Moxon (171*) and R J Blakey (71) v. Kent at Leeds, 1993
178	E I Lester (186) and J V Wilson (71) v. Warwickshiire at Scarborough, 1949
177	J D Love (105*) and J H Hampshire (89) v. Lancashire at Manchester, 1980
175	L Hutton (177) and W Barber (84) v. Sussex at Scarborough, 1939
175	A McGrath (188*) and J A Rudolph (82) v. Warwickshire at Birmingham, 2007

FIFTH WICKET (Qualification 150 runs)

340	E Wainwright (228) and G H Hirst (186) v. Surrey at The Oval, 1899
329	F Mitchell (194) and E Wainwright (153) v. Leicestershire at Leicester, 1899
297	A W Gale (272) and G S Ballance (141) v. Nottinghamshire at Scarborough, 2013
276	W Rhodes (104*) and R Kilner (166) v. Northamptonshire at Northampton, 1921
273	L Hutton (270*) and N W D Yardley (136) v. Hampshire at Bournemouth, 1947

CENTURY PARTNERSHIPS *(Continued)*

245*	H Sutcliffe (107*) and W Barber (128*)	v. Northamptonshire at Northampton, 1939
229	D S Lehmann (193) and C White (79)	v. Kent at Canterbury, 2006
217	D B Close (140*) and R Illingworth (107)	v. Warwickshire at Sheffield, 1962
213	T Kohler-Cadmore (176) and J A Tattersall (135*)	v. Leeds/Bradford MCCU at Weetwood, Leeds, 2019
207	G S Ballance (107) and A U Rashid (180)	v. Somerset at Leeds, 2013
200	D J Malan (219) and J A Tattersall (66)	v. Derbyshire at Leeds, 2020
198	E Wainwright (145) and R Peel (111)	v. Sussex at Bradford, 1896
198	W Barber (168) and K R Davidson (101*)	v. MCC at Lord's, 1934
196*	R Kilner (115*) and G H Hirst (82*)	v. Gloucestershire at Leeds, 1919
195	M J Lumb (93) and C White (173*)	v. Derbyshire at Derby, 2003
194*	Younus Khan (202*) and G L Brophy (100*)	v. Hampshire at Southampton, 2007
193	A Mitchell (189) and W Rhodes (88)	v. Northamptonshire at Northampton, 1926
193	J D Love (106) and S N Hartley (108)	v. Oxford University at Oxford, 1985
192	C W J Athey (114*) and J D Love (123)	v. Surrey at The Oval, 1982
191*	L Hutton (271*) and C Turner (81*)	v. Derbyshire at Sheffield, 1937
191	M G Bevan (105) and A A Metcalfe (100)	v. West Indians at Scarborough, 1995
190*	R J Blakey (204*) and J D Love (79*)	v. Gloucestershire at Leeds, 1987
189	J E Root (160) and G S Ballance (87)	v. Sussex at Scarborough 2011
188	D E V Padgett (146) and J V Wilson (72)	v. Sussex at Middlesbrough, 1960
187	J V Wilson (230) and H Halliday (74)	v. Derbyshire at Sheffield, 1952
185	G Boycott (104*) and K Sharp (99)	v. Kent at Tunbridge Wells, 1984
182	E Lockwood (208) and E Lumb (40)	v. Kent at Gravesend, 1882
182	B B Wilson (109) and W Rhodes (111)	v. Sussex at Hove, 1910
182	D B Close (164) and J V Wilson (55)	v. Combined Services at Harrogate, 1954
182	A W Gale (126*) and J A Leaning (76)	v. Middlesex at Scarborough, 2014
181	A A Metcalfe (149) and J D Love (88)	v. Glamorgan at Leeds, 1986
177	Hon F S Jackson (87) and G H Hirst (232*)	v. Surrey at The Oval, 1905
176	L Hutton (176*) and A Coxon (72)	v. Sussex at Sheffield, 1948
175	A Drake (108) and R Kilner (77)	v. Cambridge University at Cambridge, 1913
173	H Sutcliffe (206) and R Kilner (124)	v. Warwickshire at Dewsbury, 1925
170	W Rhodes (157) and R Kilner (87)	v. Derbyshire at Leeds, 1925
170	J V Wilson (130*) and N W D Yardley (67)	v. Lancashire at Manchester, 1954
169	W Watson (147) and A B Sellers (92)	v. Worcestershire at Worcester, 1947
168	A T Barber (63) and A Mitchell (122*)	v. Worcestershire at Worcester, 1929
167	J M Bairstow (136) and G S Ballance (61)	v. Somerset at Taunton 2011
165	E Oldroyd (143) and W Rhodes (110)	v. Glamorgan at Leeds, 1922
165	K Sharp (100*) and P Carrick (73)	v. Middlesex at Lord's, 1980
164	A A Metcalfe (151) and D L Bairstow (88)	v. Northamptonshire at Luton, 1986
159*	J D Love (170*) and D L Bairstow (52*)	v. Worcestershire at Worcester, 1979
159	D B Close (128) and R Illingworth (74)	v. Lancashire at Sheffield, 1959
159	J H Hampshire (183*) and C Johnson (53)	v. Sussex at Hove, 1971
158*	G Boycott (153*) and P E Robinson (74*)	v. Derbyshire at Harrogate, 1984
157	T L Taylor (135*) and G H Hirst (72)	v. An England XI at Hastings, 1901
157	G H Hirst (142) and F Smith (51)	v. Somerset at Bradford, 1903
157	W Barber (87) and N W D Yardley (101)	v. Surrey at The Oval, 1937
156	A McGrath (158) and I J Harvey (103)	v. Derbyshire at Derby, 2005
155	J M Bairstow (102) and J A Leaning (62)	v. Hampshire at Leeds, 2015
153	S N Hartley (87) and M D Moxon (112*)	v. Indians at Scarborough, 1986
152	J H Hampshire (83) and S N Hartley (106)	v. Nottinghamshire at Nottingham, 1981
151*	G H Hirst (102*) and R Kilner (50*)	v. Kent at Bradford, 1913
151	G H Hirst (120) and F Smith (55)	v. Kent at Leeds, 1903
151	W Rhodes (57) and R Kilner (90)	v. Nottinghamshire at Nottingham, 1925

SIXTH WICKET (Qualification 100)

296	A Lyth (251) and A U Rashid (159*)	v. Lancashire at Manchester, 2014
276	M Leyland (191) and E Robinson (124*)	v. Glamorgan at Swansea, 1926
252	C White (181) and R J Blakey (109*)	v. Lancashire at Leeds, 1996
248	G J Maxwell (140) and A U Rashid (127)	v. Durham at Scarborough, 2015
233	M W Booth (210) and G H Hirst (100)	v. Worcestershire at Worcester, 1911

CENTURY PARTNERSHIPS (Continued)

229	W Rhodes (267*) and N Kilner (112) v. Leicestershire at Leeds, 1921
225	E Wainwright (91) and Lord Hawke (127) v. Hampshire at Southampton, 1899
217*	H Sutcliffe (200*) and A Wood (123*) v. Worcestershire at Sheffield, 1935
214	W Watson (214*) and N W D Yardley (76) v. Worcestershire at Worcester, 1955
205	G H Hirst (125) and S Haigh (159) v. Nottinghamshire at Sheffield, 1901
200	D Denton (127) and G H Hirst (134) v. Essex at Bradford, 1902
198	M Leyland (247) and W Rhodes (100*) v. Worcestershire at Worcester, 1928
190	W Rhodes (126) and M Leyland (79) v. Middlesex at Bradford, 1923
190	J A Rudolph (122) and A U Rashid (86) v. Surrey at The Oval, 2007
188	W Watson (174) and R Illingworth (53) v. Lancashire at Sheffield, 1955
188	M P Vaughan (161) and R J Blakey (92) v. Essex at Ilford, 1997.
188	G S Ballance (111) and A U Rashid (82) v. Warwickshire at Birmingham 2011
184	R Kilner (104) and M W Booth (79) v. Leicestershire at Leeds, 1913
183	G H Hirst (131) and E Smith (129) v. Hampshire at Bradford, 1899
183	W Watson (139*) and R Illingworth (78) v. Somerset at Harrogate, 1956
178*	D Denton (108*) and G H Hirst (112*) v. Lancashire at Manchester, 1902
178*	N W D Yardley (100*) and R Illingworth (71*) v. Gloucestershire at Bristol, 1955
178	E Robinson (100) and D C F Burton (83) v. Derbyshire at Hull, 1921
178	H Sutcliffe (135) and P A Gibb (157*) v. Nottinghamshire at Sheffield, 1935
175	G M Fellows (88) and R J Blakey (103) v. Warwickshire at Birmingham, 2002
174	D S Lehmann (136) and G M Hamilton (73) v. Kent at Maidstone, 1998
173	T Kohler-Cadmore (81) and A J Hodd (85) v. Somerset at Leeds, 2018
172	A J Dalton (119*) and D L Bairstow (62) v. Worcestershire at Dudley, 1971
170*	A U Rashid 103*) and A J Hodd (68*) v. Somerset at Taunton, 2013
170	A W Gale (101) and T T Bresnan (97) v. Worcestershire at Worcester, 2009
169	W Barber (124) and H Verity (78*) v. Warwickshire at Birmingham, 1933
169	R Illingworth (162) and J Birkenshaw (37) v. Indians at Sheffield, 1959
166	E Wainwright (116) and E Smith (61) v. Kent at Catford, 1900
166	D B Close (161) and F S Trueman (104) v. Northamptonshire at Northampton, 1963
162*	G Boycott (220*) and J G Binks (70*) v. Northamptonshire at Sheffield, 1967
161*	D L Bairstow (100*) and P Carrick (59*) v. Middlesex at Leeds, 1983
159*	D S Lehmann (187*) and R J Blakey (78*) v. Somerset at Bath, 2001
159	J M Bairstow (182) and A McGrath (90) v. Leicestershire at Scarborough, 2012
156	W Rhodes (82*) and E Robinson (94) v. Derbyshire at Chesterfield, 1919
154	C Turner (84) and A Wood (79) v. Glamorgan at Swansea, 1936
153*	J A Rudolph (92*) and A U Rashid (73*) v. Worcestershire at Kidderminster, 2009
153	J A Rudolph (69*) and J M Bairstow (81) v. Warwickshire at Birmingham, 2010
151	D Denton (91) and W Rhodes (76) v. Middlesex at Sheffield, 1904
151	G Boycott (152*) and P Carrick (75) v. Warwickshire at Leeds, 1982
150	G Ulyett (199*) and J M Preston (93) v. Derbyshire at Sheffield, 1887

SEVENTH WICKET (Qualification 125 runs)

366*	J M Bairstow (219*) and T T Bresnan (169*) v. Durham at Chester-le-Street, 2015
254	W Rhodes (135) and D C F Burton (142*) v. Hampshire at Dewsbury, 1919
247	P Holmes (285) and W Rhodes (79) v. Nottinghamshire at Nottingham, 1929
227	J M Bairstow (246) and L E Plunkett (126) v. Hampshire at Leeds, 2016
215	E Robinson (135*) and D C F Burton (110) v. Leicestershire at Leicester, 1921
197	G S Ballance (165*) and T T Bresnan (78) v. Sussex at Hove, 2015
185	E Wainwright (100) and G H Hirst (134) v. Gloucestershire at Bristol, 1897
183	G H Hirst (341) and H Myers (57) v. Leicestershire at Leicester, 1905
183	J A Rudolph (220) and T T Bresnan (101*) v. Warwickshire at Scarborough, 2007
180	C Turner (130) and A Wood (97) v. Somerset at Sheffield, 1936
170	G S Blewett (190) and G M Hamilton (84*) v. Northamptonshire at Scarborough, 1999
168	G L Brophy (99) and A U Rashid (157*) v. Lancashire at Leeds, 2009
166	R Peel (55) and I Grimshaw (122*) v. Derbyshire at Holbeck, 1886
162	E Wainwright (100) and S Haigh (73) v. Somerset at Taunton, 1900
162	R J Blakey (90) and R K J Dawson (87) v. Kent at Canterbury, 2002
162	A W Gale (149) and G L Brophy (97) v. Warwickshire at Scarborough, 2006

281

CENTURY PARTNERSHIPS *(Continued)*

161	R G Lumb (118) and C M Old (89) v. Worcestershire at Bradford, 1980
160	J Tunnicliffe (158) and D Hunter (58*) v. Worcestershire at Worcester, 1900
157*	F A Lowson (259*) and R Booth (53*) v. Worcestershire at Worcester, 1953
157	K S Wiiliamson (189) and T T Bresnan (61) v. Sussex at Scarborough, 2014
155	D Byas (122*) and P Carrick (61) v. Leicestershire at Leicester.1991.
154*	G H Hirst (76*) and J T Newstead (100*) v. Nottinghamshire at Nottingham, 1908
148	J Rowbotham (113) and J Thewlis (50) v. Surrey at The Oval, 1873
147	E Wainwright (78) and G Ulyett (73) v. Somerset at Taunton, 1893
147	M P Vaughan (153) and R J Harden (64) v. Kent at Scarborough, 1999
143	C White (135*) and A K D Gray (60) v. Durham at Chester-le-Street, 2003
141	G H Hirst (108*) and S Haigh (48) v. Worcestershire at Worcester, 1905
141	J H Hampshire (149*) and J G Binks (72) v. MCC at Scarborough, 1965
140	E Wainwright (117) and S Haigh (54) v. CI Thornton's XI at Scarborough, 1900
140	D Byas (67) and P J Hartley (75) v. Derbyshire at Chesterfield, 1990
138	D Denton (78) and G H Hirst (103*) v. Sussex at Leeds, 1905
136	GH Hirst (93) and S Haigh (138) v. Warwickshire at Birmingham, 1904
136	E Robinson (77*) and A Wood (65) v. Glamorgan at Scarborough, 1931
133*	W Rhodes (267*) and N Kilner (52*) v. Leicestershire at Leeds, 1921
133*	E I Lester (86*) and A B Sellers (73*) v. Northamptonshire at Northampton, 1948
133	D Byas (100) and P W Jarvis (80) v. Northamptonshire at Scarborough, 1992
132	W Rhodes (196) and S Haigh (59*) v. Worcestershire at Worcester, 1904
132	A J Hodd (96*) and Azeem Rafiq (74) v. Nottinghamshire at Scarborough, 2016
131*	D L Bairstow (79*) and A Sidebottom (52*) v. Oxford University at Oxford, 1981
130	P J Sharpe (64) and J V Wilson (134) v. Warwickshire at Birmingham, 1962
128	W Barber (66) and T F Smailes (86) v. Cambridge University at Cambridge, 1938
128	D B Close (88*) and A Coxon (59) v. Essex at Leeds, 1949
126	E Wainwright (171) and R Peel (46) v. Middlesex at Lord's, 1897
126	W Rhodes (91) and G G Macaulay (63) v. Hampshire at Hull, 1925
126	J C Balderstone (58) and J G Binks (95) v. Middlesex at Lord's, 1964
126	J M Bairstow (70) and A U Rashid (59) v. Kent at Canterbury, 2010
125	A B Sellers (109) and T F Smailes (65) v. Kent at Bradford, 1937

EIGHTH WICKET (Qualification 125 runs)

292	R Peel (210*) and Lord Hawke (166) v. Warwickshire at Birmingham, 1896
238	I J Harvey (209*) and T T Bresnan (74) v. Somerset at Leeds, 2005
192*	W Rhodes (108*) and G G Macaulay (101*) v. Essex at Harrogate, 1922
192	A U Rashid (117*) and A Shahzad (78) v. Hampshire at Basingstoke, 2009
180	W Barber (191) and T F Smailes (58) v. Sussex at Leeds, 1935
167	J A Leaning (118) and J A Brooks (109*) v. Lancashire at Manchester, 2017
165	S Haigh (62) and Lord Hawke (126) v. Surrey at The Oval, 1902
163	G G Macaulay (67) and A Waddington (114) v. Worcestershire at Leeds, 1927
159	E Smith (95) and W Rhodes (105) v. MCC at Scarborough, 1901
157	A Shahzad (88) and D J Wainwright (85*) v. Sussex at Hove, 2009
156	G S Ballance (112) and R J Sidebottom (40) v. Leeds/Bradford MCCU at Leeds, 2013
152	W Rhodes (98) and J W Rothery (70) v. Hampshire at Portsmouth, 1904
151	W Rhodes (201) and Lord Hawke (51) v. Somerset at Taunton, 1905
151	R J Blakey (80*) and P J Hartley (89) v. Sussex at Eastbourne, 1996
149	G L Brophy (177*) and R J Sidebottom (61) v. Worcestershire at Worcester 2011
147	J P G Chadwick (59) and F S Trueman (101) v. Middlesex at Scarborough, 1965
146	S Haigh (159) and Lord Hawke (89) v. Nottinghamshire at Sheffield, 1901
144	G L Brophy (85) and D J Wainwright (102*) v. Warwickshire at Scarborough, 2009
138	E Wainwright (100) and Lord Hawke (81) v. Kent at Tonbridge, 1899
137	E Wainwright (171) and Lord Hawke (75) v. Middlesex at Lord's, 1897
135	P W Jarvis (55) and P J Hartley (69) v. Nottinghamshire at Scarborough, 1992
133	R Illingworth (61) and F S Trueman (74) v. Leicestershire at Leicester, 1955
132	G H Hirst (103) and E Smith (59) v. Middlesex at Sheffield, 1904
132	W Watson (119) and J H Wardle (65) v. Leicestershire at Leicester, 1949
131	P E Robinson (85) and P Carrick (64) v. Surrey at Harrogate, 1990
130	E Smith (98) and Lord Hawke (54) v. Lancashire at Leeds, 1904

CENTURY PARTNERSHIPS *(Continued)*

128	H Verity (96*) and T F Smailes (77) v. Indians at Bradford, 1936
128	D L Bairstow (145) and G B Stevenson (11) v. Middlesex at Scarborough, 1980
127	E Robinson (70*) and A Wood (62) v. Middlesex at Leeds, 1928
126	R Peel (74) and E Peate (61) v. Gloucestershire at Bradford, 1883
126	M W Booth (56) and E R Wilson (104*) v. Essex at Bradford, 1913
126	J D Middlebrook (84) and C E W Silverwood (70) v. Essex at Chelmsford, 2001
126	M J Lumb (115*) and D Gough (72) v. Hampshire at Southampton, 2003

NINTH WICKET (Qualification 100 runs)

246	T T Bresnan (116) and J N Gillespie (123*) v. Surrey at The Oval, 2007
192	G H Hirst (130*) and S Haigh (85) v. Surrey at Bradford, 1898
179	R A Hutton (189) and G A Cope (30*) v. Pakistanis at Bradford, 1971
176*	R Moorhouse (59*) and G H Hirst (115*) v. Gloucestershire at Bristol, 1894
173	S Haigh (85) and W Rhodes (92*) v. Sussex at Hove, 1902
171	G S Ballance (194) and J A Brooks (82) v. Worcestershire at Worcester, 2018
167	H Verity (89) and T F Smailes (80) v. Somerset at Bath, 1936
162	W Rhodes (94*) and S Haigh (84) v. Lancashire at Manchester, 1904
161	E Smith (116*) and W Rhodes (79) v. Sussex at Sheffield, 1900
154	R M Pyrah (117) and R J Sidebottom (52) v. Lancashire at Leeds 2011
151	J M Bairstow (205) and R J Sidebottom (45*) v. Nottinghamshire at Nottingham 2011
150	Azeem Rafiq (100) and M J Hoggard (56*) v. Worcestershire at Worcester, 2009
149*	R J Blakey (63*) and A K D Gray (74*) v. Leicestershire at Scarborough, 2002
149	G H Hirst (232*) and D Hunter (40) v. Surrey at The Oval, 1905
146	G H Hirst (214) and W Rhodes (53) v. Worcestershire at Worcester, 1901
144	T T Bresnan (91) and J N Gillespie (44) v. Hampshire at Leeds, 2006
140	A U Rashid (111) and D J Wainwright (104) v. Sussex at Hove, 2008
136	R Peel (210*) and G H Hirst (85) v. Warwickshire at Birmingham, 1896
125*	L Hutton (269*) and A Coxon (65*) v. Northamptonshire at Wellingborough, 1949
124	P J Hartley (87*) and P W Jarvis (47) v. Essex at Chelmsford, 1986
120	G H Hirst (138) and W Rhodes (38) v. Nottinghamshire at Nottingham, 1899
119	A B Sellers (80*) and E P Robinson (66) v. Warwickshire at Birmingham, 1938
118	S Haigh (96) and W Rhodes (44) v. Somerset at Leeds, 1901
118	J E Root (99) and SA Patterson (47*) v. Glamorgan at Cardiff 2021
114	E Oldroyd (194) and A Dolphin (47) v. Worcestershire at Worcester, 1923
114	N Kilner (102*) and G G Macaulay (60) v. Gloucestershire at Bristol, 1923
113	G G Macaulay (125*) and A Waddington (44) v. Nottinghamshire at Nottingham, 1921
113	A Wood (69) and H.Verity (45*) v. MCC at Lord's, 1938
112	G H Hirst (78) and Lord Hawke (61*) v. Essex at Leyton, 1907
109	Lees Whitehead (60) and W Rhodes (81*) v. Sussex at Harrogate, 1899
108	A McGrath (133*) and C E W Silverwood (80) v. Durham at Chester-le-Street, 2005
106	L E Plunkett (86) and S A Patterson (43) v. Warwickshire at Leeds, 2014
105	J V Wilson (134) and A G Nicholson (20*) v. Nottinghamshire at Leeds, 1962
105	C M Old (100*) and H P Cooper (30) v. Lancashire at Manchester, 1978
105	C White (74*) and J D Batty (50) v. Gloucestershire at Sheffield, 1993
104	L Hall (129*) and R Moorhouse (86) v. Gloucestershire at Clifton, 1888
100	G Pollitt (51) and Lees Whitehead (54) v. Hampshire at Bradford, 1899

TENTH WICKET (Qualification 100 runs)

149	G Boycott (79) and G B Stevenson (115*) v. Warwickshire at Birmingham, 1982
148	Lord Hawke (107*) and D Hunter (47) v. Kent at Sheffield, 1898
144	A Sidebottom (124) and A L Robinson (30*) v. Glamorgan at Cardiff, 1977
121	J T Brown (141) and D Hunter (25*) v. Liverpool & District at Liverpool, 1894
118	Lord Hawke (110*) and D Hunter (41) v. Kent at Leeds, 1896
113	P J Hartley (88*) and R D Stemp (22) v. Middlesex at Lord's, 1996
110	C E W. Silverwood (45*) and R D Stemp (65) v. Durham at Chester-le-Street, 1996
109	A Shahzad (70) and R J Sidebottom (28*) v. Worcestershire at Scarborough, 2010
108	Lord Hawke (79) and Lees Whitehead (45*) v. Lancashire at Manchester, 1903
108	G Boycott (129) and M K Bore (37*) v. Nottinghamshire at Bradford, 1973
106	A B Sellers (79) and D V Brennan (30) v. Worcestershire at Worcester, 1948
103	A Dolphin (62*) and E Smith (49) v. Essex at Leyton, 1919
102	D Denton (77*) and D Hunter (45) v. Cambridge University at Cambridge, 1895

FIFTEEN WICKETS OR MORE IN A MATCH

A complete list of 12, 13 and 14 wickets in a match up to and including 2007 is to be found in the 2008 edition

W E BOWES (1)
16 for 35 (8 for 18 and 8 for 17) v. Northamptonshire at Kettering, 1935

A DRAKE (1)
15 for 51 (5 for 16 and 10 for 35) v. Somerset at Weston-super-Mare, 1914

T EMMETT (1)
16 for 38 (7 for 15 and 9 for 23) v. Cambridgeshire at Hunslet, 1869

G H HIRST (1)
15 for 63 (8 for 25 and 7 for 38) v. Leicestershire at Hull, 1907

R ILLINGWORTH (1)
15 for 123 (8 for 70 and 7 for 53) v. Glamorgan at Swansea, 1960

R PEEL (1)
15 for 50 (9 for 22 and 6 for 28) v. Somerset at Leeds, 1895

W RHODES (1)
15 for 56 (9 for 28 and 6 for 28) v. Essex at Leyton, 1899

H VERITY (4)
17 for 91 (8 for 47 and 9 for 44) v. Essex at Leyton, 1933
15 for 129 (8 for 56 and 7 for 73) v. Oxford University at Oxford, 1936
15 for 38 (6 for 26 and 9 for 12) v. Kent at Sheffield, 1936
15 for 100 (6 for 52 and 9 for 48) v. Essex at Westcliffe-on-Sea, 1936

J H WARDLE (1)
16 for 112 (9 for 48 and 7 for 64) v. Sussex at Hull, 1954

TEN WICKETS IN A MATCH
(including best analysis)

61	W Rhodes	15 for 56	v Essex	at Leyton	1899
48	H Verity	17 for 91	v Essex	at Leyton	1933
40	G H Hirst	15 for 63	v Leicestershire	at Hull	1907
31	G G Macaulay	14 for 92	v Gloucestershire	at Bristol	1926
28	S Haigh	14 for 43	v Hampshire	at Southampton	1898
27	R Peel	14 for 33	v Nottinghamshire	at Sheffield	1888
25	W E Bowes	16 for 35	v Northamptonshire	at Kettering	1935
25	J H Wardle	16 for 112	v Sussex	at Hull	1954
22	E Peate	14 for 77	v Surrey	at Huddersfield	1881
20	F S Trueman	14 for 123	v Surrey	at The Oval	1960
19	T Emmett	16 for 38	v Cambridgeshire	at Hunslet	1869
17	R Appleyard	12 for 43	v Essex	at Bradford	1951
15	E Wainwright	14 for 77	v Essex	at Bradford	1896
11	R Illingworth	15 for 123	v Glamorgan	at Swansea	1960
10	A Waddington	13 for 48	v Northamptonshire	at Northampton	1920
9	M W Booth	14 for 160	v Essex	at Leyton	1914
9	R Kilner	12 for 55	v Sussex	at Hove	1924
8	W Bates	11 for 47	v Nottinghamshire	at Nottingham	1881
8	G Freeman	13 for 60	v Surrey	at Sheffield	1869
7	E P Robinson	13 for 115	v Lancashire	at Leeds	1939
7	D Wilson	13 for 52	v Warwickshire	at Middlesbrough	1967
6	G A Cope	12 for 116	v Glamorgan	at Cardiff (Sophia Gardens)	1968
6	A Hill	12 for 59	v Surrey	at The Oval	1871

TEN WICKETS IN A MATCH (Including best analysis) *(Continued)*

6 T F Smailes	14 for 58	v Derbyshire	at Sheffield	1939
5 P Carrick	12 for 89	v Derbyshire	at Sheffield (Abbeydale Pk)	1983
5 J M Preston	13 for 63	v MCC	at Scarborough	1888
5 E Robinson	12 for 95	v Northamptonshire	at Huddersfield	1927
4 J T Newstead	11 for 72	v Worcestershire	at Bradford	1907
3 T W Foster	11 for 93	v Liverpool & District	at Liverpool	1894
3 G P Harrison	11 for 76	v Kent	at Dewsbury	1883
3 F S Jackson	12 for 80	v Hampshire	at Southampton	1897
3 P W Jarvis	11 for 92	v Middlesex	at Lord's	1986
3 S P Kirby	13 for 154	v Somerset	at Taunton	2003
3 A G Nicholson	12 for 73	v Glamorgan	at Leeds	1964
3 R K Platt	10 for 87	v Surrey	at The Oval	1959
3 A Sidebottom	11 for 64	v Kent	at Sheffield (Abbeydale Pk)	1980
3 R J Sidebottom	11 for 43	v Kent	at Leeds	2000
3 G Ulyett	12 for 102	v Lancashire	at Huddersfield	1889
2 T Armitage	13 for 46	v Surrey	at Sheffield	1876
2 R Aspinall	14 for 65	v Northamptonshire	at Northampton	1947
2 J T Brown (Darfield)	12 for 109	v Gloucestershire	at Huddersfield	1899
2 R O Clayton	12 for 104	v Lancashire	at Manchester	1877
2 D B Close	11 for 116	v Kent	at Gillingham	1965
2 B O Coad	10 for 102	v. Warwickshire	at Birmingham	2017
2 M J Cowan	12 for 87	v Warwickshire	at Birmingham	1960
2 A Coxon	10 for 57	v Derbyshire	at Chesterfield	1949
2 D Gough	10 for 80	v Lancashire	at Leeds	1995
2 G M Hamilton	11 for 72	v Surrey	at Leeds	1998
2 P J Hartley	11 for 68	v Derbyshire	at Chesterfield	1995
2 R A Hutton	11 for 62	v Lancashire	at Manchester	1971
2 E Leadbeater	11 for 162	v Nottinghamshire	at Nottingham	1950
2 K A Maharaj	10 for 127	v. Somerset	at Leeds	2019
2 M A Robinson	12 for 124	v Northamptonshire	at Harrogate	1993
2 M Ryan	10 for 77	v Leicestershire	at Bradford	1962
2 E Smith (Morley)	10 for 97	v MCC	at Scarborough	1893
2 G B Stevenson	11 for 74	v Nottinghamshire	at Nottingham	1980
2 S Wade	11 for 56	v Gloucestershire	at Cheltenham	1886
2 E R Wilson	11 for 109	v Sussex	at Hove	1921
1 A B Bainbridge	12 for 111	v Essex	at Harrogate	1961
1 J Birkenshaw	11 for 134	v Middlesex	at Leeds	1960
1 A Booth	10 for 91	v Indians	at Bradford	1946
1 H P Cooper	11 for 96	v Northamptonshire	at Northampton	1976
1 A Drake	15 for 51	v Somerset	at Weston-Super-Mare	1914
1 L Greenwood	11 for 71	v Surrey	at The Oval	1867
1 P M Hutchinson	11 for 102	v Pakistan 'A'	at Leeds	1997
1 L Hutton	10 for 101	v Leicestershire	at Leicester (Aylestone Rd)	1937
1 R Iddison	10 for 68	v Surrey	at Sheffield	1864
1 M Leyland	10 for 94	v Leicestershire	at Leicester (Aylestone Rd)	1933
1 J D Middlebrook	10 for 170	v Hampshire	at Southampton	2000
1 F W Milligan	12 for 110	v Sussex	at Sheffield	1897
1 H Myers	12 for 192	v Gloucestershire	at Dewsbury	1904
1 C M Old	11 for 46	v Gloucestershire	at Middlesbrough	1969
1 D Pickles	12 for 133	v Somerset	at Taunton	1957
1 A U Rashid	11 for 114	v Worcestershire	at Worcester	2011
1 W Ringrose	11 for 135	v Australians	at Bradford	1905
1 C E W Silverwood	12 for 148	v Kent	at Leeds	1997
1 W Slinn	12 for 53	v Nottinghamshire	at Nottingham	1864
1 J Waring	10 for 63	v Lancashire	at Leeds	1966
1 F Wilkinson	10 for 129	v Hampshire	at Bournemouth	1938
1 A C Williams	10 for 66	v Hampshire	at Dewsbury	1919

TEN WICKETS IN AN INNINGS

Bowler				Year
A Drake	10 for 35	v.	Somerset at Weston-super-Mare	1914
H Verity	10 for 36	v.	Warwickshire at Leeds	1931
*H Verity	10 for 10	v.	Nottinghamshire at Leeds	1932
T F Smailes	10 for 47	v.	Derbyshire at Sheffield	1939

*Includes the hat trick.

EIGHT WICKETS OR MORE IN AN INNINGS

(Ten wickets in an innings also listed above)

A complete list of seven wickets in an innings up to and including 2007 is to be found in the 2008 edition

R APPLEYARD (1)

8 for 76 v. MCC at Scarborough, 1951

R ASPINALL (1)

8 for 42 v. Northamptonshire at Northampton, 1947

W BATES (2)

8 for 45 v. Lancashire at Huddersfield, 1878
8 for 21 v. Surrey at The Oval, 1879

M W BOOTH (4)

8 for 52 v. Leicestershire at Sheffield, 1912
8 for 47 v. Middlesex at Leeds, 1912
8 for 86 v. Middlesex at Sheffield, 1913
8 for 64 v. Essex at Leyton, 1914

W E BOWES (9)

8 for 77 v. Leicestershire at Dewsbury, 1929
8 for 69 v. Middlesex at Bradford, 1930
9 for 121 v. Essex at Scarborough, 1932
8 for 62 v. Sussex at Hove, 1932
8 for 69 v. Gloucestershire at Gloucester, 1933
8 for 40 v. Worcestershire at Sheffield, 1935
8 for 18 v. Northamptonshire at Kettering, 1935
8 for 17 v. Northamptonshire at Kettering, 1935
8 for 56 v. Leicestershire at Scarborough, 1936

J T BROWN (Darfield) (1)

8 for 40 v. Gloucestershire at Huddersfield, 1899

P CARRICK (2)

8 for 33 v. Cambridge University at Cambridge, 1973
8 for 72 v. Derbyshire at Scarborough, 1975

R O CLAYTON (1)

8 for 66 v. Lancashire at Manchester, 1877

D B CLOSE (2)

8 for 41 v. Kent at Leeds, 1959
8 for 43 v. Essex at Leeds, 1960

H P COOPER (1)

8 for 62 v. Glamorgan at Cardiff, 1975

EIGHT WICKETS OR MORE IN AN INNINGS *(Continued)*

G A COPE (1)

8 for 73 v. Gloucestershire at Bristol, 1975

M J COWAN (1)

9 for 43 v. Warwickshire at Birmingham, 1960

A COXON (1)

8 for 31 v. Worcestershire at Leeds, 1946

A DRAKE (2)

8 for 59 v. Gloucestershire at Sheffield, 1913
10 for 35 v. Somerset at Weston-super-Mare, 1914

T EMMETT (8)

9 for 34 v. Nottinghamshire at Dewsbury, 1868
9 for 23 v. Cambridgeshire at Hunslet, 1869
8 for 31 v. Nottinghamshire at Sheffield, 1871
8 for 46 v. Gloucestershire at Clifton, 1877
8 for 16 v. MCC at Scarborough, 1877
8 for 22 v. Surrey at The Oval, 1881
8 for 52 v. MCC at Scarborough, 1882
8 for 32 v. Sussex at Huddersfield, 1884

S D FLETCHER (1)

8 for 58 v. Essex at Sheffield, 1988

T W FOSTER (1)

9 for 59 v. MCC at Lord's, 1894

G FREEMAN (2)

8 for 11 v. Lancashire at Holbeck, 1868
8 for 29 v. Surrey at Sheffield, 1869

L GREENWOOD (1)

8 for 35 v. Cambridgeshire at Dewsbury, 1867

S HAIGH (5)

8 for 78 v. Australians at Bradford, 1896
8 for 35 v. Hampshire at Harrogate, 1896
8 for 21 v. Hampshire at Southampton, 1898
8 for 33 v. Warwickshire at Scarborough, 1899
9 for 25 v. Gloucestershire at Leeds, 1912

P J HARTLEY (2)

8 for 111 v. Sussex at Hove, 1992
9 for 41 v. Derbyshire at Chesterfield, 1995

G H HIRST (8)

8 for 59 v. Warwickshire at Birmingham, 1896
8 for 48 v. Australians at Bradford, 1899
8 for 25 v. Leicestershire at Hull, 1907
9 for 45 v. Middlesex at Sheffield, 1907
9 for 23 v. Lancashire at Leeds, 1910
8 for 80 v. Somerset at Sheffield, 1910
9 for 41 v. Worcestershire at Worcester, 1911
9 for 69 v. MCC at Lord's, 1912

EIGHT WICKETS OR MORE IN AN INNINGS *(Continued)*

R ILLINGWORTH (5)

8 for 69 v. Surrey at The Oval, 1954
9 for 42 v. Worcestershire at Worcester, 1957
8 for 70 v. Glamorgan at Swansea, 1960
8 for 50 v. Lancashire at Manchester, 1961
8 for 20 v. Worcestershire at Leeds, 1965

R KILNER (2)

8 for 26 v. Glamorgan at Cardiff, 1923
8 for 40 v. Middlesex at Bradford, 1926

S P KIRBY (1)

8 for 80 v. Somerset at Taunton, 2003

E LEADBEATER (1)

8 for 83 v. Worcestershire at Worcester, 1950

M LEYLAND (1)

8 for 63 v. Hampshire at Huddersfield, 1938

G G MACAULAY (3)

8 for 43 v. Gloucestershire at Bristol, 1926
8 for 37 v. Derbyshire at Hull, 1927
8 for 21 v. Indians at Harrogate, 1932

H MYERS (1)

8 for 81 v. Gloucestershire at Dewsbury, 1904

A G NICHOLSON (2)

9 for 62 v. Sussex at Eastbourne, 1967
8 for 22 v. Kent at Canterbury, 1968

E PEATE (6)

8 for 24 v. Lancashire at Manchester, 1880
8 for 30 v. Surrey at Huddersfield, 1881
8 for 69 v. Sussex at Hove, 1881
8 for 32 v. Middlesex at Sheffield, 1882
8 for 5 v. Surrey at Holbeck, 1883
8 for 63 v. Kent at Gravesend, 1884

R PEEL (6)

8 for 12 v. Nottinghamshire at Sheffield, 1888
8 for 60 v. Surrey at Sheffield, 1890
8 for 54 v. Cambridge University at Cambridge, 1893
9 for 22 v. Somerset at Leeds, 1895
8 for 27 v. South of England XI at Scarborough, 1896
8 for 53 v. Kent at Halifax, 1897

J M PRESTON (2)

8 for 27 v. Sussex at Hove, 1888
9 for 28 v. MCC at Scarborough, 1888

EIGHT WICKETS OR MORE IN AN INNINGS *(Continued)*

W RHODES (18)

9 for 28 v. Essex at Leyton, 1899
8 for 38 v. Nottinghamshire at Nottingham, 1899
8 for 68 v. Cambridge University at Cambridge, 1900
8 for 43 v. Lancashire at Bradford, 1900
8 for 23 v. Hampshire at Hull, 1900
8 for 72 v. Gloucestershire at Bradford, 1900
8 for 28 v. Essex at Harrogate, 1900
8 for 53 v. Middlesex at Lord's, 1901
8 for 55 v. Kent at Canterbury, 1901
8 for 26 v. Kent at Catford, 1902
8 for 87 v. Worcestershire at Worcester, 1903
8 for 61 v. Lancashire at Bradford, 1903
8 for 90 v. Warwickshire at Birmingham, 1905
8 for 92 v. Northamptonshire at Northampton, 1911
8 for 44 v. Warwickshire at Bradford, 1919
8 for 39 v. Sussex at Leeds, 1920
8 for 48 v. Somerset at Huddersfield, 1926
9 for 39 v. Essex at Leyton, 1929

W RINGROSE (1)

9 for 76 v. Australians at Bradford, 1905

E ROBINSON (3)

9 for 36 v. Lancashire at Bradford, 1920
8 for 32 v. Northamptonshire at Huddersfield, 1927
8 for 13 v. Cambridge University at Cambridge, 1928

E P ROBINSON (2)

8 for 35 v. Lancashire at Leeds, 1939
8 for 76 v. Surrey at The Oval, 1946

M A ROBINSON (1)

9 for 37 v. Northamptonshire at Harrogate, 1993

A SIDEBOTTOM (1)

8 for 72 v. Leicestershire at Middlesbrough, 1986

T F SMAILES (2)

8 for 68 v. Glamorgan at Hull, 1938
10 for 47 v. Derbyshire at Sheffield, 1939

G B STEVENSON (2)

8 for 65 v. Lancashire at Leeds, 1978
8 for 57 v. Northamptonshire at Leeds, 1980

F S TRUEMAN (8)

8 for 70 v. Minor Counties at Lord's, 1949
8 for 68 v. Nottinghamshire at Sheffield, 1951
8 for 53 v. Nottinghamshire at Nottingham, 1951
8 for 28 v. Kent at Dover, 1954
8 for 84 v. Nottinghamshire at Worksop, 1962
8 for 45 v. Gloucestershire at Bradford, 1963
8 for 36 v. Sussex at Hove, 1965
8 for 37 v. Essex at Bradford, 1966

EIGHT WICKETS OR MORE IN AN INNINGS *(Continued)*

H VERITY (20)

9 for 60 v. Glamorgan at Swansea, 1930
10 for 36 v. Warwickshire at Leeds, 1931
8 for 33 v. Glamorgan at Swansea, 1931
8 for 107 v. Lancashire at Bradford, 1932
8 for 39 v. Northamptonshire at Northampton, 1932
10 for 10 v. Nottinghamshire at Leeds, 1932
8 for 47 v. Essex at Leyton, 1933
9 for 44 v. Essex at Leyton, 1933
9 for 59 v. Kent at Dover, 1933
8 for 28 v. Leicestershire at Leeds, 1935
8 for 56 v. Oxford University at Oxford, 1936
8 for 40 v. Worcestershire at Stourbridge, 1936
9 for 12 v. Kent at Sheffield, 1936
9 for 48 v. Essex at Westcliff-on-Sea, 1936
8 for 42 v. Nottinghamshire at Bradford, 1936
9 for 43 v. Warwickshire at Leeds, 1937
8 for 80 v. Sussex at Eastbourne, 1937
8 for 43 v. Middlesex at The Oval, 1937
9 for 62 v. MCC at Lord's, 1939
8 for 38 v. Leicestershire at Hull, 1939

A WADDINGTON (3)

8 for 34 v. Northamptonshire at Leeds, 1922
8 for 39 v. Kent at Leeds, 1922
8 for 35 v. Hampshire at Bradford, 1922

E WAINWRIGHT (3)

8 for 49 v. Middlesex at Sheffield, 1891
9 for 66 v. Middlesex at Sheffield, 1894
8 for 34 v. Essex at Bradford, 1896

J H WARDLE (4)

8 for 87 v. Derbyshire at Chesterfield, 1948
8 for 26 v. Middlesex at Lord's, 1950
9 for 48 v. Sussex at Hull, 1954
9 for 25 v. Lancashire at Manchester, 1954

C WHITE (1)

8 for 55 v. Gloucestershire at Gloucester, 1998

A C WILLIAMS (1)

9 for 29 v. Hampshire at Dewsbury, 1919

R WOOD (1)

8 for 45 v. Scotland at Glasgow, 1952

SIX WICKETS IN AN INNINGS AT LESS THAN FOUR RUNS EACH

A complete list of 5 wickets at less than 4 runs each up to and including 2007 is to be found in the 2008 edition

R APPLEYARD (2)

6 for 17 v. Essex at Bradford, 1951
6 for 12 v. Hampshire at Bournemouth, 1954

T ARMITAGE (1)

6 for 20 v. Surrey at Sheffield, 1876

R ASPINALL (1)

6 for 23 v. Northamptonshire at Northampton, 1947

W BATES (5)

6 for 11 v. Middlesex at Huddersfield, 1879
6 for 22 v. Kent at Bradford, 1881
6 for 17 v. Nottinghamshire at Nottingham, 1881
6 for 12 v. Kent at Sheffield, 1882
6 for 19 v. Lancashire at Dewsbury, 1886

A BOOTH (1)

6 for 21 v. Warwickshire at Birmingham, 1946

W E BOWES (4)

6 for 17 v. Middlesex at Lord's, 1934
6 for 16 v. Lancashire at Bradford, 1935
6 for 20 v. Gloucestershire at Sheffield, 1936
6 for 23 v. Warwickshire at Birmingham, 1947

J T BROWN (Darfield) (1)

6 for 19 v. Worcestershire at Worcester, 1899

R.O CLAYTON (1)

6 for 20 v. Nottinghamshire at Sheffield, 1876

A COXON (1)

6 for 17 v. Surrey at Sheffield, 1948

T EMMETT (6)

6 for 7 v. Surrey at Sheffield, 1867
6 for 13 v. Lancashire at Holbeck, 1868
6 for 21 v. Middlesex at Scarborough, 1874
6 for 12 v. Derbyshire at Sheffield, 1878
6 for 19 v. Derbyshire at Bradford, 1881
6 for 22 v. Australians at Bradford, 1882

H FISHER (1)

6 for 11 v. Leicestershire at Bradford, 1932

SIX WICKETS IN AN INNINGS AT LESS THAN FOUR RUNS EACH *(Continued)*

S HAIGH (10)

6 for 18 v. Derbyshire at Bradford, 1897
6 for 22 v. Hampshire at Southampton, 1898
6 for 21 v. Surrey at The Oval, 1900
6 for 23 v. Cambridge University at Cambridge, 1902
6 for 19 v. Somerset at Sheffield, 1902
6 for 22 v. Cambridge University at Sheffield, 1903
6 for 21 v. Hampshire at Leeds, 1904
6 for 21 v. Nottinghamshire at Sheffield, 1905
6 for 13 v. Surrey at Leeds, 1908
6 for 14 v. Australians at Bradford, 1912

A HILL (2)

6 for 9 v. United South of England XI at Bradford, 1874
6 for 18 v. MCC at Lord's, 1881

G H HIRST (7)

6 for 23 v. MCC at Lord's, 1893
6 for 20 v. Lancashire at Bradford, 1906
6 for 12 v. Northamptonshire at Northampton, 1908
6 for 7 v. Northamptonshire at Northampton, 1908
6 for 23 v. Surrey at Leeds, 1908
6 for 23 v. Lancashire at Manchester, 1909
6 for 20 v. Surrey at Sheffield, 1909

R ILLINGWORTH (2)

6 for 15 v. Scotland at Hull, 1956
6 for 13 v. Leicestershire at Leicester, 1963

F S JACKSON (1)

6 for 19 v. Hampshire at Southampton, 1897

R KILNER (5)

6 for 22 v. Essex at Harrogate, 1922
6 for 13 v. Hampshire at Bournemouth, 1922
6 for 14 v. Middlesex at Bradford, 1923
6 for 22 v. Surrey at Sheffield, 1923
6 for 15 v. Hampshire at Portsmouth, 1924

G G MACAULAY (10)

6 for 10 v. Warwickshire at Birmingham, 1921
6 for 3 v. Derbyshire at Hull, 1921
6 for 8 v. Northamptonshire at Northampton, 1922
6 for 12 v. Glamorgan at Cardiff, 1922
6 for 18 v. Northamptonshire at Bradford, 1923
6 for 19 v. Northamptonshire at Northampton, 1925
6 for 22 v. Leicestershire at Leeds, 1926
6 for 11 v. Leicestershire at Hull, 1930
6 for 22 v. Leicestershire at Bradford, 1933
6 for 22 v. Middlesex at Leeds, 1934

SIX WICKETS IN AN INNINGS AT LESS THAN FOUR RUNS EACH *(Continued)*

E PEATE (5)

6 for 14 v. Middlesex at Huddersfield, 1879
6 for 12 v. Derbyshire at Derby, 1882
6 for 13 v. Gloucestershire at Moreton-in-Marsh, 1884
6 for 16 v. Sussex at Huddersfield, 1886
6 for 16 v. Cambridge University at Sheffield, 1886

R PEEL (4)

6 for 21 v. Nottinghamshire at Sheffield, 1888
6 for 19 v. Australians at Huddersfield, 1888
6 for 22 v. Gloucestershire at Bristol, 1891
6 for 19 v. Leicestershire at Scarborough, 1896

A C RHODES (1)

6 for 19 v. Cambridge University at Cambridge, 1932

W RHODES (12)

6 for 21 v. Somerset at Bath, 1898
6 for 16 v. Gloucestershire at Bristol, 1899
6 for 4 v. Nottinghamshire at Nottingham, 1901
6 for 15 v. MCC at Lord's, 1902
6 for 16 v. Cambridge University at Cambridge, 1905
6 for 9 v. Essex at Huddersfield, 1905
6 for 22 v. Derbyshire at Glossop, 1907
6 for 17 v. Leicestershire at Leicester, 1908
6 for 13 v. Sussex at Hove, 1922
6 for 23 v. Nottinghamshire at Leeds, 1923
6 for 22 v. Cambridge University at Cambridge, 1924
6 for 20 v. Gloucestershire at Dewsbury, 1927

W RINGROSE (1)

6 for 20 v. Leicestershire at Dewsbury, 1903

R J SIDEBOTTOM (1)

6 for 16 v. Kent at Leeds, 2000

W SLINN (1)

6 for 19 v. Nottinghamshire at Nottingham, 1864

G B STEVENSON (1)

6 for 14 v. Warwickshire at Sheffield, 1979

F S TRUEMAN (4)

6 for 23 v. Oxford University at Oxford, 1955
6 for 23 v. Oxford University at Oxford, 1958
6 for 18 v. Warwickshire at Birmingham, 1963
6 for 20 v. Leicestershire at Sheffield, 1968

H VERITY (5)

6 for 11 v. Surrey at Bradford, 1931
6 for 21 v. Glamorgan at Swansea, 1931
6 for 12 v. Derbyshire at Hull, 1933
6 for 10 v. Essex at Ilford, 1937
6 for 22 v. Hampshire at Bournemouth, 1939

SIX WICKETS IN AN INNINGS AT LESS THAN FOUR RUNS EACH *(Continued)*

A WADDINGTON (2)

6 for 21 v. Northamptonshire at Harrogate, 1921
6 for 21 v. Northamptonshire at Northampton, 1923

S WADE (1)

6 for 18 v. Gloucestershire at Dewsbury, 1887

E WAINWRIGHT (4)

6 for 16 v. Sussex at Leeds, 1893
6 for 23 v. Sussex at Hove, 1893
6 for 18 v. Sussex at Dewsbury, 1894
6 for 22 v. MCC at Scarborough, 1894

J H WARDLE (8)

6 for 17 v. Sussex at Sheffield, 1948
6 for 10 v. Scotland at Edinburgh, 1950
6 for 12 v. Gloucestershire at Hull, 1950
6 for 20 v. Kent at Scarborough, 1950
6 for 23 v. Somerset at Sheffield, 1951
6 for 21 v. Glamorgan at Leeds, 1951
6 for 18 v. Gloucestershire at Bristol, 1951
6 for 6 v. Gloucestershire at Bristol, 1955

D WILSON (3)

6 for 22 v. Sussex at Bradford, 1963
6 for 15 v. Gloucestershire at Middlesbrough, 1966
6 for 22 v. Middlesex at Sheffield, 1966

FOUR WICKETS IN FOUR BALLS

A Drake v. Derbyshire at Chesterfield, 1914

FOUR WICKETS IN FIVE BALLS

F S Jackson v. Australians at Leeds, 1902
A Waddington v. Northamptonshire at Northampton, 1920
G G Macaulay v. Lancashire at Manchester, 1933
P J Hartley v. Derbyshire at Chesterfield, 1995
D Gough v. Kent at Leeds, 1995
J D Middlebrook v. Hampshire at Southampton, 2000

BEST BOWLING ANALYSES IN A MATCH
FOR AND AGAINST YORKSHIRE

Best For Yorkshire:
17 for 91 (8 for 47 and 9 for 44) H Verity v Essex at Leyton, 1933

Against Yorkshire:
17 for 91 (9 for 62 and 8 for 29) H Dean for Lancashire at Liverpool, 1913
(non-championship)

County Championship
16 for 114 (8 for 48 and 8 for 66) G Burton for Middlesex at Sheffield, 1888

Yorkshire versus:

Derbyshire	*For Yorkshire:*	14 for 58 (4 for 11 and 10 for 47) T F Smailes at Sheffield, 1939
	Against:	13 for 65 (7 for 33 and 6 for 32) W Mycroft at Sheffield, 1879
Most 10 wickets in a match	*For Yorkshire:*	P Carrick and E Peate 4 each
	Against:	W Mycroft 3
Durham	*For Yorkshire:*	10 for 101 (6 for 57 and 4 for 44) M A Robinson at Durham, 1992
	Against:	10 for 144 (7 for 81 and 3 for 63) O D Gibson at Chester-le-Street, 2007
Most 10 wickets in a match	*For Yorkshire:*	M A Robinson 1
	Against:	G R Breese and O D Gibson 1 each
Essex	*For Yorkshire:*	17 for 91 (8 for 47 and 9 for 44) H Verity at Leyton, 1933
	Against:	14 for 127 (7 for 37 and 7 for 90) W Mead at Leyton, 1899
Most 10 wickets in a match	*For Yorkshire:*	W Rhodes 7
	Against:	J K Lever, W Mead 2 each
Glamorgan	*For Yorkshire:*	15 for 123 (8 for 70 and 7 for 53) R Illingworth at Swansea. 1960
	Against:	12 for 76 (7 for 30 and 5 for 46) D J Shepherd at Cardiff, 1957
Most 10 wickets in a match	*For Yorkshire:*	H Verity 5
	Against:	D J Shepherd, J S Pressdee 1 each
Gloucestershire	*For Yorkshire:*	14 for 64 (7 for 58 and 7 for 6) R Illingworth at Harrogate, 1967
	Against:	15 for 79 (8 for 33 and 7 for 46) W G Grace at Sheffield, 1872
Most 10 wickets in a match	*For Yorkshire:*	W Rhodes 8
	Against:	E G Dennett 5
Hampshire	*For Yorkshire:*	14 for 43 (8 for 21 and 6 for 22) S Haigh at Southampton, 1898
	Against:	12 for 145 (7 for 78 and 5 for 67) D Shackleton at Bradford, 1962
Most 10 wickets in a match	*For Yorkshire:*	W Rhodes, E Robinson, H Verity 3 each
	Against:	A S Kennedy 3

BEST BOWLING ANALYSES IN A MATCH
FOR AND AGAINST YORKSHIRE *(continued)*

Yorkshire versus

Kent	*For Yorkshire:*	15 for 38 (6 for 26 and 9 for 12) H Verity at Sheffield, 1936
	Against:	13 for 48 (5 for 13 and 8 for 35) A Hearne at Sheffield, 1885
Most 10 wickets in a match	*For Yorkshire:*	E Peate and J H Wardle 4 each
	Against:	C Blythe 6
Lancashire	*For Yorkshire:*	14 for 80 (6 for 56 and 8 for 24) E Peate at Manchester, 1880
	Against:	17 for 91 (9 for 62 and 8 for 29) H Dean at Liverpool, 1913 (non-championship) 14 for 90 (6 for 47 and 8 for 43) R Tattersall at Leeds, 1956 (championship)
Most 10 wickets in a match	*For Yorkshire:*	T Emmett 5
	Against:	J Briggs 8
Leicestershire	*For Yorkshire:*	15 for 63 (8 for 25 and 7 for 38) G H Hirst at Hull, 1907
	Against:	12 for 139 (8 for 85 and 4 for 54) A D Pougher at Leicester, 1895
Most 10 wickets in a match	*For Yorkshire:*	G H Hirst 5
	Against:	A D Pougher 2
Middlesex	*For Yorkshire:*	13 for 94 (6 for 61 and 7 for 33) S Haigh at Leeds, 1900
	Against:	16 for 114 (8 for 48 and 8 for 66) G Burton at Sheffield, 1888
Most 10 wickets in a match	*For Yorkshire:*	W Rhodes 5
	Against:	J T Hearne 7
Northamptonshire	*For Yorkshire:*	16 for 35 (8 for 18 and 8 for 17) W E Bowes at Kettering, 1935
	Against:	15 for 31 (7 for 22 and 8 for 9) G E Tribe at Northampton, 1958
Most 10 wickets in a match	*For Yorkshire:*	W E Bowes, G G Macaulay, H Verity, A Waddington 3 each
	Against:	G E Tribe 3
Nottinghamshire	*For Yorkshire:*	14 for 33 (8 for 12 and 6 for 21) R Peel at Sheffield, 1888
	Against:	14 for 94 (8 for 38 and 6 for 56) F Morley at Nottingham, 1878
Most 10 wickets in a match	*For Yorkshire:*	G H Hirst 5
	Against:	F Morley, J C Shaw 4 each
Somerset	*For Yorkshire:*	15 for 50 (9 for 22 and 6 for 28) R Peel at Leeds, 1895
	Against:	15 for 71 (6 for 30 and 9 for 41) L C Braund at Sheffield, 1902
Most 10 wickets in a match	*For Yorkshire:*	G H Hirst 7
	Against:	L C Braund 3

BEST BOWLING ANALYSES IN A MATCH
FOR AND AGAINST YORKSHIRE *(continued)*

Yorkshire versus

Surrey	*For Yorkshire:*	14 for 77 (6 for 47 and 8 for 30) E Peate at Huddersfield, 1881
	Against:	15 for 154 (7 for 55 and 8 for 99) T Richardson at Leeds, 1897
Most 10 wickets in a match	*For Yorkshire:* *Against:*	W Rhodes 7 G A Lohmann, T Richardson 6 each
Sussex	*For Yorkshire:*	16 for 112 (9 for 48 and 7 for 64) J H Wardle at Hull, 1954
	Against:	12 for 110 (6 for 71 and 6 for 39) G R Cox at Sheffield, 1907
Most 10 wickets in a match	*For Yorkshire:* *Against:*	R Peel, E Wainwright 3 each Twelve players 1 each
Warwickshire	*For Yorkshire:*	14 for 92 (9 for 43 and 5 for 49) H Verity at Leeds, 1937
	Against:	12 for 55 (5 for 21 and 7 for 34) T W Cartwright at Bradford, 1969
Most 10 wickets in a match	*For Yorkshire:* *Against:*	S Haigh 4 E F Field 4
Worcestershire	*For Yorkshire:*	14 for 211 (8 for 87 and 6 for 124) W Rhodes at Worcester, 1903
	Against:	13 for 76 (4 for 38 and 9 for 38) J A Cuffe at Bradford, 1907
Most 10 wickets in a match	*For Yorkshire:* *Against:*	S Haigh, G G Macaulay 4 each N Gifford 2
Australians	*For Yorkshire:*	13 for 149 (8 for 48 and 5 for 101) G H Hirst at Bradford, 1899
	Against:	13 for 170 (6 for 91 and 7 for 79) J M Gregory at Sheffield, 1919
Most 10 wickets in a match	*For Yorkshire:* *Against:*	S Haigh 2 C V Grimmett, F R Spofforth, C T B Turner, H Trumble 2 each

BEST BOWLING ANALYSES IN AN INNINGS
FOR AND AGAINST YORKSHIRE

Best For Yorkshire:
10 for 10 H Verity v Nottinghamshire at Leeds, 1932

Against Yorkshire:
10 for 37 C V Grimmett for Australians at Sheffield, 1930
(non-championship)

County Championship
10 for 51 H Howell for Warwickshire at Birmingham, 1923

Yorkshire versus:

Derbyshire	*For Yorkshire:*	10 for 47	T F Smailes at Sheffield, 1939
	Against:	9 for 27	J J Hulme at Sheffield, 1894
Most 5 wickets in an innings	*For Yorkshire:* *Against:*	S Haigh, E Peat, W Rhodes 11 each W Mycroft 10	

BEST BOWLING ANALYSES IN AN INNINGS
FOR AND AGAINST YORKSHIRE *(continued)*

Yorkshire versus

Durham	*For Yorkshire:*	6 for 37	R D Stemp at Durham, 1994
		6 for 37	J N Gillespie at Chester-le-Street, 2006
	Against:	7 for 58	J Wood at Leeds, 1999
Most 5 wickets	*For Yorkshire:*	D Gough and M J Hoggard 2 each	
in an innings	*Against:*	G R Breese, S J E Brown, S J Harmison and G Onions 2 each	
Essex	*For Yorkshire:*	9 for 28	W Rhodes at Leyton, 1899
	Against:	8 for 44	F G Bull at Bradford, 1896
Most 5 wickets	*For Yorkshire:*	W Rhodes 18	
in an innings	*Against:*	W Mead 14	
Glamorgan	*For Yorkshire:*	9 for 60	H Verity at Swansea, 1930
	Against:	9 for 43	J S Pressdee at Swansea, 1965
Most 5 wickets	*For Yorkshire:*	H Verity 12	
in an innings	*Against:*	D J Shepherd 6	
Gloucestershire	*For Yorkshire:*	9 for 25	S Haigh at Leeds, 1912
	Against:	9 for 36	C W L Parker at Bristol, 1922
Most 5 wickets	*For Yorkshire:*	W Rhodes 22	
in an innings	*Against:*	T W J Goddard 17	
Hampshire	*For Yorkshire:*	9 for 29	A C Williams at Dewsbury, 1919
	Against:	8 for 49	O W Herman at Bournemouth, 1930
Most 5 wickets	*For Yorkshire:*	G H Hirst 10	
in an innings	*Against:*	A S Kennedy 10	
Kent	*For Yorkshire:*	9 for 12	H Verity at Sheffield, 1936
	Against:	8 for 35	A Hearne at Sheffield, 1885
Most 5 wickets	*For Yorkshire:*	W Rhodes 12	
in an innings	*Against:*	A P Freeman 14	
Lancashire	*For Yorkshire:*	9 for 23	G H Hirst at Leeds, 1910
	Against:	9 for 41	A Mold at Huddersfield, 1890
Most 5 wickets	*For Yorkshire:*	T Emmett 16	
in an innings	*Against:*	J Briggs 19	
Leicestershire	*For Yorkshire:*	8 for 25	G H Hirst at Hull, 1907
	Against:	9 for 63	C T Spencer at Huddersfield, 1954
Most 5 wickets	*For Yorkshire:*	G H Hirst 15	
in an innings	*Against:*	H A Smith 7	
Middlesex	*For Yorkshire:*	9 for 45	G H Hirst at Sheffield 1907
	Against:	9 for 57	F A Tarrant at Leeds, 1906
Most 5 wickets	*For Yorkshire:*	W Rhodes 18	
in an innings	*Against:*	J T Hearne 21	
Northamptonshire	*For Yorkshire:*	9 for 37	M A Robinson at Harrogate, 1993
	Against:	9 for 30	A E Thomas at Bradford, 1920
Most 5 wickets	*For Yorkshire:*	G G Macaulay 14	
in an innings	*Against:*	G E Tribe, W Wells 7 each	
Nottinghamshire	*For Yorkshire:*	10 for 10	H Verity at Leeds, 1932
	Against:	8 for 32	J C Shaw at Nottingham, 1865
Most 5 wickets	*For Yorkshire:*	W Rhodes 17	
in an innings	*Against:*	F Morley 17	

BEST BOWLING ANALYSES IN AN INNINGS
FOR AND AGAINST YORKSHIRE (continued)

Yorkshire versus

Somerset	*For Yorkshire:*	10 for 35	A Drake at Weston-super-Mare, 1914
	Against:	9 for 41	L C Braund at Sheffield, 1902
Most 5 wickets	*For Yorkshire:*	G H Hirst 16	
in an innings	*Against:*	E J Tyler 8	
Surrey	*For Yorkshire:*	8 for 5	E Peate at Holbeck, 1883
	Against:	9 for 47	T Richardson at Sheffield, 1893
Most 5 wickets	*For Yorkshire:*	W Rhodes 17	
in an innings	*Against:*	W Southerton 19	
Sussex	*For Yorkshire:*	9 for 48	J H Wardle at Hull, 1954
	Against:	9 for 34	James Langridge at Sheffield, 1934
Most 5 wickets	*For Yorkshire:*	W Rhodes 14	
in an innings	*Against:*	G R Cox, J A Snow 6 each	
Warwickshire	*For Yorkshire:*	10 for 36	H Verity at Leeds, 1930
	Against:	10 for 51	H Howell at Birmingham, 1923
Most 5 wickets	*For Yorkshire:*	W Rhodes 18	
in an innings	*Against:*	E F Field, W E Hollies 7 each	
Worcestershire	*For Yorkshire:*	9 for 41	G H Hirst at Worcester, 1911
	Against:	9 for 38	J A Cuffe at Bradford, 1907
Most 5 wickets	*For Yorkshire:*	S Haigh, W Rhodes 11 each	
in an innings	*Against:*	R T D Perks 7	
Australians	*For Yorkshire:*	9 for 76	W Ringrose at Bradford, 1905
	Against:	10 for 37	C V Grimmett at Sheffield, 1930
Most 5 wickets	*For Yorkshire:*	R Peel 7	
in an innings	*Against:*	F R Spofforth 7	

HAT-TRICKS

G Freeman v. Lancashire at Holbeck, 1868
G Freeman v. Middlesex at Sheffield, 1868
A Hill v. United South of England XI at Bradford, 1874
A Hill v. Surrey at The Oval, 1880
E Peate v. Kent at Sheffield, 1882
G Ulyett v. Lancashire at Sheffield, 1883
E Peate v. Gloucestershire at Moreton-in-Marsh, 1884
W Fletcher v. MCC at Lord's, 1892
E Wainwright v. Sussex at Dewsbury, 1894
G H Hirst v. Leicestershire at Leicester, 1895
J T Brown v. Derbyshire at Derby, 1896
R Peel v. Kent at Halifax, 1897
S Haigh v. Derbyshire at Bradford, 1897
W Rhodes v. Kent at Canterbury, 1901
S Haigh v. Somerset at Sheffield, 1902
H A Sedgwick v. Worcestershire at Hull, 1906
G Deyes v. Gentlemen of Ireland at Bray, 1907
G H Hirst v. Leicestershire at Hull, 1907
J T Newstead v. Worcestershire at Bradford, 1907
S Haigh v. Lancashire at Manchester, 1909
M W Booth v. Worcestershire at Bradford, 1911
A Drake v. Essex at Huddersfield, 1912

HAT-TRICKS *(Continued)*

M W Booth v. Essex at Leyton, 1912
A Drake v. Derbyshire at Chesterfield, 1914 (4 in 4)
W Rhodes v. Derbyshire at Derby, 1920
A Waddington v. Northamptonshire at Northampton, 1920 (4 in 5)
G G Macaulay v. Warwickshire at Birmingham, 1923
E Robinson v. Sussex at Hull, 1928
G G Macaulay v. Leicestershire at Hull, 1930
E Robinson v. Kent at Gravesend, 1930
H Verity v. Nottinghamshire at Leeds, 1932
H Fisher v. Somerset at Sheffield, 1932 (all lbw)
G G Macaulay v. Glamorgan at Cardiff, 1933
G G Macaulay v. Lancashire at Manchester, 1933 (4 in 5)
M.Leyland v. Surrey at Sheffield, 1935
E Robinson v. Kent at Leeds, 1939
A Coxon v. Worcestershire at Leeds, 1946
F S Trueman v. Nottinghamshire at Nottingham, 1951
F S Trueman v. Nottinghamshire at Scarborough, 1955
R Appleyard v. Gloucestershire at Sheffield, 1956
F S.Trueman v. MCC at Lord's, 1958
D Wilson v. Nottinghamshire at Middlesbrough, 1959
F S Trueman v. Nottinghamshire at Bradford, 1963
D Wilson v. Nottinghamshire at Worksop, 1966
D Wilson v. Kent at Harrogate, 1966
G A Cope v. Essex at Colchester, 1970
A L Robinson v. Nottinghamshire at Worksop, 1974
P W Jarvis v. Derbyshire at Chesterfield, 1985
P J Hartley v. Derbyshire at Chesterfield, 1995 (4 in 5)
D Gough v. Kent at Leeds, 1995 (4 in 5)
C White v. Gloucestershire at Gloucester, 1998
M J Hoggard v. Sussex at Hove, 2009

52 Hat-Tricks: G G Macaulay and F S Trueman took four each, S Haigh and D Wilson three each. There have been seven hat-tricks versus Kent and Nottinghamshire, and six versus Derbyshire.

200 WICKETS IN A SEASON

Bowler	Season	Overs	Maidens	Runs	Wickets	Average
W Rhodes	1900	1366.4	411	3054	240	12.72
W Rhodes	1901	1455.3	474	3497	233	15.00
G H Hirst	1906	1111.1	262	3089	201	15.36
G G Macaulay	1925	1241.2	291	2986	200	14.93
R Appleyard†	1951	1323.2	394	2829	200	14.14

† First full season in First-Class cricket.

100 WICKETS IN A SEASON

Bowler		Wickets taken	Wickets taken	Wickets taken
R Appleyard	(3)	200 in 1951	141 in 1954	110 in 1956
A Booth	(1)	111 in 1946	—	—
M W Booth	(3)	104 in 1912	167 in 1913	155 in 1914
W E Bowes	(8)	117 in 1931	168 in 1932	130 in 1933
		109 in 1934	154 in 1935	113 in 1936
		106 in 1938	107 in 1939	—

100 WICKETS IN A SEASON *(Continued)*

Bowler		Wickets taken	Wickets taken	Wickets taken
D B Close	(2)	105 in 1949	114 in 1952	—
A Coxon	(2)	101 in 1949	129 in 1950	—
A Drake	(2)	115 in 1913	158 in 1914	—
T Emmett	(1)	112 in 1886	—	—
S Haigh	(10)	100 in 1898	160 in 1900	154 in 1902
		102 in 1903	118 in 1904	118 in 1905
		161 in 1906	120 in 1909	100 in 1911
		125 in 1912	—	—
G H Hirst	(12)	150 in 1895	171 in 1901	121 in 1903
		114 in 1904	100 in 1905	201 in 1906
		169 in 1907	164 in 1908	138 in 1910
		130 in 1911	113 in 1912	100 in 1913
R Illingworth	(5)	103 in 1956	120 in 1961	116 in 1962
		122 in 1964	105 in 1968	—
R Kilner	(4)	107 in 1922	143 in 1923	134 in 1924
		123 in 1925	—	—
G G Macaulay	(10)	101 in 1921	130 in 1922	163 in 1923
		184 in 1924	200 in 1925	133 in 1926
		130 in 1927	117 in 1928	102 in 1929
		141 in 1933	—	—
J T Newstead	(1)	131 in 1908	—	—
A G Nicholson	(2)	113 in 1966	101 in 1967	—
E Peate	(3)	131 in 1880	133 in 1881	165 in 1882
R Peel	(6)	118 in 1888	132 in 1890	106 in 1892
		134 in 1894	155 in 1895	108 in 1896
W Rhodes	(22)	141 in 1898	153 in 1899	240 in 1900
		233 in 1901	174 in 1902	169 in 1903
		118 in 1904	158 in 1905	113 in 1906
		164 in 1907	100 in 1908	115 in 1909
		105 in 1911	117 in 1914	155 in 1919
		156 in 1920	128 in 1921	100 in 1922
		127 in 1923	102 in 1926	111 in 1928
		100 in 1929	—	—
E Robinson	(1)	111 in 1928	—	—
E P Robinson	(4)	104 in 1938	120 in 1939	149 in 1946
		108 in 1947	—	—
T F Smailes	(4)	105 in 1934	125 in 1936	120 in 1937
		104 in 1938	—	—
F S Trueman	(8)	129 in 1954	140 in 1955	104 in 1959
		150 in 1960	124 in 1961	122 in 1962
		121 in 1965	107 in 1966	—
H Verity	(9)	169 in 1931	146 in 1932	168 in 1933
		100 in 1934	199 in 1935	185 in 1936
		185 in 1937	137 in 1938	189 in 1939
A Waddington	(5)	100 in 1919	140 in 1920	105 in 1921
		132 in 1922	105 in 1925	—
E Wainwright	(3)	114 in 1893	157 in 1894	102 in 1896
J H Wardle	(10)	148 in 1948	100 in 1949	172 in 1950
		122 in 1951	169 in 1952	126 in 1953
		122 in 1954	159 in 1955	146 in 1956
		106 in 1957	—	—
D Wilson	(3)	100 in 1966	107 in 1968	101 in 1969

BOWLERS WHO HAVE TAKEN OVER 500 WICKETS

Player	M	Runs	Wkts	Av'ge	Best
W Rhodes	883	57634	3598	16.01	9 for 28
G H Hirst	717	44716	2481	18.02	9 for 23
S Haigh	513	29289	1876	15.61	9 for 25
G G Macaulay	445	30554	1774	17.22	8 for 21
F S Trueman	459	29890	1745	17.12	8 for 28
H Verity	278	21353	1558	13.70	10 for 10
J H Wardle	330	27917	1539	18.13	9 for 25
R Illingworth	496	26806	1431	18.73	9 for 42
W E Bowes	301	21227	1351	15.71	9 for 121
R Peel	318	20638	1311	15.74	9 for 22
T Emmett	299	15465	1216	12.71	9 for 23
D Wilson	392	22626	1104	20.49	7 for 19
P Carrick	425	30530	1018	29.99	8 for 33
E Wainwright	352	17744	998	17.77	9 for 66
D B Close	536	23489	967	24.29	8 for 41
Emmott Robinson	413	19645	893	21.99	9 for 36
A G Nicholson	282	17296	876	19.74	9 for 62
R Kilner	365	14855	857	17.33	8 for 26
A Waddington	255	16203	835	19.40	8 for 34
T F Smailes	262	16593	802	20.68	10 for 47
E Peate	154	9986	794	12.57	8 for 5
Ellis P Robinson	208	15141	735	20.60	8 for 35
C M Old	222	13409	647	20.72	7 for 20
R Appleyard	133	9903	642	15.42	8 for 76
W Bates	202	10692	637	16.78	8 for 21
G A Cope	230	15627	630	24.80	8 for 73
P J Hartley	195	17438	579	30.11	9 for 41
A Sidebottom	216	13852	558	24.82	8 for 72
M W Booth	144	11017	557	19.17	8 for 47
A Hill	140	7002	542	12.91	7 for 14
Hon F S Jackson	207	9690	506	19.15	7 for 42

BOWLERS UNCHANGED IN A MATCH
(IN WHICH THE OPPONENTS WERE DISMISSED TWICE)

**There have been 31 instances. The first and most recent are listed below.
A complete list is to be found in the 2008 edition.**

First: L Greenwood (11 for 71) and G Freeman (8 for 73) v. Surrey
at The Oval, 1867
Yorkshire won by an innings and 111 runs

Most Recent: E Robinson (8 for 65) and G G Macaulay (12 for 50) v. Worcestershire
at Leeds, 1927
Yorkshire won by an innings and 106 runs

FIELDERS (IN MATCHES FOR YORKSHIRE)

MOST CATCHES IN AN INNINGS

6	E P Robinson	v. Leicestershire	at Bradford, 1938
6	T Kohler- Cadmore		
		v. Kent	at Canterbury, 2019
5	J Tunnicliffe	v. Leicestershire	at Leeds, 1897
5	J Tunnicliffe	v. Leicestershire	at Leicester, 1900
5	J Tunnicliffe	v. Leicestershire	at Scarborough, 1901
5	A B Sellers	v. Essex	at Leyton, 1933
5	D Wilson	v. Surrey	at The Oval, 1969
5	R G Lumb	v. Gloucestershire	at Middlesbrough, 1972

MOST CATCHES IN A MATCH

7	J Tunnicliffe	v. Leicestershire	at Leeds, 1897
7	J Tunnicliffe	v. Leicestershire	at Leicester, 1900
7	A B Sellers	v Essex	at Leyton, 1933
7	E P Robinson	v. Leicestershire	at Bradford, 1938
7	A Lyth	v. Middlesex	at Scarborough, 2014
7	T Kohler-Cadmore		
		v. Hampshire	at West End, Southampton, 2019

MOST CATCHES IN A SEASON

70	J Tunnicliffe	in 1901
70	P J Sharpe	in 1962
61	J Tunnicliffe	in 1895
60	J Tunnicliffe	in 1904
59	J Tunnicliffe	in 1896
57	J V Wilson	in 1955
54	J V Wilson	in 1961
53	J V Wilson	in 1957
51	J V Wilson	in 1951

MOST CATCHES IN A CAREER

665	J Tunnicliffe	(1.40 per match)
586	W Rhodes	(0.66 per match)
564	D B Close	(1.05 per match)
525	P J Sharpe	(1.27 per match)
520	J V Wilson	(1.09 per match)
518	G H Hirst	(0.72 per match)

WICKET-KEEPERS IN MATCHES FOR YORKSHIRE

MOST DISMISSALS IN AN INNINGS

7	(7ct)	D L Bairstow	v. Derbyshire	at Scarborough	1982
6	(6ct)	J Hunter	v. Gloucestershire	at Gloucester	1887
6	(5ct,1st)	D Hunter	v. Surrey	at Sheffield	1891
6	(6ct)	D Hunter	v. Middlesex	at Leeds	1909
6	(2ct,4st)	W R Allen	v. Sussex	at Hove	1921
6	(5ct,1st)	J G Binks	v. Lancashire	at Leeds	1962
6	(6ct)	D L Bairstow	v. Lancashire	at Manchester	1971
6	(6ct)	D L Bairstow	v. Warwickshire	at Bradford	1978
6	(5ct,1st)	D L Bairstow	v. Lancashire	at Leeds	1980
6	(6ct)	D L Bairstow	v. Derbyshire	at Chesterfield	1984
6	(6ct)	R J Blakey	v. Sussex	at Eastbourne	1990
6	(5ct,1st)	R J Blakey	v. Gloucestershire	at Cheltenham	1992
6	(5ct,1st)	R J Blakey	v. Glamorgan	at Cardiff	1994
6	(6ct)	R J Blakey	v. Glamorgan	at Leeds	2003
6	(6ct)	G L Brophy	v. Durham	at Chester-le-Street	2009
6	(6ct)	J M Bairstow	v. Middlesex	at Leeds	2013
6	(6ct)	J M Bairstow	v. Sussex	at Arundel	2014
6	(6ct)	H G Duke	v. Nottinghamshire	at Nottingham	2021

MOST DISMISSALS IN A MATCH

11	(11ct)	D L Bairstow (Equalled World Record)	v. Derbyshire	at Scarborough	1982
9	(9ct)	J.Hunter	v. Gloucestershire	at Gloucester	1887
9	(8ct,1st)	A Dolphin	v. Derbyshire	at Bradford	1919
9	(9ct)	D L Bairstow	v. Lancashire	at Manchester	1971
9	(9ct)	R J Blakey	v. Sussex	at Eastbourne	1990
8	(2ct,6st)	G Pinder	v. Lancashire	at Sheffield	1872
8	(2ct,6st)	D Hunter	v. Surrey	at Bradford	1898
8	(7ct,1st)	A Bairstow	v. Cambridge University	at Cambridge	1899
8	(8ct)	A Wood	v. Northamptonshire	at Huddersfield	1932
8	(8ct)	D L Bairstow	v. Lancashire	at Leeds	1978
8	(7ct,1st)	D L Bairstow	v. Derbyshire	at Chesterfield	1984
8	(6ct,2st)	D L Bairstow	v. Derbyshire	at Chesterfield	1985
8	(8ct)	R J Blakey	v. Hampshire	at Southampton	1989
8	(8ct)	R J Blakey	v. Northamptonshire	at Harrogate	1993
8	(8ct)	A J Hodd	v. Glamorgan	at Leeds	2012
8	(8ct)	J M Bairstow	v. Middlesex	at Leeds	2013

MOST DISMISSALS IN A SEASON

107	(96ct,11st)	J G Binks, 1960
94	(81ct,13st)	JG Binks, 1961
89	(75ct,14st)	A Wood, 1934
88	(80ct,8st)	J G Binks, 1963
86	(70ct,16st)	J G Binks, 1962
82	(52ct,30st)	A Dolphin, 1919
80	(57ct,23st)	A. Wood, 1935

MOST DISMISSALS IN A CAREER

1186	(863ct,323st)	D Hunter (2.29 per match)
1044	(872ct,172st)	J G Binks (2.12 per match)
1038	(907ct,131st)	D L Bairstow (2.41 per match)
855	(612ct,243st)	A Wood (2.09 per match)
829	(569ct,260st)	A Dolphin (1.94 per match)
824	(768ct, 56st)	R J Blakey (2.43 per match)

YORKSHIRE PLAYERS WHO HAVE COMPLETED THE "DOUBLE"

(all First-Class matches)

Player	Year	Runs	Average	Wickets	Average
M W Booth (1)	1913	1,228	27.28	181	18.46
D B Close (2)	†1949	1,098	27.45	113	27.87
	1952	1,192	33.11	114	24.08
A Drake (1)	1913	1,056	23.46	116	16.93
S Haigh (1)	1904	1,055	26.37	121	19.85
G H Hirst (14)	1896	1,122	28.20	104	21.64
	1897	1,535	35.69	101	23.22
	1901	1,950	42.39	183	16.38
	1903	1,844	47.28	128	14.94
	1904	2,501	54.36	132	21.09
	1905	2,266	53.95	110	19.94
	††1906	2,385	45.86	208	16.50
	1907	1,344	28.38	188	15.20
	1908	1,598	38.97	114	14.05
	1909	1,256	27.30	115	20.05
	1910	1,840	32.85	164	14.79
	1911	1,789	33.12	137	20.40
	1912	1,133	25.75	118	17.37
	1913	1,540	35.81	101	20.13
R Illingworth (6)	1957	1,213	28.20	106	18.40
	1959	1,726	46.64	110	21.46
	1960	1,006	25.79	109	17.55
	1961	1,153	24.53	128	17.90
	1962	1,612	34.29	117	19.45
	1964	1,301	37.17	122	17.45
F S Jackson (1)	1898	1,566	41.21	104	15.67
R Kilner (4)	1922	1,198	27.22	122	14.73
	1923	1,404	32.24	158	12.91
	1925	1,068	30.51	131	17.92
	1926	1,187	37.09	107	22.52
R Peel (1)	1896	1,206	30.15	128	17.50
W Rhodes (16)	1903	1,137	27.07	193	14.57
	1904	1,537	35.74	131	21.59
	1905	1,581	35.93	182	16.95
	1906	1,721	29.16	128	23.57
	1907	1,055	22.93	177	15.57
	1908	1,673	31.56	115	16.13
	1909	2,094	40.26	141	15.89
	1911	2,261	38.32	117	24.07
	1914	1,377	29.29	118	18.27
	1919	1,237	34.36	164	14.42
	1920	1,123	28.07	161	13.18
	1921	1,474	39.83	141	13.27
	1922	1,511	39.76	119	12.19
	1923	1,321	33.02	134	11.54
	1924	1,126	26.18	109	14.46
	1926	1,132	34.30	115	14.86
T F Smailes (1)	1938	1,002	25.05	113	20.84
E Wainwright (1)	1897	1,612	35.82	101	23.06

† First season in First-Class cricket.
†† The only instance in First-Class cricket of 2,000 runs and 200 wickets in a season.

H Sutcliffe (194) and M Leyland (45) hit 102 off six consecutive overs for Yorkshire v. Essex at Scarborough in 1932.

From 1898 to 1930 inclusive, Wilfred Rhodes took no less than 4,187 wickets, and scored 39,969 runs in First-Class cricket at home and abroad, a remarkable record. He also took 100 wickets and scored 1,000 in a season 16 times, and G H Hirst 14 times.

Of players with a qualification of not less than 50 wickets, Wilfred Rhodes was first in bowling in First-Class cricket in 1900, 1901, 1919, 1920, 1922, 1923 and 1926; Schofield Haigh in 1902, 1905, 1908 and 1909; Mr E R Wilson in 1921; G G Macaulay in 1924; H Verity in 1930, 1933, 1935, 1937 and 1939; W E Bowes in 1938; A Booth in 1946; R Appleyard in 1951 and 1955, and F S Trueman in 1952 and 1963.

The highest aggregate of runs made in one season in First-Class cricket by a Yorkshire player is 3,429 by L Hutton in 1949. This total has been exceeded three times, viz: D C S Compton 3,816 and W J Edrich 3,539 in 1947, and 3,518 by T Hayward in 1906. H Sutcliffe scored 3,336 in 1932.

Three players have taken all 10 Yorkshire wickets in an innings. G Wootton, playing for All England XI at Sheffield in 1865, took all 10 wickets for 54 runs. H Howell performed the feat for Warwickshire at Edgbaston in 1923 at a cost of 51 runs; and C V Grimmett, Australia, took all 10 wickets for 37 runs at Sheffield in 1930.

The match against Sussex at Dewsbury on June 7th and 8th, 1894, was brought to a summary conclusion by a remarkable bowling performance on the part of Edward Wainwright. In the second innings of Sussex, he took the last five wickets in seven balls, including the "hat trick". In the whole match he obtained 13 wickets for only 38 runs.

M D Moxon has the unique distinction of scoring a century in each of his first two First-Class matches in Yorkshire — 116 (2nd inns.) v. Essex at Leeds and 111 (1st inns.) v. Derbyshire at Sheffield, June 1981).

In the Yorkshire v. Norfolk match — played on the Hyde Park Ground, Sheffield, on July 14th to 18th, 1834 — 851 runs were scored in the four innings, of which no fewer than 128 were extras: 75 byes and 53 wides. At that time wides were not run out, so that every wide included in the above total represents a wide actually bowled. This particular achievement has never been surpassed in the annals of county cricket.

L Hutton reached his 1,000 runs in First-Class cricket in 1949 as early as June 9th.

W Barber reached his 1,000 runs in 1934 on June 13th. P Holmes reached his 1,000 in 1925 on June 16th, as also did H Sutcliffe in 1932. J T Brown reached his 1,000 in 1899 on June 22nd. In 1905, D Denton reached his 1,000 runs on June 26th; and in 1906 G H Hirst gained the same total on June 27th.

In 1912, D Denton scored over 1,000 runs during July, while M Leyland and H Sutcliffe both scored over 1,000 runs in August 1932.

L Hutton scored over 1,000 in June and over 1,000 runs in August in 1949.

H Verity took his 100th wicket in First-Class cricket as early as June 19th in 1936 and on June 27th in 1935. In 1900, W Rhodes obtained his 100th wicket on June 21st, and again on the same date in 1901, while G H Hirst obtained his 100th wicket on June 28th, 1906.

In 1930, Yorkshiremen (H Sutcliffe and H Verity) occupied the first places by English players in the batting and the bowling averages of First-Class cricket, which is a record without precedent. H Sutcliffe was also first in the batting averages in 1931 and 1932.

G Boycott was the first player to have achieved an average of over 100 in each of two English seasons. In 1971, he scored 2,503 runs for an average of 100.12, and in 1979 he scored 1,538 runs for an average of 102.53.

FIRST-CLASS MATCHES BEGUN AND FINISHED IN ONE DAY

Yorkshire v. Somerset, at Huddersfield, July 9th, 1894.
Yorkshire v. Hampshire, at Southampton, May 27th, 1898.
Yorkshire v. Worcestershire, at Bradford, May 7th, 1900

For England

YORKSHIRE TEST CRICKETERS 1877–2022 (Correct to January 17, 2022)

Player	M.	I	NO	Runs	HS.	Av'ge.	100s	50s	Balls	R	W	Av'ge	Best	5wI	10wM	c/st
APPLEYARD, R ...1954-56	9	9	6	51	19*	17.00	—	—	1,596	554	31	17.87	5-51	1	—	4
ARMITAGE, T.......1877	2	3	0	33	21	11.00	—	—	12	15	0	—	—	—	—	0
ATHEY, C W J ...1980-88	23	41	1	919	123	22.97	—	4	—	—	—	—	—	—	—	13
BAIRSTOW, D L ...1979-81	4	7	1	125	59	20.83	—	1	—	—	—	—	—	—	—	12/1
BAIRSTOW, J M .2012-21/22	80	142	8	4,575	167*	34.14	7	22	—	—	—	—	—	—	—	196/13
BALLANCE, G S 2013/14-17	23	42	2	1,498	156	37.45	4	7	—	—	—	—	—	—	—	22
BARBER, W 1935	2	4	0	83	44	20.75	—	—	12	5	0	—	—	—	—	1
BATES, W 1881-87	15	26	2	656	64	27.33	—	5	2,364	821	50	16.42	7-28	4	1	9
BESS D M 2018-20/21	14	19	5	319	57	22.78	—	1	2,502	1,223	36	33.97	5-30	2	—	3
BINKS, J G 1964	2	4	0	91	55	22.75	—	—	—	—	—	—	—	—	—	8/0
BLAKEY, R J 1993	2	4	0	7	6	1.75	—	—	—	—	—	—	—	—	—	2/0
BOOTH, M W ...1913-14	2	2	0	46	32	23.00	—	—	312	130	7	18.57	4-49	—	—	0
BOWES, W E ...1932-46	15	11	5	28	10*	4.66	—	—	3,655	1,519	68	22.33	6-33	6	—	2
†BOYCOTT, G ...1964-82	108	193	23	8,114	246*	47.72	22	42	944	382	7	54.57	3-47	—	—	33
BRENNAN, D V 1951	2	2	0	16	16	8.00	—	—	—	—	—	—	—	—	—	0/1
BRESNAN, T T .2009-13/14	23	26	4	575	91	26.13	—	3	4,674	2,357	72	32.73	5-48	1	—	8
BROWN, J T ...1894-99	8	16	3	470	140	36.15	1	1	35	22	0	—	—	—	—	7
†CLOSE, D B ...1949-76	22	37	2	887	70	25.34	—	4	1,212	532	18	29.55	4-35	—	—	24
COPE, G A 1977-78	3	3	0	40	22	13.33	—	—	864	277	8	34.62	3-102	—	—	1
COXON, A 1948	1	2	0	19	19	9.50	—	—	378	172	3	57.33	2-90	—	—	0
DAWSON, R K J ..2002-03	7	13	3	114	19*	11.40	—	—	1,116	677	11	61.54	4-134	—	—	3
DENTON, D ...1905-10	11	22	1	424	104	20.19	1	1	—	—	—	—	—	—	—	8
DOLPHIN, A 1921	1	2	0	1	1	0.50	—	—	—	—	—	—	—	—	—	1/0
EMMETT, T ...1877-82	7	13	1	160	48	13.33	—	—	728	284	9	31.55	7-68	1	—	9
GIBB, P A 1938-46	8	13	0	581	120	44.69	2	3	—	—	—	—	—	—	—	3/1

307

For England

YORKSHIRE TEST CRICKETERS 1877-2022 (Continued)

Player	M.	I	NO	Runs	HS.	Av'ge.	100s	50s	Balls	R	W	Av'ge	Best	5wI	10wM	c/st
GOUGH, D 1994-2003	58	86	18	855	65	12.57	—	2	11,821	6,503	229	28.39	6-42	9	—	13
GREENWOOD, A 1877	2	4	0	77	49	19.25	—	—	—	—	—	—	—	—	—	2
HAIGH, S 1899-1912	11	18	3	113	25	7.53	—	—	1,294	622	24	25.91	6-11	1	—	8
HAMILTON, G.M. 1999	1	2	0	0	0	0.00	—	—	90	63	0	—	—	—	—	0
HAMPSHIRE, J H ..1969-75	8	16	1	403	107	26.86	1	2	—	—	—	—	—	—	—	9
†HAWKE, LORD ..1896-99	5	8	1	55	30	7.85	—	—	—	—	—	—	—	—	—	3
HILL, A 1877	2	4	2	101	49	50.50	—	—	340	130	7	18.57	4-27	—	—	1
HIRST, G H 1897-1909	24	38	3	790	85	22.57	—	5	3,967	1,770	59	30.00	5-48	3	—	18
HOGGARD, M J .2000-2008	67	92	27	473	88	7.27	—	—	13,909	7,564	248	30.50	7-61	7	1	24
HOLMES, P 1921-32	7	14	1	357	88	27.46	—	4	—	—	—	—	—	—	—	3
HUNTER, J 1884-85	5	7	2	93	39*	18.60	—	—	—	—	—	—	—	—	—	8/3
†HUTTON, L 1937-55	79	138	15	6,971	364	56.67	19	33	260	232	3	77.33	1-2	—	—	57
HUTTON, R A 1971	5	8	2	219	81	36.50	—	2	738	257	9	28.55	3-72	—	—	9
†ILLINGWORTH, R .1958-73	61	90	11	1,836	113	23.24	2	5	11,934	3,807	122	31.20	6-29	3	—	45
†JACKSON, Hon F S 1893-1905	20	33	4	1,415	144*	48.79	5	6	1,587	799	24	33.29	5-52	1	—	10
JARVIS, P W 1988-93	9	15	2	132	29*	10.15	—	—	1,912	965	21	45.95	4-107	—	—	2
KILNER, R 1924-26	9	8	1	233	74	33.28	—	2	2,368	734	24	30.58	4-51	—	—	6
LEADBEATER, E ..1951-52	2	2	0	40	38	20.00	—	—	289	218	2	109.00	1-38	—	—	3
LEYLAND, M 1928-38	41	65	5	2,764	187	46.06	9	10	1,103	585	6	97.50	3-91	—	—	13
LOWSON, F A 1951-55	7	13	0	245	68	18.84	—	2	—	—	—	—	—	—	—	5
LYTH A 2015	7	13	0	265	107	20.38	1	—	6	0	0	—	—	—	—	8
McGRATH, A 2003	4	5	0	201	81	40.20	—	2	102	56	4	14.00	3-16	—	—	3
MACAULAY, G G ..1923-33	8	10	4	112	76	18.66	—	1	1,701	662	24	27.58	5-64	1	—	5
MALAN, D J ...2017-21/22	22	39	0	1,074	140	27.53	1	9	222	131	2	65.50	2-33	—	—	13
MILLIGAN, F W 1899	2	4	0	58	38	14.50	—	—	45	29	0	—	—	—	—	1
MITCHELL, A 1933-36	6	10	0	298	72	29.80	—	2	6	4	0	—	—	—	—	9

For England

YORKSHIRE TEST CRICKETERS 1877-2022 (Continued)

Player	M.	I	NO	Runs	HS.	Av'ge.	100s	50s	Balls	R	W	Av'ge	Best	5wI	10wM	c/st
*MITCHELL, F 1899	2	4	0	88	41	22.00	—	—	—	—	—	—	—	—	—	2
MOXON, M D 1986-89	10	17	1	455	99	28.43	—	3	48	30	0	—	—	—	—	10
OLD, C M 1972-81	46	66	9	845	65	14.82	—	2	8,858	4,020	143	28.11	7-50	4	—	22
PADGETT, D E V 1960	2	4	0	51	31	14.82	—	—	12	8	0	—	—	—	—	0
PEATE, E 1881-86	9	14	8	70	13	11.66	—	—	2,096	682	31	22.00	6-85	2	—	2
PEEL, R 1884-96	20	33	4	427	83	14.72	—	3	5,216	1,715	101	16.98	7-31	5	1	17
PLUNKETT, L E 2005/6-2014	13	20	5	238	55*	15.86	—	1	2,659	1,536	41	37.46	5-64	1	—	3
RASHID, A U 2015/16-19	19	33	0	540	61	19.28	—	2	3,816	2,390	60	39.83	5-49	1	—	4
RHODES, W 1899-1930	58	98	21	2,325	179	30.19	2	11	8,231	3,425	127	26.96	8-68	6	1	60
†ROOT, J E 2012-21/22	114	210	15	9,600	254	49.23	23	53	3,719	1,977	44	44.93	5- 8	1	—	148
SHARPE, P J 1963-69	12	21	4	786	111	46.23	1	4	—	—	—	—	—	—	—	17
SHAHZAD, A 2010	1	1	1	5	5	5.00	—	—	102	63	4	15.75	3-45	—	—	2
SIDEBOTTOM, A 1985	1	1	0	2	2	2.00	—	—	112	65	1	65.00	1-65	—	—	0
SIDEBOTTOM, R J 2001-10	22	31	11	313	31	15.65	—	—	4,812	2,231	79	28.24	7-47	5	—	5
SILVERWOOD, CEW1997-2003	6	7	3	29	10	7.25	—	—	828	444	11	40.36	5-91	—	—	2
SMAILES, T F 1946	1	1	0	25	25	25.00	—	—	120	62	3	20.66	3-44	—	—	0
SMITHSON, G A 1948	2	3	0	70	35	23.33	—	—	—	—	—	—	—	—	—	0
†STANYFORTH, R T 1927-28	4	6	1	13	6*	2.60	—	—	—	—	—	—	—	—	—	7/2
STEVENSON, G B .1980-81	2	2	1	28	27*	28.00	—	—	312	183	5	36.60	3-111	—	—	0
SUTCLIFFE, H ...1924-35	54	84	9	4,555	194	60.73	16	23	—	—	—	—	—	—	—	23
TAYLOR, K 1959-64	3	5	0	57	24	11.40	—	—	12	6	0	—	—	—	—	1
TRUEMAN, F S ..1952-65	67	85	14	981	39*	13.81	—	—	15,178	6,625	307	21.57	8-31	17	3	64
ULYETT, G 1877-90	25	39	0	949	149	24.33	1	7	2,627	1,020	50	20.40	7-36	1	—	19
†VAUGHAN M P .1999-2008	82	147	9	5,719	197	41.44	18	18	978	561	6	93.50	2-71	—	—	44
VERITY, H 1931-39	40	44	12	669	66*	20.90	—	3	11,173	3,510	144	24.37	8-43	5	2	30
WADDINGTON, A ..1920-21	2	4	0	16	7	4.00	—	—	276	119	1	119.00	1-35	—	—	1

309

YORKSHIRE TEST CRICKETERS 1877-2022 (Continued)

For England

Player	M.	I	NO	Runs	HS.	Av'ge.	100s	50s	Balls	R	W	Av'ge	Best	5wI	10wM	c/st
WAINWRIGHT, E 1893-98	5	9	0	132	49	14.66	—	—	127	73	0	—	—	—	—	2
WARDLE, J H 1948-57	28	41	8	653	66	19.78	—	2	6,597	2,080	102	20.39	7-36	5	1	12
WATSON, W 1951-59	23	37	3	879	116	25.85	2	3	—	—	—	—	—	—	—	8
WHITE, C 1994-2002	30	50	7	1,052	121	24.46	1	5	3,959	2,220	59	37.62	5-32	3	—	14
WILSON, C E M 1899	2	4	1	42	18	14.00	—	—	—	—	—	—	—	—	—	0
WILSON, E R 1921	1	2	0	10	5	5.00	—	—	123	36	3	12.00	2-28	—	—	1
WOOD, A 1938-39	4	5	1	80	53	20.00	—	1	—	—	—	—	—	—	—	10/1
†YARDLEY, N W D ..1938-50	20	34	2	812	99	25.37	—	4	1,662	707	21	33.66	3-67	—	—	14

†Captained England
*Also represented and captained South Africa

For South Africa

†MITCHELL, F 1912	3	6	0	28	12	4.66	—	—	—	—	—	—	—	—	—	0

†Captained South Africa

Overseas Players

(Qualification: 20 first-class matches for Yorkshire)

For Australia

BEVAN, M G 1994-98	18	30	3	785	91	29.07	—	6	1,285	703	29	24.24	6-82	1	1	8
GILLESPIE, J N ..1996-2006	71	93	28	1,218	201*	18.73	1	2	14,234	6,770	259	26.13	7-37	8	—	27
JAQUES, P A 2005-2008	11	19	0	902	150	47.47	3	6	—	—	—	—	—	—	—	7
LEHMANN, D S ...1999-2004	27	42	2	1,798	177	44.95	5	10	974	412	15	27.46	3-42	—	—	11

For South Africa

OLIVIER, D ...2016/17-21/22	12	14	7	37	10*	5.28	0	0	1,782	1,119	53	21.11	6-37	3	1	2
RUDOLPH, J A ..2003-12/13	48	83	9	2,622	222*	35.43	6	11	664	432	4	108.00	1- 1	—	—	29

For West Indies

RICHARDSON, R B 1983-84/95	86	146	12	5,949	194	44.39	16	27	66	18	0	—	—	—	—	90

CENTURIES FOR ENGLAND

C W J ATHEY (1)
123 v Pakistan at Lord's, 1987

J M BAIRSTOW (7)
150* v. South Africa at Cape Town, 2016
167* v. Sri Lanka at Lord's, 2016
101 v. New Zealand at Christchurch, 2018
113 v. Australia at Sydney, 2022
140 v. Sri Lanka at Leeds, 2016
119 v. Australia at Perth, 2017
110 v. Sri Lanka at Colombo (SSC), 2018

G S BALLANCE (4)
104* v. Sri Lanka at Lord's, 2014
256 v. India at Southampton, 2014
110 v. India at Lord's, 2014
122 v. West Indies at North Sound, 2015

G BOYCOTT (22)
113 v. Australia at The Oval, 1964
117 v. South Africa at Port Elizabeth, 1965
246* v. India at Leeds, 1967
116 v. West Indies at Georgetown, 1968
128 v. West Indies at Manchester, 1969
106 v. West Indies at Lord's, 1969
142* v. Australia at Sydney, 1971
119* v. Australia at Adelaide, 1971
121* v. Pakistan at Lord's, 1971
112 v. Pakistan at Leeds, 1971
115 v. New Zealand at Leeds, 1973
112 v West Indies at Port-of-Spain, 1974
107 v. Australia at Nottingham, 1977
191 v. Australia at Leeds, 1977
100* v. Pakistan at Hyderabad, 1978
131 v. New Zealand at Nottingham, 1978
155 v. India at Birmingham, 1979
125 v. India at The Oval, 1979
128* v. Australia at Lord's, 1980
104* v. West Indies at St John's, 1981
137 v. Australia at The Oval, 1981
105 v. India at Delhi, 1981

J T BROWN (1)
140 v. Australia at Melbourne, 1895

D DENTON (1)
104 v. South Africa at Old Wanderers, Johannesburg, 1910

P A GIBB (2)
106 v. South Africa at Old Wanderers, Johannesburg, 1938
120 v. South Africa at Kingsmead, Durban, 1939

J H HAMPSHIRE (1)
107 v. West Indies at Lord's, 1969

L HUTTON (19)
100 v. New Zealand at Manchester, 1937
100 v. Australia at Nottingham, 1938
364 v. Australia at The Oval, 1938
196 v. West Indies at Lord's, 1939
165* v. West Indies at The Oval, 1939
122* v. Australia at Sydney, 1947
100 v. South Africa at Leeds, 1947
158 v. South Africa at Ellis Park, J'b'rg, 1948
123 v. South Africa at Ellis Park, J'b'rg, 1949
101 v. New Zealand at Leeds, 1949
206 v. New Zealand at The Oval, 1949
202* v. West Indies at The Oval, 1950
156* v. Australia at Adelaide, 1951
100 v. South Africa at Leeds, 1951
150 v. India at Lord's, 1952
104 v. India at Manchester, 1952
145 v. Australia at Lord's, 1953
169 v. West Indies at Georgetown, 1954
205 v. West Indies at Kingston, 1954

R ILLINGWORTH (2)
113 v. West Indies at Lord's, 1969
107 v. India at Manchester, 1971

Hon. F S JACKSON (5)
103 v. Australia at The Oval, 1893
118 v. Australia at The Oval, 1899
128 v. Australia at Manchester, 1902
144* v. Australia at Leeds, 1905
113 v. Australia at Manchester, 1905

CENTURIES FOR ENGLAND

M LEYLAND (9)

- 137 v. Australia at Melbourne, 1929
- 102 v. South Africa at Lord's, 1929
- 109 v. Australia at Lord's, 1934
- 153 v. Australia at Manchester, 1934
- 110 v. Australia at The Oval, 1934
- 161 v. South Africa at The Oval, 1935
- 126 v. Australia at Woolloongabba, Brisbane, 1936
- 111* v. Australia at Melbourne, 1937
- 187 v. Australia at The Oval, 1938

A LYTH (1)

107 v. New Zealand at Leeds 2015

W RHODES (2)

179 v. Australia at Melbourne, 1912
152 v. South Africa at Old Wanderers, Johannesburg, 1913

J E ROOT (23)

- 104 v. New Zealand at Leeds, 2013
- 200* v. Sri Lanka at Lord's, 2014
- 149* v. India at The Oval, 2014
- 134 v. Australia at Cardiff 2015
- 110 v. South Africa at Johannesburg, 2016
- 124 v. India at Rajkot, 2016
- 136 v. West Indies at Birmingham, 2017
- 124 v. Sri Lanka at Pallekele, 2018
- 226 v, New Zealand at Hamilton, 2019
- 186 v. Sri Lanka at Galle, 2021
- 109 v. India at Nottingham, 2021
- 121 v. India at Leeds, 2021
- 180 v. Australia at Lord's, 2013
- 154* v. India at Nottingham, 2014
- 182* v. West Indies at St George's, 2015
- 130 v. Australia at Nottingham, 2015
- 254 v. Pakistan at Manchester, 2016
- 190 v. South Africa at Lord's, 2017
- 125 v. India at The Oval, 2018
- 122 v. West Indies at Gros Islet, 2019
- 228 v. Sri Lanka at Galle, 2021
- 218 v. India at Chennai, 2021
- 180 *v. India at Lord's, 2021

P J SHARPE (1)

111 v. New Zealand at Nottingham, 1969

H SUTCLIFFE (16)

- 122 v. South Africa at Lord's, 1924
- 115 v. Australia at Sydney, 1924
- 176 v. Australia at Melbourne, 1925 (1st Inns)
- 127 v. Australia at Melbourne, 1925 (2nd Inns)
- 143 v. Australia at Melbourne, 1925
- 161 v. Australia at The Oval, 1926
- 102 v. South Africa at Old Wanderers, Jbg.1927
- 135 v. Australia at Melbourne, 1929
- 114 v. South Africa at Birmingham, 1929
- 100 v. South Africa at Lord's, 1929
- 104 v. South Africa at The Oval, 1929 (1st inns)
- 109* v. South Africa at The Oval, 1929 (2nd inns)
- 161 v. Australia at The Oval, 1930
- 117 v. New Zealand at The Oval, 1931
- 109* v. New Zealand at Manchester, 1931
- 194 v. Australia at Sydney, 1932

G ULYETT (1)

149 v. Australia at Melbourne, 1882

CENTURIES FOR ENGLAND *(Continued)*

M P VAUGHAN (18)

120 v. Pakistan at Manchester, 2001
115 v. Sri Lanka at Lord's, 2002
100 v. India at Lord's, 2002
197 v. India at Nottingham, 2002
195 v. India at The Oval, 2002
177 v. Australia at Adelaide, 2002
145 v. Australia at Melbourne, 2002
183 v. Australia at Sydney, 2003
156 v. South Africa at Birmingham, 2003
105 v. Sri Lanka at Kandy, 2003
140 v. West Indies at Antigua, 2004
103 v. West Indies at Lord's (1st inns) 2004
101* v. West Indies at Lord's (2nd inns) 2004
120 v. Bangladesh at Lord's, 2005
166 v. Australia at Manchester, 2005
103 v. West Indies at Leeds, 2007
124 v. India at Nottingham, 2007
106 v. New Zealand at Lord's, 2008

W WATSON (2)

109 v. Australia at Lord's, 1953
116 v. West Indies at Kingston, 1954

C WHITE (1)

121 v. India at Ahmedabad, 2001

Summary of the Centuries

versus	Total	In England	Away
Australia	44	23	21
Bangladesh	1	1	0
India	22	18	4
New Zealand	13	11	2
Pakistan	6	5	1
South Africa	21	11	10
Sri Lanka	10	5	5
West Indies	21	11	10
Totals	138	85	53

For Australia

J N GILLESPIE (1)

201* v. Bangladesh at Chittagong, 2006

P A JAQUES (3)

100 v. Sri Lanka at Brisbane, 2007
150 v. Sri Lanka at Hobart, 2007
108 v. West Indies at Bridgetown, 2008

D S LEHMANN (5)

160 v. West Indies at Port of Spain, 2003
110 v. Bangladesh at Darwin, 2003
177 v. Bangladesh at Cairns, 2003
129 v. Sri Lanka at Galle, 2004
153 v. Sri Lanka at Columbo, 2004

For South Africa

J A RUDOLPH (6)

222* v. Bangladesh at Chittagong, 2003
101 v West Indies at Cape Town, 2004
154* v. New Zealand at Auckland, 2004
102 v. Sri Lanka at Galle, 2004
102* v Australia at Perth, 2005
105* v. New Zealand at Dunedin, 2012

10 WICKETS IN A MATCH FOR ENGLAND

W BATES (1)
14 for 102 (7 for 28 and 7 for 74) v. Australia at Melbourne, 1882

M J HOGGARD (1)
12 for 205 (5 for 144 and 7 for 61) v. South Africa at Johannesburg, 2005

R PEEL (1)
11 for 68 (7 for 31 and 4 for 37) v. Australia at Manchester, 1888

Note: The scorebook for the Australia v. England Test match at Sydney in February 1888 shows that the final wicket to fall was taken by W Attewell, and not by Peel
Peel therefore took 9, and not 10 wickets, in the match
His career totals have been amended to take account of this alteration

W RHODES (1)
15 for 124 (7 for 56 and 8 for 68) v. Australia at Melbourne, 1904

R J SIDEBOTTOM (1)
10 for 139 (4 for 90 and 6 for 49) v. New Zealand at Hamilton, 2008

F S TRUEMAN (3)
11 for 88 (5 for 58 and 6 for 30) v. Australia at Leeds, 1961
11 for 152 (6 for 100 and 5 for 52) v. West Indies at Lord's, 1963*
12 for 119 (5 for 75 and 7 for 44) v. West Indies at Birmingham, 1963*
consecutive Tests

H VERITY (2)
11 for 153 (7 for 49 and 4 for 104) v. India at Chepauk, Madras, 1934
15 for 104 (7 for 61 and 8 for 43) v. Australia at Lord's, 1934

J H WARDLE (1)
12 for 89 (5 for 53 and 7 for 36) v. South Africa at Cape Town, 1957

Summary of Ten Wickets in a Match

versus	Total	In England	Away
Australia	5	3	2
India	1	—	1
New Zealand	1	—	1
Pakistan	—	—	—
South Africa	2	—	2
Sri Lanka	—	—	—
West Indies	2	2	—
Totals	11	5	6

For Australia

M G BEVAN (1)
10 for 113 (4 for 31and 6 for 82) v. West Indies at Adelaide, 1997

5 WICKETS IN AN INNINGS FOR ENGLAND

R APPLEYARD (1)
5 for 51 v. Pakistan at Nottingham, 1954

W BATES (4)
7 for 28 v. Australia at Melbourne, 1882   5 for 31 v. Australia at Adelaide, 1884
7 for 74 v. Australia at Melbourne, 1882   5 for 24 v. Australia at Sydney, 1885

D M BESS (2)
5 for 51 v. South Africa at Port Elizabeth, 2020   5 for 30 v. Sri Lanka at Galle 2021

5 WICKETS IN AN INNINGS FOR ENGLAND *(Continued)*

W E BOWES (6)

6-34	v. New Zealand	at Auckland	1933	5-100	v. South Africa	at Manchester	1935
6-142	v. Australia	at Leeds	1934*	5-49	v. Australia	at The Oval	1938
5-55	v. Australia	at The Oval	1934*	6-33	v. West Indies	at Manchester	1939

consecutive Test matches

T T BRESNAN (1)

5-48   v. India   at Nottingham   2011

T EMMETT (1)

7-68   v. Australia   at Melbourne   1879

D GOUGH (9)

6-49	v. Australia	at Sydney	1995	5-70	v. South Africa	at Johannesburg	1999
5-40	v. New Zealand	at Wellington	1997	5-109	v. West Indies	at Birmingham	2000
5-149	v. Australia	at Leeds	1997	5-61	v. Pakistan	at Lord's	2001
6-42	v. South Africa	at Leeds	1998	5-103	v. Australia	at Leeds	2001
5-96	v. Australia	at Melbourne	1998				

S HAIGH (1)

6-11   v. South Africa   at Cape Town   1909

G H HIRST (3)

5-77	v. Australia	at The Oval	1902	5-58	v. Australia	at Birmingham	1909
5-48	v. Australia	at Melbourne	1904				

M J HOGGARD (7)

7-63	v. New Zealand	at Christchurch	2002	5-73	v. Bangladesh	at Chester-le-Street	2005
5-92	v. Sri Lanka	at Birmingham	2002				
5-144	v. South Africa	at Johannesburg	2005*	6-57	v. India	at Nagpur	2006
7-61	v. South Africa	at Johannesburg	2005*	7-109	v. Australia	at Adelaide	2006

Consecutive Test innings

R ILLINGWORTH (3)

6-29	v. India	at Lord's	1967	5-70	v. India	at The Oval	1971
6-87	v. Australia	at Leeds	1968				

Hon F S JACKSON (1)

5-52   v. Australia   at Nottingham   1905

G G MACAULAY (1)

5-64   v. South Africa   at Cape Town   1923

C M OLD (4)

5-113	v. New Zealand	at Lord's	1973	6-54	v. New Zealand	at Wellington	1978
5-21	v. India	at Lord's	1974	7-50	v. Pakistan	at Birmingham	1978

E PEATE (2)

5-43   v. Australia   at Sydney   1882   6-85   v. Australia   at Lord's   1884

R PEEL (5)

5-51	v. Australia	at Adelaide	1884	6-67	v. Australia	at Sydney	1894
5-18	v. Australia	at Sydney	1888	6-23	v. Australia	at The Oval	1896
7-31	v. Australia	at Manchester	1888				

L E PLUNKETT (1)

5-64   v. Sri Lanka   at Leeds   2014

A U RASHID (2)

5-64   v. Pakistan   at Abu Dhabi   2015   5-49   v. Sri Lanka   at Colombo (SSC)   2018

5 WICKETS IN AN INNINGS FOR ENGLAND *(Continued)*

W RHODES (6)

7-17	v. Australia	at Birmingham	1902	7-56	v. Australia	at Melbourne	1904*
5-63	v. Australia	at Sheffield	1902	8-68	v. Australia	at Melbourne	1904*
5-94	v. Australia	at Sydney	1903*	5-83	v. Australia	at Manchester	1909

consecutive Test innings

J E ROOT (1)

5- 8 v. India at Ahmedabad 2021

C E W SILVERWOOD (1)

5-91 v. South Africa at Cape Town 2000

R J SIDEBOTTOM (5)

5-88	v. West Indies	at Chester-le-Street		5-105	v. New Zealand	at Wellington	2008
			2007	7-47	v. New Zealand	at Napier	2008
6-49	v. New Zealand	at Hamilton	2008	6-47	v. New Zealand	at Nottingham	2008

F S TRUEMAN (17)

8-31	v. India	at Manchester	1952	6-31	v. Pakistan	at Lord's	1962
5-48	v. India	at The Oval	1952	5-62	v. Australia	at Melbourne	1963
5-90	v. Australia	at Lord's	1956	7-75	v. New Zealand	at Christchurch	1963
5-63	v. West Indies	at Nottingham	1957	6-100	v. West Indies	at Lord's	1963*
5-31	v. New Zealand	at Birmingham	1958	5-52	v. West Indies	at Lord's	1963*
5-35	v. West Indies	at Port-of-Spain	1960	5-75	v. West Indies	at Birmingham	1963*
5-27	v. South Africa	at Nottingham	1960	7-44	v. West Indies	at Birmingham	1963*
5-58	v. Australia	at Leeds	1961*	5-48	v. Australia	at Lord's	1964
6-30	v. Australia	at Leeds	1961*				

G ULYETT (1)

7-36 v. Australia at Lord's 1884

H VERITY (5)

5-33	v. Australia	at Sydney	1933	8-43	v. Australia	at Lord's	1934*
7-49	v. India	at Chepauk, Madras	1934	5-70	v. South Africa	at Cape Town	1939
7-61	v. Australia	at Lord's	1934*				

J H WARDLE (5)

7-56	v. Pakistan	at The Oval	1954	7-36	v. South Africa	at Cape Town	1957*
5-79	v. Australia	at Sydney	1955	5-61	v. South Africa	at Kingsmead Durban	1957*
5-53	v. South Africa	at Cape Town	1957*				

C WHITE (3)

5-57	v. West Indies	at Leeds	2000	5-32	v. West Indies	at The Oval	2000
	5-127	v. Australia	at Perth	2002			

consecutive Test innings

5 WICKETS IN AN INNINGS *(Continued)*

Summary of Five Wickets in an Innings

versus	Total	In England	Away
Australia	42	22	20
Bangladesh	1	1	0
India	9	6	3
New Zealand	11	3	8
Pakistan	6	5	1
South Africa	14	3	11
Sri Lanka	4	2	2
West Indies	11	10	1
Totals	98	52	46

For Australia

M G BEVAN (1)

6-82	v. West Indies	at Adelaide	1997

J N GILLESPIE (8)

5-54	v. South Africa	at Port Elizabeth	1997
7-37	v. England	at Leeds	1997
5-88	v. England	at Perth	1998
5-89	v. West Indies	at Adelaide	2000
6-40	v. West Indies	at Melbourne	2000
5-53	v. England	at Lord's	2001
5-39	v. West Indies	at Georgetown	2003
5-56	v. India	at Nagpur	2004

For South Africa

D OLIVIER (3)

6-37	v. Pakistan (1st innings)	at Centurion	2018
5-59	v. Pakistan (2nd innings)	at Centurion	2018
5-51	v. Pakistan	at Johannesburg	2019

HAT-TRICKS

W Bates	v. Australia	at Melbourne	1882
D Gough	v. Australia	at Sydney	1998
M J Hoggard	v. West Indies	at Bridgetown	2004
R J Sidebottom	v. New Zealand	at Hamilton	2008

FOUR WICKETS IN FIVE BALLS

C M Old	v. Pakistan	at Birmingham	1978

THREE WICKETS IN FOUR BALLS

R Appleyard	v. New Zealand	at Auckland	1955
D Gough	v. Pakistan	at Lord's	2001

YORKSHIRE PLAYERS WHO PLAYED ALL THEIR TEST CRICKET AFTER LEAVING YORKSHIRE

For England

Player	M.	I	NO	Runs	HS.	Av.'ge.	100s	50s	Balls	R	W	Av.'ge.	Best	5wI	10wM	c/st
BALDERSTONE, J C ...1976	2	4	0	39	35	9.75	—	—	96	80	1	80.00	1:80	—	—	1
BATTY G J ...2003/4-16/17	9	12	2	149	38	14.90	—	1	1,714	914	15	60.93	3-55	—	—	3
BIRKENSHAW, J ...1973-74	5	7	0	148	64	21.14	—	1	1,017	469	13	36.07	5:57	1	—	3
BOLUS, J B ...1963-64	7	12	0	496	88	41.33	—	4	18	16	0	—	—	—	—	2
†PARKIN, C H ...1920-24	10	16	3	160	36	12.30	—	—	2,095	1,128	32	35.25	5:38	2	—	3
RHODES, S J ...1994-95	11	17	5	294	65*	24.50	—	1	—	—	—	—	—	—	—	46/3
†SUGG, F H ...1888	2	2	0	55	31	27.50	—	—	—	—	—	—	—	—	—	0
WARD, A ...1893-95	7	13	0	487	117	37.46	1	3	—	—	—	—	—	—	—	1
WOOD, B ...1972-78	12	21	0	454	90	21.61	—	2	98	50	0	—	—	—	—	6

For South Africa

Player	M.	I	NO	Runs	HS.	Av.'ge.	100s	50s	Balls	R	W	Av.'ge.	Best	5wI	10wM	c/st
THORNTON, P G 1902	1	1	1	1	1*	—	—	—	24	20	1	20.00	1:20	—	—	1

†Born outside Yorkshire

CENTURIES FOR ENGLAND

A WARD (1)
117 v. Australia at Sydney, 1894

5 WICKETS IN AN INNINGS FOR ENGLAND

J BIRKENSHAW (1)
5 : 57 v. Pakistan at Karachi, 1973

C H PARKIN (2)
5 : 60 v. Australia at Adelaide, 1921
5 : 38 v. Australia at Manchester, 1921

YORKSHIRE'S TEST CRICKET RECORDS

R APPLEYARD

Auckland 1954-55: took 3 wickets in 4 balls as New Zealand were dismissed for the lowest total in Test history (26).

C W J ATHEY

Perth 1986-87: shared an opening stand of 223 with B C Broad – England's highest for any wicket at the WACA Ground.

J M BAIRSTOW

Cape Town, January 2016: scored his maiden Test Century (150*). His sixth- wicket partnership of 399 with B A Stokes (258) was the highest in Test cricket and the highest First Class partnership for any wicket at Newlands. There was only one higher partnership for England. This was 411 by P B H May and M C Cowdrey for the fourth wicket against the West Indies at Birmingham in 1957.

Chittagong, October 2016: scored 52 in the first innings, which passed his 1,000 Test runs in a calendar year. He became only the third Yorkshire player to do this after M P Vaughan with 1,481 in 2002 and J E Root 1,385 in 2015. He was only the second Test wicket-keeper to pass this mark. His first scoring shot in the second inning broke a 16-year record set by Zimbabwe's A Flower (1,045 in 2000) to give him the highest total of runs scored in a calendar year by a Test wicket-keeper. His final tally for 2016 was 1,470.

Mohali, November 2016: his third catch of India's first innings (U T Yadav) was his 68th dismissal of the year to pass the previous best in a calendar year (67) by I A Healy (Australia) in 1991 and M V Boucher (South Africa) in 1998. Bairstow's final tally for the calendar year was 70 (66 caught and 4 stumped).

W BATES

Melbourne 1882-83 (Second Test): achieved the first hat-trick for England when he dismissed P S McDonnell, G Giffen and G J Bonnor in Australia's first innings. Later in the match, he became the first player to score a fifty (55) and take 10 or more wickets (14 for 102) in the same Test.

W E BOWES

Melbourne 1932-33: enjoyed the unique satisfaction of bowling D G Bradman first ball in a Test match (his first ball to him in Test cricket).

G BOYCOTT

Leeds 1967: scored 246 not out off 555 balls in 573 minutes to establish the record England score against India. His first 100 took 341 minutes (316 balls) and he was excluded from the next Test as a disciplinary measure; shared in hundred partnerships for three successive wickets.

Adelaide 1970-71: with J H Edrich, became the third opening pair to share hundred partnerships in both innings of a Test against Australia.

Port-of-Spain 1973-74: first to score 99 and a hundred in the same Test.

Nottingham 1977: with A P E Knott, equalled England v. Australia sixth-wicket partnership record of 215 – the only England v. Australia stand to be equalled or broken since 1938. Batted on each day of the five-day Test (second after M L Jaisimha to achieve this feat).

Leeds 1977: first to score his 100th First Class hundred in a Test; became the fourth England player to be on the field for an entire Test.

YORKSHIRE'S TEST CRICKET RECORDS *(Continued)*

G BOYCOTT *(Continued)*

Perth: 1978-79: eighth to score 2,000 runs for England against Australia.

Birmingham 1979: emulated K F Barrington by scoring hundreds on each of England's six current home grounds.

Perth: 1979-80: fourth to carry his bat through a completed England innings (third v. Australia) and the first to do so without scoring 100; first to score 99 not out in a Test.

Lord's 1981: 100th Test for England – second after M C Cowdrey (1968).

The Oval, 1981: second after Hon F S Jackson to score five hundreds v. Australia in England.

Gained three Test records from M C Cowdrey: exceeded England aggregate of 7,624 runs in 11 fewer Tests (Manchester 1981); 61st fifty – world record (The Oval 1981); 189th innings – world record (Bangalore 1981-82).

Delhi, 4.23p.m. on 23 December 1981: passed G St.A Sobers's world Test record of 8,032 runs, having played 30 more innings and batted over 451 hours (cf. 15 complete five-day Tests); his 22nd hundred equalled the England record.

J T BROWN

Melbourne 1894-95: his 28-minute fifty remains the fastest in Test cricket, and his 95-minute hundred was a record until 1897-98; his third-wicket stand of 210 with A Ward set a Test record for any wicket.

D B CLOSE

Manchester 1949: at 18 years 149 days he became – and remains – the youngest to represent England.

Melbourne 1950-51: became the youngest (19 years 301 days) to represent England against Australia.

T EMMETT

Melbourne 1878-79: first England bowler to take seven wickets in a Test innings.

P A GIBB

Johannesburg 1938-39: enjoyed a record England debut, scoring 93 and 106 as well as sharing second-wicket stands of 184 and 168 with E Paynter.

Durban 1938-39: shared record England v. South Africa second-wicket stand of 280 with W J Edrich, his 120 in 451 minutes including only two boundaries.

D GOUGH

Sydney 1998-99: achieved the 23rd hat-trick in Test cricket (ninth for England and first for England v. Australia since 1899).

Lord's 2001: took 3 wickets in 4 balls v. Pakistan.

S HAIGH

Cape Town 1898-99: bowled unchanged through the second innings with A E Trott, taking 6 for 11 as South Africa were dismissed for 35 in the space of 114 balls.

J H HAMPSHIRE

Lord's 1969: became the first England player to score 100 at Lord's on his debut in Tests.

A HILL

Melbourne 1876-77: took the first wicket to fall in Test cricket when he bowled N Thompson, and held the first catch when he dismissed T P Horan.

YORKSHIRE'S TEST CRICKET RECORDS *(Continued)*

G H HIRST

The Oval: 1902: helped to score the last 15 runs in a match-winning tenth-wicket partnership with W Rhodes.

Birmingham 1909: shared all 20 Australian wickets with fellow left-arm spinner C Blythe (11 for 102).

M J HOGGARD

Bridgetown 2004: became the third Yorkshire player to take a hat-trick in Test cricket (see W Bates and D Gough). It was the 10th hat-trick for England and the third for England versus West Indies.

L HUTTON

Nottingham 1938: scored 100 in his first Test against Australia.

The Oval 1938: his score (364) and batting time (13 hours 17 minutes – the longest innings in English First-Class cricket) remain England records, and were world Test records until 1958. It remains the highest Test score at The Oval. His stand of 382 with M Leyland is the England second-wicket record in all Tests and the highest for any wicket against Australia. He also shared a record England v. Australia sixth-wicket stand of 216 with J Hardstaff Jr. – the first instance of a batsman sharing in two stands of 200 in the same Test innings. 770 runs were scored during his innings (Test record) which was England's 100th century against Australia, and contained 35 fours. England's total of 903 for 7 declared remains the Ashes Test record.

Lord's 1939: added 248 for the fourth wicket with D C S Compton in 140 minutes.

The Oval 1939: shared (then) world-record third-wicket stand of 264 with W R Hammond, which remains the record for England v. West Indies. Hutton's last eight Tests had brought him 1,109 runs.

The Oval 1948: last out in the first innings, he was on the field for all but the final 57 minutes of the match.

Johannesburg 1948-49: shared (then) world-record first-wicket stand of 359 in 310 minutes with C Washbrook on the opening day of Test cricket at Ellis Park; it remains England's highest opening stand in all Tests.

The Oval 1950: scored England's first 200 in a home Test v. West Indies, and remains alone in carrying his bat for England against them; his 202 not out (in 470 minutes) is the highest score by an England batsman achieving this feat.

Adelaide 1950-51: only England batsman to carry his bat throughout a complete Test innings twice, and second after R Abel (1891-92) to do so for any country against Australia.

Manchester 1951: scored 98 not out, just failing to become the first to score his 100th First Class hundred in a Test match.

The Oval 1951: became the only batsman to be out 'obstructing the field' in Test cricket.

1952: first professional to be appointed captain of England in the 20th Century.

The Oval 1953: first captain to win a rubber after losing the toss in all five Tests.

Kingston 1953-54: scored the first 200 by an England captain in a Test overseas.

R ILLINGWORTH

Manchester 1971: shared record England v. India eighth-wicket stand of 168 with P Lever.

YORKSHIRE'S TEST CRICKET RECORDS *(Continued)*

Hon. F S JACKSON

The Oval 1893: his 100 took 135 minutes, and was the first in a Test in England to be completed with a hit over the boundary (then worth only four runs).

The Oval 1899: his stand of 185 with T W Hayward was then England's highest for any wicket in England, and the record opening partnership by either side in England v. Australia Tests.

Nottingham 1905: dismissed M A Noble, C Hill and J Darling in one over (W01W0W).

Leeds 1905: batted 268 minutes for 144 not out – the first hundred in a Headingley Test.

Manchester 1905: first to score five Test hundreds in England.

The Oval 1905: first captain to win every toss in a five-match rubber.

M LEYLAND

Melbourne 1928-29: scored 137 in his first innings against Australia.

1934: first to score three hundreds in a rubber against Australia in England.

Brisbane 1936-37: scored England's only 100 at 'The Gabba' before 1974-75.

The Oval 1938: contributed 187 in 381 minutes to the record Test total of 903 for 7 declared, sharing in England's highest stand against Australia (all wickets) and record second-wicket stand in all Tests: 382 with L Hutton. First to score hundreds in his first and last innings against Australia.

G G MACAULAY

Cape Town 1922-23: fourth bowler (third for England) to take a wicket (G A L Hearne) with his first ball in Test cricket. Made the winning hit in the fourth of only six Tests to be decided by a one-wicket margin.

Leeds 1926: shared a match-saving ninth-wicket stand of 108 with G Geary.

C M OLD

Birmingham 1978: took 4 wickets in 5 balls in his 19th over (0WW no-ball WW1) to emulate the feat of M J C Allom.

R PEEL

Took his 50th wicket in his ninth Test and his 100th in his 20th Test – all against Australia.

W RHODES

Birmingham 1902: his first-innings analysis of 7 for 17 remains the record for all Tests at Edgbaston.

The Oval 1902: helped to score the last 15 runs in a match-winning tenth-wicket partnership with G H Hirst.

Sydney 1903-04: shared record England v. Australia tenth-wicket stand of 130 in 66 minutes with R E Foster.

Melbourne 1903-04: first to take 15 wickets in England v. Australia Tests; his match analysis of 15 for 124 remains the record for all Tests at Melbourne.

Melbourne 1911-12: shared record England v. Australia first-wicket stand of 323 in 268 minutes with J B Hobbs.

Johannesburg 1913-14: took his 100th wicket and completed the first 'double' for England (in 44

Sydney 1920-21: first to score 2,000 runs and take 100 wickets in Test cricket.

Adelaide 1920-21: third bowler to take 100 wickets against Australia.

YORKSHIRE'S TEST CRICKET RECORDS *(Continued)*

W RHODES *(Continued)*

The Oval 1926: set (then) record of 109 wickets against Australia.

Kingston 1929-30: ended the world's longest Test career (30 years 315 days) as the oldest Test cricketer (52 years 165 days).

J E ROOT

Chittagong, October 2016: with his score (40) in England's first innings he passed 1,000 runs in a calendar year. He also did this in 2015 (1,385) and became the first Yorkshire player to do this twice. His final tally (1,477) in 2016 left him four short of M P Vaughan's total in 2002

Visakhapatnam, November 2016: Played his 50th Test match, which was also his 100th first-class match

Lord's, July 2017 v. West Indies: His first innings (190) was the highest by an England captain in his first innings in this role.

Galle, January 2021 v. Sri Lanka. In the second Test match Root's first-innings score of 186 took him passed G Boycott's England Test runs total of 8,114, and by the end of that match Root's total runs for England stood at 8,249, leaving him in fourth place behind A N Cook (12,472), G A Gooch (8,900) and A J Stewart (8,463).

Chennai, February 2021 First Test Match v. India. Root with scores of 218 and 40 became the first player to score a double-hundred in their 100th Test Match. Eight others including two England players, M C Cowdrey (1968) and A J Stewart (2000) passed the century mark in their 100th Test Match. Root is now England's third all-time run-scorer.

Root scored a total of 1,708 Test runs in the calendar year 2021 to become the highest England player on this list. M P Vaughan with 1,481 runs in 2002 was the previous best. Only two other players have scored more runs in a calendar year, Mohammad Yousuf (Pakistan) with 1,788 runs and I V A Richards (West Indies) with 1,710.

The Ashes Test Match at Sydney in January 2022 saw Root become the player to captain England most times (60) passing A N Cook (59).

At the end of the fifth Ashes Test at Hobart he had scored 5,006 runs as captain, the first England captain to do this.

H SUTCLIFFE

Birmingham 1924: shared the first of 15 three-figure partnerships with J B Hobbs at the first attempt.

Lord's 1924: shared stand of 268 with J B Hobbs, which remains the first-wicket record for all Lord's Tests, and was then the England v. South Africa record.

Sydney 1924-25: his first opening stands against Australia with J B Hobbs realised 157 and 110.

Melbourne 1924-25 (Second Test): with J B Hobbs achieved the first instance of a batting partnership enduring throughout a full day's Test match play; they remain the only England pair to achieve this feat, and their stand of 283 in 289 minutes remains the longest for the first wicket in this series. Became the first to score 100 in each innings of a Test against Australia, and the first Englishman to score three successive hundreds in Test cricket.

Melbourne 1924-25 (Fourth Test): first to score four hundreds in one rubber of Test matches; it was his third 100 in successive Test innings at Melbourne. Completed 1,000 runs in fewest Test innings (12) – since equalled.

Sydney 1924-25: his aggregate of 734 was the record for any rubber until 1928-29.

YORKSHIRE'S TEST CRICKET RECORDS *(Continued)*

H SUTCLIFFE *(Continued)*

The Oval 1926: shared first-wicket stand of 172 with J B Hobbs on a rain-affected pitch.

The Oval 1929: first to score hundreds in each innings of a Test twice; only England batsman to score four hundreds in a rubber twice.

Sydney 1932-33: his highest England innings of 194 overtook J B Hobbs's world record of 15 Test hundreds.

F S TRUEMAN

Leeds 1952: reduced India to 0 for 4 in their second innings by taking 3 wickets in 8 balls on his debut.

Manchester 1952: achieved record England v. India innings analysis of 8 for 31.

The Oval 1952: set England v. India series record with 29 wickets.

Leeds 1961: took 5 for 0 with 24 off-cutters at a reduced pace v. Australia.

Lord's 1962: shared record England v. Pakistan ninth-wicket stand of 76 with T W Graveney.

Christchurch 1962-63: passed J B Statham's world Test record of 242 wickets; his analysis of 7-75 remains the record for Lancaster Park Tests and for England in New Zealand.

Birmingham 1963: returned record match analysis (12-119) against West Indies in England and for any Birmingham Test, ending with a 6-4 spell from 24 balls.

The Oval 1963: set England v. West Indies series record with 34 wickets.

The Oval 1964: first to take 300 wickets in Tests.

G ULYETT

Sydney 1881-82: with R G Barlow shared the first century opening partnership in Test cricket (122).

Melbourne 1881-82: his 149 was the first Test hundred for England in Australia, and the highest score for England on the first day of a Test in Australia until 1965-66.

M P VAUGHAN

Scored 1481 runs in 2002 – more than any other England player in a calendar year, surpassing the 1379 scored by D L Amiss in 1979. It was the fourth highest in a calendar year.

Scored 633 runs in the 2002-3 series versus Australia – surpassed for England in a five Test series versus Australia only by W R Hammond, who scored 905 runs in 1928-29, H Sutcliffe (734 in 1924-25), J B Hobbs (662 in 1911-12) and G Boycott (657 in 1970-71), when he played in five of the six Tests.

Scored six Test Match centuries in 2002 to equal the record set for England by D C S Compton in 1947.

Lord's 2004: scored a century in each innings (103 and 101*) versus West Indies and so became the third player (after G A Headley and G A Gooch) to score a century in each innings of a Test match at Lord's.

Lord's 2005: only the second player (J B Hobbs is the other) to have scored centuries in three consecutive Test match innings at Lord's. Scored the 100th century for England by a Yorkshire player.

YORKSHIRE'S TEST CRICKET RECORDS *(Continued)*

H VERITY

Lord's 1934: took 14 for 80 on the third day (six of them in the final hour) to secure England's first win against Australia at Lord's since 1896. It remains the most wickets to fall to one bowler in a day of Test cricket in England. His match analysis of 15 for 104 was then the England v. Australia record, and has been surpassed only by J C Laker.

W WATSON

Lord's 1953: scored 109 in 346 minutes in his first Test against Australia.

N W D YARDLEY

Melbourne 1946-47: dismissed D G Bradman for the third consecutive innings without assistance from the field. Became the first to score a fifty in each innings for England and take five wickets in the same match.

Nottingham 1947: shared record England v. South Africa fifth-wicket stand of 237 with D C S Compton.

* * *

Facts adapted by Bill Frindall from his *England Test Cricketers – The Complete Record from 1877* (Collins Willow, 1989). With later additions.

TEST MATCHES AT HEADINGLEY, LEEDS 1899-2021

1899 **Australia 172** (J Worrall 76) and **224** (H Trumble 56, J T Hearne hat-trick). **England 220** (A F A Lilley 55, H Trumble 5 for 60) and **19 for 0 wkt.**
Match drawn *Toss: Australia*

1905 **England 301** (Hon F S Jackson 144*) and **295 for 5 wkts dec** (J T Tyldesley 100, T W Hayward 60, W W Armstrong 5 for 122). **Australia 195** (W W Armstrong 66, A R Warren 5 for 57) and **224 for 7 wkts** (M A Noble 62).
Match drawn *Toss: England*

1907 **England 76** (G A Faulkner 6 for 17) and **162** (C B Fry 54). **South Africa 110** (C Blythe 8 for 59) and **75** (C Blythe 7 for 40).
England won by 53 runs *Toss: England*

1909 **Australia 188** (S F Barnes 6 for 63). **England 182** (J Sharp 61, J T Tyldesley 55, C G Macartney 7 for 58) and **87** (A Cotter 5 for 38).
Australia won by 126 runs *Toss: Australia*

1912 **England 242** (F E Woolley 57) and **238** (R H Spooner 82, J B Hobbs 55). **South Africa 147** (S F Barnes 6 for 52) and **159**.
England won by 174 runs *Toss: England*

1921 **Australia 407** (C G Macartney 115, W W Armstrong 77, C E Pellew 52, J M Taylor 50) and **273 for 7 wkts dec** (T J E Andrew 92). **England 259** (J W H T Douglas 75, Hon L H Tennyson 63, G Brown 57) and **202**.
Australia won by 219 runs *Toss: Australia*

1924 **England 396** (E H Hendren 132, H Sutcliffe 83) and **60 for 1 wkt**. **South Africa 132** (H W Taylor 59*, M W Tate 6 for 42) and **323** (H W Taylor 56, R H Catterall 56).
England won by 9 wickets *Toss: England*

1926 **Australia 494** (C G Macartney 151, W M Woodfull 141, A J Richardson 100). **England 294** (G G Macaulay 76, C V Grimmett 5 for 88) and **254 for 3 wkts** (H Sutcliffe 94, J B Hobbs 88).
Match drawn *Toss: England*

1929 **South Africa 236** (R H Catterall 74, C L Vincent 60, A P Freeman 7 for 115) and **275** (H G Owen-Smith 129). **England 328** (F E Woolley 83, W R Hammond 65, N A Quinn 6 for 92) and **186 for 5 wkts** (F E Woolley 95*).
England won by 5 wickets *Toss: South Africa*

1930 **Australia 566** (D G Bradman 334, A F Kippax 77, W M Woodfull 50, M W Tate 5 for 124). **England 391** (W R Hammond 113, C V Grimmett 5 for 135) and **95 for 3 wkts**.
Match drawn *Toss: Australia*

1934 **England 200** and **229 for 6 wkts**. **Australia 584** (D G Bradman 304, W H Ponsford 181, W E Bowes 6 for 142).
Match drawn *Toss: England*

1935 **England 216** (W R Hammond 63, A Mitchell 58) and **294 for 7 wkts dec** (W R Hammond 87*, A Mitchell 72, D Smith 57). **South Africa 171** (E A B Rowan 62) and **194 for 5 wkts** (B Mitchell 58).
Match drawn *Toss: England*

1938 **England 223** (W R Hammond 76, W J O'Reilly 5 for 66) and **123** (W J O'Reilly 5 for 56). **Australia 242** (D G Bradman 103, B A Barnett 57) and **107 for 5 wkts**.
Australia won by 5 wickets *Toss: England*

1947 **South Africa 175** (B Mitchell 53, A Nourse 51) and **184** (A D Nourse 57). **England 317 for 7 wkts dec** (L Hutton 100, C Washbrook 75) and **47 for 0 wkt**.
England won by 10 wickets *Toss: South Africa*

1948 **England 496** (C Washbrook 143, W J Edrich 111, L Hutton 81, A V Bedser 79) and **365 for 8 wkts dec** (D C S Compton 66, C Washbrook 65, L Hutton 57, W J Edrich 54). **Australia 458** (R N Harvey 112, S J E Loxton 93, R R Lindwall 77, K R Miller 58) and **404 for 3 wkts** (A R Morris 182, D G Bradman 173*).
Australia won by 7 wickets *Toss: England*

1949 **England 372** (D C S Compton 114, L Hutton 101, T B Burtt 5 for 97, J Cowie 5 for 127) and **267 for 4 wkts dec** (C Washbrook 103*, W J Edrich 70). **New Zealand 341** (F B Smith 96, M P Donnelly 64, T E Bailey 6 for 118) and **195 for 2 wkts** (B Sutcliffe 82, F Smith 54*).
Match drawn   Toss: England

1951 **South Africa 538** (E A B Rowan 236, P N F Mansell 90, C B. van Ryneveld 83, R A McLean 67) and **87 for 0 wkt** (E A B Rowan 60*). **England 505** (P B H May 138, L Hutton 100, T E Bailey 95, F A Lowson 58, A M B Rowan 5 for 174).
Match drawn   Toss: South Africa

1952 **India 293** (V L Manjrekar 133, V S Hazare 89) and 165 (D G Phadkar 64, V S Hazare 56). **England 334** (T W Graveney 71, T G Evans 66, Ghulam Ahmed 5 for 100) and **128 for 3 wkts** (R T Simpson 51).
England won by 7 wickets   Toss: India

1953 **England 167** (T W Graveney 55, R R Lindwall 5 for 54) and 275 (W J Edrich 64, D C S Compton 61). **Australia 266** (R N Harvey 71, G B Hole 53, A V Bedser 6 for 95) and **147 for 4 wkts**.
Match drawn   Toss: Australia

1955 **South Africa 171** and **500** (D J McGlew 133, W R Endean 116*, T L Goddard 74, H J Keith 73). **England 191** (D C S Compton 61) and **256** (P B H May 97, T L Goddard 5 for 69, H J Tayfield 5 for 94).
South Africa won by 224 runs   Toss: South Africa

1956 **England 325** (P B H May 101, C Washbrook 98). **Australia 143** (J C Laker 5 for 58) and **140** (R N Harvey 69, J C Laker 6 for 55).
England won by an innings and 42 runs   Toss: England

1957 **West Indies 142** (P J Loader 6 for 36, including hat-trick) and **132**. **England 279** (P B H May 69, M C Cowdrey 68, Rev D S Sheppard 68, F M M Worrell 7 for 70).
England won by an innings and 5 runs   Toss: West Indies

1958 **New Zealand 67** (J C Laker 5 for 17) and **129** (G A R Lock 7 for 51). **England 267 for 2 wkts dec** (P B H May 113*, C A Milton 104*).
England won by an innings and 71 runs   Toss: New Zealand

1959 **India 161** and **149**. **England 483 for 8 wkts dec** (M C Cowdrey 160, K F Barrington 80, W G A Parkhouse 78, G Pullar 75).
England won by an innings and 173 runs   Toss: India

1961 **Australia 237** (R N Harvey 73, C C McDonald 54, F S Trueman 5 for 58) and **120** (R N Harvey 53, F S Trueman 6 for 30); **England 299** (M C Cowdrey 93, G Pullar 53, A K Davidson 5 for 63) and **62 for 2 wkts**.
England won by 8 wickets   Toss: Australia

1962 **England 428** (P H Parfitt 119, M J Stewart 86, D A Allen 62, Munir Malik 5 for 128). **Pakistan 131** (Alimuddin 50) and **180** (Alimuddin 60, Saeed Ahmed 54).
England won by an innings and 117 runs   Toss: Pakistan

1963 **West Indies 397** (G St A Sobers 102, R B Kanhai 92, J S Solomon 62) and **229** (B F Butcher 78, G St.A Sobers 52). **England 174** (G A R Lock 53, C C Griffith 6 for 36) and **231** (J M Parks 57, D B Close 56).
West Indies won by 221 runs   Toss: West Indies

1964 **England 268** (J M Parks 68, E R Dexter 66, N J N Hawke 5 for 75) and **229** (K F Barrington 85). **Australia 389** (P J P Burge 160, W M Lawry 78) and **111 for 3 wkts** (I R Redpath 58*).
Australia won by 7 wickets   Toss: England

1965 **England 546 for 4 wkts dec** (J H Edrich 310*, K F Barrington 163). **New Zealand 193** (J R Reid 54) and **166** (V Pollard 53, F J Titmus 5 for 19).
England won by an innings and 187 runs   Toss: England

1966 **West Indies 500 for 9 wkts dec** (G St A Sobers 174, S M Nurse 137). **England 240** (B L D'Oliveira 88, G St A Sobers 5 for 41) and **205** (R W Barber 55, L R Gibbs 6 for 39).
West Indies won by an innings and 55 runs   Toss: West Indies

1967 **England 550 for 4 wkts dec** (G Boycott 246*, B L D'Oliveira 109, K F Barrington 93, T W Graveney 59) and **126 for 4 wkts. India 164** (Nawab of Pataudi jnr 64) and **510** (Nawab of Pataudi jnr 148, A L Wadekar 91, F M Engineer 87, Hanumant Singh 73).
England won by 6 wickets Toss: England

1968 **Australia 315** (I R Redpath 92, I M Chappell 65) and **312** (I M Chappell 81, K D Walters 56, R Illingworth 6 for 87). **England 302** (R M Prideaux 64, J H Edrich 62, A N Connolly 5 for 72) and **230 for 4 wkts** (J H Edrich 65).
Match drawn Toss: Australia

1969 **England 223** (J H Edrich 79) and **240** (G.St A Sobers 5 for 42). **West Indies 161** and **272** (B F Butcher 91, G S Camacho 71).
England won by 30 runs Toss: England

1971 **England 316** (G Boycott 112, B L D'Oliveira 74) and **264** (B L D'Oliveira 72, D L Amiss 56) **Pakistan 350** (Zaheer Abbas 72, Wasim Bari 63, Mushtaq Mohammad 57) and **205** (Sadiq Mohammad 91).
England won by 25 runs Toss: England

1972 **Australia 146** (K R Stackpole 52) and **136** (D L Underwood 6 for 45). **England 263** (R Illingworth 57, A A Mallett 5 for 114) and **21 for 1 wkt.**
England won by 9 wickets Toss: Australia

1973 **New Zealand 276** (M G Burgess 87, V Pollard 62) and **142** (G M Turner 81, G G Arnold 5 for 27). **England 419** (G Boycott 115, K W R Fletcher 81, R Illingworth 65, RO Collinge 5 for 74).
England won by an innings and 1 run Toss: New Zealand

1974 **Pakistan 285** (Majid Khan 75, Safraz Nawaz 53) and **179. England 183** and **238 for 6 wkts** (J H Edrich 70, K W R Fletcher 67*).
Match drawn Toss: Pakistan

1975 **England 288** (D S Steele 73, J H Edrich 62, A W Greig 51, G J Gilmour 6 for 85) and **291** (D Steele 92). **Australia 135** (P H Edmonds 5 for 28) and **220 for 3 wkts** (R B McCosker 95*, I M Chappell 62).
Match drawn Toss: England

1976 **West Indies 450** (C G Greenidge 115, R C Fredericks 109, I V A Richards 66, L G Rowe 50) and **196** (C L King 58, R G D Willis 5 for 42). **England 387** (A W Greig 116, A P E Knott 116) and **204** (A W Greig 76*).
West Indies won by 55 runs Toss: West Indies

1977 **England 436** (G Boycott 191, A P E Knott 57). **Australia 103** (I T Botham 5 for 21) and **248** (R W Marsh 63).
England won by an innings and 85 runs Toss: England

1978 **Pakistan 201** (Sadiq Mohammad 97). **England 119 for 7 wkts** (Safraz Nawaz 5 for 39).
Match drawn Toss: Pakistan

1979 **England 270** (I T Botham 137). **India 223 for 6 wkts** (S M Gavaskar 78, D B Vengsarkar 65*).
Match drawn Toss: England

1980 **England 143** and **227 for 6 wkts dec** (G A Gooch 55). **West Indies 245.**
Match drawn Toss: West Indies

1981 **Australia 401 for 9 wkts dec** (J Dyson 102, K J Hughes 89, G N Yallop 58, I T Botham 6 for 95) and **111** (R G D Willis 8 for 43). **England 174** (I T Botham 50) and **356** (I T Botham 149*, G R Dilley 56, T M Alderman 6 for 135).
England won by 18 runs Toss: Australia

1982 **Pakistan 275** (Imran Khan 67*, Mudassar Nazar 65, Javed Miandad 54) and **199** (Javed Miandad 52, I T Botham 5 for 74). **England 256** (D I Gower 74, I T Botham 57, Imran Khan 5 for 49) and **219 for 7 wkts** (G Fowler 86).
England won by 3 wickets Toss: Pakistan

1983 **England 225** (C J Tavaré 69, A J Lamb 58, B L Cairns 7 for 74) and **252** (D I Gower 112*, E J Chatfield 5 for 95). **New Zealand 377** (J G Wright 93, B A Edgar 84, R J Hadlee 75) and **103 for 5 wkts** (R G D Willis 5 for 35).
New Zealand won by 5 wickets Toss: New Zealand

1984 **England 270** (A J Lamb 100) and **159** (G Fowler 50, M D Marshall 7 for 53). **West Indies 302** (H A Gomes 104*, M A Holding 59, P J W Allott 6 for 61) and **131 for 2 wkts**.
West Indies won by 8 wickets   Toss: England

1985 **Australia 331** (A M J Hilditch 119) and **324** (W B Phillips 91, A M J Hilditch 80, K C Wessels 64, J E Emburey 5 for 82). **England 533** (R T Robinson 175, I T Botham 60, P R Downton 54, M W Gatting 53) and **123 for 5 wkts**.
England won by 5 wickets   Toss: Australia

1986 **India 272** (D B Vengsarkar 61) and **237** (D B Vengsarkar 102*). **England 102** (R M H Binny 5 for 40) and **128**.
India won by 279 runs   Toss: India

1987 **England 136** (D J Capel 53) and **199** (D I Gower 55, Imran Khan 7 for 40). **Pakistan 353** (Salim Malik 99, Ijaz Ahmed 50, N A Foster 8 for 107).
Pakistan won by an innings and 18 runs   Toss: England

1988 **England 201** (A J Lamb 64*) and **138** (G A Gooch 50). **West Indies 275** (R A Harper 56, D L Haynes 54, D R Pringle 5 for 95) and **67 for 0 wkt**.
West Indies won by 10 wickets   Toss: West Indies

1989 **Australia 601 for 7 wkts dec** (S R Waugh 177*, M A Taylor 136, D M Jones 79, M G Hughes 71, A R Border 66) and **230 for 3 wkts dec** (M A Taylor 60, A R Border 60*). **England 430** (K J Barnett 80, R A Smith 66, T M Alderman 5 for 107) and **191**. (G A Gooch 68, T M Alderman 5 for 44).
Australia won by 210 runs   Toss: England

1991 **England 198** (R A Smith 54) and **252** (G A Gooch 154*, C E L Ambrose 6 for 52). **West Indies 173** (I V A Richards 73) and **162** (R B Richardson 68).
England won by 115 runs   Toss: West Indies

1992 **Pakistan 197** (Salim Malik 82*) and **221** (Salim Malik 84*, Ramiz Raja 63, N A Mallinder 5 for 50). **England 320** (G A Gooch 135, M A Atherton 76, Waqar Younis 5 for 117) and **99 for 4 wkts**.
England won by 6 wickets   Toss: Pakistan

1993 **Australia 653 for 4 wkts dec** (A R Border 200*, S R Waugh 157*, D C Boon 107, M J Slater 67, M E Waugh 52). **England 200** (G A Gooch 59, M A Atherton 55, P R Reiffel 5 for 65) and **305** (A J Stewart 78, M A Atherton 63).
Australia won by an innings and 148 runs   Toss: Australia

1994 **England 477 for 9 wkts dec** (M A Atherton 99, A J Stewart 89, G P Thorpe 72, S J Rhodes 65*) and **267 for 5 wkts dec** (G A Hick 110, G P Thorpe 73). **South Africa 447** (P N Kirsten 104, B M McMillan 78, C R Matthews 62*) and **116 for 3 wkts** (G Kirsten 65).
Match drawn   Toss: England

1995 **England 199** (M A Atherton 81, I R Bishop 5 for 32) and **208** (G P Thorpe 61). **West Indies 282** (S L Campbell 69, J C Adams 58, B C Lara 53) and **129 for 1 wkt** (C L Hooper 73*).
West Indies won by 9 wickets   Toss: West Indies

1996 **Pakistan 448** (Ijaz Ahmed 141, Mohin Khan 105, Salim Malik 55, Asif Mujtaba 51, D G Cork 5 for 113) and **242 for 7 wkts dec** (Inzamam-ul-Haq 65, Ijaz Ahmed sen 52) **England 501** (A J Stewart 170, N V Knight 113, J P Crawley 53).
Match drawn   Toss: England

1997 **England 172** (J N Gillespie 7 for 37) and **268** (N Hussain 105, J P Crawley 72, P R Reiffel 5 for 49). **Australia 501 for 9 wkts dec** (M T G Elliott 199, R T Ponting 127, P R Reiffel 54*, D Gough 5 for 149).
Australia won by an innings and 61 runs   Toss: Australia

1998 **England 230** (M A Butcher 116) and **240** (N Hussain 94, S M Pollock 5 for 53, A A Donald 5 for 71). **South Africa 252** (W J. Cronje 57, A R C Fraser 5 for 42) and **195** (J N Rhodes 85, B M McMillan 54, D Gough 6 for 42).
England won by 23 runs   Toss: South Africa

2000 **West Indies 172** (R R Sarwan 59*, C White 5 for 57) and **61** (A R Caddick 5 for 14). **England 272** (M P Vaughan 76, G A Hick 59).
England won by an innings and 39 runs   Toss: West Indies

2001 **Australia 447** (R T Ponting 144, D R Martyn 118, M E Waugh 72, D Gough 5 for 103) and **176 for 4 wkts dec** (R T Ponting 72). **England 309** (A J Stewart 76*, G D McGrath 7 for 76) and **315 for 4 wkts** (M A Butcher 173*, N Hussain 55).
England won by 6 wickets   Toss: Australia

2002 **India 628 for 8 wkts dec** (S R Tendulkar 193, R S Dravid 148, S C Ganguly 128, S B Bangar 68). **England 273** (A J Stewart 78*, M P Vaughan 61) and **309** (N Hussain 110.)
India won by an innings and 46 runs   Toss: India

2003 **South Africa 342** (G Kirsten 130, M Zondeki 59, J A Rudolph 55) and **365** (A J Hall 99*, G Kirsten 60). **England 307** (M A Butcher 77, M E Trescothick 59, A Flintoff 55) and **209** (M A Butcher 61, A Flintoff 50, J H Kallis 6 for 54.)
South Africa won by 191 runs   Toss: South Africa

2004 **New Zealand 409** (S P Fleming 97, M H W Papps 86, B B McCullum 54) and **161**. **England 526** (M E Trescothick 132, G O Jones 100, A Flintoff 94, A J Strauss 62) and **45 for 1 wkt**
England won by 9 wickets   Toss: England

2006 **England 515** (K P Pietersen 135, I R Bell 119, Umar Gul 5 for 123) and **345** (A J Strauss 116, M E Trescothick 58, C M W Reid 55). **Pakistan 538** (Mohammad Yousuf 192, Younis Khan 173) and **155**.
England won by 167 runs   Toss: Pakistan

2007 **England 570 for 7 wkts dec** (K P Pietersen 226, M P Vaughan 103, M J Prior 75). **West Indies 146** and **141** (D J Bravo 52).
England won by an innings and 283 runs   Toss: England

2008 **England 203** and **327** (S C J Broad 67*, A N Cook 60). **South Africa 522** (A B de Villiers 174, A G Prince 149) and **9 for 0 wkt**.
South Africa won by 10 wickets   Toss: South Africa

2009 **England 102** (P M Siddle 5 for 21) and **263** (G P Swann 62, S C J Broad 61, M G Johnson 5 for 69). **Australia 445** (M J North 110, M J Clarke 93, R T Ponting 78, S R Watson 51, S C J Broad 6 for 91).
Australia won by an innings and 80 runs   Toss: England

2010 **Australia 88** and **349** (R T Ponting 66, M J Clarke 77, S P D Smith 77). **Pakistan 258** (S R Watson 6-33) and **180-7** (Imran Farhat 67, Azhar Ali 51).
Pakistan won by 3 wickets   Toss: Australia
(This was a Home Test Match for Pakistan)

2012 **South Africa 419** (A N Petersen 182, G C Smith 52) and **258-9 dec** (J A Rudolph 69, GC Smith 52, S C J Broad 5-69). **England 425** (K P Pietersen 149, M J Prior 68) and **130-4**.
Match drawn   Toss: England

2013 **England 354** (J E Root 104, J M Bairstow 64, T A Boult 5-57) and **287-5 dec** (A N Cook 130, I J L Trott 76). **New Zealand 174** and **220** (L R P L Taylor 70, G P Swann 6-90)
England won by 247 runs   Toss: England

2014 **Sri Lanka 257** (K C Sangakkara 79, L E Plunkett 5-64) and **457** (K C Sangakkara 55, DPMD Jayawardene 79, A D Mathews 160). **England 365** (S D Robson 127, G S Ballance 74, I R Bell 64) and **249** (M M Ali 108*, K T G D Prasad 5-50).
Sri Lanka won by 100 runs   Toss: England

2015 **New Zealand 350** (T W M Latham 84, L Ronchi 88, S C J Broad 5-109) and **454-8 dec** (M J Guptill 70, B B McCullum 55, B J Watling 120, M D Craig 58*). **England 350** (A Lyth 107, A N Cook 75) and **255** (A N Cook 56, J C Buttler 73)
New Zealand won by 199 runs   Toss: England

2016 **England 298** (A D Hales 86, J M Bairstow 140). **Sri Lanka 91** (J M Anderson 5-16) and **119** (B K G Mendis 53, J N Anderson 5-29)
England won by an innings and 88 runs   Toss: Sri Lanka

2017 **England 258** (J E Root 58, B A Stokes100) and **490-8 dec** (M D Stoneman 52, J E Root 72, D J Malan 61, B A Stokes 58, M M Ali 84, C R Woakes 61*). **West Indies** 427 (K C Brathwaite 134, S D Hope 147, J M Anderson 5-76) and 322-5 (K C Brathwaite 95, S D Hope 118*).
West Indies won by 5 wickets   Toss: England

2018 **Pakistan** 174 (Shadab Khan 56) and **134**. **England** 363 (J C Buttler 80*)
England won by an innings and 55 runs　　　　　　　　　　　　　　　Toss: Pakistan
2019 **Australia** 179 (M Labuschagne 74, J C Archer 6-45) and **246** (M Labuschagne 80). **England** 67 (J R Hazlewood 5-65) and **362-9** (J E Root 77, J L Denly 50, B A Stokes 135*)
England won by 1 wicket　　　　　　　　　　　　　　　　　　　　Toss: England
2019 **Australia** 179 (M Labuschagne 74, J C Archer 6-45) and **246** (M Labuschagne 80).
2021 **India** 78 and **278** (R G Sharma 59, C A Pujara 91, V Kohli 55, O E Robinson 5-65). **England** 432 (R J Burns 61, H Hameed 68, D J Malan 70, J E Root 121)
England won by an innings and 76 runs　　　　　　　　　　　　　　　Toss: India

SUMMARY OF RESULTS

ENGLAND	First played	Last played	Played	Won	Lost	Drawn
v. Australia	1899	2019	25	8	9	8
v. India	1952	2021	7	4	2	1
v. New Zealand	1949	2015	8	5	2	1
v. Pakistan	1962	2018	10	6	1	3
v. South Africa	1907	2012	13	6	3	4
v. Sri Lanka	2014	2016	2	1	1	0
v. West Indies	1957	2017	13	5	7	1
Totals	1899	2021	78	35	25	18

SIX HIGHEST AGGREGATES

Runs	Wkts	
1723	31	in 1948 (England 496 and 365 for 8 wkts dec; Australia 458 and 404 for 3 wkts)
1553	40	in 2006 (England 515 and 345; Pakistan 538 and 155)
1497	33	in 2017 (England 258 and 490-8 dec; West Indies 427 and 322-5)
1452	30	in 1989 (Australia 601 for 7 wkts dec and 230 for 3 wkts dec; England 430 and 191)
1409	40	in 2015 (New Zealand 350 and 454 for 8 wkts dec; England 350 and 255)
1350	28	in 1967 (England 550 for 4 wkts dec and 126 for 4 wkts; India 164 and 510)

Note: The highest aggregate prior to the Second World War

| 1141 | 37 | in 1921 (Australia 407 and 272 for 7 wkts dec; England 259 and 202) |

SIX LOWEST AGGREGATES

Runs	Wkts	
423	40	in 1907 (England 76 and 162; South Africa 110 and 75)
463	22	in 1958 (New Zealand 67 and 129; England 267 for 2 wkts)
505	30	in 2000 (West Indies 172 and 61; England 272)
508	30	in 2016 (England 298; Sri Lanka 91 and 119)
553	30	in 1957 (West Indies 142 and 132; England 279)
566	31	in 1972 (Australia 146 and 136; England 263 and 21 for 1 wkt)

SIX HIGHEST TOTALS

653 for 4 wkts dec	Australia	v. England, 1993
608 for 8 wkts dec	India	v. England, 2002
601 for 7 wkts dec	Australia	v. England, 1989
584	Australia	v. England, 1934
570 for 7 wkts dec	England	v. West Indies, 2007
566	Australia	v. England, 1930

SIX LOWEST TOTALS

61	West Indies	v. England, 2000
67	New Zealand	v. England, 1958
67	England	v. Australia, 2019
75	South Africa	v. England, 1907
76	England	v. South Africa, 1907
78	India	v. England, 2021

SIX HIGHEST INDIVIDUAL SCORES
For England

310*	J H Edrich versus New Zealand, 1965
246*	G Boycott versus India, 1967
226	K P Pietersen versus West Indies, 2007
191	G Boycott versus Australia, 1977
175	R T Robinson versus Australia, 1985
173*	M A Butcher versus Australia, 2001

For Australia

334	D G Bradman, 1930
304	D G Bradman, 1934
200*	A R Border, 1993
199	M T G Elliott, 1997
182	A R Morris, 1948
181	W H Ponsford, 1934

For Pakistan

192	Mohammad Yousuf, 2006
173	Younis Khan, 2006
141	Ijaz Ahmed, 1996
105	Moin Khan, 1996
99	Salim Malik, 1987
97	Sadiq Mohammad, 1978

For India

193	S R Tendulkar, 2002
148	Nawab of Pataudi jnr, 1967
148	R S Dravid, 2002
133	V L Manjrekar, 1952
128	S C Ganguly, 2002
102*	D B Vengsarkar, 1986

For South Africa

236	E A B Rowan, 1951
182	A N Petersen, 2012
174	A B de Villiers, 2008
149	A G Prince, 2008
133	D J McGlew, 1955
130	G Kirsten, 2003

For New Zealand

120	B J Watling , 2015
97	S P Fleming, 2004
96	F B Smith, 1949
93	J G Wright, 1983
88	L Ronchi, 2015
87	M G Burgess, 1973

For Sri Lanka

160*	A D Mathews, 2014
79	K C Sangakkara, 2014
55	K C Sangakkara, 2014
53*	B K G Mendis, 2016
48	H M R K B Herath, 2014
45	L D Chandimal, 2014
45	F D M Karunaratne, 2014

For West Indies

174	G St.A Sobers, 1966
147	S D Hope, 2017 (1st innings)
137	S M Nurse, 1966
134	K C Brathwaite, 2017
118*	S D Hope, 2017 (2nd innings)
115	C G Greenidge, 1976

S D Hope was the first player to score centuries in both innings of a First Class match at Headingley

HUNDRED BEFORE LUNCH

First day
112*	C G Macartney for Australia, 1926
105*	D G Bradman for Australia, 1930

Third day
102	(from 27* to 129) H G Owen-Smith for South Africa, 1929

CARRYING BAT THROUGH A COMPLETED INNINGS

154* out of 252 G A Gooch, England v. West Indies, 1991

MOST CENTURIES IN AN INNINGS

3	1926	C G Macartney (151), W M Woodfull (141) and A J Richardson for Australia
3	1993	A R Border (200*), S R Waugh (157*) and D C Boon (107) for Australia
3	2002	S R Tendulkar (193), R S Dravid (148) and S C Ganguly (128) for India

MOST CENTURIES IN A MATCH

5	1948	C Washbrook (143) and W J Edrich (111) for England; R N Harvey (112), A R Morris (182) and D G Bradman (173*) for Australia
5	2006	K P Pietersen (135), I R Bell (119) and A J Strauss (116) for England: Younis Khan (173) and Mohammad Yousuf (192) for Pakistan
4	1976	C G Greenidge (115) and R C Fredericks (109) for West Indies; A W Greig (116) and A P E Knott (116) for England
4	1996	Ijaz Ahmed (141) and Moin Khan (105) for Pakistan; A J Stewart (170) and N V Knight (113) for England
4	2002	S R Tendulkar (193), R S Dravid (148) and S C Ganguly (128) for India; N Hussain (110) for England
4	2017	B A Stokes (100) for England; K C Brathwaite (134), S D Hope (147 and 118*) for West Indies

CENTURY PARTNERSHIPS

For England
(six highest)
For the 1st wicket

177	A Lyth (107) and A N Cook (75) v. New Zealand, 2015
168	L Hutton (81) and C Washbrook (143) v. Australia, 1948 (1st inns)
168	G A Gooch (135) and M A Atherton (76) v. Pakistan, 1992
158	M E Trescothick (58) and A J Strauss (116) v. Pakistan, 2006
156	J B Hobbs (88) and H Sutcliffe (94) v. Australia, 1926
153	M E Trescothick (132) and A J Strauss (62) v. New Zealand, 2004

For all other wickets

369	(2nd wkt) J H Edrich (310*) and K F Barrington (163) v. New Zealand, 1965
252	(4th wkt) G Boycott (246*) and B L D'Oliveira (109) v. India, 1967
194*	(3rd wkt) C A Milton (104*) and P B H May (113*) v. New Zealand, 1958
193	(4th wkt) M C Cowdrey (160) and K F Barrington (80) v. India, 1959
187	(4th wkt) P B H May (101) and C Washbrook (98) v. Australia, 1956
181	(3rd wkt) M A Butcher (173*) and N Hussain (55) v. Australia, 2001

For Australia
(six highest)
For the 1st wkt – none

For all other wickets

388	(4th wkt) W H Ponsford (181) and D G Bradman (304), 1934
332*	(5th wkt) A R Border (200*) and S R Waugh (157*), 1993
301	(2nd wkt) A R Morris (182) and D G Bradman (173*), 1948
268	(5th wkt) M T G Elliott (199) and R T Ponting (127), 1997
235	(2nd wkt) W M Woodfull (141) and C G Macartney (151), 1926
229	(3rd wkt) D G Bradman (334) and A F Kippax (77), 1930

For other countries in total
India

249	(4th wkt) S R Tendulkar (193) and S C Ganguly (128), 2002
222	(4th wkt) V S Hazare (89) and V L Manjrekar (133), 1952
170	(2nd wkt) S B Bangar (68) and R S Dravid (148), 2002
168	(2nd wkt) F M Engineer (87) and A L Wadekar (91), 1967
150	(3rd wkt) R S Dravid (148) and S R Tendulkar (193), 2002
134	(5th wkt) Hanumant Singh (73) and Nawab of Pataudi jnr (148), 1967
105	(6th wkt) V S Hazare (56) and D G Phadkar (64), 1952

CENTURY PARTNERSHIPS *(Continued)*

New Zealand

169	(2nd wkt) M H W Papps (86) and S P Fleming (97), 2004	
121	(5th wkt) B B McCullum (55) and B J Watling (120), 2015	
120	(5th wkt) M P Donnelly (64) and F B Smith (96), 1949	
120	(6th wkt) T W M Latham (84) and L Ronchi (88), 2015	
116	(2nd wkt) J G Wright (93) and M D Crowe (37), 1983	
112	(1st wkt) B Sutcliffe (82) and V J Scott (43), 1949	
106	(5th wkt) M G Burgess (87) and V Pollard (62), 1973	

Pakistan

363	(3rd wkt) Younis Khan (173) and Mohammad Yousuf (192), 2006
130	(4th wkt) Ijaz Ahmed (141) and Salim Malik (55), 1996
129	(3rd wkt) Zaheer Abbas (72) and Mushtaq Mohammed (57), 1971
112	(7th wkt) Asif Mujtaba (51) and Moin Khan (105), 1996
110	(2nd wkt) Imran Farhat (67) and Azhar Ali (51), 2010 v. Australia
100	(3rd wkt) Mudassar Nazar (65) and Javed Miandad (54), 1982
100	(4th wkt) Majid Khan (75) and Zaheer Abbas (48), 1974

South Africa

212	(5th wkt)	A G Prince (149)	and A B de Villiers (174)	2008
198	(2nd wkt)	E A B Rowan (236)	and C B van Ryneveld (83)	1951
176	(1st wkt)	D J McGlew (133)	and T L Goddard (74)	1955
150	(8th wkt)	G Kirsten (130)	and M Zondeki (59)	2003
120	(1st wkt)	A N Petersen (182)	and G C Smith (52)	2012
120	(1st wkt)	J A Rudolph (69)	and G C Smith (52)	2012
117	(6th wkt)	J N Rhodes (85)	and B M McMillan (54)	1998
115	(7th wkt)	P N Kirsten (104)	and B M McMillan (78)	1994
108	(5th wkt)	E A B Rowan (236)	and R A McLean (67)	1951
103	(10th wkt)	H G Owen-Smith (129)	and A J Bell (26*)	1929

Sri Lanka

149	(8th wkt)	A D Mathews (160)	and H M R K B Herath (48)	2014

West Indies

265	(5th wkt)	S M Nurse (137)	and G St A Sobers (174)	1966
246	(4th wkt)	K C Brathwaite (134)	and S D Hope (147)	2017
192	(1st wkt)	R C Fredericks (109)	and C G Greenidge (115)	1976
144	(3rd wkt)	K C Brathwaite (95)	and S D Hope (118*)	2017
143	(4th wkt)	R B Kanhai (92)	and G St A Sobers (102)	1963
118*	(4th wkt)	C L Hooper (73*)	and B C Lara (48*)	1995
108	(3rd wkt)	G S Camacho (71)	and B F Butcher (91)	1969
106	(1st wkt)	C G Greenidge (49)	and D L Haynes (43)	1984

6 BEST INNINGS ANALYSES

For England

8-43	R G D Willis	v. Australia	1981
8-59	C Blythe	v. South Africa	1907 (1st inns)
8-107	N A Foster	v. Pakistan	1987
7-40	C Blythe	v. South Africa	1907 (2nd inns)
7-51	G A R Lock	v. New Zealand	1958
7-115	A P Freeman	v. South Africa	1929

For Australia

7-37	J N Gillespie	1997	
7-58	C G Macartney	1909	
7-76	G D McGrath	2001	
6-33	S R Watson	2010	v. Pakistan
6-85	G J Gilmour	1975	
6-135	T M Alderman	1981	

5 WICKETS IN AN INNINGS

For India (2)
5-40	R M H Binny	1986
5-100	Ghulam Ahmed	1952

For New Zealand (6)
7-74	B L Cairns	1983
5-57	T A Boult	2013
5-74	R O Collinge	1973
5-95	E J Chatfield	1983
5-97	T B Burtt	1949
5-127	J Cowie	1949

For Pakistan (6)
7-40	Imran Khan	1987
5-39	Sarfraz Nawaz	1978
5-49	Imran Khan	1982
5-117	Waqar Younis	1992
5-123	Umar Gul	2006
5-128	Munir Malik	1962

For South Africa (8)
6-17	G A Faulkner	1907
6-92	N A Quinn	1929
6-54	J H Kallis	2003
5-53	S M Pollock	1998
5-69	T L Goddard	1955
5-71	A A Donald	1998
5-94	H J Tayfield	1955
5-174	A M B Rowan	1951

For Sri Lanka
5-50	K T G D Prasad	2014

For West Indies (8)
7-53	M D Marshall	1984
7-70	F M Worrell	1957
6-36	C C Griffith	1963
6-39	L R Gibbs	1996
6-52	C E L Ambrose	1991
5-32	I R Bishop	1995
5-41	G.St.A Sobers	1966
5-42	G.St A Sobers	1969

10 WICKETS IN A MATCH

For England (8)
15-99	(8-59 and 7-40)	C Blythe	v. South Africa	1907
11-65	(4-14 and 7-51)	G A R Lock	v. New Zeland	1958
11-88	(5-58 and 6-30)	F S Trueman	v. Australia	1961
11-113	(5-58 and 6-55)	J C Laker	v. Australia	1956
10-45	(5-16 and 5-29)	J M Anderson	v. Sri Lanka	2016
10-82	(4-37 and 6-45)	D L Underwood	v. Australia	1972
10-115	(6-52 and 4-63)	S F Barnes	v. South Africa	1912
10-132	(4-42 and 6-90)	G P Swann	v. New Zealand	2013
10-207	(7-115 and 3-92)	A P Freeman	v. South Africa	1929

For Australia (3)
11-85	(7-58 and 4-27)	C G Macartney	1909
10-122	(5-66 and 5-56)	W J O'Reilly	1938
10-151	(5-107 and 5-44)	T M Alderman	1989

For New Zealand (1)
10-144	(7-74 and 3-70)	B L Cairns	1983

For Pakistan (1)
10-77	(3-37 and 7-40)	Imran Khan	1987

Note: Best bowling in a match for:

India	7-58	(5-40 and 2-18)	R M H Binny	1986
Sri Lanka	6-125	(1-75 and 5-50)	K T G D Prasad	2014
South Africa	9-75	(6-17 and 3-58)	G A Faulkner	1907
West Indies	9-81	(6 -36 and 3-45)	C C Griffith	1963

HAT-TRICKS

J T Hearne	v. Australia	1899
P J Loader	v. West Indies	1957
S C J Broad	v. Sri Lanka	2014

TEST MATCH AT BRAMALL LANE, SHEFFIELD 1902

1902 **Australia 194** (S F Barnes 6 for 49) and **289** (C Hill 119, V T Trumper 62, W Rhodes 5 for 63) **England 145** (J V Saunders 5 for 50, M A Noble 5 for 51) and **195** (A C MacLaren 63, G L Jessop 55, M A Noble 6 for 52).
Australia won by 143 runs   Toss: Australia

LIST OF PLAYERS AND CAREER AVERAGES IN ALL FIRST-CLASS MATCHES FOR YORKSHIRE 1863-2021

Based on research by John T Potter, Paul E Dyson, Mick Pope and the late Roy D Wilkinson and Anthony Woodhouse

Career records date from the foundation of Yorkshire County Cricket Club in 1863. The Club welcome any help in keeping this list up to date. The compilers do not believe that we should alter the status of matches from that determined when they were played. These averages include the match versus Gentlemen of Scotland in 1878, and exclude those versus Liverpool and District in 1889, 1891, 1892 and 1893 in line with what appear to have been the decisions of the Club.

* Played as an amateur   © Awarded County Cap   § Born outside Yorkshire

Player	Date of Birth	Date of Death (if known)	First Played	Last Played	M	Inns	NO	Runs	HS	Av'ge	100s	Runs	Wkts	Av'ge	Ct/St
Ackroyd, A *	Aug. 29, 1858	Oct. 3, 1927	1879	1879	1	1	0	2	2*	—	0	7	0	—	0
Allen, S *	Dec 20, 1893	Oct 9, 1978	1924	1924	1	2	0	8	6	4.00	0	116	2	58.00	0
Allen, W R	Apr14, 1893	Oct 14, 1950	1921	1925	30	32	10	475	95*	21.59	—	—	—	—	45/21
Ambler, F	Feb 12, 1860	Feb 10 1886	1886	1886	4	7	0	68	25	9.71	—	22	0	—	2
Anderson, G	Jan 20, 1826	Nov 27, 1902	1863	1869	19	31	0	520	99*	20.80	0	—	—	—	19
Anderson, P N	Apr. 28, 1966		1988	1988	1	1	1	0	0*	0.00	0	47	1	47.00	1
Anson, C E *	Oct 14, 1889	Mar 26, 1969	1924	1924	1	2	0	27	14	13.50	0	—	—	—	1
Appleton, C *	May15, 1844	Feb 26, 1925	1865	1865	3	6	1	56	18	11.20	0	0	0	—	0
Appleyard, R	©June 27, 1924	Mar 17, 2015	1950	1958	133	122	43	679	63	8.59	0	9,903	642	15.42	70
Armitage, C1 *	Apr. 28, 1849	Apr 24, 1917	1873	1878	3	5	0	26	12	5.20	0	29	0	—	0
Armitage, T	Apr. 25, 1848	Sept 21, 1922	1872	1878	52	85	6	1,053	95	13.67	0	1,614	107	15.08	20
Ash, D L	Feb 18, 1944		1965	1965	3	3	0	22	12	7.33	—	22	0	—	1
Ashman, J R	May 20, 1926	Mar 4, 2019	1951	1951	1	1	—	—	—	—	—	116	4	29.00	0
Ashraf, Moin A	Jan 5, 1992		2010	2013	21	19	5	56	10*	4.00	0	1,268	43	29.48	2
Aspinall, R	©Oct 26, 1918	Aug 16, 1999	1946	1950	36	48	8	763	75*	19.07	0	2,670	131	20.38	18
Aspinall, W	Mar 24, 1858	Jan 27, 1910	1880	1880	2	3	0	16	14	5.33	0	—	—	—	1
Asquith, F T	Feb 5, 1870	Jan 11, 1916	1903	1903	1	2	0	0	0	0.00	0	—	—	—	2
Athey, C W J	©Sept 27, 1957		1976	1983	151	246	16	6,320	134	28.08	10	1,003	21	47.76	144/2
Atkinson, G R	Sept 21, 1830	May 3, 1906	1863	1870	27	38	8	399	44	13.30	—	1,146	54	21.22	14
Atkinson, H T	Feb 1, 1881	Dec 23, 1959	1907	1907	1	2	0	0	0	0.00	0	17	—	—	0
§ Azeem Rafiq	©Feb 27, 1991		2009	2017	35	41	4	814	100	22.00	1	2,511	63	39.85	14
Backhouse, E N	May 13, 1901	Nov 1, 1936	1931	1931	1	2	0	4	2	2.00	0	—	—	—	0
Badger, H D *	Mar 7, 1900	Aug 10, 1975	1921	1922	1	4	2	6	6*	3.00	0	145	6	24.16	1
Bainbridge, A B	Oct 15, 1932		1961	1963	5	10	0	93	24	9.30	0	358	20	17.90	3

336

LIST OF PLAYERS AND CAREER AVERAGES IN ALL FIRST-CLASS MATCHES FOR YORKSHIRE (Continued)

Player	Date of Birth	Date of Death (if known)	First Played	Last Played	M	Inns	NO	Runs	HS	Av'ge	100s	Runs	Wkts	Av'ge	Ct/St
Baines, F E *	June 18, 1864	Nov 17, 1948	1888	1888	1	1	0	0	0	0.00	0	—	—	—	0
Bairstow, A	Aug 14, 1868	Dec 7, 1945	1896	1900	24	24	10	69	12	4.92	0	—	—	—	41/18
Bairstow, D L	Sept 1, 1951	Jan 5, 1998	1970	1990	429	601	113	12,985	145	26.60	9	192	6	32.00	907/131
§ Bairstow, J M	Sept 26, 1989		2009	2020	94	149	22	6,445	246	50.74	15	1	0	—	240/10
Baker, G R	Apr 18, 1862	Feb 6, 1938	1884	1884	7	11	1	42	13	4.20	0	—	—	—	5
Baker, R *	July 3, 1849	June 21, 1896	1874	1875	3	5	1	45	22	11.25	0	43	2	21.35	3
Balderstone, J C	Nov 16, 1940	Mar 6, 2000	1961	1969	68	81	6	1,332	82	17.76	0	790	37		24
§ **Ballance, G S**	**Nov 22, 1989**		**2008**	**2021**	**127**	**202**	**21**	**8,507**	**203***	**47.00**	**27**	**143**	**0**	—	**70**
Barber, A T *	June 17, 1905	Mar 10, 1985	1929	1930	42	54	3	1,050	100	20.58	1	0	0	—	40
Barber, W	Apr 18, 1901	Sept 10, 1968	1926	1947	354	495	48	15,315	255	34.26	27	404	14	28.85	169
Barraclough, E S	Mar 30, 1923	May 21, 1999	1949	1950	2	4	2	43	24*	21.50	0	136	4	34.00	0
Bates, W	Nov 19, 1855	Jan 8, 1900	1877	1887	202	331	12	6,499	136	20.37	8	10,692	637	16.78	163
Bates, W E	Mar 5, 1884	Jan 17, 1957	1907	1913	113	167	15	2,634	81	17.32	0	57	2	28.50	64
Batty G J	Oct 13, 1977		1997	1997	1	2	1	18	18	9.00	0	70	2	35.00	0
Batty, J D	May 15, 1971		1989	1994	64	67	20	703	51	14.95	0	5,286	140	37.75	25
Bayes, G W	Feb 27, 1884	Dec 6, 1960	1910	1921	18	24	11	165	36	12.69	0	1,534	48	31.95	7
Beaumont, H	Oct 14, 1916	Nov. 15, 2003	1946	1947	28	46	6	716	60	17.90	0	236	9	26.22	11
Beaumont, J	Sept 16, 1854	May 1, 1920	1877	1878	5	9	4	50	24	10.00	0	50	2	25.00	0
Bedford, H	July 17, 1907	July, 5, 1968	1928	1928	5	5	1	57	24	14.25	0	179	8	22.37	0
Bedford, R	Feb 24, 1879	July, 28 1939	1903	1903	2	2	1	38	30*	38.00	0	117	2	58.50	1
Bell, J T	June 16, 1895	Aug 8, 1974	1921	1923	7	8	1	125	54	17.85	0	—	—	—	2
Berry, John	Jan 10, 1823	Feb 26, 1895	1864	1867	18	32	2	492	78	16.40	0	149	8	18.62	12
Berry, Joseph	Nov 29, 1829	Apr 20, 1894	1863	1874	3	7	1	68	30	17.00	0	—	—	—	1
Berry, P J	Dec 28, 1966		1986	1990	4	7	6	76	31*	76.00	0	401	7	57.28	6
§ **Bess, D M**	**July 22, 1997**		**2019**	**2021**	**18**	**25**	**2**	**555**	**91**	**24.13**	**0**	**1,146**	**35**	**32.74**	**5**
Best T L	Aug 26, 1981		2010	2010	9	9	0	86	40	9.55	0	793	18	44.05	4
Betts, G	Sept 19, 1841	Sept. 26, 1902	1873	1874	2	4	1	56	44*	18.66	0	—	—	—	0
§ Bevan, M G	May 8, 1970		1995	1996	32	56	8	2,823	160*	58.81	9	720	10	72.00	24
§ Binks, J G	Oct 5, 1935		1955	1969	491	587	128	6,745	95	14.69	0	66	—	—	872/172
Binns, J	Mar 31, 1870	Dec 8, 1934	1898	1898	1	1	0	4	4	4.00	0	—	—	—	0/3

337

LIST OF PLAYERS AND CAREER AVERAGES IN ALL FIRST-CLASS MATCHES FOR YORKSHIRE (Continued)

Player	Date of Birth	Date of Death (if known)	First Played	Last Played	M	Inns	NO	Runs	HS	Av'ge	100s	Runs	Wkts	Av'ge	Ct/St
Bird, H D	Apr 19, 1933		1956	1959	14	25	2	613	181*	26.65	1	—	—	—	3
Birkenshaw, J	Nov 13, 1940		1958	1960	30	42	5	588	42	16.80	0	1,819	69	26.36	21
Birtles, T J D	Oct 26, 1886		1913	1924	37	57	11	876	104	19.04	1	—	—	—	19
Blackburn, J D H *	Oct 27, 1924		1956	1956	1	2	0	18	15	9.00	0	20	0	—	0
Blackburn, J S	Sept 24, 1852	July 8, 1922	1876	1877	6	11	1	102	28	10.20	0	—	—	—	4
§ Blackburn, W E *	Nov 24, 1888	June 3, 1941	1919	1920	10	13	6	26	6*	3.71	0	173	45	24.71	4
§ Blain J A R	Jan 4, 1979		2004	2010	15	17	8	137	28*	15.22	0	1,113	45	24.73	9
Blake, W	Nov 29, 1854	Nov 28, 1931	1880	1880	2	3	0	44	21	14.66	0	1,312	38	34.52	4
Blakey, R J	July 15, 1967		1985	2003	339	541	84	14,150	223*	30.96	12	17	1	17.00	768/56
Blamires, E	July 31, 1850	Mar 22, 1886	1877	1877	1	2	0	23	17	11.50	0	68.00	5	16.40	0
§ Blewett, G S	Oct 28, 1971		1999	1999	1	2	1	12	6	2.00	0	82	5	42.40	5
Bloom, G R	Sept 13, 1941		1964	1964	1	1	0	6	6	6.00	0	212			2
Bocking, H	Dec 10, 1835	Feb 22, 1907	1865	1865	2	1	1	—	—	2.00	0	—	—	—	1
Boden, J G *	Dec 27, 1848	Jan 3, 1928	1878	1878	1	2	0	14	11	7.00	0	—	—	—	0
Bolton, B C *	Sept 23, 1861	Nov 18, 1910	1890	1891	4	6	0	25	11	4.16	0	252	13	19.38	2
Bolus, J B	Jan 31, 1934		1956	1962	107	179	18	4,712	146*	29.26	7	407	13	31.30	45
Booth, A	Nov 3, 1902	Aug 17, 1974	1931	1947	36	36	16	114	29	5.70	0	1,684	122	13.80	10
Booth, M W	Dec 10, 1886	July 1, 1916	1908	1914	144	218	31	4,244	210	22.69	4	11,017	557	19.77	114
Booth, P A	Sept 5, 1965		1982	1989	23	29	9	193	33*	9.65	0	1,517	35	43.34	7
Booth, R	Oct 1, 1926	May 2, 2017	1951	1955	65	76	28	730	53*	15.20	0	—	—	—	79/29
Bore, M K	June 2, 1947		1969	1977	74	78	21	481	37*	8.43	0	4,866	162	30.03	27
Borrill, P D	July 4, 1951		1971	1971	2	2	0	—	—	—	—	61	5	12.20	0
Bosomworth W E	Mar 8, 1847	June 7, 1891	1872	1880	4	7	1	20	7	3.33	0	140	9	15.55	2
Bottomley, I H *	Apr 9, 1855	Apr 23, 1922	1878	1880	9	12	0	166	32	13.83	0	75	1	75.00	7
Bottomley, T	Dec 26, 1910	Feb 19, 1977	1934	1935	9	7	0	142	51	20.28	0	188	1	188.00	5
Bower, W H	Oct 17, 1857	Jan 31, 1943	1883	1883	1	2	0	10	5	5.00	0	—	—	—	0
Bowes, W E	July 25, 1908	Sept 4, 1987	1929	1947	301	257	117	1,251	43*	8.93	0	21,227	1,351	15.71	118
§ Boycott, G	Oct 21, 1940		1962	1986	414	674	111	32,570	260*	57.85	103	665	28	23.75	200
Brackin, T	Jan 5, 1859	Oct 7, 1924	1882	1882	3	2	1	9	9	2.00	0	—	—	—	0
§ Brathwaite, K C	Dec 1, 1992		2017	2017	2	4	0	40	18	10.00	0	—	—	—	1

338

LIST OF PLAYERS AND CAREER AVERAGES IN ALL FIRST-CLASS MATCHES FOR YORKSHIRE (Continued)

Player	Date of Birth	Date of Death (if known)	First Played	Last Played	M	Inns	NO	Runs	HS	Av'ge	100s	Runs	Wkts	Av'ge	Ct/St
Brayshay, P B *	Oct 14, 1916	July 6, 2004	1952	1952	2	3	0	20	13	6.66	0	104	3	34.66	0
Brearley, H *	June 26, 1913	Aug 14, 2007	1937	1937	1	2	0	17	9	8.50	0	—	—	—	0
Brennan, D V * ©	Feb 10, 1920	Jan 9, 1985	1947	1953	204	221	66	1,653	47	10.66	0	—	—	—	280/100
Bresnan, T T * ©	Feb 28, 1985		2003	2019	163	232	35	5,594	169*	28.39	5	13,663	445	30.70	89
Briton, G	Feb 7, 1843	Jan 3, 1910	1867	1867	1	2	0	3	3	1.50	0	—	—	—	0
Broadbent, A	June 7, 1879	July 19, 1958	1909	1910	3	5	0	66	29	13.20	0	252	5	50.40	1
Broadhead, W B	May 31, 1903	Apr 2, 1986	1929	1929	3	2	0	5	3	2.50	0	—	—	—	0
Broadhurst, M	June 20, 1974		1991	1994	5	3	0	7	6	2.33	0	231	7	33.00	0
Brook, H C * ©	**Feb 22, 1999**		**2016**	**2021**	**47**	**76**	**2**	**2,082**	**124**	**28.13**	**4**	**375**	**8**	**46.87**	**36**
Brook, J W	Feb 1, 1897	Mar 3, 1989	1923	1923	1	1	1	0	0*	0.00	0	—	—	—	0
Brooke, B	Mar 3, 1930	Apr 19, 2021	1950	1950	2	4	0	16	14	4.00	0	191	2	95.50	0
§ Brooks, J A ©	June 4, 1984		2013	2018	81	102	34	1,229	109*	18.07	0	8,341	316	26.39	21
§ Brophy, G L ©	Nov 26, 1975		2006	2012	73	112	12	3,012	177*	30.12	3	6	0	—	176/15
Broughton, P N	Oct 22, 1935		1956	1956	6	5	2	19	12	6.33	0	365	16	22.81	2
Brown, A	June 10, 1854	Nov 2, 1900	1872	1872	2	3	0	9	5	3.00	0	47	3	15.66	4
Brown, J T (Driffield) ©	Aug 20, 1869	Nov 4, 1904	1889	1904	345	567	41	15,694	311	29.83	23	5,183	177	29.28	188
Brown, J T (Darfield) ©	Nov 24, 1874	Apr 12, 1950	1897	1903	30	32	3	333	37*	11.48	0	2,071	97	21.35	18
Brown, W	Nov 19, 1876	July 27, 1945	1902	1908	2	2	1	2	2	2.00	0	—	—	—	0
Brownhill, T	Oct 10, 1838	Jan 6, 1915	1863	1871	14	20	3	185	25	10.88	0	84	4	21.00	7
Brumfitt, J	Feb 18, 1917	Mar 16, 1987	1938	1938	1	1	0	9	9	9.00	0	—	—	—	0
Buller, J S	Aug 23, 1909	Aug 7, 1970	1930	1930	1	2	0	5	3	2.50	0	—	—	—	2
Bulmer, J R L	Dec 28, 1867	Jan 20, 1917	1891	1891	1	2	1	0	0*	0.00	0	79	1	79.00	0
Burgess, T	Oct 1, 1859	Feb 15, 1922	1895	1895	1	2	1	0	0*	0.00	0	—	—	—	2
Burgin, E	Jan 4, 1924	Nov 16, 2012	1952	1953	12	10	3	92	32	13.14	0	795	31	25.64	2
Burman, J	Oct 5, 1838	May 14, 1900	1867	1867	1	2	1	1	1*	1.00	0	—	—	—	0
Burnet, J R *	Oct 11, 1918	Mar 6, 1999	1958	1959	54	75	6	889	54	12.88	0	26	1	26.00	7
§ Burrows, M	Aug 18, 1855	May 29, 1893	1880	1880	6	10	0	82	23	8.20	0	—	—	—	2
Burton, D C F * ©	Sept 13, 1887	Sept 24, 1971	1907	1921	104	130	15	2,273	142*	19.76	2	—	—	—	44
Burton, R C *	Apr 11, 1891	Apr 30, 1971	1914	1914	2	2	0	47	47	23.50	0	73	6	12.16	2
Butterfield, E B *	Oct 22, 1848	May 6, 1899	1870	1870	1	2	0	18	10	9.00	0	—	—	—	0

339

LIST OF PLAYERS AND CAREER AVERAGES IN ALL FIRST-CLASS MATCHES FOR YORKSHIRE (Continued)

Player	Date of Birth	Date of Death (if known)	First Played	Last Played	M	Inns	NO	Runs	HS	Av'ge	100s	Runs	Wkts	Av'ge	Ct/St
Byas, D .... ⓒ	Aug. 26, 1963		1986	2001	268	449	42	14,398	213	35.37	28	727	12	60.58	351
Byrom, J L *	July 20, 1851	Aug. 24, 1931	1874	1874	2	4	0	19	11	4.75	0	—	—	—	1
Callis, E	Nov. 8, 1994		2016	2017	2	3	1	131	84	65.50	0	—	—	—	1
Cammish, J W	May 21, 1921	July 16, 1974	1954	1954	2	3	1	0	0	0.00	0	155	3	51.66	0
Carrick, P	July, 16, 1952	Jan 11, 2000	1970	1993	425	543	102	9,994	131*	22.66	3	30,530	1,018	29.99	183
Carter, Rev E S *	Feb 3, 1845	May 23, 1923	1876	1881	14	21	2	210	39*	11.05	0	104	8	13.00	4
Cartman, W H	June 20, 1861	Jan 16, 1935	1891	1891	3	6	0	57	49	9.50	0	—	—	—	0
Carver, K	Mar 26, 1996		2014	2018	8	13	6	108	20	15.42	0	543	18	30.16	4
Cawthray, G	Sept. 28, 1913	Jan 5, 2001	1939	1952	4	5	1	114	30	19.00	0	304	4	76.00	1
Chadwick, J P G ..	Nov 8, 1934		1960	1965	6	9	3	106	59	17.66	0	67	2	33.50	7
Chapman, A	Dec 27, 1851	June 26, 1909	1876	1879	14	23	4	148	29	7.78	0	17	1	17.00	7
Chapman, C A	June 8, 1971		1990	1998	8	13	2	238	80	21.63	0	—	—	—	13/3
Charlesworth, A P	Feb 19, 1865	May 11, 1926	1894	1895	7	12	1	241	63	21.90	0	—	—	—	2
§ Chichester- Constable, R C J *	Dec 21, 1890	May 26, 1963	1919	1919	1	1	0	0	0	0.00	0	6	0	—	0
Clarkson, A	Sept 5, 1939		1963	1963	6	8	1	80	30	11.42	0	92	5	18.40	5
Claughton, H M ..	Dec 24, 1891	Oct 17, 1980	1914	1919	4	6	0	39	15	6.50	0	176	3	58.66	1
§ Claydon, M E ...	Nov 25, 1982		2005	2006	3	2	0	38	38	19.00	0	263	3	87.66	0
§ Clayton, R O	Jan 1, 1844	Nov 26, 1901	1870	1879	70	115	23	992	62	10.78	0	2,478	153	16.19	26
§ Cleary, M F	July 19, 1980		2005	2005	2	2	0	23	12	11.50	0	250	8	31.25	0
Clegg, H	Dec 8, 1850	Dec 30, 1920	1881	1881	6	8	1	63	25*	9.00	0	—	—	—	2
Clifford, C C	July, 5, 1942		1972	1972	11	12	4	39	12*	4.87	0	666	26	25.61	5
Close, D B .... ⓒ	Feb 24, 1931	Sept 14, 2015	1949	1970	536	811	102	22,650	198	31.94	33	23,489	967	24.29	564
Clough, G D	May 23, 1978		1998	1998	1	2	0	34	34	17.00	0	41	2	20.50	0
Coad, B O ..... ⓒ	**Jan 10, 1994**		**2016**	**2021**	**48**	**63**	**21**	**603**	**48**	**14.35**	**0**	**3,896**	**192**	**20.29**	**2**
Collinson, R W *	Nov 6, 1875	Dec 26, 1963	1897	1897	2	3	0	58	34	19.33	0	—	—	—	0
Cooper, H P	Apr 17, 1949		1971	1980	98	107	29	1,159	56	14.85	0	6,327	227	27.87	60
Cooper, P E *	Feb 19, 1885	May 21, 1950	1910	1910	1	2	0	0	0	0.00	0	—	—	—	0
Cope, G A .... ⓒ	Feb 23, 1947		1966	1980	230	249	89	2,241	78	14.00	0	15,627	630	24.80	64
Corbett, A M	Nov 25, 1855	Oct 7, 1934	1881	1881	1	2	0	—	—	—	0	—	—	—	1

340

LIST OF PLAYERS AND CAREER AVERAGES IN ALL FIRST-CLASS MATCHES FOR YORKSHIRE (Continued)

Player	Date of Birth	Date of Death (if known)	First Played	Last Played	M	Inns	NO	Runs	HS	Av'ge	100s	Runs	Wkts	Av'ge	Ct/St
Coverdale, S P	Nov 20, 1954		1973	1980	6	4	0	31	18	7.75	0	—	—	—	11/4
Coverdale, W *	July 8, 1862	Sept 23, 1934	1888	1888	2	2	0	2	1	1.00	0	—	—	—	2
Cowan, M J	© June 10, 1933		1953	1962	91	84	48	170	19*	4.72	0	6,389	266	24.01	37
Cownley, J M	Feb 24, 1929	Nov 7, 1998	1952	1952	2	2	1	19	19	19.00	0	119	1	119.00	0
Coxon, A	© Jan 18, 1916	Jan 22, 2006	1945	1950	142	182	33	2,747	83	18.43	0	9,528	464	20.53	124
Craven, V J	July 31, 1980		2000	2004	33	55	6	1,206	81*	24.61	0	584	15	38.93	18
Crawford, G H	Dec 15, 1890	June 28, 1975	1914	1926	9	8	0	46	22	5.75	0	541	21	25.76	3
Crawford, M G *	July 30, 1920	Dec 2, 2012	1951	1951	1	2	0	22	13	11.00	0	—	—	—	1
Creighton, E	July 9, 1859	Feb 17, 1931	1888	1888	4	8	0	22	10	5.50	0	181	10	18.10	0
Crick, H	Jan 29, 1910	Feb 10, 1960	1937	1947	8	10	0	88	20	8.80	0	—	—	—	18/4
Crookes, R	Oct 9, 1846	Feb 15, 1897	1879	1879	1	1	0	2	2*	2.00	0	14	0	—	0
Crossland, S M	Aug 16, 1851	April 11, 1906	1883	1886	4	6	2	32	20	8.00	0	—	—	—	3/5
Crowther, A	Aug 1, 1878	June 4, 1946	1905	1905	1	2	0	0	0	0.00	0	—	—	—	1
Cuttell, W	Jan 28, 1835	June 10, 1896	1863	1871	15	27	6	271	56	12.90	0	596	36	16.55	4
Dalton, A J	Mar 14, 1947		1969	1972	21	31	2	710	128	24.48	3	—	—	—	6
§ Darnton, T	Feb 12, 1836	Oct 18, 1874	1864	1868	13	22	1	314	81*	14.95	0	349	12	29.08	3
Davidson, K R	Dec 24, 1905	Dec 25, 1954	1933	1935	30	46	5	1,331	128	32.46	2	—	—	—	18
Dawes, J	Feb 14, 1836	Not known	1865	1865	5	9	2	93	28	13.28	0	196	5	39.20	3
Dawood, I	July 23, 1976		2004	2005	20	31	9	636	75	26.50	0	—	—	—	46/3
Dawson, E	May 1, 1835	Dec 1, 1888	1863	1874	16	25	1	224	30	9.33	0	—	—	—	5
Dawson, R K J	Aug 4, 1980		2001	2006	72	106	9	2,179	87	22.46	0	6,444	157	41.04	39
Dawson, W A *	Dec 3, 1850	Mar 6, 1916	1870	1870	1	2	0	0	0	0.00	0	—	—	—	1
Day, A G *	© Sept 20, 1865	Oct 16, 1908	1885	1888	6	10	0	78	25	7.80	0	—	—	—	3
Dennis, F	© June 11, 1907	Nov 21, 2000	1928	1933	89	150	28	1,332	67	18.50	0	—	—	—	58
Dennis, S J	© Oct 18, 1960		1980	1988	67	62	24	338	53*	8.89	0	4,517	156	28.95	19
Denton, D	© July 4, 1874	Feb 16, 1950	1894	1920	676	1,058	61	33,282	221	33.38	61	5,548	173	32.06	360/1
Denton, J	Feb 3, 1865	July 18, 1946	1887	1888	15	24	1	222	59	9.65	0	957	34	28.14	6
Dewse, H	Feb 23, 1836	July 8, 1910	1873	1873	1	2	0	14	12	7.00	0	15	0	—	1
Deyes, G	Feb 11, 1878	Jan 11, 1963	1905	1907	17	24	4	44	12	2.20	0	944	41	23.02	6
Dick, R D *	Apr 16, 1889	Dec 14, 1983	1911	1911	1	1	0	2	2	2.00	0	37	2	18.50	1

341

LIST OF PLAYERS AND CAREER AVERAGES IN ALL FIRST-CLASS MATCHES FOR YORKSHIRE (Continued)

Player	Date of Birth	Date of Death (if known)	First Played	Last Played	M	Inns	NO	Runs	HS	Av'ge	100s	Runs	Wkts	Av'ge	Ct/St
Dobson, A	Feb 22, 1854	Sept 17, 1932	1879	1879	2	3	0	1	1	0.33	0	—	—	—	1
Doidge, M J	July 2, 1970		1990	1990	1	—	—	—	—	—	—	106	0	—	0
Dolphin, A	Dec 24, 1885	Oct 23, 1942	1905	1927	427	446	157	3,325	66	11.50	0	28	1	28.00	569/260
Douglas, J S	Apr 4, 1903	Dec 27, 1971	1925	1934	23	26	8	125	19	6.94	0	1,310	49	26.73	14
Drake, A	Apr 16, 1884	Feb 14, 1919	1909	1914	156	244	24	4,789	147*	21.76	3	8,623	479	18.00	93
Drake, J	Sept 1, 1893	May 22, 1967	1923	1924	3	4	1	21	10	7.00	0	117	1	117.00	1
Driver, J	May 16, 1861	Dec 10, 1946	1889	1889	2	4	1	24	8	8.00	0	—	—	—	2
Dury, T S *	June 12, 1854	Mar 20, 1932	1878	1881	13	24	1	329	46	14.30	0	21	0	—	2
Duke, H G	**Sep 6, 2001**		**2021**	**2021**	**9**	**13**	**1**	**197**	**54**	**16.41**	**0**	**0**	**0**	—	**31**
Dyson, W L	Dec 11, 1857	May 1, 1936	1887	1887	2	4	0	8	6	2.00	0	—	—	—	2
Earnshaw, W	Sept 20, 1867	Nov 24, 1941	1893	1896	6	7	3	44	23	11.00	0	349	11	31.72	6/2
Eastwood, D	Mar 30, 1848	May 17, 1903	1870	1877	29	51	2	591	68	12.06	0	—	—	—	16
Eckersley, S	Sept 4, 1925	May 30, 2009	1945	1945	1	2	0	9	9*	—	0	62	0	—	0
Elam, F W *	Sept 13, 1871	Mar 19, 1943	1900	1902	2	3	1	48	24	24.00	0	—	—	—	0
§ Elliott, M T G	Sept 28, 1971		2002	2002	5	10	1	487	127	54.11	1	77	1	77.00	7
Ellis, J E	Nov 10, 1864	Dec 1, 1927	1888	1892	11	15	6	14	4*	1.55	0	—	—	—	11/10
Ellis, S *	Nov 23, 1851	Oct 28, 1930	1880	1880	1	3	0	12	9	4.00	0	—	—	—	2
Elms, J S	Dec 24, 1874	Nov 1, 1951	1905	1905	1	2	0	20	20	10.00	0	28	1	28.00	0
Elstub, C J	Feb 3, 1981		2000	2002	6	2	0	28	18*	28.00	0	356	9	39.55	2
Emmett, T	Sept 3, 1841	June 29, 1904	1866	1888	299	484	65	6,315	104	15.07	1	15,465	1,216	12.71	179
Farrar, A	Apr 29, 1883	Dec 25, 1954	1906	1906	1	1	0	2	2	2.00	0	—	—	—	1
Fearnley, M C	Aug 21, 1936	July 7, 1979	1962	1964	3	4	2	19	11*	9.50	0	133	6	22.16	0
Featherby, W D	Aug 18, 1888	Nov 20, 1958	1920	1920	1	1	0	—	—	—	0	12	0	—	0
Fellows, G M	July 30, 1978		1998	2003	46	71	6	1,526	109	23.47	1	1,202	32	37.56	23
Fiddling, K	Oct 13, 1917	June 19, 1992	1938	1946	18	24	6	182	25	10.11	0	—	—	—	24/13
§ Finch, A J	Nov 17, 1986		2014	2015	8	10	1	415	110	46.11	1	40	1	40.00	4
Firth, A *	Sept 3, 1847	Jan 16, 1927	1869	1869	1	1	0	4	4	4.00	0	—	—	—	0
Firth, Rev E B *	Apr 11, 1863	July 25, 1905	1894	1894	1	1	0	1	1	1.00	0	—	—	—	0
§ Firth, E L *	Mar 7, 1886	Jan 8, 1949	1912	1912	2	4	0	43	37	10.75	0	—	—	—	1

342

LIST OF PLAYERS AND CAREER AVERAGES IN ALL FIRST-CLASS MATCHES FOR YORKSHIRE (Continued)

Player	Date of Birth	Date of Death (if known)	First Played	Last Played	M	Inns	NO	Runs	HS	Av'ge	100s	Runs	Wkts	Av'ge	Ct/St
Firth, J	June 26, 1917	Sept. 6, 1981	1949	1950	8	8	5	134	67*	44.66	0	—	—	—	14/2
Fisher, H	Aug 3, 1903	Apr 16, 1974	1928	1936	52	58	14	681	76*	15.47	0	2,621	93	28.18	22
Fisher, I D	Mar 31, 1976		1996	2001	24	32	9	545	68*	23.69	0	1,382	43	32.13	1
Fisher, M D	**Nov 9, 1997**		**2015**	**2021**	**18**	**24**	**5**	**297**	**47***	**15.63**	**0**	**1,518**	**56**	**27.10**	**6**
Flaxington, S	Oct 14, 1860		1882	1882	4	8	0	121	57	15.12	0	—	—	—	1
§ Fleming, S P	Apr 1, 1973		2003	2003	9	14	2	469	98	39.08	0	—	—	—	13
Fletcher, S D	June 8, 1964		1983	1991	107	91	31	414	28*	6.90	0	7,966	234	34.04	25
Fletcher, W	Feb 16, 1866	June 1, 1935	1892	1892	5	8	1	80	31*	11.42	0	157	7	22.42	4
Foord, C W	June 11, 1924	July 8, 2015	1947	1953	51	34	16	114	35	6.33	0	3,412	126	27.07	19
Foster, E J	Nov 23, 1873	April 16, 1956	1901	1901	1	1	0	2	2	2.00	0	27	0	—	0
§ Foster, T W *	Sept 17, 1972		1993	1994	5	7	1	165	63*	27.50	0	150	6	25.00	6
Foster, R	Nov 12, 1871	Jan 31, 1947	1894	1895	14	20	5	138	25*	9.20	0	952	58	16.41	8
Fraine, W A R	**June 13, 1996**		**2019**	**2021**	**14**	**25**	**1**	**460**	**106**	**19.16**	**1**	—	—	—	**10**
Frank, J *	Dec 27, 1857	Oct 22, 1940	1881	1881	1	2	0	10	10	5.00	0	17	1	17.00	3
© Frank, R W *	May 29, 1864	Sept 9, 1950	1889	1903	18	28	4	298	58	12.41	0	9	0	—	8
Freeman, G	July 27, 1843	Nov 18, 1895	1865	1880	32	54	5	752	53	14.46	0	2,079	209	9.94	16
© Gale, A W	Nov 28, 1983		2004	2016	149	235	17	7,726	272	35.44	19	238	1	238.00	46
Geldart, C J	Dec 17, 1991		2010	2011	2	2	0	51	34	25.50	0	—	—	—	1
© Gibb, P A *	July 11, 1913	Dec 7, 1977	1935	1946	36	54	4	1,545	157*	32.87	2	82	3	27.33	25/8
Gibson, B P **	Mar 31, 1996		2011	2011	1	1	0	0	0	0.00	0	1*	—	—	6/0
Gibson, R	Jan 22, 1996		2016	2016	1	1	0	0	0	0.00	0	42	1	42.00	1
§ Gifkins, C J *	Feb 19, 1856	Jan 31, 1897	1880	1880	2	3	0	30	23	10.00	0	—	—	—	1
Gilbert, C R	Apr 16, 1984		2007	2007	1	1	0	64	64	64.00	0	—	—	—	1
Gill, F	Sept 3, 1883	Nov 1, 1917	1906	1906	2	4	0	18	11	4.50	0	11	0	—	0
§ Gillespie, J N	©April 19, 1975		2006	2007	26	34	11	640	123*	27.82	1	2,013	59	34.11	4
§ Gillhouley, K	Aug 8, 1934		1961	1961	24	31	7	323	56	13.45	0	1,702	77	22.10	16
© Gough, D	Sept 18, 1970		1989	2008	146	188	29	2,922	121	18.37	0	12,487	453	27.56	30
Goulder, A	Aug 16, 1907	June 11, 1986	1929	1929	2	1	0	3	3	3.00	0	90	3	30.00	0

** At 15 years and 27 days on April 27, 2011, First Day of Yorkshire's match v. Durham MCCU, he became the youngest ever English First Class cricketer.

343

LIST OF PLAYERS AND CAREER AVERAGES IN ALL FIRST-CLASS MATCHES FOR YORKSHIRE (Continued)

Player	Date of Birth	Date of Death (if known)	First Played	Last Played	M	Inns	NO	Runs	HS	Av'ge	100s	Runs	Wkts	Av'ge	Ct/St
§ Gray, A K D	May 19, 1974		2001	2004	18	26	3	649	104	28.21	1	1,357	30	45.23	16
Grayson, A P	Mar 31, 1971		1990	1995	52	80	10	1,958	100	27.97	1	846	13	65.07	36
Greenwood, A	Aug 20, 1847	Feb 12, 1889	1869	1880	95	166	8	2,762	91	17.93	0	9	0	—	33
Greenwood, F E *	Sept 28, 1905	July 30, 1963	1929	1932	57	66	4	1,558	104*	26.86	1	36	2	18.00	37
Greenwood, L	July 13, 1834	Nov 1, 1909	1864	1874	50	84	3	885	83	12.29	0	1,615	85	19.00	24
Grimshaw, C H	May 12, 1880	Sept 25, 1947	1904	1908	54	75	7	1,219	85	17.92	0	221	7	31.57	42
Grimshaw, I	May 4, 1857	Jan 18, 1911	1880	1887	125	194	14	3,354	129*	18.63	4	—	—	—	76/3
Guy S M	Nov 17, 1978		2000	2011	37	52	6	742	52*	16.13	0	8	0	—	98/12
Haggas, S	Apr 18, 1856		1878	1882	31	47	3	478	43	10.86	0	—	—	—	10
Haigh S	Mar 19, 1871	Feb 27, 1921	1895	1913	513	687	110	10,993	159	19.05	4	29,289	1,876	15.61	276
Hall, B	Sept 16, 1929	Feb 27, 1989	1952	1952	1	2	0	14	10	7.00	0	55	1	55.00	1
Hall, C H	Apr 5, 1906	Dec 11, 1976	1928	1934	23	22	9	67	15*	5.15	0	1,226	45	27.24	11
§ Hall, J	Nov 11, 1815	Apr 17, 1888	1863	1863	1	2	0	4	3	2.00	0	—	—	—	2
Halliday, L	Nov 1, 1852	Nov 19, 1915	1873	1894	275	477	58	9,757	160	23.28	9	781	15	52.06	173
Halliday, H	Feb 9, 1920	Aug 27, 1967	1938	1953	182	279	18	8,361	144	32.03	12	3,119	101	30.88	140
Halliley, C	Dec 5, 1852	Mar 23, 1929	1872	1872	3	5	0	27	17	5.40	0	—	—	—	2
Hamer, D	Dec 8, 1916	Nov 3, 1993	1938	1938	2	2	0	3	3	1.50	0	64	1	64.00	2
§ Hamilton, G M	Sept 16, 1974		1994	2003	73	108	18	2,228	125	24.75	1	5,479	222	24.68	25
Hampshire, A W	Oct 5, 1913	May 23, 1997	1975	1975	1	2	0	18	17	9.00	0	—	—	—	1
Hampshire, J	Feb 10, 1941	March 1, 2017	1961	1981	456	724	89	21,979	183*	34.61	34	109	5	21.80	1
§ Handscomb, P S P	Apr 26, 1991		2017	2017	9	14	1	441	109	33.92	1	1,108	24	46.16	367
Hannon-Dalby, O J	Jun 20, 1989		2008	2012	24	25	10	45	11*	3.00	0	1,938	43	45.06	7
§ Harbord, W E *	Dec 15, 1908	July 28, 1992	1929	1935	16	21	1	411	109	20.55	1	—	—	—	2
§ Harden, R J	Aug 16, 1965		1999	2000	12	22	2	439	69	21.95	0	—	—	—	7
Hardisty, C H	Dec 12, 1885	Mar 2, 1968	1906	1909	38	55	5	991	84	19.82	0	—	—	—	18
§ Hargreaves, H S	Mar 22, 1912	Sept 29, 1990	1934	1938	18	20	6	51	9	3.64	0	1,145	55	20.81	3
§ Harrison, S J	Oct 23, 1978		2012	2012	3	3	0	25	23	8.33	0	195	8	24.37	1
Harris, W	Nov 21, 1861	May 23, 1923	1884	1887	4	8	2	45	23	7.50	0	18	0	—	1
Harrison, G P	Feb 11, 1862	Sept 14, 1940	1883	1892	59	87	26	407	28	6.67	0	3,276	226	14.49	36

LIST OF PLAYERS AND CAREER AVERAGES IN ALL FIRST-CLASS MATCHES FOR YORKSHIRE (Continued)

Player	Date of Birth	Date of Death (if known)	First Played	Last Played	M	Inns	NO	Runs	HS	Av'ge	100s	Runs	Wkts	Av'ge	Ct/St
Harrison, H	Jan 26, 1885	Feb 11, 1962	1907	1907	2	1	1	4	4*	—	0	39	2	19.50	1
Harrison, W H	May 27, 1863	July 15, 1939	1888	1888	3	6	1	12	6	2.40	0	—	—	—	0
Hart, H W *	Sept 21, 1859	Nov 2, 1895	1888	1888	1	2	0	6	6	3.00	0	—	—	—	0
Hart, P R	Jan 12, 1947		1981	1981	3	5	0	23	11	4.60	0	32	2	16.00	2
Hartington, H E	Sept 18, 1881	Feb 16, 1950	1910	1911	10	10	4	51	16	8.50	0	140	2	70.00	1
Hartley, P J	Apr 18, 1960		1985	1997	195	237	51	3,844	127*	20.66	2	764	23	33.21	2
Hartley, S N	Mar 18, 1956		1978	1988	133	199	27	4,193	114	24.37	2	17,438	579	30.11	60
§ Hartley, I J	Apr 10, 1972		2004	2005	20	31	2	1,045	209	36.03	2	2,052	42	48.85	47
Hatton, A G	Mar 25, 1937		1960	1961	3	3	1	4	4*	—	0	1,218	37	32.91	12
§ Hawke, Lord *	Aug 16, 1860	Oct 10, 1938	1881	1911	510	739	91	13,133	166	20.26	10	202	6	33.66	159
Hayley, H	Feb 22, 1860	June 3, 1922	1884	1898	7	12	1	122	24	11.09	0	16	0	—	3
Haywood, W J	Feb 25, 1841	Jan 7, 1912	1878	1878	1	2	0	7	7	3.50	0	48	0	—	0
§ Head, T M	Dec 29, 1993		2016	2016	1	2	0	56	54	28.00	0	14	1	14.00	0
Hicks, J	Dec 10, 1850	June 10, 1912	1872	1876	15	25	3	313	66	14.22	0	16	0	—	12
Higgins, J	Mar 13, 1877	July 19, 1954	1901	1905	9	14	5	93	28	10.33	0	17	0	—	10/3
Hill, A	Nov 15, 1843	Aug 28, 1910	1871	1882	140	223	25	1,705	49	8.61	0	7,002	542	12.91	91
Hill, G G H	**Jan 24, 2001**		**2020**	**2021**	**9**	**13**	**1**	**296**	**71**	**24.66**	**0**	**182**	**8**	**22.75**	**1**
Hill, H *	Nov 29, 1858	Aug 14, 1935	1888	1891	14	27	2	337	39	13.48	0	—	—	—	10
Hill, L G *	Nov 2, 1860	Aug 27, 1940	1882	1882	1	2	0	13	8	6.50	0	—	—	—	0
Hirst, E T *	May 6, 1857	Oct 26, 1914	1877	1888	21	33	2	328	87*	10.58	0	—	—	—	7
Hirst, E W *	Feb 27, 1855	Oct 24, 1933	1881	1881	2	3	0	33	28	11.00	0	3	0	—	0
Hirst, G H	Sept 7, 1871	May 10, 1954	1891	1921*	717	1,050	128	32,024	341	34.73	56	44,716	2,481	18.02	518
Hirst, P	May 21, 1865	Apr 3, 1927	1899	1899	1	1	0	5	5*	—	0	27	0	—	1
§ Hodd, A J	Jan 12, 1984		2012	2018	57	79	10	1,803	96*	26.13	0	14	0	—	165/11
Hodgson, D M	Feb 26, 1990		2014	2015	2	3	0	72	35	24.00	0	—	—	—	2
Hodgson, G	July 24, 1938		1964	1964	1	1	0	4	4	4.00	0	—	—	—	0/2
Hodgson, I	Nov 15, 1828	Nov 24, 1867	1863	1866	21	35	14	164	21*	7.80	0	1,537	88	17.46	11
Hodgson, L J	Jun 29, 1986		2009	2010	3	3	0	99	34	33.00	0	158	2	79.00	1
Hodgson, P	Sept 21, 1935	Mar 30, 2015	1954	1956	13	6	2	33	8*	8.25	0	648	22	29.45	6
Hoggard, M J	Dec 31, 1976		1996	2009	102	120	34	956	89*	11.11	0	8,956	331	27.05	23

345

LIST OF PLAYERS AND CAREER AVERAGES IN ALL FIRST-CLASS MATCHES FOR YORKSHIRE (Continued)

Player	Date of Birth	Date of Death (if known)	First Played	Last Played	M	Inns	NO	Runs	HS	Av'ge	100s	Runs	Wkts	Av'ge	Ct/St
Holdsworth, W E N	Sept 17, 1928	July 31, 2016	1952	1953	27	26	12	111	22*	7.92	0	1,598	53	30.15	7
Holgate, G	June 23, 1839	July 11, 1895	1865	1867	12	19	0	174	38	9.15	0	—	—	—	17/1
Holmes, P	Nov 25, 1886	Sept 3, 1971	1913	1933	485	699	74	26,220	315*	41.95	60	124	1	124.00	319
Horner, N F	May 10, 1926	Dec 24, 2003	1950	1955	222	411	24	9,523	181	24.53	11	35	0	—	117
Houseman I J	Oct 12, 1969		1989	1991	5	2	1	18	18	18.00	0	311	3	103.66	2
Hoyle, T H	Mar 19, 1884	June 2, 1953	1919	1919	2	2	0	7	7	3.50	0	—	—	—	0/1
Hudson, B	June 29, 1851	Nov 11, 1901	1880	1880	3	4	0	13	7	3.25	0	—	—	—	2
Hunter, D	Feb 23, 1860	Jan 11, 1927	1888	1909	517	681	323	4,177	58*	11.66	0	43	0	—	863/323
Hunter, J	Aug 3, 1855	Jan 4, 1891	1878	1888	143	213	61	1,183	60*	7.78	0	—	—	—	207/102
Hutchison, P M	June 9, 1977		1996	2001	39	39	23	187	30	11.68	0	3,244	143	22.68	8
Hutton, L	June 23, 1916	Sept 6, 1990	1934	1955	341	527	62	24,807	280*	53.34	85	4,221	154	27.40	278
Hutton, R A	Sept 6, 1942		1962	1974	208	292	45	4,986	189	20.18	4	10,254	468	21.91	160
Iddison, R	Sept 15, 1834	Mar 19, 1890	1863	1876	72	108	15	1,916	112	20.60	1	1,540	102	15.09	70
Illingworth, R	June 8, 1932	Dec 25, 2021	1951	1983	496	668	131	14,986	162	27.90	14	26,806	1,431	18.73	285
§ Imran Tahir	Mar 27, 1979		2007	2007	1	2	0	5	5	2.50	0	141	0	—	0
Ingham, P G	Sept 28, 1956		1979	1981	8	14	0	290	64	20.71	0	—	—	—	0
Inglis, J W	Oct 19, 1979		2000	2000	1	2	0	4	2	2.00	0	—	—	—	0
§ Inzamam-ul-Haq	Mar 3, 1970		2007	2007	3	4	0	89	51	22.25	0	—	—	—	5
Jackson, Hon F S *	Nov 21, 1870	Mar 9, 1947	1890	1907	207	328	22	10,371	160	33.89	21	9,690	506	19.15	129
Jackson, S R *	July 15, 1859	July 19, 1941	1891	1891	1	2	0	9	9	4.50	0	—	—	—	0
Jacques, T A *	Feb 19, 1905	Feb 23, 1995	1927	1936	28	20	7	162	35*	12.46	0	1,786	57	31.33	12
Jakeman, F	Jan 10, 1921	May 17, 1986	1946	1947	10	16	2	262	51	18.71	0	—	—	—	3
James, B	Apr 23, 1934	May 26, 1999	1954	1954	4	5	3	22	11*	11.00	0	228	8	28.50	0
§ Jaques, P A	May 3, 1979		2004	2013	53	82	3	4,039	243	51.12	11	112	1	112.00	46
Jarvis, P W	June 29, 1965		1981	1993	138	160	46	1,898	80	16.64	0	11,990	449	26.70	36
Johnson, C	Sept 5, 1947		1969	1979	100	152	14	2,960	107	21.44	2	265	4	66.25	50
Johnson, M	May 16, 1916	Jan 16, 2011	1936	1939	3	3	2	5	4*	5.00	0	27	5	5.40	1
Johnson, M	Apr 23, 1958		1981	1981	4	4	2	2	2	1.00	0	301	7	43.00	0
Joy, J	Dec 29, 1825	Sept 27, 1889	1863	1867	3	5	0	107	74	21.40	0	5	0	—	3

346

LIST OF PLAYERS AND CAREER AVERAGES IN ALL FIRST-CLASS MATCHES FOR YORKSHIRE (Continued)

Player	Date of Birth	Date of Death (if known)	First Played	Last Played	M	Inns	NO	Runs	HS	Av'ge	100s	Runs	Wkts	Av'ge	Ct/St
Judson, A	July 10, 1885		1920	1920	1	—	—	—	—	—	—	5	0	—	0
§ Karich, S M	Aug 21, 1975		2002	2002	1	2	0	37	21	18.50	0	25	0	—	1
Kaye, Harold S *	May 9, 1882	Nov. 6, 1953	1907	1908	18	25	1	243	37	10.12	0	—	—	—	9
Kaye, James	June 11, 1846	Jan 24, 1892	1872	1873	8	14	0	117	33	8.35	0	—	—	—	3
Keedy, G	Nov 27, 1974		1994	1994	1	1	0	1	1	1.00	0	—	—	—	0
§ Keighley, W G * ©	Jan 10, 1925	June 14, 2005	1947	1951	35	51	5	1,227	110	26.67	1	18	0	—	12
Kellett, S A	Oct 16, 1967		1989	1995	86	147	10	4,204	125*	30.68	7	7	0	—	74
Kennie, G	May 17, 1904	Apr 11, 1994	1927	1927	1	2	0	6	6	3.00	0	—	—	—	0
Kettleborough, R A	Mar 15, 1973		1994	1997	13	19	2	446	108	26.23	1	—	—	—	9
Kilburn, S	Oct 16, 1868	Sept 25, 1940	1896	1896	1	1	0	8	8	8.00	0	153	3	51.00	0
Kilner, N	July 21, 1895	Apr 28, 1979	1919	1923	69	73	7	1,253	112	18.98	2	—	—	—	34
Kilner, R ©	Oct 17, 1890	Apr 5, 1928	1911	1927	365	478	46	13,018	206*	30.13	15	14,855	857	17.33	231
King, A M	Oct 8, 1932		1955	1955	1	1	0	12	12	12.00	0	—	—	—	0
Kippax, P J	Oct 15, 1940		1961	1962	4	7	2	37	12	7.40	0	279	8	34.87	1
§ Kirby, S P	Oct 4, 1977		2001	2004	47	61	14	342	57	7.27	0	5,143	182	28.25	11
§§ Kohler-Cadmore, T©	**Apr 19, 1994**		**2017**	**2021**	**40**	**66**	**4**	**2,049**	**176**	**33.04**	**5**	—	—	—	**61**
§ Kruis, G J	May 9, 1974		2005	2009	54	64	31	617	50*	18.69	0	5,431	154	35.26	11
§ Lambert, G A	Jan 4, 1980		2000	2000	2	3	2	6	3*	6.00	0	133	4	33.25	1
Lancaster, W W	Feb 4, 1873	Dec 30, 1938	1895	1895	7	10	0	163	51	16.30	0	29	0	—	1
§ Landon, C W *	May 30, 1850	Mar 5, 1903	1878	1882	9	13	0	51	18	3.92	0	74	0	—	7
Law, W *	Apr 9, 1851	Dec 20, 1892	1871	1873	4	7	0	51	22	7.28	0	—	—	—	3
Lawson, M A K	Oct 24, 1985		2004	2007	15	21	5	197	44	12.31	0	—	—	—	7
Leadbeater, B ©	Aug 14, 1943		1966	1979	144	236	27	5,247	140*	25.10	7	1,699	42	40.45	80
Leadbeater, E	Aug 15, 1927	Apr 17, 2011	1949	1956	81	94	29	898	91	13.81	0	5,657	201	28.14	49
Leadbeater, H *	Dec 31, 1863	Oct 9, 1928	1884	1890	6	10	2	141	65	17.62	0	5	1	5.00	4
§ Leaning, J A ©	Oct 18, 1993		2013	2019	68	108	11	2,955	123	30.46	4	11	0	—	52
Leatham, G A B *	Apr 30, 1851	June 19, 1932	1874	1886	12	18	5	61	14	4.69	0	455	8	56.87	21/7
Leather, R S *	Aug 17, 1880	Jan 3, 1913	1906	1906	1	2	0	19	14	9.50	0	—	—	—	0
Lee, C	Mar 17, 1924	Sept 4, 1999	1952	1952	2	4	0	98	74	24.50	0	—	—	—	1

347

LIST OF PLAYERS AND CAREER AVERAGES IN ALL FIRST-CLASS MATCHES FOR YORKSHIRE (Continued)

Player	Date of Birth	Date of Death (if known)	First Played	Last Played	M	Inns	NO	Runs	HS	Av'ge	100s	Runs	Wkts	Av'ge	Ct/St
Lee, G ©	Nov 18, 1856	Sept 13, 1896	1882	1890	105	182	10	3,622	165	21.05	3	—	—	—	53/1
Lee, G H	Aug 24, 1854	Oct 4, 1919	1879	1879	1	2	0	13	9	6.50	0	—	—	—	0
Lee, Herbert	July 2, 1856	Feb 4, 1908	1885	1885	5	6	0	20	12	3.33	0	—	—	—	2
Lee, J E *	Mar 23, 1838	Apr 2, 1880	1867	1867	2	3	0	9	6	3.00	0	—	—	—	0
Lee, J E	Dec 23, 1988		2006	2009	2	3	1	24	21*	12.00	0	149	2	74.50	1
Lees, D J	**Jan 10, 2001**		**2020**	**2021**	**3**	**2**	**1**	**1**	**1***	**1.00**	**0**	**213**	**4**	**53.25**	**0**
Lees, A Z	Apr 14, 1993		2010	2018	82	140	11	4,528	275*	35.10	11	77	2	38.50	56
Legard, A D *	June 19, 1878	Aug 15, 1939	1910	1910	4	5	0	50	15	10.00	0	26	0	—	1
§ Lehmann, D S ©	Feb 5, 1970		1997	2006	88	137	8	8,871	339	68.76	26	1,952	61	32.00	35
§ Lehmann, J S	Jul 8, 1992		2016	2016	5	8	1	384	116	54.85	1	—	—	—	0
Leyland, M ©	Feb 18, 1923	Mar 23, 2015	1945	1956	228	339	27	10,616	186	34.02	24	160	3	53.33	106
Lilley, A E	July 20, 1900	Jan 1, 1967	1920	1946	548	720	82	26,180	263	41.03	62	11,079	409	27.08	204
Linaker, L	Apr 17, 1992		2011	2011	1	—	—	—	—	—	—	34	0	—	0
Lister, B	Apr 8, 1885	Nov 17, 1961	1909	1909	1	2	0	0	0	0.00	0	28	1	28.00	0
Lister, J *	Dec 9, 1850	Dec 3, 1919	1874	1878	7	11	0	36	10	3.60	0	—	—	—	2
§ Lister-Kaye, K A *	May 14, 1930	Jan 28, 1991	1954	1954	2	4	0	35	16	8.75	0	—	—	—	0
Lockwood, E	Apr 4, 1845	Feb 28, 1955	1928	1928	1	2	1	13	7*	13.00	0	64	1	64.00	2
Lockwood, H	Oct 20, 1855	Dec 19, 1921	1868	1884	214	364	29	7,789	208	23.25	6	2,265	141	16.06	164/2
Lodge, J T	Apr 16, 1921	Feb 18, 1921	1877	1882	16	27	2	408	90	16.32	0	37	0	—	8
Logan, J E G	Oct 12, 1997	July 9, 2002	1948	1948	2	2	1	48	30	16.00	0	17	0	—	1
Loten, T W	**Jan 8, 1999**		**2019**	**2019**	**2**	**3**	**1**	**33**	**20***	**16.50**	**0**	**85**	**4**	**21.25**	**0**
Love, J D	Apr 22, 1955		2018	**2021**	**5**	**7**	**0**	**126**	**58**	**18.00**	**0**	—	—	—	**1**
Lowe, G E	Jan 12, 1877	Aug 15, 1932	1975	1989	247	388	58	10,263	170*	31.10	13	835	12	69.58	123
Lowe J R	Oct 19,1991		1902	1902	1	1	0	5	5*	—	0	—	0	—	0
Lowson, F A	July 1, 1925	Sept 8, 1984	2010	2010	1	1	0	5	5	5.00	0	—	0	—	0
§ Lucas, D S	Aug 19, 1978		1949	1958	252	404	31	13,897	259*	37.25	30	15	0	—	180
Lumb, E *	Sept 12, 1852	Apr 5, 1891	2005	2005	1	—	—	—	—	—	—	84	8	10.50	0
§ Lumb, M J	Sept 12, 1980		1872	1886	14	23	4	311	70*	16.36	0	—	—	—	5
Lumb, R G	Feb 27, 1950		2000	2006	78	135	12	4,194	144	34.09	8	199	5	39.80	43
			1970	1984	239	395	30	11,525	165*	31.57	22	5	0	—	129

348

LIST OF PLAYERS AND CAREER AVERAGES IN ALL FIRST-CLASS MATCHES FOR YORKSHIRE (Continued)

Player	Date of Birth	Date of Death (if known)	First Played	Last Played	M	Inns	NO	Runs	HS	Av'ge	100s	Runs	Wkts	Av'ge	Ct/St
Lupton, A W * ....©	Feb 23, 1879	Apr 14, 1944	1908	1927	104	79	15	668	43*	10.43	0	88	0	—	25
Lynas, G G	Sept 7, 1832	Dec 8, 1896	1867	1867	2	3	1	4	4*	2.00	0	—	—	—	2
Lyth, A ....**©**	**Sept 25, 1987**		**2007**	**2021**	**180**	**301**	**16**	**11,085**	**251**	**38.89**	**26**	**1,633**	**35**	**46.65**	**249**
Macaulay, G G ....©	Dec 7, 1897	Dec 13, 1940	1920	1935	445	430	112	5,717	125*	17.97	0	30,554	1,774	17.22	361
McGrath, A	Oct 6, 1975		1995	2012	242	405	29	14,091	211	37.47	34	4,652	128	36.34	168
McHugh, F P	Nov 15, 1925		1949	1949	3	1	0	0	0	0.00	0	147	4	36.75	1
§ Maharaj, K A	Feb 7, 1990		2019	2019	5	9	0	239	85	26.55	0	719	38	18.92	1
§ Malan, D J ....**©**	**Sept 3,1987**		**2020**	**2021**	**5**	**8**	**0**	**552**	**219**	**69.00**	**2**	**24**	**2**	**12.00**	**4**
§ Marsh, S E	Jul 9, 1983		2017	2017	2	3	1	225	125*	112.50	1	—	—	—	1
Marshall, S	July 10, 1849	Aug 3, 1891	1874	1874	1	2	1	2	1	1.00	0	11	0	—	2
§ Martyn, D R	Oct 21, 1971		2003	2003	1	2	0	342	238	171.00	1	—	—	—	2
Mason, A	May 2, 1921		1947	1950	18	19	3	105	22	6.56	0	1,473	51	28.88	6
Maude, E *	Dec 31, 1839	Mar 22, 2006	1866	1866	2	2	0	17	16	8.50	0	—	—	—	0
§ Maxwell, G J	Oct 14, 1988	July 2, 1876	2015	2015	4	7	1	244	140	40.66	1	144	4	36.00	3
Metcalfe, A A ....©	Dec 25, 1963		1983	1995	184	317	19	10,465	216*	35.11	25	344	3	114.66	72
Micklethwait, W H * ..	Dec 13, 1885	Oct 7, 1947	1911	1911	1	1	0	44	44	44.00	0	—	—	—	0
Middlebrook, J D	May 13, 1977		1998	2015	29	38	3	534	84	15.25	0	1,899	66	28.77	17
Middlebrook, W	May 23, 1858	Apr 26, 1919	1888	1889	17	27	7	88	19*	4.40	0	895	50	17.90	17
Midgley, C A *	May 24, 1877	June 24, 1942	1906	1906	4	6	2	115	59	28.75	0	149	8	18.62	3
Milburn, S M	Sept 29, 1972		1992	1995	6	8	2	22	7	3.66	0	431	14	30.78	0
§ Milligan, F W * .....©	Mar 19, 1870	Mar 31, 1900	1894	1898	81	113	10	1,879	74	18.24	0	2,736	112	24.42	40
Mitchell, A ....©	Sept 13, 1902	Dec 25, 1976	1922	1945	401	550	69	18,189	189	37.81	39	291	5	58.20	406
Mitchell, F * ....©	Aug 13, 1872	Oct 11, 1935	1894	1904	83	125	5	4,104	194	34.20	10	16	1	16.00	52
Monks, G D	Sept 3, 1929	Jan 3, 2011	1952	1952	1	1	0	3	3	3.00	0	—	—	—	0
Moorhouse, R ....©	Sept 7, 1866	Jan 7, 1921	1888	1899	206	315	45	5,217	113	19.32	8	1,232	43	28.65	92
§ Morkel, M	Oct 6, 1984		2008	2008	1	2	0	8	8	4.00	0	33	1	33.00	0
Morris, A C	Oct 4, 1976		1995	1997	16	23	2	362	60	17.23	0	508	9	56.44	12
§ Mosley, H	Mar 8, 1850	Nov 29, 1933	1881	1881	2	2	0	1	1	0.25	0	34	3	11.33	1
Motley, A *	Feb 5, 1858	Sept 28, 1897	1879	1879	2	2	1	10	8*	10.00	0	135	7	19.28	1

349

LIST OF PLAYERS AND CAREER AVERAGES IN ALL FIRST-CLASS MATCHES FOR YORKSHIRE (Continued)

Player	Date of Birth	Date of Death (if known)	First Played	Last Played	M	Inns	NO	Runs	HS	Av'ge	100s	Runs	Wkts	Av'ge	Ct/St
Mounsey, J T	Aug 30, 1871	Apr 6, 1949	1891	1897	92	145	21	1,939	64	15.63	0	444	10	44.40	45
Moxon, M D ©	May 4, 1960		1981	1997	277	476	42	18,973	274*	43.71	41	1,213	22	55.13	190
Myers, H ©	Jan 2, 1875	June 12, 1944	1901	1910	201	289	46	4,450	91	18.31	0	7,095	282	25.15	106
Myers, M	Apr 12, 1847	Dec 8, 1919	1876	1878	22	40	4	537	49	14.91	0	20	—	—	11
§ Naved-ul-Hasan, Rana	Feb 28, 1978		2008	2009	11	16	3	207	32	15.92	0	1,018	26	39.15	3
Naylor, J E	Dec 11, 1930	June 27, 1996	1953	1953	1	—	—	—	—	—	—	88	0	—	0
Newstead, J T	Sept 8, 1877	Mar 25, 1952	1903	1913	96	128	17	1,791	100*	16.13	1	5,555	297	18.70	75
Nicholson, A G	June 25, 1938	Nov 3, 1985	1962	1975	282	267	125	1,667	50	11.73	0	17,296	876	19.74	85
Nicholson, N G ©	Oct 17, 1963		1988	1989	5	8	3	134	56*	26.80	0	25	0	—	5
§ Northeast, S A	Oct 16, 1989		2021	2021	2	2	0	4	3	2.00	0	0	0	—	2
Oates, William	Jan 1, 1852	Dec 9, 1940	1874	1875	7	13	7	34	14*	5.66	0	—	—	—	5/1
Oates, W F	June 11, 1929	May 15, 2001	1956	1956	3	3	0	20	10	6.66	0	—	—	—	0
Old, C M ©	Dec 22, 1948		1966	1982	222	262	56	4,785	116	23.22	5	13,409	647	20.72	131
Oldham, S	July 26, 1948		1974	1985	59	39	18	212	50	10.09	0	3,849	130	29.60	18
Oldroyd, E	Oct 1, 1888	Dec 27, 1964	1910	1931	383	509	58	15,891	194	35.23	37	1,658	42	39.47	203
§ Olivier, D ©	May 9, 1992		2019	2021	25	32	17	224	24	14.93	0	2,432	75	32.42	7
Oyston, C	May 12, 1869	July 15, 1942	1900	1909	15	21	8	96	22	7.38	0	872	31	28.12	3
Padgett, D E V ©	July 20, 1934		1951	1971	487	774	63	20,306	161*	28.55	29	208	6	34.66	250
Padgett, G H	Oct 9, 1931		1952	1952	7	7	4	56	32*	18.66	0	336	4	84.00	5
Padgett, J	Nov 15, 1860	Aug 2, 1943	1882	1889	6	9	0	92	22	10.22	0	—	—	—	2
Parker, B	June 23, 1970		1992	1998	44	71	10	1,839	138*	30.14	2	3	0	—	19
§ Parkin, C H	Feb 18, 1886	June 15, 1943	1906	1906	1	1	0	0	0	0.00	0	25	2	12.50	0
Parratt, J	Mar 24, 1859	May 6, 1905	1888	1890	2	2	0	11	11	5.50	0	75	1	75.00	4
§ Parton, J W	Jan 31, 1863	Jan. 30, 1906	1889	1889	2	2	0	16	14	8.00	0	4	0	—	0
§ Patel, A Y ©	Oct 3, 1988		2019	2019	2	2	1	20	20	20.00	0	231	2	115.50	0
Patterson, S A ©	**Oct 3, 1983**		**2005**	**2021**	**172**	**207**	**45**	**2,568**	**63***	**15.85**	**0**	**12,466**	**452**	**27.57**	**34**
Pearson, H E	Aug 7, 1851	July 8, 1903	1878	1880	4	7	5	31	10*	15.50	0	90	5	18.00	1
Pearson, J H	May 14, 1915	May 13, 2007	1934	1936	3	3	0	54	44	18.00	0	—	—	—	0
Peate, E	Mar 2, 1855	Mar 11, 1900	1879	1887	154	226	61	1,793	95	10.86	0	9,986	794	12.57	97

350

LIST OF PLAYERS AND CAREER AVERAGES IN ALL FIRST-CLASS MATCHES FOR YORKSHIRE (Continued)

Player	Date of Birth	Date of Death (if known)	First Played	Last Played	M	Inns	NO	Runs	HS	Av'ge	100s	Runs	Wkts	Av'ge	Ct/St
Peel, R ©.......	Feb 12, 1857	Aug 12, 1941	1882	1897	318	510	42	9,322	210*	19.91	6	20,638	1,311	15.74	141
Penny, J H	Sept 29, 1856	July 29, 1902	1891	1891	1	1	1	8	8*	—	0	31	2	15.50	1
Pickles, C S ...	Jan 30, 1966	June 22, 2020	1985	1992	58	76	21	1,336	66	24.29	0	3,638	83	43.83	24
Pickles, D	Nov 16, 1935		1957	1960	41	40	20	74	12	3.70	0	2,062	96	21.47	10
§ Pillans, M W	**Jul 4, 1991**		**2018**	**2019**	**2**	**2**	**0**	**11**	**8**	**5.50**	**0**	**189**	**2**	**94.50**	**0**
Pinder, G	July 15, 1841	Jan 15, 1903	1867	1880	125	199	44	1,639	57	10.57	0	325	19	17.10	145/102
Platt, R K	Dec 26, 1932		1955	1963	96	103	47	405	57*	7.23	0	6,389	282	22.65	35
Plunkett, L E ©	Apr 6, 1985		2013	2017	36	51	7	1,241	126	28.20	1	2,925	98	29.84	20
Pollard, G	Aug 7, 1835	Mar 26, 1909	1865	1865	1	2	0	3	3	1.50	0	19	0	—	0
Pollitt, G	June 3, 1874	May 19, 1942	1899	1899	1	1	0	51	51	51.00	0	—	—	—	1
§ Poysden, J E	Aug 8, 1991		2018	2018	3	5	2	25	20*	8.33	0	259	7	37.00	0
Prest, C H * ...	Dec 9, 1841	Mar 4, 1875	1864	1864	2	4	0	57	31	14.25	0	—	—	—	3
Preston, J M ... ©	Aug 23, 1864	Nov 26, 1890	1885	1889	79	134	11	1,935	93	15.73	0	3,232	178	18.15	36
Pride, T	July 23, 1864	Feb 16, 1919	1887	1887	1	1	0	1	1	1.00	0	—	—	—	4/3
Priestley, I M .	Sept 25, 1967		1989	1989	1	2	0	25	23	12.50	0	119	4	29.75	1
Pullan, P	Mar 29, 1857	Mar 3, 1901	1884	1884	1	2	0	14	14	14.00	0	5	0	—	1
§ Pujara, C A .. ©	Jan 25, 1988		2015	2018	10	18	1	436	133*	25.64	1	—	—	—	6
Pyrah, R M .... ©	Nov 1, 1982		2004	2015	51	61	8	1,621	134*	30.58	3	2527	55	45.94	22
§ Radcliffe, E J R H * ©	Jan 27, 1884	Nov 23, 1969	1909	1911	64	89	13	826	54	10.86	0	134	2	67.00	21
Ramage, A	Nov 29, 1957		1979	1983	23	22	9	219	52	16.84	0	1,649	44	37.47	2
Ramsden, G ...	Mar 2, 1983		2000	2000	1	1	1	0	0*	—	0	68	1	68.00	1
Randhawa, G S	Jan 25, 1992		2011	2011	1	1	0	5	5	5.00	0	62	2	31.00	0
Raper, J R S *	Aug 9, 1909	Mar 9, 1997	1936	1947	3	4	0	24	15	6.00	0	—	—	—	0
Rashid, A U .... ©	**Feb 17, 1988**		**2006**	**2017**	**140**	**196**	**33**	**5,620**	**180**	**34.47**	**10**	**14,136**	**420**	**33.65**	**70**
§ Rawlin, J A .. ©	May 22, 1988		2018	2018	4	7	0	84	71	12.00	0	—	—	—	3
Rawlin, E R	Oct 14, 1897	Jan 11, 1943	1927	1936	8	10	2	72	35	8.00	0	498	21	23.71	2
Rawlin, J T	Nov 10, 1856	Jan 19, 1924	1880	1885	27	36	2	274	30	8.05	0	258	11	23.45	13
Rawlinson, E B	Apr 10, 1837	Feb 17, 1892	1867	1875	37	68	5	991	55	15.73	0	62	5	12.40	16
Read, J	Feb 2, 1998		2016	2016	1	1	0	14	14	14.00	0	—	—	—	4
Redfearn, J	May 13, 1862	Jan 14, 1931	1890	1890	1	1	0	5	5	5.00	0	—	—	—	0

351

LIST OF PLAYERS AND CAREER AVERAGES IN ALL FIRST-CLASS MATCHES FOR YORKSHIRE (Continued)

Player	Date of Birth	Date of Death (if known)	First Played	Last Played	M	Inns	NO	Runs	HS	Av'ge	100s	Runs	Wkts	Av'ge	Ct/St
Render, G W A	Jan 5, 1887	Sept 17, 1922	1919	1919	1	1	0	5	5	5.00	0	—	—	—	0
Revis, M L	**Nov 15, 2001**		**2019**	**2021**	**2**	**4**	**0**	**43**	**34**	**10.75**	**0**	**19**	**2**	**9.50**	**1**
Rhodes, A C	Oct 14, 1906	May 21, 1957	1932	1934	61	70	19	917	64*	17.98	0	3,026	107	28.28	45
§ Rhodes, H E *	Jan 11, 1852	Sept 10, 1889	1878	1883	10	16	1	269	64	17.93	0	—	—	—	1
Rhodes, S J	June 17, 1964		1981	1984	3	2	1	41	35	41.00	0	—	—	—	3
© Rhodes, Wilfred	Oct 29, 1877	July 8, 1973	1898	1930	883	1,195	162	31,075	267*	30.08	46	57,634	3,598	16.01	586
§ Rhodes, William	Mar 4, 1883	Aug 5, 1941	1911	1911	1	1	0	—	1*	—	0	40	0	—	0
Richardson, J A *	Mar 2, 1995		2015	2016	15	25	2	689	95	29.95	0	551	16	34.43	8
§ Richardson, R B	Aug 4, 1908	Apr 2, 1985	1936	1947	7	12	2	308	61	30.80	0	90	2	45.00	3
© Richardson, S A	Jan 12, 1962		1993	1994	23	39	1	1,310	112	34.47	1	23	1	23.00	18
§ Richardson, S A	Sept 5, 1977		2000	2003	13	23	1	377	69	17.95	0	—	—	—	11
Riley, H	Aug 17, 1875	Nov 6, 1922	1895	1900	4	5	1	36	25*	9.00	0	54	1	54.00	1
Riley, M *	Apr 5, 1851	June 1, 1899	1878	1882	17	28	1	361	92	13.37	0	10	0	—	3
© Ringrose, W	Sept 2, 1871	Sept 14, 1943	1901	1906	57	66	9	353	23	6.19	0	3,224	155	20.80	25
© Robinson, A L	Aug 17, 1946		1971	1977	84	69	31	365	30*	9.60	0	4,927	196	25.13	48
Robinson, B L H	May 12, 1858	Dec 14, 1909	1879	1879	1	2	1	5	4	2.50	0	20	1	20.00	0
Robinson, Edward *	Dec 27, 1862	Sept 3, 1942	1887	1887	1	2	1	23	23*	23.00	0	—	—	—	0
Robinson, Emmott	Nov 16, 1883	Nov 17, 1969	1919	1931	413	455	77	9,651	135*	25.53	7	19,645	893	21.99	318
© Robinson, E P	Aug 10, 1911	Nov 10, 1998	1934	1949	208	253	46	2,596	75*	12.54	0	15,141	735	20.60	189
Robinson, M A	Nov 23, 1966		1991	1995	90	93	36	240	23	4.21	0	6,866	218	31.49	17
© Robinson, P E	Aug 3, 1963		1984	1991	132	217	31	6,668	189	35.84	7	238	1	238.00	96
Robinson, W	Nov 29, 1851	Aug 14, 1919	1876	1877	7	14	1	151	68	11.61	0	—	—	—	3
Roebuck C G	Aug 14, 1991		2010	2010	1	1	0	23	23	23.00	0	—	—	—	0
© **Root, J E**	**Dec 30, 1990**		**2010**	**2021**	**52**	**86**	**9**	**3,410**	**236**	**44.28**	**8**	**901**	**18**	**50.05**	**32**
Roper, E *	Apr 8, 1851	Apr 27, 1921	1878	1880	5	7	1	85	68	14.16	0	—	—	—	2
© Rothery, J W	Sept 5, 1876	June 2, 1919	1903	1910	150	236	18	4,614	161	21.16	3	44	2	22.00	45
Rowbotham, J	July 8, 1831	Dec 22, 1899	1863	1876	94	162	9	2,624	113	17.15	3	37	3	12.33	52
© Rudolph J A	May 4, 1981		2007	2011	68	112	8	5,429	228*	52.20	18	311	1	311.00	79
Rudston, H	Nov 22, 1878	Apr 14, 1962	1902	1907	21	30	6	609	164	20.30	1	—	—	—	3

LIST OF PLAYERS AND CAREER AVERAGES IN ALL FIRST-CLASS MATCHES FOR YORKSHIRE (Continued)

Player	Date of Birth	Date of Death (if known)	First Played	Last Played	M	Inns	NO	Runs	HS	Av'ge	100s	Runs	Wkts	Av'ge	Ct/St
Ryan, M	©June 23, 1933	Nov 16, 2015	1954	1965	150	149	58	682	26*	7.49	0	9,466	413	22.92	59
Ryder, L	Aug 28, 1900	Jan 24, 1955	1924	1924	2	2	1	1	1	1.00	0	151	4	37.75	2
Sanderson B W	Jan 3, 1989		2008	2010	3	2	1	6	6	6.00	0	190	6	31.66	0
Savile, G*	Apr 26, 1847	Sept 4, 1904	1867	1874	5	7	0	140	65	20.00	0				2
Sayers, J J	©Nov 5, 1983		2004	2013	97	161	13	4,855	187	32.80	9	166	6	27.66	60
Schofield, C J	Mar 21, 1976		1996	1996	1	1	0	25	25	25.00	0				0
Schofield, D	Oct 9, 1947		1970	1974	3	4	4	13	6*	—	0	112	5	22.40	0
Scott, E	July 6, 1834	Dec 3, 1898	1864	1864	1	1	0	8	8	8.00	0	27	2	13.50	1
Sedgwick, H A	Apr 8, 1883	Dec 28, 1957	1906	1906	3	5	2	53	34	17.66	0	327	16	20.43	2
Sellers, Arthur*	©May 31, 1870	Sept 25, 1941	1890	1899	49	88	5	1,643	105	18.88	2	84	2	42.00	40
Sellers, A B *	©Mar 5, 1907	Feb 20, 1981	1932	1948	334	437	51	8,949	204	23.18	4	653	8	81.62	264
Shackleton, W A	Mar 9, 1908	Nov 16, 1971	1928	1934	5	6	0	49	25	8.16	0	130	6	21.66	3
Shahzad, Ajmal	©July 27, 1985		2006	2012	45	58	14	1,145	88	26.02	0	4,196	125	33.56	5
Sharp, K	©Apr. 6, 1959		1976	1990	195	320	35	8,426	181	29.56	11	836	12	69.66	95
§ Sharpe, C M *	Sept 6, 1851	June 25, 1935	1875	1875	1	1	0	15	15	15.00	0	17		—	0
Sharpe, P J	©Dec 27, 1936	May 19, 2014	1958	1974	411	666	71	17,685	203*	29.72	23	140	2	70.00	526
Shaw C	Feb 17, 1964		1984	1988	61	58	27	340	31	10.96	0	4,101	123	33.34	9
Shaw, James	Mar 12, 1865	Jan 22, 1921	1896	1897	3	3	0	8	7	2.66	0	181	7	25.85	2
Shaw, Joshua	Jan 3, 1996		2016	2019	8	11	2	144	42	16.00	0	617	12	51.41	1
Sheepshanks, E R *	Mar 22, 1910	Dec 31, 1937	1929	1929	1	1	0	26	26	26.00	0			—	1
Shepherd, D A *	Mar 10, 1916	May 29, 1998	1938	1938	1	1	1	0	0	0.00	0			—	0
Shotton, W	Dec 1, 1840	May 26, 1909	1865	1874	2	4	0	13	7	3.25	0			—	0
Shutt, J W	**June 24, 1997**		**2020**	**2020**	**3**	**4**	**3**	**7**	**7***	**7.00**	**0**	**104**	**2**	**52.00**	**2**
Sidebottom, A	©Apr 1, 1954		1973	1991	216	249	50	4,243	124	22.33	1	13,852	558	24.82	60
Sidebottom, R J	©Jan 15, 1978		1997	2017	137	172	55	1,674	61	14.30	0	10,128	450	22.50	37
Sidgwick, R*	Aug 7, 1851	Oct 23, 1933	1882	1882	9	13	0	64	17	4.92	0			—	2
Silverwood, C E W	©Mar 5, 1975		1993	2005	131	179	33	2,369	80	16.22	0	11,413	427	27.62	30
Silvester, S	Mar 12, 1951		1976	1977	6	7	4	30	14	10.00	0	313	12	26.08	2
Simpson, E T B *	Mar 5, 1867	Mar 20, 1944	1889	1889	1	2	0	1	1	0.50	0			—	0

LIST OF PLAYERS AND CAREER AVERAGES IN ALL FIRST-CLASS MATCHES FOR YORKSHIRE (Continued)

Player	Date of Birth	Date of Death (if known)	First Played	Last Played	M	Inns	NO	Runs	HS	Av'ge	100s	Runs	Wkts	Av'ge	Ct/St
§ Sims, Rev H M *	Mar 15, 1853	Oct 5, 1885	1875	1877	5	10	1	109	35*	12.11	0	—	—	—	2
Slinn, W	Dec 13, 1826	June 17, 1888	1863	1864	9	14	3	22	11	2.00	0	742	48	15.45	5
Smailes, T F ....©	Mar 27, 1910	Dec 1, 1970	1932	1948	262	339	42	5,686	117	19.14	3	16,593	802	20.68	153
Smales, K	Sept 15, 1927	Mar 10, 2015	1948	1950	13	19	3	165	45	10.31	0	766	22	34.81	4
Smith, A F	Mar 7, 1847	Jan 6, 1915	1868	1874	28	49	4	692	89	15.37	0	—	—	—	11
Smith, E (Morley) * ©	Oct 19, 1869	April 9, 1945	1888	1907	154	234	18	4,453	129	20.61	2	6,278	248	25.31	112
Smith, E (Barnsley)	July 11, 1888	Jan 2, 1972	1914	1926	16	21	5	169	49	10.56	0	1,090	46	23.69	5
Smith, Fred (Yeadon)	Dec 18, 1879	Oct 20, 1905	1903	1903	13	19	1	292	55	16.22	0	—	—	—	6
Smith, Fred (Idle)	Dec 26, 1885	Not known	1911	1911	1	1	0	11	11	11.00	0	45	2	22.50	0
Smith, G	Jan 19, 1875	Jan 16, 1929	1901	1906	2	1	0	7	7	7.00	0	62	0	—	0
Smith, J	Mar 23, 1833	Feb 12, 1909	1865	1865	1	2	0	28	16	9.33	0	72	6	12.00	3
Smith, N	Apr 1, 1949		1970	1971	8	11	0	82	20	13.66	0	—	—	—	14/3
Smith, R	Apr 6, 1944		1969	1970	5	8	3	99	37*	19.80	0	—	—	—	0
Smith, Walter	Aug 19, 1845	June 2, 1926	1874	1874	5	9	0	152	59	16.88	0	—	—	—	3
§ Smith, William	Nov 1, 1839	Apr 19, 1897	1865	1874	11	19	3	260	90	16.25	0	—	—	—	8
Smithson, G A ....©	Nov 1, 1926	Sept 6, 1970	1946	1950	39	60	5	1,449	169	26.34	2	84	1	84.00	21
Smurthwaite, J	Oct 17, 1916	Oct 20, 1989	1938	1939	7	9	5	29	20*	7.25	0	237	12	19.75	4
Sowden, N	Dec 1, 1853	July 5, 1921	1878	1887	7	8	1	87	37	12.45	0	22	0	—	1
Squire, H	Dec 31, 1864	Apr 28, 1922	1893	1893	1	2	0	0	0	0.00	0	25	0	—	0
Squires, P J	Aug 4, 1951		1972	1976	49	84	8	1,271	70	16.72	0	32	0	—	14
Stanley, H C *	Feb 16, 1888	May 18, 1934	1911	1913	8	13	0	155	42	11.92	0	—	—	—	6
§ Stanyforth, R T *	May 30, 1892	Feb 20, 1964	1928	1928	3	3	1	26	10	8.66	0	—	—	—	2
Starc, M A	Jan 30, 1990		2012	2012	2	1	1	28	28*	—	0	153	7	21.85	0
Stead, B	June 21, 1939	Apr 15, 1980	1959	1959	2	3	0	8	8	2.66	0	115	7	16.42	0
§ Stemp, R D ....©	Dec 11, 1967		1993	1998	104	135	36	1,267	65	12.79	0	8,557	241	35.50	49
Stephenson, E	June 5, 1832	July 5, 1898	1863	1873	36	61	5	803	67	14.33	0	—	—	—	30/27
Stephenson, J S *	Nov 10, 1903	Oct 7, 1975	1923	1926	16	19	2	182	60	10.70	0	65	0	—	6
Stevenson, G B ....©	Dec 16, 1955	Jan 21, 2014	1973	1986	177	217	32	3,856	115*	20.84	2	13,254	464	28.56	73
Stott, W B ....©	July 18, 1934		1952	1963	187	309	19	9,168	186	31.61	17	112	7	16.00	91

354

LIST OF PLAYERS AND CAREER AVERAGES IN ALL FIRST-CLASS MATCHES FOR YORKSHIRE (Continued)

Player	Date of Birth	Date of Death (if known)	First Played	Last Played	M	Inns	NO	Runs	HS	Av'ge	100s	Runs	Wkts	Av'ge	Ct/St
Stringer, P M	Feb 23, 1943		1967	1969	19	17	8	101	15*	11.22	0	696	32	21.75	7
Stuchbury, S	June 22, 1954		1978	1981	3	3	2	11	7*	7.00	0	236	8	29.50	0
§ Sugg, F H	Jan 11, 1862	May 29, 1933	1883	1883	8	12	4	80	13*	10.00	0	—	—	—	4/1
§ Sugg, W	May 21, 1860	May 21, 1933	1881	1881	1	1	0	9	9	9.00	0	—	—	—	0
Sullivan, J H B *	Sept 21, 1890	Feb 8, 1932	1912	1912	1	2	0	41	26	20.50	0	43	0	—	0
Sutcliffe, H ......©	Nov 24, 1894	Jan 22, 1978	1919	1945	602	864	96	38,558	313	50.20	112	381	8	47.62	402
Sutcliffe, W H H * ..©	Oct 10, 1926		1948	1957	177	273	34	6,247	181	26.13	6	152	6	25.33	80
Swallow, I G	Dec 18, 1962		1983	1989	61	82	18	1,296	114	20.25	1	3,270	64	51.09	28
§ Swanepoel, P J	Mar 30, 1977		2003	2003	2	3	0	20	17	6.66	0	129	3	43.00	1
§ Tait, T	Oct 7, 1872	Sept 6, 1954	1898	1899	2	3	1	7	3	3.50	0	—	—	—	1
Tasker, J * ....©	Feb 4, 1887	Aug 24, 1975	1912	1913	31	43	4	586	67	15.02	0	—	—	—	14
Tattersall, G *	Apr 21, 1882	June 29, 1972	1905	1905	1	2	0	26	26	13.00	0	—	—	—	0
Tattersall, J A	**Dec 15, 1994**		**2018**	**2021**	**32**	**49**	**5**	**1,374**	**135***	**31.22**	**1**	—	—	—	**80/4**
Taylor, C R	Feb 21, 1981		2001	2008	16	27	3	416	52*	17.33	0	—	—	—	8
Taylor, H	Dec 18, 1900	Oct 28, 1988	1924	1925	9	13	0	153	36	11.76	0	—	—	—	1
Taylor, H S	Dec 11, 1856	Nov 16, 1896	1879	1879	3	5	0	36	22	7.20	0	—	—	—	0
Taylor, J	Apr 2, 1850	May 27, 1924	1880	1881	9	13	1	107	44	8.91	0	—	—	—	4
Taylor, K	Aug 21, 1935		1953	1968	303	505	35	12,864	203*	27.37	16	3,680	129	28.52	146
Taylor, N S	June 2, 1963		1982	1983	8	6	4	10	4	5.00	0	720	22	32.72	2
Taylor, T L * ....©	May 25, 1878	Mar. 16, 1960	1899	1906	82	122	10	3,933	156	35.11	8	—	—	—	47/2
§ Tendulkar, S R ...©	Apr 24, 1973		1992	1992	16	25	2	1,070	100	46.52	1	195	4	48.75	10
Thewlis, H	Aug 31, 1865	Nov 30, 1920	1888	1888	2	4	1	4	2*	1.33	0	—	—	—	2
Thewlis, John Sen.	Mar 11, 1828	Dec 29, 1899	1863	1875	44	80	3	1,280	108	16.62	1	—	—	—	21/1
Thewlis, John Jun.	Sept 21, 1850	Aug 9, 1901	1879	1879	3	4	0	21	10	5.25	0	—	—	—	0
Thompson, J A	**Oct 8, 1996**		**2019**	**2021**	**20**	**29**	**1**	**681**	**98**	**24.32**	**0**	**1,300**	**66**	**19.69**	**6**
Thornicroft, N D	Jan 23, 1985		2002	2007	7	10	4	50	30	8.33	0	545	16	34.06	2
Thornton, A	July 20, 1854	Apr 18, 1915	1881	1881	3	4	0	21	7	5.25	0	—	—	—	2
Thornton, G *	Dec 24, 1867	Jan 31, 1939	1891	1891	3	4	0	21	16	5.25	0	74	2	37.00	0

LIST OF PLAYERS AND CAREER AVERAGES IN ALL FIRST-CLASS MATCHES FOR YORKSHIRE (Continued)

Player	Date of Birth	Date of Death (if known)	First Played	Last Played	M	Inns	NO	Runs	HS	Av'ge	100s	Runs	Wkts	Av'ge	Ct/St
Thorpe, G	Feb 20, 1834	Mar 2, 1899	1864	1864	1	2	1	14	9*	14.00	0	—	—	—	2
Threapleton, J W	July 20, 1857	July 30, 1918	1881	1881	1	1	0	8	8*	—	0	—	—	—	2/1
Tinsley, H J	Feb 20, 1865	Dec 10, 1938	1890	1891	9	13	0	56	15	4.30	0	57	4	14.25	1
Townsley, R A J	June 24, 1952		1974	1975	2	4	0	22	12	5.50	0	0	0	—	—
Towse, A D	Apr 22, 1968		1988	1988	1	1	0	1	1	1.00	0	50	3	16.66	1
Trueman, F S	Feb 6, 1931	July 1, 2006	1949	1968	459	533	81	6,852	104	15.15	2	29,890	1,745	17.12	325
Tunnicliffe, J	Aug 26, 1866	July 11, 1948	1891	1907	472	768	57	19,435	243	27.33	22	388	7	55.42	665
Turner, A	Sept 2, 1885	Aug 29, 1951	1910	1911	9	16	1	163	37	10.86	0	—	—	—	7
Turner, B	July 25, 1938	Dec 27, 2015	1960	1961	2	4	2	7	3*	3.50	0	47	4	11.75	2
Turner, C	Jan 11, 1902	Nov 19, 1968	1925	1946	200	266	32	6,132	130	26.20	2	5,320	173	30.75	181
Turner, F I	Sept 3, 1894	Oct 18, 1954	1924	1924	5	7	0	33	12	4.71	0	—	—	—	2
Tyson, C T	Jan 24, 1889	Apr 3, 1940	1921	1921	3	5	2	232	100*	77.33	1	—	—	—	1
Ullathorne, C E	Apr 11, 1845	May 2, 1904	1868	1875	27	46	8	283	7	7.44	0	—	—	—	19
Ulyett, G	Oct 21, 1851	June 18, 1898	1873	1893	355	618	31	14,157	199*	24.11	15	8,181	457	17.90	235
§ Usher, J	Feb 26, 1859	Aug 9, 1905	1888	1888	1	2	0	7	5	3.50	0	31	2	15.50	1
van Geloven, J	Jan 4, 1934	Aug 21, 2003	1955	1955	3	3	1	17	16	17.00	0	224	6	37.33	2
§ Vaughan, M P	Oct 29, 1974		1993	2009	151	267	14	9,160	183	36.20	20	4,268	92	46.39	55
§ Verelst, H W *	July 2, 1846	Apr 5, 1918	1868	1869	3	4	1	66	33*	22.00	0	—	—	—	1
Verity, H	May 18, 1905	July 31, 1943	1930	1939	278	294	77	3,898	101	17.96	1	21,353	1,558	13.70	191
Waddington, A	Feb 4, 1893	Oct 28, 1959	1919	1927	255	250	65	2,396	114	12.95	0	16,203	835	19.40	222
Wade, S	Feb 8, 1858	Nov 5, 1931	1886	1890	65	11	20	1,438	74*	15.80	0	2,498	133	18.78	31
Wainwright D J	Mar 21, 1985		2004	2011	29	36	11	914	104*	36.56	0	2,480	69	35.94	6
Wainwright, E	Apr 8, 1865	Oct 28, 1919	1888	1902	352	545	30	11,092	228	21.53	18	17,744	998	17.77	327
Wainwright, W	Jan 21, 1882	Dec 31, 1961	1903	1905	24	38	6	648	62	19.63	0	582	19	30.63	21
Waite, M J	**Dec 24, 1995**		**2017**	**2019**	**8**	**11**	**1**	**160**	**42**	**16.00**	**0**	**583**	**23**	**25.34**	**2**
Wake, W R *	May 21, 1852	Mar 14, 1896	1881	1881	3	3	0	13	11	4.33	0	—	—	—	2
Walker, A *	June 22, 1844	May 26, 1927	1863	1870	9	16	1	138	26	9.20	0	74	1	74.00	3

LIST OF PLAYERS AND CAREER AVERAGES IN ALL FIRST-CLASS MATCHES FOR YORKSHIRE (Continued)

Player	Date of Birth	Date of Death (if known)	First Played	Last Played	M	Inns	NO	Runs	HS	Av'ge	100s	Runs	Wkts	Av'ge	Ct/St
Walker, C	June 27, 1919	Dec 3, 1992	1947	1948	5	9	2	268	91	38.28	0	71	2	35.50	1
Walker, T	Apr 3, 1854	Aug 28, 1925	1879	1880	14	22	2	179	30	8.95	0	7	0	—	3
Waller, G	Dec 3, 1864	Dec 11, 1937	1893	1894	3	4	0	17	13	4.25	0	70	4	17.50	1
Wallgate, L *	Nov 12, 1849	May 9, 1887	1875	1878	3	3	0	9	6	3.00	0	17	1	17.00	3
Ward, A	Nov 21, 1865	Jan 6, 1939	1886	1886	4	7	1	41	22	6.83	0	1	0	—	0
Ward, F	Aug 31, 1881	Feb 28, 1948	1903	1903	1	1	1	0	0	0.00	0	—	—	—	0
Ward, H P *	Jan 20, 1899	Dec 16, 1946	1920	1920	1	1	0	10	10*	—	0	16	0	—	1
Wardall, T A	Apr 19, 1862	Dec 20, 1932	1884	1894	43	73	2	1,003	106	14.12	2	489	23	21.26	25
Wardlaw, I	Jun 29, 1985		2011	2012	4	3	2	31	17*	31.00	0	368	4	92.00	2
Wardle, J H ©	Jan 8, 1923	July 23, 1985	1946	1958	330	418	57	5,765	79	15.96	0	27,917	1,539	18.13	210
Waring, J S	Oct 1, 1942		1963	1966	28	27	15	137	26	11.41	0	1,122	53	21.16	17
Waring, S *	Nov 4, 1838	Apr 17, 1919	1870	1870	1	1	0	9	9	9.00	0	—	—	—	0
Warner, J D	Nov 14, 1996		2020	2020	1	1	0	4	4	4.00	0	23	1	23.00	0
Washington, W A ©	Dec 11, 1879	Oct 20, 1927	1900	1902	44	62	6	1,290	100*	23.03	1	—	—	—	18
Watson, H	Sept 26, 1880	Nov 24, 1951	1908	1914	29	35	11	141	41	5.87	0	—	—	—	46/10
Watson, W ©	Mar 7, 1920	Apr 24, 2004	1939	1957	283	430	65	13,953	214*	38.22	26	75	0	—	170
Waud, B W *	June 4, 1837	May 31, 1889	1863	1864	6	10	1	165	42	18.33	0	—	—	—	2
Webster, C	June 9, 1838	Jan 6, 1881	1868	1868	3	5	1	30	10	7.50	0	—	—	—	1
Webster, H H	May 8, 1844	Mar 5, 1915	1868	1868	2	3	0	10	10	3.33	0	—	—	—	0
§ Weekes, L C	July 19, 1971		1994	2000	2	2	0	20	10	10.00	0	191	10	19.10	1
West, J	Oct 16, 1844	Jan 27, 1890	1868	1876	38	64	13	461	41	9.03	0	853	53	16.09	14
Wharf, A G	June 4, 1975		1994	1997	7	9	1	186	62	23.25	0	454	11	41.27	2
Whatmough, F J	Dec 4, 1856	June 3, 1904	1878	1882	7	11	1	51	20	5.10	0	111	5	22.20	4
Wheater, C H *	Mar 4, 1860	May 11, 1885	1880	1880	2	4	1	45	27	15.00	0	—	—	—	2
White, Sir A W *	Oct 14, 1877	Dec 16, 1945	1908	1920	97	128	28	1,457	55	14.57	0	7	0	—	50
White, J ©	Dec 16, 1969		1990	2007	221	350	45	10,376	186	34.01	19	7,649	276	27.71	140
Whitehead, J P ©	Sept 3, 1925	Aug 15, 2000	1946	1951	37	38	17	387	58*	18.42	0	2,610	96	27.47	11
Whitehead, Lees ©	Mar 14, 1864	Nov 22, 1913	1889	1904	119	172	38	2,073	67*	15.47	0	2,408	99	24.32	68

357

LIST OF PLAYERS AND CAREER AVERAGES IN ALL FIRST-CLASS MATCHES FOR YORKSHIRE (Continued)

Player	Date of Birth	Date of Death (if known)	First Played	Last Played	M	Inns	NO	Runs	HS	Av'ge	100s	Runs	Wkts	Av'ge	Ct/St
Whitehead, Luther	June 25, 1869	Jan 17, 1931	1893	1893	2	4	0	21	13	5.25	0	—	—	—	0
Whiteley, J P	Feb 28, 1955		1978	1982	45	38	17	231	20	11.00	0	2,410	70	34.42	21
Whiting, C P	Apr 18, 1888	Jan 14, 1959	1914	1920	6	10	2	92	26	11.50	0	416	15	27.73	2
Whitwell, J F *	Feb 22, 1869	Nov 6, 1932	1890	1890	1	2	0	8	4	4.00	0	11	1	11.00	0
§ Whitwell, W F *	Dec 12, 1867	Apr 12, 1942	1890	1890	10	14	2	67	26	5.58	0	518	25	20.72	2
Widdup, S	Nov 10, 1977		2000	2001	11	18	1	245	44	14.41	0	22	1	22.00	5
Wigley, D H	Oct 26, 1981		2002	2002	7	2	1	19	15	19.00	0	116	1	116.00	0
§ Wilkinson, A J A *	May 28, 1835	Dec 11, 1905	1865	1868	5	6	0	129	53	21.50	0	57	0	—	1
Wilkinson, F	May 23, 1914	Mar 26, 1984	1937	1939	14	14	1	73	18*	5.61	0	590	26	22.69	12
Wilkinson, H *	© Dec 11, 1877	Apr 15, 1967	1903	1905	48	75	3	1,382	113	19.19	1	121	3	40.33	19
Wilkinson, R	Nov 11, 1977		1998	1998	1	1	0	9	9	9.00	0	35	1	35.00	0
Wilkinson, W H	© Mar 12, 1881	June 4, 1961	1903	1910	126	192	14	3,812	103	21.41	1	971	31	31.32	93
§ Willey, D J	© Feb 28, 1990		2016	2021	19	26	6	463	46	23.15	0	1,494	50	29.88	4
Williams, A C	Mar 1, 1887	June 1, 1966	1911	1919	12	14	10	95	48*	23.75	0	678	30	22.60	6
§ Williamson, K S	© Aug 8, 1990		2013	2018	19	32	3	1,292	189	44.55	1	475	11	43.18	20
Wilson, B B	© Dec 11, 1879	Sept 14, 1957	1906	1914	185	308	12	8,053	208	27.50	15	278	2	139.00	53
Wilson, C E M *	May 15, 1875	Feb 8, 1944	1896	1899	9	13	3	256	91*	25.60	0	257	12	21.41	3
Wilson, D	Aug 7, 1937	July 21, 2014	1957	1974	392	502	85	5,788	83	13.88	0	22,626	1,104	20.49	235
Wilson, E R *	© Mar 25, 1879	July 21, 1957	1899	1923	66	72	18	902	104*	16.70	1	3,106	197	15.76	30
Wilson, Geoffrey *	© Aug 21, 1895	Nov 29, 1960	1919	1924	92	94	14	983	70	12.28	0	11	0	—	33
Wilson, G A *	Feb 2, 1916	Sept 24, 2002	1936	1939	15	25	5	352	55*	17.60	0	138	1	138.00	7
Wilson, John *	June 30, 1857	Nov 11, 1931	1887	1888	4	5	1	17	13*	4.25	0	165	12	13.75	3
Wilson, J P *	Apr 3, 1889	Oct 3, 1959	1911	1912	9	14	1	81	36	6.23	0	24	1	24.00	2
Wilson, J V	Jan 17, 1921	June 5, 2008	1946	1962	477	724	75	20,548	230	31.66	29	313	3	104.33	520
Wood, A	© Aug 25, 1898	Apr 1, 1973	1927	1946	408	481	80	8,579	123*	21.39	1	33	1	33.00	612/243
Wood, B	Dec 26, 1942		1964	1964	5	7	2	63	35	12.60	0	—	—	—	4
Wood, C H	July 23, 1934	June 28, 2006	1959	1959	4	4	1	22	10	7.33	0	319	11	29.00	1
Wood, G W	Nov 18, 1862	Dec 4, 1948	1895	1895	2	2	0	2	2	1.00	0	—	—	—	0/1

358

LIST OF PLAYERS AND CAREER AVERAGES IN ALL FIRST-CLASS MATCHES FOR YORKSHIRE (Continued)

Player	Date of Birth	Date of Death (if known)	First Played	Last Played	M	Inns	NO	Runs	HS	Av'ge	100s	Runs	Wkts	Av'ge	Ct/St
Wood, H *	Mar 22, 1855	July 31, 1941	1879	1880	10	16	1	156	36	10.40	0	212	10	21.20	8
Wood, J H *			1881	1881	2	1	0	14	14	14.00	0	—	—	—	0
Wood, M J ....©	Apr 6, 1977		1997	2007	128	222	20	6,742	207	33.37	16	27	2	13.50	113
Wood, R	June 3, 1929	May 22, 1990	1952	1956	22	18	4	60	17	4.28	0	1,346	51	26.39	5
Woodford, J D	Sept 9, 1943		1968	1972	38	61	2	1,204	101	20.40	1	185	4	46.25	12
Woodhead, F E *	May 29, 1868	Aug 25, 1943	1893	1894	4	8	0	57	18	7.12	0	—	—	—	3
Woodhouse, W H *	Apr 16, 1856	Mar 4, 1938	1884	1885	9	13	0	218	63	16.76	0	—	—	—	6
Wormall, A	May 10, 1855	Feb 6, 1940	1885	1891	7	11	3	161	80	20.12	0	—	—	—	10/2
Worsley, W A * ...©	Apr 5, 1890	Dec 4, 1973	1928	1929	60	50	4	722	56	15.69	0	—	—	—	32
Wrathmell, L F	Jan 22, 1855	Sept 16, 1928	1886	1886	1	2	0	18	17	9.00	0	—	—	—	0
Wright, R	July 19, 1852	Jan 2, 1891	1877	1877	2	4	1	28	22	9.33	0	—	—	—	0
Wright, T J *	Mar 5, 1900	Nov 7, 1962	1919	1919	1	1	0	12	12	12.00	0	—	—	—	0
Yardley, N W D ... ©	Mar 19, 1915	Oct 3, 1989	1936	1955	302	420	56	11,632	183*	31.95	17	5,818	195	29.83	220
Yeadon, J	Dec 10, 1861	May 30, 1914	1888	1888	3	6	2	41	22	10.25	0	—	—	—	5/3
§ Younus Khan ......©	Nov 29, 1977		2007	2007	13	19	2	824	217*	48.47	3	342	8	42.75	11
§ Yuvraj Singh	Dec 12, 1981		2003	2003	7	12	2	145	56	14.50	0	130	3	43.33	12

In the career averages it should be noted that the bowling analysis for the second Cambridgeshire innings at Ashton-under-Lyne in 1865 has not been found. G R Atkinson took 3 wickets, W Cuttell 2, G Freeman 4 and R Iddison 1. The respective bowling averages have been calculated excluding these wickets.

MOST FIRST-CLASS APPEARANCES FOR YORKSHIRE

Matches	Player	Matches	Player
883	W Rhodes (1898-1930)	477	J V Wilson (1946-1962)
717	G H Hirst (1891-1929)	472	J Tunnicliffe (1891-1907)
676	D Denton (1894-1920)	459	F S Trueman (1949-1968)
602	H Sutcliffe (1919-1945)	456	J H Hampshire (1961-1981)
548	M Leyland (1920-1947)	445	G G Macaulay (1920-1935)
536	D B Close (1949-1970)	429	D L Bairstow (1970-1990)
517	D Hunter (1888-1909)	427	A Dolphin (1905-1927)
513	S Haigh (1895-1913)	425	P Carrick (1970-1993)
510	Lord Hawke (1881-1911)	414	G Boycott (1962-1986)
496	R Illingworth (1951-1983)	413	E. Robinson (1919-1931)
491	† J G Binks (1955-1969)	411	P J Sharpe (1958-1974)
487	D E V Padgett (1951-1971)	408	A Wood (1927-1946)
485	P Holmes (1913-1933)	401	A Mitchell (1922-1945)

† Kept wicket in 412 consecutive Championship matches 1955-1969

MOST TOTAL APPEARANCES FOR YORKSHIRE
(First-Class, Domestic List A and t20)

Matches	Player	Matches	Player
883	W Rhodes (1898-1930)	513	S Haigh (1895-1913)
832	D L Bairstow (1970-1990)	510	Lord Hawke (1881-1911)
729	P Carrick (1970-1993)	502	P J Sharpe (1958-1974)
719	R J Blakey (1985-2004)	485	P Holmes (1913-1933)
717	G H Hirst (1891-1929)	477	J V Wilson (1946-1962)
690	J H Hampshire (1961-1981)	472	J Tunnicliffe (1891-1907)
678	G Boycott (1962-1986)	470	F S Trueman (1949-1968)
676	D Denton (1894-1920)	467	J D Love (1975-1989)
602	H Sutcliffe (1919-1945)	453	D Wilson (1957-1974)
583	A McGrath (1995-2012)	452	A Sidebottom (1973-1991)
581	D Byas (1986-2001)	445	G G Macaulay (1920-1935)
568	D B Close (1949-1970)	443	C M Old (1966-1982)
548	M Leyland (1920-1947)	427	A Dolphin (1905-1927)
546	C White (1990-2007)	414	P J Hartley (1985-1997)
544	D E V Padgett (1951-1971)	413	E Robinson (1919-1931)
537	R Illingworth (1951-1983)	408	A Wood (1927-1946)
521	J G Binks (1955-1969)	402	A G Nicholson (1962-1975)
517	D Hunter (1888-1909)	401	A Mitchell (1922-1945)
514	M D Moxon (1980-1997)		

ONE DAY RECORDS SECTION

Yorkshire County Cricket Club thanks Statistician JOHN T. POTTER, who in 2014 revamped and streamlined Yorkshire's One-Day Records Section. John's symbols in the pages that follow are:

$ = Sunday and National Leagues, Pro 40, Clydesdale Bank 40 and Yorkshire Bank 40

\# = Benson & Hedges Cup

\+ = Gillette Cup, NatWest Trophy, Cheltenham & Gloucester Trophy, Friends Provident Trophy and Royal London Cup

Yorkshire played no List A matches in 2020 because of the Covid-19 pandemic

WINNERS OF THE GILLETTE CUP, NATWEST TROPHY, CHELTENHAM & GLOUCESTER TROPHY FRIENDS PROVIDENT TROPHY AND ROYAL LONDON ONE-DAY CUP

Yorkshire's Position

GILLETTE CUP

Year	Opponent	Yorkshire's Position
1963	Sussex	Quarter-Final
1964	Sussex	Round 2
1965	**Yorkshire**	**Winner**
1966	Warwickshire	Round 2
1967	Kent	Quarter-Final
1968	Warwickshire	Round 2
1969	**Yorkshire**	**Winner**
1970	Lancashire	Round 1
1971	Lancashire	Round 2
1972	Lancashire	Round 1
1973	Gloucestershire	Round 1
1974	Kent	Quarter-Final
1975	Lancashire	Round 2
1976	Northamptonshire	Round 2
1977	Middlesex	Round 2
1978	Sussex	Quarter-Final
1979	Somerset	Quarter-Final
1980	Middlesex	Semi-Final

NATWEST TROPHY

1981	Derbyshire	Round 1
1982	Surrey	Semi-Final
1983	Somerset	Round 2
1984	Middlesex	Round 1
1985	Essex	Round 2
1986	Sussex	Quarter-Final
1987	Nottinghamshire	Quarter-Final
1988	Middlesex	Round 2
1989	Warwickshire	Round 2
1990	Lancashire	Quarter-Final
1991	Hampshire	Round 1
1992	Northamptonshire	Round 2
1993	Warwickshire	Quarter-Final
1994	Worcestershire	Round 2
1995	Warwickshire	Semi-Final
1996	Lancashire	Semi-Final
1997	Essex	Quarter-Final
1998	Lancashire	Round 2
1999	Gloucestershire	Semi-Final
2000	Gloucestershire	Round 4

CHELTENHAM & GLOUCESTER TROPHY

2001	Somerset	Quarter-Final
2002	**Yorkshire**	**Winner**
2003	Gloucestershire	Round 4
2004	Gloucestershire	Semi-Final
2005	Hampshire	Semi-Final
2006	Sussex	North 7 (10)

FRIENDS PROVIDENT TROPHY

2007	Durham	North 5 (10)
2008	Essex	Semi-Final
2009	Hampshire	Group C 3 (5)

ROYAL LONDON ONE-DAY CUP

2014	Durham	Quarter-Final
2015	Gloucestershire	Semi-Final
2016	Warwickshire	Semi-Final
2017	Nottinghamshire	Quarter-Final
2018	Hampshire	Semi-Final
2019	Somerset	North 6 (9)
2020	*Not played: COVID-19 restrictions*	
2021	Glamorgan	Quarter-Final

WINNERS OF THE NATIONAL AND SUNDAY LEAGUES, PRO 40, CLYDESDALE BANK 40 AND YORKSHIRE BANK 40 1969-2014

Yorkshire's Position

SUNDAY LEAGUE

1969	Lancashire	8th
1970	Lancashire	14th
1971	Worcestershire	15th
1972	Kent	4th
1973	Kent	2nd
1974	Leicestershire	=6th
1975	Hampshire	=5th
1976	Kent	15th
1977	Leicestershire	=13th
1978	Hampshire	7th
1979	Somerset	=4th
1980	Warwickshire	=14th
1981	Essex	=7th
1982	Sussex	16th
1983	**Yorkshire**	**1st**
1984	Essex	=14th
1985	Essex	6th
1986	Hampshire	8th
1987	Worcestershire	=13th
1988	Worcestershire	8th
1989	Lancashire	11th
1990	Derbyshire	6th
1991	Nottinghamshire	7th
1992	Middlesex	15th
1993	Glamorgan	9th
1994	Warwickshire	5th
1995	Kent	12th
1996	Surrey	3rd
1997	Warwickshire	10th
1998	Lancashire	9th

NATIONAL LEAGUE

1999	Lancashire	5th Div 1
2000	Gloucestershire	2nd Div 1
2001	Kent	6th Div 1
2002	Glamorgan	4th Div 1
2003	Surrey	8th Div 1
2004	Glamorgan	4th Div 2
2005	Essex	8th Div 2
2006	Essex	9th Div 2
2007	Worcestershire	6th Div 2
2008	Sussex	2nd Div 2
2009	Sussex	7th Div 1

CLYDESDALE BANK 40

2010	Warwickshire	Group B 1 (7) (Semi-Final)
2011	Surrey	Group A 6 (7)
2012	Hampshire	Group C 5 (7)
2013	Nottinghamshire	Group C 6 (7)

BENSON & HEDGES WINNERS 1972-2002

Yorkshire's Position

1972	Leicestershire	Final
1973	Kent	Group N 3 (5)
1974	Surrey	Quarter-Final
1975	Leicestershire	Quarter-Final
1976	Kent	Group D 3 (5)
1977	Gloucestershire	Group D 3 (5)
1978	Kent	Group D 4 (5)
1979	Essex	Semi-Final
1980	Northamptonshire	Group B 4 (5)
1981	Somerset	Quarter-Final
1982	Somerset	Group A 5 (5)
1983	Middlesex	Group B 5 (5)
1984	Lancashire	Semi-Final
1985	Leicestershire	Group B 3 (5)
1986	Middlesex	Group B 3 (5)
1987	**Yorkshire**	**Winner**
1988	Hampshire	Group B 4 (5)
1989	Nottinghamshire	Group C 3 (5)
1990	Lancashire	Group C 3 (5)
1991	Worcestershire	Semi-Final
1992	Hampshire	Group C 5 (5)
1993	Derbyshire	Round One
1994	Warwickshire	Round One
1995	Lancashire	Quarter-Final
1996	Lancashire	Semi-Final
1997	Surrey	Quarter-Final
1998	Essex	Semi-Final
1999	Gloucestershire	Final
2000	Gloucestershire	Quarter-Final
2001	Surrey	Semi-Final
2002	Warwickshire	Quarter-Final

SEASON-BY-SEASON RECORD OF ALL LIST A MATCHES PLAYED BY YORKSHIRE 1963-2021

Season	Played	Won	Lost	Tie	N R	Abd	Season	Played	Won	Lost	Tie	N R	Abd
1963	2	1	1	0	0	0	1994	19	11	8	0	0	1
1964	1	0	1	0	0	0	1995	27	15	11	0	1	1
1965	4	4	0	0	0	1	1996	27	18	9	0	0	0
1966	1	0	1	0	0	0	1997	25	14	10	1	0	0
1967	2	1	1	0	0	0	1998	25	14	10	0	1	0
1968	1	0	1	0	0	0	1999	23	13	10	0	0	0
1969	19	12	7	0	0	2	2000	24	13	10	0	1	0
1970	17	5	10	0	2	0	2001	26	13	13	0	0	0
1971	15	5	10	0	0	2	2002	27	16	11	0	0	1
1972	25	15	8	0	2	1	2003	18	6	12	0	0	0
1973	21	14	7	0	0	0	2004	23	13	8	0	2	0
1974	22	12	9	0	1	1	2005	22	8	14	0	0	0
1975	22	12	10	0	0	0	2006	15	4	10	0	1	2
1976	22	9	13	0	0	0	2007	17	8	7	0	2	1
1977	19	5	10	0	4	2	2008	18	10	4	1	3	0
1978	22	10	11	0	1	2	2009	16	6	9	0	1	0
1979	21	12	6	0	3	3	2010	13	10	3	0	0	0
1980	23	9	14	0	0	0	2011	12	5	7	0	0	0
1981	19	9	8	0	2	3	2012	11	4	7	0	0	1
1982	23	7	14	1	1	1	2013	13	4	9	0	0	0
1983	19	11	7	0	1	3	2014	10	6	4	0	0	0
1984	23	10	13	0	0	0	2015	10	5	3	0	2	0
1985	19	9	9	0	1	3	2016	10	5	4	0	1	0
1986	22	11	9	1	1	1	2017	10	6	3	0	1	0
1987	24	14	9	0	1	2	2018	9	6	3	0	0	1
1988	21	9	9	0	3	1	2019	8	2	3	2	0	0
1989	23	10	13	0	0	0	2020	No matches played due to Covid-19					
1990	22	13	9	0	0	1	2021	9	4	3	0	2	0
1991	24	13	10	0	1	0							
1992	21	8	13	0	0	2		1007	499	458	6	44	40
1993	21	10	10	1	0	0							

Abandoned matches are not included in the list of matches played.

ABANDONED LIST A MATCHES (40)

1965	v. South Africa at Bradford
1969 (2)	v. Warwickshire at Harrogate $
	v. Lancashire at Manchester $
1971 (2)	v. Gloucestershire at Sheffield $
	v. Somerset at Weston-Super-Mare $
1972	v. Sussex at Leeds $
1974	v. Warwickshire at Leeds $
1977 (2)	v. Warwickshire at Birmingham $
	v. Surrey at Leeds $
1978 (2)	v. Essex at Bradford $
	v. Gloucestershire at Hull $
1979 (3)	v. Leicestershire at Middlesbrough $
	v. Kent at Huddersfield $
	v. Worcestershire at Worcester $
1981 (3)	v. Warwickshire at Birmingham $
	v. Lancashire at Leeds #
	v. Sussex at Hove $
1982	v. Glamorgan at Bradford $
1983 (3)	v. Derbyshire at Chesterfield #
	v. Surrey at Leeds $
	v. Essex at Chelmsford $
1985 (3)	v. Derbyshire at Scarborough $
	v. Warwickshire at Birmingham $
	v. Lancashire at Leeds $
1986	v. Kent at Canterbury $
1987 (2)	v. Sussex at Hull $
	v. Hampshire at Leeds $
1988	v. Northamptonshire at Northampton $
1990	v. Glamorgan at Newport $
1992 (2)	v. Sussex at Hove $
	v. Durham at Darlington $
1994	v. Essex at Leeds $
1995	v. Derbyshire at Chesterfield #
1997	v. Sussex at Scarborough $
2002	v. Nottinghamshire at Nottingham $
2006 (2)	v. Nottinghamshire at Leeds +
	v. Derbyshire at Derby $
2007	v. Warwickshire at Birmingham +
2012	v. Northamptonshire at Leeds $
2018	v. Nottinghamshire at Leeds +

ANALYSIS OF LIST A RESULTS V. ALL TEAMS 1963-2021
DOMESTIC MATCHES

		HOME				AWAY				
Opponents	Played	Won	Lost	Tied	N. R	Won	Lost	Tied	N. R	Abd
Derbyshire	66	20	9	1	1	21	9	1	4	4
Durham	31	10	5	0	1	7	7	0	1	1
Essex	48	12	12	0	0	11	13	0	0	3
Glamorgan	40	9	8	0	0	10	13	0	0	2
Gloucestershire	55	12	12	0	2	8	19	0	2	2
Hampshire	45	11	9	0	1	9	15	0	0	1
Kent	55	13	11	0	1	10	20	0	0	2
Lancashire	64	10	17	0	2	15	18	0	2	3
Leicestershire	69	20	16	0	0	14	16	1	2	1
Middlesex	48	14	4	0	3	9	16	0	2	0
Northamptonshire	61	18	11	0	4	20	7	0	1	2
Nottinghamshire	61	19	8	1	3	10	17	0	3	3
Somerset	55	13	14	0	1	11	16	0	0	1
Surrey	57	12	16	0	0	11	18	0	0	2
Sussex	46	11	11	0	1	11	12	0	0	5
Warwickshire	64	12	18	1	2	13	17	1	0	6
Worcestershire	65	13	20	0	2	17	13	0	0	1
Bedfordshire	1	0	0	0	0	1	0	0	0	0
Berkshire	2	0	0	0	0	2	0	0	0	0
Cambridgeshire	3	2	0	0	0	1	0	0	0	0
Cheshire	1	0	0	0	0	1	0	0	0	0
Combined Universities	3	0	2	0	0	1	0	0	0	0
Devon	4	0	0	0	0	4	0	0	0	0
Dorset	1	0	0	0	0	1	0	0	0	0
Durham (M C)	3	1	1	0	0	1	0	0	0	0
Herefordshire	1	0	0	0	0	1	0	0	0	0
Ireland	4	3	0	0	0	1	0	0	0	0
Minor Counties	11	6	0	0	0	5	0	0	0	0
Netherlands	4	1	1	0	0	1	1	0	0	0
Norfolk	2	1	0	0	0	1	0	0	0	0
Northumberland	1	1	0	0	0	0	0	0	0	0
Scotland	16	8	0	0	0	8	0	0	0	0
Shropshire	2	0	0	0	0	1	1	0	0	0
Unicorns	4	2	0	0	0	2	0	0	0	0
Wiltshire	1	0	0	0	0	1	0	0	0	0
Yorkshire Cricket Board	1	0	0	0	0	1	0	0	0	0
Total	**995**	**254**	**205**	**3**	**24**	**241**	**248**	**3**	**17**	**39**

OTHER MATCHES

Australia	3	0	1	0	2	0	0	0	0	0
Bangladesh A	1	1	0	0	0	0	0	0	0	0
South Africa	0	0	0	0	0	0	0	0	0	1
South Africa A	1	0	0	0	1	0	0	0	0	0
Sri Lanka A	3	0	3	0	0	0	0	0	0	0
West Indies	1	1	0	0	0	0	0	0	0	0
West Indies A	1	0	1	0	0	0	0	0	0	0
Young Australia	1	1	0	0	0	0	0	0	9	0
Zimbabwe	1	1	0	0	0	0	0	0	0	0
Total	**12**	**4**	**5**	**0**	**3**	**0**	**0**	**0**	**0**	**1**
Grand Total	**1007**	**258**	**210**	**3**	**27**	**241**	**248**	**3**	**17**	**40**

Abandoned matches are not included in the list of matches played.

LIST A HIGHEST AND LOWEST SCORES BY AND AGAINST YORKSHIRE
PLUS INDIVIDUAL BEST BATTING AND BOWLING

The lowest score is the lowest all-out total or the lowest score at completion of the allotted overs, 10-over matches not included

Yorkshire versus:

Derbyshire

	By Yorkshire			Against Yorkshire		
Highest Score:	In Yorkshire	349:7		at Leeds 2017 +	334:8	at Leeds 2017 +
	Away	288:6		at Derby 2002 #	268:8	at Chesterfield 2010 $
Lowest Score:	In Yorkshire	117		at Huddersfield 1978 $	87	at Scarborough 1973 $
	Away	132		at Chesterfield 1986 #	127	at Chesterfield 1972 #
Best Batting:	In Yorkshire	140	P S P Handscomb	at Leeds 2017 +	112 W L Madsen	at Leeds 2017 +
	Away	115*	M J Wood	at Derby 2002 #	109* C J Adams	at Derby 1997 $
Best Bowling:	In Yorkshire	6-32	S A Patterson	at Leeds 2010 $	4-20 F E Rumsey	at Bradford 1973 #
	Away	5-35	C W J Athey	at Chesterfield 1981 $	5-24 C J Tunnicliffe	at Derby 1981 #

Durham

Highest Score:	In Yorkshire	339:4		at Leeds 2017 +	335:5	at Leeds 2017 +
	Away	328:4		at Chester-le-Street 2018 +	281:7	at Chester-le-Street 2016 +
Lowest Score:	In Yorkshire	133		at Leeds 1995 $	121	at Scarborough 1997 $
	Away	122		at Chester-le-Street 2007 $	136	at Chester-le-Street 1996 $
Best Batting:	In Yorkshire	174	J M Bairstow	at Leeds 2017 +	114 W Larkins	at Leeds 1993 $
	Away	164	T Kohler-Cadmore	at Chester-le-Street 2018 +	124* J P Maher	at Chester-le-Street 2006 +
Best Bowling	In Yorkshire	4-18	C White	at Scarborough 1997 $	4-20 S J E Brown	at Leeds 1995 $
	Away	4-26	C E W Silverwood	at Chester-le-Street 1996 $	4-31 P D Collingwood	at Chester-le-Street 2000 #

Essex

Highest Score:	In Yorkshire	290:6		at Scarborough 2014 +	291:5	at Scarborough 2014 +
	Away	307:3		at Chelmsford 1995 +	317:7	at Chelmsford 2021 +
Lowest Score:	In Yorkshire	54		at Leeds 2003 $	108	at Leeds 1996 $
	Away	119:8		at Colchester 1987 $	123	at Colchester 1974 $
Best Batting:	In Yorkshire	111*	J A Leaning	at Scarborough 2014 +	119* R N ten Doeschate	at Scarborough 2014 +
	Away	125*	A W Gale	at Chelmsford 2010 $	136* N Hussain	at Chelmsford 2002 #
Best Bowling:	In Yorkshire	4-20	G B Stevenson	at Barnsley 1977 #	6-18 R E East	at Hull 1969 $
	Away	4-31	A L Robinson	at Leyton 1976 $	5-20 R E East	at Colchester 1979 $

LIST A HIGHEST AND LOWEST SCORES BY AND AGAINST YORKSHIRE
PLUS INDIVIDUAL BEST BATTING AND BOWLING (Continued)

Yorkshire versus:

Glamorgan

		By Yorkshire			Against Yorkshire	
Highest Score:	In Yorkshire	253:4		at Leeds 2013 $	216:6	at Leeds 2013 $
	Away	257		at Colwyn Bay 2013 $	285:7	at Colwyn Bay 2013 $
Lowest Score:	In Yorkshire	139		at Hull 1981 $	83	at Leeds 1987 +
	Away	93-8		at Swansea 1985 $	90	at Neath 1969 $
Best Batting:	In Yorkshire	96	A A Metcalfe	at Leeds 1991 $	97* G P Ellis	at Leeds 1976 $
	Away	141*	M D Moxon	at Cardiff 1991 #	127 A R Butcher	at Cardiff 1991 #
Best Bowling:	In Yorkshire	5-22	P Carrick	at Leeds 1991 $	5-26 D S Harrison	at Leeds 2002 $
	Away	6-40	R J Sidebottom	at Cardiff 1998 $	5-16 G C Holmes	at Swansea 1985 $

Gloucestershire

Highest Score:	In Yorkshire	263:9		at Leeds 2015 +	269	at Leeds 2009 +
	Away	262:7		at Bristol 1996 $	294:6	at Cheltenham 2010 $
Lowest Score:	In Yorkshire	115		at Leeds 1973 $	91	at Scarborough 2001 $
	Away	133		at Cheltenham 1999 $	90	at Tewkesbury 1972 $
Best Batting:	In Yorkshire	118	J A Rudolph	at Leeds 2009 +	146* S Young	at Leeds 1997 $
	Away	100*	J D Love	at Gloucester in 1985 $	143* C M Spearman	at Bristol 2004 $
		100*	R J Blakey	at Cheltenham 1990 $		
Best Bowling:	In Yorkshire	5-42	N D Thornicroft	at Leeds 2003 $	5-33 M C J Ball	at Leeds 2003 $
	Away	4-25	R D Stemp	at Bristol 1996 $	5-42 M C J Ball	at Cheltenham 1999 $

Hampshire

Highest Score:	In Yorkshire	259:4		at Middlesbrough 1985 $	257:6	at Middlesbrough 1985 $
	Away	264:2		at Southampton 1995 $	348:9	at West End, Southampton, 2018 +
Lowest Score:	In Yorkshire	74:9		at Hull 1970 $	50	at Leeds 1991 #
	Away	118		at Leeds 1999 #	133	at Bournemouth 1976 $
Best Batting:	In Yorkshire	104*	D Byas	at Leeds 1999 #	155* B A Richards	at Hull 1970 $
	Away	97*	M G Bevan	at Southampton 1995 $	171 J M Vince	at West End, Southampton, 2018 +
Best Bowling:	In Yorkshire	5-16	G M Hamilton	at Leeds 1998 $	5-33 A J Murtagh	at Huddersfield 1977 $
	Away	5-33	A U Rashid	at Southampton 2014 +	5-31 D W White	at Southampton 1969 $

LIST A HIGHEST AND LOWEST SCORES BY AND AGAINST YORKSHIRE
PLUS INDIVIDUAL BEST BATTING AND BOWLING *(Continued)*

Yorkshire versus:

Kent

		By Yorkshire		Against Yorkshire	
Highest Score:	In Yorkshire	299:3	at Leeds 2002 $	232:8	at Leeds 2011 $
	Away	263:3	at Maidstone 1998 $	266:5	at Maidstone 1998 $
Lowest Score:	In Yorkshire	75	at Leeds 1995 $	133	at Leeds 1974 $
				133	at Leeds 1979 #
Best Batting:	Away	114	at Canterbury 1978 #	105	at Canterbury 1969 $
	In Yorkshire	130*	R J Blakey	at Scarborough 1991 $	118* M H Denness	at Scarborough 1976 $
	Away	102	A McGrath	at Canterbury 2001 $	118* C J Tavare	at Canterbury 1981 +
Best Bowling:	In Yorkshire	4-15	A G Nicholson	at Leeds 1974 $	6-32 M T Coles	at Leeds 2012 $
	Away	6-18	D Wilson	at Canterbury 1969 $	5-25 B D Julien	at Canterbury 1971 +

Lancashire

Highest Score:	In Yorkshire	310		at Leeds 2019 +	311:6		at Leeds 2019 +
	Away	379:7		at Manchester 2018 +	363		at Manchester 2018 +
Lowest Score:	In Yorkshire	81		at Leeds 1998 $	68		at Leeds 2000 $
		81		at Leeds 2002 +			
	Away	125		at Manchester 1973 #	84		at Manchester 2016 +
Best Batting:	In Yorkshire	111*	D Byas	at Leeds 1996 $	102* N J Speak	at Leeds 1992 $
	Away	144	A Lyth	at Manchester 2018 +	141* B J Hodge	at Manchester 2007 +
Best Bowling:	In Yorkshire	5-25	C White	at Leeds 2000 #	6-25 G Chapple	at Leeds 1998 $
	Away	4-18	G S Blewett	at Manchester 1999 +	5-49 M Watkinson	at Manchester 1991 #

Leicestershire

Highest Score:	In Yorkshire	379:7		at Leeds 2019 +	302:7		at Leeds 2008 $
	Away	376:3		at Leicester 2016 +	327:7		at Leicester 2021 +
Lowest Score:	In Yorkshire	93		at Leeds 1998 $	141		at Hull 1975 $
	Away	89:9		at Leicester 1989 $	53		at Leicester 2000 $
Best Batting:	In Yorkshire	156	G S Ballance	at Leeds 2019 +	108 N E Briers	at Bradford 1984 $
	Away	176	T M Head	at Leicester 2016 +	127 M S Harris	at Leicester 2021 +
Best Bowling:	In Yorkshire	5-29	M W Pillans	at Leeds 2019 +	5-24 C W Henderson	at Leeds 2004 $
	Away	5-16	S Stuchbury	at Leicester 1982 $	4-25 J Ormond	at Leicester 2001 #

LIST A HIGHEST AND LOWEST SCORES BY AND AGAINST YORKSHIRE
PLUS INDIVIDUAL BEST BATTING AND BOWLING (Continued)

Yorkshire versus:

	Middlesex	**By Yorkshire**			**Against Yorkshire**		
Highest Score:	In Yorkshire	271:7		at Scarborough 1990 $	245:8		at Scarborough 2010 $
	Away	275:4		at Lord's 2011 $	273:6		at Southgate 2004 $
Lowest Score:	In Yorkshire	148		at Leeds 1974 $	23		at Leeds 1974 $
	Away	90		at Lord's 1964 +	107		at Lord's 1979 #
Best Batting:	In Yorkshire	124*	J A Rudolph	at Scarborough 2010 $	104	P N Weekes	at Leeds 1996 +
	Away	116	A A Metcalfe	at Lord's 1991	125*	O A Shah	at Southgate 2004 $
Best Bowling:	In Yorkshire	4-6	R Illingworth	at Hull 1983 $	4-24	N G Cowans	at Leeds 1986 +
	Away	4-28	H P Cooper	at Lord's 1979 #	5-44	T M Lamb	at Lord's 1975 #

	Northamptonshire						
Highest Score:	In Yorkshire	314:8		at Scarborough 2016 +	314:4		at Leeds 2007 +
	Away	341:3		at Northampton 2006 +	351		at Northampton 2019 +
Lowest Score:	In Yorkshire	129		at Leeds 2000 $	127		at Huddersfield 1974 $
	Away	112		at Northampton 1975 $	109		at Northampton 2000 $
Best Batting:	In Yorkshire	125	A Lyth	at Scarborough 2016 +	132	U Afzaal	at Leeds 2007 +
	Away	152*	G S Ballance	at Northampton in 2017 +	161	D J G Sales	at Northampton 2006 +
Best Bowling:	In Yorkshire	5-38	C M Old	at Sheffield 1972 $	5-16	B S Crump	at Bradford 1969 $
	Away	5-29	P W Jarvis	at Northampton 1992 $	5-15	Sarfraz Nawaz	at Northampton 1975 $

	Nottinghamshire						
Highest Score:	In Yorkshire	352:6		at Scarborough 2001 $	251:5		at Scarborough 1996 $
					251:9		at Scarborough 2016 +
	Away	280:4		at Nottingham 2007 +	291:6		at Nottingham 2004 +
Lowest Score:	In Yorkshire	120:9		at Scarborough 1998 $	66		at Bradford 1969 $
	Away	147		at Nottingham 1975 $	134:8		at Nottingham 1973 $
Best Batting:	In Yorkshire	191	D S Lehmann	at Scarborough 2001 $	101	M J Harris	at Hull 1973 #
	Away	103	R B Richardson	at Nottingham 1993 $	123	D W Randall	at Nottingham 1987 $
Best Bowling:	In Yorkshire	5-17	A G Nicholson	at Hull 1972 $	5-41	C L Cairns	at Scarborough 1996 $
	Away	4-12	C M Old	at Nottingham 1977 $	5-30	F D Stephenson	at Nottingham 1991 #

LIST A HIGHEST AND LOWEST SCORES BY AND AGAINST YORKSHIRE PLUS INDIVIDUAL BEST BATTING AND BOWLING (*Continued*)

Yorkshire versus:

Somerset

	By Yorkshire			Against Yorkshire		
Highest Score:	In Yorkshire	283:9			338;5		at Leeds 2013 $
	Away	343:9			345;4		at Taunton 2005 $
Lowest Score:	In Yorkshire	110			103		at Sheffield 1972 $
	Away	120			63		at Taunton 1965 +
Best Batting:	In Yorkshire	127	J A Rudolph		113	R T Ponting	at Scarborough 2004 $
	Away	148	A McGrath		140*	P D Trego	at Taunton 2006 $
Best Bowling:	In Yorkshire	6-36	A G Nicholson		4-10	I T Botham	at Scarborough 1979 $
	Away	6-15	F S Trueman		5-27	J Garner	at Bath 1985 $

Surrey

Highest Score:	In Yorkshire	289.9			375:4		at Scarborough 1994 $
	Away	334;5			329;8		at The Oval 2009 +
Lowest Score:	In Yorkshire	76			90		at Leeds 1996 $
	Away	128:8			134		at The Oval 1969 +
Best Batting:	In Yorkshire	118*	J D Love		136	M A Lynch	at Bradford 1985 $
	Away	146	G Boycott		177	S A Newman	at The Oval 2009 +
Best Bowling:	In Yorkshire	5-25	D Gough		7-33	R D Jackman	at Harrogate 1970 +
	Away	5-29	R Illingworth		5-22	R D Jackman	at The Oval 1978 $

Sussex

Highest Score:	In Yorkshire	302:4			267		at Scarborough 2011 $
	Away	270			292		at Hove 1963 +
Lowest Score:	In Yorkshire	89:7			85		at Huddersfield 1969 $
	Away	89			108		at Hove 1998 $
Best Batting:	In Yorkshire	132*	J A Rudolph		129	A W Greig	at Scarborough 1976 $
	Away	111*	J H Hampshire		103	L J Wright	at Hastings 1973 $
Best Bowling:	In Yorkshire	5-34	G M Hamilton		4-15	Imran Khan	at Sheffield 1985 $
	Away	5-13	D Gough		4-10	M H Yardy	at Hove 2011 $

LIST A HIGHEST AND LOWEST SCORES BY AND AGAINST YORKSHIRE
PLUS INDIVIDUAL BEST BATTING AND BOWLING (Continued)

Yorkshire versus:

		By Yorkshire			Against Yorkshire	
Warwickshire						
Highest Score:	In Yorkshire	320-7		at York 2021 +	283:6	at Leeds 2016 +
	Away	281:8		at Birmingham 2017 +	309-3	at Birmingham 2005 $
Lowest Score:	In Yorkshire	158		at Scarborough 2012 $	59	at Leeds 2001 $
	Away	56		at Birmingham 1995 $	158:9	at Birmingham 2003 $
Best Batting:	In Yorkshire	139*	S P Fleming	at Leeds 2003 $	118	I J L Trott	at Leeds 2016 +
	Away	100*	J H Hampshire	at Birmingham 1975 $	137	I R Bell	at Birmingham 2005 $
Best Bowling:	In Yorkshire	5-31	M D Moxon	at Leeds 1991 #	4-16	N M Carter	at Scarborough 2012 $
	Away	4-27	H P Cooper	at Birmingham 1973 $	7-32	R G D Willis	at Birmingham 1981 #
Worcestershire						
Highest Score:	In Yorkshire	346:9		at Leeds 2018 +	350:6		at Leeds 2018 +
	Away	346:6		at Worcester 2015 +	342		at Worcester 2017 +
Lowest Score:	In Yorkshire	88		at Leeds 1995 #	86		at Leeds 1969 $
	Away	90		at Worcester 1987 $	122		at Worcester 1975 $
Best Batting:	In Yorkshire	101	M G Bevan	at Scarborough 1995 $	113*	G A Hick	at Scarborough 1995 $
	Away	101	C A Pujara	at Leeds 2018 +	115	Younis Ahmed	at Worcester 1980 #
	Away	142	G Boycott	at Worcester 1980 #			
Best Bowling:	In Yorkshire	7-15	R A Hutton	at Leeds 1969 $	5-36	Kabir Ali	at Leeds 2002 $
	Away	6-14	H P Cooper	at Worcester 1976 $	5-25	W D Parnell	at Worcester 2019 +
Bedfordshire +						
Highest Score:	Away	212:6		at Luton 2001	211:9		at Luton 2001
Best Batting:	Away	88	D S Lehmann	at Luton 2001	34	O J Clayton	at Luton 2001
Best Bowling:	Away	4-39	R J Sidebottom	at Luton 2001	4-54	S R Rashid	at Luton 2001
Berkshire +						
Highest Score:	Away	131:3		at Reading 1983	128:9		at Reading 1983
Lowest Score:	Away				105		at Finchampstead 1988
Best Batting:	Away	74*	A A Metcalfe	at Finchampstead 1988	29	G R J Roope	at Reading 1983
Best Bowling:	Away	5-27	G B Stevenson	at Reading 1983	1-15	M Lickley	at Reading 1983

370

LIST A HIGHEST AND LOWEST SCORES BY AND AGAINST YORKSHIRE PLUS INDIVIDUAL BEST BATTING AND BOWLING *(Continued)*

Yorkshire versus:

Cambridgeshire + By Yorkshire   Against Yorkshire

		By Yorkshire			Against Yorkshire		
Highest Score:	In Yorkshire	177:1		at Leeds 1986	176: 8		at Leeds 1986
	Away	299:5		at March 2003	214:8		at March 2003
Lowest Score:	In Yorkshire			at March 2003	176: 8		at Leeds 1986
	Away	299:5			214:8		at March 2003
Best Batting:	In Yorkshire	75	M D Moxon	at Leeds 1986	85	J D R Benson	at Leeds 1986
	Away	118*	M J Wood	at March 2003	53	N T Gadsby	at March 2003
Best Bowling:	In Yorkshire	3-11	A G Nicholson	at Castleford 1967	2-8	D H Fairey	at Castleford 1967
	Away	3-37	A K D Gray	at March 2003	3-53	Ajaz Akhtar	at March 2003

Cheshire +

Highest Score:	Away	160:0		at Oxton 1985	159:7		at Oxton 1985
Best Batting:	Away	82*	M D Moxon	at Oxton 1985	46	K Teasdale	at Oxton 1985
Best Bowling:	Away	2-17	G B Stevenson	at Oxton 1985			

Combined Universities

Highest Score:	In Yorkshire	197:8		at Leeds 1990	200:8		at Leeds 1990
	Away	151:1		at Oxford 1980	150:7		at Oxford 1980
Lowest Score:	In Yorkshire	197:8		at Leeds 1990	200:8		at Leeds 1990
	Away	151:1		at Oxford 1980	150:7		at Oxford 1980
Best Batting:	In Yorkshire				63	S P James	at Leeds 1990
	Away	74*	C W J Athey	at Oxford 1980	63	J O D Orders	at Oxford 1980
Best Bowling:	In Yorkshire	3-34	P J Hartley	at Leeds 1990	3-44	M E W Brooker	at Barnsley 1976
	Away	2-43	H P Cooper	at Oxford 1980	1-16	C J Ross	at Oxford 1980

Devon +

Highest Score:	Away	411:6		at Exmouth 2004	279-8		at Exmouth 2004
Lowest Score:	Away	259:5		at Exmouth 2002	80		at Exmouth 1998
Best Batting:	Away	160	M J Wood	at Exmouth 2004	83	P M Roebuck	at Exmouth 1994
Best Bowling:	Away	4-26	D S Lehmann	at Exmouth 2002	2-42	A O F Le Fleming	at Exmouth 1994

371

LIST A HIGHEST AND LOWEST SCORES BY AND AGAINST YORKSHIRE
PLUS INDIVIDUAL BEST BATTING AND BOWLING (Continued)

Yorkshire versus:

Dorset +

	By Yorkshire			Against Yorkshire		
Highest Score: Away	101.2		at Bournemouth 2004	97		at Bournemouth 2004
Best Batting: Away	71*	M J Wood	at Bournemouth 2004	23	C L Park	at Bournemouth 2004
Best Bowling: Away	4-18	C E W Silverwood	at Bournemouth 2004	2-31	D J Worrad	at Bournemouth 2004

Durham M C +

Highest Score: In Yorkshire	249.6		at Middlesbrough 1978	138:5		at Middlesbrough 1978
Away	214.6		at Chester-le-Street 1979	213:9		at Chester-le-Street 1979
Lowest Score: In Yorkshire	135		at Harrogate 1973	136:7		at Middlesbrough 1978
Away				213:9		at Chester-le-Street 1979
Best Batting: In Yorkshire	110	J H Hampshire	at Middlesbrough 1978	52	N A Riddell	at Middlesbrough 1978
Away	92	G Boycott	at Chester-le-Street 1979	52	Wasim Raja	at Chester-le-Street 1979
Best Bowling: In Yorkshire	4-9	C M Old	at Middlesbrough 1978	5-15	B R Lander	at Harrogate 1973
Away	3-39	H P Cooper	at Chester-le-Street 1979	2-35	B L Cairns	at Chester-le-Street 1979

Herefordshire +

Highest Score: Away	275.8		at Kington 1999	124.5		at Kington 1999
Best Batting: Away	77	G S Blewett	at Kington 1999	39	R D Hughes	at Kington 1999
Best Bowling: Away	2-22	G M Hamilton	at Kington 1999	2-41	C W Boroughs	at Kington 1999

Ireland +

Highest Score: In Yorkshire	299.6		at Leeds 1995	228:7		at Leeds 1995
Away	202.4		at Belfast 2005	201:7		at Belfast 2005
Lowest Score: In Yorkshire	249		at Leeds 1997	53		at Leeds 1997
Away				201:7		at Belfast 2005
Best Batting: In Yorkshire	113	C White	at Leeds 1995	82	S J S Warke	at Leeds 1995
Away	58	M P Vaughan	at Belfast 2005	59	E J G Morgan	at Belfast 2005
Best Bowling: In Yorkshire	7-27	D Gough	at Leeds 1997	3-26	P McCrum	at Leeds 1997
Away	4-43	C White	at Belfast 2005	1-29	W K McCallan	at Belfast 2005

LIST A HIGHEST AND LOWEST SCORES BY AND AGAINST YORKSHIRE PLUS INDIVIDUAL BEST BATTING AND BOWLING (*Continued*)

Yorkshire versus:

Minor Counties

		By Yorkshire		Against Yorkshire	
Highest Score:	In Yorkshire	309:5		206:6	at Leeds 1988
	Away	218:3		182	at Scunthorpe 1975
		218:9	at Scunthorpe 1975		
Lowest Score:	In Yorkshire	309:5	at Leeds 1997	109	at Leeds 1974
	Away	218:3	at Scunthorpe 1975	85	at Jesmond 1979
		218:9	at Jesmond 1979		
Best Batting:	In Yorkshire	109*	A McGrath	at Leeds 1997	80* J D Love	at Leeds 1991
	Away	83*	G Boycott	at Chester-le-Street 1973	61 N A Folland	at Jesmond 1989
Best Bowling:	In Yorkshire	6-27	A G Nicholson	at Middlesbrough 1972	3-37 S Oakes	at Leeds 1997
	Away	5-32	S Oldham	at Scunthorpe 1975	3-27 I E Conn	at Jesmond 1989

Netherlands $

		By Yorkshire		Against Yorkshire	
Highest Score:	In Yorkshire	204:6		200:8	at Leeds 2010
	Away	158:5		154:9	at Rotterdam 2010
Lowest Score:	In Yorkshire	188:5		190:8	at Leeds 2011
	Away	123		154:9	at Amsterdam 2011
Best Batting:	In Yorkshire	83*	J A Rudolph	at Leeds 2010	62 M G Dighton	at Leeds 2010
	Away	46*	J M Bairstow	at Rotterdam 2010	34 P W Borren	at Amsterdam 2011
Best Bowling:	In Yorkshire	3-34	S A Patterson	at Leeds 2010	3-26 Mudassar Bukhari	at Leeds 2011
	Away	4-24	R M Pyrah	at Rotterdam 2010	3-28 Mudassar Bukhari	at Amsterdam 2011

Norfolk +

		By Yorkshire		Against Yorkshire	
Highest Score:	In Yorkshire	106:0		104	at Leeds 1990
	Away	167		78	at Lakenham 1969
Lowest Score:	In Yorkshire			104	at Leeds 1990
	Away	167		78	at Lakenham 1969
Best Batting:	In Yorkshire	56*	M D Moxon	at Leeds 1990	25 R J Finney	at Leeds 1990
	Away	55	J H Hampshire	at Lakenham 1969	21 G J Donaldson	at Lakenham 1969
Best Bowling:	In Yorkshire	3-8	P Carrick	at Leeds 1990		
	Away	3-14	C M Old	at Lakenham 1969	6-48 T I Moore	at Lakenham 1969

373

LIST A HIGHEST AND LOWEST SCORES BY AND AGAINST YORKSHIRE
PLUS INDIVIDUAL BEST BATTING AND BOWLING (Continued)

Yorkshire versus:

Northumberland +

		By Yorkshire		Against Yorkshire		
Highest Score:	In Yorkshire	138: 2		137		at Leeds 1992
Best Batting:	In Yorkshire	38	S A Kellett	47	G R Morris	at Leeds 1992
Best Bowling:	In Yorkshire	3-18	M A Robinson	2-22	S Greensword	at Leeds 1992

Scotland

Highest Score:	In Yorkshire	317:5		at Leeds 1986 #	244		at Leeds 2008 +
	Away	259:8		at Edinburgh 2007 +	217		at Edinburgh 2007 +
Lowest Score:	In Yorkshire	228:6		at Bradford 1981 #	142		at Leeds 1996 #
	Away	199:8		at Edinburgh 2004 $	129		at Glasgow 1995 #
Best Batting:	In Yorkshire	118*	J D Love	at Leeds 1986 #	73	I L Philip	at Leeds 1989 +
	Away	91	A A Metcalfe	at Bradford 1981 #	78	J A Beukes	at Edinburgh 2005 $
Best Bowling:	In Yorkshire	5-28	C E W Silverwood	at Leeds 1996 #	2-22	P J C Hoffman	at Leeds 2006 +
	Away	4-20	R K J Dawson	at Edinburgh 2004 $	3-42	Asim Butt	at Linlithgow 1998 #

Shropshire +

Highest Score:	Away	192			229:5		at Telford 1984
Lowest Score:	Away	192			185		at Telford 1984
Best Batting:	Away	59	J H Hampshire	at Wellington 1976	80	Mushtaq Mohammad	at Wellington 1976
Best Bowling:	Away	3-17	A L Robinson	at Wellington 1976	3-26	Mushtaq Mohammad	at Telford 1984

Unicorns $

		By Yorkshire		Against Yorkshire		
Highest Score:	In Yorkshire	266:6		at Leeds 2013	234		at Leeds 2013
	Away	191:5		at Chesterfield 2013	189:9		at Chesterfield 2013
Lowest Score:	In Yorkshire				150:6		at Leeds 2012
	Away				184		at Scarborough 2012
Best Batting:	In Yorkshire	139	G S Ballance	at Leeds 2013	107	M S Lineker	at Leeds 2013
	Away	103*	G S Ballance	at Scarborough 2012	83*	T J New	at Scarborough 2012
Best Bowling:	In Yorkshire	5-22	J A Leaning	at Leeds 2013	2-25	R J Woolley	at Leeds 2012
	Away	3-34	R M Pyrah	at Chesterfield 2013	2-31	W W Lee	at Chesterfield 2013

374

LIST A HIGHEST AND LOWEST SCORES BY AND AGAINST YORKSHIRE PLUS INDIVIDUAL BEST BATTING AND BOWLING (*Continued*)

Yorkshire versus:

Wiltshire +

		By Yorkshire		Against Yorkshire	
Highest Score:	Away	304:7		175	at Trowbridge 1987
Best Batting:	Away	85	A A Metcalfe	62 J J Newman	at Trowbridge 1987
Best Bowling:	Away	4-40	K Sharp	2-38 R C Cooper	at Trowbridge 1987

Yorkshire Cricket Board +

Highest Score:	Away	240:5		110		at Harrogate 2000
Best Batting:	Away	70	M P Vaughan	31	R A Kettleborough	at Harrogate 2000
Best Bowling:	Away	5-30	D Gough	1-25	A E McKenna	at Harrogate 2000

Australians

Highest Score:	In Yorkshire	188		297:3		at Leeds 1989
Lowest Score:	In Yorkshire	140		297:3		at Leeds 1989
Best Batting:	In Yorkshire	105	G Boycott	172	D C Boon	at Leeds 1989
Best Bowling:	In Yorkshire	2-23	D Wilson	3-30	D J Colley	at Bradford 1972

Bangladesh A

Highest Score:	In Yorkshire	198		191		at Leeds 2013
Best Batting:	In Yorkshire	47*	L E Plunkett	69	Anamul Haque	at Leeds 2013
Best Bowling:	In Yorkshire	5-30	Azeem Rafiq	3-25	Elias Sunny	at Leeds 2013

South Africa A

Highest Score:	In Yorkshire			129:4		at Leeds 2017
Best Batting:	In Yorkshire			56*	K Zonda	at Leeds 2017
Best Bowling:	In Yorkshire	2-16	S A Patterson			at Leeds 2017

Sri Lanka A

Highest Score:	In Yorkshire	249		275:9		at Leeds 2014
Lowest Score:	In Yorkshire	179:7				at Leeds 2004
Best Batting:	In Yorkshire	81	A W Gale	100	L D Chandimal	at Leeds 2014
Best Bowling:	In Yorkshire	5-51	A Shahzad	4-42	S Prasanna	at Leeds 2014

LIST A HIGHEST AND LOWEST SCORES BY AND AGAINST YORKSHIRE
PLUS INDIVIDUAL BEST BATTING AND BOWLING (Continued)

Yorkshire versus:

West Indians

		By Yorkshire			Against Yorkshire		
Highest Score:	In Yorkshire	253-4		at Scarborough 1995	242		at Scarborough 1995
Best Batting:	In Yorkshire	106	A McGrath	at Scarborough 1995	54	R B Richardson	at Scarborough 1995
Best Bowling:	In Yorkshire	3-42	G M Hamilton	at Scarborough 1995	3-48	R Dhanraj	at Scarborough 1995

West Indians A

Highest Score:	In Yorkshire	139		at Leeds 2002	140-2		at Leeds 2002
Best Batting:	In Yorkshire	48	M J Wood	at Leeds 2002	57	D Ganga	at Leeds 2002
Best Bowling:	In Yorkshire	1-31	C J Elstub	at Leeds 2002	4-24	J J C Lawson	at Leeds 2002

Young Australians

Highest Score:	In Yorkshire	224-6		at Leeds 1995	156		at Leeds 1995
Best Batting:	In Yorkshire	76	M P Vaughan	at Leeds 1995	51	A C Gilchrist	at Leeds 1995
Best Bowling:	In Yorkshire	5-32	A C Morris	at Leeds 1995	2-21	S Young	at Leeds 1995

Zimbabwe

Highest Score:	In Yorkshire	203-7		at Sheffield 1982	202		at Sheffield 1982
Best Batting:	In Yorkshire	98*	G Boycott	at Sheffield 1982	53	D A G Fletcher	at Sheffield 1982
Best Bowling:	In Yorkshire	3-47	P W Jarvis	at Sheffield 1982	3-30	D A G Fletcher	at Sheffield 1982

LIST A HIGHEST TEAM TOTALS

BY YORKSHIRE

411:6	v.	Devon at Exmouth	2004 +
379:7	v.	Lancashire at Manchester	2018 +
379:7	v.	Leicestershire at Leeds	2019 +
376:3	v.	Leicestershire at Leicester	2016 +
352:6	v.	Nottinghamshire at Scarborough	2001 $
349:7	v.	Derbyshire at Leeds	2017 +
346:9	v.	Worcestershire at Leeds	2018 +
345:5	v.	Nottinghamshire at Leeds	1996 +
345:6	v.	Worcestershire at Worcester	2015 +
343:9	v.	Somerset at Taunton	2005 $
341:3	v.	Northamptonshire at Northampton	2006 +
339:4	v.	Durham at Leeds	2017 +
334:5	v.	Surrey at The Oval	2005 $
330:6	v	Surrey at The Oval	2009 +
329:3	v.	Leicestershire at Leicester	2021 +
328:4	v.	Durham at Chester-le-Street	2018 +
325:7	v.	Lancashire at Manchester	2016 +
324:7	v.	Lancashire at Manchester	2014 +
320:7	v.	Warwickshire at York	2021 +
318:7	v.	Leicestershire at Leicester	1993 $
317:4	v.	Surrey at Lord's	1965 +
317:5	v.	Scotland at Leeds	1986 #
314:8	v.	Northamptonshire at Scaboough	2016 +
310:5	v.	Leicestershire at Leicester	1997 +
310	v.	Lancashire at Leeds	2019 +
309:5	v.	Minor Counties at Leeds	1997 #
307:3	v.	Essex at Chelmsford	1995 +
307:4	v.	Somerset at Taunton	2002 $
304:7	v.	Wiltshire at Trowbridge	1986 +

AGAINST YORKSHIRE

375:4	for Surrey at Scarborough	1994 $
363	for Lancashire at Manchester	2018 +
351	for Northamptonshire at Northampton	2019 +
350:6	for Worcestershire at Leeds	2018 +
348:9	for Hampshire at West End	2018 +
345:4	for Somerset at Taunton	2005 $
342	for Worcestershire at Worcester	2017 +
339:7	for Northamptonshire at Northampton	2006 +
338:5	for Somerset at Leeds	2013 $
335:5	for Durham at Leeds	2017 +
334:8	for Derbyshire at Leeds	2017 +
329:8	for Surrey at The Oval	2009 +
327:7	for Leicestershire at Leicester	2021 +
325:7	for Northamptonshire at Northampton	1992 $
317:7	for Essex at Chelmsford	2021 +
314:4	for Northamptonshire at Leeds	2007 +
313:7	for Surrey at Leeds	2017 +
311:6	for Lancashire at Leeds	2019 +
310:7	for Northamptonshire at Scarborough	2016 +
309:3	for Warwickshire at Birmingham	2005 $
308:6	for Surrey at The Oval	1995 $
306:8	for Somerset at Taunton	2002 $
302:7	for Leicestershire at Leeds	2008 $
298:9	for Leicestershire at Leicester	1997 $
297:3	for Australians at Leeds	1989
294:6	for Gloucestershire at Cheltenham	2010 $

LIST A HIGHEST INDIVIDUAL SCORES

BY YORKSHIRE

191	D S Lehmann	v.	Nottinghamshire at Scarborough	2001 $
175	T M Head	v.	Leicestershire at Leicester	2016 +
174	J M Bairstow	v.	Durham at Leeds	2017 +
164	T Kohler-Cadmore	v.	Durham at Chester-le-Street	2018 +
160	M J Wood	v.	Devon at Exmouth	2004 +
156	G S Ballance	v.	Leicestershire at Leeds	2019 +
152 *	G S Ballance	v.	Northamptonshire at Northampton	2017 +
148	C White	v.	Leicestershire at Leicester	1997 $
148	A McGrath	v.	Somerset at Taunton	2006 $
146	G Boycott	v.	Surrey at Lord's	1965 +
144	A Lyth	v.	Lancashire at Manchester	2018 +
142	G Boycott	v.	Worcestershire at Worcester	1980 #
141*	M D Moxon	v	Glamorgan at Cardiff	1991 #
140	P S P Handscomb	v.	Derbyshire at Leeds	2017 +
139*	S P Fleming	v.	Warwickshire at Leeds	2003 $
139	G S Ballance	v.	Unicorns at Leeds	2013 $

AGAINST YORKSHIRE

177	S A Newman	for	Surrey at The Oval	2009 +
172	D C Boon	for	Australia at Leeds	1989
171	J M Vince	for	Hampshire at West End	2018 +
161	D J G Sales	for	Northamptonshire at Northampton	2006 +
155*	B A Richards	for	Hampshire at Hull	1970 $
146*	S Young	for	Gloucestershire at Leeds	1997 $
143*	C M Spearman	for	Gloucestershire at Bristol	2004 $
141*	B J Hodge	for	Lancashire at Manchester	2007 +
140*	P D Trego	for	Somerset at Taunton	2013 $
137*	M Klinger	for	Gloucestershire at Leeds	2015 +
137	I R Bell	for	Warwickshire at Birmingham	2005 $
136*	N Hussain	for	Essex at Chelmsford	2002 #
136	M A Lynch	for	Surrey at Bradford	1985 $
135*	D J Bicknell	for	Surrey at The Oval	1989 $
133	A D Brown	for	Surrey at Scarborough	1994 $

MOST RUNS IN LIST A MATCHES

742	v.	Lancashire at Manchester	2018 +	Y 379:7	L 363
696	v.	Worcestershire at Leeds	2018 +	W 350:6	Y 346:9
690	v.	Devon at Exmouth	2004 +	Y 411:6	D 279:8
688	v.	Somerset at Taunton	2005 $	S 345:4	Y 343:9
683	v.	Derbyshire at Leeds	2017 +	Y 349:7	D 334:8
680	v.	Northamptonshire at Northampton	2006 +	Y 342:3	N 339:7
674	v.	Durham at Leeds	2017 +	D 335:5	Y: 339-4
659	v.	Surrey at The Oval	2009 +	S 329:8	Y 330:6
656	v.	Leicestershire at Leicester	2021 +	L 327:7	Y 329:3
633	v.	Worcestershire at Worcester	2017 +	W 342	Y 291
625	v.	Surrey at The Oval	2005 $	Y 334:5	S 291
624	v.	Northamptonshire at Scarborough	2016 +	N 310:7	Y 314:8
621	v.	Lancashire at Leeds	2019 +	L 311:6	Y 310
613	v.	Somerset at Taunton	2002 $	Y 307:4	S 306:8
605	v.	Leicestershire at Leeds	2008 $	Y 303:4	L 302:7
604	v.	Surrey at The Oval	1995 $	S 308:6	Y 296:6
602	v.	Surrey at Leeds	2017 +	S 313:7	Y 289:9
601	v.	Lancashire at Manchester	2014 +	Y 324:7	L 277
601	v.	Warwickshire at York	2021+	Y 320:7	W 281

LIST A BEST BOWLING

BY YORKSHIRE

7-15	R A Hutton	v.	Worcestershire at Leeds	1969 $
7-27	D Gough	v.	Ireland at Leeds	1997 +
6-14	H P Cooper	v.	Worcestershire at Worcester	1975 $
6-15	F S Trueman	v.	Somerset at Taunton	1965 +
6-18	D Wilson	v.	Kent at Canterbury	1969 $
6-27	A G Nicholson	v.	Minor Counties at Middlesbrough	1972 #
6-27	P W Jarvis	v.	Somerset at Taunton	1989 $
6-32	S A Patterson	v.	Derbyshire at Leeds	2010 $
6-36	A G Nicholson	v	Somerset At Sheffield	1972 $
6-40	R J Sidebottom	v.	Glamorgan at Cardiff	1998 $
5-13	D Gough	v.	Sussex at Hove	1994 $
5-16	S Stuchbury	v.	Leicestershire at Leicester	1982 $
5-16	G M Hamilton	v.	Hampshire at Leeds	1998 $
5-17	A G Nicholson	v.	Nottinghamshire at Hull	1972 $
5-18	P W Jarvis	v.	Derbyshire at Leeds	1990 $

AGAINST YORKSHIRE

7-32	R G D Willis	for	Warwickshire at Birmingham	1981 #
7-33	R D Jackman	for	Surrey at Harrogate	1970 +
6-15	A A Donald	for	Warwickshire at Birmingham	1995 $
6-18	R E East	for	Essex at Hull	1969 $
6-25	G Chapple	for	Lancashire at Leeds	1998 $
6-32	M T Coles	for	Kent at Leeds	2012 $
6-48	T I Moore	for	Norfolk at Lakenham	1969 +
5-15	B R Lander	for	Durham M C at Harrogate	1973 +
5-15	Sarfraz Nawaz	for	Northamptonshire at Northampton	1975 $
5-16	B S Crump	for	Northamptonshire at Bradford	1969 $
5-16	G C Holmes	for	Glamorgan at Swansea	1985 $
5-20	R E East	for	Essex at Colchester	1979 $
5-22	R D Jackman	for	Surrey at The Oval	1978 $
5-24	C J Tunnicliffe	for	Derbyshire at Derby	1981 #
5-24	C W Henderson	for	Leicestershire at Leeds	2004 $

LIST A ECONOMICAL BOWLING

BY YORKSHIRE

| 11-9-3-1 | C M Old | v. | Middlesex at Lord's | 1979 # |
| 8-5-3-3 | A L Robinson | v. | Derbyshire at Scarborough | 1973 $ |

AGAINST YORKSHIRE

| 8-4-6-2 | P J Sainsbury | for | Hampshire at Hull | 1970 $ |
| 8-5-6-3 | M J Procter | for | Gloucestershire at Cheltenham | 1979 $ |

LIST A MOST EXPENSIVE BOWLING

BY YORKSHIRE

| 9-0-87-1 | T T Bresnan | v. | Somerset at Taunton | 2005 $ |

AGAINST YORKSHIRE

| 12-1-96-0 | M E Waugh | for | Essex at Chelmsford | 1995 + |

LIST A HAT-TRICKS FOR YORKSHIRE (4)

P W Jarvis	v.	Derbyshire	at Derby	1982 $	D Gough	v. Ireland at Leeds	1997 +
D Gough	v.	Lancashire	at Leeds	1998 $	C White	v. Kent at Leeds	2000 $

LIST A MAN-OF-THE-MATCH AWARDS (137)

M D Moxon	12	M P Vaughan	5	M J Wood		3
G Boycott	11	A Sidebottom	4	R J Blakey		2
D L Bairstow	8	C E W Silverwood	4	G L Brophy		2
C White	8	D Byas	3	P Carrick		2
A A Metcalfe	7	D Gough	3	R A Hutton		2
J H Hampshire	6	P J Hartley	3	L E Plunkett		2
D S Lehmann	6	J D Love	3	P J Sharpe		2
C W J Athey	5	A McGrath	3	G B Stevenson		2
M G Bevan	5	C M Old	3			

One each: T T Bresnan, D B Close, M T G Elliott, G M Fellows, S D Fletcher, G M Hamilton, S N Hartley, P M Hutchinson, R Illingworth, C Johnson, S A Kellett, B Leadbeater, M J Lumb, A G Nicholson, S Oldham, S A Patterson, R M Pyrah, P E Robinson, R D Stemp, F S Trueman and D Wilson.

ALL LIST A CENTURIES 1963-2021 (118)

C W J ATHEY (2)

118	v.	Leicestershire	at Leicester	1978 $
115	v.	Kent	at Leeds	1980 +

D L BAIRSTOW (1)

103 *	v.	Derbyshire	at Derby	1981 #

J M BAIRSTOW (2)

114	v.	Middlesex	at Lord's	2011 $
174	v.	Durham	at Leeds	2017 +

G S BALLANCE (4)

139	v.	Unicorns	at Leeds	2013 $
103 *	v.	Unicorns	at Scarborough	2012 $
152 *	v.	Northamptonshire	at Northampton	2017 +
156	v.	Leicestershire	at Leeds	2019 +

M G BEVAN (2)

103 *	v.	Gloucestershire	at Middlesbrough	1995 $
101	v.	Worcestershire	at Scarborough	1995 $

G BOYCOTT (7)

146	v.	Surrey	at Lord's	1965 +
142	v.	Worcestershire	at Worcester	1980 #
108 *	v.	Northamptonshire	at Huddersfield	1974 $
106	v.	Northamptonshire	at Bradford	1984 #
105	v.	Australians	at Bradford	1972
104 *	v.	Glamorgan	at Colwyn Bay	1973 $
102	v.	Northamptonshire	at Middlesbrough	1977 #

R J BLAKEY (3)

130	v.	Kent	at Scarborough	1991 $
105 *	v.	Warwickshire	at Scarborough	1992 $
100 *	v.	Gloucestershire	at Cheltenham	1990 $

ALL LIST A CENTURIES 1963-2021 *(Continued)*

H C BROOK (1)

| 103 | v. | Leicestershire | at Leeds | 2019 + |

D BYAS (5)

116 *	v.	Surrey	at The Oval	1996 #
111 *	v.	Lancashire	at Leeds	1996 $
106 *	v.	Derbyshire	at Chesterfield	1993 $
104 *	v.	Hampshire	at Leeds	1999 #
101 *	v.	Nottinghamshire	at Leeds	1994 $

H G DUKE (1)

| 125 | v. | Leicestershire | at Leicester | 2021 + |

M T G ELLIOTT (3)

128 *	v.	Somerset	at Lord's	2002 +
115 *	v.	Kent	at Leeds	2002 $
109	v.	Leicestershire	at Leicester	2002 $

S P FLEMING (1)

| 139 * | v. | Warwickshire | at Leeds | 2003 $ |

M J FOSTER (1)

| 118 | v. | Leicestershire | at Leicester | 1993 $ |

A W GALE (2)

| 125 * | v. | Essex | at Chelmsford | 2010 $ |
| 112 | v. | Kent | at Canterbury | 2011 $ |

J H HAMPSHIRE (7)

119	v.	Leicestershire	at Hull	1971 $
114 *	v.	Northamptonshire	at Scarborough	1978 $
111 *	v.	Sussex	at Hastings	1973 $
110	v.	Durham M C	at Middlesbrough	1978 +
108	v.	Nottinghamshire	at Sheffield	1970 $
106 *	v.	Lancashire	at Manchester	1972 $
100 *	v.	Warwickshire	at Birmingham	1975 $

P S P HANDSCOMB (1)

| 140 | v. | Derbyshire | at Leeds | 2017 + |

T M HEAD (1))

| 175 | v. | Leicestershire | at Leicester | 2016 + |

P A JAQUES (1)

| 105 | v. | Sussex | at Leeds | 2004 $ |

S A KELLETT (2)

| 118 * | v. | Derbyshire | at Leeds | 1992 $ |
| 107 | v. | Ireland | at Leeds | 1995 + |

T KOHLER-CADMORE (1)

| 164 | v. | Durham | at Chester-le-Street | 2018 + |

J A LEANING (2)

| 131 * | v. | Leicestershire | at Leicester | 2016 + |
| 111 * | v. | Essex | at Scarborough | 2014 + |

A Z LEES (1)

| 102 | v. | Northamptonshire | at Northampton | 2014 + |

ALL LIST A CENTURIES 1963-2021 *(Continued)*

D S LEHMANN (8)

191	v. Nottinghamshire	at Scarborough	2001 $
119	v. Durham	at Leeds	1998 #
118 *	v. Northamptonshire	at Northampton	2006 +
105	v. Glamorgan	at Cardiff	1995 +
104	v. Somerset	at Taunton	2002 $
103	v. Derbyshire	at Leeds	2001 #
103	v. Leicestershire	at Scarborough	2001 $
102 *	v. Derbyshire	ar Derby	1998 #

J D LOVE (4)

118 *	v. Scotland	at Bradford	1981 #
118 *	v. Surrey	at Leeds	1987 $
104 *	v. Nottinghamshire	at Hull	1986 $
100 *	v. Gloucestershire	at Gloucester	1985 $

R G LUMB (1)

101	v. Nottinghamshire	at Scarborough	1976 $

A LYTH (5)

144	v. Lancashire	at Manchester	2018 +
136 §	v. Lancashire	at Manchester	2016 +
132*	v. Leicestershire	at Leicester	2018 +
125 §	v. Northamptonshire	at Scarborough	2016 +
109 *	v. Sussex	at Scarborough	2009 $

(§ consecutive days)

A McGRATH (7)

148	v. Somerset	at Taunton	2006 $
135 *	v. Lancashire	at Manchester	2007 +
109 *	v. Minor Counties	at Leeds	1997 #
106	v. West Indies	at Scarborough	1995
105 *	v. Scotland	at Leeds	2008 +
102	v. Kent	at Canterbury	2001 $
100	v. Durham	at Leeds	2007 +

G J MAXWELL (1)

111	v. Worcestershire	at Worcester	2015 +

A A METCALFE (4)

127 *	v. Warwickshire	at Leeds	1990 +
116	v. Middlesex	at Lord's	1991 $
115 *	v. Gloucestershire	at Scarborough	1984 $
114	v. Lancashire	at Manchester	1991 #

M D MOXON (7)

141 *	v. Glamorgan	at Cardiff	1991 #
137	v. Nottinghamshire	at Leeds	1996+
129 *	v. Surrey	at The Oval	1991 $
112	v. Sussex	at Middlesbrough	1991 $
107 *	v. Warwickshire	at Leeds	1990 +
106 *	v. Lancashire	at Manchester	1986 #
105	v. Somerset	at Scarborough	1990 $

ALL LIST A CENTURIES 1963-2021 *(Continued)*

C A PUJARA (1)

101	v. Worcestershire	at Leeds	2018 +

R B RICHARDSON (1)

103	v. Nottinghamshire	at Nottingham	1993 $

J A RUDOLPH (9)

132 *	v. Sussex	at Scarborough	2011 $
127	v. Somerset	at Scarborough	2007 $
124 *	v. Middlesex	at Scarborough	2010 $
120	v. Leicestershire	at Leeds	2008 $
118	v. Gloucestershire	at Leeds	2009 +
106	v. Warwickshire	at Scarborough	2010 $
105	v. Derbyshire	at Chesterfield	2010 $
101 *	v. Essex	at Chelmsford	2010 $
100	v. Leicestershire	at Leeds	2007 +

K SHARP (3)

114	v. Essex	at Chelmsford	1985 $
112 *	v. Worcestershire	at Worcester	1985 $
105 *	v. Scotland	at Leeds	1984 #

S R TENDULKAR (1)

107	v. Lancashire	at Leeds	1992 $

M P VAUGHAN (3)

125 *	v. Somerset	at Taunton	2001 #
116 *	v. Lancashire	at Manchester	2004 +
116 *	v. Kent	at Leeds	2005 $

C WHITE (5)

148	v. Leicestershire	at Leicester	1997 $
113	v. Ireland	at Leeds	1995 +
112	v. Northamptonshire	at Northampton	2006 +
101 *	v. Durham	at Chester-le-Street	2006 +
100 *	v. Surrey	at Leeds	2002 +

D J WILLEY (1)

131	v. Lancashire	at Manchester	2018 +

M J WOOD (5)

160	v. Devon	at Exmouth	2004 +
118 *	v. Cambridgeshire	at March	2003 +
115 *	v. Derbyshire	at Derby	2002 #
111	v. Surrey	at The Oval	2005 $
105 *	v. Somerset	at Taunton	2002$

YOUNUS KHAN (1)

100	v. Nottinghamshire	at Nottingham	2007 +

LIST A PARTNERSHIPS OF 150 AND OVER 1963-2019 (51)

274	3rd wkt T M Head (175)	and J A Leaning (131*)	v. Leicestershire at Leicester	2016+
242*	1st wkt M D Moxon (107*)	and A A Metcalfe (127*)	v. Warwickshire at Leeds	1990 +
235	2nd wkt A Lyth (144)	and D J Willey (131)	v. Lancashire at Manchester	2018 +
233*	1st wkt A W Gale (125*)	and J A Rudolph (101*)	v. Essex at Chelmsford	2010 $
213	1st wkt M D Moxon (141*)	and A A Metcalfe (84)	v. Glamorgan at Cardiff	1991 #
211*	1st wkt M D Moxon (93*)	and A A Metcalfe (94*)	v. Warwickshire at Birmingham	1987 #
211	4th wkt H C Brook (103)	and G S Ballance (156)	v. Leicestershire at Leeds	2019 +
207	4th wkt S A Kellett (107)	and C White (113)	v. Ireland at Leeds	1995 +
202	2nd wkt G Boycott (87)	and C W J Athey (115)	v. Kent at Leeds	1980 +
201	1st wkt J H Hampshire (86)	and C W J Athey (118)	v. Leicestershire at Leicester	1978 $
198*	4th wkt M T G Elliott (115*)	and A McGrath (85*)	v. Kent at Leeds	2002 $
195	1st wkt A Lyth (84)	and A Z Lees (102)	v. Northamptonshire at Northampton	2014 +
192	2nd wkt G Boycott (146)	and D B Close (79)	v. Surrey at Lord's	1965 +
190	1st wkt G Boycott (89*)	and R G Lumb (101)	v. Nottinghamshire at Scarborough	1976 $
190	5th wkt R J Blakey (96)	and M J Foster (118)	v. Leicestershire at Leicester	1993 $
189	2nd wkt J M Bairstow (174)	and J E Root (55)	v. Durham at Leeds	2017 +
186	1st wkt G Boycott (99)	and J H Hampshire (92*)	v. Gloucestershire at Scarborough	1975 $
186	1st wkt G S Blewett (71)	and D Byas (104*)	v. Hampshire at Leeds	1999 #
184	3rd wkt M P Vaughan (70)	and D S Lehmann (119)	v. Durham at Leeds	1998 #
181	5th wkt M T G Elliott (109)	and A McGrath (78)	v. Leicestershire at Leicester	2002 $
176	3rd wkt R J Blakey (86)	and S R Tendulkar (107)	v. Lancashire at Leeds	1992 $
176	2nd wkt T Kohler-Cadmore (164)	and C A Pujara (82)	v. Durham at Chester-le-Street	2018 +
172	2nd wkt D Byas (86)	and D S Lehmann (99)	v. Kent at Maidstone	1998 $
172	3rd wkt A McGrath (38)	and D S Lehmann (191)	v. Nottinghamshire at Scarborough	2001 $
171	1st wkt M D Moxon (112)	and A A Metcalfe (68)	v. Sussex at Middlesbrough	1991 $
170	4th wkt M J Wood (105*)	and D S Lehmann (104)	v. Somerset at Taunton	2002 $
170	1st wkt A W Gale (89)	and J A Rudolph (120)	v. Leicestershire at Leeds	2008 $
167*	6th wkt M G Bevan (95*)	and R J Blakey ((80*)	v. Lancashire at Manchester	1996 #
167*	1st wkt C White (100*)	and M J Wood (57*)	v. Surrey at Leeds	2002 +
167	1st wkt M D Moxon(64)	and A A Metcalfe (116)	v. Middlesex at Lord's	1991 $
167	1st wkt M J Wood (65)	and S P Fleming (139*)	v. Warwickshire at Leeds	2003 $
166	1st wkt M D Moxon (82*)	and A A Metcalfe (70)	v. Northamptonshire at Leeds	1988 #
165	1st wkt M D Moxon (80)	and D Byas (106*)	v. Derbyshire at Chesterfield	1993 $
165	1st wkt M D Moxon (70)	and D Byas (88*)	v. Northamptonshire at Leeds	1993 $
164*	2nd wkt G Boycott (91*)	and C W J Athey (79*)	v. Worcestershire at Worcester	1981 $

LIST A PARTNERSHIPS OF 150 AND OVER *(Continued)*

164	3rd wkt	A McGrath (105*)	and J A Rudolph (82)	v. Scotland at Leeds	2008 +
164	3rd wkt	J A Rudolph (84)	and A McGrath (73)	v. Glamorgan at Scarborough	2008 $
161	1st wkt	M D Moxon (74)	and A A Metcalfe (85)	v. Wiltshire at Trowbridge	1987 +
160*	1st wkt	G Boycott (70*)	and M D Moxon (82*)	v. Cheshire at Oxton	1985 +
160*	5th wkt	G M Fellows (80*)	and C White (73*)	v. Surrey at Leeds	2001 +
160*	3rd wkt	A Lyth (60*)	and G S Ballance (103*)	v. Unicorns at Scarborough	2012 +
160	1st wkt	G Boycott (67)	and J H Hampshire (84)	v. Warwickshire at Birmingham	1973 $
159	2nd wkt	G Boycott (92)	and D B Close (96)	v. Surrey at The Oval	1969 +
157	2nd wkt	K Sharp (71)	and R J Blakey (79)	v. Worcestershire at Worcester	1990 $
157	1st wkt	T Kohler-Cadmore (79)	and A Lyth (78)	v. Derbyshire at Leeds	2019 +
156	4th wkt	P S P Handscomb (140)	and G S Ballance (63)	v. Derbyshire at Leeds	2017 +
155*	1st wkt	A Lyth (67*)	and A Z Lees (69*)	v. Derbyshire at Scarborough	2014 +
154*	2nd wkt	J H Hampshire (111*)	and B Leadbeater (57*)	v. Sussex at Hove	1973 $
153	4th wkt	Younus Khan (100)	and A W Gale ((69*)	v. Nottinghamshire at Nottingham	2007 +
153	1st wkt	A Lyth (132*)	and T Kohler-Cadmore (74)	v. Leicestershire at Leicester	2018 +
150*	5th wkt	S N Hartley (67*)	and J D Love (82*)	v. Hampshire at Middlesbrough	1983 $

LIST A HIGHEST PARTNERSHIPS FOR EACH WICKET

1st wkt	242*	M D Moxon (107*)	and A A Metcalfe (127*)	v Warwickshire at Leeds	1990 +
2nd wkt	235	A Lyth (144)	and D J Willey (131)	v. Lancashire at Manchester	2018 +
3rd wkt	274	T M Head (175)	and J A Leaning (131*)	v. Leicestershire at Leicester	2016+
4th wkt	211	H C Brook (103)	and G S Ballance (156)	v. Leicestershire at Leeds	2019 +
5th wkt	190	R J Blakey (96)	and M J Foster (118)	v. Leicestershire at Leicester	1993 $
6th wkt	167*	M G Bevan (95*)	and R J Blakey ((80*)	v. Lancashire at Manchester	1996 #
7th wkt	149*	J D Love (118*)	and C M Old (78*)	v. Scotland at Bradford	1981 #
8th wkt	89	R J Blakey (60)	and R K J Dawson (41)	v. Leicestershire at Scarborough	2002 $
9th wkt	88	S N Hartley (67)	and A Ramage (32*)	v. Middlesex at Lord's	1982 $
10th wkt	80*	D L Bairstow (103*)	and M Johnson (4*)	v. Derbyshire at Derby	1981 #

ALL LIST A 5 WICKETS IN AN INNINGS 1963-2021 (58)

C W J ATHEY (1)

| 5-35 | v | Derbyshire | at Chesterfield | 1981 $ |

AZEEM RAFIQ (1)

| 5-30 | v | Bangladesh A | at Leeds | 2013 |

M G BEVAN (1)

| 5-29 | v | Sussex | at Eastbourne | 1996 $ |

P CARRICK (2)

| 5-22 | v | Glamorgan | at Leeds | 1991 $ |
| 5-40 | v | Sussex | at Middlesbrough | 1991 $ |

H P COOPER (2)

| 6-14 | v | Worcestershire | at Worcester | 1975 $ |
| 5-30 | v | Worcestershire | at Middlesbrough | 1978 $ |

D GOUGH (4)

5-13	v	Sussex	at Hove	1994 $
7-27	v	Ireland	at Leeds	1997 +
5-25	v	Surrey	at Leeds	1998 $
5-30	v	Yorkshire C B	at Harrogate	2000 +

G M HAMILTON (2)

| 5-16 | v | Hampshire | at Leeds | 1998 $ |
| 5-34 | v | Sussex | at Scarborough | 2000 $ |

P J HARTLEY (4)

5-36	v	Sussex	at Scarborough	1993 $
5-38	v	Worcestershire	at Worcester	1990 $
5-43	v	Scotland	at Leeds	1986 #
5-46	v	Hampshire	at Southampton	1990 +

M J HOGGARD (3)

5-28	v	Leicestershire	at Leicester	2000 $
5-30	v	Northamptonshire	at Northampton	2000 $
5-65	v	Somerset	at Lord's	2002 +

R A HUTTON (1)

| 7-15 | v | Worcestershire | at Leeds | 1969 $ |

R ILLINGWORTH (1)

| 5-29 | v | Surrey | at Lord's | 1965 + |

P W JARVIS (3)

6-27	v	Somerset	at Taunton	1989 $
5-18	v	Derbyshire	at Leeds	1990 $
5-29	v	Northamptonshire	at Northampton	1992 $

J A LEANING (1)

| 5-22 | v | Unicorns | at Leeds | 2013 $ |

A C MORRIS (1)

| 5-32 | v | Young Australia | at Leeds | 1995 |

M D MOXON (1)

| 5-31 | v | Warwickshire | at Leeds | 1991 # |

A G NICHOLSON (4)

6-27	v	Minor Counties	at Middlesbrough	1972 #
6-36	v	Somerset	at Sheffield	1972 $
5-17	v	Nottinghamshire	at Hull	1972 $
5-24	v	Derbyshire	at Bradford	1975 #

ALL LIST A 5 WICKETS IN AN INNINGS *(Continued)*

C M OLD (2)

| 5-33 | v | Sussex | at Hove | 1971 $ |
| 5-38 | v | Northamptonshire | at Sheffield | 1972 $ |

S OLDHAM (1)

| 5-32 | v | Minor Counties | at Scunthorpe | 1975 # |

S A PATTERSON (2)

| 6-32 | v | Derbyshire | at Leeds | 2010 $ |
| 5-24 | v | Worcestershire | at Worcester | 2015 + |

M W PILLANS (1)

| 5-29 | v | Leicestershire | Leeds | 2019 + |

A U RASHID (1)

| 5-33 | v | Hampshire | at Southampton | 2014 + |

A SHAHZAD (1)

| 5-51 | v | Sri Lanka A | at Leeds | 2007 |

C SHAW (1)

| 5-41 | v | Hampshire | at Bournemouth | 1984 $ |

A SIDEBOTTOM (2)

| 5-27 | v | Worcestershire | at Bradford | 1985 # |
| 5-27 | v | Glamorgan | at Leeds | 1987 + |

R J SIDEBOTTOM (2)

| 6-40 | v | Glamorgan | at Cardiff | 2003 $ |
| 5-42 | v | Leicestershire | at Leicester | 2003 $ |

C E W SILVERWOOD (1)

| 5-28 | v | Scotland | at Leeds | 1996 # |

G B STEVENSON (4)

5-27	v	Berkshire	at Reading	1983 +
5-28	v	Kent	at Canterbury	1978 #
5-41	v	Leicestershire	at Leicester	1976 $
5-50	v	Worcestershire	at Leeds	1982 #

S STUCHBURY (1)

| 5-16 | v | Leicestershire | at Leicester | 1982 $ |

N D THORNICROFT (1)

| 5-42 | v | Gloucestershire | at Leeds | 2003 $ |

F S TRUEMAN (1)

| 6-15 | v | Somerset | at Taunton | 1965 + |

M J WAITE (1)

| 5-50 | v. | Leicestershire | at Leicester | 2021 + |

C WHITE (2)

| 5-19 | v | Somerset | at Scarborough | 2002 $ |
| 5-25 | v | Lancashire | at Leeds | 2000 # |

D WILSON (2)

| 6-18 | v | Kent | at Canterbury | 1969 $ |
| 5-25 | v | Lancashire | at Bradford | 1972 # |

ALL LIST A PLAYERS WHO HAVE TAKEN 4 WICKETS IN AN INNINGS 1963-2021 (170) AND BEST FIGURES

11	C M Old	4-9	v	Durham M C	at Middlesbrough	1978 +
10	C White	4-14	v	Lancashire	at Leeds	2000 $
		4-14	v	Surrey	at The Oval	2005 $
9	A Sidebottom	4-15	v	Worcestershire	at Leeds	1987 $
8	P W Jarvis	4-13	v	Worcestershire	at Leeds	1986 $
8	D Gough	4-17	v	Nottinghamshire	at Nottingham	2000 #
8	G B Stevenson	4-20	v	Essex	at Barnsley	1977 #
7	S D Fletcher	4-11	v	Kent	at Canterbury	1988 $
6	C E W Silverwood	4-11	v	Leicestershire	at Leicester	2000 $
6	H P Cooper	4-18	v	Leicestershire	at Leeds	1975 +
5	S Oldham	4-13	v	Nottinghamshire	at Nottingham	1989 $
5	R M Pyrah	4-24	v	Netherlands	at Rotterdam	2010 $
4	P Carrick	4-13	v	Derbyshire	at Bradford	1983 $
4	R K J Dawson	4-13	v	Derbyshire	at Derby	2002 #
4	T T Bresnan	4-25	v	Somerset	at Leeds	2005 $
4	G M Hamilton	4-27	v	Warwickshire	at Birmingham	1995 $
3	R A Hutton	4-18	v	Surrey	at The Oval	1972 $
3	A G Nicholson	4-15	v	Kent	at Leeds	1974 $
3	P J Hartley	4-21	v	Scotland	at Glasgow	1995 #
3	A L Robinson	4-25	v	Surrey	at The Oval	1974 $
3	R D Stemp	4-25	v	Gloucestershire	at Bristol	1996 $
3	M P Vaughan	4-27	v	Gloucestershire	at Bristol	2000 $
3	S A Patterson	4-28	v	Worcestershire	at Worcester	2011 $
3	A U Rashid	4-38	v	Northamptonshire	at Northampton	2012 $
2	M K Bore	4-21	v	Sussex	at Middlesbrough	1970 $
		4-21	v	Worcestershire	at Worcester	1970 $
2	J D Woodford	4-23	v	Northamptonshire	at Northampton	1970 $
		4-23	v	Warwickshire	at Middlesbrough	1971 $
2	G J Kruis	4-17	v	Derbyshire	at Leeds	2007 $
2	D Wilson	4-22	v	Nottinghamshire	at Bradford	1969 $
2	V J Craven	4-22	v	Kent	at Scarborough	2003 $
2	M A Robinson	4-23	v	Northamptonshire	at Leeds	1993 $
2	M W Pillans	4-26	v.	Nottinghamshire	at York	2021 +
2	S N Hartley	4-32	v	Derbyshire	at Leeds	1989 #
2	A U Rashid	4-38	v	Northamptonshire	at Northampton	2012 $
2	A McGrath	4-41	v	Surrey	at Leeds	2003 $
2	D J Willey	4-47	v	Derbyshire	at Derby	2018 +
1	R Illingworth	4-6	v	Middlesex	at Hull	1983 $
1	J R Sullivan	4-11	v	Derbyshire	at Chesterfield	2021 +
1	M Johnson	4-18	v	Scotland	at Bradford	1981 #
1	G S Blewett	4-18	v	Lancashire	at Manchester	1999 +
1	G M Fellows	4-19	v	Durham	at Leeds	2002 $
1	A P Grayson	4-25	v	Glamorgan	at Cardiff	1994 $
1	C J Elstub	4-25	v	Surrey	at Leeds	2001 $
1	D S Lehmann	4-26	v	Devon	at Exmouth	2002 +
1	C Shaw	4-29	v	Middlesex	at Leeds	1988 $
1	A G Wharf	4-29	v	Nottinghamshire	at Leeds	1996 #
1	F S Trueman	4-30	v	Nottinghamshire	at Middlesbrough	1963 +
1	J D Batty	4-33	v	Kent	at Scarborough	1991 $

ALL LIST A PLAYERS WHO HAVE TAKEN 4 WICKETS IN AN INNINGS 1963-2021 (170) AND BEST FIGURES *(Continued)*

1	P M Hutchinson	4-34	v	Gloucestershire	at Gloucester	1998 $
1	A K D Gray	4-34	v	Kent	at Leeds	2002 $
1	A Shahzad	4-34	v	Middlesex	at Lord's	2010 $
1	P M Stringer	4-35	v	Derbyshire	at Sheffield	1969 $
1	C S Pickles	4-36	v	Somerset	at Scarborough	1990 $
1	M J Hoggard	4-39	v	Surrey	at Leeds	2000 #
1	R J Sidebottom	4-39	v	Bedfordshire	at Luton	2001 +
1	K Sharp	4-40	v	Wiltshire	at Trowbridge	1987 +
1	T L Best	4-46	v	Essex	at Chelmsford	2010 $
1	Azeem Rafiq	4-47	v.	Lancashire	at Leeds	2017 +
1	A C Morris	4-49	v	Leicestershire	at Leicester	1997 $
1	L E Plunkett	4-52	v	Kent	Canterbury	2016 +
1	D B Close	4-60	v	Sussex	at Hove	1963 +
1	B O Coad	4-63	v.	Derbyshire	at Leeds	2017 +
1	M J Waite	4-65	v.	Worcestershire	at Worcester	2017 +

CAREER AVERAGES FOR YORKSHIRE
ALL LIST A MATCHES OF 40 TO 65 OVERS 1963-2021

Player	M	Inns	NO	Runs	HS	Av'ge	100s	50s	Runs	Wkts	Av'ge	Ct/St
Ashraf, M A ...	22	6	4	3	3*	1.50	0	0	895	23	38.91	4
Athey, C W J ...	140	129	14	3,662	118	31.84	2	25	431	19	22.68	46
Azeem Rafiq ..	30	21	8	222	52*	17.07	0	1	1,160	41	28.29	12
Bairstow, D L ..	403	317	71	5,180	103*	21.05	1	19	17	0	—	390/31
Bairstow, J M .	**43**	**39**	**4**	**1,051**	**174**	**30.02**	**2**	**3**	**0**	**0**	**—**	**33/3**
Baker, T M	4	1	0	3	3	3.00	0	0	89	4	22.25	3
Balderstone, J C	13	11	2	173	46	19.22	0	0	38	2	19.00	3
Ballance, G S ..	**76**	**70**	**10**	**3,033**	**156**	**50.55**	**4**	**19**	**0**	**0**	**—**	**32**
Batty, J D	38	16	7	50	13*	5.55	0	0	1,297	42	30.88	18
Berry, P J	1	0	0	0	0	—	0	0	28	0	—	0
Bess, D M	**4**	**3**	**0**	**19**	**7**	**6.33**	**0**	**0**	**188**	**1**	**188.00**	**1**
Best, T L	5	1	1	8	8*	—	0	0	166	10	16.60	1
Bevan, M G	48	45	12	2,110	103*	63.93	2	19	540	28	19.28	11
Binks, J G	30	21	3	247	34	13.72	0	0	0	0	—	26/8
Birkhead, B D .	**1**	**0**	**0**	**0**	**—**	**—**	**0**	**0**	**0**	**0**	**—**	**1**
Blain, J A R	15	8	3	34	11*	6.80	0	0	462	14	33.00	3
Blakey, R J	373	319	84	7,361	130*	31.32	3	35	0	0	—	369/59
Blewett, G S ...	17	17	0	345	77	20.29	0	2	196	11	17.81	7
Booth, P A	5	2	1	7	6*	7.00	0	0	147	3	49.00	1
Bore, M K	55	24	10	90	15	6.42	0	0	1,600	50	32.00	15
Boycott, G	264	255	38	8,699	146	40.08	7	63	1,095	25	43.80	92
Bresnan, T T ...	181	130	31	2,124	95*	21.45	0	8	6,536	196	33.34	52
Broadhurst, M ..	1	0	0	0	—	—	0	0	27	0	—	0
Brook, H C	**15**	**12**	**1**	**343**	**103**	**31.18**	**1**	**1**	**19**	**0**	**—**	**4**
Brooks, J A	12	4	1	7	6	2.33	0	0	461	15	30.73	3
Brophy, G L	68	57	12	1,240	93*	27.55	0	9	0	0	—	67/14
Byas, D	313	301	35	7,782	116*	29.25	5	44	659	25	26.36	128
Callis, E	1	1	0	0	0	0.00	0	0	0	0	—	0
Carrick, P	304	206	53	2,159	54	14.11	0	2	7,408	236	31.38	70
Carver, K	15	4	4	52	35*	—	0	0	440	14	31.42	2
Chapman, C A ..	10	7	4	94	36*	31.33	0	0	0	0	—	7
Claydon, M E ..	7	2	0	15	9	7.50	0	0	293	8	36.62	0
Cleary, M F	4	3	1	50	23*	25.00	0	0	159	2	79.50	0
Close, D B	32	31	2	631	96	21.75	0	3	475	23	20.65	14
Coad, B O	**25**	**10**	**7**	**27**	**10**	**9.00**	**0**	**0**	**1,033**	**28**	**36.89**	**6**
Cooper, H P ...	142	74	34	483	29*	12.07	0	0	4,184	177	23.63	26
Cope, G A	37	20	13	96	18*	13.71	0	0	1,020	24	42.50	9
Coverdale, S P .	3	3	2	18	17*	18.00	0	0	0	0	—	3
Craven, V J	42	39	5	580	59	17.05	0	2	353	21	16.80	9
Dalton, A J	17	16	1	280	55	18.66	0	1	0	0	—	7
Dawson, I	25	20	4	260	57	16.25	0	1	0	0	—	18/8
Dawson, R K J .	92	58	12	431	41	9.36	0	0	2,784	91	30.59	31
Dennis, S J	56	24	11	114	16*	8.76	0	0	1,736	42	41.33	7
Duke, H G	**9**	**7**	**0**	**206**	**125**	**29.42**	**1**	**0**	**0**	**0**	**—**	**4/1**
Elliott, M T G ..	6	6	3	394	128*	131.33	3	0	0	0	—	0
Elstub, C J	10	4	4	6	4*	—	0	0	290	12	24.16	0
Fellows, G M ..	95	79	15	1,342	80*	20.96	0	6	836	22	38.00	27
Fisher, I D	28	12	3	68	20	7.55	0	0	708	29	24.41	6
Fisher, M D ...	**27**	**14**	**9**	**201**	**36***	**40.20**	**0**	**0**	**1,039**	**27**	**38.48**	**7**
Fleming, S P ...	7	7	1	285	139*	47.50	1	1	0	0	—	3
Fletcher, S D ...	129	32	18	109	16*	7.78	0	0	4,686	164	28.57	34
Foster, M J	20	14	1	199	118	15.30	1	0	370	6	61.66	6

ALL LIST A MATCHES OF 40 TO 65 OVERS 1963-2021 *(Continued)*

Player	M	Inns	NO	Runs	HS	Av'ge	100s	50s	Runs	Wkts	Av'ge	Ct/St
Fraine, W A R .	**10**	**8**	**1**	**227**	**69***	**32.42**	**0**	**1**	**0**	**0**	**—**	**4**
Gale, A W	125	116	11	3,256	125*	31.00	2	17	0	0	—	24
Gibson, R	6	4	1	19	9	6.33	0	0	158	5	31.60	1
Gilbert, C R . . .	5	4	0	55	37	13.75	0	0	199	8	24.87	2
Gillespie, J N . .	18	4	1	29	15*	9.66	0	0	601	18	33.38	6
Gough, D	214	120	33	1,280	72*	14.71	0	1	6,798	291	23.36	43
Gray, A K D . .	31	19	7	130	30*	10.83	0	0	843	25	33.72	8
Grayson, A P . .	66	49	8	587	55	14.31	0	1	1,441	39	36.94	19
Guy, S M	32	23	4	282	40	14.84	0	0	0	0	—	35/11
Hamilton, G M .	101	70	18	1,059	57*	20.36	0	2	2,803	121	23.16	15
Hampshire, A W	4	3	0	3	3	1.00	0	0	0	0	—	1
Hampshire, J H .	234	223	24	6,296	119	31.63	7	36	26	1	26.00	69
Hannon-Dalby, O J	5	1	1	21	21*	—	0	0	202	5	40.40	3
Handscomb, P S P	9	9	1	504	140	63.00	1	3	0	0	—	5
Harden, R J	19	16	2	230	42	16.42	0	0	0	0	—	1
Hartley, P J	219	145	49	1,609	83	16.76	0	4	7,476	283	26.41	40
Hartley, S N . . .	171	154	31	2,815	83*	22.88	0	13	2,153	67	32.13	52
Harvey, I J	28	27	2	637	74	25.48	0	3	950	30	31.66	8
Head, T M	4	4	0	277	175	69.25	1	1	0	0	—	0
Hill, G C H	**9**	**7**	**1**	**222**	**90***	**37.00**	**0**	**2**	**249**	**10**	**24.90**	**1**
Hodd, A J	32	23	5	368	69*	20.44	0	1	0	0	—	39/8
Hodgson, D M .	12	10	1	272	90	30.22	0	3	0	0	—	10/2
Hodgson, L J . .	6	2	0	9	9	4.50	0	0	161	4	40.25	1
Hoggard, M J . .	83	28	19	41	7*	4.55	0	0	2,682	118	22.72	7
Hutchison, P M .	32	11	8	18	4*	6.00	0	0	844	43	19.62	3
Hutton, R A	107	80	25	1,075	65	19.54	0	4	3,000	128	23.43	27
Illingworth, R . .	41	15	11	171	45	42.75	0	0	793	40	19.82	14
Ingham, P G . . .	12	10	4	312	87*	52.00	0	2	0	0	—	2
Inzamam ul Haq	3	3	0	69	53	23.00	0	1	0	0	—	0
Jaques, P A	43	42	2	1,588	105	39.70	1	13	0	0	—	16
Jarvis, P W	144	74	28	529	42	11.50	0	0	4,684	213	21.99	33
Johnson, C	129	102	22	1,615	73*	20.18	0	4	28	2	14.00	33
Johnson, N	14	6	3	34	15*	11.33	0	0	455	12	37.91	2
Katich, S M	3	3	2	79	40*	79.00	0	0	0	0	—	2
Kellett, S A	56	51	3	1,207	118*	25.14	2	4	16	0	—	13
Kettleborough, R A	10	6	3	71	28	23.66	0	0	72	3	24.00	4
Kirby, S P	29	12	3	38	15	4.22	0	0	1,061	24	44.20	6
Kohler-Cadmore, T .	**17**	**16**	**0**	**762**	**164**	**47.62**	**1**	**6**	**0**	**0**	**—**	**16**
Kruis, G J	55	22	11	138	31*	12.54	0	0	1,793	62	28.91	9
Lawson, M A K .	4	4	0	30	20	7.50	0	0	141	3	47.00	1
Leadbeater, B . .	105	100	19	2,245	90	27.71	0	11	95	5	19.00	26
Leaning, J A . . .	47	40	7	1,024	131*	31.03	2	5	204	7	29.14	24
Lee, J E	4	0	0	0	—	—	0	0	116	7	16.57	0
Lees, A Z	42	39	2	1,109	102	29.97	1	8	0	0	—	15
Lehmann, D S . .	130	126	20	5,229	191	49.33	8	38	1,990	79	25.18	41
Lester, E I	1	1	0	0	0	0.00	0	0	0	0	—	0
Loten, T W	**1**	**0**	**0**	**0**	**—**	**—**	**0**	**0**	**0**	**0**	**—**	**0**
Love, J D	220	203	33	4,298	118*	25.28	4	18	129	5	25.80	44
Lucas, D S	5	2	0	40	32	20.00	0	0	187	3	62.33	1
Lumb, M J	104	98	8	2,606	92	28.95	0	18	28	0	—	31
Lumb, R G	137	123	13	2,784	101	25.30	1	16	0	0	—	21
Luxton, W	**7**	**6**	**1**	**165**	**68**	**33.00**	**0-**	**1**	**0**	**0**	**—**	**1**
Lyth, A	121	114	8	3,754	144	35.41	5	18	373	6	62.16	53

ALL LIST A MATCHES OF 40 TO 65 OVERS 1963-2021 *(Continued)*

Player	M	Inns	NO	Runs	HS	Av'ge	100s	50s	Runs	Wkts	Av'ge	Ct/St
McGrath, A	275	253	39	7,220	148	33.73	7	44	2,514	79	31.82	91
Maxwell, G J	8	7	1	312	111	52.00	1	2	144	3	48.00	4
Metcalfe, A A	194	189	15	5,584	127*	32.09	4	36	44	2	22.00	44
Middlebrook, J D	18	11	3	61	15*	7.62	0	0	530	13	40.76	5
Milburn, S M	4	2	1	14	13*	14.00	0	0	118	2	59.00	1
Miller, D A	3	3	0	45	44	15.00	0	0	0	0	—	3
Morris, A C	27	17	5	212	48*	17.66	0	0	464	21	22.09	5
Moxon, M D	237	229	21	7,380	141*	35.48	7	49	1,202	34	35.35	77
Nicholson, A G	120	46	22	155	15*	6.45	0	0	2,951	173	17.05	16
Nicholson, N G	2	2	1	1	1*	1.00	0	0	0	0	—	2
Old, C M	221	169	38	2,572	82*	19.63	0	10	5,841	308	18.96	56
Oldham, S	106	40	21	192	38*	10.10	0	0	3,136	142	22.08	17
Olivier, D	**6**	**3**	**3**	**17**	**8***	**—**	**0**	**0**	**322**	**3**	**107.33**	**2**
Padgett, D E V	57	54	3	1,069	68	20.96	0	2	25	1	25.00	13
Parker, B	73	61	8	965	69	18.20	0	1	18	0	—	12
Patterson, S A	**95**	**40**	**20**	**249**	**25***	**12.45**	**0-**	**0-**	**3,436**	**118**	**29.11**	**7**
Pickles, C S	71	48	5	375	37*	13.39	0	0	2,403	63	38.14	23
Pillans, M W	**14**	**8**	**2**	**115**	**40**	**19.16**	**0**	**0**	**595**	**24**	**24.79**	**3**
Plunkett, L E	28	21	10	327	53	29.72	0	1	1,060	33	32.12	17
Poysden, J E	8	4	1	2	1	0.66	0	0	303	6	50.50	1
Pyrah, R M	114	75	20	978	69	17.78	0	2	3,572	133	26.85	35
Pujara, C A	8	8	1	370	101	52.85	1	3	0	0	—	4
Ramage, A	34	17	8	134	32*	14.88	0	0	1,178	30	39.26	9
Ramsden, G	1	0	0	0	—	—	0	0	26	2	13.00	0
Rana Naved-ul-Hasan	17	16	1	375	74	25.00	0	3	681	26	26.19	5
Rashid, A U	**107**	**75**	**22**	**1,063**	**71**	**20.05**	**0**	**1**	**3,986**	**137**	**29.09**	**34**
Read, J	1	0	0	0	—	—	0	0	0	0	—	0
Revis, M L	**9**	**7**	**1**	**186**	**58***	**31.00**	**0**	**1**	**229**	**5**	**45.80**	**5**
Rhodes, S J	2	1	0	6	6	6.00	0	0	0	0	—	3
Rhodes, W M H	21	17	2	252	46	16.80	0	0	364	11	33.09	8
Richardson. R B	28	28	6	993	103	45.13	1	8	0	0	—	5
Richardson, S A	1	1	0	7	7	7.00	0	0	0	0	—	0
Robinson, A L	92	36	19	127	18*	7.47	0	0	2,588	105	24.64	14
Robinson, M A	89	30	16	41	7	2.92	0	0	2,795	91	30.71	7
Robinson, O E	3	2	2	16	12*	—	0	0	66	0	—	4
Robinson, P E	135	123	15	2,738	78*	25.35	0	14	0	0	—	47
Root, J E	**23**	**22**	**3**	**747**	**83**	**39.31**	**0**	**5**	**280**	**7**	**40.00**	**10**
Rudolph, J A	65	62	9	3,090	132*	59.42	9	19	37	0	—	32
Ryan, M	3	2	1	7	6*	7.00	0	0	149	5	29.80	3
Sadler, J L	1	1	0	19	19	19.00	0	0	0	0	—	0
Sanderson, B W	10	2	1	14	12*	14.00	0	0	247	8	30.87	0
Sayers, J J	31	30	2	594	62	21.21	0	5	79	1	79.00	2
Scofield, D	3	1	0	0	0	0.00	0	0	111	2	55.50	1
Shahzad. A	30	22	7	243	59*	16.20	0	1	1,182	34	34.76	7
Sharp, K	206	191	18	4,776	114	27.60	3	28	48	4	12.00	68
Sharpe, P J	91	86	4	1,515	89*	18.47	0	8	11	0	—	53
Shaw, C	48	20	10	127	26	12.70	0	0	1,396	58	24.06	8
Shutt, J W	**5**	**2**	**2**	**2**	**1***	**—**	**0**	**0**	**88**	**1**	**88.00**	**3**
Sidebottom, A	236	131	47	1,279	52*	15.22	0	1	6,918	260	26.60	51
Sidebottom, R J	113	51	22	303	30*	10.44	0	0	3,631	124	29.28	24
Silverwood, C E W	166	94	33	892	61	14.62	0	4	5,212	224	23.26	25
Smith, N	7	2	1	5	5	5.00	0	0	0	0	—	2

ALL LIST A MATCHES OF 40 TO 65 OVERS 1963-2021 *(Continued)*

Player	M	Inns	NO	Runs	HS	Av'ge	100s	50s	Runs	Wkts	Av'ge	Ct/St
Smith, R	3	2	0	17	17	8.50	0	0	0	0	—	1
Squires, P J	56	48	5	708	79*	16.46	0	3	4	0	—	10
Starc, M A	4	2	0	5	4*	—	0	0	181	8	22.62	1
Stemp, R D	88	28	10	118	23	6.55	0	0	2,996	100	29.96	14
Stevenson, G B	217	158	23	1,710	81*	12.66	0	2	6,820	290	23.51	38
Stott, W B	2	2	0	30	30	15.00	0	0	0	0	—	0
Stringer, P M	11	8	6	29	13*	14.50	0	0	256	15	17.06	0
Stuchbury, S	22	8	4	21	9*	5.25	0	0	677	29	23.34	2
Sullivan, J R	**3**	**1**	**0**	**6**	**6**	**6.00**	**0**	**0**	**79**	**5**	**15.80**	**0**
Swallow, I G	8	5	3	37	17*	18.50	0	0	198	2	99.00	5
Swanepoel, P J	3	2	2	9	8*	—	0	0	100	3	33.33	0
Tattersall, J	**24**	**18**	**3**	**528**	**89**	**35.20**	**0**	**6**	**0**	**0**	**—**	**21/3**
Taylor, C R	6	5	0	102	28	20.40	0	0	0	0	—	0
Taylor, K	10	10	0	135	30	13.50	0	0	168	11	15.27	3
Taylor, N S	1	0	0	0	0	—	0	0	45	1	45.00	1
Tendulkar, S R	17	17	2	540	107	36.00	1	1	167	6	27.83	3
Thompson, J A	**1**	**0**	**0**	**0**	**—**	**—**	**0**	**0**	**43**	**0**	**—**	**0**
Thornicroft, N	14	7	4	52	20	17.33	0	0	591	17	34.76	3
Townsley, R A J	5	4	1	81	34	27.00	0	0	62	0	—	1
Trueman, F S	11	9	1	127	28	15.87	0	0	348	21	16.57	5
Vaughan, M P	183	178	13	4,966	125*	30.09	3	29	1,860	60	31.00	56
Wainman, J C	4	3	1	51	33	25.50	0	0	201	5	40.20	1
Wainwright, D J	48	21	13	150	26	18.75	0	0	1,427	38	37.55	16
Waite, M E	**22**	**16**	**4**	**437**	**71**	**36.41**	**0**	**1**	**842**	**28**	**30.07**	**0**
Wardlaw, I	17	10	4	56	18	9.33	0	0	686	24	28.58	3
Waring, J	1	1	1	1	1*	—	0	0	11	0	—	0
Warner, J D	1	0	0	0	—	—	0	0	32	0	—	0
Warren, A C	1	1	0	3	3	3.00	0	0	35	1	35.00	0
Wharf, A G	6	1	1	2	2*	—	0	0	176	8	22.00	1
White, C	292	266	39	6,384	148	28.12	5	28	6,120	248	24.67	84
Whiteley, J P	6	4	0	19	14	4.75	0	0	195	2	97.50	3
Widdup, S	4	4	0	49	38	12.25	0	0	0	0	—	2
Wigley, D H	1	1	0	0	0	0.00	0	0	38	0	—	0
Willey, D J	**20**	**16**	**2**	**448**	**131**	**32.00**	**1**	**2**	**808**	**33**	**24.48**	**5**
Williamson, K A	13	11	0	279	70	25.36	0	1	42	1	42.00	6
Wilson, D	61	47	8	430	46	11.02	0	0	1,527	76	20.09	22
Wood, G L	1	1	0	26	26	26.00	0	0	0	0	—	0
Wood, M J	145	134	14	3,270	160	27.25	5	14	76	3	25.33	57
Woodford, J D	72	57	14	890	69*	20.69	0	2	1,627	77	21.12	25
Younus Khan	11	8	0	248	100	31.00	1	0	144	2	72.00	5
Yuvraj Singh	9	9	0	196	50	21.77	0	1	197	3	65.66	1

LIMITED-OVERS INTERNATIONAL MATCHES AT NORTH MARINE ROAD, SCARBOROUGH 1976-1978

1976 **England 202 for 8 wkts** (55 overs) (G D Barlow 80*, A M E Roberts 4 for 32).
West Indies 207 for 4 wkts (41 overs) (I V A Richards 119*).
West Indies won by 6 wickets **Award: I V A Richards**

1978 **England 206 for 8 wkts** (55 overs) (G A Gooch 94, B L Cairns 5 for 28).
New Zealand 187 for 8 wkts (55 overs) (B E Congdon 52*).
England won by 19 runs **Award: G A Gooch**

For England   **YORKSHIRE ONE-DAY INTERNATIONAL CRICKETERS 1971-2021** (Correct to October 19, 2021)

Player	M	I	NO	Runs	HS	Av'ge	100s	50s	Balls	Runs	W	Av'ge	Best	4wI	Ct/St
ATHEY, C W J 1980-88	31	30	3	848	142*	31.40	2	4	—	—	—	—	—	0	16
BAIRSTOW, D L 1979-84	21	20	8	206	23*	14.71	0	0	—	—	—	—	—	0	17/4
BAIRSTOW, J M 2011-21	89	81	8	3,498	141*	47.91	11	14	—	—	—	—	—	0	45/3
BALLANCE, G S 2013-14/15	16	15	1	297	79	21.21	0	2	—	—	—	—	—	0	8
BLAKEY, R J 1992-93	3	2	0	25	25	12.50	0	0	—	—	—	—	—	0	2/1
BOYCOTT, G 1971-81	36	34	4	1,082	105	36.06	1	9	168	105	5	21.00	2-14	0	5
BRESNAN, T T 2006-15	85	64	20	871	80	19.79	0	0	4,221	3,813	109	34.98	5-48	4	20
COPE, G A 1977-78	2	1	1	1	1*	—	0	0	112	35	2	17.50	1-16	0	0
GOUGH, D 1994-2006	158	87	38	609	46*	12.42	0	0	8,422	6,154	234	26.29	5-44	10	24
HAMPSHIRE, J H .1971-72	3	3	1	48	25*	24.00	0	0	—	—	—	—	—	0	0
HOGGARD, M J ...2001-06	26	6	2	17	7	4.25	0	0	1,306	1,152	32	36.00	5-49	1	5
JARVIS, P W 1988-93	16	8	2	31	16*	5.16	0	0	879	672	24	28.00	5-35	2	1
LOVE, J D 1981	3	3	0	61	43	20.33	0	0	—	—	—	—	—	0	1
MALAN, D J 2019-21	6	6	2	158	68*	39.50	0	2	—	—	—	—	—	0	3
McGRATH, A 2003-04	14	12	2	166	52	16.60	0	1	228	175	4	43.75	1-13	0	4
MOXON, M D 1985-88	8	8	0	174	70	21.75	0	1	—	—	—	—	—	0	5
OLD, C M 1973-81	32	25	7	338	51*	18.77	0	1	1,755	999	45	22.20	4-8	2	8
PLUNKETT, L E 2005/6-2019	89	50	19	646	56	20.83	0	1	4,137	4,010	135	29.70	5-52	7	24
RASHID, A U 2009-21	112	50	14	663	69	18.41	0	1	5,573	5,251	159	33.02	5-27	9	35
ROOT, J E 2012/13-20	149	140	21	5,962	133*	50.10	16	33	1,552	1,491	26	57.34	3-52	0	74
SHAHZAD, A 2010-11	11	8	2	39	9	6.50	0	0	588	490	17	28.82	3-41	0	4
SIDEBOTTOM, R J .2001-10	25	18	8	133	24	13.30	0	0	1,277	1,039	29	35.82	3-19	0	6
SILVERWOOD, C E W 1996-2001	7	4	0	17	12	4.25	0	0	306	244	6	40.66	3-43	0	0
STEVENSON, G B .1980-81	4	4	1	43	28*	43.00	0	0	192	125	7	17.85	4-33	1	2
VAUGHAN, M P ...2001-07	86	83	10	1,982	90*	27.15	0	16	796	649	16	40.56	4-22	0	25
WHITE, C 1994-2003	51	41	5	568	57*	15.77	0	1	2,364	1,726	65	26.55	5-21	2	12
WILLEY, D J ...2015-2021	52	29	13	377	51	23.56	0	2	2,305	2,181	69	31.60	5-30	4	23

YORKSHIRE ONE-DAY INTERNATIONAL CRICKETERS 1971-2020 (Correct to December 8, 2020)

For Scotland

Player	M	I	NO	Runs	HS	Av'ge	100s	50s	Balls	Runs	W	Av'ge	Best	4wI	Ct/St
BLAIN, J A R 1999-2009	33	25	6	284	41	14.94	0	0	1,329	1,173	41	28.60	5-22	4	8
HAMILTON, G M .1999-2010	38	38	3	1,231	119	35.17	2	7	220	160	3	53.33	2-36	0	6/1
WARDLAW, I ...2012/14/15	22	14	8	21	7*	3.50	0	0	1,108	1,036	36	28.77	4-22	2	1

YORKSHIRE PLAYERS WHO PLAYED ALL THEIR ONE-DAY INTERNATIONAL CRICKET AFTER LEAVING YORKSHIRE

For England

Player	M	I	NO	Runs	HS	Av'ge	100s	50s	Balls	Runs	W	Av'ge	Best	4wI	Ct/St
BATTY, G J 2002-09	10	8	2	30	17	5.00	0	0	440	366	5	73.20	2-40	—	4
CLOSE, D B 1972	3	3	0	49	43	16.33	0	0	18	21	0	—	—	—	1
GRAYSON, A P ...2000-01	2	2	0	6	6	3.00	0	0	90	60	3	20.00	3-40	—	1
ILLINGWORTH, R .1971-72	2	2	0	5	4	2.50	0	0	130	84	4	21.00	3-50	—	1
LUMB, M J 2013/14	3	3	0	165	106	55.00	1	0							—
RHODES, S J 1989-95	9	8	2	107	56	17.83	0	1							9/2
WHARF, A G 2004-05	13	5	3	19	9	9.50	0	0	584	428	18	23.77	4-24	1	1
WOOD, B 1972-82	13	12	2	314	78*	31.40	0	2	420	224	9	24.88	2-14	—	6

Overseas Players
(Qualification: 20 List A matches for Yorkshire)

For Australia

Player	M	I	NO	Runs	HS	Av'ge	100s	50s	Balls	Runs	W	Av'ge	Best	4wI	Ct/St
BEVAN, M G 1994-2004	232	196	67	6,912	108*	53.58	6	46	1,966	1,655	36	45.97	3-36	—	128
HARVEY, I J ...1997/98-2004	73	51	11	715	48*	17.87	0	0	3,279	2,577	85	30.31	4-16	4	17
JAQUES, P A ...2006-2007	6	6	0	125	94	20.83	0	1							3
LEHMANN, D S .1996-2005	117	101	22	3,078	119	38.96	4	17	1,793	1,445	52	27.78	4-7	1	26

For South Africa

Player	M	I	NO	Runs	HS	Av'ge	100s	50s	Balls	Runs	W	Av'ge	Best	4wI	Ct/St
RUDOLPH, J A 2003-06	43	37	6	1,157	81	37.32	0	7	24	26	0	—	—	—	11

For West Indies

Player	M	I	NO	Runs	HS	Av'ge	100s	50s	Balls	Runs	W	Av'ge	Best	4wI	Ct/St
RICHARDSON, R B .1983-96	224	217	30	6,248	122	33.41	5	44	58	46	1	46.00	1-4	—	75

YORKSHIRE PLAYERS IN WORLD CUPS FOR ENGLAND

BATTING AND FIELDING

Player	Seasons	M	I	NO	Runs	HS	100s	50s	Avge	SR	ct/st
J M Bairstow	2019	11	11	0	532	111	2	2	48.36	92.84	9
G S Ballance	2015	4	4	0	36	10	0	0	9.00	50.70	1
G Boycott	1979	5	5	1	92	57	0	1	23.00	42.90	0
T T Bresnan	2011	7	5	1	41	20*	0	0	10.25	82.00	0
D Gough	1996										
	&1999	11	6	2	95	26*	0	0	23.75	73.07	2
C M Old	1975										
	&1979	9	7	2	91	51*	0	1	18.20	122.97	2
A U Rashid	2019	11	5	1	45	25	0	0	11.25	118.42	3
J E Root *	2015										
	&2019	17	16	2	758	121	3	3	54.14	88.03	20
A Shahzad	2011	2	2	1	7	6*	0	0	7.00	140.00	0
M P Vaughan	2003										
	&2007	14	14	0	348	79	0	3	24.85	71.02	3
C White	1996										
	&2003	7	5	1	92	35	0	0	23.00	98.92	1

* Joe Root's catching tally is an England record. Collingwood has 13, so he is way out in front. Only Ricky Ponting, of Australia, on 28, is ahead.

BOWLING

Player	Overs	Mdns	Runs	Wkts	Avge	BpW	Best	4wi	RPO
G Boycott	27	1	94	5	18.80	32.40	2-14	0	3.48
T T Bresnan	63	5	309	9	34.33	42.00	5-48	1	4.90
D Gough	99.4	8	430	15	28.66	39.86	4-34	1	4.31
C M Old	90.3	18	243	16	15.18	33.93	4- 8	1	2.68
A U Rashid	92	0	526	11	47.81	50.18	3-54	0	5.71
J E Root	19	0	111	3	37.00	38.00	2-27	0	5.84
A Shahzad	18	0	96	3	32.00	36.00	3-43	0	5.33
M P Vaughan	30	0	128	4	32.00	45.00	3-39	0	4.26
C White	51.3	6	202	9	22.44	34.33	3-33	0	3.91

Paul E Dyson

LIMITED-OVERS INTERNATIONAL MATCHES
AT HEADINGLEY, LEEDS 1973-2019

1973 **West Indies 181** (54 overs) (R B Kanhai 55). **England 182 for 9 wkts** (54.3 overs) (M H Denness 66).
England won by 1 wicket   **Award: M H Denness**

1974 **India 265** (53.5 overs) (B P Patel 82, A L Wadekar 67). **England 266 for 6 wkts** (51.1 overs) (J H Edrich 90).
England won by 4 wickets   **Award: J H Edrich**

1975 **Australia 278 for 7 wkts** (60 overs) (R Edwards 80*). **Pakistan 205** (53 overs) (Majid Khan 65, Asif Iqbal 53, D K Lillee 5 for 34).
Australia won by 73 runs   **Award: D K Lillee**

1975 **East Africa 120** (55.3 overs). **India 123 for 0 wkt** (29.5 overs) (S M Gavaskar 65* F M Engineer 54*).
India won by 10 wickets   **Award: F M Engineer**

1975 **England 93** (36.2 overs) (G J Gilmour 6 for 14). **Australia 94 for 6 wkts** (28.4 overs).
Australia won by 4 wickets   **Award: G J Gilmour**

1979 **Canada 139 for 9 wkts** (60 overs). **Pakistan 140 for 2 wkts** (40.1 overs) (Sadiq Mohammed 57*).
Pakistan won by 8 wickets   **Award: Sadiq Mohammed**

1979 **India 182 (55.5 overs)** (S M Gavaskar 55). **New Zealand 183 for 2 wkts** (57 overs) (B A Edgar 84*).
New Zealand won by 8 wickets   **Award: B A Edgar**

1979 **England 165 for 9 wkts** (60 overs). **Pakistan 151** (56 overs) (Asif Iqbal 51, M Hendrick 4 for 15)
England won by 14 runs   **Award: M Hendrick**

1980 **West Indies 198** (55 overs) (C G Greenidge 78). **England 174** (51.2 overs) (C J Tavaré 82*).
West Indies won by 24 runs   **Award: C J Tavaré**

1981 **Australia 236 for 8 wkts** (55 overs) (G M Wood 108). **England 165** (46.5 overs) (R M Hogg 4 for 29).
Australia won by 71 runs   **Award: G M Wood**

1982 **India 193** (55 overs) (Kapil Dev 60, I T Botham 4 for 56). **England 194 for 1 wkt** (50.1 overs) (B Wood 78*, C J Tavaré 66).
England won by 9 wickets   **Award: B Wood**

1983 **West Indies 252 for 9 wkts** (60 overs) (H A Gomes 78). **Australia 151** (30.3 overs) (W W Davis 7 for 51).
West Indies won by 101 runs   **Award: W W Davis**

1983 **Pakistan 235 for 7 wkts** (60 overs) (Imran Khan 102*, Shahid Mahboob 77, A L F de Mel 5 for 39). **Sri Lanka 224** (58.3 overs) (S Wettimuny 50, Abdul Qadir 5 for 44).
Pakistan won by 11 runs   **Award: Abdul Qadir**

1983 **Sri Lanka 136** (50.4 overs). **England 137 for 1 wkt** (24.1 overs) (G Fowler 81*).
England won by 9 wickets   **Award: R G D Willis**

1986 **New Zealand 217 for 8 wkts** (55 overs) (J J Crowe 66). **England 170** (48.2 overs).
New Zealand won by 47 runs   **Award: J J Crowe**

1988 **England 186 for 8 wkts** (55 overs). **West Indies 139** (46.3 overs).
England won by 9 wickets   **Award: D R Pringle**

1990 **England 295 for 6 wkts** (55 overs) (R A Smith 128, G A Gooch 55). **New Zealand 298 for 6 wkts** (54.5 overs) (M J Greatbatch 102*, J G Wright 52, A H Jones 51).
New Zealand won by 4 wickets   **Award: M J Greatbatch**

1990 **England 229** (54.3 overs) (A J Lamb 56, D I Gower 50). **India 233 for 4 wkts** (53 overs) (S V Manjrekar 82, M Azharuddin 55*)
India won by 6 wickets   **Award: A Kumble**

LIMITED-OVERS INTERNATIONAL MATCHES
AT HEADINGLEY, LEEDS 1973-2019 *(Continued)*

1996 **India 158** (40.2 overs). **England 162 for 4 wkts** (39.3 overs) (G P Thorpe 79*).
England won by 6 wickets **Award: G P Thorpe**

1997 **Australia 170 for 8 wkts** (50 overs).**England 175 for 4 wkts** (40.1 overs) (G P Thorpe 75*, A J Hollioake 66*).
England won by 6 wickets **Award: G P Thorpe**

1998 **South Africa 205 for 8 wkts** (50 overs) (S M Pollock 56). **England 206 for 3 wkts** (35 overs) (A D Brown 59, N V Knight 51).
England won by 7 wickets **Award: A D Brown**

1999 **Pakistan 275 for 8 wkts** (50 overs) (Inzamam-ul-Haq 81, Abdur Razzaq 60). **Australia 265** (49.5 overs) (M G Bevan 61, Wasim Akram 4-40).
Pakistan won by 10 runs **Award: Inazmam-ul-Haq**

1999 **Zimbabwe 175** (49.3 overs) (M A Goodwin 57). **New Zealand 70 for 3 wkts** (15 overs).
No result **No Award**

1999 **South Africa 271 for 7 wkts** (50 overs) (H H Gibbs 101, D J Cullinan 50). **Australia 275 for 5 wkts** (49.4 overs) (S R. Waugh 120*, R T Ponting 69).
Australia won by 5 wickets **Award: S R Waugh**

2001 **England 156 (45.2 overs)** (B C Hollioake 53, Waqar Younis 7 for 36). **Pakistan 153 for 4 wkts** (39.5 overs) (Abdur Razzaq 75).
Pakistan won — England conceding the match following a pitch invasion.
Award: Waqar Younis

2002 **Sri Lanka 240 for 7 wkts** (32 overs) (S T Jayasuriya 112). **England 241 for 7 wkts** (31.2 overs) (M E Trescothick 82).
England won by 3 wkts **Award: S T Jayasuriya**

2003 **England 81 for 4 wkts. Zimbabwe did not bat.**
No result **No Award**

2004 **West Indies 159** (40.1 overs). **England 160 for 3 wkts** (22 overs) (M E Trescothick 55).
England won by 7 wickets **Award: S J Harmison**

2005 **Bangladesh 208 for 7 wkts** (50 overs) (Belim 81, A Flintoff 4-29). **England 209 for 5 wkts** (38.5 overs) (A J Strauss 98)
England won by 5 wickets **Award: A J Strauss**

Australia 219 for 7 wkts (50 overs) (P D Collingwood 4-34). **England 221 for 1 wkt** (46 overs) (M E Trescothick 104*, M P Vaughan 59*).
England won by 9 wickets **Award: M E Trescothick**

2006 **England 321 for 7 wkts** (50 overs) (M E Trescothick 121, S L Malinga 4-44). **Sri Lanka 324 for 2 wkts** (37.3 overs) (S T Jayasuriya 152, W U Tharanga 109).
Sri Lanka won by 8 wickets **Award: S T Jayasuriya**

2007 **India 324 for 6 wkts** (50 overs) (Yuvraj Singh 72, S R Tendulkar 71, S C Ganguly 59, G Gambhir 51). **England 242 for 8 wkts** (39 overs) (P D Collingwood 91*).
India won by 38 runs *(D/L Method)* **Award: S C Ganguly**

2008 **England 275 for 4 wkts** (50 overs) (K P Pietersen 90*, A Flintoff 78). **South Africa 255** (J H Kallis 52).
England won by 20 runs **Award: K P Pietersen**

2009 **England v. West Indies** **Match abandoned without a ball bowled**

2010 **Pakistan 294 for 8 wkts** (50 overs) (Kamran Akmal 74, Asad Shafiq 50, S C J Broad 4-81). **England 295 for 6 wkts** (A J Strauss 126, I J L Trott 53)
England won by 4 wickets **Award: A J Strauss**

2011 **Sri Lanka 309 for 5 wkts** (50 overs) (D P M D Jayawardene 144, K C Sangakkara 69) **England 240 all out** (E J G Morgan 52)
Sri Lanka won by 69 runs **Award: D P M D Jayawardene**

2012 **England v. West Indies** **Match abandoned without a ball bowled**

2013 **England v. Australia** **Match abandoned without a ball bowled**

LIMITED-OVERS INTERNATIONAL MATCHES
AT HEADINGLEY, LEEDS 1973-2019 *(Continued)*

2014 **England 294 for 7 wkts** (50 overs) (J E Root 113). **India 253 all out** (48.4 overs) (R A Jadeja 87)
England won by 41 runs   **Award: J E Root**

2015 **Australia 299 for 7 wkts** (50 overs) (G J Bailey 75, G J Maxwell 85, M S Wade 50*). **England 304 for 7 wkts** (48.2 overs) (E J G Morgan 92, P J Cummins 4-49)
England won by 7 wickets   **Award: E J G Morgan**

2016 **Pakistan 247 for 8 wkts** (50 overs) (Azhar Ali 80, Imad Wasim 57*); **England 252 for 6 wkts** (48 overs) (B A Stokes 69, J M Bairstow 61)
England won by 6 wickets   **Award: J M Bairstow**

2017 **England 339 for 6 wkts** (50 overs) (A D Hales 61, E J G Morgan 107, M M Ali 77*). **South Africa 267** (45 overs) (H M Amla 72, F du Plessis 67, C R Woakes 4-38)
England won by 72 runs   **Award M M Ali**

2018 **India 256 for 8 wkts** (50 overs) (V Kohli 71). **England 260 for 2 wkts** (44.3 overs) (J E Root 100*, E J G Morgan 88*)
England won by 8 wickets   **Award: A U Rashid**

2019 **England 351 for 9 wkts** (50 overs) (J E Root 84, E J G Morgan 76, Shaheen Afridi 4-82). **Pakistan 297** (46.5 overs) (Babar Azam 80, Sarfaraz Ahmed 97, C R Woakes 5-54)
England won by 54 runs   **Award: C R Woakes**

2019 **Sri Lanka 232 for 9 wkts** (50 overs) (A D Mathews 85*). **England 212** (47 overs) (B A Stokes 82*, S L Malinga 4-43)
Sri Lanka won by 20 runs   **Award: S L Malinga**

2019 **Afghanistan 227 for 9 wkts** (50 overs) (Shaheen Afridi 4-47). **Pakistan 230 for 7 wkts** (49.4 overs)
Pakistan won by 3 wickets   **Award: Imad Wasim**

2019 **West Indies 311 for 6 wkts** (50 overs) (E Lewis 58, S D Hope 77). **Afghanistan 288** (50 overs) (Rahmat Shah 62, Ikram Ali Khil 86, C R Brathwaite 4-63)
West Indies won by 23 runs   **Award: S D Hope**

2019 **Sri Lanka 264 for 7 wkts** (50 overs) (A D Mathews 113). **India 265 for 3 wkts** (43.3 overs) (K L Rahul 111, R G Sharma 103)
India won by 7 wickets   **Award: R G Sharma**

SUMMARY OF RESULTS

ENGLAND	Played	Won	Lost
v. Australia	5	3	2
v. Bangladesh	1	1	0
v. India	7	5	2
v. New Zealand	2	0	2
v. Pakistan	5	4	1
v. South Africa	3	3	0
v. Sri Lanka	5	2	3
v. West Indies	4	3	1
v. Zimbabwe	1*	0	0
Totals	33	21	11

*No result. In addition to two matches v. West Indies abandoned and one match v. Australia abandoned

AFGHANISTAN	Played	Won	Lost
v. Pakistan	1	0	1
v. West Indies	1	0	1
Totals	2	0	2

SUMMARY OF RESULTS *(Continued)*

AUSTRALIA	Played	Won	Lost
v. England	5	2	3
v. Pakistan	2	1	1
v. South Africa	1	1	0
v. West Indies	1	0	1
Totals	9	4	5

In addition to one match abandoned

BANGLADESH	Played	Won	Lost
v. England	1	0	1

INDIA	Played	Won	Lost
v. England	7	2	5
v. East Africa	1	1	0
v. New Zealand	1	0	1
v. Sri Lanka	1	1	0
Totals	10	4	6

NEW ZEALAND	Played	Won	Lost
v. England	2	2	0
v. India	1	1	0
v. Zimbabwe	1*	0	0
Totals	4	3	0

*No result

PAKISTAN	Played	Won	Lost
v. Afghanistan	1	1	0
v. Australia	2	1	1
v. Canada	1	1	0
v. England	5	1	4
v. Sri Lanka	1	1	0
Totals	10	5	5

SOUTH AFRICA	Played	Won	Lost
v. Australia	1	0	1
v. England	2	0	2
Totals	3	0	3

SRI LANKA	Played	Won	Lost
v. England	5	3	2
v. India	1	0	1
v. Pakistan	1	0	1
Totals	7	3	4

WEST INDIES	Played	Won	Lost
v. Afghanistan	1	1	0
v. Australia	1	1	0
v. England	4	1	3
Totals	6	3	3

In addition to two matches abandoned

SUMMARY OF RESULTS *(Continued)*

ZIMBABWE	Played	Won	Lost
v. England	1*	0	0
v. New Zealand	1*	0	0
Totals	2*	0	0

*No result

CANADA	Played	Won	Lost
v. Pakistan	1	0	1
EAST AFRICA	**Played**	**Won**	**Lost**
v. India	1	0	1

CENTURIES

152	S J Jayasuriya	for Sri Lanka	v. England	2006
144	D P M D Jayawardene	for Sri Lanka	v. England	2011
128	R A Smith	for England	v. New Zealand	1990
126	A J Strauss	for England	v. Pakistan	2010
121	M E Trescothick	for England	v. Sri Lanka	2006
120*	S R Waugh	for Australia	v. South Africa	1999
113	J E Root	for England	v. India	2014
113	A M Mathews	for Sri Lanka	v. India	2019
112	S J Jayasuriya	for Sri Lanka	v. England	2002
111	K L Rahul	for India	v. Sri Lanka	2019
109	W U Tharanga	for Sri Lanka	v. England	2006
108	G M Wood	for Australia	v. England	1981
104*	M E Trescothick	for England	v. Australia	2005
103	R G Sharma	for India	v. Sri Lanka	2019
102*	Imran Khan	for Pakistan	v. Sri Lanka	1983
102*	M J Greatbatch	for New Zealand	v. England	1990
101	H H Gibbs	for South Africa	v. Australia	1999
100*	J E Root	for England	v. India	2018

4 WICKETS IN AN INNINGS

7-36	Waqar Younis	for Pakistan	v. England	2001
7-51	W W Davis	for West Indies	v. Australia	1983
6-14	G J Gilmour	for Australia	v. England	1975
5-34	D K Lillee	for Australia	v. Pakistan	1975
5-39	A L F de Mel	for Sri Lanka	v. Pakistan	1983
5-44	Abdul Qadir	for Pakistan	v. Sri Lanka	1983
5-54	C R Woakes	for England	v. Pakistan	2019
4-15	M Hendrick	for England	v. Pakistan	1979
4-29	R M Hogg	for Australia	v England	1981
4-29	A Flintoff	for England	v. Bangladesh	2005
4-34	P D Collingwood	for England	v. Australia	2005
4-38	C R Woakes	for England	v. South Africa	2017
4-40	Wasim Akram	for Pakistan	v. Australia	1999
4-43	S L Malinga	for Sri Lanka	v. England	2019
4-44	S L Malinga	for Sri Lanka	v. England	2006
4-47	Shaheen Afridi	for Pakistan	v. Afghanistan	2019
4-49	P J Cummins	Australia	v. England	2015
4-56	I T Botham	for England	v. India	1982
4-81	S J C Broad	for England	v. Pakistan	2010

For England YORKSHIRE T20i CRICKETERS 2003-2021 (Correct to November 12, 2021)

Player	M	I	NO	Runs	HS	Av'ge	100s	50s	Balls	Runs	W	Av'ge	Best	4wI	Ct/St
BAIRSTOW, J M ...2011-21	63	57	12	1,190	86*	26.44	0	7	0	0	0	—	—	0	44/1
BRESNAN, T T ..2006-13/14	34	22	9	216	47*	16.61	0	0	663	887	24	36.95	3-10	0	10
BROOK, H C ...2021/22	1	1	0	10	10	10.00	0	0	—	—	—	—	—	0	0
MALAN, D J ...2017-2021	36	35	5	1,239	103*	41.30	1	11	12	27	1	27.00	1-27	0	14
PLUNKETT, L E ...2006-19	22	11	4	42	18	6.00	0	0	476	627	25	25.08	3-21	0	7
RASHID, A U ...2009-21/22	73	26	14	85	22	7.08	0	0	1,520	1,840	81	22.71	4-2	2	17
ROOT, J E ...2012-19	32	30	5	893	90*	35.72	0	5	84	139	6	23.16	2-9	0	18
SHAHZAD, A ...2010-11	3	1	1	0	0*	—	0	0	66	97	3	32.33	2-38	0	1
VAUGHAN, M P ...2005-7	2	2	0	27	27	13.50	0	0	0	0	0	—	—	0	0
WILLEY, D J ...2015-21	32	21	8	182	29*	14.00	0	0	641	854	34	38.00	4-7	1	15

For Scotland

BLAIN, J A R ...2007-8	6	3	1	4	3*	2.00	0	0	120	108	6	18.00	2-23	0	1
HAMILTON, G M ...2007-10	12	8	0	90	32	11.25	0	0	0	0	0	—	—	0	3
WARDLAW, I .2012/13-13/14	4	1	0	1	1	1.00	0	0	96	145	9	16.11	4-40	0	0

YORKSHIRE PLAYERS WHO PLAYED ALL THEIR T20i CRICKET AFTER LEAVING YORKSHIRE

For England

BATTY, G J ...2009	1	1	0	4	4	4.00	0	0	18	17	0	—	—	0	0
GOUGH, D ...2005-06	2	0	0	0	—	—	0	—	41	49	3	16.33	3-16	0	0
LUMB, M J ...2010-13/14	27	27	1	552	63	21.23	0	3	0	0	0	—	—	0	8
SIDEBOTTOM, R J .2007-10	18	1	1	5	5*	—	0	0	367	437	23	19.00	3-16	0	5

Overseas Players
(Qualification: 20 t20 matches for Yorkshire)

For South Africa

RUDOLPH, J A 2006	1	1	1	6	6*	—	0	0	—	—	—	—	—	0	0

T20 RECORDS SECTION
TROPHY WINNERS 2003-2021

		Yorkshire's Position			*Yorkshire's Position*
2003	Surrey	Group N 2 (6)	2013	Northamptonshire	Group N 6 (6)
2004	Leicestershire	Group N 5 (6)	2014	Warwickshire	Group N 5 (9)
2005	Somerset	Group N 4 (6)	2015	Lancashire	Group N 8 (9)
2006	Leicestershire	Quarter-Final	2016	Northamptonshire	Semi-Final
2007	Kent	Quarter-Final	2017	Nottinghamshire	Group N 5 (9)
2008	Middlesex	Group N 3 (6)	2018	Worcestershire	Group N 5 (9)
2009	Sussex	Group N 5 (9)	2019	Essex	Group N 5 (9)
2010	Hampshire	Group N 6 (9)	2020	Nottinghamshire	Group N 5 (6)
2011	Leicestershire	Group N 6 (9)	2021	Kent	Quarter-Final
2012	Hampshire	Final			

SEASON-BY-SEASON RECORD OF ALL T20 MATCHES PLAYED BY YORKSHIRE 2003-2021

Season	Played	Won	Lost	Tie	N R	Abd	Season	Played	Won	Lost	Tie	N R	Abd
2003	5	3	2	0	0	0	2013	10	2	7	1	0	0
2004	5	2	3	0	0	0	2014	11	6	5	0	0	3
2005	8	3	5	0	0	0	2015	14	5	8	1	0	0
2006	9	4	4	0	1	0	2016	15	8	6	0	1	1
2007	8	4	4	0	0	1	2017	12	6	5	1	0	2
2008	9	5	3	1	0	1	2018	16	8	8	0	0	0
2009	10	4	6	0	0	0	2019	10	4	5	1	0	4
2010	16	6	9	1	0	0	2020	8	3	5	0	0	2
2011	15	6	7	0	2	1	2021	13	7	6	0	0	1
2012	12	9	2	0	1	1		212	97	103	6	6	17
2012/13	6	2	3	0	1	0							

ANALYSIS OF T20 RESULTS V. ALL TEAMS 2003-2021
DOMESTIC MATCHES

		HOME				AWAY				
Opponents	Played	Won	Lost	Tied	N. R.	Won	Lost	Tied	N. R.	Abd
Derbyshire	32	10	8	0	0	9	4	0	1	0
Durham	35	10	5	1	0	8	10	0	1	2
Essex	1	0	0	0	0	0	1	0	0	0
Glamorgan	1	0	0	0	0	1	0	0	0	0
Hampshire	1	0	0	0	0	0	1	0	0	0
Lancashire	32	9	6	1	0	4	11	1	0	4
Leicestershire	25	6	5	0	0	4	9	1	0	2
Northamptonshire	14	5	3	0	0	4	1	1	0	3
Nottinghamshire	32	6	7	0	1	4	14	0	0	3
Sussex	3	0	1	0	0	1	1	0	0	0
Warwickshire	16	5	3	1	0	1	4	0	2	2
Worcestershire	12	5	2	0	0	2	3	0	0	1
Total	**204**	**56**	**40**	**3**	**1**	**38**	**59**	**3**	**4**	**17**

Abandoned matches are not included in the list of matches played.

ANALYSIS OF T20 RESULTS V. ALL TEAMS 2003-2021 *(Cont)*
OTHER MATCHES

		HOME				AWAY				
Opponents	*Played*	*Won*	*Lost*	*Tied*	*N. R*	*Won*	*Lost*	*Tied*	*N. R*	*Abd*
Uva	1	0	0	0	0	1	0	0	0	0
Trinidad and Tobago	1	0	0	0	0	1	0	0	0	0
Sydney Sixers	1	0	0	0	0	0	1	0	0	0
Mumbai	1	0	0	0	0	0	0	0	1	0
Highveld	1	0	0	0	0	0	1	0	0	0
Chennai	1	0	0	0	0	0	1	0	0	0
Lahore Qalandars	1	0	0	0	0	0	1	0	0	0
Hobart Hurricanes	1	0	0	0	1	0	0	0	0	0
Total	**8**	**0**	**0**	**0**	**1**	**3**	**4**	**0**	**1**	**0**
Grand Total	212	56	40	3	1	41	63	3	5	17

Abandoned matches are not included in matches played

ABANDONED T20 MATCHES (17)

2007	v. Lancashire at Leeds		v. Warwickshire at Birmingham
2008	v. Leicestershire at Leeds	2019	v. Nottinghamshire at Leeds
2011	v. Northamptonshire at Leeds		v. Northamptonshire at Northampton
2012	v. Lancashire at Manchester		
2014	v. Warwickshire at Birmingham		v. Lancashire at Manchester
	v. Lancashire at Leeds		v. Durham at Leeds
	v. Worcestershire at Worcester	2020	v. Nottinghamshire at Leeds
2016	v. Nottinghamshire at Leeds		v. Leicestershire at Leeds
2017	v. Northamptonshire at Northampton	2021	v. Durham at Leeds

T20 HIGHEST TEAM TOTALS

BY YORKSHIRE

260-4	v.	Northamptonshire at Leeds	2017
255:2	v.	Leicestershire at Leicester	2019
240:4	v.	Leicestershire at Leeds	2021
233-6	v.	Worcestershire at Leeds	2017
227-5	v.	Nottinghamshire at Leeds	2017
226:8	v.	Birmingham Bears at Leeds	2018
224:3	v.	Northamptonshire at Leeds	2021
223-5	v.	Nottinghamshire at Nottingham	2017
223:6	v.	Durham at Leeds	2016
220:5	v.	Derbyshire at Leeds	2020
216:6	v.	Worcestershire at Worcester	2021
215:6	v.	Northamptonshire at Leeds	2016
213:7	v.	Worcestershire at Leeds	2010
212:5	v.	Worcestershire at Leeds	2012
211:6	v.	Leicestershire at Leeds	2004
210:3	v.	Derbyshire at Derby	2006
209:4	v.	Nottinghamshire at Leeds	2015
207:7	v.	Nottinghamshire at Nottingham	2004
202:8	v.	Lancashire at Manchester	2015

T20 HIGHEST TEAM TOTALS
AGAINST YORKSHIRE

231:6	for Lancashire at Manchester	2015
225:5	for Nottinghamshire at Nottingham	2017
222:6	for Derbyshire at Leeds	2010
222:8	for Leicestershire at Leeds	2021
221:3	for Leicestershire at Leeds	2004
215:6	for Nottinghamshire at Nottingham	2011
215:6	for Durham at Chester-le-Street	2013
212:5	for Nottinghamshire at Nottingham	2018
210:7	for Nottinghamshire at Nottingham	2004
208:7	for Worcestershire at Worcester	2010
207:3	for Leicestershire at Leicester	2021
207:5	for Derbyshire at Leeds	2019
207:6	for Lancashire at Manchester	2005
201:4	for Leicestershire at Leicester	2019
201:5	for Nottinghamshire at Leeds	2014
204:7	for Lancashire at Manchester	2016
196:7	for Worcestershire at Leeds	2017
195:8	for Derbyshire at Leeds	2005
195:4	for Nottinghamshire at Nottingham	2006

T20 HIGHEST INDIVIDUAL SCORES
BY YORKSHIRE

161	A Lyth	v.	Northamptonshire at Leeds	2017
118	D J Willey	v.	Worcestershire at Leeds	2017
112	J M Bairstow	v.	Worcestershire at Worcester	2021
109	I J Harvey	v.	Derbyshire at Leeds	2005
108*	I J Harvey	v.	Lancashire at Leeds	2004
102*	J M Bairstow	v.	Durham at Chester-le-Street	2014
101*	H H Gibbs	v.	Northamptonshire at Northampton	2010
96*	M J Wood	v.	Nottinghamshire at Nottingham	2004
96*	T Kohler-Cadmore	v.	Leicestershire at Leicester	2019
94*	T Kohler-Cadmore	v.	Birmingham Bears at Birmingham	2019
92*	G J Maxwell	v.	Nottinghamshire at Leeds	2015
92*	J E Root	v.	Lancashire at Manchester	2016
92*	A Lyth	v.	Durham at Leeds	2018
92	P A Jaques	v.	Leicestershire at Leeds	2004
92	J M Bairstow	v.	Durham at Leeds	2015
91*	H C Brook	v.	Lancashire at Leeds	2021
91	A W Gale	v.	Nottinghamshire at Leeds	2009
89	A J Finch	v.	Nottinghamshire at Leeds	2014
88	A J Finch	v.	Lancashire at Manchester	2014
87	A Lyth	v.	Durham at Leeds	2017

T20 HIGHEST INDIVIDUAL SCORES

AGAINST YORKSHIRE

111	D L Maddy	for	Leicestershire at Leeds	2004
101	S G Law	for	Lancashire at Manchester	2005
101	A D Hales	for	Nottinghamshire at Nottingham	2017
100*	G M Smith	for	Derbyshire at Leeds	2008
100	Sohail Akhtar	for	Lahore Qalandars at Abu Dhabi	2018
99*	A M Lilley	for	Leicestershire at Leicester	2021
97	B J Hodge	for	Leicestershire at Leicester	2003
96*	A B McDonald	for	Leicestershire at Leeds	2011
94	L E Bosman	for	Derbyshire at Leeds	2010
91*	G Clark	for	Durham at Leeds	2015
91*	R A Whiteley	for	Worcestershire at Leeds	2015
91	M A Ealham	for	Nottinghamshire at Nottingham	2004
91	P Mustard	for	Durham at Chester-le-Street	2013
91	M H Wessels	for	Worcestershire at Leeds	2019
90*	S R Patel	for	Nottinghamshire at Leeds	2015
90*	B A Stokes	for	Durham at Leeds	2018
88*	P D Collingwood	for	Durham at Chester-le-Street	2017
85*	B M Duckett	for	Nottinghamshire at Nottingham	2020
85	A Flintoff	for	Lancashire at Leeds	2004

T20 BEST BOWLING

BY YORKSHIRE

6-19	T T Bresnan	v.	Lancashire at Leeds	2017
5-11	J W Shutt	v.	Durham at Chester-le-Street	2019
5-16	R M Pyrah	v.	Durham at Scarborough	2011
5-19	Azeem Rafiq	v.	Northamptonshire at Leeds	2017
5-22	M D Fisher	v.	Derbyshire at Leeds	2015
5-21	J A Brooks	v.	Leicestershire at Leeds	2013
5-31	A Lyth	v.	Nottinghamshire at Nottingham	2019
4-18	M A Ashraf	v.	Derbyshire at Derby	2012
4-18	D J Willey	v.	Northamptonshire at Leeds	2019
4-19	A U Rashid	v.	Durham at Leeds	2017
4-20	R M Pyrah	v.	Durham at Leeds	2008
4-20	A U Rashid	v.	Leicestershire at Leeds	2010
4-21	R M Pyrah	v.	Worcestershire at Leeds	2011
4-21	B W Sanderson	v.	Derbyshire at Derby	2011
4-21	J A Brooks	v.	Derbyshire at Leeds	2013
4-23	Rana Naved	v.	Nottinghamshire at Leeds	2009
4-24	A U Rashid	v.	Nottinghamshire at Nottingham	2008
4-24	L H Ferguson	v.	Lancashire at Leeds	2021
4-25	R J Sidebottom	v.	Durham at Chester-le-Street	2012

T20 BEST BOWLING

AGAINST YORKSHIRE

5-43	L J Fletcher	for	Nottinghamshire at Nottingham	2020
4- 9	C K Langeveldt	for	Derbyshire at Leeds	2008
4-17	L V van Beek	for	Derbyshire at Leeds	2019
4-19	K H D Barker	for	Warwickshire at Birmingham	2010
4-19	J S Patel	for	Warwickshire at Leeds	2014
4-19	R Rampaul	for	Derbyshire at Chesterfield	2018
4-19	M R J Watt	for	Derbyshire at Chesterfield	2019
4-20	L Wood	for	Lancashire at Manchester	2021
4-21	J Needham	for	Derbyshire at Leeds	2009
4-23	A J Hall	for	Northamptonshire at Northampton	2011
4-23	M W Parkinson	for	Lancashire at Leeds	2017
4-24	D Y Pennington	for	Worcestershire at Leeds	2021
4-25	J A Morkel	for	Derbyshire at Chesterfield	2013
4-25	I G Butler	for	Northamptonshire at Leeds	2014
4-25	M A Wood	for	Durham at Birmingham	2016
4-31	Shakib al Hasan	for	Worcestershire at Worcester	2011
4-31	B J Dwarshuis	for	Worcestershire at Worcester	2021
4-32	C A Ingram	for	Glamorgan at Cardiff	2016
4-35	C F Parkinson	for	Leicestershire at Leicester	2021

T20 ECONOMICAL BOWLING

BY YORKSHIRE

4-0-11-5	J W Shutt	v. Durham at Chester-le-Street	2019

AGAINST YORKSHIRE

4-0-9-4	C K Langeveldt	for Derbyshire at Leeds	2008

T20 MOST EXPENSIVE BOWLING

BY YORKSHIRE

4-0-65-2	M J Hoggard	v.	Lancashire at Leeds	2005

AGAINST YORKSHIRE

4-0-77-0	B W Sanderson	for Northamptonshire at Leeds	2017

T20 MAN OF THE MATCH AWARDS (99)

A W Gale	8	Azeem Rafiq	4	A J Finch	2
A Lyth	8	I J Harvey	3	H H Gibbs	2
A McGrath	6	J A Leaning	3	P A Jaques	2
T Kohler-Cadmore	6	D A Miller	3	A Z Lees	2
D J Willey	6	A U Rashid	3	M J Lumb	2
J M Bairstow	5	J A Thompson	3	J E Root	2
T T Bresnan	5	K S Williamson	3		
R M Pyrah	5	H C Brook	2		

One each: G S Ballance, J A Brooks, M E Claydon, M D Fisher, S P Fleming, D S Lehmann, G J Maxwell, J A Rudolph, B W Sanderson, J J Sayers, A Shahzad, J W Shutt, D J Wainwright and C White

T20 HIGHEST AND LOWEST SCORES BY AND AGAINST YORKSHIRE PLUS INDIVIDUAL BEST BATTING AND BOWLING 2003-2021

The lowest score is the lowest all-out score or the lowest score at completion of the allotted overs, five-over matches not included.

Yorkshire versus:

Derbyshire

	By Yorkshire			Against Yorkshire		
Highest Score:	In Yorkshire	220:5	at Leeds 2020	222:5		at Leeds 2010
	Away	210:3	at Derby 2006	170:5		at Chesterfield 2018
Lowest Score:	In Yorkshire	102	at Leeds 2018	124		at Chesterfield 2014
	Away	109	at Derby 2012	119:7		at Leeds 2007
Best Batting:	In Yorkshire	109	I J Harvey	at Leeds 2005	100*	G M Smith	at Leeds 2008
	Away	79*	A W Gale	at Chesterfield 2009	71*	B A Godleman	at Chesterfield 2018
Best Bowling:	In Yorkshire	5-22	M D Fisher	at Leeds 2015	4-9	C K Langeveldt	at Leeds 2008
	Away	4-18	M A Ashraf	at Derby 2012	4-19	R Rampaul	at Chesterfield 2018
				4-19	M R J Watt	at Chesterfield 2019

Durham

Highest Score:	In Yorkshire	223:6	at Leeds 2016	191:6		at Leeds 2015
	Away	198:3	at Chester-le-Street 2020	215:6		at Chester-le-Street 2013
Lowest Score:	In Yorkshire	95	at Leeds 2014	116:8		at Leeds 2009
	Away	90:9	at Chester-le-Street 2009	98		at Chester-le-Street 2006
Best Batting:	In Yorkshire	92	J M Bairstow	at Leeds 2015	91*	G Clark	at Leeds 2015
	Away	102*	J M Bairstow	at Chester-le-Street 2014	91	P Mustard	at Chester-le-Street 2013
Best Bowling:	In Yorkshire	5-16	R M Pyrah	at Scarborough 2011	4-38	S J Harmison	at Leeds 2008
	Away	5-11	J W Shutt	at Chester-le-Street 2019	4-25	M A Wood	at Birmingham 2016

Essex

Highest Score:	Away	143:7		at Chelmsford 2006	149:5		at Chelmsford 2006
Best Batting:	Away	43	G L Brophy	at Chelmsford 2006	48*	J S Foster	at Chelmsford 2006
Best Bowling:	Away	2-22	A Shahzad	at Chelmsford 2006	2-11	T J Phillips	at Chelmsford 2006

Glamorgan

Highest Score:	Away	180:8		at Cardiff 2016	90		at Cardiff 2016
Best Batting:	Away	79	D J Willey	at Cardiff 2016	26	J A Rudolph	at Cardiff 2016
Best Bowling:	Away	4-26	A U Rashid	at Cardiff 2016	4-32	C A Ingram	at Cardiff 2016

T20 HIGHEST AND LOWEST SCORES BY AND AGAINST YORKSHIRE
PLUS INDIVIDUAL BEST BATTING AND BOWLING 2003-2021 (Continued)

The lowest score is the lowest all-out score or the lowest score at completion of the allotted overs, five-over matches not included.

Yorkshire versus:

		By Yorkshire		Against Yorkshire	
Hampshire					
Highest Score:	Away	140:6	at Cardiff 2012	150:6	at Cardiff 2012
Best Batting:	Away	72*	D A Miller at Cardiff 2012	43	J H K Adams at Cardiff 2012
Best Bowling:	Away	2-20	R J Sidebottom at Cardiff 2012	3-26	C P Wood at Cardiff 2012
Lancashire					
Highest Score:	In Yorkshire	185:8	at Leeds 2015	186:6	at Leeds 2015
	Away	202:8	at Manchester 2015	231:4	at Manchester 2015
Lowest Score:	In Yorkshire	111:8	at Leeds 2009	131:9	at Leeds 2004
	Away	97	at Manchester 2005	104:3	at Manchester 2003
Best Batting:	In Yorkshire	108*	I J Harvey	85	A Flintoff at Leeds 2004
	Away	92*	J E Root at Manchester 2016	101	S G Law at Manchester 2005
Best Bowling	In Yorkshire	6-19	T T Bresnan at Leeds 2017	4-23	M W Parkinson at Leeds 2017
	Away	3-15	Azeem Rafiq at Manchester 2011	4-20	L Wood at Manchester 2021
Leicestershire					
Highest Score:	In Yorkshire	240:4	at Leeds 2021	221:3	at Leeds 2004
	Away	255:2	at Leicester 2019	207:3	at Leicester 2021
Lowest Score:	In Yorkshire	134	at Leeds 2006	113:9	at Leeds 2013
	Away	105	at Leicester 2013	147:9	at Leicester 2012
Best Batting:	In Yorkshire	92	P A Jaques at Leeds 2004	111	D L Maddy at Leeds 2004
	Away	96*	T Kohler-Cadmore at Leicester 2019	99*	A M Lilley at Leicester 2019
Best Bowling:	In Yorkshire	5-21	J A Brooks at Leeds 2013	3-3	J K H Naik at Leeds 2011
	Away	3-42	L E Plunkett at Leicester 2017	4-35	C F Parkinson at Leicester 2021

409

T20 HIGHEST AND LOWEST SCORES BY AND AGAINST YORKSHIRE
PLUS INDIVIDUAL BEST BATTING AND BOWLING 2003-2021 *(Continued)*

The lowest score is the lowest all-out score or the lowest score at completion of the allotted overs, five-over matches not included.

Yorkshire versus:

Northamptonshire

		By Yorkshire		Against Yorkshire	
Highest Score:	In Yorkshire	260:4	at Leeds 2017	165:7	at Leeds 2014
	Away	181:3	at Northampton 2014	180:5	at Northampton 2010
Lowest Score:	In Yorkshire	162:7	at Leeds 2014	107	at Leeds 2019
	Away	144	at Northampton 2011	132:7	at Northampton 2011
Best Batting:	In Yorkshire	161	A Lyth at Leeds 2017	65	R E Levi at Leeds 2017
	Away	101*	H H Gibbs at Northampton 2010	76	R E Levi at Northampton 2014
Best Bowling:	In Yorkshire	5-19	Azeem Rafiq at Leeds 2017	4-25	I G Butler at Leeds
	Away	3-15	T T Bresnan at Northampton 2016	4-23	A J Hall at Northampton 2011

Nottinghamshire

Highest Score:	In Yorkshire	227:5	at Leeds 2017	201:4	at Leeds 2014
	Away	223:5	at Nottingham 2017	225:5	at Nottingham 2017
Lowest Score:	In Yorkshire	141:8	at Leeds 2008	155:6	at Leeds 2009
	Away	112:7	at Nottingham 2010	136:6	at Nottingham 2008
Best Batting:	In Yorkshire	92*	G J Maxwell at Leeds 2015	90*	S R Patel at Leeds 2014
	Away	96*	M J Wood at Nottingham 2004	101	A D Hales at Nottingham 2017
Best Bowling:	In Yorkshire	4-23	Rana Naved-ul-Hasan at Leeds 2009	3-38	J T Ball at Leeds 2014
	Away	5-31	A Lyth at Nottingham 2019	5-43	L J Fletcher at Nottingham 2020

Sussex

Highest Score:	Home	177:7	at Chester-l-Street 2021	178:5	at Chester-le-Street 2021
	Away	172:6	at Cardiff 2012	193:5	at Hove 2007
Lowest Score:	Home	155	at Hove 2007	136:8	at Cardiff 2012
	Away	55	T Kohler-Cadmore and G S Ballance at Chester-le-Street 2021	54	L J Wright at Chester-le-Street 2021
Best Batting:	Away	68*	J M Bairstow at Cardiff 2012	80*	C D Nash at Cardiff 2012
	Home		J A Thompson at Chester-le-Street 2021		
Best Bowling:	Away	3-28		3-39	T S Mills at Chester-le-Street 2021
	Away	2-22	T T Bresnan at Cardiff 2012	3-22	S B Styris at Cardiff 2012

T20 HIGHEST AND LOWEST SCORES BY AND AGAINST YORKSHIRE
PLUS INDIVIDUAL BEST BATTING AND BOWLING 2003-2021 (Continued)

The lowest score is the lowest all-out score or the lowest score at completion of the allotted overs, five-over matches not included.

Yorkshire versus:

		By Yorkshire		Against Yorkshire	
	Warwickshire				
Highest Score:	In Yorkshire	226:8	at Leeds 2018	177:4	at Leeds 2019
	Away	200:3	at Birmingham 2019	158:2	at Birmingham 2018
Lowest Score:	In Yorkshire	121:9	at Leeds 2010	145	at Leeds 2015
	Away	81	at Birmingham 2021	181:5	at Birmingham 2019
Best Batting:	In Yorkshire	76*	T Kohler-Cadmore	at Leeds 2019	69* L J Evans	at Leeds 2019
	Away	94*	T Kohler-Cadmore	at Birmingham 2019	64* S R Hain	at Birmingham 2019
Best Bowling:	In Yorkshire	3-21	T T Bresnan	at Leeds 2017	4-19 J S Patel	at Leeds 2014
	Away	3-25	S A Patterson	at Birmingham 2010	4-19 K H D Barker	at Birmingham 2010
	Worcestershire				
Highest Score:	In Yorkshire	233:6	at Leeds 2017	196:7	at Leeds 2017
	Away	216:6	at Worcester 2021	208:7	at Worcester 2010
Lowest Score:	In Yorkshire	117	at Leeds 2015	109	at Leeds 2010
	Away	142	at Worcester 2011	120	at Worcester 2021
Best Batting:	In Yorkshire	118	D J Willey	at Leeds 2017	91* R A Whiteley	at Leeds 2015
	Away	112	J M Bairstow	at Worcester 2021	91 M H Wessels	at Leeds 2019
Best Bowling:	In Yorkshire	4-21	R M Pyrah	at Leeds 2011	56 A N Kervezee	at Worcester 2011
	Away	3-30	A Shahzad	at Worcester 2011	4-24 D Y Pennington	at Leeds 2021
				4-31 Shakib al Hasan	at Worcester 2011
				4-31 B J Dwarshuis	at Worcester 2021
	Chennai				
Highest Score:	Away	140:6	at Durban 2012	141:6	at Durban 2012
Best Batting:	Away	58	G S Ballance	at Durban 2012	47 S Badrinath	at Durban 2012
Best Bowling:	Away	3-23	I Wardlaw	at Durban 2012	2-12 J A Morkel	at Durban 2012
	Highveld				
Highest Score:	Away	131:7	at Johannesburg 2012	134:5	at Johannesburg
Best Batting:	Away	31	P A Jaques	at Johannesburg 2012	32 Q de Kock	at Johannesburg 2012
Best Bowling:	Away	2-21	S A Patterson	at Johannesburg 2012	2-23 A M Phangiso	at Johannesburg

411

T20 HIGHEST AND LOWEST SCORES BY AND AGAINST YORKSHIRE
PLUS INDIVIDUAL BEST BATTING AND BOWLING 2003-2021 (Continued)

The lowest score is the lowest all-out score or the lowest score at completion of the allotted overs, five-over matches not included.

Yorkshire versus:

Hobart Hurricanes

		By Yorkshire		Against Yorkshire	
Highest Score:	Away	144:1	at Abu Dhabi 2018	140:7	at Abu Dhabi 2018
Best Batting:	Away	72* T Kohler-Cadmore	at Abu Dhabi 2018	38 C P Jewell	at Abu Dhabi 2018
Best Bowling:	Away	2-29 K Carver	at Abu Dhabi 2018	1-24 J Clark	at Abu Dhabi 2018

Lahore Qalandars

Highest Score:	Away	184:5	at Abu Dhabi 2018	189:4	at Abu Dhabi 2018
Best Batting:	Away	37 H C Brook	at Abu Dhabi 2018	100 Sohail Akhtar	at Abu Dhabi 2018
Best Bowling:	Away	2-26 J E Poysden	at Abu Dhabi 2018	2-36 Shaheen Shah Afridi	at Abu Dhabi 2018

Mumbai

Highest Score:	Away			156: 6	at Cape Town 2012
Best Batting:	Away			37 D R Smith	at Cape Town
Best Bowling:	Away	2-36 Azeem Rafiq	at Cape Town 2012		

Sydney Sixers

Highest Score:	Away	96:9	at Cape Town 2012	98:2	at Cape Town 2012
Best Batting:	Away	25 J E Root	at Cape Town 2012	43* M J Lumb	at Cape Town 2012
Best Bowling:	Away	1-21 Azeem Rafiq	at Cape Town 2012	3-22 M A Starc	at Cape Town 2012

Trinidad and Tobago

Highest Score:	Away	154:4	at Centurion 2012	148:9	at Centurion 2012
Best Batting:	Away	64* G S Ballance	at Centurion 2012	59 D Ramdin	at Centurion 2012
Best Bowling:	Away	3-13 R J Sidebottom	at Centurion 2012	1-16 K Y G Ottley	at Centurion 2012

Uva

Highest Score:	Away	151:5	at Johannesburg 2012	150:7	at Johannesburg 2012
Best Batting:	Away	39* D A Miller	at Johannesburg 2012	29 S H T Kandamby	at Johannesburg 2012
Best Bowling:	Away	2-29 M A Ashraf	at Johannesburg 2012	3-32 E M D Y Munaweera	at Johannesburg 2012

T20 PARTNERSHIPS OF 100 AND OVER 2003-2021 (28)

150	2nd wkt	A Lyth	(66)	and D J Willey	(79)	v. Northamptonshire at Northampton 2018
146	3rd wkt	J M Bairstow (112)		and T Kohler-Cadmore (53)		v.Worcestershire at Worcester 2021
141*	6th wkt	H C Brook (83*)		and J A Thompson (66*)		v. Worcestershire at Leeds 2021
137*	2nd wkt	A W Gale	(60*)	and H H Gibbs	(76*)	v. Durham at Leeds 2010
131	1st wkt	A Lyth	(78)	and P A Jaques	(64)	v. Derbyshire at Leeds 2012
129	2nd wkt	A W Gale	(91)	and M P Vaughan	(41*)	v. Nottinghamshire at Leeds 2009
129	2nd wkt	T Kohler-Cadmore	(46)	and D J Willey	(80)	v. Lancashire at Leeds 2018
127	1st wkt	A Lyth	(161)	and T Kohler-Cadmore	(41)	v. Northamptonshire at Leeds 2017
124	2nd wkt	I J Harvey	(109)	and P A Jaques	(37)	v. Derbyshire at Leeds 2005
124	2nd wkt	A Lyth	(161)	and D J Willey	(40)	v. Northamptonshire at Leeds 2017
121	3rd wkt	J A Rudolph	(56)	and A McGrath	(59)	v. Leicestershire at Leicester 2008
121	2nd wkt	T Kohler-Cadmore	(96*)	and N Pooran	(67)	v. Leicestershire at Leicester 2019
116	1st wkt	A W Gale	(70)	and P A Jaques	(48)	v. Leicestershire at Leeds 2012
113	1st wkt	A Lyth (51)		and J M Bairstow (82)		v. Leicestershire at Leeds 2021
116	1st wkt	A Lyth	(69)	and T Kohler-Cadmore	(96*)	v. Leicestershire at Leicester 2019
110*	4th wkt	A Lyth	(92*)	and J A Tattersall (53*)		v. Durham at Leeds 2018
108	2nd wkt	I J Harvey	(108*)	and P A Jaques	(39)	v. Lancashire at Leeds 2004
108	2nd wkt	A Lyth	(59)	and H H Gibbs	(40)	v. Worcestershire at Leeds 2010
106	2nd wkt	D J Willey	(74)	and A Z Lees	(35)	v. Northamptonshire at Leeds 2016
104	1st wkt	A W Gale	(43)	and J A Rudolph	(61)	v. Leicestershire at Leicester 2009
104	2nd wkt	A Z Lees	(63)	and J A Leaning	(60*)	v. Warwickshire at Leeds 2015
104	1st wkt	A Lyth	(68)	and T Kohler-Cadmore	(40)	v. Worcestershire at Leeds 2019
103*	5th wkt	G S Ballance	(64*)	and A U Rashid	(33*)	v. Trinidad & Tobago at Centurion 2012/13
103	1st wkt	A W Gale	(65*)	and J A Rudolp	(53)	v. Leicestershire at Leicester 2010
102	1st wkt	T Kohler-Cadmore	(94*)	and A Lyth	(42)	v. Birmingham Bears at Birmingham 2019
101	2nd wkt	M J Wood	(57)	and M J Lumb	(55)	v. Nottinghamshire at Leeds 2003
101	3rd wkt	A J Hodd	(70)	and G J Maxwell (92*)		v. Nottinghamshire at Leeds 2015
100	4th wkt	A Z Lees	(59)	and J A Leaning	(64)	v. Northamptonshire at Northampton 2016

T20 HIGHEST PARTNERSHIPS FOR EACH WICKET

1st wkt	131	A Lyth	(78)	and P A Jaques	(64)	v. Derbyshire at Leeds	2012
2nd wkt	150	A Lyth	(66)	and D J Willey	(79)	v. Northamptonshire at Northampton	2018
3rd wkt	146	J M Bairstow (112)		and T Kohler-Cadmore	(53)	v.Worcestershire at Worcester	2021
4th wkt	100	A Z Lees	(59)	and J A Leaning	(64)	v. Northamptonshire at Northampton	2016
5th wkt	103*	G S Ballance	(64*)	and A U Rashid	(33*)	v. Trinidad & Tobago at Centurion	2012/13
6th wkt	141*	H C Brook	(83*)	and J A Thompson (66*)		v. Worcestershire at Leeds	2021
7th wkt	68*	T T Bresnan	(45*)	and A U Rashid	(29*)	v. Warwickshire at Leeds	2014
8th wkt	54	T T Bresnan	(51)	and J D Middlebrook	(29*)	v. Lancashire at Manchester	2015
9th wkt	33*	A U Rashid	(5*)	and D Gough	(20*)	v. Lancashire at Leeds	2008
10th wkt	28*	A U Rashid	(28*)	and G J Kruis	(12*)	v. Durham at Chester-le-Street	2009

ALL WHO HAVE TAKEN 4 WICKETS IN AN INNINGS (24)

M A ASHRAF (1)
4-18	v. Derbyshire	at Derby	2012

AZEEM RAFIQ (1)
5-19	v. Northamptonshire	at Leeds	2017

T T BRESNAN (1)
6-19	v. Lancashire	at Leeds	2017

J A BROOKS (2)
5-21	v. Leicestershire	at Leeds	2013
4-21	v. Derbyshire	at Leeds	2013

L H FERGUSON (1)
4-24	v. Lancashire	at Leeds	2021

M D FISHER (1)
5-22	v. Derbyshire	at Leeds	2015

A LYTH (1)
5-31	v. Nottinghamshire	at Nottingham	2019

C J MCKAY (1)
4-33	v. Derbyshire	at Leeds	2010

RANA NAVED-UL-HASAN (1)
4-23	v. Nottinghamshire	at Leeds	2009

S A PATTERSON (1)
4-30	v. Lancashire	at Leeds	2010

R M PYRAH (3)
5-16	v. Durham	at Scarborough	2011
4-20	v. Durham	at Leeds	2006
4-21	v. Worcestershire	at Leeds	2011

A U RASHID (5)
4-19	v. Durham	at Leeds	2017
4-20	v. Leicestershire	at Leeds	2011
4-24	v. Nottingham	at Nottingham	2008
4-26	v. Lancashire	at Leeds	2011
4-26	v. Glamorgan	at Cardiff	2016

B W SANDERSON (1)
4-21	v. Derbyshire	at Derby	2011

J W SHUTT (1)
5-11	v. Durham	at Chester-le-Street	2019

R J SIDEBOTTOM (1)
4-25	v. Durham	at Chester-le-Street	2012

J A THOMPSON (1)
4-44	v. Durham	at Chester-le-Street	2021

D J WILLEY
4-18	v. Northamptonshire	at Leeds	2019

CAREER AVERAGES FOR YORKSHIRE

ALL t20 MATCHES 2003-2021

Player	M	Inns	NO	Runs	HS	Av'ge	100s	50s	Runs	Wkts	Av'ge	Ct/St
Ashraf, M A ...	17	1	0	4	4	4.00	0	0	462	17	27.17	1
Azeem Rafiq ...	95	37	24	153	21*	11.76	0	0	2,489	102	24.40	36
Bairstow, J M .	67	62	11	1,526	112	29.92	2	6	0	0	—	29/8
Ballance, G S ..	88	76	9	1,549	79	23.11	0	5	0	0	—	43
Bess, D M ...	15	7	3	40	24	10.00	0	0	375	15	25.00	2
Best, T L	8	3	2	10	10*	10.00	0	0	243	7	34.71	4
Birkhead, B D .	1	0	0	0	—	—	0	0	0	0	—	1
Blakey, R J ...	7	5	1	119	32	29.75	0	0	0	0	—	5/1
Bresnan, T T ..	118	91	35	1,208	51	21.57	0	1	2,918	118	24.72	41
Brook, H C ...	38	38	11	1,042	91*	38.59	0	3	26	1	26.00	23
Brooks, J A	23	0	0	0	—	—	0	0	582	22	26.45	11
Brophy, G L ...	54	46	9	717	57*	19.37	0	2	0	0	—	25/7
Carver, K	10	2	1	2	2	2.00	0	0	208	8	26.00	5
Claydon, M E ..	7	2	2	14	12*	—	0	0	188	5	37.60	2
Coad, B O	12	4	1	14	7	4.66	0	0	323	13	24.84	6
Craven, V J	6	6	4	76	44*	38.00	0	0	67	0	—	3
Dawood, I	11	8	3	44	15	8.80	0	0	0	0	—	5/2
Dawson, R K J .	22	8	3	71	22	14.20	0	0	558	24	23.25	7
Duke, H G	4	0	0	0	—	—	0	0	0	0	—	3
Ferguson, L H ..	10	2	1	2	2	2.00	0	0	269	14	19.21	1
Finch, A J	16	16	0	332	89	20.75	0	2	24	1	24.00	16
Fisher, M D ..	38	11	5	61	19	10.16	0	0	1,102	43	25.62	12
Fleming, S P ...	4	4	0	62	58	15.50	0	1	0	0	—	1
Fraine, W A R .	19	18	7	272	44*	24.72	0	0	0	0	—	13
Gale, A W	104	97	8	2,260	91	25.39	0	16	0	0	—	30
Gibbs, H H	15	15	3	443	101*	36.91	1	2	0	0	—	8
Gibson, R	3	2	0	32	18	16.00	0	0	30	0	—	1
Gilbert, C R	13	9	2	107	38*	15.28	0	0	0	0	—	7
Gillespie, J N ...	17	4	2	14	8*	7.00	0	0	422	17	24.82	5
Gough, D	17	7	3	42	20*	10.50	0	0	416	16	26.00	2
Gray, A K D ...	8	3	0	17	13	5.66	0	0	211	9	23.44	4
Guy, S M	10	6	1	44	13	8.80	0	0	0	0	—	4
Hamilton, G M .	3	3	1	41	41*	20.50	0	0	0	0	—	1
Handscomb, P S P	7	6	0	97	31	16.16	0	0	0	0	—	3/3
Hannon-Dalby, O J	2	0	0	0	—	—	0	0	58	3	19.33	4
Harvey, I J	10	10	1	438	109	48.66	2	2	258	10	25.80	4
Head, T M	4	4	0	113	40	28.25	0	0	4	0	—	0
Hill, G C H	10	7	1	57	19*	9.50	0	0	50	1	50.00	3
Hodd, A J	26	17	4	147	70	11.30	0	1	0	0	—	9/6
Hodgson, D M .	16	14	2	213	52*	17.75	0	1	0	0	—	9/1
Hodgson, L J ...	2	1	1	39	39*	—	0	0	59	2	29.50	1
Hoggard, M J ..	15	2	1	19	18	19.00	0	0	472	13	36.30	4
Jaques, P A	34	32	3	907	92	31.27	0	6	15	0	—	5
Kirby, S P	3	0	0	0	—	—	0	0	119	4	29.75	1
Kohler-Cadmore, T												
	46	45	6	1,394	96*	35.74	0	13	0	0	—	24
Kruis, G J	20	5	3	41	22	20.50	0	0	486	19	25.57	6
Lawson, M A K .	2	1	1	4	4*	—	0	0	87	3	29.00	1
Leaning, J A ...	52	45	11	952	64	28.00	0	2	45	1	45.00	25
Lees, A Z	37	36	2	857	67*	25.20	0	4	0	0	—	12
Lehmann, D S ..	9	9	3	252	48	42.00	0	0	180	8	22.50	4
Lumb, M J	26	26	3	442	84*	19.21	0	4	65	3	21.66	8
Lyth, A	132	123	3	3,159	161	26.32	1	19	605	22	27.50	69

415

CAREER AVERAGES FOR YORKSHIRE
ALL t20 MATCHES 2003-2021 *(Continued)*

Player	M	Inns	NO	Runs	HS	Av'ge	100s	50s	Runs	Wkts	Av'ge	Ct/St
McGrath, A	66	61	12	1,403	73*	28.63	0	8	698	23	30.34	26
McKay, C J	8	6	3	54	21*	18.00	0	0	258	10	25.80	1
Maharaj, K A	5	2	2	10	10*	—	0	0	126	2	63.00	2
Malan, D J	**8**	**8**	**0**	**77**	**27**	**9.62**	**0**	**0**	**16**	**0**	**—**	**1**
Marsh, S E	11	11	4	289	60*	41.28	0	2	0	0	—	1
Maxwell, G J	12	12	1	229	92*	20.81	0	1	264	12	22.00	6
Middlebrook, J D	4	2	2	33	29*	—	0	0	101	4	25.25	1
Miller, D A	14	13	4	457	74*	50.77	0	4	0	0	—	7
Northeast, S A	1	1	1	0	0*	—	0	0	0	0	—	0
Olivier, D	**8**	**3**	**0**	**10**	**8**	**3.33**	**0**	**0**	**264**	**11**	**24.00**	**1**
Patterson, S A	63	9	4	9	3*	1.80	0	0	1,811	61	29.68	10
Pillans, M W	9	3	0	18	8	6.00	0	0	246	5	49.20	2
Plunkett, L E	42	31	10	353	36	16.80	0	0	1,146	44	26.04	13
Pooran, N	3	3	0	122	67	40.66	0	1	0	0	—	2
Poysden, J E	8	1	1	0	0*	—	0	0	205	8	25.62	2
Pyrah, R M	105	71	21	593	42	11.86	0	0	2,315	108	21.43	40
Rana Naved-ul-Hasan	8	8	2	63	20*	10.50	0	0	159	11	14.45	2
Rashid, A U	**108**	**63**	**20**	**577**	**36***	**13.41**	**0**	**0**	**2,817**	**115**	**24.49**	**34**
Revis, M L	**2**	**1**	**1**	**0**	**0***	**—**	**0**	**0**	**0**	**0**	**—**	**0**
Rhodes, W M H	18	16	3	128	45	9.84	0	0	283	13	21.76	2
Robinson, O E	7	3	0	5	3	1.66	0	0	162	6	27.00	3
Root, J E	**42**	**38**	**8**	**1,008**	**92***	**33.60**	**0**	**8**	**470**	**14**	**33.57**	**15**
Rudolph, J A	39	35	5	710	61	23.66	0	3	145	6	24.16	7
Sanderson, B W	4	0	0	0	—	—	0	0	74	6	12.33	0
Sarfraz Ahmed	5	4	0	53	42	13.25	0	0	0	0	—	3/1
Sayers, J J	17	14	0	253	44	18.07	0	0	0	0	—	5
Shahzad, A	22	16	4	129	20	10.75	0	0	576	17	33.88	5
Shaw, J	5	2	1	1	1	1.00	0	0	138	2	69.00	0
Shutt, J W	**11**	**4**	**3**	**0**	**0***	**0.00**	**0**	**0**	**271**	**12**	**22.58**	**7**
Sidebottom, R J	40	16	10	87	16*	14.50	0	0	1,069	42	25.45	9
Silverwood, C E W	9	5	2	32	13*	10.66	0	0	264	7	37.71	4
Starc, M A	10	2	1	0	0*	0.00	0	0	218	21	10.38	1
Stoneman, M D	4	4	0	58	50	14.50	0	1	0	0	—	2
Swanepoel, P J	2	1	1	2	2*	—	0	0	60	3	20.00	1
Tattersall, J A	**35**	**25**	**8**	**382**	**53***	**22.47**	**0**	**1**	**0**	**0**	**—**	**23/6**
Taylor, C R	2	2	1	10	10*	10.00	0	0	0	0	—	0
Thompson, J A	38	30	10	417	74	20.85	0	3	936	34	27.52	15
Vaughan, M P	16	16	1	292	41*	19.46	0	1	81	1	81.00	2
Wainman, J C	2	1	1	12	12*	—	0	0	49	1	49.00	0
Wainwright, D J	26	9	6	23	6*	7.66	0	0	551	21	26.23	9
Waite, M J	**17**	**9**	**5**	**52**	**19***	**13.00**	**0**	**0**	**345**	**11**	**31.36**	**3**
Wardlaw, I	10	1	1	1	1	—	0	0	179	5	35.80	0
Warren, A C	2	0	0	0	—	—	0	0	70	4	17.50	0
Wharton, J H	**2**	**2**	**0**	**12**	**8**	**6.00**	**0**	**0**	**0**	**0**	**—**	**0**
White, C	33	31	0	570	55	18.38	0	2	132	2	66.00	8
Willey, D J	50	46	3	1,340	118	31.16	1	7	1,342	50	26.84	24
Williamson, K S	12	11	0	302	65	27.45	0	1	37	3	12.33	3
Wisniewski, S A	**2**	**0**	**0**	**0**	**—**	**—**	**0**	**0**	**32**	**0**	**—**	**0**
Wood, M J	15	15	3	328	96*	27.33	0	2	32	2	16.00	11
Younus Khan	2	2	0	55	40	27.50	0	0	32	2	16.00	0
Yuvraj Singh	5	5	0	154	71	30.80	0	1	51	5	10.20	0

SECOND ELEVEN CHAMPIONS

In the seasons in which Yorkshire have competed.

From 2009 the Championship was divided into two groups, each team playing each other once. The two group winners played for the Championship.

For 2021 the Championship reverted to one league of 18 teams, each team playing between seven and 12 games Final positions were decided on average points per game.

Season	Champions	Yorkshire's Position	Season	Champions	Yorkshire's Position
1959	Gloucestershire	7th	1999	Middlesex	14th
1960	Northamptonshire	14th	2000	Middlesex	5th
1961	Kent	11th	2001	Hampshire	2nd
1975	Surrey	4th	2002	Kent	3rd
1976	Kent	5th	**2003**	**Yorkshire**	**1st**
1977	**Yorkshire**	**1st**	2004	Somerset	8th
1978	Sussex	5th	2005	Kent	10th
1979	Warwickshire	3rd	2006	Kent	3rd
1980	Glamorgan	5th	2007	Sussex	10th
1981	Hampshire	11th	2008	Durham	5th
1982	Worcestershire	14th	2009	Surrey	A 2nd
1983	Leicestershire	2nd	2010	Surrey	A 8th
1984	**Yorkshire**	**1st**	2011	Warwickshire	A 10th
1985	Nottinghamshire	12th	2012	Kent	(North) 9th
1986	Lancashire	5th	2013	Lancashire & Middlesex	(North) 4th
1987	**Yorkshire and Kent**	**1st**	2014	Leicestershire	(North) 4th
1988	Surrey	9th	2015	Nottinghamshire	(North) 7th
1989	Middlesex	9th	2016	Durham	(North) 5th
1990	Sussex	17th	2017	Lancashire	(North) 4th
1991	**Yorkshire**	**1st**	2018	Durham	(North) 5th
1992	Surrey	5th	2019	Leicestershire	(North) 2nd
1993	Middlesex	3rd	2020	*No Second Eleven*	
1994	Somerset	2nd		*Championship fixtures*	
1995	Hampshire	5th		*were played because of*	
1996	Warwickshire	4th		*the Coronavirus outbreak*	
1997	Lancashire	2nd			
1998	Northamptonshire	9th	2021	Hampshire	5th

SECOND ELEVEN CHAMPIONSHIP 1959-1961 AND 1975-2021

SUMMARY OF RESULTS BY SEASON

Season	Played	Won	Lost	Drawn	Tied	Abandoned	Position in Championship
1959	10	4	1	5	0	0	7
1960	10	1	3	6	0	0	14
1961	9	2	2	5	0	1	11
1975	14	4	0	10	0	0	4
1976	14	5	5	4	0	0	5
1977	**16**	**9**	**0**	**7**	**0**	**1**	**1**
1978	15	5	2	8	0	1	4
1979	16	5	0	11	0	0	3
1980	14	5	2	7	0	1	5
1981	16	2	3	11	0	0	11
1982	16	2	3	11	0	0	14 =
1983	11	5	1	5	0	3	2
1984	**15**	**9**	**3**	**3**	**0**	**0**	**1**
1985	14	3	3	8	0	1	12
1986	16	5	1	10	0	0	5
1987	**15**	**5**	**2**	**8**	**0**	**1**	**1 =**
1988	16	4	1	11	0	0	9
1989	17	2	3	12	0	0	9 =
1990	16	1	6	9	0	0	17
1991	**16**	**8**	**1**	**7**	**0**	**0**	**1**
1992	17	5	2	10	0	0	5
1993	17	6	1	10	0	0	3
1994	17	6	2	9	0	0	2
1995	17	7	1	9	0	0	5
1996	17	6	3	8	0	0	4
1997	16	8	5	3	0	1	2
1998	15	4	2	9	0	0	9
1999	16	3	8	5	0	1	14
2000	14	5	2	7	0	1	5
2001	12	8	2	2	0	1	2
2002	12	5	1	6	0	0	3
2003	**10**	**7**	**1**	**2**	**0**	**0**	**1**
2004	7	2	0	5	0	1	8
2005	12	2	4	6	0	0	10
2006	14	6	4	4	0	0	3
2007	12	4	5	3	0	0	10
2008	12	4	4	4	0	2	5
2009	9	5	0	4	0	0	(Group A) 2
2010	9	2	4	3	0	0	(Group A) 8
2011	9	0	4	4	1	0	(Group A) 10
2012	7	1	2	4	0	2	(North) 9
2013	9	3	4	2	0	0	(North) 4
2014	9	2	1	6	0	0	(North) 4
2015	9	2	4	3	0	0	(North) 7
2016	9	2	3	4	0	0	(North) 5
2017	8	2	0	6	0	1	(North) 4
2018	9	3	1	5	0	0	(North) 5
2019	8	3	1	4	0	0	(North) 2
2021	11	4	1	6	0	1	5
Totals	628	202	113	311	1	22	

Matches abandoned without a ball bowled are not counted as matches played. The 1976 match between Yorkshire and Northamptonshire at Bradford was cancelled after the fixtures had been published.

ANALYSIS OF RESULTS AGAINST EACH OPPONENT

County	Played	Won	Lost	Drawn	Tied	Abandoned	First Played
Derbyshire	61	14	8	39	0	3	1959
Durham	35	11	6	18	0	3	1992
Essex	14	10	2	2	0	0	1990
Glamorgan	41	11	3	27	0	2	1975
Gloucestershire	11	4	3	4	0	0	1990
Hampshire	12	4	1	7	0	0	1990
Kent	26	5	4	17	0	1	1981
Lancashire	74	14	20	40	0	3	1959
Leicestershire	34	15	8	10	1	2	1975
MCC Young Cricketers	8	4	1	3	0	0	2005
MCC Universities	4	1	1	2	0	0	2011
Middlesex	18	7	2	9	0	0	1977
Northamptonshire	52	16	6	30	0	2	1959
Nottinghamshire	62	17	13	32	0	4	1959
Scotland	2	1	0	1	0	0	2007
Somerset	18	9	3	6	0	0	1988
Surrey	37	9	9	19	0	2	1976
Sussex	16	6	5	5	0	0	1990
Warwickshire	66	25	13	28	0	0	1959
Worcestershire	45	21	6	18	0	0	1961
Totals	636	204	1	114	317	22	

Note: Matches abandoned are not included in the total played.

Largest Victory   An innings and 230 runs v. Glamorgan at Headingley, 1986
Largest Defeat   An innings and 124 runs v. Gloucestershire at Bradford, 1994
Narrowest Victory   By 1 run v. Lancashire at Old Trafford, 2003
Narrowest Defeat   By 8 runs v. Derbyshire at Harrogate, 1982

Highest Total

By Yorkshire: 602 for 8 wkts dec v. Gloucestershire at Bristol, 2021
Against Yorkshire: 567 for 7 wkts dec by Middlesex at RAF Vine Lane, Uxbridge, 2000

Lowest Total

By Yorkshire 66 v Nottinghamshire at Trent College, 2016
Against Yorkshire: 36 by Lancashire at Elland, 1979

Highest Match Aggregate

1,470 for 39 wkts   v. Gloucestershire at Cheltenham, 2001

Highest Individual Score

For Yorkshire: 273* by R J Blakey v. Northamptonshire at Northampton, 1986
Against Yorkshire: 235 by O A Shah for Middlesex at Leeds, 1999

Century in Each Innings

For Yorkshire:
C White	209* and 115*	v. Worcestershire at Worcester, 1990
	(The only instance of two unbeaten centuries in the same match)	
K Sharp	150* and 127	v. Essex at Elland, 1991
A A Metcalfe	109 and 136*	v. Somerset at North Perrott, 1994
R A Kettleborough	123 and 192*	v. Nottinghamshire at Todmorden, 1996
C R Taylor	201* and 129	v. Sussex at Hove, 2005
A W Gale	131 and 123	v. Somerset at Taunton, 2006
J J Sayers	157 and 105	v. Lancashire at Leeds, 2007

Century in Each Innings *(Continued)*

Against Yorkshire:
N Nannan	100	and 102*	for Nottinghamshire at Harrogate, 1979
G D Lloyd	134	and 103	for Lancashire at Scarborough, 1989
A J Swann	131	and 100	for Northamptonshire at York, 1998
G J Kennis	114	and 114	for Somerset at Taunton, 1999

Most Career Runs

         B Parker   7,450 in 122 matches (average 40.48)

Best Bowling in an Innings

For Yorkshire: 9 for 27 by G A Cope v. Northamptonshire at Northampton, 1979
Against Yorkshire: 8 for 15 by I Folley for Lancashire at Heywood, 1983

Best Bowling in a Match

For Yorkshire: 13 for 92 (6 for 48 and 7 for 44) by M K Bore v. Lancashire at Harrogate, 1976
Against Yorkshire: 13 for 100 (7 for 45 and 6 for 55) by N J Perry for Glamorgan at Cardiff, 1978

Most Career Wickets

         Paul A Booth   248 in 85 matches, average 29.33

Totals of 450 and over

By Yorkshire (32)

Score	Versus	Ground	Season
602 for 8 wkts dec	Gloucestershire	Bristol	2021
585 for 8 wkts dec	Lancashire	Scarborough	2017
538 for 9 wkts dec	Worcestershire	Stamford Bridge	2007
534 for 5 wkts dec	Lancashire	Stamford Bridge	2003
530 for 8 wkts dec	Nottinghamshire	Middlesbrough	2000
526 for 8 wkts dec	MCC Young Cricketers	High Wycombe	2017
514 for 3 wkts dec	Somerset	Taunton	1988
509 for 4 wkts dec	Northamptonshire	Northampton	1986
508	Durham	Riverside	2017
505 for 6 wkts dec	Worcestershire	Scarborough	2021
502	Derbyshire	Chesterfield	2003
501 for 5 wkts dec	MCC Young Cricketers	Stamford Bridge	2009
497	Derbyshire	Chesterfield	2005
495 for 5 wkts dec	Somerset	Taunton	2006
488 for 8 wkts dec	Warwickshire	Harrogate	1984
486 for 6 wkts dec	Glamorgan	Leeds	1986
480	Leicestershire	Market Harborough	2013
476 for 3 wkts dec	Glamorgan	Gorseinon	1984
475 for 9 wkts dec	Nottinghamshire	Nottingham	1995
474 for 3 wkts dec	Glamorgan	Todmorden	2003
474	Durham	Stamford Bridge	2003
470	Lancashire	Leeds	2006
469	Warwickshire	Castleford	1999
462	Scotland	Stamford Bridge	2007
461 for 8 wkts dec	Essex	Stamford Bridge	2006
459 for 5 wkts dec	Leicestershire	Oakham	1997
459 for 6 wkts dec	Glamorgan	Bradford	1992
457 for 9 wkts dec	Kent	Canterbury	1983
456 for 5 wkts dec	Gloucestershire	Todmorden	1990
456 for 6 wkts dec	Nottinghamshire	York	1986
454 for 9 wkts dec	Derbyshire	Chesterfield	1959
452 for 9 wkts dec	Glamorgan	Cardiff	2005

Totals of 450 and over

Against Yorkshire (14)

Score	For	Ground	Season
567 for 7 wkts dec	Middlesex	RAF Vine Lane, Uxbridge	2000
555 for 7 wkts dec	Derbyshire	Stamford Bridge	2002
530 for 9 wkts dec	Leicestershire	Hinckley	2015
525 for 7 wkts dec	Sussex	Hove	2005
502 for 4 wkts dec	Warwickshire	Edgbaston Community Foundation Sports Ground	2016
493 for 8 wkts dec	Nottinghamshire	Lady Bay, Nottingham	2002
488 for 8 wkts dec	Warwickshire	Castleford	1999
486	Essex	Chelmsford	2000
485	Gloucestershire	North Park, Cheltenham	2001
477	Lancashire	Headingley	2006
471	Warwickshire	Clifton Park, York	2010
458	Lancashire	Bradford	1997
454 for 7 wkts dec	Lancashire	Todmorden	1993
450 for 7 wkts (inns closed)	Derbyshire	Bradford	1980

Completed Innings under 75

By Yorkshire (6)

Score	Versus	Ground	Season
66	Nottinghamshire	Trent College	2016
67	Worcestershire	Barnt Green (1st inns)	2013
68	Worcestershire	Barnt Green (2nd inns)	2013
69	Lancashire	Heywood	1983
72	Leicestershire	Kibworth	2019
74	Derbyshire	Chesterfield	1960
74	Nottinghamshire	Bradford	1998

Against Yorkshire (10)

Score	By	Ground	Season
36	Lancashire	Elland	1979
49	Leicestershire	Leicester	2008
50	Lancashire	Liverpool	1984
60	Derbyshire	Bradford	1977
60	Surrey	Sunbury-on-Thames	1977
62	MCC YC	High Wycombe	2005
64	Nottinghamshire	Brodsworth	1959
66	Leicestershire	Lutterworth	1977
72	Sussex	Horsham	2003
74	Worcestershire	Barnsley	1978

Individual Scores of 150 and over (71)

Score	Player	Versus	Ground	Season
273*	R J Blakey	Northamptonshire	Northampton	1986
238*	K Sharp	Somerset	Taunton	1988
233	P E Robinson	Kent	Canterbury	1983
230	T Kohler-Cadmore	Derbyshire	York	2017
221*	K Sharp	Gloucestershire	Todmorden	1990
219	G M Hamilton	Derbyshire	Chesterfield	2003
218*	A McGrath	Surrey	Elland	1994
212	G S Ballance	MCC Young Cricketers	Stamford Bridge	2009
209*	C White	Worcestershire	Worcester	1990
207	G C H Hill	Gloucestershire	Bristol	2021
205	C R Taylor	Glamorgan	Todmorden	2003
204	B Parker	Gloucestershire	Bristol	1993
203	A McGrath	Durham	Headingley	2005
202*	J M Bairstow	Leicestershire	Oakham	2009
202	A Z Lees	Durham	Riverside	2017
202	M J Wood	Essex	Stamford Bridge	2006
201*	C R Taylor	Sussex	Hove	2005
200*	D Byas	Worcestershire	Worcester	1992
200*	A McGrath	Northamptonshire	Northampton	2012
192*	R A Kettleborough	Nottinghamshire	Todmorden	1996
191	P E Robinson	Warwickshire	Harrogate	1984
191	M J Wood	Derbyshire	Rotherham	2000
191	M J Lumb	Nottinghamshire	Middlesbrough	2000
189*	C S Pickles	Gloucestershire	Bristol	1991
186	A McGrath	MCC Universities	York	2011
186	W A R Fraine	Gloucestershire	Bristol	2021
184	J D Love	Worcestershire	Headingley	1976
183	A W Gale	Durham	Stamford Bridge	2006
174	G L Brophy	Worcestershire	Stamford Bridge	2007
173	S N Hartley	Warwickshire	Edgbaston	1980
173	A A Metcalfe	Glamorgan	Gorseinon	1984
173	B Parker	Sussex	Hove	1996
173	R A Kettleborough	Leicestershire	Oakham School	1997
173	T Kohler-Cadmore	Northamptonshire	Desborough	2018
172	A C Morris	Lancashire	York	1995
170*	R A J Townsley	Glamorgan	Harrogate	1975
170	M J Waite	Essex	Billericay	2021
169	J E Root	Warwickshire	York	2010
168	M J Wood	Leicestershire	Oakham School	1997
166	A A Metcalfe	Lancashire	York	1984
166	C A Chapman	Northamptonshire	York	1998
165*	A Lyth	Durham	Stamford Bridge	2006
165	J J Sayers	Sussex	Hove	2006
164*	A W Gale	Leicestershire	Harrogate	2002
164	J C Balderstone	Nottinghamshire	Harrogate	1960
163*	J E Root	Leicestershire	Oakham	2009
163	A A Metcalfe	Derbyshire	Chesterfield	1992
162*	D Byas	Surrey	Scarborough	1987
162*	R Gibson	Leicestershire	York	2016
161	H C Brook	Lancashire	Scarborough	2017
160	A A Metcalfe	Somerset	Bradford	1993
157*	W A R Fraine	Worcestershire	Kidderminster	2019
157	J J Sayers	Lancashire	Headingley	2007
155	S M Guy	Derbyshire	Chesterfield	2005

Individual Scores of 150 and over *(Continued)*

Score	Player	Versus	Ground	Season
154*	C R Taylor	Surrey	Whitgift School	2005
153*	A A Metcalfe	Warwickshire	Bingley	1995
153	C White	Worcestershire	Marske-by-the-Sea	1991
153	R A Stead	Surrey	Todmorden	2002
152	A A Metcalfe	Gloucestershire	Bristol	1993
151*	P E Robinson	Nottinghamshire	York	1986
151*	S J Foster	Kent	Elland	1992
151*	J J Sayers	Durham	Stamford Bridge	2004
151	P J Hartley	Somerset	Clevedon	1989
151	A McGrath	Somerset	Elland	1995
151	V J Craven	Glamorgan	Todmorden	2003
150*	K Sharp	Essex	Elland	1991
150*	G M Fellows	Hampshire	Todmorden	1998
150*	S M Guy	Nottinghamshire	Headingley	2005
150*	J A Leaning	Worcestershire	Worcester	2011
150	K Sharp	Glamorgan	Ebbw Vale	1983
150	S N Hartley	Nottinghamshire	Worksop	1988
150	C R Taylor	Derbyshire	Chesterfield	2003

7 Wickets in an Innings (31)

Analysis	Player	Versus	Ground	Season
9 for 27	G A Cope	Northamptonshire	Northampton	1977
9 for 62	M K Bore	Warwicshire	Scarborough	1976
8 for 33	B O Coad	MCC Young Cricketers	York	2018
8 for 53	S J Dennis	Nottinghamshire	Nottingham	1983
8 for 57	M K Bore	Lancashire	Manchester	1977
8 for 79	P J Berry	Derbyshire	Harrogate	1991
7 for 13	P Carrick	Northamptonshire	Marske-by-the-Sea	1977
7 for 21	S Silvester	Surrey	Sunbury-on-Thames	1977
7 for 22	J A R Blain	Surrey	Purley	2004
7 for 32	P W Jarvis	Surrey	The Oval	1984
7 for 34	P Carrick	Glamorgan	Leeds	1986
7 for 37	P M Hutchison	Warwickshire	Coventry	2001
7 for 39	G M Hamilton	Sussex	Leeds	1995
7 for 40	M K Bore	Worcestershire	Old Hill	1976
7 for 44	M K Bore	Lancashire	Harrogate	1976
7 for 44	J P Whiteley	Worcestershire	Leeds	1979
7 for 51	J D Middlebrook	Derbyshire	Rotherham	2000
7 for 53	J P Whiteley	Warwickshire	Birmingham	1980
7 for 55	C White	Leicestershire	Bradford	1990
7 for 58	K Gillhouley	Derbyshire	Chesterfield	1960
7 for 58	P J Hartley	Lancashire	Leeds	1985
7 for 63	M J Hoggard	Worcestershire	Harrogate	1998
7 for 65	M K Bore	Nottinghamshire	Steetley	1976
7 for 70	J D Batty	Leicestershire	Bradford	1992
7 for 71	J D Batty	Hampshire	Harrogate	1994
7 for 81	K Gillhouley	Lancashire	Scarborough	1960
7 for 84	I J Houseman	Kent	Canterbury	1989
7 for 88	I G Swallow	Nottinghamshire	Nottingham	1983
7 for 90	A P Grayson	Kent	Folkestone	1991
7 for 93	D Pickles	Nottinghamshire	Nottingham	1960
7 for 94	K Gillhouley	Northamptonshire	Redcar	1960

12 Wickets in a Match (6)

Analysis		Player	Versus	Ground	Season
13 for 92	(6-48 and 7-44)	M K Bore	Lancashire	Harrogate	1976
13 for 110	(7-70 and 6-40)	J D Batty	Leicestershire	Bradford	1992
13 for 111	(4-49 and 9-62)	M K Bore	Warwickshire	Scarborough	1976
12 for 69	(5-32 and 7-37)	P M Hutchison	Warwickshire	Coventry	2001
12 for 120	(5-39 and 7-81)	K Gillhouley	Lancashire	Scarborough	1960
12 for 162	(5-78 and 7-84)	I J Houseman	Kent	Canterbury	1989

Hat-tricks (4)

Player	Versus	Ground	Season
I G Swallow	Warwickshire	Harrogate	1984
S D Fletcher	Nottinghamshire	Marske-by-the-Sea	1987
I G Swallow	Derbyshire	Chesterfield	1988
M Broadhurst	Essex	Southend-on-Sea	1992

Second Eleven Performance Of The Year Award

The Trophy was instituted in 2013 to reward a Second Eleven performance with either bat or ball that stood out from the ordinary and turned the course of the game.

2013	M D Fisher	6-25	v. Leicestershire (One-Day Trophy)	
2014	J A Leaning	102	v. Nottinghamshire (T20)	Grace Road, Leicester
2015	M J Waite	143	v. Lancashire (Friendly)	Trent College, Nottingham
2016	W M H Rhodes	137		Scarborough
		and 114*	v Lancashire (Friendly)	Liverpool
2017	J W Jack Shutt	4-19	v. Middlesex in the Trophy Final	Headingley
		and 4-12	v. Derbyshire in the T20	Alvaston and Boulton
		to secure two victories.		
2018	J H Wharton	162	v. Leicestershire (Friendly)	Kibworth CC
		in only his second Second Eleven match.		
2019	M L Revis	177	v Sussex (Friendly)	Hove
2020	No Award	The Coronoviris epidemic prevented any Second Eleven cricket being played in 2020		
2021	G C H Hill	207	v. Gloucestershire. His maiden Championship century	

SECOND ELEVEN TROPHY

WINNERS 1986-2019

1986	**Northamptonshire,** who beat Essex by 14 runs
1987	**Derbyshire,** who beat Hampshire by 7 wickets
1988	**Yorkshire,** who beat Kent by 7 wickets
1989	**Middlesex,** who beat Kent by 6 wickets
1990	**Lancashire,** who beat Somerset by 8 wickets
1991	**Nottinghamshire,** who beat Surrey by 8 wickets
1992	**Surrey,** who beat Northamptonshire by 8 wickets
1993	**Leicestershire,** who beat Sussex by 142 runs
1994	**Yorkshire,** who beat Leicestershire by 6 wickets
1995	**Leicestershire,** who beat Gloucestershire by 3 runs
1996	**Leicestershire,** who beat Durham by 46 runs
1997	**Surrey,** who beat Gloucestershire by 3 wickets
1998	**Northamptonshire,** who beat Derbyshire by 5 wickets
1999	**Kent,** who beat Hampshire by 106 runs.
2000	**Leicestershire,** who beat Hampshire by 25 runs.
2001	**Surrey,** who beat Somerset by 6 wickets
2002	**Kent,** who beat Hampshire by 5 wickets
2003	**Hampshire,** who beat Warwickshire by 8 wickets
2004	**Worcestershire,** who beat Essex by 8 wickets
2005	**Sussex,** who beat Nottinghamshire by 6 wickets
2006	**Warwickshire,** who beat Yorkshire by 93 runs
2007	**Middlesex,** who beat Somerset by 1 run
2008	**Hampshire,** who beat Essex by 7 runs
2009	**Yorkshire,** who beat Lancashire by 2 wickets
2010	**Essex,** who beat Lancashire by 14 runs
2011	**Nottinghamshire,** who beat Lancashire by 4 wickets
2012	**Lancashire,** who beat Durham by 76 runs
2013	**Lancashire,** who beat Nottinghamshire by 76 runs
2014	**Leicestershire,** who beat Lancashire by 168 runs
2015	**Derbyshire,** who beat Durham by 10 runs
2016	**Lancashire,** who beat Somerset by 10 wickets *(DLS)*
2017	**Yorkshire,** who beat Middlesex by 99 runs *(DLS)*
2018	**Middlesex,** who beat Somerset by 1 wicket
2019	**Kent,** who beat Durham by 16 runs

SECOND ELEVEN TWENTY20

WINNERS 2011-2021

2011	**Sussex,** who beat Durham by 24 runs
2012	**England Under-19s,** who beat Sussex by eight wickets
2013	**Surrey,** who beat Middlesex by six runs
2014	**Leicesterhire,** who beat Middlesex by 11 runs
2015	**Middlesex,** who beat Kent by four wickets
2016	**Middlesex,** who beat Somerset by two wickets
2017	**Sussex,** who beat Hampshire by 24 runs
2018	**Lancashire,** who beat Essex by 25 runs
2019	**Glamorgan,** who beat Hampshire by 1 run
2021	**110,** who beat Sussex by 54 runs